PEARSON ALWAYS LEARNING

S.A. Hummelbrunner • K. Suzanne Coombs

Contemporary Business Mathematics with Canadian Applications

Custom Edition for Georgian College

Taken from:
Contemporary Business Mathematics with Canadian Applications
by S.A. Hummelbrunner and K. Suzanne Coombs

Cover Art: Chicago 53, Chicago 74, Chicago 77 by Patrick Linehan.

Taken from:

Contemporary Business Mathematics with Canadian Applications
by S.A. Hummelbrunner and K. Suzanne Coombs
Copyright © 2012, 2009, 2008, 2001, 1998 by Pearson Canada Inc.
Published by Pearson Canada
Toronto, Ontario

All rights reserved. No part of this book may be reproduced, in any form or by any means, without permission in writing from the publisher.

This special edition published in cooperation with Pearson Learning Solutions.

All trademarks, service marks, registered trademarks, and registered service marks are the property of their respective owners and are used herein for identification purposes only.

Pearson Learning Solutions, 501 Boylston Street, Suite 900, Boston, MA 02116
A Pearson Education Company
www.pearsoned.com

Printed in the United States of America

5 6 7 8 9 10 V0CR 17 16 15 14 13

000200010271726953

SH

ISBN 10: 1-256-93956-0
ISBN 13: 978-1-256-93956-6

BRIEF CONTENTS

CONTENTS

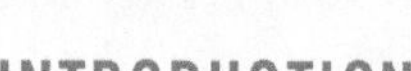

PREFACE

INTRODUCTION

Contemporary Business Mathematics with Canadian Applications is intended for use in introductory mathematics of finance courses in post-secondary business management, marketing, accounting, and finance programs. It also provides a review of basic mathematics.

The primary objective of the text is to increase the student's knowledge and skill in the solution of practical financial and operational problems encountered in operating a business.

ORGANIZATION

Contemporary Business Mathematics with Canadian Applications is a teaching text using problem-identification and problem-solving approaches. The systematic and sequential development of the material is illustrated by examples that show a step-by-step approach to solving the problem. The detailed solutions are presented in a visually clear and colourful layout that allows learners to monitor their own progress in the classroom or in independent study.

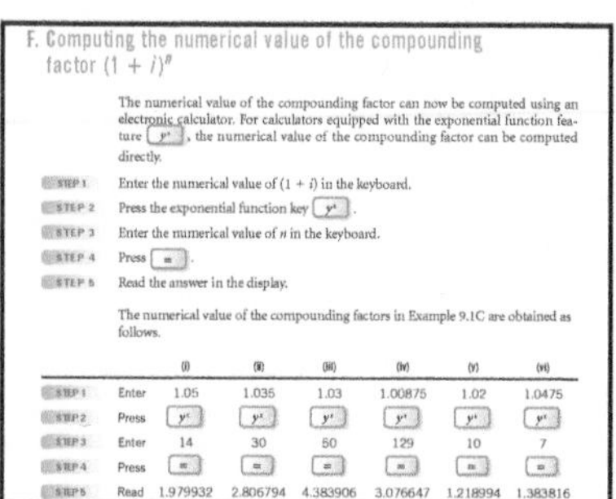

F. Computing the numerical value of the compounding factor $(1 + i)^n$

The numerical value of the compounding factor can now be computed using an electronic calculator. For calculators equipped with the exponential function feature y^x, the numerical value of the compounding factor can be computed directly.

STEP 1 Enter the numerical value of $(1 + i)$ in the keyboard.
STEP 2 Press the exponential function key y^x.
STEP 3 Enter the numerical value of n in the keyboard.
STEP 4 Press =.
STEP 5 Read the answer in the display.

The numerical value of the compounding factors in Example 9.1C are obtained as follows.

		(i)	(ii)	(iii)	(iv)	(v)	(vi)
STEP 1	Enter	1.05	1.035	1.03	1.00875	1.02	1.0475
STEP 2	Press	y^x	y^x	y^x	y^x	y^x	y^x
STEP 3	Enter	14	30	50	129	10	7
STEP 4	Press	=	=	=	=	=	=
STEP 5	Read	1.979932	2.806794	4.383906	3.076647	1.218994	1.383816

Each topic in each chapter is followed by practice exercises containing numerous drill questions and application problems. At the end of each chapter, Review Exercises, Self-Test, and Case Studies integrate the material presented.

The first four chapters and Appendix I (Further Review of Basic Algebra) are intended for students with little or no background in algebra and provide an opportunity to review arithmetic and algebraic processes.

The text is based on Canadian practice, and reflects current trends using available technology—specifically the availability of preprogrammed financial calculators. Students using this book should have access to calculators having a power function and a natural logarithm function. The use of such calculators eliminates the constraints associated with manually calculating results using formulas.

In solving problems involving multiple steps, often values are determined that will be used in further computations. Such values should not be rounded and all available digits should be retained in the calculator. Using the memory functions of the calculator enables the student to retain such non-rounded values.

When using the memory the student needs to be aware that the number of digits retained in the registers of the calculator is greater than the number of digits displayed. Depending on whether the memory or the displayed digits are used, slight differences may occur.

Students are encouraged to use preprogrammed financial calculators. The use of these preprogrammed calculators facilitates the solving of most financial problems and is demonstrated extensively in Chapters 9 to 16.

NEW TO THIS EDITION

The Ninth Edition of Hummelbrunner/Coombs, *Contemporary Business Mathematics with Canadian Applications*, includes updates based on changes in current practices in Canadian finance and business and the needs of students and instructors using this book.

- This edition continues to clarify the consistent approach to rounding rules. The **Student's Reference Guide to Rounding and Special Notation** (pages xix–xxii) gives a clear explanation of the rounding conventions used throughout the text.
- The text and solutions manual have been thoroughly technically checked for accuracy and consistency with the rounding approach.
- Tables, charts, and further diagrams have been added to enable the learner to visualize the problems and the solutions.
- Numerous new examples and exercises have been added.
- Chapter 5 has been significantly revised with standardized formulas and wording, illustrated by visual approaches to solving the problems.
- Chapter 6 has been significantly revised with emphasis on the relationships between parts of CVP. Break-even charts are integrated with theory by introducing them after explanations of revenue and cost behaviour.
- Canadian references have been emphasized in *Business Math News Boxes* and Website references.
- Interest rates reflect current investment and borrowing rates.

Many examples and exercises have been updated, rewritten, and expanded. To enhance the building-block approach, exercises are ordered to link the topics and the solved examples. Help references have been expanded to link selected exercises to solved examples.

Specifically, in Chapter 1 (Review of Arithmetic), revised rates and calculations for GST/PST/HST have been included to incorporate new legislation for 2010, and property tax terminology and valuations have been updated.

In Chapter 2 (Review of Algebra), new exercises have been added to utilize formulas for simple and compound interest.

In Chapter 3 (Ratio, Proportion, and Percent), currency conversion rates, CPI numbers, and personal income taxes have been updated, and new examples and exercises have been added.

In Chapter 4 (Linear Systems), the algebraic approach has been included to illustrate the existing discussion of graphing.

Chapter 5 (Trade Discount, Cash Discount, Markup, and Markdown) has significantly changed. To emphasize the building-block approach, visuals have been added to show step-by-step components. Further explanation for these steps has been added. For consistency and clarity, terminology and explanations have been simplified and formulas have been standardized. To reflect current industry practice, coverage of EOM and ROG dating has been reduced. Many examples have been revised, and new exercises have been added.

Chapter 6 (Break-Even and Cost-Volume-Profit Analysis) has been significantly changed. Relationships between the parts of cost, volume, and profit have been clarified. To enhance learning of the concepts, break-even charts have been introduced after explanations of cost and revenue behaviours, enabling integration of theory and graphing. A new section has been added to explain analysis of break-even with unknown unit prices or unit costs. Visuals have been added to show the components of the analysis.

In Chapter 7 (Simple Interest) and Chapter 8 (Simple Interest Applications), interest rates and dates have been updated, and examples and exercises have been simplified. The explanation of interest-bearing and non-interest-bearing notes has been separated and clarified. New exercises have been added.

In Chapter 9 (Compound Interest—Future Value and Present Value), further explanation of rounding has been included, formulas have been simplified by reducing use of the symbols S and P, the step-by-step approach has been expanded, interest rates and dates have been updated, and many examples and exercises have been updated or added. There is reduced emphasis on n as a fractional value.

Chapter 10 (Compound Interest—Further Topics) continues the changes from Chapter 9. Visual analysis in the form of tables has been added.

In Chapter 11 (Ordinary Simple Annuities) and in Chapter 12 (Ordinary General Annuities), terms and definitions for annuities have been revised and formulas have been standardized and simplified. Subscripts on formulas remain but are omitted on examples and exercises. The step-by-step approach continues, with clarified and enhanced explanations of numbered sequential steps. A chart of questions has been added to aid the learner in identifying types of annuities. Visual features in the form of tables have been added and diagrams clarified. Long paragraphs and sections have been replaced by numbered and lettered explanations. To reflect a more logical flow, some calculator explanations have been changed. Many new examples and exercises have been added.

In Chapter 13 (Annuities Due, Deferred Annuities, and Perpetuities), explanations of annuities due are simplified, as are formulas, where $(1 + i)$ has been placed consistently at the end of the formula. The step-by-step approach has been increased and further explained. Additional timelines are included, and duplicate examples have been replaced. The order of the end-of-chapter questions has changed to vary the types of annuity questions. Numerous new exercises, many on deferred annuities, have been added. Canadian and student-friendly topics have been added. Deferred perpetuities have been separated into a new section.

In Chapter 14 (Amortization of Loans, Including Residential Mortgages), explanations of the retrospective and prospective approaches have been simplified, with less emphasis on the prospective method. Further explanation on the rounding approach is included, and sections on CMHC and mortgages have been updated to reflect changes in legislation. New examples and exercises are included.

In Chapter 15 (Bond Valuation and Sinking Funds), bond rates have been updated to reflect current rates, formulas have been simplified for consistency with earlier chapters, tables have been added for visual analysis, and new exercises have been added.

In Chapter 16 (Investment Decision Applications), explanations and instructions for the calculator functions NPV and IRR have been added. Solutions using these calculator functions have been included.

In general, interest rates used reflect the current economic climate in Canada. Calculator tips and solutions have been updated or clarified. Spreadsheet instructions and Internet Website references have been updated. *Pitfalls and Pointers* have been included to assist in performing tasks and interpreting word problems, and sections have been rewritten to clarify the explanations. Many more word problems have been added and references to solved examples have been added. *Business Math News Boxes* and Case Studies have been updated. Examples involving both business and personal situations are included. The pedagogical elements of the previous edition have been retained. In response to requests and suggestions by users of the book, a number of new features for this edition have been included. They are described below.

FEATURES

- A new colourful and student-friendly design has been created for the book, making it more accessible and less intimidating to learners at all levels.
- Any preprogrammed financial calculator may be used, but this edition includes extensive instructions for using the Texas Instruments BAII Plus financial calculator. Equivalent instructions are given in Appendix II for the Sharp EL-733A and the Hewlett Packard 10B financial calculators.

Table 9.3 Financial Calculator Function Keys that Correspond to Variables Used in Compound Interest Calculations

Variable	Algebraic Symbol	Function Key: TI BAII+	Function Key: Sharp EL-733A	Function Key: HP 10B
The number of compounding periods	n	N	n	N
The rate of interest[1]	i	I/Y C/Y	i	I/YR
The periodic annuity payment[2]	R	PMT	PMT	PMT
The present value or principal	P	PV	PV	PV
The future value or maturity value	S	FV	FV	FV

- To reduce the amount of "translation" required to go from the formulas in the text to the keystrokes on the preprogrammed financial calculator, the compounding and annuity formulas in Chapters 9 to 16 have been restated in this edition. From the beginning of Chapter 9, the P has been replaced with PV, S has been replaced with FV, and A has been replaced with PMT in these formulas. In addition, the compounding interval, C/Y, has been identified within the calculator solutions.

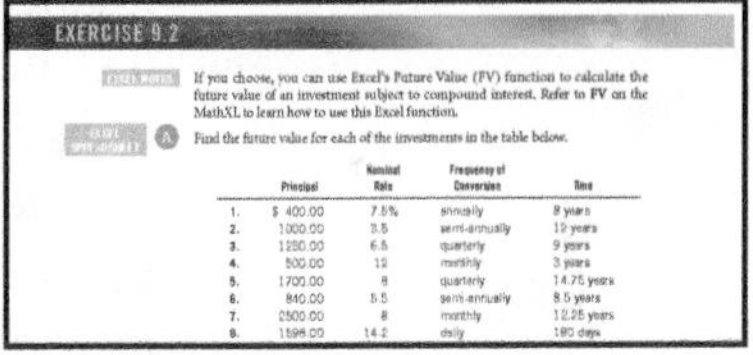

EXERCISE 9.2

If you choose, you can use Excel's Future Value (FV) function to calculate the future value of an investment subject to compound interest. Refer to FV on the MathXL to learn how to use this Excel function.

A Find the future value for each of the investments in the table below.

	Principal	Nominal Rate	Frequency of Conversion	Time
1.	$ 400.00	7.5%	annually	8 years
2.	1000.00	3.5	semi-annually	12 years
3.	1250.00	6.5	quarterly	9 years
4.	500.00	12	monthly	3 years
5.	1700.00	8	quarterly	14.75 years
6.	840.00	5.5	semi-annually	8.5 years
7.	2500.00	8	monthly	12.25 years
8.	1596.00	14.2	daily	180 days

EXCEL SPREADSHEET

- An Excel Spreadsheet icon in the text highlights the questions in the text that can be solved using an Excel spreadsheet function featured on MathXL (see p. xvii). Three appendices are also included on MathXL.
- A set of learning objectives is listed at the beginning of each chapter.
- Each chapter opens with a description of a situation familiar to students to emphasize the practical applications of the material to follow.

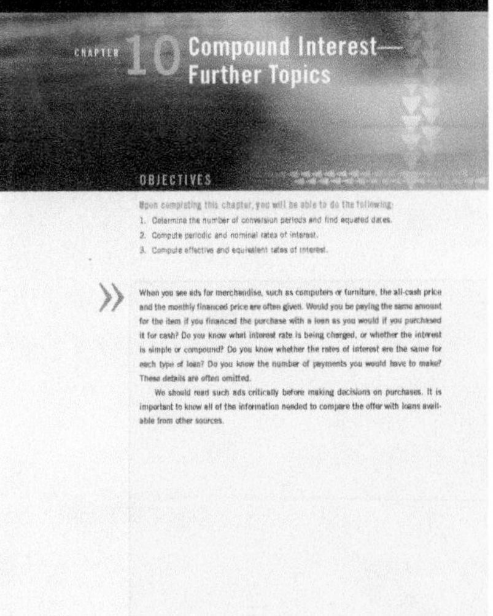

CHAPTER 10 Compound Interest—Further Topics

OBJECTIVES

Upon completing this chapter, you will be able to do the following:

1. Determine the number of conversion periods and find equated dates.
2. Compute periodic and nominal rates of interest.
3. Compute effective and equivalent rates of interest.

When you see ads for merchandise, such as computers or furniture, the all-cash price and the monthly financed price are often given. Would you be paying the same amount for the item if you financed the purchase with a loan as you would if you purchased it for cash? Do you know what interest rate is being charged, or whether the interest is simple or compound? Do you know whether the rates of interest are the same for each type of loan? Do you know the number of payments you would have to make? These details are often omitted.

We should read such ads critically before making decisions on purchases. It is important to know all of the information needed to compare the offer with loans available from other sources.

- A *Business Math News Box* is presented in every chapter. This element consists of short excerpts based on material appearing in newspapers, magazines, or Websites, followed by a set of questions. These boxes demonstrate how widespread business math applications are in the real world.

BUSINESS MATH NEWS BOX

National Salary Comparisons

Knowing how much you are worth in the job market is critical for not being underpaid. Successful salary negotiations are accomplished by having accurate information. In today's electronic age, the Internet offers a variety of Websites focusing on salary information.

Three popular job functions along with the respective salaries are listed below by major metropolitan location.

Financial Controller

Responsible for directing an organization's accounting functions. These functions include establishing and maintaining the organization's accounting principles, practices, and procedures. Prepares financial reports and presents findings and recommendations to top management.

Bank Branch Manager

Oversees the daily activities of the bank branch. Provides guidance on more complex issues. Familiar with a variety of the field's concepts, practices, and procedures. Relies on extensive experience and judgment to plan and accomplish goals.

Marketing Manager

Develops and implements strategic marketing plan for an organization. Generally manages a group of marketing professionals. Typically reports to an executive.

[illegible]*	[illegible]	Salary Comparison (Average) [illegible]	[illegible]	[illegible]	[illegible]
Financial Controller	$98 576	$118 207	$102 750	$89 580	$94 882
Bank Branch Manager	$81 601	$83 749	$77 352	$76 973	$77 021
Marketing Manager	$68 460	$78 989	$77 243	$65 202	$73 026

* Represents salary and not necessarily total compensation.

Source: Data represent the high range number found for each job title per city from "PayScale" at **www.payscale.com/resources.aspx?nc=ip_calculator_canada01&mode=none**, accessed August 1, 2010.

- The *Pointers and Pitfalls* boxes emphasize good practices, highlight ways to avoid common errors, show how to use a financial calculator efficiently, or give hints for tackling business math situations to reduce math anxiety.

POINTERS AND PITFALLS

You can use the BREAKEVEN function of a financial calculator to determine the break-even point. In this function, FC refers to the total fixed cost for the period, VC refers to the unit variable cost, P refers to the unit price, PFT is the resulting profit and Q is used to input or calculate the quantity or number of units. For example, for Example 6.1D press:

2nd Brkevn FC = 8640.00 Enter ↓

VC = 30.00 Enter ↓

P = 50.00 Enter ↓

PFT = 0 Enter ↓

CPT Q = 432 units

- Numerous Examples with worked-out Solutions are provided throughout the book, offering easy-to-follow, step-by-step instructions.

EXAMPLE 8.1B

You have applied for and received a credit card. The interest rate charged is 18.9% per annum. You note the following transactions for the month of September.

September 6 Purchased textbooks and supplies for a total of $250.
September 10 Withdrew $100 as a cash advance through your credit card.
September 30 Received the credit card statement, showing a minimum balance owing of $25. A payment date of October 10 is stated on the statement.

(i) Compute the amount of interest charged on the cash advance from September 10 until September 30.

(ii) You decide to pay the amount owing, in full, on October 1. How much must you pay?

(iii) Instead of paying the full amount, you decide to pay the minimum, $25, on October 1. What would be the balance owing after the payment?

(iv) If there are no further transactions during October, how much is owing at the end of October?

SOLUTION

(i) Interest charged (on cash advance):
September 10 to September 30 inclusive: $100 at 18.9% for 21 days.

$$I = 100.00(0.189)\left(\frac{21}{365}\right) = \$1.09$$

(ii) $250.00 + 100.00 + 1.09 = $351.09

- Programmed solutions using the Texas Instruments BAII Plus calculator are offered for all examples in Chapters 9 to 16. Since this calculator display can be pre-set, it is suggested that the learner set the display to show six decimal places to match the mathematical calculations in the body of the text. Both mathematical and calculator solutions for all Exercises, Review Exercises, and Self-Tests are included in the Instructor's Solutions Manual. An icon highlights information on the use of the BAII Plus calculator.

- Key Terms are introduced in the text in boldface type. A Glossary at the end of each chapter lists each term with its definition and a page reference to where the term was first defined in the chapter.

11.1 INTRODUCTION TO ANNUITIES

A. Basic concepts

An **annuity** is a series of payments, usually of equal size, made at periodic intervals. The length of time between the successive payments is called the **payment interval** or **payment period**. The length of time from the beginning of the first payment interval to the end of the last payment interval is called the **term of an annuity**. The size of each of the regular payments is the **periodic rent**.

When performing annuity calculations, the timing of payments must be con-

GLOSSARY

Cash discount a reduction in the amount of an invoice, usually to encourage prompt payment of the invoice *(p. 186)*

Credit period the time period at the end of which an invoice has to be paid *(p. 186)*

Discount a reduction from the original price *(p. 180)*

Discount period the time period during which a cash discount applies *(p. 186)*

Discount series two or more discounts taken off a list price in succession *(p. 180)*

End-of-month dating (E.O.M.) payment terms based on the last day of the month in which the invoice is dated *(p. 187)*

Gross profit *see* **Markup**

List price price printed in a catalogue or in a list of prices *(p. 177)*

Manufacturer's suggested retail price (MSRP) catalogue

Net factor *see* **Net price factor (NPF)**

Net price the difference between a list price and the amount of discount *(p. 178)*

Net price factor (NPF) the difference between 100% and a percent discount—the net price expressed as a fraction of the list price *(p. 179)*

Ordinary dating payment terms based on the date of an invoice *(p. 187)*

Partial payment part payment of an invoice *(p. 189)*

Payment terms a statement of the conditions under which a cash discount may be taken *(p. 186)*

Rate of discount a reduction in price expressed as a percent of the original price *(pp. 177, 186)*

Receipt-of-goods dating (R.O.G.) payment terms based on the date the merchandise is received *(p. 187)*

Regular selling price the price of an article sold to the consumer before any markdown is applied *(p. 203)*

Sale price the price of an article sold to the consumer after a markdown has been applied *(p. 203)*

- Main Equations are highlighted in the chapters and repeated in a Summary of Formulas at the ends of the chapters. Each main formula is presented in colour and labelled numerically (with the letter A suffix if equivalent forms of the formula are presented later). By contrast, equivalent formulae are presented in black and labelled with the number of the related main formula followed by the letter B or C.

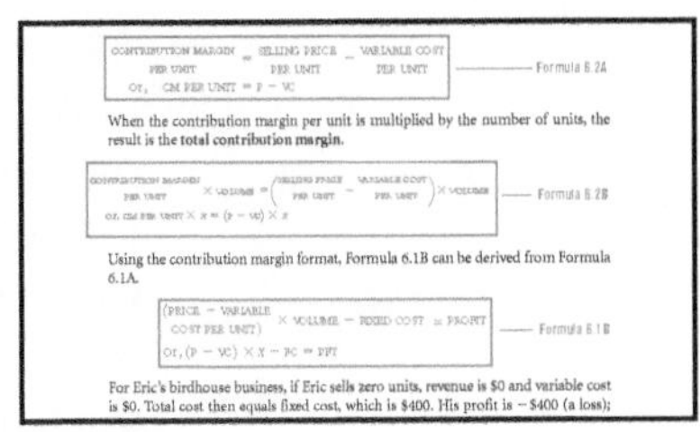

CONTRIBUTION MARGIN PER UNIT = SELLING PRICE PER UNIT − VARIABLE COST PER UNIT —— Formula 6.2A
Or, CM PER UNIT = P − VC

When the contribution margin per unit is multiplied by the number of units, the result is the **total contribution margin**.

CONTRIBUTION MARGIN PER UNIT × VOLUME = (SELLING PRICE PER UNIT − VARIABLE COST PER UNIT) × VOLUME —— Formula 6.2B
Or, CM PER UNIT × x = (P − VC) × x

Using the contribution margin format, Formula 6.1B can be derived from Formula 6.1A.

(PRICE − VARIABLE COST PER UNIT) × VOLUME − FIXED COST = PROFIT —— Formula 6.1B
Or, (P − VC) × X − FC = PFT

For Eric's birdhouse business, if Eric sells zero units, revenue is $0 and variable cost is $0. Total cost then equals fixed cost, which is $400. His profit is −$400 (a loss);

- A list of the Main Formulas can be found on the study card bound into this text.

- An Exercise set is provided at the end of each section in every chapter. If students choose, they can use the suggested Excel spreadsheet functions to answer those questions marked with the Excel Spreadsheet icon. In addition, each chapter contains a Review Exercise set and a Self-Test. If students choose, they can use an Excel spreadsheet function to answer those questions marked with Excel Spreadsheet icon, but they must decide which function to use. Answers to all the odd-numbered Exercises, Review Exercises, and Self-Tests are given at the back of the book.

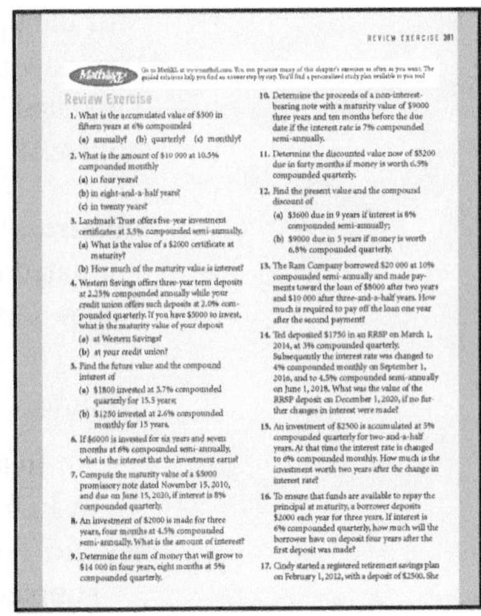

REVIEW EXERCISE 281

Go to MathXL at www.mathxl.com. You can practise many of this chapter's exercises as often as you want. The guided solutions help you find an answer step by step. You'll find a personalized study plan available to you too!

Review Exercise

1. What is the accumulated value of $500 in fifteen years at 6% compounded
   (a) annually? (b) quarterly? (c) monthly?
2. What is the amount of $10 000 at 10.5% compounded monthly
   (a) in four years?
   (b) in eight-and-a-half years?
   (c) in twenty years?
3. Landmark Trust offers five-year investment certificates at 3.5% compounded semi-annually.
   (a) What is the value of a $2000 certificate at maturity?
   (b) How much of the maturity value is interest?
4. Western Savings offers three-year term deposits at 2.25% compounded annually while your credit union offers such deposits at 2.0% compounded quarterly. If you have $5000 to invest, what is the maturity value of your deposit
   (a) at Western Savings?
   (b) at your credit union?
5. Find the future value and the compound interest of
   (a) $1800 invested at 3.7% compounded quarterly for 15.5 years;
   (b) $1250 invested at 2.6% compounded monthly for 15 years.
6. If $6000 is invested for six years and seven months at 6% compounded semi-annually, what is the interest that the investment earns?
7. Compute the maturity value of a $5000 promissory note dated November 15, 2010, and due on June 15, 2020, if interest is 8% compounded quarterly.
8. An investment of $2000 is made for three years, four months at 4.5% compounded semi-annually. What is the amount of interest?
9. Determine the sum of money that will grow to $14 000 in four years, eight months at 5% compounded quarterly.
10. Determine the proceeds of a non-interest-bearing note with a maturity value of $9000 three years and ten months before the due date if the interest rate is 7% compounded semi-annually.
11. Determine the discounted value now of $5200 due in forty months if money is worth 6.5% compounded quarterly.
12. Find the present value and the compound discount of
    (a) $3600 due in 9 years if interest is 8% compounded semi-annually;
    (b) $9000 due in 5 years if money is worth 6.8% compounded quarterly.
13. The Ram Company borrowed $20 000 at 10% compounded semi-annually and made payments toward the loan of $8000 after two years and $10 000 after three-and-a-half years. How much is required to pay off the loan one year after the second payment?
14. Ted deposited $1750 in an RRSP on March 1, 2014, at 3% compounded quarterly. Subsequently the interest rate was changed to 4% compounded monthly on September 1, 2016, and to 4.5% compounded semi-annually on June 1, 2018. What was the value of the RRSP deposit on December 1, 2020, if no further changes in interest were made?
15. An investment of $2500 is accumulated at 5% compounded quarterly for two-and-a-half years. At that time the interest rate is changed to 6% compounded monthly. How much is the investment worth two years after the change in interest rate?
16. To ensure that funds are available to repay the principal at maturity, a borrower deposits $2000 each year for three years. If interest is 6% compounded quarterly, how much will the borrower have on deposit four years after the first deposit was made?
17. Cindy started a registered retirement savings plan on February 1, 2012, with a deposit of $2500. She

- Also included in this edition are references to solved Examples from the chapter, which are provided at the end of key exercises. Students are directed to specific examples so they can check their work and review fundamental problem types.

- A set of Challenge Problems is provided in each chapter. These problems give users the opportunity to apply the skills learned in the chapter to questions that are pitched at a higher level than the Exercises.

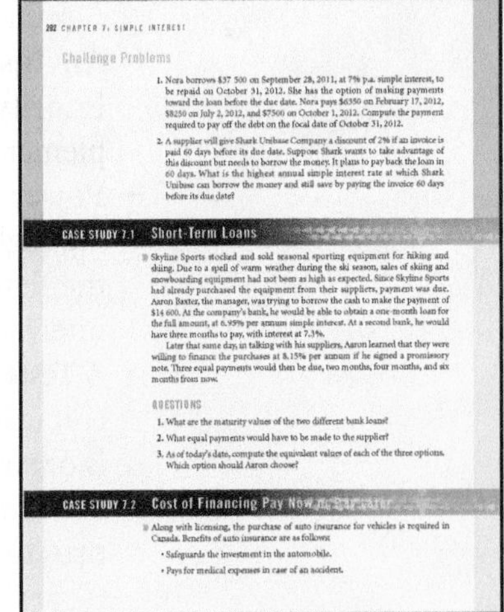

282 CHAPTER 7: SIMPLE INTEREST

Challenge Problems

1. Nora borrows $37 500 on September 28, 2011, at 7% p.a. simple interest, to be repaid on October 31, 2012. She has the option of making payments toward the loan before the due date. Nora pays $6350 on February 17, 2012, $8250 on July 2, 2012, and $7500 on October 1, 2012. Compute the payment required to pay off the debt on the focal date of October 31, 2012.
2. A supplier will give Shark Unibase Company a discount of 2% if an invoice is paid 60 days before its due date. Suppose Shark wants to take advantage of this discount but needs to borrow the money. It plans to pay back the loan in 60 days. What is the highest annual simple interest rate at which Shark Unibase can borrow the money and still save by paying the invoice 60 days before its due date?

CASE STUDY 7.1 Short-Term Loans

Skyline Sports stocked and sold seasonal sporting equipment for hiking and skiing. Due to a spell of warm weather during the ski season, sales of skiing and snowboarding equipment had not been as high as expected. Since Skyline Sports had already purchased the equipment from their suppliers, payment was due. Aaron Baxter, the manager, was trying to borrow the cash to make the payment of $14 600. At the company's bank, he would be able to obtain a one-month loan for the full amount, at 6.95% per annum simple interest. At a second bank, he would have three months to pay, with interest at 7.3%.

Later that same day, in talking with his suppliers, Aaron learned that they were willing to finance the purchases at 8.15% per annum if he signed a promissory note. Three equal payments would then be due, two months, four months, and six months from now.

QUESTIONS

1. What are the maturity values of the two different bank loans?
2. What equal payments would have to be made to the supplier?
3. As of today's date, compute the equivalent values of each of the three options. Which option should Aaron choose?

CASE STUDY 7.2 Cost of Financing Pay Now

Along with licensing, the purchase of auto insurance for vehicles is required in Canada. Benefits of auto insurance are as follows:

- Safeguards the investment in the automobile.
- Pays for medical expenses in case of an accident.

- Thirty-two Case Studies are included in the book, two near the end of each chapter. They present comprehensive realistic scenarios followed by a set of questions and illustrate some of the important types of practical applications of the chapter material.

- An updated set of Useful Internet Sites is provided at the end of each chapter, with the URL and a brief description provided for each site. These sites are related to the chapter topic or to companies mentioned in the chapter, or they show how business math is important to the day-to-day operations of companies and industries.

USEFUL INTERNET SITES

www.csi.ca
CSI Global Education Inc. CSI provides training for the Canadian financial services industry. Many courses are offered for careers in financial planning, banking, and estate management, starting with the Canadian Securities Course.

www.toolkit.com/tools
Business Owner's Toolkit This small-business guide includes analysis of starting and planning your business, marketing and managing your finances. A discussion is included on improving your bottom line by helping to improve the environment by "going green."

SUPPLEMENTS

The Instructor's Solutions Manual and Student's Solutions Manual have been revised for the update of the Ninth Edition. The updated Instructor's Solutions Manual can be downloaded from Pearson's online catalogue at **http://vig.pearsoned.ca**. The updated Student Solutions Manual (0-13-216522-8) is available from your college or university bookstore.

Instructors: To acquire a copy of the Instructor's Resource CD-ROM with the updated Instructor's Solutions Manual, please see your Pearson Education Canada Sales Representative.

The following supplements are available to accompany *Contemporary Business Mathematics with Canadian Applications.*

- An **Instructor's Resource CD-ROM** includes the Instructor's Solutions Manual in PDF format, the Instructor's Resource Manual, PowerPoint® Lecture Slides, and TestGen. Instructions to access each item are given on the CD-ROM. Each supplement is described in more detail below.
- An **Instructor's Solutions Manual** provides complete mathematical and calculator solutions to all the Exercises, Review Exercises, Self-Tests, *Business Math News Box* questions, Challenge Problems, and Case Studies in the textbook.
- An **Instructor's Resource Manual** includes Chapter Overviews, Suggested Priority of Topics, Chapter Outlines, and centralized information on all the supplements available with the text.
- **PowerPoint® Lecture Slides** present an outline of each chapter in the book, highlighting the major concepts taught. The presentation will include many of the figures and tables from the text and provides the instructor with a visually interesting summary of the entire book.
- A **TestGen**, a special computerized version of the test bank, enables instructors to edit existing questions, add new questions, and generate tests. The Test Generator is organized by chapter, with level of difficulty indicated for each question.
- **Personal Response System Slides** will help instructors to gauge students' progress with clicker questions that enable instructors to pose questions, record results, and display those results instantly in the classroom. Questions are provided in PowerPoint® format.
- A **Student's Solutions Manual** provides complete solutions to all the odd-numbered Exercises, Review Exercises, and Self-Test questions in the textbook.
- A complete **Answer Key** for all of the exercise and self-test questions will be included on the IRCD and available for instructors to download from Pearson's online catalogue at **http://vig.pearsoned.ca.**

MathXL

MathXL is a powerful online homework, tutorial, and assessment system tied directly to *Contemporary Business Mathematics with Canadian Applications*, Ninth Edition. Ideal for use in a lecture, self-paced, or distance-learning course, MathXL

- Diagnoses students' weaknesses and creates a personalized study plan based on their test results.
- Provides students with unlimited practice using a database of algorithmically generated exercises correlated to the exercises in the textbook.
- Offers an interactive guided solution and a sample problem with each tutorial exercise, to help students improve their skills independently.
- Includes an interactive eBook that links directly to supplemental multimedia resources such as Excel spreadsheet templates.
- Provides narrated, animated PowerPoints to reinforce core concepts.

Instructors can use MathXL to create online homework assignments, quizzes, and tests that are automatically graded and tracked. Instructors can view and manage all students' homework and test results, study plans, and tutorial work in MathXL's flexible online Gradebook.

To learn more about how MathXL can enhance the use of *Contemporary Business Mathematics with Canadian Applications*, please contact your Pearson Education Canada Sales and Editorial Representative.

ACKNOWLEDGMENTS

Thanks to Bruce M. Coombs of Kwantlen University College for his help in creating and updating the Excel spreadsheet templates. Also, thanks go to Kelly Halliday of Georgian College, who contributed the *Business Math News Boxes*.

We would like to express our thanks to the many people who offered thoughtful suggestions and recommendations for updating and improving the book. We would particularly like to thank the following instructors for providing formal reviews for the Ninth Edition:

Douglas A. Leatherdale, Georgian College
Peter Au, George Brown College
Michael Conte, Durham College
Midori Kobayashi, Humber College
Helen Catania, Centennial College
Harry Matsugu, Humber College
Hoshiar Gosal, Langara College
Lorne Jeal, Medicine Hat College
Jim Watson, Humber Institute of Technology and Advanced Learning
Dan Miron, Georgian College
Hang Lau, McGill University
Tom Fraser, Niagara College
Thambyrajah Kugathasan, Seneca College
Minli Lian, Kwantlen Polytechnic University

Stephen Peplow
Kelly Halliday, Georgian College
Deborah Sauer, Capilano University
Alexander Dyke, Nova Scotia Community College
Carollyne Guidera, University of the Fraser Valley
Allen Zhu, Capilano University
Melanie Christian, St. Lawrence College

We would also like to thank the many people at Pearson Canada Inc. who helped with the development and production of this book, especially to the acquisitions editor, Nick Durie; the developmental editor, Victoria Naik; the project manager, Cherly Jackson; the freelance production editor, Heather Sangster; the copy editor, Cat Haggert; the technical checkers, Carolina Ayala and Andreas J. Guelzow; and the proofreader, Linda Jenkins.

STUDENT'S REFERENCE GUIDE TO ROUNDING AND SPECIAL NOTATIONS

Developed by Jean-Paul Olivier, based on the textbook authored by Suzanne Coombs

Universal Principle of Rounding: When performing a sequence of operations, never round any interim solution until the final answer is achieved. Only apply rounding principles to the final answer. Interim solutions should only be rounded where common practice would require rounding.

Note: Due to space limitations, the textbook only shows the first 6 decimals (rounded) of any number. Starting in Chapter 11, because the calculator display may not have sufficient space for all 6 decimals, as many decimals as possible will be shown. However, the Universal Principle of Rounding still applies.

Section 1.2

1. For repeating decimals, use the notation of placing a period above the repeating sequence. E.g. $\frac{1}{3} = 0.333333\ldots = 0.\dot{3}$
2. For terminating decimals, if they terminate within the first 6 decimal places, then carry all the decimals in your final answer.
3. For non-terminating decimals, round to 6 decimals unless specified or logically sound to do so otherwise. If the final digits would be zeros, the zeros are generally not displayed.
4. Calculations involving money are rounded to 2 decimals as their final answer. Interim solutions may be rounded to 2 decimals if the situation dictates (for example, if you withdraw money from an account). If the calculation does not involve cents, it is optional to display the decimals.

Section 1.3

1. Calculations involving percentages will only involve 4 decimal positions since there are only 6 decimals in decimal format.

Section 1.5

1. Hourly rate calculations for salaried employees require that all the decimals should be carried until the final answer is achieved. If the solution is to express the hourly rate or overtime rate itself, then rounding to 2 decimals is appropriate.
2. Overtime hourly wage rate calculations should carry all decimals of the overtime rate until the final answer is achieved.

Section 3.6

1. Larger sums of money usually are involved in currency exchanges. Therefore, the two decimal rule for money is insufficient. To produce a more accurate result, currency exchange rates need to carry at least four decimals.
2. It needs to be recognized that not all currencies utilize the same decimals when expressing amounts.
   (a) Final currency amounts for the Canadian Dollar, U.S. Dollar, British Pound, Euro, and Swiss Franc should be rounded to the standard two decimal places.

(b) Final currency amounts for the Japanese Yen should be rounded to the nearest integer, as there are no decimal amounts in their currency.

3. Price per litre of gasoline is generally expressed to three decimal points (129.9¢/L = $1.299/L)

Section 3.7

1. As indexes are similar to percentages, an index will only have 4 decimals.

Section 6.1

1. When calculating break-even units, remember that the solution is the *minimum* number of units that must be sold. As such, any decimals must be rounded upwards to the next integer, regardless of the actual value of the decimal. For example, 38.05 units means 39 units must be sold to at least break even.

Section 7.2D

1. t is always an integer. It is important to note in this calculation that in most instances the interest (I) earned or charged to the account has been rounded to two decimals. This will cause the calculation of t to be slightly imprecise. Therefore, when calculating t it is possible that decimals close to an integer (such as 128.998 days or 130.012 days) may show up. These decimals should be rounded to the nearest integer to correct for the rounded interest amount.

Section 9.2D

1. In determining when it is appropriate to round, it is important to recognize that if the money remains inside an account (deposit or loan), all of the decimals need to carry forward into the next calculation. For example, if a bank deposit of $2000 earns 6% p.a. compounded monthly for 4 years, and then earns 7% p.a. compounded quarterly for three more years, then the money remained in the account the whole time. We can solve this in one step as follows:

$$FV = 2000.00(1.005)^{48}\ (1.0175)^{12} = \$3129.06$$

Or two steps as follows:

$$FV = 2000.00(1.005)^{48} = \$2540.978322$$

$$FV = 2540.978322(1.0175)^{12} = \$3129.06$$

Note that the first step is an interim calculation, for which we must carry forward all the decimals to the next step where the solution can then be rounded.

(a) If money is withdrawn/transferred from the account at any time, then only 2 decimals can be carried forward to any further steps (since a currency payout can only involve 2 decimals).

Section 9.4C

1. In promissory notes, the FV solution in the first step must be rounded to 2 decimals before discounting as this is the amount of the debt that will be repaid on the maturity date.

Section 9.5B

2. When calculating equivalent values for more than one payment, each payment is a separate transaction (one could make each payment separate from

any other payment) and therefore any equivalent value is rounded to two decimals before summing multiple payments.

Section 10.1

1. When determining the n for non-annuity calculations (lump-sum amounts), generally the solution would not be rounded off since n can be fractional in nature (we can get 4.5632 quarters).
   - **(a)** However, when n is discussed, the n may be simplified to 2 decimals so that it is easier to communicate. For example, if $n = 5.998123$ years this would mean a term of slightly under 6 years. However, when discussed it may be spoken simply as a term of 6.00 years. Alternatively if $n = 17.559876$ months this would mean a little more than half way through the 17th month. However, when discussed it may be spoken as a term of approximately 17.56 months.
   - **(b)** An exception to this rule is when the n gets converted into days. As interest generally is not accrued more than daily, a fraction of a day is not possible. The fraction shows up most likely due to rounding in the numbers being utilized in the calculation. Since we do not know how these numbers were rounded, it is appropriate for our purposes to round n to the nearest integer.

Section 11.5A

1. When determining the n for annuity calculations, remember that n represents the number of payments. Therefore, n must be a whole number and should always be rounded upwards. Whether a partial or full payment is made, it is still a payment. For example, if $n = 21.34$ payments, this would indicate 21 full payments and a smaller last payment (which is still a payment). Therefore, 22 payments are required.
   - **(a)** In most cases, the payment (*PMT*) has been rounded to two decimals. This may cause insignificant decimals to show up in the calculations. As a result, an exception to this rule would be when n is extremely close to a whole number. This would mean that no significant digits show up in the first two decimals. For example, if $n = 23.001$, it can be reasonably concluded that n is 23 payments since the 0.001 is probably a result of the rounded payment.

Section 13.1E

1. When working with the n for an annuity due, n represents the number of payments and must be a whole number. Therefore, n will always round upward. However, it is important to distinguish whether the question is asking about the term of the annuity due or when the last payment of the annuity due occurs.
   - **(a)** If the term is being asked, n can be used to figure out the timeline. For example, a yearly apartment rental agreement would have $n = 12$ monthly payments, thus the term ends 12 months from now.
   - **(b)** If the last payment is being asked, $n - 1$ can be used to figure out the timeline. In the same example, the last rental payment would occur at

the beginning of the 12th month. The last payment would be 12 − 1 = 11 months from now.

Section 14.1

1. The payment must be rounded to the two decimal standard for currency.
2. When constructing an amortization schedule, it is important to recognize that all numbers in the schedule need to be rounded to two decimals (since it is currency). However, since the money remains in the account at all times, all decimals are in fact being carried forward throughout. As such, calculated numbers may sometimes be off by a penny due to the rounding of the payment or the interest.

Section 15.1

1. When determining the purchase price for a bond, it is important to carry all the decimals until the calculation is complete. When completing the calculation by formula, the present value of the bond's face value and interest payments along with any accrued interest must be calculated. For simplicity reasons, the text shows each of these values rounded to two decimals and then summed to get the purchase price. Remember though that all decimals are being carried forward until the final answer.

Section 15.5

1. A sinking fund schedule has the same characteristics as an amortization schedule and may also experience a penny difference due to the rounding of the payment or the interest.

Section 16.1

1. When making choices between various alternatives, it is sufficient to calculate answers rounded to the nearest dollar. There are two rationales for this. First, in most cases future cash flows are not entirely certain (they are estimates) and therefore may be slightly inaccurate themselves. Second, as cents have little value, most decisions would not be based on cents difference; rather decisions would be based on dollars difference.

Section 16.2

1. In choosing whether to accept or reject a contract using the net present value method, remember that future cash flows are estimates. Therefore, when an NPV is calculated that is within \$500 of \$0, it can be said that the result does not provide a clear signal to accept or reject. Although the desired rate of return has barely been met (or not), this may be a result of the estimated cash flows. In this case, a closer examination of the estimates to determine their accuracy may be required before any decision could be made.

Section 16.3

1. Performance indexes are generally rounded to one decimal in percentage format.
2. This unknown rate of return (d) is generally rounded to 2 decimals in percentage format.
3. A rate of return is generally rounded to one decimal in percentage format.

CHAPTER 1 Review of Arithmetic

Objectives are a "roadmap" showing what will be covered and what is especially important in each chapter.

OBJECTIVES

Upon completing this chapter, you will be able to do the following:

1. Simplify arithmetic expressions using the basic order of operations.
2. Determine equivalent fractions and convert fractions to decimals.
3. Convert percents to common fractions and to decimals, and change decimals and fractions to percents.
4. Through problem solving, compute simple arithmetic and weighted averages.
5. Determine gross earnings for employees remunerated by the payment of salaries, hourly wages, or commissions.
6. Through problem solving, compute GST, HST, PST, sales taxes, and property taxes.

Each chapter opens with a description of a familiar situation to help you understand the practical applications of the material to follow.

Being able to perform arithmetic calculations is important in business operations. The use of arithmetic expressions, fractions, and percent is common in today's business environment. Competence in problem solving, including calculation of averages, is essential. When you employ people in operating a business, you must determine the amounts to pay them in the form of salaries or wages, and you must deduct and pay payroll taxes such as Canada Pension Plan, Employment Insurance, and employee income taxes. You are responsible for paying your employees and submitting the tax amounts to the federal government. Operating a business also means that you must determine the amount of goods and services tax (GST) or harmonized sales tax (HST) to collect on almost everything you sell. The amount you must remit to the federal government, or the refund you are entitled to, is calculated on the basis of the GST or HST you pay when you make purchases of goods and services. By using arithmetic and problem-solving approaches in this chapter you should be able to determine the amounts owed.

INTRODUCTION

The basics of fraction, decimal, and percent conversions are vital skills for dealing with situations you face, not only as a small-business owner, but as a consumer and investor. Although calculators and computers have become common tools for solving business problems, it is still important to understand clearly the process behind the conversions between number forms, the rounding of answers, and the correct order of operations.

1.1 BASICS OF ARITHMETIC

A. The basic order of operations

Boldfaced words are Key Terms that are explained here and defined in the Glossary section at the end of the chapter.

To ensure that arithmetic calculations are performed consistently, we must follow the **order of operations**.

If an arithmetic expression contains brackets on exponents, multiplication, division, addition, and subtraction, we use the following procedure:

1. Perform all operations *inside* a bracket first (the operations inside the bracket must be performed in proper order).
2. Perform exponents.
3. Perform multiplication and division in order as they appear from left to right.
4. Perform addition and subtraction in order as they appear from left to right.

Numerous Examples, often with worked-out Solutions, offer you easy-to-follow, step-by-step instructions.

The following "BEDMAS" rule might help you to more easily remember the order of operations:

B	E	D	M	A	S
Brackets	Exponents	Division	Multiplication	Addition	Subtraction

EXAMPLE 1.1A

(i) $(9 - 4) \times 2 = 5 \times 2 = 10$ — work inside the bracket first

(ii) $9 - 4 \times 2 = 9 - 8 = 1$ — do multiplication before subtraction

(iii) $18 \div 6 + 3 \times 2 = 3 + 6 = 9$ — do multiplication and division before adding

(iv) $(13 + 5) \div 6 - 3 = 18 \div 6 - 3 = 3 - 3 = 0$ — work inside the bracket first, then do division before subtraction

(v) $18 \div (6 + 3) \times 2 = 18 \div 9 \times 2 = 2 \times 2 = 4$ — work inside the bracket first, then do division and multiplication in order

(vi) $18 \div (3 \times 2) + 3 = 18 \div 6 + 3 = 3 + 3 = 6$ — work inside the bracket first, then divide before adding

(vii) $8(9 - 4) - 4(12 - 5) = 8(5) - 4(7)$ — work inside the brackets first, then multiply before subtracting
$= 40 - 28$
$= 12$

(viii) $\dfrac{12 - 4}{6 - 2} = (12 - 4) \div (6 - 2)$ — the fraction line indicates brackets as well as division
$= 8 \div 4$
$= 2$

(ix) $128 \div (2 \times 4)^2 - 3 = 128 \div 8^2 - 3$ — work inside the bracket first, do the exponent, then divide before subtracting
$= 128 \div 64 - 3$
$= 2 - 3$
$= -1$

(x) $128 \div (2 \times 4^2) - 3 = 128 \div (2 \times 16) - 3$ — start inside the bracket and do the exponent first, then multiply, then divide before subtracting
$= 128 \div 32 - 3$
$= 4 - 3$
$= 1$

EXERCISE 1.1

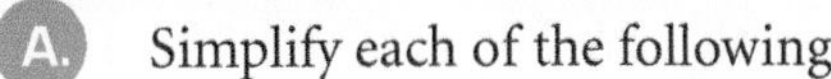

A. Simplify each of the following.

Each section in the chapter ends with an Exercise that allows you to review and apply what you've just learned. And you can find the solutions to the odd-numbered exercises at the back of the text.

1. $12 + 6 \div 3$

2. $(3 \times 8 - 6) \div 2$

3. $(7 + 4) \times 5 - 2$

4. $5 \times 3 + 2 \times 4$

5. $(3 \times 9 - 3) \div 6$

6. $6(7 - 2) - 3(5 - 3)$

7. $8(9 - 6) + 4(6 + 5)$

8. $\dfrac{16 - 8}{8 - 4}$

9. $\dfrac{20 - 16}{15 + 5}$

10. $4(8 - 5)^2 - 5(3 + 2^2)$

11. $(3 \times 4 - 2)^2 + (2 - 2 \times 7^2)$

12. $250(1 + 0.08)^{10}$

13. $(1 + 0.04)^4 - 1$

14. $7 \times 340 + 5400 + 10 \times 340$

15. $30 \times 600 - 2500 - 12 \times 600$

16. $1 - [(1 - 0.40)(1 - 0.25)(1 - 0.05)]$

Reference Example 1.1A

References to Examples direct you back to the chapter for help in answering the questions.

1.2 FRACTIONS

A. Common fractions

A **common fraction** is used to show a part of the whole. The fraction ⅔ means two parts out of a whole of three. The number written *above* the dividing line is the *part* and is called the **numerator.** The number written *below* the dividing line is the *whole* and is called the **denominator.** The numbers 2 and 3 are called the **terms of the fraction.**

A **proper fraction** has a numerator that is *less* than the denominator. An **improper fraction** has a numerator that is *greater* than the denominator.

EXAMPLE 1.2A

$\frac{3}{8}$ ← numerator / ← denominator — a proper fraction, since the numerator is less than the denominator

$\frac{6}{5}$ ← numerator / ← denominator — an improper fraction, since the numerator is greater than the denominator

B. Equivalent fractions

Equivalent fractions are obtained by changing the *terms* of a fraction without changing the value of the fraction.

Equivalent fractions in higher terms can be obtained by multiplying both the numerator and the denominator of a fraction by the same number. For any fraction, we can obtain an unlimited number of equivalent fractions in higher terms.

Equivalent fractions in lower terms can be obtained if both the numerator and denominator of a fraction are divisible by the same number or numbers. The process of obtaining such equivalent fractions is called *reducing to lower terms.*

EXAMPLE 1.2B

(i) Convert $\frac{3}{4}$ into higher terms by multiplying successively by 2, 6, and 25.

SOLUTION

$$\frac{3}{4} = \frac{3 \times 2}{4 \times 2} = \frac{6}{8} = \frac{6 \times 6}{8 \times 6} = \frac{36}{48} = \frac{36 \times 25}{48 \times 25} = \frac{900}{1200}$$

$$\text{Thus } \frac{3}{4} = \frac{6}{8} = \frac{36}{48} = \frac{900}{1200}$$

(ii) Reduce $\frac{210}{252}$ to lower terms.

SOLUTION

$$\frac{210}{252} = \frac{210 \div 2}{252 \div 2} = \frac{105}{126}$$

$$= \frac{105 \div 3}{126 \div 3} = \frac{35}{42}$$

$$= \frac{35 \div 7}{42 \div 7} = \frac{5}{6}$$

The fractions $\frac{105}{126}$, $\frac{35}{42}$, and $\frac{5}{6}$ are lower-term equivalents of $\frac{210}{252}$.

The terms of the fraction $\frac{5}{6}$ cannot be reduced any further. It represents the simplest form of the fraction $\frac{210}{252}$. It is the **fraction in lowest terms.**

C. Converting common fractions into decimal form

Common fractions are converted into decimal form by performing the indicated division to the desired number of decimal places or until the decimal terminates or repeats. We place a dot above a decimal number to show that it repeats. For example, $0.\dot{5}$ stands for 0.555. . . .

EXAMPLE 1.2C

(i) $\frac{9}{8} = 9 \div 8 = 1.125$

(ii) $\frac{1}{3} = 1 \div 3 = 0.333333\ldots = 0.\dot{3}$

(iii) $\frac{7}{6} = 7 \div 6 = 1.166666\ldots = 1.1\dot{6}$

D. Converting mixed numbers to decimal form

Mixed numbers consist of a whole number and a fraction, such as $5\frac{3}{4}$. Such numbers represent the *sum* of a whole number and a common fraction and can be converted into decimal form by changing the common fraction into decimal form.

EXAMPLE 1.2D

(i) $5\frac{3}{4} = 5 + \frac{3}{4} = 5 + 0.75 = 5.75$

(ii) $6\frac{2}{3} = 6 + \frac{2}{3} = 6 + 0.666\ldots = 6.6666\ldots = 6.\dot{6}$

(iii) $7\frac{1}{12} = 7 + \frac{1}{12} = 7 + 0.083333\ldots = 7.083333\ldots = 7.08\dot{3}$

E. Rounding

Answers to problems, particularly when obtained with the help of a calculator, often need to be rounded to a desired number of decimal places. In most business problems involving money values, the rounding needs to be done to the nearest cent, that is, to two decimal places.

While different methods of rounding are used, for most business purposes the following procedure is suitable.

1. If the first digit in the group of decimal digits that is to be dropped is the digit 5 or 6 or 7 or 8 or 9, the last digit retained is *increased* by 1.
2. If the first digit in the group of decimal digits that is to be dropped is the digit 0 or 1 or 2 or 3 or 4, the last digit retained is left *unchanged.*

EXAMPLE 1.2E

Round each of the following to two decimal places.

(i) 7.384 → 7.38 — drop the digit 4

(ii) 7.385 → 7.39 — round the digit 8 up to 9

(iii) 12.9448 → 12.94 — discard 48

(iv) 9.32838 → 9.33 — round the digit 2 up to 3

(v) 24.8975 → 24.90 — round the digit 9 up to 0; this requires rounding 89 to 90

(vi) 1.996 ⟶ 2.00 — round the second digit 9 up to 0; this requires rounding 1.99 to 2.00

(vii) 3199.99833 ⟶ 3200.00 — round the second digit 9 up to 0; this requires rounding 3199.99 to 3200.00

F. Complex fractions

Complex fractions are mathematical expressions containing one or more fractions in the numerator or denominator or both. Certain formulas used in simple interest and simple discount calculations result in complex fractions. When you encounter such fractions, take care to follow the order of operations properly.

EXAMPLE 1.2F

(i) $\frac{420}{1600 \times \frac{315}{360}} = \frac{420}{1600 \times 0.875} = \frac{420}{1400} = 0.3$

(ii) $\$500\left(1 + 0.16 \times \frac{225}{365}\right)$

$= \$500(1 + 0.098630)$ — multiply 0.16 by 225 and divide by 365

$= \$500(1.098630)$ — add inside bracket

$= \$549.32$

(iii) $\$1000\left(1 - 0.18 \times \frac{288}{365}\right) = \$1000(1 - 0.142027)$

$= \$1000(0.857973)$

$= \$857.97$

(iv) $\frac{\$824}{1 + 0.15 \times \frac{73}{365}} = \frac{\$824}{1 + 0.03} = \frac{\$824}{1.03} = \$800$

(v) $\frac{\$1755}{1 - 0.21 \times \frac{210}{365}} = \frac{\$1755}{1 - 0.120822} = \frac{\$1755}{0.879178} = \$1996.18$

Pointers and Pitfalls boxes emphasize good practices, highlight ways to avoid common errors, show how to use a financial calculator efficiently, or give hints for business math situations.

A calculator icon highlights information on the use of the Texas Instruments BAII Pluscalculator.

POINTERS AND PITFALLS

When using a calculator to compute business math formulas involving complicated denominators, consider using the reciprocal key ([1/x] or [x^{-1}]) to simplify calculations. Start by solving the denominator. Enter the fraction first, then multiply, change the sign, and add. Press the reciprocal key and multiply by the numerator. For example, to calculate part (v) of Example 1.2F above, the following calculator sequence would apply:

$$\frac{\$1755}{1 - 0.21 \times \frac{210}{365}}$$

210 [÷] 365 [×] 0.21 [±] [+] 1 [=] [1/x] [×] 1755 [=]

The result is $1996.18.

EXERCISE 1.2

EXCEL SPREADSHEET

An Excel Spreadsheet icon in the margin highlights a question that can be solved using one of the question-specific Excel spreadsheets on MathXL at www.mathxl.com.

A. Reduce each of the following fractions to lowest terms.

1. $\frac{24}{36}$ **2.** $\frac{28}{56}$ **3.** $\frac{210}{360}$ **4.** $\frac{330}{360}$

5. $\frac{360}{225}$ **6.** $\frac{360}{315}$ **7.** $\frac{144}{360}$ **8.** $\frac{360}{288}$

9. $\frac{25}{365}$ **10.** $\frac{115}{365}$ **11.** $\frac{365}{73}$ **12.** $\frac{365}{219}$

B. Convert each of the following fractions into decimal form. If appropriate, place a dot above a decimal number to show that it repeats.

1. $\frac{11}{8}$ **2.** $\frac{7}{4}$ **3.** $\frac{5}{3}$ **4.** $\frac{5}{6}$

5. $\frac{11}{6}$ **6.** $\frac{7}{9}$ **7.** $\frac{13}{12}$ **8.** $\frac{19}{15}$

C. Convert each of the following mixed numbers into decimal form.

1. $3\frac{3}{8}$ **2.** $3\frac{2}{5}$ **3.** $8\frac{1}{3}$ **4.** $16\frac{2}{3}$

5. $33\frac{1}{3}$ **6.** $83\frac{1}{3}$ **7.** $7\frac{7}{9}$ **8.** $7\frac{1}{12}$

D. Round each of the following to two decimal places.

1. 5.633 **2.** 17.449 **3.** 18.0046 **4.** 253.4856

5. 57.69875 **6.** 3.09475 **7.** 12.995 **8.** 39.999

E. Simplify each of the following.

1. $\frac{\$54}{0.12 \times \frac{225}{365}}$ **2.** $\frac{264}{4400 \times \frac{146}{365}}$

3. $\$620\left(1 + 0.14 \times \frac{45}{365}\right)$ **4.** $\$375\left(1 + 0.16 \times \frac{292}{365}\right)$

5. $\frac{\$250\,250}{1 + 0.15 \times \frac{330}{365}}$ **6.** $\frac{\$2358}{1 + 0.12 \times \frac{146}{365}}$

7. $1000\left[\frac{(1 + 0.03)^{24} - 1}{0.03}\right]$ **8.** $70(1 + 0.02)\left[\frac{(1 + 0.02)^{20} - 1}{0.02}\right]$

9. $1500 + \frac{1500}{0.05}$ **10.** $50\left[\frac{1 - (1 + 0.075)^{-8}}{0.075}\right]$

11. $25\,000(15 - 8) - 146\,000$ **12.** $(300 \times 8000) - (180 \times 8000) - 63\,000$

13. $1 - [(1 - 0.4)(1 - 0.25)(1 - 0.08)]$

14. $1 - [(1 - 0.32)(1 - 0.15)(1 - 0.12)]$

1.3 PERCENT

A. The meaning of percent

Fractions are used to compare the quantity represented by the numerator with the quantity represented by the denominator. The easiest method of comparing the two quantities is to use fractions with denominator 100. The preferred form of writing such fractions is the *percent* form. **Percent** means "per hundred," and the symbol % is used to show "parts of one hundred."

PERCENT means HUNDREDTHS

% means $\frac{}{100}$

Accordingly, any fraction involving "hundredths" may be written as follows:

(i) as a common fraction $\frac{13}{100}$

(ii) as a decimal 0.13

(iii) in percent form 13%

B. Changing percents to common fractions

When speaking or writing, we often use percents in the percent form. However, when computing with percents, we use the corresponding common fraction or decimal fraction. To convert a percent into a common fraction, replace the symbol % by the symbol $\frac{}{100}$. Then reduce the resulting fraction to lowest terms.

EXAMPLE 1.3A

(i) $24\% = \frac{24}{100}$ ——— replace % by $\frac{}{100}$

$= \frac{6}{25}$ ——— reduce to lowest terms

(ii) $175\% = \frac{175}{100} = \frac{7 \times 25}{4 \times 25} = \frac{7}{4}$

(iii) $6.25\% = \frac{6.25}{100}$

$= \frac{625}{10\,000}$ ——— multiply by 100 to change the numerator to a whole number

$= \frac{125}{2000} = \frac{25}{400} = \frac{5}{80}$ ——— reduce gradually or in one step

$= \frac{1}{16}$

(iv) $0.025\% = \frac{0.025}{100} = \frac{25}{100\,000} = \frac{1}{4000}$

(v) $\frac{1}{4}\% = \frac{\frac{1}{4}}{\frac{100}{1}}$ ——— replace % by $\frac{}{\frac{100}{1}}$

$= \frac{1}{4} \times \frac{1}{100}$ ——— invert and multiply

$= \frac{1}{400}$

(vi) $33\frac{1}{3}\% = \frac{33\frac{1}{3}}{100}$ ——— replace % by $\frac{}{100}$

$= \frac{\frac{100}{3}}{\frac{100}{1}}$ ——— convert the mixed number $33\frac{1}{3}$ into a common fraction

$= \frac{100}{3} \times \frac{1}{100} = \frac{100}{300}$

$= \frac{1}{3}$

(vii) $216\frac{2}{3}\% = \frac{216\frac{2}{3}}{100} = \frac{\frac{650}{3}}{\frac{100}{1}} = \frac{\overset{13}{\cancel{650}}}{3} \times \frac{1}{\underset{2}{\cancel{100}}} = \frac{13}{6}$

Alternatively

$216\frac{2}{3}\% = 200\% + 16\frac{2}{3}\%$ ——— separate the multiple of 100% (i.e., 200%) from the remainder

$= 2 + \frac{\frac{50}{3}}{\frac{100}{1}}$

$= 2 + \frac{50}{3} \times \frac{1}{100}$

$= 2 + \frac{1}{6}$

$= \frac{13}{6}$

C. Changing percents to decimals

Replacing the % symbol by $\frac{}{100}$ indicates a division by 100. Since division by 100 is performed by moving the decimal point *two places to the left*, changing a percent to a decimal is easy to do. Simply drop the % symbol and move the decimal point two places to the left.

EXAMPLE 1.3B

(i) 52% = 0.52 —— drop the percent symbol and move the decimal point two places to the left

(ii) 175% = 1.75

(iii) 6% = 0.06

(iv) 0.75% = 0.0075

(v) $\frac{1}{4}\% = 0.25\%$ —— first change the fraction to a decimal

$= 0.0025$ —— drop the percent symbol and move the decimal point two places to the left

(vi) $\frac{1}{3}\% = 0.\dot{3}\%$ —— change the fraction to a repeating decimal

$= 0.00\dot{3}$ —— drop the percent symbol and move the decimal point two places to the left

D. Changing decimals to percents

Changing decimals to percents is the inverse operation of changing percents into decimals. It is accomplished by multiplying the decimal by 100. Since multiplication by 100 is performed by moving the decimal point *two places to the right*, a decimal is easily changed to a percent. Move the decimal point two places to the right and add the % symbol.

EXAMPLE 1.3C

(i) 0.36 = 0.36(100)%
= 36% —— move the decimal point two places to the right and add the % symbol

(ii) 1.65 = 165%

(iii) 0.075 = 7.5%

(iv) 0.4 = 40%

(v) 0.001 = 0.1%

(vi) 2 = 200%

(vii) 0.0005 = 0.05%

(viii) $0.\dot{3} = 33.\dot{3}\%$

(ix) $1.1\dot{6} = 116.\dot{6}\%$

(x) $1\frac{5}{6} = 1.8\dot{3} = 183.\dot{3}\%$

E. Changing fractions to percents

When changing a fraction to a percent, it is best to convert the fraction to a decimal and then to change the decimal to a percent.

EXAMPLE 1.3D

(i) $\frac{1}{4} = 0.25$ —— convert the fraction to a decimal

$= 25\%$ —— convert the decimal to a percent

(ii) $\frac{7}{8} = 0.875 = 87.5\%$ (iii) $\frac{9}{5} = 1.8 = 180\%$

(iv) $\frac{5}{6} = 0.8\dot{3} = 83.\dot{3}\%$ (v) $\frac{5}{9} = 0.\dot{5} = 55.\dot{5}\%$

(vi) $1\frac{2}{3} = 1.\dot{6} = 166.\dot{6}\%$

POINTERS AND PITFALLS

There is a foolproof method of determining the lowest common denominator (LCD) for a given group of fractions:

STEP 1 Divide the given denominators by integers of 2 or greater until they are all reduced to 1. Make sure the integer divides into at least one of the denominators evenly.

STEP 2 Multiply all of the resultant integers (divisors) to find the LCD.

To illustrate, find the LCD for (i) $\frac{4}{5}, \frac{7}{9}, \frac{5}{6}$

(ii) $\frac{3}{4}, \frac{2}{3}, \frac{13}{22}, \frac{11}{15}$

Solution: (i)

	5	9	6	← denominators
÷ 2 =	5	9	3	← 2 divides into 6 evenly
÷ 3 =	5	3	1	← 3 divides into 9 and 3 evenly
÷ 3 =	5	1	1	← 3 divides into 3 evenly
÷ 5 =	1	1	1	← 5 divides into 5 evenly

$\text{LCD} = 2 \times 3 \times 3 \times 5 = 90$

(ii)

	4	3	22	15
÷ 2 =	2	3	11	15
÷ 2 =	1	3	11	15
÷ 3 =	1	1	11	5
÷ 5 =	1	1	11	1
÷ 11 =	1	1	1	1

$\text{LCD} = 2 \times 2 \times 3 \times 5 \times 11 = 660$

EXERCISE 1.3

A. Change each of the following percents into a decimal.

1. 64% **2.** 300% **3.** 2.5% **4.** 0.1% **5.** 0.5%

6. 85% **7.** 250% **8.** 4.8% **9.** 7.5% **10.** 0.9%

11. 6.25% **12.** 99% **13.** 225% **14.** 0.05% **15.** $8\frac{1}{4}\%$

16. $\frac{1}{2}\%$ **17.** $112\frac{1}{2}\%$ **18.** $9\frac{3}{8}\%$ **19.** $\frac{3}{4}\%$ **20.** $162\frac{1}{2}\%$

21. $\frac{2}{5}\%$ **22.** $\frac{1}{4}\%$ **23.** $\frac{1}{40}\%$ **24.** $137\frac{1}{2}\%$ **25.** $\frac{5}{8}\%$

26. 0.875% **27.** $2\frac{1}{4}\%$ **28.** $16\frac{2}{3}\%$ **29.** $116\frac{2}{3}\%$ **30.** $183\frac{1}{3}\%$

31. $83\frac{1}{3}\%$ **32.** $66\frac{2}{3}\%$

B. Change each of the following percents into a common fraction in lowest terms.

1. 25% **2.** $62\frac{1}{2}\%$ **3.** 175% **4.** 5% **5.** $37\frac{1}{2}\%$

6. 75% **7.** 4% **8.** 8% **9.** 40% **10.** $87\frac{1}{2}\%$

11. 250% **12.** 2% **13.** $12\frac{1}{2}\%$ **14.** 60% **15.** 2.25%

16. 0.5% **17.** $\frac{1}{8}\%$ **18.** $33\frac{1}{3}\%$ **19.** $\frac{3}{4}\%$ **20.** $66\frac{2}{3}\%$

21. 6.25% **22.** 0.25% **23.** $16\frac{2}{3}\%$ **24.** 7.5% **25.** 0.75%

26. $\frac{7}{8}\%$ **27.** 0.1% **28.** $\frac{3}{5}\%$ **29.** 2.5% **30.** $133\frac{1}{3}\%$

31. $183\frac{1}{3}\%$ **32.** $166\frac{2}{3}\%$

C. Express each of the following as a percent.

1. 3.5 **2.** 0.075 **3.** 0.005 **4.** 0.375 **5.** 0.025

6. 2 **7.** 0.125 **8.** 0.001 **9.** 0.225 **10.** 0.008

11. 1.45 **12.** 0.0225 **13.** 0.0025 **14.** 0.995 **15.** 0.09

16. 3 **17.** $\frac{3}{4}$ **18.** $\frac{3}{25}$ **19.** $\frac{5}{3}$ **20.** $\frac{7}{200}$

21. $\frac{9}{200}$ **22.** $\frac{5}{8}$ **23.** $\frac{3}{400}$ **24.** $\frac{5}{6}$ **25.** $\frac{9}{800}$

26. $\frac{7}{6}$ **27.** $\frac{3}{8}$ **28.** $\frac{11}{40}$ **29.** $\frac{4}{3}$ **30.** $\frac{9}{400}$

31. $\frac{13}{20}$ **32.** $\frac{4}{5}$

1.4 APPLICATIONS—AVERAGES

A. Basic problems

When calculators are used, the number of decimal places used for intermediate values often determines the accuracy of the final answer. To avoid introducing rounding errors, keep intermediate values unrounded.

EXAMPLE 1.4A A coffee company received 36 ¾ kilograms of coffee beans at $240 per kilogram. Sales for the following five days were:

3⅝ kilograms, 4¾ kilograms, 7⅔ kilograms, 5½ kilograms, and 6⅜ kilograms.

What was the value of inventory at the end of Day 5?

SOLUTION

$$\begin{aligned}
\text{Total sales (in kilograms)} &= 3\tfrac{5}{8} + 4\tfrac{3}{4} + 7\tfrac{2}{3} + 5\tfrac{1}{2} + 6\tfrac{3}{8} \\
&= 3.625 + 4.75 + 7.\dot{6} + 5.5 + 6.375 \\
&= 27.91\dot{6} \\
\text{Inventory (in kilograms)} &= 36\tfrac{3}{4} - 27.91\dot{6} = 36.75 - 27.91\dot{6} = 8.8\dot{3} \\
\text{Value of inventory} &= 8.8\dot{3} \times 240 = \$2120.00
\end{aligned}$$

EXAMPLE 1.4B

Complete the following excerpt from an invoice.

Quantity	Unit Price	Amount
72	\$0.875	\$______
45	$66\frac{2}{3}$¢	______
54	$83\frac{1}{3}$¢	______
42	$\$1.3\dot{3}$	______
32	\$1.375	______
	Total	\$______

SOLUTION

$$
\begin{aligned}
72 \times \$0.875 &= & \$\ 63.00 \\
45 \times 66\tfrac{2}{3}¢ &= 45 \times \$0.\dot{6} & \\
&= 45 \times \$0.666667 = & \$\ 30.00 \\
54 \times 83\tfrac{1}{3}¢ &= 54 \times \$0.8\dot{3} & \\
&= 54 \times \$0.833333 = & \$\ 45.00 \\
42 \times \$1.3\dot{3} &= 42 \times \$1.\dot{3} \quad = & \$\ 56.00 \\
32 \times \$1.375 &= & \$\ 44.00 \\
& \text{TOTAL} & \$238.00
\end{aligned}
$$

POINTERS AND PITFALLS

The display on the calculator shows a limited number of decimal places, depending on how the calculator is formatted. By choosing the format function, you can change the setting to show a different number of decimal places. In continuous calculations, the calculator uses unrounded numbers.

To format the calculator to six decimal places:

[2nd] [Format] DEC = 6 [Enter] [2nd] [QUIT]

B. Problems involving simple arithmetic average

The **arithmetic average** or **mean** of a set of values is a widely used average found by adding the values in the set and dividing by the number of those values.

EXAMPLE 1.4C

The marks obtained by Byung Kang for the seven tests that make up Section 1 of his Mathematics of Finance course were 82, 68, 88, 72, 78, 96, and 83.

(i) If all tests count equally, what was his average mark for Section 1?

(ii) If his marks for Section 2 and Section 3 of the course were 72.4 and 68.9 respectively and all section marks have equal value, what was his course average?

SOLUTION

(i) $\text{Section average} = \dfrac{\text{Sum of the test marks for the section}}{\text{Number of tests}}$

$= \dfrac{82 + 68 + 88 + 72 + 78 + 96 + 83}{7}$

$= \dfrac{567}{7}$

$= 81.0$

(ii) $\text{Course average} = \dfrac{\text{Sum of the section marks}}{\text{Number of sections}}$

$= \dfrac{81.0 + 72.4 + 68.9}{3}$

$= \dfrac{222.3}{3}$

$= 74.1$

EXAMPLE 1.4D

Monthly sales of Sheridan Service for last year were:

January	$13 200	July	$13 700
February	11 400	August	12 800
March	14 600	September	13 800
April	13 100	October	15 300
May	13 600	November	14 400
June	14 300	December	13 900

What were Sheridan's average monthly sales for the year?

SOLUTION

Total sales = $164 100

$$\text{Average monthly sales} = \frac{\text{Total sales}}{\text{Number of months}} = \frac{\$164\,100}{12} = \$13\,675$$

POINTERS AND PITFALLS

Instead of trying to remember the numbers that you have calculated, you may store them in the calculator. After a calculation has been performed, the unrounded number can be stored and later recalled. The TI BAII Plus has the capability of storing 10 different numbers. To perform a calculation, store, and recall the results, follow the steps below:

To calculate $\frac{1}{3} + \frac{1}{7}$:

1 [÷] 3 [=] Result will show 0.333333 (when set to six decimal places)

To store the results: press [STO] 1

1 [÷] 7 [=] Result will show 0.142857 (when set to six decimal places)

To store the results: press [STO] 2

To recall the results, and to add them together:

[RCL] 1 [+] [RCL] 2 [=] Result will show 0.476190 (rounded to six decimal places)

C. Weighted average

If the items to be included in computing an arithmetic mean are arranged in groups or if the items are not equally important, a **weighted arithmetic average** should be obtained. Multiply each item by the numbers involved or by a weighting factor representing its importance.

EXAMPLE 1.4E

During last season, Fairfield Farms sold strawberries as follows: 800 boxes at \$1.25 per box in the early part of the season; 1600 boxes at \$0.90 per box and 2000 boxes at \$0.75 per box at the height of the season; and 600 boxes at \$1.10 per box during the late season.

(i) What was the average price charged?

(ii) What was the average price per box?

SOLUTION

(i) The average price charged is a simple average of the four different prices charged during the season.

$$\text{Average price} = \frac{1.25 + 0.90 + 0.75 + 1.10}{4} = \frac{4.00}{4} = \$1.00$$

(ii) To obtain the average price per box, the number of boxes sold at each price must be taken into account; that is, a weighted average must be computed.

800 boxes @ \$1.25 per box		⟶	\$1000.00
1600 boxes @ \$0.90 per box		⟶	1440.00
2000 boxes @ \$0.75 per box		⟶	1500.00
600 boxes @ \$1.10 per box		⟶	660.00
5000 boxes	⟵ TOTALS	⟶	\$4600.00

$$\text{Average price per box} = \frac{\text{Total value}}{\text{Number of boxes}} = \frac{\$4600.00}{5000} = \$0.92$$

EXAMPLE 1.4F

The specialty tea shop creates its house brand by mixing 13 kilograms of tea priced at \$7.50 per kilogram, 16 kilograms of tea priced at \$6.25 per kilogram, and 11 kilograms of tea priced at \$5.50 per kilogram. At what price should the store sell its house blend to realize the same revenue it could make by selling the three types of tea separately?

SOLUTION

13 kg @ \$7.50 per kg		⟶	\$ 97.50
16 kg @ \$6.25 per kg		⟶	100.00
11 kg @ \$5.50 per kg		⟶	60.50
40 kg	⟵ TOTALS	⟶	\$258.00

$$\text{Average value} \frac{\text{Total value}}{\text{Number of units}} = \frac{\$258.00}{40} = \$6.45$$

The house blend should sell for \$6.45 per kilogram.

EXAMPLE 1.4G

The credit hours and grades for Dana's first-term courses are listed here.

Course	Credit Hours	Grade
Accounting	5	A
Economics	3	B
English	4	C
Law	2	D
Marketing	4	A
Mathematics	3	A
Elective	2	D

According to the grading system, A's, B's, C's, and D's are worth 4, 3, 2, and 1 grade points respectively. On the basis of this information, determine

(i) Dana's average course grade;

(ii) Dana's grade-point average (average per credit hour).

SOLUTION

(i) The average course grade is the average grade points obtained:

$$\frac{4+3+2+1+4+4+1}{7} = \frac{19}{7} = 2.71$$

(ii) The average course grade obtained in part (i) is misleading since the credit hours of the courses are not equal. The grade-point average is a more appropriate average because it is a weighted average allowing for the number of credit hours per course.

Course	Credit Hours	×	Grade Points	=	Weighted Points
Accounting	5	×	4	=	20
Economics	3	×	3	=	9
English	4	×	2	=	8
Law	2	×	1	=	2
Marketing	4	×	4	=	16
Mathematics	3	×	4	=	12
Elective	2	×	1	=	2
	23 ←		Totals	→	69

$$\text{Grade-point average} = \frac{\text{Total weighted points}}{\text{Total credit hours}} = \frac{69}{23} = 3.00$$

EXAMPLE 1.4H

A partnership agreement provides for the distribution of the yearly profit or loss on the basis of the partners' average monthly investment balance. The investment account of one of the partners shows the following entries:

Balance, January 1	$25 750
April 1, withdrawal	3 250
June 1, investment	4 000
November 1, investment	2 000

Determine the partner's average monthly balance in the investment account.

SOLUTION

To determine the average monthly investment, determine the balance in the investment account after each change and weight this balance by the number of months invested.

Date	Change	Balance	×	Invested	=	Value
January 1		25 750	×	3	=	77 250
April 1	−3250	22 500	×	2	=	45 000
June 1	+4000	26 500	×	5	=	132 500
November 1	+2000	28 500	×	2	=	57 000
		Totals		12		311 750

$$\text{Average monthly investment} = \frac{\text{Total weighted value}}{\text{Number of months}} = \frac{\$311\ 750}{12} = \$25\ 979.17$$

EXAMPLE 1.41

Several shoe stores in the city carry the same make of shoes. The number of pairs of shoes sold and the price charged by each store are shown below.

Store	Number of Pairs Sold	Price per Pair ($)
A	60	43.10
B	84	38.00
C	108	32.00
D	72	40.50

(i) What was the average number of pairs of shoes sold per store?

(ii) What was the average price per store?

(iii) What was the average sales revenue per store?

(iv) What was the average price per pair of shoes?

SOLUTION

(i) The average number of pairs of shoes sold per store

$$= \frac{60 + 84 + 108 + 72}{4} = \frac{324}{4} = 81$$

(ii) The average price per store

$$= \frac{43.10 + 38.00 + 32.00 + 40.50}{4} = \frac{153.60}{4} = \$38.40$$

(iii) The average sales revenue per store

$$\begin{aligned} 60 \times 43.10 &= \$\ 2\ 586.00 \\ 84 \times 38.00 &= \ 3\ 192.00 \\ 108 \times 32.00 &= \ 3\ 456.00 \\ 72 \times 40.50 &= \ 2\ 916.00 \\ &\ \$12\ 150.00 \end{aligned}$$

$$\text{Average} = \frac{\$12\ 150.00}{4} = \$3037.50$$

(iv) The average price per pair of shoes

$$= \frac{\text{Total sales revenue}}{\text{Total pairs sold}} = \frac{\$12\,150.00}{324} = \$37.50$$

EXERCISE 1.4

Answer each of the following questions.

1. Rae sold four pieces of gold when the price was $1125 per ounce. If the pieces weighed, in ounces, $1\frac{1}{3}$, $2\frac{3}{4}$, $1\frac{5}{8}$, and $3\frac{5}{6}$ respectively, what was the total selling value of the four pieces?

2. Five carpenters worked $15\frac{1}{2}$, $13\frac{3}{4}$, $18\frac{1}{2}$, $21\frac{1}{4}$, and $22\frac{3}{4}$ hours respectively. What was the total cost of labour if the carpenters were each paid $12.75 per hour?

3. A piece of property valued at $56 100 is assessed for property tax purposes at $\frac{6}{11}$ of its value. If the property tax rate is $3.75 on each $100 of assessed value, what is the amount of tax levied on the property?

4. A retailer returned 2700 defective items to the manufacturer and received a credit for the retail price of $\$0.8\dot{3}$ or $83\frac{1}{3}$¢ per item less a discount of $\frac{3}{8}$ of the retail price. What was the amount of the credit received by the retailer?

5. Extend the following invoice.

Quantity	Description	Unit Price	$
64	A	$0.75	______
54	B	$83\frac{1}{3}$¢	______
72	C	$0.375	______
42	D	$\$1.3\dot{3}$	______
		Total	______

6. Complete the following inventory sheet.

Item	Quantity	Cost per Unit	Total
1	96	$0.875	______
2	330	$16\frac{2}{3}$¢	______
3	144	$1.75	______
4	240	$\$1.6\dot{6}$	______
		Total	______

An Excel Notes icon highlights information on the use of Excel to solve problems, and directs you to a tutorial or an Excel spreadsheet template on MathXL at **www.mathxl.com**.

EXCEL NOTES

Excel provides the Simple Arithmetic Average (AVERAGE) function to calculate the average of a group of numbers. Refer to AVERAGE on MathXL to learn how to use this Excel function.

B. Solve each of the following problems involving an arithmetic average.

1. Records of Montes Service's fuel oil consumption for the last six-month period show that Montes paid 38.5 cents per litre for the first 1100 litres, 41.5 cents per litre for the next 1600 litres, and 42.5 cents per litre for the last delivery of 1400 litres. Determine the average cost of fuel oil per litre for the six-month period.
2. On a trip, a motorist purchased gasoline as follows: 56 litres at $0.99 per litre; 64 litres at $1.065 cents per litre; 70 litres at $1.015 cents per litre; and 54 litres at $1.045 cents per litre.

EXCEL SPREADSHEET

   (a) What was the average number of litres per purchase?
   (b) What was the average cost per litre?
   (c) If the motorist averaged 8.75 km per litre, what was the average cost of gasoline per kilometre?
3. The course credit hours and grades for Bill's fall semester are given below. At his college, an A is worth six grade points, a B four points, a C two points, and a D one point.

Credit hours:	3	5	2	4	4	2
Grade:	B	C	A	C	D	A

   What is Bill's grade-point average?
4. Kim Blair invested $7500 in a business on January 1. She withdrew $900 on March 1, reinvested $1500 on August 1, and withdrew $300 on September 1. What is Kim's average monthly investment balance for the year?
5. Neuer started a systematic investment program by buying $200.00 worth of mutual funds on the first day of every month starting on February 1. When you purchase mutual funds, you purchase units in the fund. Neuer purchased as many units as he could with his $200.00, including fractions of units. Unit prices for the first six months were $10.00, $10.60, $11.25, $9.50, $9.20, and $12.15 respectively.
   (a) What is the simple average of the unit prices?

EXCEL SPREADSHEET

   (b) What is the total number of units purchased during the first six months (correct to three decimals)?
   (c) What is the average cost of the units purchased?
   (d) What is the value of Neuer's mutual fund holdings on July 31 if the unit price on that date is $11.90?

1.5 APPLICATIONS—PAYROLL

Employees can be remunerated for their services in a variety of ways. The main methods of remuneration are salaries, hourly wage rates, and commission. While the computations involved in preparing a payroll are fairly simple, utmost care is needed to ensure that all calculations are accurate.

A. Salaries

Compensation of employees by **salary** is usually on a monthly or a yearly basis. Monthly salaried personnel get paid either monthly or semi-monthly. Personnel on a yearly salary basis may get paid monthly, semi-monthly, every two weeks, weekly, or according to special schedules such as those used by some boards of education to pay their teachers. If salary is paid weekly or every two weeks, the year is assumed to consist of exactly 52 weeks.

Calculations of **gross earnings** per pay period is fairly simple. Computing overtime for salaried personnel can be problematic since overtime is usually paid on an hourly basis.

EXAMPLE 1.5A

An employee with an annual salary of $23 296 is paid every two weeks. The regular workweek is 40 hours.

(i) What is the gross pay per pay period?

(ii) What is the hourly rate of pay?

(iii) What are the gross earnings for a pay period in which the employee worked six hours of overtime and is paid one-and-a-half times the regular hourly rate of pay?

SOLUTION

(i) An employee paid every two weeks receives the annual salary over 26 pay periods.

$$\text{Gross pay per two-week period} = \frac{23\,296.00}{26} = \$896.00$$

(ii) Given a 40-hour week, the employee's compensation for two weeks covers 80 hours.

$$\text{Hourly rate of pay} = \frac{896.00}{80} = \$\ 11.20$$

(iii) Regular gross earnings for two-week period $896.00

Overtime pay

6 hours @ $11.20 × 1.5 = 6 × 11.20 × 1.5 = 100.80

Total gross earnings for pay period $996.80

EXAMPLE 1.5B

Mike Paciuc receives a monthly salary of $2080 paid semi-monthly. Mike's regular workweek is 37.5 hours. Any hours worked over 37.5 hours in a week are overtime and are paid at time-and-a-half regular pay. During the first half of October, Mike worked 7.5 hours overtime.

(i) What is Mike's hourly rate of pay?

(ii) What are his gross earnings for the pay period ending October 15?

SOLUTION

(i) When computing the hourly rate of pay for personnel employed on a monthly salary basis, the correct approach requires that the yearly salary be determined first. The hourly rate of pay may then be computed on the basis of 52 weeks per year.

$$\text{Yearly gross earnings} = 2080.00 \times 12 = \$24\,960.00$$

$$\text{Weekly gross earnings} = \frac{24\,960.00}{52} = \$480.00$$

$$\text{Hourly rate of pay} = \frac{480.00}{37.5} = \$12.80$$

(ii) Regular semi-monthly gross earnings $= \frac{2080.00}{2} = \$1040.00$

Overtime pay $= 7.5 \times 12.80 \times 1.5 =$ 144.00

Total gross earnings for pay period $1184.00

EXAMPLE 1.5C

Teachers with the Northern Manitoba Board of Education are under contract for 200 teaching days per year. They are paid according to the following schedule:

8% of annual salary on the first day of school
4% of annual salary for each of 20 two-week pay periods
12% of annual salary at the end of the last pay period in June

Alicia Nowak, a teacher employed by the board, is paid an annual salary of $65 200.

(i) What is Alicia's daily rate of pay?

(ii) What is Alicia's gross pay
  (a) for the first pay period?
  (b) for the last pay period?
  (c) for all other pay periods?

(iii) If Alicia takes an unpaid leave of absence for three days during a pay period ending in April, what is her gross pay for that pay period?

SOLUTION

(i) Daily rate of pay $= \frac{65\ 200}{200} = \$326.00$

(ii) (a) First gross pay $= 0.08 \times 65\ 200.00 = \$5216.00$
  (b) Last gross pay $= 0.12 \times 65\ 200.00 = \$7824.00$
  (c) All other gross pay $= 0.04 \times 65\ 200.00 = \$2608.00$

(iii) Gross pay for pay period ending in April = $2608.00
  Less 3 days of pay $= \frac{3}{200}$ of $65 200.00 = 978.00
  Gross pay $1630.00

B. Commission

Persons engaged in the buying and selling functions of a business are often compensated by a **commission.** Of the various types of commission designed to meet the specific circumstances of a particular business, the most commonly encountered are straight commission, graduated (or sliding-scale) commission, and base salary plus commission.

Straight commission is usually calculated as a percent of net sales for a given time period. **Net sales** are the difference between the gross sales for the time period and any sales returns and allowances, or sales discounts.

Graduated commission usually involves paying an increasing percent for increasing sales levels during a given time period.

Salary plus commission is a method that guarantees a minimum income per pay period to the salesperson. However, the rate of commission in such cases is either at a lower rate or is not paid until a minimum sales level (called a **quota**) for a time period has been reached.

Sales personnel on commission often have a drawing account with their employer. The salesperson may withdraw funds from such an account in advance to meet business and personal expenses. However, any money advanced is deducted from the commission earned when the salesperson is paid.

EXAMPLE 1.5D

Javier receives a commission of 11.5% on his net sales and is entitled to drawings of up to $1500 per month. During August, Javier's gross sales amounted to $25 540 and sales returns and allowances were $360.

(i) What are Javier's net sales for August?

(ii) How much is his commission for August?

(iii) If Javier drew $1400 in August, what is the amount due to him?

SOLUTION

(i)	Gross sales	$25 540.00
	Less sales returns and allowances	360.00
	Net sales	$25 180.00

(ii) Commission = 11.5% of net sales
= 0.115 × 25 180.00
= $2895.70

(iii)	Gross commission earned	$2895.70
	Less drawings	1400.00
	Amount due	$1495.70

EXAMPLE 1.5E

Valerie works as a salesperson for the local Minutemen Press. She receives a commission of 7.5% on monthly sales up to $8000, 9.25% on the next $7000, and 11% on any additional sales during the month. If Valerie's September sales amounted to $18 750, what is her gross commission for the month?

SOLUTION

Commission on the first $8000.00 = 0.075 × 8000.00 =	$ 600.00
Commission on the next $7000.00 = 0.0925 × 7000.00 =	647.50
Commission on sales over $15 000.00 = 0.11 × 3750.00 =	412.50
Total commission for September	$1660.00

EXAMPLE 1.5F

Ana is employed as a salesclerk in a fabric store. She receives a weekly salary of $575 plus a commission of 6¼% on all weekly sales over the weekly sales quota of $5000. Derek works in the shoe store located next door. He receives a minimum of $500 per week or a commission of 12.5% on all sales for the week, whichever is the greater. If both Ana and Derek had sales of $5960 last week, how much compensation did each receive for the week?

SOLUTION

Ana's compensation

Base salary	$575.00
Plus commission = 6¼% on sales over $5000.00	
= 0.0625 × 960.00	60.00
Total compensation	$635.00

Derek's compensation

Minimum weekly pay	$500.00
Commission = 12.5% of $5960.00 = 0.125 × 5960.00 =	$745.00

Since the commission is greater than the guaranteed minimum pay of $500, Derek's compensation is $745.

C. Wages

The term **wages** usually applies to compensation paid to *hourly* rated employees. Their gross earnings are calculated by multiplying the number of hours worked by the hourly rate of pay plus any overtime pay. Overtime is most often paid at time-and-a-half the regular hourly rate for any hours exceeding an established number of regular hours per week or per day. The number of regular hours is often established by agreement between the employer and employees. The most common regular workweek is 40 hours. If no agreement exists, federal or provincial employment standards legislation provides for a maximum number of hours per week, such as 44 hours for most employers. Any hours over the set maximum must be paid at least at time-and-a-half of the regular hourly rate.

When overtime is involved, gross earnings can be calculated by either of two methods.

Method A

The most common method, and the easiest for the wage earner to understand, determines total gross earnings by adding overtime pay to the gross pay for a regular workweek.

Method B

In the second method, the overtime excess (or **overtime premium**) is computed separately and added to gross earnings for all hours (including the overtime hours) at the regular rate of pay. Computation of the excess labour cost due to overtime emphasizes the additional expense due to overtime and provides management with information that is useful for cost control.

EXAMPLE 1.5G

Mario is a machinist with Scott Tool and Die and is paid $14.40 per hour. The regular workweek is 40 hours and overtime is paid at time-and-a-half the regular hourly rate. If Mario worked 46½ hours last week, what were his gross earnings?

SOLUTION

Method A

Gross earnings for a regular workweek = 40 × 14.40 = \$576.00
Overtime pay = 6.5 × 14.40 × 1.5 = 140.40
Gross pay \$716.40

Method B

Earnings at the regular hourly rate = 46.5 × 14.40 = \$669.60
Overtime premium = $6.5 \times \left(\frac{1}{2} \text{ of } 14.40\right)$ = 6.5 × 7.20 = 46.80
Gross pay \$716.40

EXAMPLE 1.5H

Hasmig works for \$8.44 per hour under a union contract that provides for daily overtime for all hours worked over eight hours. Overtime includes hours worked on Saturdays and is paid at time-and-a-half of the regular rate of pay. Hours worked on Sundays or holidays are paid at double the regular rate of pay. Use both methods to determine Hasmig's gross earnings for a week in which she worked the following hours:

Monday	9 hours	Tuesday	10½ hours
Wednesday	7 hours	Thursday	9½ hours
Friday	8 hours	Saturday	6 hours
Sunday	6 hours		

Day	Mon	Tue	Wed	Thu	Fri	Sat	Sun	Total
Regular hours	8	8	7	8	8			39
Overtime at time-and-a-half	1	2.5		1.5		6		11
Overtime at double time							6	6
Total hours worked	9	10.5	7	9.5	8	6	6	56

SOLUTION

Method A

Gross earnings for regular hours = 39 × 8.44 = \$329.16
Overtime pay
at time-and-a-half = 11 × 8.44 × 1.5 = \$139.26
at double time = 6 × 8.44 × 2 = 101.28 240.54
Total gross pay \$569.70

Method B

Earnings at regular hourly rate = 56 × 8.44 = \$472.64
Overtime pay
at time-and-a-half = $11\left(\frac{1}{2} \text{ of } \$8.44\right)$
= 11 × 4.22 = \$46.42
at double time = 6 × 8.44 = 50.64 97.06
Total gross pay \$569.70

EXERCISE 1.5

Answer each of the following questions.

1. R. Burton is employed at an annual salary of $31 824 paid semi-monthly. The regular workweek is 36 hours.
   (a) What is the regular salary per pay period?
   (b) What is the hourly rate of pay?
   (c) What is the gross pay for a pay period in which the employee worked 11 hours overtime at time-and-a-half of regular pay?
2. C. Bernal receives a yearly salary of $23 868.00. She is paid bi-weekly and her regular workweek is 37.5 hours.
   (a) What is the gross pay per pay period?
   (b) What is the hourly rate of pay?
   (c) What is the gross pay for a pay period in which she works 8½ hours overtime at time-and-a-half regular pay?
3. Carole is paid a monthly salary of $1101.10. Her regular workweek is 35 hours.
   (a) What is Carole's hourly rate of pay?
   (b) What is Carole's gross pay for May if she worked 7¾ hours overtime during the month at time-and-a-half regular pay?
4. Dimitri receives a semi-monthly salary of $863.20 and works a regular workweek of 40 hours.
   (a) What is Dimitri's hourly rate of pay?
   (b) If Dimitri's gross earnings in one pay period were $990.19, for how many hours of overtime was he paid at time-and-a-half regular pay?
5. An employee of a Board of Education is paid an annual salary in 22 biweekly payments of $1123.00 each. If the employee is under contract for 200 workdays of 7½ hours each,
   (a) what is the hourly rate of pay?
   (b) what is the gross pay for a pay period in which the employee was away for two days at no pay?
6. Geraldine Moog is paid a commission of 9¾% on her net sales and is authorized to draw up to $800 a month. What is the amount due to Geraldine at the end of a month in which she drew $720, had gross sales of $12 660, and sales returns of $131.20?
7. What is a salesperson's commission on net sales of $16 244 if the commission is paid on a sliding scale of 8¼% on the first $6000, 9¾% on the next $6000, and 11.5% on any additional net sales?
8. A sales representative selling auto parts receives a commission of 4.5% on net sales up to $10 000, 6% on the next $5000, and 8% on any further sales. If his gross sales for a month were $24 250 and sales returns were $855, what was his commission for the month?
9. A salesclerk at a local boutique receives a weekly base salary of $825 on a quota of $8500 per week plus a commission of 6½% on sales exceeding the quota.
   (a) What are the gross earnings for a week if sales are $8125?
   (b) What are the gross earnings for a week if sales amount to $10 150?

10. Sandra, working in sales at a clothing store, is paid a weekly salary of $400 or a commission of 6.5% of her sales, whichever is greater. What is her salary for a week in which her sales were
    (a) $5830?
    (b) $8830?

11. Manny's commission was $1590.90 on gross sales of $31 240.00. If returns and allowances were 3% of gross sales, what is his rate of commission based on net sales?

12. For last week, Tony's gross earnings were $466.25. He earns a base salary of $350 on a weekly quota of $5000. If his sales for the week were $6550, what is his commission rate?

13. Wilson's commission for March was $2036.88. If his rate of commission is 11.25% of net sales, and returns and allowances were 8% of gross sales, what were Wilson's gross sales for the month?

14. Debra had gross earnings of $637.50 for the week. If she receives a base salary of $464 on a quota of $4800 and a commission of 8.75% on sales exceeding the quota, what were Debra's sales for the week?

15. Chandra's hourly rate of pay is $11.58. The regular workweek is 40 hours and overtime is paid at time-and-a-half regular pay. Using the two methods illustrated in the chapter, compute Chandra's gross earnings for a week in which he worked 47 hours.

16. Kim earns $12.60 per hour. Overtime for the first five days in a week worked is paid at time-and-a-half pay for hours worked greater than 8 in a day. If more than five days are worked in a week, those hours are paid at double the regular rate of pay. Last week, for each day, Kim worked 8 hours, 9 hours, 8 hours, 10½ hours, 8 hours, and 6 hours. Determine Kim's gross wages by each of the two methods.

17. An employee of a repair shop receives a gross pay of $451.44 for a regular workweek of 44 hours. What is the hourly rate of pay?

18. Mario's wage statement showed 45 hours of work, resulting in $537.70 in gross earnings. What is the hourly rate of pay if the regular workweek is 40 hours and overtime is paid at time-and-a-half the regular rate of pay?

1.6 APPLICATIONS—TAXES

A **tax** is a fee charged on sales, services, property, or income by a government to pay for services provided by the government. As consumers, we encounter the **provincial sales tax (PST)**, the **goods and services tax (GST)**, or the **harmonized sales tax (HST)**. As homeowners, we encounter property taxes, and as employees and workers, we encounter income taxes. All of these taxes are expressed as a percent of the amount to be taxed. PST, GST, and HST are expressed as a percent of the value of the items or services purchased. Property taxes are determined by a percent of the value of the property. These two types of taxes are discussed in this chapter. Income taxes are also based on percent calculations, and are discussed in Chapter 3.

A. Sales and service taxes

1. Goods and Services Tax (GST)

The goods and services tax (GST) is a federal tax charged on the cost of almost all goods and services. Businesses and organizations carrying out commercial activities in Canada must register with the Canada Revenue Agency (CRA) for the purpose of collecting the GST if their annual revenue from GST-taxable goods and services exceeds \$30 000. Below that level of revenue, registration is optional.

Effective January 1, 2008, GST-taxable goods and services are taxed at 5%. Registered businesses and organizations will charge the 5% GST on taxable sales of goods and services to their customers, and they pay the 5% GST on their business purchases. Depending on the volume of taxable sales, a GST return must be submitted by each registrant to the CRA at selected intervals (monthly, quarterly, annually), showing the amount of tax collected and the amount of tax paid. If the amount of GST collected is more than the amount of GST paid, the difference must be remitted to the CRA. If the amount of GST collected is less than the amount of GST paid, a refund can be claimed. (While most consumers do not have this option, the government has provided GST rebate cheques to Canadians with earnings below a particular annual income level.)

EXAMPLE 1.6A

Suppose you had your car repaired at your local Canadian Tire repair shop. Parts amounted to \$165.00 and labour to \$246. Since both parts and labour are GST-taxable, what is the amount of GST that Canadian Tire must collect from you?

SOLUTION

The GST-taxable amount = \$165.00 + \$246.00 = \$411.00
GST = 5% of \$411.00 = 0.05(\$411.00) = \$20.55
Canadian Tire must collect GST of \$20.55.

EXAMPLE 1.6B

Canadian Colour Company (CCC) purchased GST-taxable supplies from Kodak Canada worth \$35 000 during 2008. CCC used these supplies to provide prints for its customers. CCC's total GST-taxable sales for the year were \$50 000. How much tax must CCC remit to the Canada Revenue Agency?

SOLUTION

GST collected = 0.05(\$50 000) = \$2500
GST paid = 0.05(\$35 000) = \$1750
GST payable = \$2500 − \$1750 = \$750

2. Provincial Sales Tax (PST)

The provincial sales tax (PST) is a provincial tax imposed by certain provinces on the price of most goods. In Manitoba and Saskatchewan, the PST is applied as a percent of the retail price, in the same way as the GST. In Quebec and Prince Edward Island, the sales tax is applied after adding the GST to the retail price.

NWT	0% PST	Manitoba	7% PST
Nunavut	0% PST	Saskatchewan	5% PST
Yukon	0% PST	Quebec	8.5% PST
Alberta	0% PST	Prince Edward Island	10% PST

3. Harmonized Sales Tax (HST)

For the remaining provinces, the PST and GST are blended to form the Harmonized Sales Tax or HST. For British Columbia and Ontario, the HST came into effect on July 1, 2010.

British Columbia	12% HST
Newfoundland	13% HST
New Brunswick	13% HST
Nova Scotia	15% HST
Ontario	13% HST

EXAMPLE 1.6C

Determine the amount of provincial sales tax on an invoice of taxable items totalling $740 before taxes

(i) in Saskatchewan;

(ii) in Quebec.

SOLUTION

(i) In Saskatchewan, the PST = 5% of $740.00 = 0.05(740.00) = $37.00.

(ii) In Quebec, the PST = 8.5% of $740.00 + 8.5% of the GST on $740.00.

Since the GST = 5% of $740.00 = 0.05(740.00) = $37.00, the PST = 0.085(740.00) + 0.085(37.00) = 62.90 + 3.15 = $66.05.

EXAMPLE 1.6D

In Ontario, restaurant meals are subject to the 13% HST on food items. Alcoholic beverages are also subject to 13% HST. You take your friend out for dinner and spend $60 on food items and $32 on a bottle of wine. You also tip the waiter 15% of the combined cost of food items and wine, for good service. How much do you spend?

SOLUTION

Cost of food items	$60.00
Cost of wine	32.00
Total cost of meal	$92.00

HST on food = 13% of $60.00 = 0.13(60.00) = $7.80
HST on wine = 13% of $32.00 = 0.13(32.00) = $4.16

Total cost including taxes = 92.00 + 7.80 + 4.16	= $103.96
Tip = 15% of $92.00 = 0.15(92.00)	= 13.80
Total amount spent	= $117.76

B. Property tax

To pay for their services, municipalities charge a **property tax** based on the **assessed value** of real estate, both residential and commercial. Some education taxes are also calculated using this method. The property tax is determined by applying a percent to the assessed value of the property. In some municipalities, the assessed value is divided by 1000, and then the percent is applied.

EXAMPLE 1.6E

The municipality of Vermeer requires a budget of \$650 million to operate next year. Provincial and federal grants, fees, and commercial taxes will cover \$450 million, leaving \$200 million to be raised by a tax on residential assessments.

(i) Calculate the rate per \$1000 to raise the \$200 million if the total assessed residential value for taxation purposes is \$8 billion.

(ii) Determine the taxes on a building lot in Vermeer if it is assessed at \$72 800.

SOLUTION

(i) $\text{Rate} = \dfrac{\text{Tax revenue required from residential assessments}}{\text{Current assessed value}}$

$= \dfrac{\$200\ 000\ 000}{\$8\ 000\ 000\ 000} = \$0.025$

For each dollar of assessed value on a residential property, each owner must pay 2.5 cents.

(ii) Property taxes on the building lot = 0.025(72 800) = \$1820.00

EXAMPLE 1.6F

The municipality of Cranberry lists the following property tax rates for various local services:

Service	Rate per \$1000
General city	3.20
Garbage collection	0.99
Schools	10.51
Capital development	1.20

If a homeowner's property has been assessed at \$250 000, determine the property taxes payable.

SOLUTION

Total rate per \$1000 = 3.20 + 0.99 + 10.51 + 1.20 = 15.90
Tax payable = Total rate per \$1000 × 0.001 × Assessed value
Tax payable = 15.90 × 0.001 × 250 000 = \$3975.00

EXERCISE 1.6

Answer each of the following questions.

1. Cook's Department Store files GST returns monthly. If the figures in the following table represent the store's GST taxable sales and GST is paid on its purchases for the last five months, calculate Cook's monthly GST bills. Determine if Cook's owes the government money or is entitled to a refund.

Month	Sales	Purchases
January	$546 900	$147 832
February	244 000	69 500
March	588 000	866 000
April	650 300	450 000
May	156 800	98 098

2. Riza's Home Income Tax business operates only during tax season. Last season Riza grossed $28 350 including GST. During that season she spent $8000 before GST on her paper and supply purchases. How much does Riza owe the Canada Revenue Agency for GST?

3. "Save the GST" is a popular advertising gimmick. How much would you save on the purchase of a TV with a list price of $780 in a Manitoba store during a "Save the GST" promotion?

4. How much would a consumer pay for a T-shirt with a list price of $15 if the purchase was made in Regina, Saskatchewan?

5. During an early season promotion, a weekend ski pass was priced at $84 plus HST at Blackcomb Mountain, B.C., and at $84 plus PST and GST at Mont Tremblant, Quebec. What is the difference in the total price paid by skiers at the two ski resorts?

6. A retail chain sells snowboards for $625 plus tax. What is the price difference for consumers in Toronto, Ontario, and Calgary, Alberta?

7. Calculate the property taxes on a property assessed at $125 000 if the rate per $1000 is 22.751.

8. The town of Eudora assesses property at market value. How much will the owner of a house valued at $225 000 owe in taxes if this year's property tax rate has been set at 0.019368?

9. The City of Mississauga sent a semi-annual tax bill to a resident who owns a house assessed at $196 000. If the semi-annual tax bill is $1420.79, what is the annual mill rate in Mississauga?

10. A town has an assessed residential property value of $250 000 000. The town council must meet the following expenditures:

Education	$10 050 000
General purposes	$2 000 000
Recreation	$250 000
Public works	$700 000
Police and fire protection	$850 000

(a) Suppose 80% of the expenditures are charged against residential real estate. Calculate the total property taxes that must be raised.
(b) What is the tax rate per $1000?
(c) What is the property tax on a property assessed at $175 000?

BUSINESS MATH NEWS BOX

HST Will Not Effect Purchase Price of Resale Homes

In March 2009, the Ontario Liberal government announced the introduction of a harmonized sales tax (HST) for implementation in the province starting July 1, 2010. This levy blended the current 5% federal goods and services tax (GST) and the 8% Ontario provincial sales tax (PST) into a single 13% value-added sales tax. Although the government has been careful to note that only 17% of all taxable goods will see an increase in price, some items that were previously taxed with only GST are now taxed with HST.

Ontario consumers will notice price increases in a long list of goods and services, including utilities (heating, hydro, electricity), gasoline, hotels, domestic air travel, personal services (hair stylists, massage therapists), and many recreation and entertainment activities. Therefore, the Ontario government is providing a one-time Ontario GST rebate of $1000 to families with an income below $160 000 to offset the initial tax burden for everyday purchases.

One major purchase that has been affected significantly is housing. The HST has become a major consideration for homebuyers in Ontario because the HST applies differently depending on the type of real estate—whether it is resale housing or newly constructed housing.

Resale housing, which was never subject to GST or PST, continues to be exempt from both taxes now combined under the HST. However, newly constructed homes, which have always been subject to the GST, will now be subject to PST as well, meaning thousands of extra tax dollars for homebuyers choosing this option.

A new provincial housing rebate provides relief on 75% of the provincial component of the HST on the first $400 000 paid for new housing purchased as primary residences, up to a maximum rebate of $24 000.

QUESTIONS

1. Prior to July 1, 2010, how much more did a homebuyer pay for a $500 000 new versus resale home in Ontario?
2. Calculate the HST on a new Ontario home priced at $500 000.
3. Beginning on July 1, 2010, how much additional tax does the new homebuyer face from the provincial portion of the HST, after the rebate is applied?

Source: Bill Johnston, "HST will not effect purchase price of resale homes," *Toronto Star*, July 7, 2010, **www.yourhome.ca/homes/realestate/article/830966--treb-hst-will-not-effect-purchase-price-of-resale-homes.**

Business Math News boxes show you how widely business math applications are used in the real world.

Go to MathXL at www.mathxl.com. You can practise many of this chapter's exercises as often as you want. The guided solutions help you find an answer step by step. You'll find a personalized study plan available to you too!

Review Exercise

The Review Exercise provides you with numerous questions that cover all the chapter content. Solutions to the odd-numbered exercises are given at the back of the text.

1. Simplify each of the following.
   (a) $32 - 24 \div 8$
   (b) $(48 - 18) \div 15 - 10$
   (c) $(8 \times 6 - 4) \div (16 - 4 \times 3)$
   (d) $9(6 - 2) - 4(3 + 4)$
   (e) $\dfrac{108}{0.12 \times \frac{216}{365}}$
   (f) $\dfrac{288}{2400 \times \frac{292}{365}}$
   (g) $320\left(1 + 0.10 \times \frac{225}{365}\right)$
   (h) $1000\left(1 - 0.12 \times \frac{150}{365}\right)$
   (i) $\dfrac{660}{1 + 0.14 \times \frac{144}{365}}$
   (j) $\dfrac{1120.00}{1 - 0.13 \times \frac{292}{365}}$

2. Change each of the following percents into a decimal.
   (a) 185% (b) 7.5% (c) 0.4%
   (d) 0.025% (e) $1\frac{1}{4}\%$ (f) $\frac{3}{4}\%$
   (g) $162\frac{1}{2}\%$ (h) $11\frac{3}{4}\%$ (i) $8\frac{1}{3}\%$
   (j) $83\frac{1}{3}\%$ (k) $266\frac{2}{3}\%$ (l) $10\frac{3}{8}\%$

3. Change each of the following percents into a common fraction in lowest terms.
   (a) 50% (b) $37\frac{1}{2}\%$ (c) $16\frac{2}{3}\%$
   (d) $166\frac{2}{3}\%$ (e) $\frac{1}{2}\%$ (f) 7.5%
   (g) 0.75% (h) $\frac{5}{8}\%$

4. Express each of the following as a percent.
   (a) 2.25 (b) 0.02 (c) 0.009
   (d) 0.1275 (e) $\frac{5}{4}$ (f) $\frac{11}{8}$
   (g) $\frac{5}{200}$ (h) $\frac{7}{25}$

5. Sales of a particular make and size of nails during a day were $4\frac{1}{3}$ kg, $3\frac{3}{4}$ kg, $5\frac{1}{2}$ kg, and $6\frac{5}{8}$ kg.
   (a) How many kilograms of nails were sold?
   (b) What is the total sales value at $1.20 per kilogram?
   (c) What was the average weight per sale?
   (d) What was the average sales value per sale?

6. Extend and total the following invoice.

Quantity	Description	Unit Price	Amount
56	Item A	$0.625	?
180	Item B	$83\frac{1}{3}$¢	?
126	Item C	$\$1.1\dot{6}$	?
144	Item D	$1.75	?
		Total	

7. The basic pay categories, hourly rates of pay, and the number of employees in each category for the machining department of a company are shown below.

Category	Hourly Pay	No. of Employees
Supervisors	$15.45	2
Machinists	12.20	6
Assistants	10.40	9
Helpers	9.50	13

   (a) What is the average rate of pay for all categories?
   (b) What is the average rate of pay per employee?

8. Hélène Gauthier invested $15 000 on January 1 in a partnership. She withdrew $2000 on June 1, withdrew a further $1500 on August 1, and reinvested $4000 on November 1. What was her average monthly investment balance for the year?

Reference Example 1.4H

9. Brent DeCosta invested $12 000 in a business on January 1 and an additional $2400 on April 1. He withdrew $1440 on June 1 and invested $2880 on October 1. What was Brent's average monthly investment balance for the year?

10. Casey receives an annual salary of $17 472.00, is paid monthly, and works 35 regular hours per week. Overtime is paid at time-and-a-half regular pay.

(a) What is Casey's gross remuneration per pay period?

(b) What is his hourly rate of pay?

(c) How many hours overtime did Casey work during a month for which his gross pay was $1693.60?

11. Tim is employed at an annual salary of $20 292.48. His regular workweek is 36 hours and he is paid semi-monthly.

(a) What is Tim's gross pay per period?

(b) What is his hourly rate of pay?

(c) What is his gross pay for a period in which he worked 12 ½ hours overtime at time-and-a-half regular pay?

12. Artemis is paid a weekly commission of 4% on net sales of $6000, 8% on the next $3000, and 12.5% on all further sales. Her gross sales for a week were $11 160 and sales returns and allowances were $120.

(a) What were her gross earnings for the week?

(b) What was her average hourly rate of pay for the week if she worked 43 hours?

13. Last week June worked 44 hours. She is paid $10.20 per hour for a regular workweek of 37.5 hours and overtime at time-and-a-half regular pay.

(a) What were June's gross wages for last week?

(b) What is the amount of the overtime premium?

14. Vacek is paid a monthly commission on a graduated basis of 7 ½% on net sales of $7000, 9% on the next $8000, and 11% on any additional sales. If sales for April were $21 500 and sales returns were $325, what were his gross earnings for the month?

15. Margit is paid on a weekly commission basis. She is paid a base salary of $240 on a weekly quota of $8000 and a commission of 4.75% on any sales in excess of the quota.

(a) If Margit's sales for last week were $11 340, what were her gross earnings?

(b) What were Margit's average hourly earnings if she worked 35 hours?

16. Last week Lisa had gross earnings of $321.30. Lisa receives a base salary of $255 and a commission on sales exceeding her quota of $5000. What is her rate of commission if her sales were $6560?

17. Costa earned a gross commission of $2101.05 during July. What were his sales if his rate of commission is 10.5% of net sales and sales returns and allowances for the month were 8% of his gross sales?

18. Edith worked 47 hours during a week for which her gross remuneration was $577.72. Based on a regular workweek of 40 hours and overtime payment at time-and-a-half regular pay, what is Edith's hourly rate of pay?

19. Hong is paid a semi-monthly salary of $1088.75. Regular hours are 37 ½ per week and overtime is paid at time-and-a-half regular pay.

(a) What is Hong's hourly rate of pay?

(b) How many hours overtime did Hong work in a pay period for which his gross pay was $1252.55?

20. Silvio's gross earnings for last week were $328.54. His remuneration consists of a base salary of $280 plus a commission of 6% on net sales exceeding his weekly quota of $5000. What were Silvio's gross sales for the week if sales returns and allowances were $136?

21. Sean's gross wages for a week were $541.20. His regular workweek is 40 hours and overtime is paid at time-and-a-half regular pay. What is Sean's regular hourly wage if he worked 47 ½ hours?

22. Aviva's pay stub shows gross earnings of $662.30 for a week. Her regular rate of pay is $7.80 per hour for a 35-hour week and overtime is paid at time-and-a-half regular pay. How many hours did she work?

23. Ramona's Dry Cleaning shows sales revenue of \$76 000 for the year. Ramona's GST-taxable expenses were \$14 960. How much should she remit to the government at the end of the year?

24. When Fred of Fred's Auto Repair tallied up his accounts at the end of the year, he found he had paid GST on parking fees of \$4000, supplies of \$55 000, utilities of \$2000, and miscellaneous eligible costs of \$3300. During this same time, he found he had charged his customers GST on billings that totalled \$75 000 for parts and \$65 650 for labour. How much GST must Fred send to the government?

25. A store located in Kelowna, B.C., sells a computer for \$1868 plus HST. If the same model is sold at the same price in a store in Kenora, Ontario, what is the difference in the prices paid by consumers in the two stores?

26. Two people living in different communities build houses of the same design on lots of equal size. If the person in Ripley has his house and lot assessed at \$150 000 with a rate per \$1000 of 20.051, will his taxes be more or less than the person in Amberly with an assessment of \$135 000 and a rate per \$1000 of 22.124?

27. A town has a total residential property assessment of \$975 500 000. It is originally estimated that \$45 567 000 must be raised through residential taxation to meet expenditures.
    - **(a)** What tax rate must be set to raise \$45 567 000 in property taxes?
    - **(b)** What is the property tax on a property assessed at \$35 000?
    - **(c)** The town later finds that it underestimated building costs. An additional \$2 000 000 in taxes must be raised. Find the increase in the tax rate required to meet these additional costs.
    - **(d)** How much more will the property taxes be on the property assessed at \$35 000?

Self-Test

You can test your understanding of the chapter content by completing the Self-Test. Again, the solutions to the odd-numbered questions are at the back of the text.

1. Evaluate each of the following.
   - **(a)** $4320\left(1 + 0.18 \times \frac{45}{365}\right)$
   - **(b)** $2160\left(0.15 \times \frac{105}{365}\right)$
   - **(c)** $2880\left(1 - 0.12 \times \frac{285}{365}\right)$
   - **(d)** $\dfrac{410.40}{0.24 \times \frac{135}{365}}$
   - **(e)** $\dfrac{5124}{1 - 0.09 \times \frac{270}{365}}$

2. Change each of the following percents into a decimal.
   - **(a)** 175%
   - **(b)** $\frac{3}{8}\%$

3. Change each of the following percents into a common fraction in lowest terms.
   - **(a)** $2\frac{1}{2}\%$
   - **(b)** $116\frac{2}{3}\%$

4. Express each of the following as a percent.
   - **(a)** 1.125
   - **(b)** $\dfrac{9}{400}$

5. The following information is shown in your investment account for last year: balance on January 1 of \$7200; a withdrawal of \$480 on March 1; and deposits of \$600 on August 1 and \$120 on October 1. What was the account's average monthly balance for the year?

6. Extend each of the following and determine the total.

Quantity	Unit Price	Total Amount
72	\$1.25	?
84	$16\frac{2}{3}$¢	?
40	\$0.875	?
48	\$1.33	?

7. Purchases of an inventory item during the last accounting period were as follows:

No. of Items	Unit Price	Total Amount
5	\$9.00	?
6	\$7.00	?
3	\$8.00	?
6	\$6.00	?

What was the average price per item?

8. Hazzid Realty sold lots for \$15 120 per 1000 square metre. What is the total sales value if the lot sizes, in 1000 square metre, were $5\frac{1}{4}$, $6\frac{1}{3}$, $4\frac{3}{8}$, and $3\frac{5}{6}$?

9. Property valued at \$130 000 is assessed at $\frac{2}{13}$ of its value. What is the amount of tax due for this year if the tax rate is \$32.50 per \$1000 of assessed value?

10. A salesperson earned a commission of \$806.59 for last week on gross sales of \$5880. If returns and allowances were 11.5% of gross sales, what is his rate of commission based on net sales?

11. A.Y. receives an annual salary of \$26 478.40. She is paid monthly on a 38-hour workweek. What is the gross pay for a pay period in which she works 8.75 hours overtime at time-and-a-half regular pay?

12. J.B. earns \$16.60 an hour with time-and-a-half for hours worked over 8 a day. His hours for a week are 8.25, 8.25, 9.5, 11.5, and 7.25. Determine his gross earnings for that week.

13. A wage earner receives a gross pay of \$699.93 for 52.5 hours of work. What is his hourly rate of pay if a regular workweek is 42 hours and overtime is paid at time-and-a-half the regular rate of pay?

14. A salesperson receives a weekly base salary of \$400 on a quota of \$4500. On the next \$2000, she receives a commission of 11%. On any additional sales, the commission rate is 15%. Calculate her gross earnings for a week in which her sales total \$8280.

15. C.D. is paid a semi-monthly salary of \$780. If her regular workweek is 40 hours, what is her hourly rate of pay?

16. Mahal of Winnipeg, Manitoba, bought a ring for \$6400. Since the jeweller is shipping the ring, she must pay a shipping charge of \$20. She must also pay PST and GST on the ring. Determine the total purchase price of Mahal's ring.

17. Ilo pays a property tax of \$2502.50. In her community the tax rate is 55 per \$1000. What is the assessed value of her property, to the nearest dollar?

18. Suppose you went shopping and bought bulk laundry detergent worth $17.95. You then received a $2.50 trade discount, and had to pay a $1.45 shipping charge. Calculate the final purchase price of the detergent if you lived in Nova Scotia.

Challenge Problems

Challenge Problems give you the opportunity to apply the skills you learned in the chapter at a higher level than the Exercises.

1. A customer in a sporting goods shop gives you a $50 bill for goods totalling $37. He asks that the change he receives include no coins worth $1 or less. Can you give this customer the correct change while meeting his request?
2. Suppose you own a small business with four employees, namely Roberto, Sandra, Petra, and Lee. At the end of the year you have set aside $1800 to divide among them as a bonus. You have two categories in place for your bonus system. An exceptional employee receives one amount and an average employee receives half that amount. You have rated Roberto and Sanda exceptional, and Petra and Lee average employees. How much bonus should each employee receive?
3. Suppose your math grade is based on the results of two tests and one final exam. Each test is worth 30% of your grade and the final exam is worth 40%. If you scored 60% and 50% on your two tests, what mark must you score on the final exam to achieve a grade of 70%?

CASE STUDY 1.1 Businesses and the GST/HST

Case Studies present comprehensive, realistic scenarios followed by a set of questions, and illustrate some of the important practical applications of the chapter material.

» Businesses providing taxable goods and services in Canada must register to collect either GST or HST, depending on where the business is registered. The federal government has set the GST rate at 5%. The HST varies by province. As of July 1, 2010, the province of Ontario has set the HST rate at 13%.

A company must remit its GST/HST collections either on a monthly, quarterly, or annual basis, depending on the amount of annual revenue. At the end of each fiscal year, registrants must file a return summarizing the collection of GST/HST, the GST/HST paid by the registrant (input tax credits or ITCs), and periodic payments made to the Canada Revenue Agency (CRA). The CRA then uses this information to calculate a business's maximum periodic installment payment for the following year.

The government gives small businesses with annual revenues of under $30 000 the option of registering to collect and remit. If businesses choose not to register, they do not have to charge GST/HST on their goods or services. The disadvantage is that they are then ineligible for a credit on the GST/HST paid on their supplies.

If a business has registered and has annual taxable revenues less than $200 000, the Quick Method can be used to calculate input tax credits (ITCs). When using the Quick Method in Ontario, the registrant charges customers 13% HST on sales of goods and services. The ITCs for the business are calculated by adding all purchases and expenses including the HST, and then subtracting employees' salaries, insurance, and land. The taxable expense amount is then multiplied by 13/113. The result is the amount of ITC.

Under the Quick Method, the numbers in the calculation vary by province.

QUESTIONS

1. Simon operates an HST-registered mobile glass repair service in Ontario. His service revenue for the year is $28 000. His HST-taxable purchases amounted to $4000. Simon does not use the Quick Method for claiming ITCs. By calculating the difference between the HST he collected and the HST he paid, determine Simon's HST remittance to the CRA.

2. Courtney operates a souvenir gift shop in Ontario. Her business is registered for the Quick Method of calculating ITCs. Her HST-taxable sales were $185 000 for the year. HST-taxable purchases of goods for resale were 47% of sales. In addition, Courtney paid $48 000 in purchases and expenses, which included $42 000 for salaries and insurance.
   - **(a)** Calculate how much HST Courtney remitted to the CRA when using the Quick Method.
   - **(b)** If she had not chosen to use the Quick Method of calculating ITCs, how much HST would she have to remit?

3. Steve has been operating Castle Creek Restaurant in Ontario for the past several years. On the basis of the information that Steve's accountant filed with the CRA during the prior year, Castle Creek Restaurant must make monthly HST payments of $3120 this year. Steve must complete the Goods and Services Tax/Harmonized Sales Tax (GST/HST) Return For Registrants online, and then make his payment. He has asked his accountant for instructions on how to do this, and was provided with this explanation:

   Line 101 reports amount of GST/HST-taxable revenues.
   Line 103 reports amount of GST/HST collected.
   Line 106 reports amount of GST/HST paid.
   Line 109 reports amount of net GST/HST payable to the CRA.
   Line 110 reports amount of GST/HST payments already made to the CRA this year.
   Line 113 reports amount of balance to be paid or to be refunded.

   When Steve checked his accounting records, he found the following information for the current fiscal year: HST-taxable revenue of $486 530 and purchases of $239 690. Referring to the form on the next page, help Steve determine the balance of HST to be paid or to be received by calculating each line of this simplified GST/HST return.

Sales and other revenue	100	00

NET TAX CALCULATION

GST and HST amounts collected or collectible	103			
Adjustments	104			
Total GST/HST and adjustments for period (add lines 103 and 104) →			105	
Input tax credits (ITCs) for the current period	106			
Adjustments	107			
Total ITCs and adjustments (add lines 106 and 107) →			108	
Net tax (subtract line 108 from line 105)			109	

OTHER CREDITS IF APPLICABLE

Installment payments and net tax already remitted	110			
Rebates	111			
Total other credits (add lines 110 and 111) →			112	
Balance (subtract line 112 from line 109)			113	

REFUND CLAIMED		PAYMENT ENCLOSED	
114		115	

CASE STUDY 1.2 How Much Are You Worth?

Eventually, most Canadians will assume the responsibility of purchasing a home. When faced with this choice, financial institutions determine whether this dream is realistic and the size of the loan that can be borrowed. To be approved, two key questions are asked to determine net worth. Net worth is calculated as the difference between a person's assets and liabilities. In layperson's terms, this is the difference between what you own and what you owe. Also measured into net worth is a consideration of your potential earnings.

Suppose you have decided to purchase a home, be it a house or condo, and you must borrow some money for the purchase. The next step is to determine whether you have the financial ability to carry the costs of a mortgage and of running the home. The two most widely accepted guidelines used to estimate how much of a homebuyer's income can be allocated to housing costs are the gross debt service ratio (GDS) and the total debt service ratio (TDS).

The formula for calculating the GDS is:

$$\left(\frac{\text{Monthly mortgage payment} + \text{Monthly property taxes} + \text{Monthly heating}}{\text{Gross monthly income}}\right) \times 100\%$$

The GDS should not exceed 32%.

The formula for calculating the TDS is:

$$\left(\frac{\text{Monthly mortage payment} + \text{Monthly property taxes} + \text{All other monthly debts}}{\text{Gross monthly income}}\right) \times 100\%$$

The TDS should not exceed 40%.

The Wong family have a combined household income of $147 000, and are considering purchasing a condominium. They have tallied up the potential costs of the condo and find that the mortgage will be $1800 per month, property taxes will be $2304 per year, and heating will be about $175 per month on equal billing. The Wongs also have a car loan of $450 per month, which has two more years to run. They find that they pay an average of $8520 per year on their credit cards.

QUESTIONS

1. Calculate the GDS and the TDS for the Wongs. If you were a bank manager, would you recommend the loan for their condo purchase?
2. Suppose the Wongs did not have the car loan and the credit card debt. How would this information affect their GDS and TDS? Would the bank manager's decision be any different?

GLOSSARY

The Glossary at the end of each chapter lists each key term with its definition and a page reference to where the term was first defined in the chapter.

Arithmetic average (mean) the average found by adding the values in the set and dividing by the number of those values *(p. 13)*

Assessed value a dollar figure applied to real estate by municipalities to be used in property tax calculations (can be a market value or a value relative to other properties in the same municipality) *(p. 28)*

Commission the term applied to remuneration of sales personnel according to their sales performance *(p. 21)*

Common fraction the division of one whole number by another whole number, expressed by means of a fraction line *(p. 3)*

Complex fraction a mathematical expression containing one or more fractions in the numerator or the denominator or both *(p. 6)*

Denominator the divisor of a fraction (i.e., the number written below the fraction line) *(p. 3)*

Equivalent fractions fractions that have the same value although they consist of different terms *(p. 4)*

Fraction in lowest terms a fraction whose terms cannot be reduced any further (i.e., whose numerator and denominator cannot be evenly divided by the same number except 1) *(p. 4)*

Goods and services tax (GST) a federal tax charged on the price of almost all goods and services *(p. 26)*

Graduated commission remuneration paid as an increasing percent for increasing sales levels for a fixed period of time *(p. 21)*

Gross earnings the amount of an employee's remuneration before deductions *(p. 20)*

Harmonized sales tax (HST) the merged GST and PST tax used in Newfoundland, Nova Scotia, New Brunswick, Ontario, and British Columbia *(p. 26)*

Improper fraction a fraction whose numerator is greater than its denominator *(p. 3)*

Mixed number a number consisting of a whole number and a fraction, such as $5\frac{1}{2}$ *(p. 5)*

Net sales gross sales less returns and allowances *(p. 21)*

Numerator the dividend of a fraction (i.e., the number written above the fraction line) *(p. 3)*

Order of operations the order in which arithmetic calculations are performed *(p. 2)*

Overtime premium extra labour cost due to overtime *(p. 23)*

Percent (%) a fraction with a denominator of 100 *(p. 8)*

Proper fraction a fraction whose numerator is less than its denominator *(p. 3)*

Property tax a municipal tax charged on the assessed value of real estate, both commercial and residential *(p. 28)*

Provincial sales tax (PST) a provincial tax charged on the price of most goods (usually a fixed percent of the cost of a good) *(p. 26)*

Quota a sales level required before the commission percent is paid; usually associated with remuneration by base salary and commission *(p. 22)*

Salary the term usually applied to monthly or annual remuneration of personnel *(p. 19)*

Salary plus commission a method of remunerating sales personnel that guarantees a minimum income per pay period *(p. 22)*

Straight commission remuneration paid as a percent of net sales for a given period *(p. 21)*

Tax a contribution levied on persons, properties, or businesses to pay for services provided by the government *(p. 26)*

Terms of the fraction the numerator and the denominator of a fraction *(p. 3)*

Wages the term usually applied to the remuneration of hourly rated employees *(p. 23)*

Weighted arithmetic average the average found by multiplying each item by the weighting factor and totalling the results *(p. 15)*

Useful Internet Sites provide URLs and brief descriptions for sites related to the chapter topic, or for companies mentioned in the chapter.

USEFUL INTERNET SITES

canada.gc.ca

Government of Canada This is the main Internet site for the Government of Canada. Information is provided on governance, services, and resources.

www.cra-arc.gc.ca

Canada Revenue Agency This Website provides general information about taxes, including GST and HST.

www.ctf.ca

Canadian Tax Foundation The Canadian Tax Foundation is an independent tax research organization whose purpose is to provide the public and the government of Canada with the benefit of expert, impartial tax research into current problems of taxation and government finance. You can check the site to see what is new in the world of tax and find Canadian tax articles written by several authors.

www.rev.gov.on.ca

Ontario Ministry of Revenue The province of Ontario Ministry of Revenue site describes the HST and its benefits for businesses and individuals.

CHAPTER 2

Review of Basic Algebra

OBJECTIVES

Upon completing this chapter, you will be able to do the following:

1. Simplify algebraic expressions using fundamental operations and substitution.
2. Simplify and evaluate powers with positive exponents, negative exponents, and exponent zero.
3. Use an electronic calculator to compute the numerical value of arithmetic expressions involving fractional exponents.
4. Write exponential equations in logarithmic form and use an electronic calculator equipped with a natural logarithm function to determine the value of natural logarithms.
5. Solve basic equations using addition, subtraction, multiplication, and division.
6. Solve equations involving algebraic simplification and formula rearrangement.
7. Solve word problems by creating and solving equations.

In operating her business, Jessie has many daily decisions to make. She must determine how much inventory to buy, what price to set to sell the inventory, how much her expenses will be, and how much money she needs to borrow to keep the business going. Knowledge and competence in algebra are necessary to solve and answer these questions. The skills developed in this chapter will help you in your decisions in business.

INTRODUCTION

An eccentric businessman wants to divide his n gold bars among his four children, so that the first child gets one-half of the bars, the second child gets one-fourth, the third child gets one-fifth, and the fourth child gets seven gold bars. How many gold bars does the eccentric businessman have?

This type of "brain teaser" is an example of the use of basic algebra. We can find the answer by letting the unknown value be represented by a letter (a variable) and applying the laws of algebraic formula manipulation. Many problems in business and finance can be solved by using predetermined formulas. When these formulas are used, we need the skills of algebraic substitution and simplification to solve them.

Many problems do not fit a predetermined formula. We must then use the basics of algebra to create our own equation, and solve it to answer the problem. An equation is a statement of equality between two algebraic expressions. Any equation that has only variables (letter symbols) to the first power is called a linear equation. Linear equations can often be created to represent business problems. When you solve the equation you solve the business problem. When you finish this chapter you should feel comfortable solving linear equations. (And if you have not already solved the brain teaser above, you should be able to figure out that the eccentric businessman has 140 gold bars.)

2.1 SIMPLIFICATION OF ALGEBRAIC EXPRESSIONS

A. Addition and subtraction

1. Simplification Involving Addition and Subtraction

In algebra, only **like terms** may be added or subtracted. This is done by *adding* or *subtracting* the **numerical coefficients** of the like terms according to the rules used for adding and subtracting signed numbers, and *retaining* the common **literal coefficient**. The process of adding and subtracting like terms is called **combining like terms** or **collecting like terms**.

EXAMPLE 2.1A

(i) $6x + 3x + 7x$ ——— all three terms are like terms

$= (6 + 3 + 7)x$ ——— add the numerical coefficients

$= 16x$ ——— retain the common literal coefficient

(ii) $-5m - (-3m) - (+6m)$

$= -5m + (+3m) + (-6m)$ ——— change the subtraction to addition

$= -5m + 3m - 6m$

$= (-5 + 3 - 6)m$

$= -8m$

(iii) $7x - 4y - 3x - 6y$ ——— the two sets of like terms are $7x$, $-3x$, and $-4y$, $-6y$, and are collected separately

$= (7 - 3)x + (-4 - 6)y$

$= 4x - 10y$

(iv) $5x^2 - 3x - 4 + 2x - 5 + x^2$
$= (5 + 1)x^2 + (-3 + 2)x + (-4 - 5)$
$= 6x^2 - x - 9$

2. Simplification Involving Brackets

When simplifying **algebraic expressions** involving brackets, remove the brackets according to the following rules and collect like terms.

(a) If the brackets are preceded by a (+) sign or no sign, drop the brackets and retain the terms inside the brackets with their signs unchanged: $(-7a + 5b - c)$ becomes $-7a + 5b - c$, because each term has been multiplied by 1.

(b) If the brackets are preceded by a (−) sign, drop the brackets and change the sign of every term inside the brackets:
$-(-7a + 5b - c)$ becomes $7a - 5b + c$, because each term has been multiplied by −1.

EXAMPLE 2.1B

(i) $(7a - 3b) - (4a + 3b)$
$= 7a - 3b - 4a - 3b$ ——— $(7a - 3b)$ becomes $7a - 3b$; $-(4a + 3b)$ becomes $-4a - 3b$
$= 3a - 6b$

(ii) $-(3x^2 - 8x - 5) + (2x^2 - 5x + 4)$
$= -3x^2 + 8x + 5 + 2x^2 - 5x + 4$
$= -x^2 + 3x + 9$

(iii) $4b - (3a - 4b - c) - (5c + 2b)$
$= 4b - 3a + 4b + c - 5c - 2b$
$= -3a + 6b - 4c$

B. Multiplication

1. Multiplication of Monomials

The product of two or more **monomials** is the product of their numerical coefficients multiplied by the product of their literal coefficients.

EXAMPLE 2.1C

(i) $5(3a)$
$= (5 \times 3)a$ ——— obtain the product of the numerical coefficients
$= 15a$

(ii) $(-7a)(4b)$
$= (-7 \times 4)(a \times b)$ ——— obtain the product of the numerical coefficients, −7 and 4, and the product of the literal coefficients, a and b
$= -28ab$

(iii) $(-3)(4x)(-5x)$
$= [(-3)(4)(-5)][(x)(x)]$
$= 60x^2$

2. Multiplication of Monomials with Polynomials

The product of a **polynomial** and a monomial is obtained by multiplying each term of the polynomial by the monomial.

EXAMPLE 2.1D

(i) $5(a-3)$
$= 5(a) + 5(-3)$ — multiply 5 by a and 5 by (-3)
$= 5a - 15$

(ii) $-4(3x^2 - 2x - 1)$
$= -4(3x^2) + (-4)(-2x) + (-4)(-1)$ — multiply each term of the trinomial by (-4)
$= (-12x^2) + (+8x) + (+4)$
$= -12x^2 + 8x + 4$

(iii) $3a(4a - 5b - 2c)$
$= (3a)(4a) + (3a)(-5b) + (3a)(-2c)$
$= (12a^2) + (-15ab) + (-6ac)$
$= 12a^2 - 15ab - 6ac$

3. Simplification Involving Brackets and Multiplication

EXAMPLE 2.1E

(i) $3(x-5) - 2(x-7)$
$= 3x - 15 - 2x + 14$ — carry out the multiplication
$= x - 1$ — collect like terms

(ii) $a(3a-1) - 4(2a+3)$
$= 3a^2 - a - 8a - 12$
$= 3a^2 - 9a - 12$

(iii) $-4(5a - 3b - 2c) + 5(-2a - 4b + c)$
$= -20a + 12b + 8c - 10a - 20b + 5c$
$= -30a - 8b + 13c$

4. Multiplication of a Polynomial by a Polynomial

The product of two polynomials is obtained by multiplying each term of one polynomial by each term of the other polynomial and collecting like terms.

EXAMPLE 2.1F

(i) $(3a + 2b)(4c - 3d)$
$= 3a(4c - 3d) + 2b(4c - 3d)$ — multiply each term of the first polynomial by the second polynomial
$= 12ac - 9ad + 8bc - 6bd$ — carry out the multiplication

(ii) $(5x - 2)(3x + 4)$
$= 5x(3x + 4) - 2(3x + 4)$
$= 15x^2 + 20x - 6x - 8$
$= 15x^2 + 14x - 8$

C. Division

1. Division of Monomials

The quotient of two monomials is the quotient of their numerical coefficients multiplied by the quotient of their literal coefficients.

EXAMPLE 2.1G

(i) $32ab \div 8b = \left(\frac{32}{8}\right)\left(\frac{ab}{b}\right) = 4a$

(ii) $24x^2 \div (-6x) = \left(\frac{24}{-6}\right)\left(\frac{x^2}{x}\right) = -4x$

2. Division of a Polynomial by a Monomial

To determine the quotient of a polynomial divided by a monomial, divide each term of the polynomial by the monomial.

EXAMPLE 2.1H

(i) $(12a + 8) \div 4 = \frac{12a + 8}{4} = \frac{12a}{4} + \frac{8}{4} = 3a + 2$

(ii) $(18x - 12) \div 6 = \frac{18x - 12}{6} = \frac{18x}{6} - \frac{12}{6} = 3x - 2$

(iii) $(12a^3 - 15a^2 - 9a) \div (-3a)$

$= \frac{12a^3 - 15a^2 - 9a}{-3a}$

$= \frac{12a^3}{-3a} + \frac{-15a^2}{-3a} + \frac{-9a}{-3a}$

$= -4a^2 + 5a + 3$

D. Substitution and evaluation

Evaluating algebraic expressions for given values of the variables requires replacing the variables with the given values. The replacement or substitution of the variables by the given values takes place each time the variables appear in the expression.

EXAMPLE 2.1I

(i) Evaluate $7x - 3y - 5$ for $x = -2, y = 3$

SOLUTION

$7x - 3y - 5$

$= 7(-2) - 3(3) - 5$ ——— replace x by (-2) and y by 3

$= -14 - 9 - 5$

$= -28$

(ii) Evaluate $\dfrac{2NC}{P(n+1)}$ for N = 12, C = 220, P = 1500, n = 15

SOLUTION

$$\frac{2NC}{P(n+1)} = \frac{2(12)(220)}{1500(15+1)} = 0.22$$

(iii) Evaluate $\dfrac{I}{rt}$ for I = \$126, r = 0.125, $t = \dfrac{328}{365}$

SOLUTION

$$\frac{I}{rt} = \frac{\$126}{0.125 \times \frac{328}{365}} = \$1121.71$$

(iv) Evaluate PV(1 + rt) for PV = \$900, r = 0.15, $t = \dfrac{244}{365}$

SOLUTION

$$\begin{aligned} PV(1+rt) &= \$900\left(1 + 0.15 \times \frac{244}{365}\right) \\ &= \$900(1 + 0.100274) \\ &= \$900(1.100274) \\ &= \$990.25 \end{aligned}$$

(v) Evaluate A(1 − dt) for A = \$800, d = 0.135, $t = \dfrac{292}{365}$

SOLUTION

$$\begin{aligned} A(1-dt) &= \$800\left(1 - 0.135 \times \frac{292}{365}\right) \\ &= \$800(1 - 0.108) \\ &= \$800(0.892) \\ &= \$713.60 \end{aligned}$$

(vi) Evaluate $\dfrac{FV}{1+rt}$ for FV = \$1644, r = 0.16, $t = \dfrac{219}{365}$

SOLUTION

$$\frac{FV}{1+rt} = \frac{\$1644}{1 + 0.16 \times \frac{219}{365}} = \frac{\$1644}{1+0.096} = \frac{\$1644}{1.096} = \$1500$$

EXERCISE 2.1

Addition and subtraction. Simplify.

1. $9a + 3a + 7a$ **2.** $6m - 2m - m$

3. $-4a - 8 + 3a - 2$ **4.** $2a - 15 - 5a + 1$

5. $2x - 3y - 4x - y$ **6.** $6p + 2q - 3p - q$

7. $12f - 9v + 2f + 5v$ **8.** $9c - 8d - 7c + 5d$

9. $x - 0.2x$ **10.** $x + 0.06x$

11. $x + 0.4x$ **12.** $x - 0.02x$

13. $x + 0.9x + 0.89x$ **14.** $3y + 2.81y - 1.76y$

15. $x^2 - 2x - 5 + x - 3 - 2x^2$ **16.** $3ax - 2x + 1 - 3 + 3x - 4ax$

17. $(2x - 3y) - (x + 4y)$ **18.** $-(4 - 5a) - (-2 + 3a)$

19. $(12b + 4c + 9) + 8 - (8b + 2c + 15)$

20. $(a^2 - ab + b^2) - (3a^2 + 5ab - 4b^2)$

21. $-(3m^2 - 4m - 5) - (4 - 2m - 2m^2)$

22. $6 - (4x - 3y + 1) - (5x + 2y - 9)$

23. $(7a - 5b) - (-3a + 4b) - 5b$

24. $(3f - f^2 + fg) - (f - 3f^2 - 2fg)$

Multiplication and division. Simplify.

1. $3(-4x)$ **2.** $-7(8a)$

3. $-5x(2a)$ **4.** $-9a(-3b)$

5. $-x(2x)$ **6.** $-6m(-4m)$

7. $-4(5x)(-3y)$ **8.** $2a(-3b)(-4c)(-1)$

9. $-2(x - 2y)$ **10.** $5(2x - 4)$

11. $a(2x^2 - 3x - 1)$ **12.** $-6x(4 - 2b - b^2)$

13. $4(5x - 6) - 3(2 - 5x)$ **14.** $-3(8a - b) - 2(-7a + 9b)$

15. $-3a(5x - 1) + a(5 - 2x) - 3a(x + 1)$

16. $8(3y - 4) - 2(2y - 1) - (1 - y)$

17. $(3x - 1)(x + 2)$

18. $(5m - 2n)(m - 3n)$

19. $(x + y)(x^2 - xy + y^2)$

20. $(a - 1)(a^2 - 2a + 1)$

21. $(5x - 4)(2x - 1) - (x - 7)(3x + 5)$

22. $2(a - 1)(2a - 3) - 3(3a - 2)(a + 1)$

23. $20ab \div 5$

24. $30xy \div (-6x)$

25. $(-12x^2) \div (-3x)$

26. $(-42ab) \div (7ab)$

27. $(20m - 8) \div 2$

28. $(14x - 21) \div (-7)$

29. $(10x^2 - 15x - 30) \div (-5)$

30. $(-a^3 - 4a^2 - 3a) \div (-a)$

C. Substitution and evaluation. Evaluate each of the following for the values given.

1. $3x - 2y - 3$ for $x = -4, y = -5$

2. $\frac{1}{2}(3x^2 - x - 1) - \frac{1}{4}(5 - 2x - x^2)$ for $x = -3$

3. $(pq - vq) - f$ for $p = 12, q = 2000, v = 7, f = 4500$

4. F/C for F = 13 000, C = 0.65

5. $(1 - d_1)(1 - d_2)(1 - d_3)$ for $d_1 = 0.35, d_2 = 0.08, d_3 = 0.02$

6. C + 0.38C + 0.24C for C = \$25.00

7. $\frac{\text{RP}(n + 1)}{2\text{N}}$ for R = 0.21, P = \$1200, $n = 77$, N = 26

8. $\frac{\text{I}}{\text{P}t}$ for I = 63, P = 840, $t = \frac{219}{365}$

9. $\frac{\text{I}}{rt}$ for I = \$198, $r = 0.165$, $t = \frac{146}{365}$

10. $\frac{2\text{NC}}{\text{P}(n + 1)}$ for N = 52, C = 60, P = 1800, $n = 25$

11. $\text{PV}(1 + rt)$ for PV = \$880, $r = 0.12$, $t = \frac{76}{365}$

12. $\text{FV}(1 - rt)$ for FV = \$1200, $r = 0.175$, $t = \frac{256}{365}$

13. $\frac{\text{P}}{1 - dt}$ for P = \$1253, $d = 0.135$, $t = \frac{284}{365}$

14. $\frac{\text{FV}}{1 + rt}$ for FV = \$1752, $r = 0.152$, $t = \frac{228}{365}$

2.2 INTEGRAL EXPONENTS

A. Basic concept and definition

If a number is to be used as a **factor** several times, the mathematical expression can be written more efficiently by using exponents:

$5 \times 5 \times 5 \times 5$ may be written as 5^4

Note: In the expression 5^4 ——→ 5 is called the **base**
——→ 4 is called the **exponent**
——→ 5^4 is called the **power**

EXAMPLE 2.2A

(i) $7 \times 7 \times 7 \times 7 \times 7 = 7^5$

(ii) $(-4)(-4)(-4) = (-4)^3$

(iii) $(1.01)(1.01)(1.01)(1.01) = (1.01)^4$

(iv) $(a)(a)(a)(a)(a)(a)(a) = a^7$

(v) $(1 + i)(1 + i)(1 + i)(1 + i)(1 + i)(1 + i) = (1 + i)^6$

Definition: When "n" is a positive integer, "a^n" represents the product of "n" equal factors whose value is "a."

$$a^n = (a)(a)(a)(a) \ldots (a) \text{ to } n \text{ factors}$$

a is called the **base**
n is called the **exponent**
a^n is called the **power**

$$\text{POWER} = \text{BASE}^{\text{to the EXPONENT}}$$

Note: If a number is raised to the exponent "1," the power equals the base.

$5^1 = 5$ and $a^1 = a$;
conversely, $6 = 6^1$ and $x = x^1$.

B. Numerical evaluation of powers with positive integral exponents

1. Evaluation When the Base Is a Positive Integer

To evaluate a power, we may rewrite the power in factored form and obtain the product by multiplication.

EXAMPLE 2.2B

(i) 2^5 ——— means that 2 is a factor 5 times
$= (2)(2)(2)(2)(2)$ ——— power rewritten in factored form
$= 32$ ——— product

(ii) $(5)^3$ ——— 5 is a factor 3 times
$= (5)(5)(5) = 125$

(iii) 1^7 ——— 1 is a factor 7 times
$= (1)(1)(1)(1)(1)(1)(1)$
$= 1$

(iv) a^n *if* $a = 4, n = 6$
$a^n = 4^6$
$= (4)(4)(4)(4)(4)(4)$
$= 4096$

2. Evaluation When the Base Is a Negative Integer

If a power has a negative base, the number of equal factors shown by the exponent determines the sign of the product.

(a) If the exponent is an even positive integer, the product is positive.
(b) If the exponent is an odd positive integer, the product is negative.

EXAMPLE 2.2C

(i) $(-4)^3$ ——— (-4) is a factor 3 times
$= (-4)(-4)(-4)$
$= -64$ ——— the answer is negative (n is odd)

(ii) $(-2)^8$ ——— (-2) is a factor 8 times
$= (-2)(-2)(-2)(-2)(-2)(-2)(-2)(-2)$
$= 256$ ——— the answer is positive (n is even)

Note: -2^8 means $-(2)^8 = -(2)(2)(2)(2)(2)(2)(2)(2) = -256$

(iii) $(-1)^{55}$
$= (-1)(-1)(-1)(-1)\ldots$ to 55 factors
$= -1$

(iv) $3a^n$ for $a = -5, n = 4$
$3a^n = 3(-5)^4$
$= 3(-5)(-5)(-5)(-5)$
$= 3(625)$
$= 1875$

3. Evaluation When the Base Is a Common Fraction or Decimal

EXAMPLE 2.2D

(i) $\left(\frac{3}{2}\right)^5$ ——— $\frac{3}{2}$ is a factor 5 times

$$= \left(\frac{3}{2}\right)\left(\frac{3}{2}\right)\left(\frac{3}{2}\right)\left(\frac{3}{2}\right)\left(\frac{3}{2}\right)$$

$$= \frac{(3)(3)(3)(3)(3)}{(2)(2)(2)(2)(2)}$$

$$= \frac{243}{32}$$

(ii) $(0.1)^4$ ——— 0.1 is a factor 4 times

$= (0.1)(0.1)(0.1)(0.1)$

$= 0.0001$

(iii) $\left(-\frac{1}{3}\right)^3$ ——— $\left(-\frac{1}{3}\right)$ is a factor 3 times

$= \left(-\frac{1}{3}\right)\left(-\frac{1}{3}\right)\left(-\frac{1}{3}\right)$

$= \frac{(-1)(-1)(-1)}{(3)(3)(3)}$

$= \frac{-1}{27}$

(iv) $(1.02)^2$

$= (1.02)(1.02)$

$= 1.0404$

(v) $(1 + i)^n$ for $i = 0.03, n = 4$

$(1 + i)^n = (1 + 0.03)^4$

$= (1.03)(1.03)(1.03)(1.03)$

$= 1.125509$

POINTERS AND PITFALLS

You can use a calculator's *power function* to evaluate powers. On most financial calculators, the power function is represented by y^x. For example, to evaluate $(-1.03)^5$ using the Texas Instruments BAII Plus, use the key sequence

1.03 [±] [y^x] 5 [=]

The answer should be −1.159274.

C. Operations with powers

1. Multiplication of Powers

To multiply powers that have the same base, retain the common base and add the exponents.

$$a^m \times a^n = a^{m+n}$$ ——— Formula 2.1A

$$a^m \times a^n \times a^p = a^{m+n+p}$$ ——— Formula 2.1B

Notice that Formula 2.1B is an extension of Formula 2.1A.

EXAMPLE 2.2E

(i) $3^5 \times 3^2$
$= 3^{5+2}$ — retain the common base 3 and add the exponents 5 and 2
$= 3^7$

(ii) $(-4)^3(-4)^7(-4)^5$
$= (-4)^{3+7+5}$ — retain the common base (-4) and add the exponents 3, 7, and 5
$= (-4)^{15}$

(iii) $\left(\frac{1}{8}\right)^5\left(\frac{1}{8}\right) = \left(\frac{1}{8}\right)^{5+1} = \left(\frac{1}{8}\right)^6$

(iv) $(x^3)(x^5)(x) = x^{3+5+1} = x^9$

(v) $(1.06)^{16}(1.06)^{14} = (1.06)^{16+14} = 1.06^{30}$

(vi) $(1+i)(1+i)^5(1+i)^{20} = (1+i)^{1+5+20} = (1+i)^{26}$

2. Division of Powers

To divide powers that have the same base, retain the common base and subtract the exponent of the divisor from the exponent of the dividend.

$$a^m \div a^n = a^{m-n}$$ — Formula 2.2

EXAMPLE 2.2F

(i) $2^8 \div 2^5$ — retain the common base 2 and subtract the exponent of the divisor, 5, from the exponent of the dividend, 8
$= 2^{8-5}$
$= 2^3$

(ii) $(-10)^8 \div (-10)^7$ — retain the common base (-10) and subtract the exponents
$= (-10)^{8-7}$
$= (-10)^1$ or -10

(iii) $\left(-\frac{2}{5}\right)^6 \div \left(-\frac{2}{5}\right)^2 = \left(-\frac{2}{5}\right)^{6-2} = \left(-\frac{2}{5}\right)^4$

(iv) $a^{15} \div a^{10} = a^{15-10} = a^5$

(v) $(1.10)^{24} \div 1.10 = (1.10)^{24-1} = 1.10^{23}$

(vi) $(1+i)^{80} \div (1+i)^{60} = (1+i)^{80-60} = (1+i)^{20}$

3. Raising a Power to a Power

To raise a power to a power, retain the base and multiply the exponents.

$$(a^m)^n = a^{mn}$$ — Formula 2.3

EXAMPLE 2.2G

(i) $(3^2)^5$
$= 3^{2\times5}$ — retain the base 3 and multiply the exponents 2 and 5
$= 3^{10}$

(ii) $[(-4)^5]^3$
$= (-4)^{5 \times 3}$ — retain the base and multiply the exponents
$= (-4)^{15}$

(iii) $\left[\left(\frac{4}{3}\right)^6\right]^{10} = \left(\frac{4}{3}\right)^{6 \times 10} = \left(\frac{4}{3}\right)^{60}$

(iv) $(a^7)^3 = a^{7 \times 3} = a^{21}$

(v) $[(1.005)^{50}]^4 = (1.005)^{50 \times 4} = 1.005^{200}$

(vi) $[(1 + i)^{75}]^2 = (1 + i)^{75 \times 2} = (1 + i)^{150}$

4. Power of a Product and Power of a Quotient

The power of a product, written in factored form, is the product of the individual factors raised to the exponent.

$$(ab)^m = a^m b^m$$ — Formula 2.4

POINTERS AND PITFALLS

Note that ab^2 is not the same as $(ab)^2$ since ab^2 means $(a)(b)(b)$ while $(ab)^2 = (ab)(ab) = (a)(a)(b)(b) = a^2b^2$.

The power of a quotient is the quotient of the dividend and the divisor raised to the exponent.

$$\left(\frac{a}{b}\right)^m = \frac{a^m}{b^m}$$ — Formula 2.5

EXAMPLE 2.2H

(i) $(2 \times 3)^5 = 2^5 \times 3^5$

(ii) $(6 \times 2^7)^4 = 6^4 \times (2^7)^4 = 6^4 \times 2^{28}$

(iii) $\left(-\frac{5}{7}\right)^3 = \frac{(-5)^3}{7^3}$

(iv) $(a^3b)^4 = (a^3)^4 \times b^4 = a^{12}b^4$

(v) $\left[\frac{(1 + i)}{i}\right]^3 = \frac{(1 + i)^3}{i^3}$

D. Zero exponent

A zero exponent results when using the law of division of powers on powers with equal exponents.

$3^5 \div 3^5$
$= 3^{5-5}$
$= 3^0$

The result may be interpreted as follows.

$$3^5 \div 3^5 = \frac{3^5}{3^5} = \frac{3 \times 3 \times 3 \times 3 \times 3}{3 \times 3 \times 3 \times 3 \times 3} = 1$$

$$\boxed{3^0 = 1}$$

Similarly, $a^6 \div a^6 = a^{6-6} = a^0$

and since $a^6 \div a^6 = \frac{a^6}{a^6} = \frac{(a)(a)(a)(a)(a)(a)}{(a)(a)(a)(a)(a)(a)} = 1$

$$\boxed{a^0 = 1}$$

In general, *any number raised to the exponent zero is 1*, except zero itself. The expression 0^0 has no meaning and is said to be *undefined.*

E. Negative exponents

A negative exponent results when the exponent of the divisor is greater than the exponent of the dividend.

$$\begin{aligned} &4^3 \div 4^5 \\ &= 4^{3-5} \\ &= 4^{-2} \end{aligned}$$

The result may be interpreted as follows.

$$4^3 \div 4^5 = \frac{4^3}{4^5} = \frac{4 \times 4 \times 4}{4 \times 4 \times 4 \times 4 \times 4} = \frac{1}{4 \times 4} = \frac{1}{4^2}$$

$$\boxed{4^{-2} = \frac{1}{4^2}}$$

Similarly, $a^5 \div a^8 = a^{5-8} = a^{-3}$

and since $a^5 \div a^8 = \frac{a^5}{a^8} = \frac{(a)(a)(a)(a)(a)}{(a)(a)(a)(a)(a)(a)(a)(a)}$

$$= \frac{1}{(a)(a)(a)} = \frac{1}{a^3}$$

$$\boxed{a^{-3} = \frac{1}{a^3}}$$

$$\boxed{a^{-m} = \frac{1}{a^m}} \quad \text{Formula 2.6}$$

In general, a base raised to a negative exponent is equivalent to "1" divided by the same base raised to the corresponding positive exponent.

EXAMPLE 2.21

(i) $2^{-3} = \frac{1}{2^3} = \frac{1}{8}$

(ii) $(-3)^{-2} = \frac{1}{(-3)^2} = \frac{1}{9}$

(iii) $\left(\frac{1}{4}\right)^{-4} = \frac{1}{(\frac{1}{4})^4} = \frac{1}{\frac{1}{256}} = \frac{1}{1} \times \frac{256}{1} = 256$

(iv) $\left(-\frac{3}{5}\right)^{-3} = \frac{1}{(-\frac{3}{5})^3} = \frac{1}{-\frac{27}{125}} = \frac{-125}{27}$

Note: Since $\frac{-125}{27} = \frac{(-5)^3}{3^3} = \left(-\frac{5}{3}\right)^3 = \left(-\frac{3}{5}\right)^{-3}$

$$\left(\frac{y}{x}\right)^{-m} = \left(\frac{x}{y}\right)^{m}$$ **Formula 2.7**

(v) $(-4)^0 = 1$

(vi) $(1.05)^{-2} = \frac{1}{1.05^2} = \frac{1}{1.1025} = 0.907029$

(vii) $(1 + i)^{-10} = \frac{1}{(1 + i)^{10}}$

(viii) $(1 + i)^{-1} = \frac{1}{1 + i}$

(ix) $(1 + i)^0 = 1$

EXERCISE 2.2

A. Evaluate each of the following.

1. 3^4 **2.** 1^5 **3.** $(-2)^4$ **4.** $(-1)^{12}$

5. $\left(\frac{2}{3}\right)^4$ **6.** $\left(\frac{5}{6}\right)^4$ **7.** $\left(-\frac{1}{4}\right)^3$ **8.** $\left(-\frac{2}{3}\right)^3$

9. $(0.5)^2$ **10.** $(2.2)^6$ **11.** $(-0.1)^3$ **12.** $(-3.2)^5$

13. $(-4)^0$ **14.** m^0 **15.** 3^{-2} **16.** 8^3

17. $(-5)^{-3}$ **18.** $(-3.6)^{-4}$ **19.** $\left(\frac{1}{5}\right)^{-3}$ **20.** $\left(\frac{2}{3}\right)^{-4}$

21. 1.01^{-1} **22.** $(1.05)^0$

B. Simplify.

1. $2^5 \times 2^3$
2. $(-4)^3 \times (-4)$
3. $4^7 \div 4^4$
4. $(-3)^9 \div (-3)^7$
5. $(2^3)^5$
6. $[(-4)^3]^6$
7. $a^4 \times a^{10}$
8. $m^{12} \div m^7$
9. $3^4 \times 3^6 \times 3$
10. $(-1)^3(-1)^7(-1)^5$
11. $\dfrac{6^7 \times 6^3}{6^9}$
12. $\dfrac{(x^4)(x^5)}{x^7}$
13. $\left(\dfrac{3}{5}\right)^4\left(\dfrac{3}{5}\right)^7$
14. $\left(\dfrac{1}{6}\right)^5 \div \left(\dfrac{1}{6}\right)^3$
15. $\left(-\dfrac{3}{2}\right)\left(-\dfrac{3}{2}\right)^6\left(-\dfrac{3}{2}\right)^4$
16. $\left(-\dfrac{3}{4}\right)^8 \div \left(-\dfrac{3}{4}\right)^7$
17. $(1.025^{80})(1.025^{70})$
18. $1.005^{240} \div 1.005^{150}$
19. $[1.04^{20}]^4$
20. $\left[\left(-\dfrac{3}{7}\right)^5\right]^3$
21. $(1 + i)^{100}(1 + i)^{100}$
22. $(1 - r)^2(1 - r)^2(1 - r)^2$
23. $[(1 + i)^{80}]^2$
24. $[(1 - r)^{40}]^3$
25. $(ab)^5$
26. $(2xy)^4$
27. $(m^3n)^8$
28. $\left(\dfrac{a^3b^2}{x}\right)^4$
29. $2^3 \times 2^5 \times 2^{-4}$
30. $5^2 \div 5^{-3}$
31. $\left(\dfrac{a}{b}\right)^{-8}$
32. $\left(\dfrac{1 + i}{i}\right)^{-n}$

2.3 FRACTIONAL EXPONENTS

A. Radicals

When the product of two or more equal factors is expressed in exponential form, one of the equal factors is called the **root of the product**. The exponent indicates the number of equal factors, that is, the **power of the root.**

For example,

$25 = 5^2$ → 5 is the second power root (square root) of 25
$8 = 2^3$ → 2 is the third power root (cube root) of 8
$81 = 3^4$ → 3 is the fourth (power) root of 81
a^5 → a is the fifth root of a^5
7^n → 7 is the nth root of 7^n
x^n → x is the nth root of x^n

The operational symbol for finding the root of an expression is $\sqrt{\ }$. This symbol represents the *positive* root only. If the negative root is desired, a minus sign is placed in front of the symbol; that is, the negative root is represented by $-\sqrt{\ }$.

The power of a root is written at the upper left of the symbol, as in $\sqrt[3]{\ }$ or $\sqrt[n]{\ }$.

The indicated root is called a **radical**, the power indicated is called the **index**, and the number under the symbol is called the **radicand**.

In $\sqrt[5]{32}$, the index is 5
the radicand is 32
the radical is $\sqrt[5]{32}$

When the square root is to be found, it is customary to omit the index 2. The symbol $\sqrt{\ }$ is understood to mean the positive square root of the radicand.

$\sqrt{49}$ means $\sqrt[2]{49}$ or 7

In special cases, such as those shown in Example 2.3A, the radicand is an integral power of the root. The root can readily be found by expressing the radicand in exponential form; the index of the root and the exponent are the same.

EXAMPLE 2.3A

(i) $\sqrt{64} = \sqrt{8^2}$ ——— the radicand 64 is expressed in exponential form as a square

$= 8$ ——— one of the two equal factors 8 is the root

(ii) $\sqrt[5]{32} = \sqrt[5]{2^5}$ ——— express the radicand 32 as the fifth power of 2

$= 2$ ——— one of the five equal factors 2 is the root

(iii) $\sqrt[3]{0.125} = \sqrt[3]{0.5^3} = 0.5$

In most cases, however, the radicand cannot be easily rewritten in exponential form. The arithmetic determination of the numerical value of these roots is a laborious process. But computating the root is easily accomplished using electronic calculators equipped with a power function.

To use the power function described in the Pointers and Pitfalls box on page 51, first rewrite the radical so it appears in exponential form. Then, as you will see in Formula 2.8 in the next section, $a^{1/n} = \sqrt[n]{a}$. Use the opposite of this formula to rewrite a radical into exponential form: $\sqrt[n]{a} = a^{1/n}$. For example, $\sqrt[5]{32}$ can be written as $32^{1/5}$. Now use the power function. The key sequence is

32 [y^x] [( ] 1 [÷] 5 [ )] [=] The solution is 2.

(Instead of using brackets, you could first calculate 1 ÷ 5, save the result in the calculator's memory, and then recall the result from memory after pressing [y^x].)

The problems in Example 2.3B are intended to ensure that you are able to use the power function. They should be done using an electronic calculator.

EXAMPLE 2.3B

(i) $\sqrt{1425} = 37.749172$ ——— *Check* $37.749172^2 = 1425$

(ii) $\sqrt[5]{12\,960} = 6.645398$ ——— *Check* $6.645398^5 = 12\,960$

(iii) $\sqrt[15]{40\,000} = 2.026768$ ——— *Check* $2.026768^{15} = 40\,000$

(iv) $\sqrt[20]{1\,048\,576} = 2$ ——— *Check* $2^{20} = 1\,048\,576$

(v) $\sqrt{0.005184} = 0.072$ ——— *Check* $0.072^2 = 0.005184$

(vi) $\sqrt[7]{0.038468} = 0.627872$ ——— *Check* $0.627872^7 = 0.038468$

(vii) $\sqrt[45]{1.954213} = 1.015$ ——— *Check* $1.015^{45} = 1.954213$

(viii) $\sqrt[36]{0.022528} = 0.9$ ——— *Check* $0.9^{36} = 0.022528$

(ix) $\sqrt{2^6} = \sqrt{64} = 8$

(x) $\sqrt[3]{5^6} = \sqrt[3]{15\,625} = 25$

Note: Many of the solutions for problems such as those above involve repeating and continuous numbers. To standardize, the number of decimal places shown in solutions will be set at six or fewer. The financial calculator can be set to show a maximum of six decimal places by following the steps:

2nd **Format** DEC = 6 **Enter** **2nd** **QUIT**

It is important to note that even though the calculator display shows six or fewer decimal places, the complete, non-rounded quantity is used in continuous calculations on the calculator.

EXAMPLE 2.3C

Calculate i in the formula $FV = PV(1 + i)^n$, where FV = 1102.50, PV = 1000.00, $n = 2$.

SOLUTION

$1102.50 = 1000.00(1 + i)^2$
$(1 + i)^2 = 1.1025$
$(1 + i) = 1.1025^{0.5}$ ——— raise both sides to the power 1/2, that is, 0.5
$(1 + i) = 1.05$
$i = 0.05$

B. Fractional exponents

Radicals may be written in exponential form and fractional exponents may be represented in radical form according to the following definitions.

(a) The exponent is a positive fraction with numerator 1.

$$a^{\frac{1}{n}} = \sqrt[n]{a}$$ ——— Formula 2.8

$$4^{\frac{1}{2}} = \sqrt{4} = 2$$

$$27^{\frac{1}{3}} = \sqrt[3]{27} = \sqrt[3]{3^3} = 3$$

$$625^{\frac{1}{4}} = \sqrt[4]{625} = \sqrt[4]{5^4} = 5$$

(b) The exponent is a negative fraction with numerator 1.

$$a^{-\frac{1}{n}} = \frac{1}{a^{\frac{1}{n}}} = \frac{1}{\sqrt[n]{a}}$$ Formula 2.9

$$8^{-\frac{1}{3}} = \frac{1}{8^{\frac{1}{3}}} = \frac{1}{\sqrt[3]{8}} = \frac{1}{\sqrt[3]{2^3}} = \frac{1}{2}$$

$$243^{-\frac{1}{5}} = \frac{1}{243^{\frac{1}{5}}} = \frac{1}{\sqrt[5]{243}} = \frac{1}{\sqrt[5]{3^5}} = \frac{1}{3}$$

(c) The exponent is a positive or negative fraction with numerator other than 1.

$$a^{\frac{m}{n}} = \sqrt[n]{a^m} = \left(\sqrt[n]{a}\right)^m$$ Formula 2.10

$$a^{-\frac{m}{n}} = \frac{1}{a^{\frac{m}{n}}} = \frac{1}{\sqrt[n]{a^m}}$$ Formula 2.11

$$16^{\frac{3}{4}} = \sqrt[4]{16^3} = (\sqrt[4]{16})^3 = (\sqrt[4]{2^4})^3 = (2)^3 = 8$$

$$27^{\frac{4}{3}} = \sqrt[3]{27^4} = (\sqrt[3]{27})^4 = (\sqrt[3]{3^3})^4 = (3)^4 = 81$$

$$36^{-\frac{3}{2}} = \frac{1}{(\sqrt[2]{36})^3} = \frac{1}{(\sqrt[2]{6^2})^3} = \frac{1}{6^3} = \frac{1}{216}$$

EXAMPLE 2.3D

(i) $36^{\frac{3}{2}} = 36^{1.5} = 216$

(ii) $3^{\frac{5}{4}} = 3^{1.25} = 3.948222$

(iii) $\sqrt[5]{12} = 12^{\frac{1}{5}} = 12^{0.2} = 1.643752$

(iv) $\sqrt[8]{325^5} = 325^{\frac{5}{8}} = 325^{0.625} = 37.147287$

(v) $\sqrt[6]{1.075} = 1.075^{\frac{1}{6}} = 1.075^{0.1\dot{6}} = 1.012126$

EXERCISE 2.3

A. Use an electronic calculator equipped with a power function to compute each of the following, correct to four decimals.

1. $\sqrt{5184}$

2. $\sqrt{205.9225}$

3. $\sqrt[7]{2187}$

4. $\sqrt[10]{1.1046221}$

5. $\sqrt[20]{4.3184}$

6. $\sqrt[16]{0.00001526}$

7. $\sqrt[6]{1.0825}$

8. $\sqrt[12]{1.15}$

B. Compute each of the following.

1. $3025^{\frac{1}{2}}$

2. $2401^{\frac{1}{4}}$

3. $525.21875^{\frac{2}{5}}$

4. $21.6^{\frac{4}{3}}$

5. $\sqrt[12]{1.125^7}$

6. $\sqrt[6]{1.095}$

7. $4^{-\frac{1}{3}}$

8. $1.06^{-\frac{1}{12}}$

9. $\frac{1.03^{60} - 1}{0.03}$

10. $\frac{1 - 1.05^{-36}}{0.05}$

11. $(1 + 0.08)^{10}$

12. $(1 + 0.045)^{-12}$

13. $26.50\,(1 + 0.043)\left[\frac{(1 + 0.043)^{30} - 1}{0.043}\right]$

14. $350.00\,(1 + 0.05)\left[\frac{(1 + 0.05)^{20} - 1}{0.05}\right]$

15. $133.00\left[\frac{1 - (1 + 0.056)^{-12}}{0.056}\right]$

16. $270.00\left[\frac{1 - (1 + 0.035)^{-8}}{0.035}\right]$

17. $5000.00\,(1 + 0.0275)^{-20} + 137.50\left[\frac{1 - (1 + 0.0275)^{-20}}{0.0275}\right]$

18. $1000.00\,(1 + 0.03)^{-16} + 300.00\left[\frac{1 - (1 + 0.03)^{-16}}{0.03}\right]$

19. $112.55 = 100.00(1 + i)^4$

20. $380.47 = 300.00(1 + i)^{12}$

21. $3036.77 = 2400.00(1 + i)^{6}$

22. $1453.36 = 800.00(1 + i)^{60}$

2.4 LOGARITHMS—BASIC ASPECTS

A. The concept of logarithm

In Section 2.2 and Section 2.3, the exponential form of writing numbers was discussed.

$64 = 2^6$ → the number 64 is represented as a power of 2
$243 = 3^5$ → the number 243 is represented as a power of 3
$10\,000 = 10^4$ → the number 10 000 is represented as a power of 10
$5 = 125^{\frac{1}{3}}$ → the number 5 is represented as a power of 125
$0.001 = 10^{-3}$ → the number 0.001 is represented as a power of 10

In general, when a number is represented as a base raised to an exponent, the exponent is called a logarithm. A **logarithm** is defined as the *exponent* to which a base must be raised to produce a given number.

Accordingly,

$64 = 2^6$ → 6 is the logarithm of 64 to the base 2, written $6 = \log_2 64$
$243 = 3^5$ → 5 is the logarithm of 243 to the base 3, written $5 = \log_3 243$
$10\,000 = 10^4$ → 4 is the logarithm of 10 000 to the base 10, written $4 = \log_{10} 10\,000$
$5 = 125^{\frac{1}{3}}$ → ⅓ is the logarithm of 5 to the base 125, written $\frac{1}{3} = \log_{125} 5$
$0.001 = 10^{-3}$ → −3 is the logarithm of 0.001 to the base 10, written $-3 = \log_{10} 0.001$

In general, if $N = b^y$ (*exponential* form)
then $y = \log_b N$ (*logarithmic* form).

EXAMPLE 2.4A

Write each of the following numbers in exponential form and in logarithmic form using the base indicated.

(i) 32 base 2	(ii) 81 base 3
(iii) 256 base 4	(iv) 100 000 base 10
(v) 6 base 36	(vi) 3 base 27
(vii) 0.0001 base 10	(viii) $\frac{1}{8}$ base 2

SOLUTION

Exponential Form	Logarithmic Form
(i) Since $32 = 2 \times 2 \times 2 \times 2 \times 2$	
$32 = 2^5$	$5 = \log_2 32$
(ii) Since $81 = 3 \times 3 \times 3 \times 3$	
$81 = 3^4$	$4 = \log_3 81$
(iii) Since $256 = 4 \times 4 \times 4 \times 4$	
$256 = 4^4$	$4 = \log_4 256$
(iv) Since $100\,000 = 10 \times 10 \times 10 \times 10 \times 10$	
$100\,000 = 10^5$	$5 = \log_{10} 100\,000$
(v) Since $6 = \sqrt{36}$	
$6 = 36^{\frac{1}{2}}$	$\frac{1}{2} = \log_{36} 6$
(vi) Since $3 = \sqrt[3]{27}$	
$3 = 27^{\frac{1}{3}}$	$\frac{1}{3} = \log_{27} 3$
(vii) Since $0.0001 = \frac{1}{10\,000} = \frac{1}{10^4}$	
$0.0001 = 10^{-4}$	$-4 = \log_{10} 0.0001$
(viii) Since $\frac{1}{8} = \frac{1}{2^3}$	
$\frac{1}{8} = 2^{-3}$	$-3 = \log_2 \frac{1}{8}$

B. Common logarithms

While the base b may be any positive number other than 1, only the numbers 10 and e are used in practice.

Logarithms with base 10 are called **common logarithms**. Obtained from the exponential function $x = 10^y$, the notation used to represent common logarithms is $y = \log x$. (The base 10 is understood and so is not written.)

By definition then, the common logarithm of a number is the exponent to which the base 10 must be raised to give that number.

$\log 1000 = 3$	since $1000 = 10^3$
$\log 1\,000\,000 = 6$	since $1\,000\,000 = 10^6$
$\log 0.01 = -2$	since $0.01 = 10^{-2}$
$\log 0.0001 = -4$	since $0.0001 = 10^{-4}$
$\log 1 = 0$	since $1 = 10^0$

Historically, common logarithms were used for numerical calculations that were required in problems involving compound interest. However, with the availability of electronic calculators equipped with a power function, the need for common logarithms as a computational tool has disappeared. Accordingly, this text gives no further consideration to common logarithms.

C. Natural logarithms

The most common exponential function is

$$y = e^x$$

where $e = \lim_{n \to \infty} \left(1 + \frac{1}{n}\right)^n = 2.718282$ approximately.

The logarithmic form of this function is $x = \log_e y$ but is always written as $\mathbf{x = \ln y}$ and called the **natural logarithm.**

Electronic calculators equipped with the universal power function are generally equipped as well with the e^x function and the $\ln x$ function (natural logarithm function). This latter function eliminates any need for common logarithms and can be used when solving equations for which the unknown quantity is an exponent. As you will see in Chapters 9 through 16, the natural logarithm function will be used to solve for n, the number of compounding periods, in mathematics of finance applications using the algebraic method.

POINTERS AND PITFALLS

In some calculator models, such as the Texas Instruments BAII Plus, the natural logarithm function is found *directly* by entering the number and pressing the [LN] key. In other calculators, the natural logarithm function is found *indirectly* by entering the number and pressing combinations of keys. For example:

For the Hewlett-Packard 10B calculator, enter the number, and then press the keys [■] [2].

For the Sharp EL-733A, enter the number, and then press [2nd F] [1/x].

EXAMPLE 2.4B

Use an electronic calculator equipped with the natural logarithm key [LN] to determine the value of each of the following.

(i) ln 2	(ii) ln 3000	(iii) ln 0.5
(iv) ln 1	(v) ln 0.0125	(vi) ln 2.718282

SOLUTION

(i) To evaluate ln 2 (using the Texas Instruments BAII Plus),
1. Key in 2.
2. Press LN.
3. Read the answer in the display.
$\ln 2 = 0.693147$

(ii) To evaluate ln 3000 (using the Sharp EL-733A), key in 3000, press 2nd F, press 1/x, and read the answer in the display.

$\ln 3000 = 8.006368$

(iii) $\ln 0.5 = -0.693147$
(iv) $\ln 1 = 0$
(v) $\ln 0.0125 = -4.382027$
(vi) $\ln 2.718282 = 1$

Note: 1. The natural logarithm of 1 is zero.

2. The natural logarithm of a number greater than 1 is positive, for example, $\ln 2 = 0.693147$.

3. The natural logarithm of a number less than 1 is negative, for example, $\ln 0.5 = -0.693147$.

D. Useful relationships

The following relationships are helpful when using natural logarithms:

1. The logarithm of a product of two or more positive numbers is the sum of the logarithms of the factors.

$$\ln (ab) = \ln a + \ln b$$ Formula 2.12A

$$\ln (abc) = \ln a + \ln b + \ln c$$ Formula 2.12B

Notice that Formula 2.12B is an extension of Formula 2.12A.

2. The logarithm of the quotient of two positive numbers is equal to the logarithm of the dividend (numerator) minus the logarithm of the divisor (denominator).

$$\ln \left(\frac{a}{b}\right) = \ln a - \ln b$$ Formula 2.13

3. The logarithm of a power of a positive number is the exponent of the power multiplied by the logarithm of the number.

$$\ln (a^k) = k(\ln a)$$ Formula 2.14

4. (i) $\ln e = 1$ since $e = e^1$

(ii) $\ln 1 = 0$ since $1 = e^0$

EXAMPLE 2.4C

Use an electronic calculator equipped with the natural logarithm function to evaluate each of the following.

(i) $\ln[3(15)(36)]$

(ii) $\ln\left[\left(\frac{5000}{1.045}\right)\right]$

(iii) $\ln[1500(1.05^6)]$

(iv) $\ln[5000(1.045^{-1})]$

(v) $\ln\left[\left(\frac{4000}{1.07^{12}}\right)\right]$

(vi) $\ln[10\,000(1.0125^{-17})]$

(vii) $\ln[1.00e^7]$

(viii) $\ln[2.00e^{-0.6}]$

(ix) $\ln\left[600\left(\frac{1.04^6 - 1}{0.04}\right)\right]$

(x) $\ln\left[\left(\frac{1 - 1.0625^{-12}}{0.0625}\right)\right]$

SOLUTION

(i) $\ln[3(15)(36)] = \ln 3 + \ln 15 + \ln 36$
$= 1.098612 + 2.708050 + 3.583519$
$= 7.390181$

Note: You can verify the answer by first simplifying.
$\ln 3(15)(36) = \ln 1620 = 7.390181$

(ii) $\ln\left[\left(\frac{5000}{1.045}\right)\right] = \ln 5000 - \ln 1.045$
$= 8.517193 - 0.044017$
$= 8.473176$

(iii) $\ln[1500(1.05^6)] = \ln 1500 + \ln 1.05^6$
$= \ln 1500 + 6(\ln 1.05)$
$= 7.313220 + 6(0.048790)$
$= 7.313220 + 0.292741$
$= 7.605961$

(iv) $\ln[5000(1.045^{-1})] = \ln 5000 + \ln 1.045^{-1}$
$= \ln 5000 - 1(\ln 1.045)$
$= 8.517193 - 1(0.044017)$
$= 8.473176$

(v) $\ln\left[\left(\frac{4000}{1.07^{12}}\right)\right] = \ln 4000 - \ln 1.07^{12}$
$= 8.294050 - 12(0.067659)$
$= 8.294050 - 0.811904$
$= 7.482146$

(vi) $\ln[10\,000(1.0125^{-17})] = \ln 10\,000 - 17(\ln 1.0125)$
$= 9.210340 - 17(0.012423)$
$= 9.210340 - 0.211183$
$= 8.999158$

(vii) $\ln[1.00e^{7}] = \ln 1.00 + \ln e^{7}$
$= \ln 1.00 + 7(\ln e)$
$= 0 + 7(1)$
$= 7$

(viii) $\ln[2.00e^{-0.6}] = \ln 2.00 + \ln e^{-0.6}$
$= \ln 2.00 - 0.6(\ln e)$
$= 0.693147 - 0.6$
$= 0.093147$

(ix) $\ln\left[600\left(\frac{1.04^{6} - 1}{0.04}\right)\right] = \ln 600 + \ln\left(\frac{1.04^{6} - 1}{0.04}\right)$
$= \ln 600 + \ln(1.04^{6} - 1) - \ln 0.04$
$= \ln 600 + \ln(1.265319 - 1) - \ln 0.04$
$= \ln 600 + \ln 0.265319 - \ln 0.04$
$= 6.396930 - 1.326822 - (-3.218876)$
$= 6.396930 - 1.326822 + 3.218876$
$= 8.288984$

(x) $\ln\left[\left(\frac{1 - 1.0625^{-12}}{0.0625}\right)\right] = \ln(1 - 1.0625^{-12}) - \ln 0.0625$
$= \ln(1 - 0.483117) - \ln 0.0625$
$= \ln 0.516883 - \ln 0.0625$
$= -0.659939 - (-2.772589)$
$= -0.659939 + 2.772589$
$= 2.112650$

EXERCISE 2.4

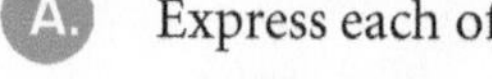

A. Express each of the following in logarithmic form.

1. $2^{9} = 512$

2. $3^{7} = 2187$

3. $5^{-3} = \frac{1}{125}$

4. $10^{-5} = 0.00001$

5. $e^{2j} = 18$

6. $e^{-3x} = 12$

B. Write each of the following in exponential form.

1. $\log_2 32 = 5$

2. $\log_3 \frac{1}{81} = -4$

3. $\log_{10} 10 = 1$

4. $\ln e^2 = 2$

C. Use an electronic calculator equipped with a natural logarithm function to evaluate each of the following.

1. $\ln 2$

2. $\ln 200$

3. $\ln 0.105$

4. $\ln[300(1.10^{15})]$

5. $\ln\left(\frac{2000}{1.09^9}\right)$

6. $\ln\left[850\left(\frac{1.01^{-120}}{0.01}\right)\right]$

BUSINESS MATH NEWS BOX

Revenue from Olympic Broadcast Partnerships

On July 2, 2003, Vancouver was elected the host city of the XXI Olympic Winter Games in 2010, becoming the largest city ever invited to host the Winter Games. It was the first time a Winter Olympics had been held at sea level, and with an average February temperature of 4.8 °C, Vancouver was also the warmest host city on record. For these reasons, Vancouver was bound to attract added interest from winter sport enthusiasts worldwide.

Although Winter Olympics attract fewer viewers than Summer Games, the Vancouver 2010 Games benefitted from the fact that the Beijing 2008 Summer Games were the most watched Games in Olympic history, with action delivered to viewers around the world via television, the Internet, and cellphones.

Ever since the London Summer Games were first broadcast into homes around the world in 1948, the Olympic movement's greatest source of revenue has come from broadcast partnerships negotiated by the International Olympic Committee (IOC). Television broadcasting rights contribute approximately 50% of the total IOC revenues. (Corporate sponsors account for 40% of the total, and ticket sales and merchandising activities account for the remainder of total revenues.)

Over the last 30 years, the global broadcast revenue for the Olympic Winter Games has increased from C$21.7 million for Lake Placid in 1980 to C$1180 million for Vancouver in 2010.

The IOC manages the broadcast program and distributes 90% of Olympic marketing revenue to organizations throughout the Olympic movement to support the staging of the Olympic Games and to promote the worldwide development of sport.

The chart below depicts the exponential growth in broadcast revenue for the Olympic Winter Games for the past 30 years. (All figures are expressed in Canadian dollars):

Olympic Winter Games	Broadcast Revenue (C$)
Lake Placid 1980	21.7 million
Sarajevo 1984	107.5 million
Calgary 1988	340 million
Albertville 1992	305.5 million
Lillehammer 1994	369.3 million
Nagano 1998	573.4 million
Salt Lake City 2002	772.4 million
Turin 2006	869.7 million
Vancouver 2010	1180 million (approximate to date)

Source: Data retrieved from **www.olympic.org** on July 12, 2010.

QUESTIONS

1. How much money did the IOC retain to cover operational and administrative costs as a result of the broadcast revenues generated by the Vancouver Winter Games?
2. Express your answer to Question 1 as an exponent in millions of Canadian dollars.
3. Estimate the total IOC revenues expected for the Vancouver Winter Games in billions of Canadian dollars.

2.5 SOLVING BASIC EQUATIONS

A. Basic terms and concepts

1. An **equation** is a statement of equality between two algebraic expressions.

$$7x = 35$$
$$3a - 4 = 11 - 2a$$
$$5(2k - 4) = -3(k + 2)$$

2. If an equation contains only one *variable* and the variable occurs with power 1 only, the equation is said to be a **linear** or **first-degree equation** in one unknown. The three equations listed above are linear equations in one unknown.
3. The two expressions that are equated are called the sides or **members of an equation**. Every equation has a left side (left member) and a right side (right member).

   In the equation $3a - 4 = 11 - 2a$,
   $3a - 4$ is the left side (left member) and
   $11 - 2a$ is the right side (right member).

4. The process of finding a replacement value (number) for the variable, which when substituted into the equation makes the two members of the equation equal, is called *solving the equation*. The replacement value that makes the two members equal is called a *solution* or **root of an equation**. A linear or first-degree equation has only one root and the root, when substituted into the equation, is said to *satisfy* the equation.

   The root (solution) of the equation $3a - 4 = 11 - 2a$
   is 3 because when 3 is substituted for a

the left side $3a - 4 = 3(3) - 4 = 9 - 4 = 5$ and
the right side $11 - 2a = 11 - 2(3) = 11 - 6 = 5$.

Thus, for $a = 3$, Left Side = Right Side and 3 satisfies the equation.

5. Equations that have the same root are called **equivalent equations**. Thus,

$$6x + 5 = 4x + 17, 6x = 4x + 12, 2x = 12, \text{ and } x = 6$$

are equivalent equations because the root of all four equations is 6; that is, when 6 is substituted for x, each of the equations is satisfied.

Equivalent equations are useful in solving equations. They may be obtained

(a) by multiplying or dividing both sides of the equation by a number other than zero; and
(b) by adding or subtracting the same number on both sides of the equation.

6. When solving an equation, the basic aims in choosing the operations that will generate useful equivalent equations are to

(a) isolate the terms containing the variable on one side of the equation (this is achieved by addition or subtraction); and
(b) make the numerical coefficient of the single term containing the variable equal to +1 (this is achieved by multiplication or division).

B. Solving equations using addition

If the same number is added to each side of an equation, the resulting equation is equivalent to the original equation.

	$x - 5 = 4$	original equation
add 3	$x - 5 + 3 = 4 + 3$	equivalent equations
or add 5	$x - 5 + 5 = 4 + 5$	

Addition is used to isolate the term or terms containing the variable when terms that have a negative coefficient appear in the equation.

EXAMPLE 2.5A

(i) $x - 6 = 4$
$x - 6 + 6 = 4 + 6$ — add 6 to each side of the equation to eliminate the term −6 on the left side of the equation
$x = 10$

(ii) $-2x = -3 - 3x$
$-2x + 3x = -3 - 3x + 3x$ — add $3x$ to each side to eliminate the term $-3x$ on the right side
$x = -3$

(iii) $-x - 5 = 8 - 2x$
$-x - 5 + 5 = 8 - 2x + 5$ — add 5 to eliminate the constant −5 on the left side
$-x = 13 - 2x$ — combine like terms
$-x + 2x = 13 - 2x + 2x$ — add $2x$ to eliminate the term $-2x$ on the right side
$x = 13$

C. Solving equations using subtraction

If the same number is subtracted from each side of an equation, the resulting equation is equivalent to the original equation.

	$x + 8 = 9$	original equation
subtract 4	$x + 8 - 4 = 9 - 4$	equivalent equations
or subtract 8	$x + 8 - 8 = 9 - 8$	

Subtraction is used to isolate the term or terms containing the variable when terms having a positive numerical coefficient appear in the equation.

EXAMPLE 2.5B

(i)

$$x + 10 = 6$$

$$x + 10 - 10 = 6 - 10 \quad \text{— subtract 10 from each side of the equation}$$

$$x = -4$$

(ii)

$$7x = 9 + 6x$$

$$7x - 6x = 9 + 6x - 6x \quad \text{— subtract } 6x \text{ from each side to eliminate the term } 6x \text{ on the right side}$$

$$x = 9$$

(iii)

$$6x + 4 = 5x - 3$$

$$6x + 4 - 4 = 5x - 3 - 4 \quad \text{— subtract 4 from each side to eliminate the term 4 on the left side}$$

$$6x = 5x - 7 \quad \text{— combine like terms}$$

$$6x - 5x = 5x - 7 - 5x \quad \text{— subtract } 5x \text{ from each side of the equation to eliminate the term } 5x \text{ on the right side}$$

$$x = -7$$

D. Solving equations using multiplication

If each side of an equation is multiplied by the same non-zero number, the resulting equation is equivalent to the original equation.

	$-3x = 6$	original equation
multiply by 2	$-6x = 12$	equivalent equations
or multiply by -1	$3x = -6$	

Multiplication is used in solving equations containing common fractions to eliminate the denominator or denominators.

EXAMPLE 2.5C

(i)

$$\frac{1}{2}x = 3 \quad \text{— original equation}$$

$$2\left(\frac{1}{2}x\right) = 2(3) \quad \text{— multiply each side by 2 to eliminate the denominator}$$

$$x = 6 \quad \text{— solution}$$

(ii) $-\frac{1}{4}x = 2$ —— original equation

$4\left(-\frac{1}{4}x\right) = 4(2)$ —— multiply each side by 4 to eliminate the denominator

$-1x = 8$

$(-1)(-x) = (-1)(8)$ —— multiply by (-1) to make the coefficient of the term in x positive

$x = -8$

(iii) $-\frac{1}{7}x = -2$

$(-7)\left(-\frac{1}{7}x\right) = (-7)(-2)$ —— multiply by (-7) to eliminate the denominator and to make the coefficient of x equal to $+1$

$x = 14$

E. Solving equations using division

If each side of an equation is divided by the same non-zero number, the resulting equation is equivalent to the original equation.

	$15x = 45$	original equation
divide by 3	$5x = 15$	equivalent equations
or divide by 5	$3x = 9$	equivalent equations
or divide by 15	$x = 3$	equivalent equations

Division is used in solving equations when the numerical coefficient of the single term containing the variable is an integer or a decimal fraction.

EXAMPLE 2.5D

(i) $12x = 36$ —— original equation

$\frac{12x}{12} = \frac{36}{12}$ —— divide each side by the numerical coefficient 12

$x = 3$ —— solution

(ii) $-7x = 42$

$\frac{-7x}{-7} = \frac{42}{-7}$ —— divide each side by the numerical coefficient -7

$x = -6$

(iii) $0.2x = 3$

$\frac{0.2x}{0.2} = \frac{3}{0.2}$

$x = 15$

(iv) $x - 0.3x = 14$

$0.7x = 14$

$\frac{0.7x}{0.7} = \frac{14}{0.7}$

$x = 20$

F. Using two or more operations to solve equations

When more than one operation is needed to solve an equation, the operations are usually applied as follows.

(a) First, use addition and subtraction to isolate the terms containing the variable on one side of the equation (usually the left side).

(b) Second, after combining like terms, use multiplication and division to make the coefficient of the term containing the variable equal to +1.

EXAMPLE 2.5E

(i)
$$\left(-\frac{3}{5}\right)x = 12$$
$$5\left(-\frac{3}{5}\right)x = 5(12) \quad \text{——— multiply by 5 to eliminate the denominator}$$
$$-3x = 60$$
$$\frac{-3x}{-3} = \frac{60}{-3} \quad \text{——— divide by } -3$$
$$x = -20$$

(ii)
$$7x - 5 = 15 + 3x$$
$$7x - 5 + 5 = 15 + 3x + 5 \quad \text{——— add 5}$$
$$7x = 20 + 3x \quad \text{——— combine like terms}$$
$$7x - 3x = 20 + 3x - 3x \quad \text{——— subtract } 3x$$
$$4x = 20$$
$$x = 5 \quad \text{——— divide by 4}$$

(iii)
$$3x + 9 - 7x = 24 - x - 3$$
$$9 - 4x = 21 - x \quad \text{——— combine like terms}$$
$$9 - 4x - 9 = 21 - x - 9$$
$$-4x = 12 - x$$
$$-4x + x = 12 - x + x$$
$$-3x = 12$$
$$x = -4$$

G. Checking equations

To check the solution to an equation, substitute the solution into each side of the equation and determine the value of each side.

EXAMPLE 2.5F

(i) For $-\frac{3}{5}x = 12$, the solution shown is $x = -20$.

Check

Left Side $= -\frac{3}{5}x = \left(-\frac{3}{5}\right)(-20) = -3(-4) = 12$

Right Side $= 12$

Since Left Side = Right Side, -20 is the solution to the equation.

(ii) For $7x - 5 = 15 + 3x$, the solution shown is $x = 5$.

Check
LS $= 7x - 5 = 7(5) - 5 = 35 - 5 = 30$
RS $= 15 + 3x = 15 + 3(5) = 15 + 15 = 30$
Since LS = RS, 5 is the solution.

(iii) For $3x + 9 - 7x = 24 - x - 3$, the solution shown is $x = -4$.

Check
LS $= 3(-4) + 9 - 7(-4) = -12 + 9 + 28 = 25$
RS $= 24 - (-4) - 3 = 24 + 4 - 3 = 25$
Since LS = RS, -4 is the solution.

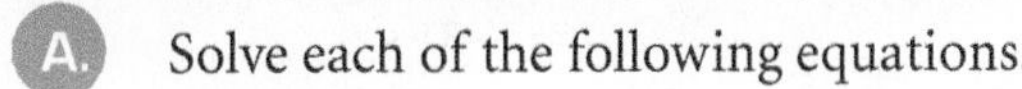

EXERCISE 2.5

A. Solve each of the following equations.

1. $15x = 45$ **2.** $-7x = 35$ **3.** $0.9x = 72$

4. $0.02x = 13$ **5.** $\frac{1}{6}x = 3$ **6.** $-\frac{1}{8}x = 7$

7. $\frac{3}{5}x = -21$ **8.** $-\frac{4}{3}x = -32$ **9.** $x - 3 = -7$

10. $-2x = 7 - 3x$ **11.** $x + 6 = -2$ **12.** $3x = 9 + 2x$

13. $4 - x = 9 - 2x$ **14.** $2x + 7 = x - 5$ **15.** $x + 0.6x = 32$

16. $x - 0.3x = 210$ **17.** $x - 0.04x = 192$ **18.** $x + 0.07x = 64.20$

B. Solve each of the following equations and check your solution.

1. $3x + 5 = 7x - 11$ **2.** $5 - 4x = -4 - x$

3. $2 - 3x - 9 = 2x - 7 + 3x$ **4.** $4x - 8 - 9x = 10 + 2x - 4$

5. $3x + 14 = 4x + 9$ **6.** $16x - 12 = 6x - 32$

7. $5 + 3 + 4x = 5x + 12 - 25$ **8.** $-3 + 2x + 5 = 5x - 36 + 14$

2.6 EQUATION SOLVING INVOLVING ALGEBRAIC SIMPLIFICATION

A. Solving linear equations involving the product of integral constants and binomials

To solve this type of equation, multiply first, then simplify.

EXAMPLE 2.6A

(i) $3(2x - 5) = -5(7 - 2x)$
$6x - 15 = -35 + 10x$ ——— expand
$6x - 10x = -35 + 15$ ——— isolate the terms in x
$-4x = -20$
$x = 5$

Check

LS = $3[2(5) - 5] = 3(10 - 5) = 3(5) = 15$

RS = $-5[7 - 2(5)] = -5(7 - 10) = -5(-3) = 15$

Since LS = RS, 5 is the solution.

(ii) $x - 4(3x - 7) = 3(9 - 5x) - (x - 11)$

$$x - 12x + 28 = 27 - 15x - x + 11 \quad \text{expand}$$
$$-11x + 28 = 38 - 16x \quad \text{combine like terms}$$
$$-11x + 16x = 38 - 28 \quad \text{isolate the terms in } x$$
$$5x = 10$$
$$x = 2$$

Check

LS = $2 - 4[3(2) - 7]$
$= 2 - 4(6 - 7)$
$= 2 - 4(-1)$
$= 2 + 4$
$= 6$

RS = $3[9 - 5(2)] - (2 - 11)$
$= 3(9 - 10) - (-9)$
$= 3(-1) + 9$
$= -3 + 9$
$= 6$

Since LS = RS, 2 is the solution.

B. Solving linear equations containing common fractions

The best approach when solving equations containing common fractions is to first create an equivalent equation without common fractions. Refer to the Pointers and Pitfalls on page 11. Multiply each term of the equation by the **lowest common denominator (LCD)** of the fractions.

EXAMPLE 2.6B

(i) $\frac{4}{5}x - \frac{3}{4} = \frac{7}{12} + \frac{11}{15}x$ — LCD = 60

$$60\left(\frac{4}{5}x\right) - 60\left(\frac{3}{4}\right) = 60\left(\frac{7}{12}\right) + 60\left(\frac{11}{15}x\right) \quad \text{multiply each term by 60}$$
$$12(4x) - 15(3) = 5(7) + 4(11x) \quad \text{reduce to eliminate the fractions}$$
$$48x - 45 = 35 + 44x$$
$$48x - 44x = 35 + 45$$
$$4x = 80$$
$$x = 20$$

Check

LS = $\frac{4}{5}(20) - \frac{3}{4} = 16 - 0.75 = 15.25$

RS = $\frac{7}{12} + \frac{11}{15}(20) = 0.58\dot{3} + 14.\dot{6} = 15.25$

Since LS = RS, 20 is the solution.

(ii) $\frac{5}{8}x - 3 = \frac{3}{4} + \frac{5x}{6}$ ——— LCD = 24

$$24\left(\frac{5x}{8}\right) - 24(3) = 24\left(\frac{3}{4}\right) + 24\left(\frac{5x}{6}\right)$$
$$3(5x) - 72 = 6(3) + 4(5x)$$
$$15x - 72 = 18 + 20x$$
$$-5x = 90$$
$$x = -18$$

Check

$$LS = \frac{5}{8}(-18) - 3 = -11.25 - 3 = -14.25$$

$$RS = \frac{3}{4} + \frac{5}{6}(-18) = 0.75 - 15 = -14.25$$

Since LS = RS, the solution is −18.

C. Solving linear equations involving fractional constants and multiplication

When solving this type of equation, the best approach is first to eliminate the fractions and then to expand.

EXAMPLE 2.6C

(i) $\frac{3}{2}(x - 2) - \frac{2}{3}(2x - 1) = 5$ ——— LCD = 6

$$6\left(\frac{3}{2}\right)(x - 2) - 6\left(\frac{2}{3}\right)(2x - 1) = 6(5)$$ ——— multiply each side by 6

$$3(3)(x - 2) - 2(2)(2x - 1) = 30$$ ——— reduce to eliminate fractions
$$9(x - 2) - 4(2x - 1) = 30$$
$$9x - 18 - 8x + 4 = 30$$
$$x - 14 = 30$$
$$x = 44$$

Check

$$LS = \frac{3}{2}(44 - 2) - \frac{2}{3}(2 \times 44 - 1) = \frac{3}{2}(42) - \frac{2}{3}(87) = 63 - 58 = 5$$

RS = 5

Since LS = RS, 44 is the solution.

(ii) $-\frac{3}{5}(4x - 1) + \frac{5}{8}(4x - 3) = -\frac{11}{10}$ ——— LCD = 40

$$40\left(\frac{-3}{5}\right)(4x - 1) + 40\left(\frac{5}{8}\right)(4x - 3) = 40\left(\frac{-11}{10}\right)$$
$$8(-3)(4x - 1) + 5(5)(4x - 3) = 4(-11)$$

$$-24(4x - 1) + 25(4x - 3) = -44$$
$$-96x + 24 + 100x - 75 = -44$$
$$4x - 51 = -44$$
$$4x = 7$$
$$x = \frac{7}{4}$$

Check

$$\text{LS} = -\frac{3}{5}\left[4\left(\frac{7}{4}\right) - 1\right] + \frac{5}{8}\left[4\left(\frac{7}{4}\right) - 3\right]$$
$$= -\frac{3}{5}(7 - 1) + \frac{5}{8}(7 - 3)$$
$$= -\frac{18}{5} + \frac{5}{2} = -\frac{36}{10} + \frac{25}{10} = -\frac{11}{10}$$
$$\text{RS} = -\frac{11}{10}$$

Since LS = RS, the solution is $\frac{7}{4}$.

POINTERS AND PITFALLS

When using a lowest common denominator (LCD) to eliminate fractions from an equation involving both fractional constants and multiplication, the LCD must be multiplied by each quantity (on *both* sides of the equation) that is preceded by a + or a − sign *outside of brackets.* (Some students multiply the LCD by each quantity inside *and* outside the brackets, which leads to an answer *much* greater than the correct answer.)

D. Formula rearrangement

Formula rearrangement, also known as **formula manipulation**, is the process of rearranging the terms of an equation. To solve for a particular variable, we want the variable to stand alone on the left side of the equation. If it does not already do so, then we have to rearrange the terms. Developing your skill in rearranging formulas is very important, as it saves a lot of time in memorization. You need only memorize one form of any particular formula. For example, consider the formula $I = Prt$. Once we have memorized this formula, there is no need to memorize equivalent forms as long as we are skilled in formula rearrangement. Thus, for example, we need not "memorize" the form $P = I/rt$.

The key to formula manipulation is the concept of *undoing operations.* Addition and subtraction are *inverse operations* (i.e., they *undo* each other). To move a number that has been added on one side of an equation, subtract the number from both sides of the equation. To move a number that has been subtracted on one side of an equation, add the number to both sides of the equation.

Multiplication and division are also inverse operations. To move a number that has been multiplied on one side of an equation, divide by that number on both sides of the equation. To move a number that has been divided on one side of an equation, multiply by that number on both sides of the equation. Powers and roots are inverses also.

Before you begin formula rearrangement, study the formula to see where the variable you wish to isolate is located and what relationship it has with other variables in the formula. Rearrange the formula so that the variable is isolated on one side of the equal sign, with all other variables on the other side.

EXAMPLE 2.6D

Given $\text{FV} = \text{PV}(1 + i)^n$, solve for PV.

$$\frac{\text{FV}}{(1+i)^n} = \text{FV}(1+i)^{-n} = \text{PV}$$ — divide both sides by $(1 + i)^n$

EXAMPLE 2.6E

Given the formula $\text{P} = (pq - vq) - \text{F}$, solve for q.

$$\text{P} = (pq - vq - \text{F})$$

$$\text{P} = q(p - v) - \text{F}$$ — isolate q

$$\text{P} + \text{F} = q(p - v)$$ — add F to both sides

$$q = \frac{\text{P} + \text{F}}{p - v}$$ — divide both sides by $(p - v)$

EXAMPLE 2.6F

Given $\text{FV} = \text{PV}(1 + i)^n$, solve for i.

$$\text{FV} = \text{PV}(1 + i)^n$$

$$\frac{\text{FV}}{\text{PV}} = (1 + i)^n$$ — divide both sides by PV

$$\sqrt[n]{\frac{\text{FV}}{\text{PV}}} = 1 + i$$ — taking a root is the undoing of a power

$$\sqrt[n]{\frac{\text{FV}}{\text{PV}}} - 1 = i$$ — subtract 1 from both sides

$$i = \sqrt[n]{\frac{\text{FV}}{\text{PV}}} - 1$$ — reverse members of the equation

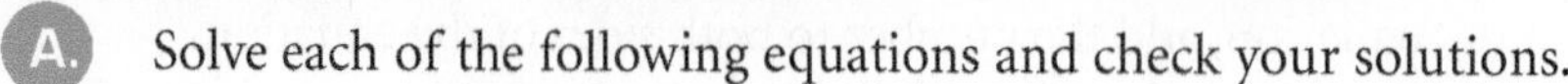

EXERCISE 2.6

A. Solve each of the following equations and check your solutions.

1. $12x - 4(9x - 20) = 320$

2. $5(x - 4) - 3(2 - 3x) = -54$

3. $3(2x - 5) - 2(2x - 3) = -15$

4. $17 - 3(2x - 7) = 7x - 3(2x - 1)$

5. $4x + 2(2x - 3) = 18$

6. $-3(1 - 11x) + (8x - 15) = 187$

7. $10x - 4(2x - 1) = 32$

8. $-2(x - 4) + 12(3 - 2x) = -8$

B. Solve each of the following equations.

1. $x - \frac{1}{4}x = 15$

2. $x + \frac{5}{8}x = 26$

3. $\frac{2}{3}x - \frac{1}{4} = -\frac{7}{4} - \frac{5}{6}x$

4. $\frac{5}{3} - \frac{2}{5}x = \frac{1}{6}x - \frac{1}{30}$

5. $\frac{3}{4}x + 4 = \frac{113}{24} - \frac{2}{3}x$

6. $2 - \frac{3}{2}x = \frac{2}{3}x + \frac{31}{9}$

C. Solve each of the following equations.

1. $\frac{3}{4}(2x - 1) - \frac{1}{3}(5 - 2x) = -\frac{55}{12}$

2. $\frac{4}{5}(4 - 3x) + \frac{53}{40} = \frac{3}{10}x - \frac{7}{8}(2x - 3)$

3. $\frac{2}{3}(2x - 1) - \frac{3}{4}(3 - 2x) = 2x - \frac{20}{9}$

4. $\frac{4}{3}(3x - 2) - \frac{3}{5}(4x - 3) = \frac{11}{60} + 3x$

D. Solve each of the following equations for the indicated variable.

1. $y = mx + b$ for x

2. $r = \frac{M}{S}$ for S

3. $\text{PV} = \frac{\text{PMT}}{i}$ for PMT

4. $\text{I} = \text{P}rt$ for t

5. $\text{A} = \text{P}(1 + rt)$ for r

6. $\text{PV} = \text{FV}(1 + i)^{-n}$ for i

2.7 SOLVING WORD PROBLEMS

One of students' biggest fears is being asked to solve a "word problem." Ironically, word problems are the answer to the "What will I ever need this math for?" question. So think of those dreaded word problems as "practical applications." There are many different types of word problems, from money, to numbers, to mixtures, to when will the train get to the station, to who did the most work. Each type of problem has a specific method of solution, but there is a series of steps that will get you through any word problem. Before you begin the series of steps, read the problem. Then read the problem again. This is not as strange as it seems. The first reading tells you what type of question you are dealing with. It may involve money, or people, or, like the brain teaser at the beginning of this chapter, gold bars. The second reading is done to find out what the question is asking you and what specific information the question is giving you. You can draw a diagram or make a chart if this will help sort out the information in the question. To solve problems by means of an algebraic equation, follow the systematic procedure outlined below.

BEFORE STEP 1 *Read the problem* to determine what type of question you are dealing with. Then *read the problem again* to determine the specific information the question is giving you.

STEP 1 *Introduce the variable* to be used by means of a complete sentence. This ensures a clear understanding and a record of what the variable is intended to represent. The variable is usually the item that you are asked to find—the item you do not know until you solve the problem.

STEP 2 *Translate* the information in the problem statement in terms of the variable. Determine what the words are telling you in relationship to the math. Watch for key words such as "more than" or "less than," "reduced by," and "half of" or "twice."

STEP 3 *Set up* an algebraic equation. This usually means matching the algebraic expressions developed in Step 2 to a specific number. Often one side of the equation represents the total number of items described in the word problem.

STEP 4 *Solve* the equation by rearranging the variables, state a conclusion, and check the conclusion against the problem statement.

EXAMPLE 2.7A

A TV set was sold during a sale for \$575. What is the regular selling price of the set if the price of the set was reduced by $\frac{1}{6}$ of the regular price?

SOLUTION

STEP 1 *Introduce the variable.* Let the regular selling price be represented by $\$x$.

STEP 2 *Translate.* The reduction in price is $\$\,\frac{1}{6}x$, and the reduced price is $\$(x - \frac{1}{6}x)$.

STEP 3 *Set up an equation.* Since the reduced price is given as \$575,

$$x - \frac{1}{6}x = 575$$

STEP 4 *Solve* the equation, state a conclusion, and check.

$$\frac{5}{6}x = 575$$

$$x = \frac{6(575)}{5}$$

$$x = 690$$

The regular selling price is \$690.

Check	Regular selling price	\$690
	Reduction: $\frac{1}{6}$ of 690	115
	Reduced price	\$575

EXAMPLE 2.7B

The material cost of a product is \$4 less than twice the cost of the direct labour, and the overhead is ⅚ of the direct labour cost. If the total cost of the product is \$157, what is the amount of each of the three elements of cost?

SOLUTION

Three values are needed, and the variable could represent any of the three. However, problems of this type can be solved most easily by representing the proper item by the variable rather than by selecting any of the other items. The *proper* item is the one to which the other item or items are *directly related.* In this problem, direct labour is that item.

Let the cost of direct labour be represented by \$$x$; then the cost of material is \$$(2x - 4)$ and the cost of overhead is \$$\frac{5}{6}x$.

The total cost is \$$(x + 2x - 4 + \frac{5}{6}x)$.

Since the total cost is given as \$157,

$$x + 2x - 4 + \frac{5}{6}x = 157$$
$$3x + \frac{5}{6}x = 161$$
$$18x + 5x = 966$$
$$23x = 966$$
$$x = 42$$

Material cost is \$80, direct labour cost is \$42, and overhead is \$35.

Check	Material cost: $2x - 4 = 2(42) - 4 =$	\$80
	Direct labour cost: $x =$	42
	Overhead cost: $\frac{5}{6}x = \frac{5}{6}(42) =$	35
	Total cost	\$157

EXAMPLE 2.7C

Nalini invested a total of \$24 000 in two mutual funds. Her investment in the Equity Fund is \$4000 less than three times her investment in the Bond Fund. How much did Nalini invest in the Equity Fund?

SOLUTION

Although the amount invested in the Equity Fund is required, it is more convenient to represent her investment in the Bond Fund by the variable since the investment in the Equity Fund is expressed in terms of the investment in the Bond Fund.

Let the amount invested in the Bond Fund be \$$x$; then the amount invested in the Equity Fund is \$$(3x - 4000)$ and the total amount invested is $(x + 3x − 4000). Since the total amount invested is $24 000,

$$\begin{aligned} x + 3x - 4000 &= 24\,000 \\ 4x &= 28\,000 \\ x &= 7000 \end{aligned}$$

The amount invested in the Equity Fund is $3x - 4000 = 3(7000) - 4000 = \$17\,000$.

Check		
	Investment in Bond Fund	$ 7 000
	Investment in Equity Fund	17 000
	Total investment	$24 000

EXAMPLE 2.7D

The Clarkson Soccer League has set a budget of $3840 for soccer balls. High-quality game balls cost $36 each, while lower-quality practice balls cost $20 each. If 160 balls are to be purchased, how many balls of each type can be purchased to use up exactly the budgeted amount?

SOLUTION

When, as in this case, the items referred to in the problem are not directly related, the variable may represent either item.

Let the number of game balls be represented by x; then the number of practice balls is $(160 - x)$.

Since the prices of the two types of balls differ, the total value of each type of ball must now be represented in terms of x.

The value of x game balls is $\$36x$;
the value of $(160 - x)$ practice balls is $\$20(160 - x)$;
the total value is $\$[36x + 20(160 - x)]$.

Since the total budgeted value is given as $3840,

$$\begin{aligned} 36x + 20(160 - x) &= 3840 \\ 36x + 3200 - 20x &= 3840 \\ 16x &= 640 \\ x &= 40 \end{aligned}$$

The number of game balls is 40 and the number of practice balls is 120.

Check

Number—40 + 120 = 160
Value—game balls: 36(40) = $1440
practice balls: 20(120) = $2400
Total value $3840

EXAMPLE 2.7E

Last year, a repair shop used 1200 small rings. The shop paid 33⅓ cents per ring for the first shipment and 37½ cents per ring for the second shipment. If the total cost was $430, how many rings did the second shipment contain?

SOLUTION

Let the number of rings in the second shipment be x; then the number of rings in the first shipment was $1200 - x$. The cost of the second shipment was $\$0.37\frac{1}{2}x$ or $\$\frac{3}{8}x$, and the cost of the first shipment was $\$0.33\frac{1}{3}(1200 - x)$ or $\$\frac{1}{3}(1200 - x)$. The total cost is $\$[\frac{3}{8}x + \frac{1}{3}(1200 - x)]$. Since the total cost is \$430,

$$\frac{3}{8}x + \frac{1}{3}(1200 - x) = 430$$

$$24\left(\frac{3}{8}x\right) + 24\left(\frac{1}{3}\right)(1200 - x) = 24(430)$$

$$3(3x) + 8(1200 - x) = 10\,320$$

$$9x + 9600 - 8x = 10\,320$$

$$x = 720$$

The second shipment consisted of 720 rings.

Check Total number of rings: $720 + 480 = 1200$

Total value: $720\left(\frac{3}{8}\right) + 480\left(\frac{1}{3}\right)$

$= 90(3) + 160(1)$

$= 270 + 160$

$= \$430$

POINTERS AND PITFALLS

Translating a Word Problem by Identifying Key Words

What are the key words in the problem and what are they asking you to do?

(a) "And" usually means "add." For example,
"Two times a number and three times a number totals \$10 000"
would be translated as
$2x + 3x = 10\,000$.

(b) "Less than" or "fewer than" usually mean "subtract." For example,
"\$3 less than ten times the amount"
would be translated as
$10x - 3$.

(c) "Reduced by" usually indicates the amount you are to subtract. For example,
"The regular selling price was reduced by 20% to compute the sale price"
would be translated as
$x - 20\%x =$ sales price, where the regular selling price would be x.

(d) "Reduced to" usually indicates the result after a subtraction. For example,
"When a regular selling price of \$589 was reduced to \$441.75, what was the discount?"
would be translated as
$589 - y\% \times 589 = 441.75$.

EXERCISE 2.7

For each of the following problems, set up an equation in one unknown and solve.

1. Sears Canada sold a sweater for $49.49. The selling price included a markup of three-fourths of the cost to the department store. What was the cost?

2. S&A Electronics sold a stereo set during a sale for $576. Determine the regular selling price of the set if the price of the set had been reduced by one-third of the original regular selling price.

3. A client at a hair salon paid a total of $36.75 for a haircut. The amount included 5% GST. What was the price of the haircut before the GST was added?

4. Some CDs were put on sale at 40% off. What was the regular price if the sale price was $11.34?

5. This month's commodity index decreased by one-twelfth of last month's index to 176. What was last month's index?

6. After an increase of one-eighth of his current hourly wage, Jean-Luc receives a new hourly wage of $10.35. How much was his hourly wage before the increase?

7. Tai's sales last week were $140 less than three times Vera's sales. What were Tai's sales if together their sales amounted to $940?

8. A metal pipe 90 centimetres long is cut into two pieces so that the longer piece is 15 centimetres longer than twice the length of the shorter piece. What is the length of the longer piece?

9. Jay purchased tickets for a concert over the Internet. To place the order, a handling charge of $5 per ticket was charged. GST of 5% was also charged on the ticket price and the handling charges. If the total charge for two tickets was $197.40, what was the cost per ticket?

10. Ken and Martina agreed to form a partnership. The partnership agreement requires that Martina invest $2500 more than two-thirds of what Ken is to invest. If the partnership's capital is to be $55 000, how much should Martina invest?

11. A furniture company has been producing 2320 chairs a day working two shifts. The second shift has produced 60 chairs fewer than four-thirds of the number of chairs produced by the first shift. Determine the number of chairs produced by the second shift.

12. An inventory of two types of floodlights showed a total of 60 lights valued at $2580. If Type A cost $40 each while Type B cost $50 each, how many Type B floodlights were in inventory?

13. A machine requires four hours to make a unit of Product A and 3 hours to make a unit of Product B. Last month the machine operated for 200 hours producing a total of 60 units. How many units of Product A were produced?

14. Alick has saved \$8.80 in nickels, dimes, and quarters. If he has four nickels fewer than three times the number of dimes, and one quarter more than three-fourths the number of dimes, how many coins of each type does Alick have?

15. The local amateur football club spent \$1475 on tickets to a professional football game. If the club bought ten more eight-dollar tickets than three times the number of twelve-dollar tickets and three fewer fifteen-dollar tickets than four-fifths the number of twelve-dollar tickets, how many of each type of ticket did the club buy?

16. Giuseppi's Pizza had orders for \$539 of pizzas. The prices for each size of pizza were: large \$18, medium \$15, and small \$11. If the number of large pizzas was one less than three times the number of medium pizzas, and the number of small pizzas was one more than twice the number of medium pizzas, how many of each size of pizza were ordered?

Go to MathXL at www.mathxl.com. You can practise many of this chapter's exercises as often as you want. The guided solutions help you find an answer step by step. You'll find a personalized study plan available to you too!

Review Exercise

1. Simplify.

(a) $3x - 4y - 3y - 5x$ (b) $2x - 0.03x$

(c) $(5a - 4) - (3 - a)$

(d) $-(2x - 3y) - (-4x + y) + (y - x)$

(e) $(5a^2 - 2b - c) - (3c + 2b - 4a^2)$

(f) $-(2x - 3) - (x^2 - 5x + 2)$

2. Simplify.

(a) $3(-5a)$ (b) $-7m(-4x)$

(c) $14m \div (-2m)$ (d) $(-15a^2b) \div (5a)$

(e) $-6(-3x)(2y)$ (f) $4(-3a)(b)(-2c)$

(g) $-4(3x - 5y - 1)$ (h) $x(1 - 2x - x^2)$

(i) $(24x - 16) \div (-4)$ (j) $(21a^2 - 12a) \div 3a$

(k) $4(2a - 5) - 3(3 - 6a)$

(l) $2a(x - a) - a(3x + 2) - 3a(-5x - 4)$

(m) $(m - 1)(2m - 5)$

(n) $(3a - 2)(a^2 - 2a - 3)$

(o) $3(2x - 4)(x - 1) - 4(x - 3)(5x + 2)$

(p) $-2a(3m - 1)(m - 4)$
$-5a(2m + 3)(2m - 3)$

3. Evaluate each of the following for the values given.

(a) $3xy - 4x - 5y$ for $x = -2, y = 5$

(b) $-5(2a - 3b) - 2(a + 5b)$
for $a = -\frac{1}{4}, b = \frac{2}{3}$

(c) $\frac{2NC}{P(n + 1)}$ for N = 12, C = 432,
P = 1800, $n = 35$

(d) $\frac{365I}{rP}$ for I = 600, $r = 0.15$, P = 7300

(e) $A(1 - dt)$ for A = \$720, $d = 0.135$, $t = \frac{280}{365}$

(f) $\frac{S}{1 + rt}$ for S = 2755, $r = 0.17$, $t = \frac{219}{365}$

4. Simplify.

(a) $(-3)^5$ (b) $\left(\frac{2}{3}\right)^4$

(c) $(-5)^0$ (d) $(-3)^{-1}$

(e) $\left(\frac{2}{5}\right)^{-4}$ (f) $(1.01)^0$

(g) $(-3)^5(-3)^4$ (h) $4^7 \div 4^2$

(i) $[(-3)^2]^5$ (j) $(m^3)^4$

(k) $\left(\frac{2}{3}\right)^3\left(\frac{2}{3}\right)^7\left(\frac{2}{3}\right)^{-6}$

(l) $\left(-\frac{5}{4}\right)^5 \div \left(-\frac{5}{4}\right)^3$

(m) $(1.03^{50})(1.03^{100})$

(n) $(1 + i)^{180} \div (1 + i)^{100}$

(o) $[(1.05)^{30}]^5$ (p) $(-2xy)^4$

(q) $\left(\frac{a^2b}{3}\right)^{-4}$ (r) $(1 + i)^{-n}$

5. Use an electronic calculator to compute each of the following.

(a) $\sqrt{0.9216}$ (b) $\sqrt[6]{1.075}$

(c) $14.974458^{\frac{1}{40}}$ (d) $1.08^{-\frac{5}{12}}$

(e) $\ln 3$ (f) $\ln 0.05$

(g) $\ln\left(\frac{5500}{1.10^{16}}\right)$

(h) $\ln\left[375(1.01)\left(\frac{1 - 1.01^{-72}}{0.01}\right)\right]$

6. Solve each of the following equations.

(a) $9x = -63$ (b) $0.05x = 44$

(c) $-\frac{1}{7}x = 3$ (d) $\frac{5}{6}x = -15$

(e) $x - 8 = -5$ (f) $x + 9 = -2$

(g) $x + 0.02x = 255$ (h) $x - 0.1x = 36$

(i) $4x - 3 = 9x + 2$

(j) $9x - 6 - 3x = 15 + 4x - 7$

(k) $x - \frac{1}{3}x = 26$ (l) $x + \frac{3}{8}x = 77$

7. Solve each of the following equations and check your answers.

(a) $-9(3x - 8) - 8(9 - 7x) = 5 + 4(9x + 11)$

(b) $21x - 4 - 7(5x - 6) = 8x - 4(5x - 7)$

(c) $\frac{5}{7}x + \frac{1}{2} = \frac{5}{14} + \frac{2}{3}x$

(d) $\frac{4x}{3} + 2 = \frac{9}{8} - \frac{x}{6}$

(e) $\frac{7}{5}(6x - 7) - \frac{3}{8}(7x + 15) = 25$

(f) $\frac{5}{9}(7 - 6x) - \frac{3}{4}(3 - 15x) = \frac{1}{12}(3x - 5) - \frac{1}{2}$

(g) $\frac{5}{6}(4x - 3) - \frac{2}{5}(3x + 4) = 5x - \frac{16}{15}(1 - 3x)$

8. Solve each of the following equations for the indicated variable.

(a) $I = Prt$ for r

(b) $S = P(1 + rt)$ for t

(c) $D = rL$ for r

(d) $FV = PMT\left[\frac{(1 + p)^n - 1}{p}\right]$ for PMT

9. For each of the following problems, set up an equation and solve.

(a) A company laid off one-sixth of its workforce because of falling sales. If the number of employees after the layoff is 690, how many employees were laid off?

(b) The current average property value is two-sevenths more than last year's average value. What was last year's average property value if the current average is $81450?

(c) The total amount paid for a banquet, including gratuities of one-twentieth of the price quoted for the banquet, was $2457. How much of the amount paid was gratuities?

(d) A piece of property with a commercial building is acquired by H & A Investments for $184 000. If the land is valued at $2000 less than one-third the value of the building, how much of the amount paid should be assigned to land?

(e) The total average monthly cost of heat, power, and water for Sheridan Service for last year was $2010. If this year's average is expected to increase by one-tenth over last year's average, and heat is $22 more than three-quarters the cost of power while water is $11 less than one-third the cost of power, how much should be budgeted on average for each month for each item?

(f) Remi Swimming Pools has a promotional budget of $87 500. The budget is to be allocated to direct selling, TV advertising, and newspaper advertising according to a formula. The formula requires that the amount spent on TV advertising be $1000 more than three times the amount spent on newspaper advertising, and that the amount spent on direct selling be three-fourths of the total spent on TV advertising and newspaper advertising combined. How much of the budget should be allocated to direct selling?

(g) A product requires processing on three machines. Processing time on Machine A is three minutes less than four-fifths of the number of minutes on Machine B, and processing time on Machine C is five-sixths of the time needed on Machines A and B together. How many minutes processing time is required on Machine C if the total processing time on all three machines is 77 minutes?

(h) Sport Alive sold 72 pairs of ski poles. Superlight poles sell at $30 per pair while ordinary poles sell at $16 per pair. If the total sales value was $1530, how many pairs of each type were sold?

(i) A cash box contains $107 made up of quarters, one-dollar coins, and two-dollar coins. How many quarters are in the box if the number of one-dollar coins is one more than three-fifths of the number of two-dollar coins, and the number of quarters is four times the number of one-dollar coins and two-dollar coins together?

Self-Test

1. Simplify.

(a) $4 - 3x - 6 - 5x$

(b) $(5x - 4) - (7x + 5)$

(c) $-2(3a - 4) - 5(2a + 3)$

(d) $-6(x - 2)(x + 1)$

2. Evaluate each of the following for the values given.

(a) $2x^2 - 5xy - 4y^2$ for $x = -3, y = 5$

(b) $3(7a - 4b) - 4(5a + 3b)$ for $a = \frac{2}{3}, b = -\frac{3}{4}$

(c) $\dfrac{2\text{NC}}{\text{P}(n + 1)}$ for $\text{N} = 12, \text{C} = 400, \text{P} = 2000, n = 24$

(d) $\dfrac{\text{I}}{\text{P}r}$ for $\text{I} = 324, \text{P} = 5400, r = 0.15$

(e) $S(1 - dt)$ for $S = 1606, d = 0.125, t = \dfrac{240}{365}$

(f) $\dfrac{S}{1 + rt}$ for $S = 1566, r = 0.10, t = \dfrac{292}{365}$

3. Simplify.

(a) $(-2)^3$

(b) $\left(\dfrac{-2}{3}\right)^2$

(c) $(4)^0$

(d) $(3)^2(3)^5$

(e) $\left(\dfrac{4}{3}\right)^{-2}$

(f) $(-x^3)^5$

4. Compute each of the following.

(a) $\sqrt[10]{1.35}$

(b) $\dfrac{1 - 1.03^{-40}}{0.03}$

(c) $\ln 1.025$

(d) $\ln[3.00e^{-0.2}]$

(e) $\ln\left(\dfrac{600}{1.06^{11}}\right)$

(f) $\ln\left[250\left(\dfrac{1.07^5 - 1}{0.07}\right)\right]$

5. Solve each of the following equations.

(a) $\dfrac{1}{81} = \left(\dfrac{1}{3}\right)^{n-2}$

(b) $\dfrac{5}{2} = 40\left(\dfrac{1}{2}\right)^{n-1}$

6. Solve each of the following equations.

(a) $-\dfrac{2}{3}x = 24$

(b) $x - 0.06x = 8.46$

(c) $0.2x - 4 = 6 - 0.3x$

(d) $(3 - 5x) - (8x - 1) = 43$

(e) $4(8x - 2) - 5(3x + 5) = 18$

(f) $x + \dfrac{3}{10}x + \dfrac{1}{2} + x + \dfrac{3}{5}x + 1 = 103$

(g) $x + \dfrac{4}{5}x - 3 + \dfrac{5}{6}\left(x + \dfrac{4}{5}x - 3\right) = 77$

(h) $\frac{2}{3}\left(3x - 1\right) - \frac{3}{4}\left(5x - 3\right) = \frac{9}{8}x - \frac{5}{6}\left(7x - 9\right)$

7. Solve each of the following equations for the indicated variable.

(a) $I = Prt$ for P (b) $S = \frac{P}{1 - dt}$ for d

8. For each of the following problems, set up an equation and solve.

(a) After reducing the regular selling price by one-fifth, Star Electronics sold a TV set for $192. What was the regular selling price?

(b) The weaving department of a factory occupies 400 square metres more than two times the floor space occupied by the shipping department. The total floor space occupied by both departments is 6700 square metres. Determine the floor space occupied by the weaving department.

(c) A machine requires three hours to make a unit of Product A and five hours to make a unit of Product B. The machine operated for 395 hours producing a total of 95 units. How many units of Product B were produced?

(d) You invested a sum of money in a bank certificate yielding an annual return of one-twelfth of the sum invested. A second sum of money invested in a credit union certificate yields an annual return of one-nineth of the sum invested. The credit union investment is $500 more than two-thirds of the bank investment, and the total annual return is $1000. What is the sum of money you invested in the credit union certificate?

Challenge Problems

1. In checking the petty cash a clerk counts "q" quarters, "d" dimes, "n" nickels, and "p" pennies. Later he discovers that x of the nickels were counted as quarters and x of the dimes were counted as pennies. (Assume that x represents the same number of nickels and dimes.) What must the clerk do to correct the original total?

2. Tom and Jerri are planning a 4000-kilometre trip in an automobile with five tires, of which four will be in use at any time. They plan to interchange the tires so that each tire will be used for the same number of kilometres. For how many kilometres will each tire be used?

3. A cheque is written for x dollars and y cents. Both x and y are two-digit numbers. In error, the cheque is cashed for y dollars and x cents, with the incorrect amount exceeding the correct amount by $17.82. Which of the following statements is correct?

(a) x cannot exceed 70.

(b) y can equal $2x$.

(c) The amount of the cheque cannot be a multiple of 5.

(d) The incorrect amount can equal twice the correct amount.

(e) The sum of the digits of the correct amount is divisible by 9.

CASE STUDY 2.1 Investing in a Tax-Free Savings Account

At the age of 25, Tasha Fellows obtained her university degree and entered the workforce. She sought the opinion of an investment advisor regarding a tax-free savings account (TFSA). The main recommendations were to start investing early, to invest the maximum allowed each year, and to stay invested. This means that someone starting a career needs to consider investing as early as possible.

The advisor provided Tasha with scenarios of investing $100 per month at 2% return at different age ranges and determining the value of her investment at age 65.

Age Started	Total Amount Contributed to Age 65	Total Value of TFSA at Age 65
25	$48 000	$82 513
35	$36 000	$53 648
45	$24 000	$31 162
55	$12 000	$13 646

Source: "TFSA Calculator," Bank of Montreal site, **www.bmo.com**, accessed August 9, 2010.

Tasha was shown that starting to contribute at a later age but still wanting to reach a goal of $82 513 would require larger monthly contributions.

Age Started	Monthly Contributions
35	$170
45	$280
55	$630

Source: "TFSA Calculator," Bank of Montreal site, **www.bmo.com**, accessed August 9, 2010.

QUESTIONS

1. How much more will Tasha have in her TFSA if she invests the $100 per month starting at age 25 compared to starting at age 35?
2. To reach a goal of $82 513, what is the total amount of contributions necessary if Tasha were to begin investing at age 45?
3. If Tasha begins her contributions at age 45, how much interest will be earned on the contributions if
   (a) her contributions are $100 per month?
   (b) her contributions are $280 per month?
4. Assume Tasha's salary is $48 000 per year. Calculate the percentage of her monthly salary that would go toward her retirement plan goal of $82 513
   (a) if she began investing $170 monthly at age 35?
   (b) if she began investing $280 monthly at age 45?
   (c) if she began investing $630 monthly at age 55?

CASE STUDY 2.2 Expenses on the Road

» Shivani Sandhu is a real estate agent's assistant in the Montreal area. The majority of his time involves travelling to different neighbourhoods showing property to potential clients.

Shivani keeps a record of his mileage, meals, and telephone calls. The real estate company reimburses him for these expenses at the end of each month. Shivani is allowed \$0.45 per kilometre for mileage and \$9 per day for telephone calls. In June, his mileage, meals, and telephone expenses totalled \$599.

QUESTIONS

1. Shivani's mileage claim was \$80 more than his claim for telephone calls, and his claim for meals was \$20 less than his mileage claim. How far did Shivani drive in June?
2. The local telephone company has decided to change its billing procedure from a \$24.50 flat rate per month to \$13.30 per month plus a service charge of \$0.35 per local call. How many local calls could Shivani make so that his new monthly telephone bill does not exceed the original June telephone bill?
3. In August, the real estate company indicated that it wanted to increase the mileage allowance to \$0.48 per kilometre and lower the daily payment for telephone calls to \$7.50. What effect would this have had on Shivani's telephone, meals, and mileage reimbursement for June?

SUMMARY OF FORMULAS

Formula 2.1A

$a^m \times a^n = a^{m+n}$ — The rule for multiplying two powers having the same base

Formula 2.1B

$a^m \times a^n \times a^p = a^{m+n+p}$ — The rule for multiplying three or more powers having the same base

Formula 2.2

$a^m \div a^n = a^{m-n}$ — The rule for dividing two powers having the same base

Formula 2.3

$(a^m)^n = a^{mn}$ — The rule for raising a power to a power

Formula 2.4

$(ab)^m = a^m b^m$ — The rule for taking the power of a product

Formula 2.5

$\left(\frac{a}{b}\right)^m = \frac{a^m}{b^m}$ — The rule for taking the power of a quotient

Formula 2.6

$$a^{-m} = \frac{1}{a^m}$$

The definition of a negative exponent

Formula 2.7

$$\left(\frac{y}{x}\right)^{-m} = \left(\frac{x}{y}\right)^m$$

The rule for a fraction with a negative exponent

Formula 2.8

$$a^{\frac{1}{n}} = \sqrt[n]{a}$$

The definition of a fractional exponent with numerator 1

Formula 2.9

$$a^{-\frac{1}{n}} = \frac{1}{a^{\frac{1}{n}}} = \frac{1}{\sqrt[n]{a}}$$

The definition of a fractional exponent with numerator −1

Formula 2.10

$$a^{\frac{m}{n}} = \sqrt[n]{a^m} = \left(\sqrt[n]{a}\right)^m$$

The definition of a positive fractional exponent

Formula 2.11

$$a^{-\frac{m}{n}} = \frac{1}{a^{\frac{m}{n}}} = \frac{1}{\sqrt[n]{a^m}}$$

The definition of a negative fractional exponent

Formula 2.12A

$$\ln(ab) = \ln a + \ln b$$

The relationship used to find the logarithm of a product

Formula 2.12B

$$\ln(abc) = \ln a + \ln b + \ln c$$

The relationship used to find the logarithm of a product

Formula 2.13

$$\ln\left(\frac{a}{b}\right) = \ln a - \ln b$$

The relationship used to find the logarithm of a quotient

Formula 2.14

$$\ln(a^k) = k(\ln a)$$

The relationship used to find the logarithm of a power

GLOSSARY

Algebraic expression a combination of numbers, variables representing numbers, and symbols indicating an algebraic operation *(p. 43)*

Base one of the equal factors in a power *(p. 49)*

Collecting like terms adding like terms *(p. 42)*

Combining like terms *see* **Collecting like terms**

Common logarithms logarithms with base 10; represented by the notation log x *(p. 62)*

Equation a statement of equality between two algebraic expressions *(p. 68)*

Equivalent equations equations that have the same root *(p. 69)*

Exponent the number of equal factors in a power *(p. 49)*

Factor one of the numbers that, when multiplied with the other number or numbers, yields a given product *(p. 49)*

First-degree equation an equation in which the variable (or variables) appears with power 1 only *(p. 68)*

Formula rearrangement (or formula manipulation) the process of rearranging the terms of an equation *(p. 76)*

Index the power of the root indicated with the radical symbol *(p. 57)*

Like terms terms having the same literal coefficient *(p. 42)*

Linear equation *see* **First-degree equation**

Literal coefficient the part of a term formed with letter symbols *(p. 42)*

Logarithm the exponent to which a base must be raised to produce a given number *(p. 61)*

Lowest common denominator (LCD) the smallest number into which a set of denominators divides without remainders *(p. 74)*

Members of an equation the two sides of an equation; the left member is the left side; the right member is the right side *(p. 68)*

Monomial an algebraic expression consisting of one term *(p. 43)*

Natural logarithms logarithms with base e; represented by the notation $\ln y$ *(p. 63)*

Numerical coefficient the part of a term formed with numerals *(p. 42)*

Polynomial an algebraic expression consisting of more than one term *(p. 44)*

Power a mathematical operation indicating the multiplication of a number of equal factors *(p. 49)*

Power of the root the exponent indicating the number of equal factors *(p. 56)*

Radical the indicated root when using the radical symbol for finding a root *(p. 57)*

Radicand the number under the radical symbol *(p. 57)*

Root of an equation the solution (replacement value) that, when substituted for the variable, makes the two sides equal *(p. 68)*

Root of the product one of the equal factors in the product *(p. 56)*

USEFUL INTERNET SITES

www.bmo.com/mutualfunds

Bank of Montreal This Website provides links to pages offering basic information on mutual funds, types of mutual funds, and investment tips.

www.bdc.ca

Business Development Bank of Canada BDC offers financial and consulting services to Canadian small businesses.

www.ic.gc.ca

Industry Canada Industry Canada's home page provides business information and statistics on markets, industries, company sourcing, business partners and alliances, products, international trade, business management, micro-economy, regulations, research laboratories, science and technology, and technology transfer.

CHAPTER 3

Ratio, Proportion, and Percent

OBJECTIVES

Upon completing this chapter, you will be able to do the following:

1. Use ratios to solve allocation and equivalence problems.
2. Find percents and percent bases to solve business problems.
3. Find rates and original quantities for increase and decrease problems.
4. Use proportions and currency cross rate tables to convert currency.
5. Use index numbers and the Consumer Price Index to compute purchasing power of the dollar.
6. Use federal income tax brackets and tax rates to calculate federal income taxes.

Every day, in newspapers and magazines, we find articles that spew figures at us. These articles include percent increases, percent decreases, sales figures, ratios, and seemingly unrelated facts. And with information available more quickly than ever from the Internet and all-day news and financial sources, figures are available up to the minute and often presented in a variety of ways. Because they are unavoidable, you *must* be able to sort through the numbers and understand what they mean—or be left behind! When you finish this chapter, you will be able to better understand and work with the numbers you read, see, and hear every day.

INTRODUCTION

Business information is often based on a comparison of related quantities stated in the form of a ratio. When two or more ratios are equivalent, a proportion equating the ratios can be set up. Allocation problems generally involve ratios, and many of the physical, economic, and financial relationships affecting businesses may be stated in the form of ratios or proportions.

The fractional form of a ratio is frequently replaced by the percent form because relative magnitudes are more easily understood as percents. This is done in business reports and articles all the time. Skill in manipulating percents, finding percents, computing rates percent, and dealing with problems of increase and decrease is fundamental to solving many business problems.

3.1 RATIOS

A. Setting up ratios

1. A **ratio** is a comparison of the *relative* values of numbers or quantities and may be written in any of the following ways:
   (a) by using the word "to," such as in "5 to 2";
   (b) by using a colon, such as in "5 : 2";
   (c) as a common fraction, such as "5/2";
   (d) as a decimal, such as "2.50";
   (e) as a percent, such as "250%."

2. When comparing more than two numbers or quantities, using the colon is preferred.
   To compare the quantities 5 kg, 3 kg, and 2 kg, the ratio is written

   5 kg : 3 kg : 2 kg

3. When using a ratio to compare quantities, the unit of measurement is usually dropped.
   If three items weigh 5 kg, 3 kg, and 2 kg respectively, their weights are compared by the ratio

   5 : 3 : 2

4. The numbers appearing in a ratio are called the **terms of the ratio**. If the terms are in different units, the terms need to be expressed in the same unit of measurement before the units can be dropped.
   The ratio of 1 quarter to 1 dollar becomes 25 cents to 100 cents or 25 : 100; the ratio of 3 hours to 40 minutes becomes 180 min : 40 min or 180 : 40.

5. When, as is frequently done, rates are expressed as ratios, ratios drop the units of measurement, even though the terms of the ratio represent different things.
   100 km/h becomes 100 : 1
   50 m in 5 seconds becomes 50 : 5
   $1.49 for 2 items becomes 1.49 : 2

6. Any statement containing a comparison of two or more numbers or quantities can be used to set up a ratio.

EXAMPLE 3.1A

(i) In a company, the work of 40 employees is supervised by five managers.
The ratio of employees to managers is 40 : 5.

(ii) Variable cost is $4000 for a sales volume of $24 000.
The ratio of variable cost to sales volume is 4000 : 24 000.

(iii) The cost of a product is made up of $30 of material, $12 of direct labour, and $27 of overhead.
The elements of cost are in the ratio 30 : 12 : 27.

B. Reducing ratios to lowest terms

When ratios are used to express a comparison, they are usually reduced to *lowest terms*. Since ratios may be expressed as fractions, ratios may be manipulated according to the rules for working with fractions. Thus, the procedure used to reduce ratios to lowest terms is the same as that used to reduce fractions to lowest terms. However, when a ratio is expressed by an improper fraction that reduces to a whole number, the denominator "1" must be written to indicate that two quantities are being compared.

EXAMPLE 3.1B

Reduce each of the following ratios to lowest terms.

(i) 80 : 35 (ii) 48 : 30 : 18

(iii) 225 : 45 (iv) 81 : 54 : 27

SOLUTION

(i) Since each term of the ratio 80 : 35 contains a common factor 5, each term can be reduced.

$80 : 35 = (16 \times 5) : (7 \times 5) = 16 : 7$

or $\frac{80}{35} = \frac{16 \times 5}{7 \times 5} = \frac{16}{7}$

(ii) The terms of the ratio 48 : 30 : 18 contain a common factor 6.
$48 : 30 : 18 = (8 \times 6) : (5 \times 6) : (3 \times 6) = 8 : 5 : 3$

(iii) $225 : 45 = (45 \times 5) : (45 \times 1) = 5 : 1$

or $\frac{225}{45} = \frac{5}{1}$

(iv) $81 : 54 : 27 = (3 \times 27) : (2 \times 27) : (1 \times 27) = 3 : 2 : 1$

C. Equivalent ratios in higher terms

Equivalent ratios in higher terms may be obtained by *multiplying* each term of a ratio by the same number. Higher-term ratios are used to eliminate decimals from the terms of a ratio.

EXAMPLE 3.1C State each of the following ratios in higher terms to eliminate the decimals from the terms of the ratios.

(i) 2.5 : 3 (ii) 1.25 : 3.75 : 7.5

(iii) $\frac{1.8}{2.7}$ (iv) $\frac{19.25}{2.75}$

SOLUTION

(i) $2.5 : 3 = 25 : 30$ — multiply each term by 10 to eliminate the decimal

$= 5 : 6$ — reduce to lowest terms

(ii) $1.25 : 3.75 : 7.5$

$= 125 : 375 : 750$ — multiply each term by 100 to eliminate the decimals

$= (1 \times 125) : (3 \times 125) : (6 \times 125)$

$= 1 : 3 : 6$

(iii) $\frac{1.8}{2.7} = \frac{18}{27} = \frac{2}{3}$

(iv) $\frac{19.25}{2.75} = \frac{1925}{275} = \frac{7 \times 275}{1 \times 275} = \frac{7}{1}$

D. Allocation according to a ratio

Allocation problems require dividing a whole into a number of parts according to a ratio. The number of parts into which the whole is to be divided is the sum of the terms of the ratio.

EXAMPLE 3.1D Allocate $480 in the ratio 5 : 3.

SOLUTION The division of $480 in the ratio 5 : 3 may be achieved by dividing the amount of $480 into (5 + 3) or 8 parts.

The value of each part = 480 ÷ 8 = 60.

The first term of the ratio consists of 5 of the 8 parts; that is,

the first term = 5 × 60 = 300 and the second term = 3 × 60 = 180.

$480 is to be divided into $300 and $180.

Alternatively

$480 in the ratio 5 : 3 may be divided by using fractions.

5 of 8 ⟶ $\frac{5}{8} \times 480 = 300$

3 of 8 ⟶ $\frac{3}{8} \times 480 = 180$

EXAMPLE 3.1E

If net income of \$72 000 is to be divided among three business partners in the ratio 4 : 3 : 2, how much should each partner receive?

SOLUTION

Divide the net income into $4 + 3 + 2 = 9$ parts;
each part has a value of $\$72\,000 \div 9 = \$8000$.

Partner 1 receives 4 of the 9 parts	$4 \times 8000 = \$32\,000$
Partner 2 receives 3 of the 9 parts	$3 \times 8000 = 24\,000$
Partner 3 receives 2 of the 9 parts	$2 \times 8000 = 16\,000$
TOTAL	\$72 000

Alternatively

$$\text{Partner 1 receives } \frac{4}{9} \text{ of } 72\,000 = \frac{4}{9} \times 72\,000 = 4 \times 8000 = \$32\,000$$

$$\text{Partner 2 receives } \frac{3}{9} \text{ of } 72\,000 = \frac{3}{9} \times 72\,000 = 3 \times 8000 = 24\,000$$

$$\text{Partner 3 receives } \frac{2}{9} \text{ of } 72\,000 = \frac{2}{9} \times 72\,000 = 2 \times 8000 = 16\,000$$

TOTAL \$72 000

EXAMPLE 3.1F

A business suffered a fire loss of \$224 640. It was covered by an insurance policy that stated that any claim was to be paid by three insurance companies in the ratio $\frac{1}{3} : \frac{3}{8} : \frac{5}{12}$. What is the amount that each of the three companies will pay?

SOLUTION

When an amount is to be allocated in a ratio whose terms are fractions, the terms need to be converted into equivalent fractions with the same denominators. The numerators of these fractions may then be used as the ratio by which the amount will be allocated.

STEP 1 Convert the fractions into equivalent fractions with the same denominators.

$$\frac{1}{3} : \frac{3}{8} : \frac{5}{12} \quad \text{——— lowest common denominator} = 24$$

$$= \frac{8}{24} : \frac{9}{24} : \frac{10}{24} \quad \text{——— equivalent fractions with the same denominators}$$

STEP 2 Allocate according to the ratio formed by the numerators.

The numerators form the ratio 8 : 9 : 10;
the number of parts is $8 + 9 + 10 = 27$;
the value of each part is $\$224\,640 \div 27 = \$8320$

First company's share of claim	$= 8320 \times 8 = \$\ 66\,560$
Second company's share of claim	$= 8320 \times 9 = 74\,880$
Third company's share of claim	$= 8320 \times 10 = 83\,200$
TOTAL	\$224 640

EXERCISE 3.1

EXCEL SPREADSHEET

A. Simplify each of the following ratios.

1. Reduce to lowest terms.

(a) 12 to 32

(b) 84 to 56

(c) 15 to 24 to 39

(d) 21 to 42 to 91

2. Set up a ratio for each of the following and reduce to lowest terms.

(a) 12 dimes to 5 quarters

(b) 15 hours to 3 days

(c) 6 seconds for 50 metres

(d) $72 per dozen

(e) $40 per day for 12 employees for 14 days

(f) 2% per month for 24 months for $5000

3. Use equivalent ratios in higher terms to eliminate decimals and fractions from the following ratios.

(a) 1.25 to 4

(b) 2.4 to 8.4

(c) 0.6 to 2.1 to 3.3

(d) 5.75 to 3.50 to 1.25

(e) $\frac{1}{2}$ to $\frac{2}{5}$

(f) $\frac{5}{3}$ to $\frac{7}{5}$

(g) $\frac{3}{8}$ to $\frac{2}{3}$ to $\frac{3}{4}$

(h) $\frac{2}{5}$ to $\frac{4}{7}$ to $\frac{5}{14}$

(i) $\frac{2}{5}$ to $\frac{3}{4}$ to $\frac{5}{16}$

(j) $\frac{3}{7}$ to $\frac{1}{3}$ to $\frac{17}{21}$

(k) $8\frac{5}{8}$ to $11\frac{1}{2}$

(l) $1\frac{3}{4}$ to $3\frac{7}{16}$

(m) $2\frac{1}{5}$ to $4\frac{1}{8}$

(n) $5\frac{1}{4}$ to $5\frac{5}{6}$

B. Set up a ratio for each of the following and reduce the ratio to lowest terms.

1. Deli Delight budgets food costs to account for 40 percent and beverage costs to account for 35 percent of total costs. What is the ratio of food costs to beverage costs?

2. At Bargain Upholstery, commissions amounted to $2500 while sales volume was $87 500 for last month. What is the ratio of commissions to sales volume?

3. A company employs 6 supervisors for 9 office employees and 36 production workers. What is the ratio of supervisors to office employees to production workers?

4. The cost of a unit is made up of $4.25 direct material cost, $2.75 direct labour cost, and $3.25 overhead. What is the ratio that exists between the three elements of cost?

5. The business school at the local college has 8 instructors and 232 students. What is the ratio that exists between the instructors and students?

6. A student spends 20 hours per week in classroom lecture time, 45 hours per week in individual study time, and 5 hours per week travelling to and from school. What is the ratio that exists between the three times?

C. Solve each of the following allocation problems.

1. A dividend of $3060 is to be distributed among three shareholders in the ratio of shares held. If the three shareholders have nine shares, two shares, and one share respectively, how much does each receive?

2. The cost of operating the Maintenance Department is to be allocated to four production departments based on the floor space each occupies. Department A occupies 1000 m^2; Department B, 600 m^2; Department C, 800 m^2; and Department D, 400 m^2. If the July cost was $21 000, how much of the cost of operating the Maintenance Department should be allocated to each production department?

EXCEL SPREADSHEET

3. Insurance cost is to be distributed among manufacturing, selling, and administration in the ratio $\frac{5}{8}$ to $\frac{1}{3}$ to $\frac{1}{6}$. If the total insurance cost was $9450, how should it be distributed?

4. Executive salaries are charged to three operating divisions on the basis of capital investment in the three divisions. If the investment is $10.8 million in the Northern Division, $8.4 million in the Eastern Division, and $14.4 million in the Western Division, how should executive salaries of $588 000 be allocated to the three divisions?

5. The cost of warehouse space is allocated to three inventories: raw materials, work-in-process, and finished goods. The inventories use the warehouse space in the ratio of one-third to one-sixth to three-eighths, respectively. If the total warehouse space is 9.6 million square metres, at a cost of $11.55 million, how much of the cost should be allocated to each of the inventories?

6. A vehicle dealership has overhead cost of $480 000. The overhead cost is allocated to new vehicle sales, used vehicle sales, vehicle servicing, and administration. The departments bear overhead cost at $\frac{1}{8}$, $\frac{1}{4}$, $\frac{1}{2}$, and $\frac{1}{16}$ respectively. How much of the overhead cost should be allocated to each of the departments?

EXCEL NOTES

You can use Excel's Lowest Common Multiplier (LCM) function to convert terms in a ratio that are fractions into equivalent fractions with the same denominator. Refer to LCM on MathXL to learn how to use this Excel function.

3.2 PROPORTIONS

A. Solving proportions

When two ratios are equal, they form a **proportion**.

$$\left.\begin{aligned} 2:3 &= 4:6 \\ x:5 &= 7:35 \\ \frac{2}{3} &= \frac{8}{x} \\ \frac{a}{b} &= \frac{c}{d} \end{aligned}\right\} \text{ are proportions}$$

Note that each proportion consists of *four terms*. These terms form an equation whose sides are common fractions.

If one of the four terms is unknown, the proportions form a linear equation in one variable. The equation can be solved by using the operations discussed in Chapter 2.

EXAMPLE 3.2A Solve the proportion $2:5 = 8:x$.

SOLUTION

$2:5 = 8:x$ — original form of proportion

$\frac{2}{5} = \frac{8}{x}$ — change the proportion into fractional form

$5x\left(\frac{2}{5}\right) = 5x\left(\frac{8}{x}\right)$ — multiply by the lowest common denominator $= 5x$

$2x = 40$

$x = 20$

Check LS $= \frac{2}{5}$, RS $= \frac{8}{20} = \frac{2}{5}$

Note: The two operations usually applied to solve proportions are multiplication and division. These operations permit the use of a simplified technique called *cross-multiplication*, which involves

(a) the multiplication of the numerator of the ratio on the left side with the denominator of the ratio on the right side of the proportion, and

(b) the multiplication of the numerator of the ratio on the right side with the denominator of the ratio on the left side.

When cross-multiplication is used to solve Example 3.2A, the value of x is obtained as follows:

$$\frac{2}{5} \times \frac{8}{x}$$

$x(2) = 5(8)$ — cross-multiply

$2x = 40$

$x = 20$

EXAMPLE 3.2B Solve each of the following proportions.

(i)

$$
\begin{aligned}
x:5 &= 7:35 && \text{original proportion}\\
\frac{x}{5} &= \frac{7}{35} && \text{in fractional form}\\
35(x) &= 5(7) && \text{cross-multiply}\\
35x &= 35\\
x &= 1
\end{aligned}
$$

(ii)

$$
\begin{aligned}
2\tfrac{1}{2}:x &= 5\tfrac{1}{2}:38\tfrac{1}{2}\\
2.5:x &= 5.5:38{:}5\\
\frac{2.5}{x} &= \frac{5.5}{38.5}\\
38.5(2.5) &= x(5.5) && \text{cross-multiply}\\
96.25 &= 5.5x\\
x &= \frac{96.25}{5.5}\\
x &= 17.5, \text{ or } 17\tfrac{1}{2}
\end{aligned}
$$

(iii)

$$
\begin{aligned}
\frac{5}{6}:\frac{14}{4} &= x:\frac{21}{10}\\
\frac{\frac{5}{6}}{\frac{14}{4}} &= \frac{\frac{x}{1}}{\frac{21}{10}} && \text{set up in fractional form}\\
\left(\frac{5}{6}\right)\left(\frac{21}{10}\right) &= \left(\frac{x}{1}\right)\left(\frac{14}{4}\right) && \text{cross-multiply}\\
\frac{105}{60} &= \frac{14x}{4}\\
(14x)(60) &= (105)(4)\\
840x &= 420\\
x &= 0.5, \text{ or } \frac{1}{2}
\end{aligned}
$$

B. Problems involving proportions

Many problems contain information that permits two ratios to be set up. These ratios are in proportion, but one term of one ratio is unknown. In such cases, a letter symbol for the unknown term is used to complete the proportion statement.

To ensure that the proportion is set up correctly, use the following procedure.

STEP 1 Use a complete sentence to *introduce* the *letter* symbol that you will use to represent the missing term.

STEP 2 Set up the *known ratio* on the *left* side of the proportion. Be sure to retain the units or a description of the quantities in the ratio.

STEP 3 Set up the ratio using the *letter symbol* on the *right* side of the proportion. Make certain that the unit or description of the numerator in the ratio on the right side corresponds to the unit or description of the numerator in the ratio on the left side.

EXAMPLE 3.2C Solve each of the following problems involving a proportion.

(i) If five kilograms of sugar cost \$9.20, what is the cost of two kilograms of sugar?

SOLUTION

STEP 1 Introduce the variable.

Let the cost of two kilograms of sugar be \$$x$.

STEP 2 Set up the known ratio retaining the units.

5 kg : \$9.20

STEP 3 Set up the ratio involving the variable.

2 kg : \$$x$

Hence, $\frac{5\text{ kg}}{\$9.20} = \frac{2\text{ kg}}{\$x}$ ——— make certain the units in the numerators and denominators correspond

$$\frac{5}{9.20} = \frac{2}{x}$$

$$x(5) = 9.20(2)$$

$$x = \frac{18.40}{5}$$

$$x = 3.68$$

Two kilograms of sugar cost \$3.68.

(ii) If your car can travel 385 km on 35 L of gasoline, how far can it travel on 24 L?

SOLUTION

Let the distance travelled on 24 L be n km;
then the known ratio is 385 km : 35 L;
the second ratio is n km : 24 L.

$$\frac{385\text{ km}}{35\text{ L}} = \frac{n\text{ km}}{24\text{ L}}$$

$$\frac{385}{35} = \frac{n}{24}$$

$$n = \frac{385 \times 24}{35}$$

$$n = 264$$

The car can travel 264 km on 24 L.

(iii) Past experience shows that a process requires \$17.50 worth of material for every \$12 spent on labour. How much should be budgeted for material if the budget for labour is \$17 760?

SOLUTION

Let the material budget be \$$k$.

The known ratio is $\dfrac{\$17.50 \text{ material}}{\$12 \text{ labour}}$;

the second ratio is $\dfrac{\$k \text{ material}}{\$17\,760 \text{ labour}}$.

$$\frac{\$17.50 \text{ material}}{\$12 \text{ labour}} = \frac{\$k \text{ material}}{\$17\,760 \text{ labour}}$$

$$\frac{17.50}{12} = \frac{k}{17\,760}$$

$$k = \frac{17.50 \times 17\,760}{12}$$

$$k = 25\,900$$

The material budget should be \$25 900.

EXAMPLE 3.2D

Two contractors agreed to share revenue from a job in the ratio 2 : 3. Contractor A, who received the smaller amount, made a profit of \$480 on the job. If contractor A's profit compared to revenue is in the ratio 3 : 8, determine

(i) contractor A's revenue;

(ii) the total revenue of the job.

SOLUTION

(i) Let \$$x$ represent contractor A's revenue.

Then $\dfrac{\text{A's profit}}{\text{A's revenue}} = \dfrac{3}{8}$ ——— known ratio

and $\dfrac{\text{A's profit}}{\text{A's revenue}} = \dfrac{\$480}{\$x}$ ——— second ratio

$$\frac{3}{8} = \frac{480}{x}$$

$$3x = 480 \times 8$$

$$x = \frac{480 \times 8}{3}$$

$$x = 1280$$

Contractor A's revenue from the job is \$1280.

(ii) Let $y represent contractor B's revenue.

$$\text{Then } \frac{\text{A's revenue}}{\text{B's revenue}} = \frac{2}{3} \text{ ——— known ratio}$$

$$\text{and } \frac{\text{A's revenue}}{\text{B's revenue}} = \frac{\$1280}{\$y} \text{ ——— second ratio}$$

$$\frac{2}{3} = \frac{1280}{y}$$

$$2y = 1280 \times 3$$

$$y = \frac{1280 \times 3}{2}$$

$$y = 1920$$

Total revenue $= x + y = 1280 + 1920 = 3200$
Total revenue on the job is $3200.

Alternatively
Let total revenue be $z.

$$\text{Then } \frac{\text{A's revenue}}{\text{Total revenue}} = \frac{2}{5} = \frac{\$1280}{\$z}$$

$$\frac{2}{5} = \frac{1280}{z}$$

$$2z = 1280 \times 5$$

$$z = 3200$$

EXERCISE 3.2

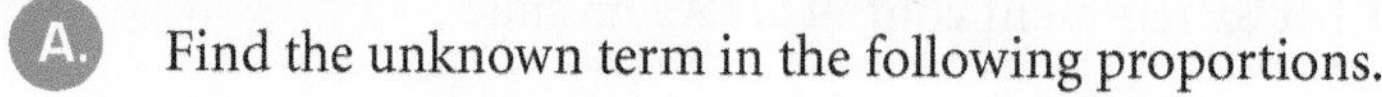

A. Find the unknown term in the following proportions.

1. $3 : n = 15 : 20$

2. $n : 7 = 24 : 42$

3. $3 : 8 = 21 : x$

4. $7 : 5 = x : 45$

5. $1.32 : 1.11 = 8.8 : k$

6. $2.17 : 1.61 = k : 4.6$

7. $m : 3.4 = 2.04 : 2.89$

8. $3.15 : m = 1.4 : 1.8$

9. $t : \frac{3}{4} = \frac{7}{8} : \frac{15}{16}$

10. $\frac{3}{4} : t = \frac{5}{8} : \frac{4}{9}$

11. $\frac{9}{8} : \frac{3}{5} = t : \frac{8}{15}$

12. $\frac{16}{7} : \frac{4}{9} = \frac{15}{14} : t$

B. Use proportions to solve each of the following problems.

1. Le Point Bookbindery pays a dividend of $1.25 per share every three months. How many months would it take to earn dividends amounting to $8.75 per share?

2. The community of Oakcrest sets a property tax rate of \$28 per \$1000 assessed valuation. What is the assessment if a tax of \$854 is paid on a property?

3. A car requires 9 litres of gasoline for 72 kilometres. At the same rate of gasoline consumption, how far can the car travel if the gas tank holds 75 litres?

4. A manufacturing process requires \$85 supervision cost for every 64 labour hours. At the same rate, how much supervision cost should be budgeted for 16 000 labour hours?

5. Suhami Chadhuri has a two-fifths interest in a partnership. She sold five-sixths of her interest for \$3000.
   (a) What was the total amount of Ms. Chadhuri's interest before selling?
   (b) What is the value of the partnership?

6. Five-eighths of Jesse Black's inventory was destroyed by fire. He sold the remaining part, which was slightly damaged, for one-third of its value and received \$1300.
   (a) What was the value of the destroyed part of the inventory?
   (b) What was the value of the inventory before the fire?

7. Last year, net profits of Herd Inc. were two-sevenths of revenue. If the company declared a dividend of \$12 800 and five-ninths of the net profit was retained in the company, what was last year's revenue?

8. Material cost of a fan belt is five-eighths of total cost, and labour cost is one-third of material cost. If labour cost is \$15, what is the total cost of the fan belt?

3.3 THE BASIC PERCENTAGE PROBLEM

A. Computing percentages

To find percentages, multiply a number by a percent.

$$50\% \text{ of } 60 = 0.50 \times 60 = 30$$

Note: 50% is called the *rate*;
60 is called the *base* or *original number*;
30 is called the *percentage* or *new number*.

$$\text{PERCENTAGE} = \text{RATE} \times \text{BASE}$$ **Formula 3.1A**

or

$$\text{NEW NUMBER} = \text{RATE} \times \text{ORIGINAL NUMBER}$$

To determine a percentage of a given number, change the percent to a decimal fraction or a common fraction and then multiply by the given number.

EXAMPLE 3.3A

(i) 80% of 400 = 0.80 × 400 = 320 — convert the percent into a decimal and multiply

(ii) 5% of 1200 = 0.05 × 1200 = 60

(iii) 240% of 15 = 2.40 × 15 = 36

(iv) 1.8% of \$600 = 0.018 × 600 = \$10.80

(v) $33\frac{1}{3}\%$ of \$45.60 = $\frac{1}{3} \times 45.60$ = \$15.20

(vi) 0.25% of \$8000 = 0.0025 × 8000 = \$20

(vii) $\frac{3}{8}\%$ of \$1800 = 0.375% of \$1800 = 0.00375 × 1800 = \$6.75

B. Computation with commonly used percents

Many of the more commonly used percents can be converted into fractions. These are easy to use when computing manually. The most commonly used percents and their fractional equivalents are listed in Table 3.1.

Table 3.1 **Commonly Used Percents and Their Fractional Equivalents**

(i)	(ii)	(iii)	(iv)	(v)
$25\% = \frac{1}{4}$	$16\frac{2}{3}\% = \frac{1}{6}$	$12\frac{1}{2}\% = \frac{1}{8}$	$20\% = \frac{1}{5}$	$8\frac{1}{3}\% = \frac{1}{12}$
$50\% = \frac{1}{2}$	$33\frac{1}{3}\% = \frac{1}{3}$	$37\frac{1}{2}\% = \frac{3}{8}$	$40\% = \frac{2}{5}$	$6\frac{2}{3}\% = \frac{1}{15}$
$75\% = \frac{3}{4}$	$66\frac{2}{3}\% = \frac{2}{3}$	$62\frac{1}{2}\% = \frac{5}{8}$	$60\% = \frac{3}{5}$	$6\frac{1}{4}\% = \frac{1}{16}$
	$83\frac{1}{3}\% = \frac{5}{6}$	$87\frac{1}{2}\% = \frac{7}{8}$	$80\% = \frac{4}{5}$	

EXAMPLE 3.3B

(i) 25% of 32 = $\frac{1}{4} \times 32 = 8$

(ii) $33\frac{1}{3}\%$ of 150 = $\frac{1}{3} \times 150 = 50$

(iii) $87\frac{1}{2}\%$ of 96 = $\frac{7}{8} \times 96 = 7 \times 12 = 84$

(iv) $83\frac{1}{3}\%$ of 48 = $\frac{5}{6} \times 48 = 5 \times 8 = 40$

$$(v)\ 116\tfrac{2}{3}\%\text{ of }240 = \left(100\% + 16\tfrac{2}{3}\%\right)\text{ of }240$$
$$= \left(1 + \frac{1}{6}\right)(240)$$
$$= \frac{7}{6} \times 240$$
$$= 7 \times 40$$
$$= 280$$

$$(vi)\ 275\%\text{ of }64 = \left(2 + \frac{3}{4}\right)(64)$$
$$= \frac{11}{4} \times 64$$
$$= 11 \times 16$$
$$= 176$$

POINTERS AND PITFALLS

Using the 1% Method

Percentages can be computed by determining 1% of the given number and then figuring the value of the given percent. While this method can be used to compute any percentage, it is particularly useful when dealing with *small* percents.

EXAMPLE 3.3C Use the 1% method to determine each of the following percentages.

(i) 3% of $1800

SOLUTION

1% of $1800 = $18
3% of $1800 = 3 × 18 = $54

(ii) $\frac{1}{2}$% of $960

SOLUTION

1% of $960 = $9.60
$\frac{1}{2}$% of $960 = $\frac{1}{2} \times 9.60$ = $4.80

(iii) $\frac{5}{8}$% of $4440

SOLUTION

1% of $4440 = $44.40
$\frac{1}{8}$% of $4440 = $\frac{1}{8} \times 44.40$ = $5.55
$\frac{5}{8}$% of $4440 = 5 × 5.55 = $27.75

(iv) $2\frac{1}{4}\%$ of \$36 500

SOLUTION

$$1\% \text{ of } \$36\,500 = \$365.00$$
$$2\% \text{ of } \$36\,500 = 2 \times 365.00 = \$730.00$$
$$\frac{1}{4}\% \text{ of } \$36\,500 = \frac{1}{4} \times 365.00 = \underline{\quad 91.25}$$
$$2\tfrac{1}{4}\% \text{ of } 36\,500 = \$821.25$$

C. Finding a rate percent

Finding a rate means *comparing* two numbers. This comparison involves a ratio that is usually written in the form of a common fraction. When the common fraction is converted to a percent, a rate percent results.

When setting up the ratio, the base (or original number) is always the denominator of the fraction, and the percentage (or new number) is always the numerator.

$$\text{RATE} = \frac{\text{PERCENTAGE}}{\text{BASE}} \text{ or } \frac{\text{NEW NUMBER}}{\text{ORIGINAL NUMBER}}$$ ——— Formula 3.1B

The problem statement indicating that a rate percent is to be found is usually in the form

(a) "What percent of x is y?" or

(b) "y is what percent of x?"

This means that y is to be compared to x and requires the setting up of the ratio $y : x$ or the fraction $\frac{y}{x}$ where x is the base (or original number) while y is the percentage (or new number).

EXAMPLE 3.3D

Answer each of the following questions.

(i) What percent of 15 is 6?

SOLUTION

$$\text{Rate} = \frac{6}{15}$$ ——— percentage (or new number) / base (or original number)

$$= 0.40$$
$$= 40\%$$

(ii) 90 is what percent of 72?

SOLUTION

$$\text{Rate} = \frac{90}{72}$$ ——— original number

$$= 1.25$$
$$= 125\%$$

(iii) What percent of \$112.50 is \$292.50?

SOLUTION

$$\text{Rate} = \frac{292.50}{112.50} = 2.60 = 260\%$$

D. Finding the base

A great number of business problems involve the relationship from Formula 3.1A,

$$\text{PERCENTAGE} = \text{RATE} \times \text{BASE}$$
$$(\text{or NEW NUMBER} = \text{RATE} \times \text{ORIGINAL NUMBER})$$

Since three variables are involved, three different problems may be solved using this relationship:

(a) finding the percentage (see Sections A and B)
(b) finding the rate percent (see Section C)
(c) finding the base (see Section D)

Of the three, the problem of finding the rate percent is the most easily recognized. However, confusion often arises in deciding whether the percentage or the base needs to be found. In such cases it is useful to represent the unknown value by a variable and set up an equation.

EXAMPLE 3.3E

Solve each of the following problems by setting up an equation.

(i) What number is 25% of 84?

SOLUTION

Introduce a variable for the unknown value and write the statement in equation form.

What number is 25% of 84

↓ ↓ ↓ ↓

$x = 25\% \text{ of } 84$

$x = \frac{1}{4} \times 84$ —— change the percent to a fraction or a decimal

$x = 21$

The number is 21.

(ii) 60% of what number is 42?

SOLUTION

60% of what number is 42

↓ ↓ ↓

$60\% \text{ of } x = 42$

$0.6x = 42$

$$x = \frac{42}{0.6}$$

$$x = 70$$

The number is 70.

(iii) How much is $16\frac{2}{3}\%$ of \$144?

SOLUTION

$x = 16\frac{2}{3}\%$ of 144

$x = \frac{1}{6} \times 144$

$x = 24$

The amount is \$24.

(iv) \$160 is 250% of what amount?

SOLUTION

$160 = 250\%$ of x

$160 = 2.5x$

$x = \frac{160}{2.5}$

$x = 64$

The amount is \$64.

POINTERS AND PITFALLS

You can calculate the percent of increase over a base with your business calculator. The function is labelled Δ%.

Press 2nd Δ%.

OLD is shown on the display. Enter the original value and press Enter ↓.

NEW is shown on the display. Enter the next number and press Enter ↓.

%CH is shown on the display. Press CPT.

Example: OLD = 150; NEW = 180; %CH = 20.0.

Press 2nd QUIT to close the worksheet.

Note: Any two of the three values can be entered into the calculator. If the NEW number is greater than the OLD number, the resulting %CH will be a positive number. If the OLD number is greater than the NEW number, the resulting %CH will be a negative number. The fourth input required by the calculator is #PD, indicating how many periods the number changes by the percent indicated. The default for this is 1.

E. Applications

EXAMPLE 3.3F Solve each of the following problems.

(i) Variable cost on monthly sales of \$48 600 amounted to \$30 375. What is the variable cost rate based on sales volume?

SOLUTION

$$\text{Rate} = \frac{\text{Variable cost}}{\text{Sales volume}}$$ ——— base for the comparison

$$= \frac{30\ 375}{48\ 600}$$
$$= 0.625$$
$$= 62.5\%$$

The variable cost is 62.5% of sales volume.

(ii) What is the annual dividend on a preferred share paying 11.5% on a par value of \$20?

SOLUTION

Let the annual dividend be \$$x$.
Since the annual dividend is 11.5% of \$20,

$$x = 11.5\% \text{ of } 20$$
$$x = 0.115 \times 20$$
$$x = 2.30$$

The annual dividend is \$2.30.

(iii) What was the amount of October sales if November sales of \$14 352 were 115% of October sales?

SOLUTION

Let October sales be represented by \$$x$.
Since November sales equal 115% of October sales,

$$14\ 352 = 115\% \text{ of } x$$
$$14\ 352 = 1.15x$$
$$x = \frac{14\ 352}{1.15}$$
$$x = 12\ 480$$

October sales amounted to \$12 480.

(iv) The 15% blended sales tax charged on the regular selling price of a computer sold in Halifax, Nova Scotia, amounted to \$201.00. What was the total cost of the computer?

SOLUTION

Let the regular selling price be \$$x$.
Since the sales tax is 15% of the regular selling price,

$$201.00 = 15\% \text{ of } x$$
$$201.00 = 0.15x$$
$$x = \frac{201.00}{0.15}$$
$$x = 1340$$

The regular selling price is	$1340.00
Add 15% of $1340	201.00
TOTAL COST	$1541.00

The total cost of the computer was $1541.00.

EXERCISE 3.3

A. Compute each of the following.

1. 40% of 90
2. 0.1% of 950
3. 250% of 120
4. 7% of 800
5. 3% of 600
6. 15% of 240
7. 0.5% of 1200
8. 300% of 80
9. 0.02% of 2500
10. $\frac{1}{2}$% of 500
11. $\frac{1}{4}$% of 800
12. 0.05% of 9000
13. 0.075% of 10 000
14. $\frac{7}{8}$% of 3600
15. 2.5% of 700
16. 0.025% of 40 000

B. Use fractional equivalents to compute each of the following (round to the highest whole number).

1. $33\frac{1}{3}$% of $48
2. $137\frac{1}{2}$% of $400
3. $162\frac{1}{2}$% of $1200
4. $66\frac{2}{3}$% of $72
5. $37\frac{1}{2}$% of $24
6. 175% of $1600
7. 125% of $160
8. $12\frac{1}{2}$% of $168
9. $83\frac{1}{3}$% of $720
10. $166\frac{2}{3}$% of $90
11. $116\frac{2}{3}$% of $42
12. $16\frac{2}{3}$% of $54
13. 75% of $180
14. $183\frac{1}{3}$% of $24
15. $133\frac{1}{3}$% of $45
16. 25% of $440

C. Find the rate percent for each of the following.

1. original amount 60; new amount 36

2. original amount 72; new amount 54

3. base $800; percentage $920

4. base \$140; percentage \$490
5. new amount \$6; original amount \$120
6. new amount \$11; original amount \$440
7. percentage \$132; base \$22
8. percentage \$30; base \$45
9. new amount \$150; base \$90
10. percentage \$39; original amount \$18

D. Answer each of the following questions.

1. \$60 is 30% of what amount?
2. \$36 is what percent of \$15?
3. What is 0.1% of \$3600?
4. 150% of what amount is \$270?
5. $\frac{1}{2}$% of \$612 is what amount?
6. 250% of what amount is \$300?
7. 80 is 40% of what amount?
8. \$120 is what percent of \$60?
9. What is $\frac{1}{8}$% of \$880?
10. \$180 is what percent of \$450?
11. \$600 is 250% of what amount?
12. What percent of \$70 is \$350?
13. \$90 is 30% of what amount?
14. 350% of what amount is \$1050?

E. Answer each of the following questions.

1. The price of a carpet was reduced by 40%. If the original price was \$70, what was the amount by which the price was reduced?
2. Labour content in the production of an article is $37\frac{1}{2}$% of total cost. How much is the labour cost if the total cost is \$72?
3. If waste is normally 6% of the material used in a production process, how much of \$25 000 worth of material will be wasted?
4. If total deductions on a yearly salary of \$18 600 amounted to $16\frac{2}{3}$%, how much was deducted?
5. If the actual sales of \$40 500 for last month were 90% of the budgeted sales, how much was the sales budget for the month?
6. The Canada Pension Plan premium deducted from an employee's wages was \$53.46. If the premium rate is 4.95% of gross wages, how much were the employee's gross wages?
7. A property was sold for 300% of what the vendors originally paid. If the vendors sold the property for \$180 000, how much did they originally pay for the property?
8. Gerry's four sons were to share equally in a prize, receiving \$28 each. How much was the total prize?
9. Shari's portion of the proceeds of a business was $\frac{1}{2}$%. If the proceeds were \$1200, how much would she receive?
10. Mei Jung paid \$18 toward a dinner that cost a total of \$45. What percent of the total was her portion?

3.4 PROBLEMS INVOLVING INCREASE OR DECREASE

A. Percent change

Problems involving a *change* (an increase or a decrease) are identifiable by such phrases as

"is 20% *more than*," "is 40% *less than*,"
"is *increased by* 150%," "is *decreased by* 30%."

The amount of change is to be added for an increase to or subtracted for a decrease from the *original number* (*base*) and is usually stated as a percent of the original number.

The existing relationship may be stated as

$$\text{ORIGINAL NUMBER} \begin{matrix} +\ \text{INCREASE} \\ -\ \text{DECREASE} \end{matrix} = \text{NEW NUMBER}$$ — **Formula 3.2**

where the change (the increase or decrease) is understood to be a *percent of the original number*.

EXAMPLE 3.4A Answer each of the following questions.

(i) 36 increased by 25% is what number?

SOLUTION

The original number is 36;
the change (increase) is 25% of 36. — **in such problems the change is a percent of the original number**
Since the original number is known,
let x represent the new number.

$$36 + 25\% \text{ of } 36 = x$$
$$36 + \frac{1}{4} \times 36 = x$$
$$36 + 9 = x$$
$$x = 45$$

The number is 45.

(ii) What number is 40% less than 75?

SOLUTION

The change (decrease) is 40% of 75.
The original number is 75.
Let x represent the new number.

$$75 - 40\% \text{ of } 75 = x$$
$$75 - 0.40 \times 75 = x$$
$$75 - 30 = x$$
$$x = 45$$

The number is 45.

(iii) How much is \$160 increased by 250%?

SOLUTION

The increase is 250% of \$160 and the original number is \$160.
Let the new amount be \$$x$.

$$160 + 250\% \text{ of } 160 = x$$
$$160 + 2.50 \times 160 = x$$
$$160 + 400 = x$$
$$x = 560$$

The amount is \$560.

B. Finding the rate of increase or decrease

This type of problem is indicated by such phrases as

(a) "20 is what percent *more than* 15?" or
(b) "What percent *less than* 96 is 72?"

In (a), the increase, which is the difference between 15, the original number, and 20, the number after the increase, is to be compared to the original number, 15.

$$\text{The rate of increase} = \frac{5}{15} = \frac{1}{3} = 33\tfrac{1}{3}\%$$

In (b), the decrease, which is the difference between 96, the number before the decrease (the original number), and 72, the number after the decrease, is to be expressed as a percent of the original number.

$$\text{The rate of decrease} = \frac{24}{96} = \frac{1}{4} = 25\%$$

In more generalized form, the problem statement is:

$$\text{“}y \text{ is what percent } \begin{Bmatrix} \text{more} \\ \text{less} \end{Bmatrix} \text{ than } x\text{?”}$$

This means the difference between x, the number before the change (the original number), and y, the number after the change, is to be expressed as a percent of the original number.

$$\text{RATE OF CHANGE} = \frac{\text{AMOUNT OF CHANGE}}{\text{ORIGINAL NUMBER}} \qquad \text{Formula 3.3}$$

EXAMPLE 3.4B

Answer each of the following questions.

(i) \$425 is what percent more than \$125?

SOLUTION

The amount before the change (the original number) is \$125.
The change (increase) = 425 − 125 = \$300.

$$\text{The rate of increase} = \frac{\text{Amount of increase}}{\text{Original amount}}$$

$$= \frac{300}{125} = 2.40 = 240\%$$

(ii) What percent less than \$210 is \$175?

SOLUTION

The amount before the decrease is \$210.
The decrease is 210 − 175 = \$35.

$$\text{The rate of decrease} = \frac{35}{210} = \frac{1}{6} = 16\tfrac{2}{3}\%$$

C. Finding the original amount

If the quantity *after* the change has taken place is known, the quantity *before* the change (the original quantity) may be found by using the relationship stated in Formula 3.2.

EXAMPLE 3.4C

Answer each of the following questions.

(i) 88 is 60% more than what number?

SOLUTION

88 is the number after the increase; the number before the increase is unknown. Let the original number be x; then the increase is 60% of x.

$x + 60\%$ of $x = 88$ ——— using Formula 3.2

$$x + 0.6x = 88$$
$$1.6x = 88$$
$$x = \frac{88}{1.6}$$
$$x = 55$$

The original number is 55.

(ii) 75 is 40% less than what number?

SOLUTION

75 is the number after the decrease.
Let the original number be x;
then the decrease is 40% of x.

$$x - 40\% \text{ of } x = 75$$
$$x - 0.4x = 75$$
$$0.6x = 75$$
$$x = \frac{75}{0.6}$$
$$x = 125$$

The original number is 125.

(iii) What sum of money increased by 175% amounts to $143?

SOLUTION

$143 is the amount after the increase.
Let the original sum of money be $\$x$;
then the increase is 175% of x.

$$x + 175\% \text{ of } x = 143$$
$$x + 1.75x = 143$$
$$2.75x = 143$$
$$x = \frac{143}{2.75}$$
$$x = 52$$

The original amount is $52.

(iv) What sum of money when diminished by $33\frac{1}{3}\%$ is $48?

SOLUTION

$48 is the amount after the decrease.
Let the original sum of money be $\$x$;
then the decrease is $33\frac{1}{3}\%$ of x.

$$x - 33\tfrac{1}{3}\% \text{ of } x = 48$$
$$x - \frac{1}{3}x = 48, \quad \text{or} \quad x - 0.\dot{3}x = 48$$
$$\frac{2}{3}x = 48, \quad \text{or} \quad 0.\dot{6}x = 48$$
$$x = \frac{48 \times 3}{2}, \quad \text{or} \quad x = \frac{48}{0.\dot{6}}$$
$$x = 72$$

The original sum of money is $72.

EXERCISE 3.4

A. Answer each of the following questions.

1. What is 120 increased by 40%?
2. What is 900 decreased by 20%?
3. How much is $1200 decreased by 5%?
4. How much is $24 increased by 200%?
5. What number is $83\frac{1}{3}\%$ more than 48?
6. What amount is $16\frac{2}{3}\%$ less than $66?

B. Find the rate of change for each of the following.

1. What percent more than 30 is 45?
2. What percent less than $90 is $72?
3. The amount of $240 is what percent more than $80?

4. The amount of \$110 is what percent less than \$165?
5. What percent less than \$300 is \$294?
6. The amount of \$2025 is what percent more than \$2000?

C. Solve each of the following equations.

1. $x + 40\%$ of $x = 28$
2. $x - 20\%$ of $x = 240$
3. $x - 5\%$ of $x = 418$
4. $x + 7\%$ of $x = 214$
5. $x + 16\frac{2}{3}\%$ of $x = 42$
6. $x - 33\frac{1}{3}\%$ of $x = 54$
7. $x + 150\%$ of $x = 75$
8. $x + 200\%$ of $x = 36$

D. Answer each of the following questions.

1. The number 24 is 25% less than what number?
2. The number 605 is $37\frac{1}{2}\%$ more than what number?
3. What amount increased by 150% equals \$325?
4. What sum of money decreased by $16\frac{2}{3}\%$ equals \$800?
5. After deducting 5% from a sum of money, the remainder is \$4.18. What was the original sum of money?
6. After an increase of 7%, the new amount is \$749. What was the original amount?

3.5 PROBLEMS INVOLVING PERCENT

A. Summary of useful relationships

Problems involving percents abound in the field of business. The terminology used varies depending on the situation. However, most problems can be solved by means of the two basic relationships

$$\text{RATE} \times \text{ORIGINAL AMOUNT} = \text{NEW AMOUNT} \qquad \textbf{Formula 3.1A}$$

and

$$\text{ORIGINAL NUMBER} \begin{array}{l} + \text{ INCREASE} \\ - \text{ DECREASE} \end{array} = \text{NEW AMOUNT} \qquad \textbf{Formula 3.2}$$

or, in the case of finding a rate percent, by means of the formulas

$$\text{RATE} = \frac{\text{NEW AMOUNT}}{\text{ORIGINAL AMOUNT}} \qquad \textbf{Formula 3.1B}$$

and

$$\text{RATE OF CHANGE} = \frac{\text{AMOUNT OF CHANGE}}{\text{ORIGINAL AMOUNT}} \qquad \textbf{Formula 3.3}$$

B. Problems involving the computation of a rate percent

EXAMPLE 3.5A Solve each of the following problems.

(i) Material content in a lighting fixture is \$40. If the total cost of the fixture is \$48, what percent of cost is the material cost?

SOLUTION

$$\frac{\text{Material cost}}{\text{Total cost}} = \frac{40}{48} = \frac{5}{6} = 83\tfrac{1}{3}\%$$

(ii) A cash discount of \$3.60 was allowed on an invoice of \$120. What was the rate of discount?

SOLUTION

$$\text{The rate of discount} = \frac{\text{Amount of discount}}{\text{Invoice amount}}$$

$$= \frac{3.60}{120.00} = \frac{360}{12\,000} = \frac{3}{100} = 3\%$$

(iii) What percent increase did Nirel Walker receive if her biweekly salary rose from \$800 to \$920?

SOLUTION

Salary before the increase (original salary) is \$800;
the raise is 920 − 800 = \$120.

$$\text{The rate of increase} = \frac{\text{Amount of increase}}{\text{Original salary}}$$

$$= \frac{120}{800} = 0.15 = 15\%$$

(iv) Expenditures for a government program were reduced from \$75 000 to \$60 000. What percent change does this represent?

SOLUTION

Expenditure before the change is \$75 000;
the change (decrease) = 75 000 − 60 000 = \$15 000.

$$\text{The rate of change} = \frac{\text{Amount of change}}{\text{Original amount}}$$

$$= \frac{15\,000}{75\,000} = 0.20 = 20\%$$

Expenditures were reduced by 20%.

C. Problems involving the basic percentage relationship

EXAMPLE 3.5B Solve each of the following problems.

(i) An electronic calculator marked \$39.95 in an Ontario bookstore is subject to 13% HST (harmonized sales tax). What will it cost you to buy the calculator?

SOLUTION

$$\begin{aligned}\text{Cash price} &= \text{Marked price} + \text{HST}\\ &= 39.95 + 13\% \text{ of } 39.95\\ &= 39.95 + 5.19\\ &= 45.14\end{aligned}$$

The calculator will cost \$45.14.

(ii) Sales for this year are budgeted at $112\frac{1}{2}\%$ of last year's sales of \$360 000. What is the sales budget for this year?

SOLUTION

$$\begin{aligned}\text{This year's sales} &= 112\tfrac{1}{2}\% \text{ of } 360\,000\\ &= 1.125 \times 360\,000\\ &= 405\,000\end{aligned}$$

Budgeted sales for this year are \$405 000.

(iii) A commission of \$300 was paid to a broker's agent for the sale of a bond. If the commission was $\frac{3}{4}\%$ of the sales value of the bond, how much was the bond sold for?

SOLUTION

$$\text{The commission paid} = \frac{3}{4}\% \text{ of the bond sale}$$

$$\begin{aligned}300 &= \frac{3}{4}\% \text{ of } x\\ 300 &= 0.75\% \text{ of } x\\ 300 &= 0.0075x\\ x &= 40\,000\end{aligned}$$

The bond was sold for \$40 000.

(iv) On the basis of past experience, Simcoe District Credit Union estimates uncollectible loans at $1\frac{1}{4}\%$ of the total loan balances outstanding. If, at the end of March, the loans account shows a balance of \$3 248 000, how much should the credit union have in reserve for uncollectible loans at the end of March?

SOLUTION

The provision for uncollectible loans = $1\frac{1}{4}\%$ of \$3 248 000

1% of \$3 248 000 ⟶ \$32 480

$\frac{1}{4}$ of 1% of \$3 248 000 ⟶ 8 120

$1\frac{1}{4}\%$ of \$3 248 000 ⟶ \$40 600

The credit union should have a reserve of \$40 600 for uncollectible loans at the end of March.

(v) The Consumer Price Index in July of this year was 225 or 180% of the index ten years ago. What was the index ten years ago?

SOLUTION

This year's index = 180% of the index ten years ago

$$225 = 180\% \text{ of } x$$
$$225 = 1.80x$$
$$x = \frac{225}{1.8}$$
$$x = 125$$

The index ten years ago was 125.

D. Problems of increase or decrease

EXAMPLE 3.5C

Solve each of the following problems.

(i) Daily car loadings for August were 5% more than for July. If August car loadings were 76 020, what were the July car loadings?

SOLUTION

Because July is earlier than August, its car loadings are the original number and are not known. Let them be represented by x.

$$x + 5\% \text{ of } x = 76\,020$$
$$x + 0.05x = 76\,020$$
$$1.05x = 76\,020$$
$$x = \frac{76\,020}{1.05}$$
$$x = 72\,400$$

Car loadings in July numbered 72 400.

(ii) The trading price of shares of Northern Gold Mines dropped 40% to \$7.20. Determine the trading price before the drop.

SOLUTION

The trading price before the drop is the original value and is not known. Let it be \$$x$.

$$x - 40\% \text{ of } x = 7.20$$
$$x - 0.4x = 7.20$$
$$0.6x = 7.20$$
$$x = \frac{7.20}{0.6}$$
$$x = 12.00$$

The trading price before the drop was \$12.00.

(iii) Dorian Guy sold his house for \$149 500. If he sold the house for $187\frac{1}{2}\%$ more than what he paid for it, how much did he gain?

SOLUTION

The base for the percent gain is the original amount paid for the house. Since this amount is not known, let it be \$$x$.

Original amount paid + Gain = Selling price

$$x + 187\tfrac{1}{2}\% \text{ of } x = 149\,500$$

$$x + 1.875x = 149\,500$$

$$2.875x = 149\,500$$

$$x = \frac{149\,500}{2.875}$$

$$x = 52\,000$$

The amount originally paid was \$52 000.
Gain = 149 500 − 52 000 = \$97 500.

(iv) The amount paid for an article, including 5% goods and services tax, was \$98.70. How much was the marked price of the article?

SOLUTION

The unknown marked price, represented by \$$x$, is the base for the sales tax.

Marked price + GST = Amount paid

$$x + 5\% \text{ of } x = 98.70$$

$$x + 0.05x = 98.70$$

$$1.05x = 98.70$$

$$x = \frac{98.70}{1.05}$$

$$x = 94.00$$

The marked price of the article was \$94.

(v) After taking off a discount of 5%, a retailer settled an invoice by paying \$532.00. How much was the amount of the discount?

SOLUTION

The unknown amount of the invoice, represented by \$$x$, is the base for the discount.

Amount of invoice − Discount = Amount paid

$$x - 5\% \text{ of } x = 532$$

$$x - 0.05x = 532$$

$$0.95x = 532$$

$$x = 560$$

Discount = 5% of 560 = 0.05×560 = \$28.

BUSINESS MATH NEWS BOX

National Salary Comparisons

Knowing how much you are worth in the job market is critical for not being underpaid. Successful salary negotiations are accomplished by having accurate information. In today's electronic age, the Internet offers a variety of Websites focusing on salary information.

Three popular job functions along with the respective salaries are listed below by major metropolitan location.

Financial Controller

Responsible for directing an organization's accounting functions. These functions include establishing and maintaining the organization's accounting principles, practices, and procedures. Prepares financial reports and presents findings and recommendations to top management.

Bank Branch Manager

Oversees the daily activities of the bank branch. Provides guidance on more complex issues. Familiar with a variety of the field's concepts, practices, and procedures. Relies on extensive experience and judgment to plan and accomplish goals.

Marketing Manager

Develops and implements strategic marketing plan for an organization. Generally manages a group of marketing professionals. Typically reports to an executive.

		Salary Comparison (Averages)			
Job Description*	Vancouver	Calgary	Toronto	Montreal	National
Financial Controller	$98 576	$118 207	$102 750	$89 580	$94 882
Bank Branch Manager	$81 601	$83 749	$77 352	$76 973	$77 021
Marketing Manager	$68 460	$78 989	$77 243	$65 202	$73 026

* Represents salary and not necessarily total compensation.

Source: Data represent the high range number found for each job title per city from "PayScale" at **www.payscale.com/resources.aspx?nc=lp_calculator_canada01&mode=none**, accessed August 1, 2010.

QUESTIONS

1. Assuming that an employee works a 40-hour week, calculate the hourly rate of each job function by location.
2. Calculate the dollar and percent difference in each city by job description.
3. What might account for the salary differences among the four cities?

EXERCISE 3.5

A. Solve each of the following problems.

1. Of FasDelivery's 1200 employees, $2\frac{1}{4}\%$ did not report to work last Friday due to an outbreak of the flu. How many employees were absent?

2. A storekeeper bought merchandise for \$1575. If she sells the merchandise at $33\frac{1}{3}\%$ above cost, how much gross profit does she make?

3. A clerk whose salary was \$280 per week was given a raise of \$35 per week. What percent increase did the clerk receive?

4. Your hydro bill for March is \$174.40. If you pay after the due date, a late payment penalty of \$8.72 is added. What is the percent penalty?

5. A sales representative receives a commission of $16\frac{2}{3}\%$ on all sales. How much must his weekly sales be so that he will make a commission of \$720 per week?

6. HRH Collection Agency retains a collection fee of 25% of any amounts collected. How much did the agency collect on a bad debt if the agency forwarded \$2490 to a client?

7. A commercial building is insured under a fire policy that has a face value of 80% of the building's appraised value. The annual insurance premium is $\frac{3}{8}\%$ of the face value of the policy and the premium for one year amounts to \$675.
   (a) What is the face value of the policy?
   (b) What is the appraised value of the building?

8. A residential property is assessed for tax purposes at 40% of its market value. The residential property tax rate is $3\frac{1}{3}\%$ of the assessed value and the tax is \$1200.
   (a) What is the assessed value of the property?
   (b) What is the market value of the property?

B. Solve each of the following problems.

1. A merchant bought an article for \$7.92. How much did the article sell for if he sold it at an increase of $83\frac{1}{3}\%$?

2. A retail outlet is offered a discount of $2\frac{1}{2}\%$ for payment in cash of an invoice of \$840. If it accepted the offer, how much was the cash payment?

3. A bicycle shop reduced its selling price on a bicycle by $33\frac{1}{3}\%$. If the regular selling price was \$195, what was the reduced price?

4. From August 2013 to June 2016, the price of gasoline increased 42%. If the price in 2013 was 75.6 cents per litre, what was the price per litre in 2016?

5. The 13% harmonized sales tax on a pair of shoes amounted to \$9.62. What was the total cost of the shoes?

6. Ms. Daisy pays $37\frac{1}{2}\%$ of her monthly gross salary as rent on a townhouse. If the monthly rent is \$660, what is her monthly salary?

7. The annual interest on a bond is $4\frac{1}{2}\%$ of its face value and amounts to \$225. What is the face value of the bond?

8. A brokerage house charges a fee of $2\frac{1}{4}$%. If its fee on a stock purchase was \$432, what was the amount of the purchase?

9. Profit last quarter decreased from \$6540 in the previous quarter to \$1090. What was the percent decrease in profit?

10. A wage earner's hourly rate of pay was increased from \$11.50 to \$11.96. What was the percent raise?

11. A property purchased for \$42 000 is now appraised at \$178 500. What is the percent gain in the value of the property?

12. The Bank of Montreal reduced its annual lending rate from 6% to 5.75%. What is the percent reduction in the lending rate?

13. After a reduction of $33\frac{1}{3}$% of the marked price, a fan was sold for \$64.46. What was the marked price?

14. A special purpose index has increased 125% during the last ten years. If the index is now 279, what was the index ten years ago?

15. After a cash discount of 5%, an invoice was settled by a payment of \$646. What was the invoice amount?

16. Sales in May increased $16\frac{2}{3}$% over April sales. If May sales amounted to \$24 535, what were April sales?

17. The working capital at the end of the third quarter was 75% higher than at the end of the second quarter. What was the amount of working capital at the end of the second quarter if the working capital at the end of the third quarter was \$78 400?

18. After real estate fees of 8% had been deducted from the proceeds of a property sale, the vendor of the property received \$88 090. What was the amount of the real estate fee?

19. A company's employee compensation expense for August, consisting of the gross pay plus 4% vacation pay based on gross pay, was \$23 400. How much was the amount of vacation pay expense?

20. In Vancouver, a car was sold for \$15 932 including 12% HST. How much was the harmonized sales tax on the car?

3.6 APPLICATIONS—CURRENCY CONVERSIONS

One practical application of proportions is currency conversion. To perform currency conversions, we use exchange rates. An **exchange rate** is the value of one nation's currency expressed in terms of another nation's currency. In other words, the exchange rate tells us how much of one currency we need to buy one unit of another currency. By using proportions and exchange rate tables (sometimes called *currency cross rate* tables), we can convert easily from one currency to another.

A. Using proportions

Suppose we were told that the U.S. dollar is worth \$1.0372 Canadian today. How would we calculate the exchange rates between the Canadian dollar and the U.S. dollar? Since there are two currencies involved, we can express the exchange rate in two different ways.

First, we can set up the exchange rate converting U.S. dollars to Canadian dollars. To do so, set up the ratio:

$$\frac{\text{Canadian dollars}}{\text{U.S. dollars}} = \frac{\$1.0372}{\$1.00} = 1.0372$$

1.0372 is the exchange rate for converting U.S. dollars to Canadian dollars

To convert U.S. dollars to Canadian dollars, multiply the number of U.S. dollars by 1.0372. Thus, to convert US\$10 to Canadian dollars, calculate: \$10.00 × 1.0372 = \$10.37.

Second, we can set up the exchange rate converting Canadian dollars to U.S. dollars. To do so, set up the ratio:

$$\frac{\text{U.S. dollars}}{\text{Canadian dollars}} = \frac{\$1.00}{\$1.0372} = 0.9641$$

0.9641 is the exchange rate for converting Canadian dollars to U.S. dollars

To convert Canadian dollars to U.S. dollars, multiply the number of Canadian dollars by 0.9641. Thus, to convert C\$10 to U.S. dollars, calculate: \$10.00 × 0.9641 = \$9.64.

In general, if we know the exchange rate from currency A to currency B (ratio $^{B}/_{A}$), then we can find the exchange rate from currency B to currency A by taking the reciprocal of the original ratio (i.e., $^{A}/_{B}$).

If both rates are known, choosing which exchange rate to use can be confusing. The best way to choose the exchange rate is to express the exchange rate as a proportion of two currencies so that the wanted currency is in the numerator of the known ratio.

EXAMPLE 3.6A

Suppose you wanted to convert C\$150 into U.S. dollars. You read in the newspaper that one U.S. dollar is worth 1.0372 Canadian dollars, and that one Canadian dollar is worth 0.9641 U.S. dollars. How much would you receive in U.S. dollars?

SOLUTION

Let the number of U.S. dollars be x. The wanted currency is U.S. dollars.

Known ratio $\quad \dfrac{\text{US}\$0.9641}{\text{C}\$1}$

Second ratio $\quad \dfrac{\text{US}\$x}{\text{C}\$150}$

Proportion $\dfrac{\text{US\$0.9641}}{\text{C\$1}} = \dfrac{\text{US\$}x}{\text{C\$150}}$

$$\frac{0.9641}{1} = \frac{x}{150}$$

Then cross-multiply:

$$x = 0.9641(150)$$
$$x = 144.62$$

Therefore, C$150 is worth US$144.62.

EXAMPLE 3.6B

While travelling in the United States, you filled your gas tank with 16.6 U.S. gallons of gas at a cost of US$50.00.

(i) How much did the fill-up cost you in Canadian funds if one Canadian dollar costs 0.96 U.S. dollars?

SOLUTION

Let the amount in Canadian dollars be x.

$$\frac{\text{C\$1}}{\text{US\$0.96}} = \frac{\text{C\$}x}{\text{US\$50.00}}$$

$$\frac{1}{0.96} = \frac{x}{50.00}$$

$$1(50.00) = x(0.96)$$

$$x = \frac{50.00}{0.96}$$

$$x = 52.08$$

The fill-up cost $52.08 in Canadian funds.

(ii) What was the cost of gas per litre in Canadian funds, if one U.S. gallon is equivalent to 3.8 litres?

SOLUTION

Since 1 U.S. gallon = 3.8 litres
16.6 U.S. gallons = 3.8(16.6) = 63.08 litres
From (i), US$50.00 = C$52.08

$$\text{Cost per litre} = \frac{52.08}{63.08} = \text{C\$0.826}$$

The cost per litre in Canadian funds was $0.826.

B. Using cross rate tables

Cross rate tables are commonly found in newspapers and business and travel magazines. They show the exchange rates between a number of currencies. One example is shown in Table 3.2. Notice that exchange rates are often given to more decimal places than the usual two places for dollars and cents. To convert currency A into currency B, first find currency A in the column headings (along the top of the table). Then find currency B in the row headings (along the left side of the table). The exchange rate is the number where the column and row intersect. For instance, from the table, the exchange rate to convert Canadian dollars to U.S. dollars is 0.9739.

EXAMPLE 3.6C

Convert $55 Canadian into Swiss francs.

SOLUTION

First, to find the exchange rate from Canadian dollars to Swiss francs, locate the Canadian dollar column in the table. Move down the Canadian dollar column until you come to the Swiss franc row. The exchange rate is 1.0413.

Conversion = 55.00 × 1.0413
= 57.27 Swiss francs

Table 3.2 **Currency Cross Rates**

(converting to)	(converting from)							
	Canada Dollar	United States Dollar	Europe Euro	United Kingdom Pound	Japan Yen	China Yuan Renminbi	Switzerland Franc	India Rupee
Canada Dollar	1.00	1.0268	1.3709	1.5315	0.0112	0.1504	0.9604	0.0226
United States Dollar	0.9739	1.00	1.3351	1.4915	0.0109	0.1465	0.9353	0.0220
Europe Euro	0.7294	0.7490	1.00	1.1171	0.0082	0.1097	0.7005	0.0165
United Kingdom Pound	0.6530	0.6705	0.8952	1.00	0.0073	0.0982	0.6271	0.0148
Japan Yen	89.4637	91.8643	122.6494	137.0124	1.00	13.4547	85.9190	2.0223
China Yuan Renminbi	6.6492	6.8277	9.1157	10.1832	0.0743	1.00	6.3858	0.1503
Switzerland Franc	1.0413	1.0692	1.4275	1.5947	0.0116	0.1566	1.00	0.0235
India Rupee	44.2379	45.4250	60.6476	67.7498	0.4945	6.6531	42.4852	1.00

EXAMPLE 3.6D

Suppose you are taking a trip from Canada to France, and then to Japan. Convert C$100 to euros, then convert the euros to Japanese yen. Use the exchange rates in Table 3.2.

SOLUTION

(i) From the table, the exchange rate for Canadian dollars to euros is 0.7294.
Conversion = 100 × 0.7294
= 72.94 euros

(ii) From the table, the exchange rate for euros to Japanese yen is 122.6494.
Conversion = 72.94 × 122.6494
= 8946 Japanese yen

You can check this answer by converting C$100 to Japanese yen. However, the answers may differ slightly due to rounding.

EXERCISE 3.6

Answer each of the following questions.

1. How many U.S. dollars can you buy for C$750 if one Canadian dollar is worth US$0.9421?
2. How many Canadian dollars can you buy for US$750 if one Canadian dollar is worth US$0.9421?
3. Suppose the exchange rate was US$0.93 for each Canadian dollar. What is the price, in Canadian dollars, of a flight to Florida costing US$299?
4. What is the price of gasoline per litre in Canadian dollars if a U.S. gallon of gasoline costs US$2.74? One U.S. dollar is worth C$1.05 and one U.S. gallon is equivalent to 3.8 litres.

Use Table 3.2 to make each of the following conversions.

1. Convert US$350 to Canadian dollars.
2. Convert C$200 to euros.
3. Convert US$175 to Swiss francs.
4. Convert 250 United Kingdom pounds to Japanese yen.
5. Convert $550 euros to Canadian dollars.

3.7 APPLICATIONS—INDEX NUMBERS

A. The nature of index numbers

An **index number** results when you compare two values of the same thing measured at different points in time. The comparison of the two values is stated as a ratio, and then expressed as a percent. When the percent symbol is dropped, the result is called an index number.

EXAMPLE 3.7A

The price of a textbook was $115 in 2010 and $125.35 in 2013. Compare the two prices to create an index number.

SOLUTION

The change in price over the time period 2010 to 2013 can be measured in relative terms by writing the ratio

$$\frac{\text{Price in 2013}}{\text{Price in 2010}} = \frac{125.35}{115} = 1.09 = 109\%$$

An index number can now be created by dropping the percent symbol. The price index is 109.

To construct an index number, you must select one of the two values as the denominator of the ratio. The point in time at which the denominator was measured is called the **base period.** In Example 3.7A, 2010 was chosen as the base period. The chronologically earlier time period is usually used as the base period.

The index for the base period is always 100. The difference between an index number and 100 indicates the relative change that has taken place. For Example 3.7A, the index number 109 indicates that the price of the book in 2013 was 9% higher than in 2010.

Indexes provide an easy way of expressing changes that occur in daily business. Converting data to indexes makes working with very large or small numbers easier and provides a basis for many types of analysis. Indexes are used in comparing and analyzing economic data and have become a widely accepted tool for measuring changes in business activity. Two of the more common indexes frequently mentioned in the media are the Consumer Price Index (CPI) and the Toronto Stock Exchange S&P/TSX Composite Index.

B. The Consumer Price Index and its uses

The **Consumer Price Index (CPI)** is the most widely accepted indicator of changes in the overall price level of goods and services. In Canada, a fixed "basket" or collection of goods and services is used to represent all Canadian goods and services. The prices of the items in this collection are monitored and are used to represent the price change of all goods and services. The CPI is currently based on 2002 price levels and is published monthly by Statistics Canada. For example, the 2008 CPI of 114.1 indicated that the price level increased 14.1% from 2002 (the base year) to 2008.

You can use the Consumer Price Index to determine the *purchasing power of the Canadian dollar* and to compute *real income.*

The **purchasing power of the dollar** is the reciprocal of the CPI, that is,

$$\text{Purchasing power of the dollar} = \frac{\$1}{\text{Consumer Price Index}}(100)$$

EXAMPLE 3.7B

The CPI was 111.5 for 2007 and 114.1 for 2008. Determine the purchasing power of the Canadian dollar for the two years, and interpret the meaning of the results.

SOLUTION

Purchasing power of the dollar for 2007

$$= \frac{\$1}{111.5}(100) = 0.896861$$

Purchasing power of the dollar for 2008

$$= \frac{\$1}{114.1}(100) = 0.876424$$

This means the dollar in 2007 could purchase only 89.7% of what it could purchase in 2002 (the base year). In 2008, the dollar could purchase even less (about 87.6% of what it could purchase in 2002).

The CPI can be used to eliminate the effect of inflation on income by adjusting **nominal income** (income stated in current dollars) to **real income** (income stated in base-period dollars).

$$\text{REAL INCOME} = \frac{\text{INCOME IN CURRENT DOLLARS}}{\text{CONSUMER PRICE INDEX}}(100)$$ —— **Formula 3.4**

EXAMPLE 3.7C

James' income was \$50 000 in 2002, \$53 000 in 2006, and \$56 000 in 2009. The Canadian CPI was 109.1 in 2006 and 114.4 in 2009. The CPI base year is 2002.

(i) Determine James' real income in 2006 and 2009.

(ii) Should James be happy about his increases in salary from 2002 to 2009?

SOLUTION

(i) $\text{Real income in 2006} = \frac{\text{Nominal income}}{(\text{CPI in 2006})}(100)$

$= \frac{\$53\,000}{109.1}(100) = \$48\,579.29$

$\text{Real income in 2009} = \frac{\text{Nominal income}}{(\text{CPI in 2009})}(100)$

$= \frac{\$56\,000}{114.4}(100) = \$48\,951.05$

(ii) To compare nominal income with real income, it is useful to determine income changes in absolute and relative terms.

Year	2002	2006	2008
Nominal income	\$50 000	\$53 000	\$56 000
Simple price index	$\frac{50\,000}{(50\,000)}(100)$	$\frac{53\,000}{(50\,000)}(100)$	$\frac{56\,000}{(50\,000)}(100)$
	= 100.00	= 106.00	= 112.00
Absolute (\$) increase		\$3000	\$6000
Relative (%) increase		6%	12%
Real income	\$50 000	\$48 579.29	\$48 951.05
Simple price index	$\frac{50\,000}{(50\,000)}(100)$	$\frac{48\,579.29}{(50\,000)}(100)$	$\frac{48\,951.05}{(50\,000)}(100)$
	= 100.00	= 97.16	= 97.90
Absolute (\$) increase (decrease)		(\$1420.71)	(\$1048.95)
Relative (%) increase (decrease)		(2.8%)	(2.1%)

While James' income in 2006 increased 6.0% over his 2002 income, his purchasing power, reflected by his 2006 real income, actually decreased by 2.8% over the four-year period. From 2002 to 2009, his nominal income increased by 12.0% over his 2002 income. His real income decreased by 2.1% during the period 2002 to 2009.

EXERCISE 3.7

Solve each of the following problems.

1. Using 2011 as a base period, compute a simple price index for each of the following commodities. Interpret your results.

Commodity	Price in 2011	Price in 2012
Bread (loaf)	\$2.49	\$2.58
Bus pass	\$199	\$220
Clothing	\$1650.00	\$1600.00

2. Using 2000 as the base period, compute a series of simple price indexes for the prices of gold and silver for the period 2004 to 2009. Interpret your results.

	2004	2005	2006	2007	2008	2009
(a) Gold price per ounce	\$409.72	\$444.74	\$603.46	\$695.39	\$871.96	\$972.35
(b) Silver price per ounce	\$6.6711	\$7.3164	\$11.5452	\$13.3836	\$14.9891	\$14.6733

3. The Consumer Price Index for 2006 was 109.1 and for 2009 it was 114.4.
   (a) Determine the purchasing power of the dollar in 2006 and 2009 relative to the base year 2002.
   (b) Compute the purchasing power of the dollar in 2009 relative to 2006.

4. Kim's annual incomes for 2002, 2005, and 2009 were \$50 000, \$60 000, and \$65 000 respectively. Given that the Consumer Price Index for the four years was 100.00, 106.11, and 114.4 respectively, compute Kim's real income for 2002, 2005, and 2009.

5. Tamara earned \$74 000 in 2003. If the Consumer Price Index in 2003 was 101.58 and in 2008 was 112.41, what did Tamara have to earn in 2008 just to keep up with inflation?

6. The S&P/TSX Composite Index was \$11 944.54 on January 6, 2010, and \$9472.09 on January 6, 2009. Josh holds an investment portfolio representative of the stocks in the index. If the value of the portfolio on January 6, 2009, was \$279 510, what was the value of the portfolio on January 6, 2010?

3.8 APPLICATIONS—PERSONAL INCOME TAXES

Personal income taxes are taxes imposed by the federal and provincial governments on the earned income of residents of Canada. The federal government collects and refunds income taxes based on the income you calculate on your income tax return each year.

Federal tax rates currently vary from 15% to 29% of taxable income. The tax rates increase as your income increases. The 2010 federal income tax brackets and tax rates are shown in Table 3.3.

Table 3.3 **2010 Federal Income Tax Brackets and Tax Rates**

Taxable Income (income tax brackets)	Tax Rates
$40 970 or less	15% of taxable income less than or equal to $40 970; plus
$40 970 to $81 941	22% of taxable income greater than $40 970 and less than or equal to $81 941; plus
$81 941 to $127 021	26% of taxable income greater than $81 941 and less than or equal to $127 021; plus
Over $127 021	29% of taxable income greater than $127 021

The income tax brackets are adjusted annually for changes in the Consumer Price Index (CPI) in excess of 3%. If the CPI increases by less than 3% during a year, there is no increase in the tax brackets.

The **marginal tax rate** is the rate at which your next dollar of earned income is taxed. Your marginal tax rate increases when your earnings increase and you move from a lower tax bracket to a higher tax bracket. It decreases if your earnings decline and you move into a lower tax bracket. Due to the variety of provincial tax rates and surtaxes, the combined federal-provincial marginal tax rates vary from province to province.

EXAMPLE 3.8A

Use the tax brackets and rates in Table 3.3 to compute the federal tax for Jim, Kulvir, and Lee, who are, respectively, declaring taxable income of

(i) $30 000
(ii) $60 000
(iii) $90 000

SOLUTION

(i) Federal tax for Jim = 15% × $30 000
= 0.15 × 30 000 = $4500.00

(ii) Federal tax for Kulvir = $15% × $40 970 + 22% × (60 000 − 40 970)
= $6145.50 + 4186.60 = $10 332.10

(iii) Federal tax for Lee = 15% × $40 970 + 22% × (81 941 − 40 970)
+ 26% × (90 000 − 81 941)
= $6145.50 + 9013.62 + 2095.34 = $17 254.46

Therefore, Jim, Kulvir, and Lee must report federal tax of $4500.00, $10 332.10, and $17 254.46, respectively.

Taxpayer	Taxable Income $	Increase in Income $	Federal Tax $	Increase in Federal Tax $
Jim	30 000		4 500.00	
Kulvir	60 000	30 000 (100%)	10 332.10	5 832.10 (130%)
Lee	90 000	60 000 (200%)	17 254.66	12 754.66 (283%)

For an increase in income of 100%, the federal tax increases 130%. For an increase in income of 200%, the federal tax increases 283%.

EXERCISE 3.8

Use the 2010 federal income tax brackets and rates in Table 3.3 to answer each of the following questions.

1. Victor calculated his 2010 taxable income to be \$49 450. How much federal income tax should he report?

2. Sonja reported a taxable income of \$86 300 on her 2010 income tax return. How much federal income tax should she report?

3. How much federal income tax should Aman report if she earned taxable income of \$32 920 and \$17 700 from her two jobs?

4. In early 2010, Mei Ling's gross pay increased from \$75 000 per year to \$83 000 per year.

(a) What was the annual percent increase in Mei Ling's pay before federal income taxes?

(b) What was the annual percent increase in Mei Ling's pay after federal income taxes were deducted?

Go to MathXL at www.mathxl.com. You can practise many of this chapter's exercises as often as you want. The guided solutions help you find an answer step by step. You'll find a personalized study plan available to you too!

Review Exercise

EXCEL SPREADSHEET

1. Set up ratios to compare each of the following sets of quantities. Reduce each ratio to its lowest terms.
   (a) twenty-five dimes and three dollars
   (b) five hours to 50 min
   (c) \$6.75 for thirty litres of gasoline
   (d) \$21 for three-and-a-half hours
   (e) 1440 words for 120 lines for 6 pages
   (f) 90 kg for 24 ha (hectares) for 18 weeks

2. Solve each of the following proportions.
   (a) $5 : n = 35 : 21$ (b) $10 : 6 = 30 : x$
   (c) $1.15 : 0.85 = k : 1.19$
   (d) $3.60 : m = 10.8 : 8.10$
   (e) $\frac{5}{7} : \frac{15}{14} = \frac{6}{5} : t$ (f) $y : \frac{9}{8} = \frac{5}{4} : \frac{45}{64}$

3. Compute each of the following.
   (a) 150% of 140 (b) 3% of 240
   (c) $9\frac{3}{4}$% of 2000 (d) 0.9% of 400

4. Use fractional equivalents to compute each of the following.
   (a) $66\frac{2}{3}$% of \$168 (b) $37\frac{1}{2}$% of \$2480
   (c) 125% of \$924 (d) $183\frac{1}{3}$% of \$720

5. Use the 1% method to determine each of the following.
   (a) $\frac{1}{4}$% of \$2664 (b) $\frac{5}{8}$% of \$1328
   (c) $1\frac{2}{3}$% of \$5400 (d) $2\frac{1}{5}$% of \$1260

6. Answer each of the following questions.
   (a) What is the rate percent if the base is 88 and the percentage is 55?
   (b) 63 is what percent of 36?
   (c) What is $\frac{3}{4}$% of \$64?
   (d) 450% of \$5 is what amount?
   (e) \$245 is $87\frac{1}{2}$% of what amount?
   (f) $2\frac{1}{4}$% of what amount is \$9.90?
   (g) What percent of \$62.50 is \$1.25?
   (h) \$30 is what percent of \$6?
   (i) $166\frac{2}{3}$% of what amount is \$220?
   (j) \$1.35 is $\frac{1}{3}$% of what amount?

7. Answer each of the following questions.
   (a) How much is \$8 increased by 125%?
   (b) What amount is $2\frac{1}{4}$% less than \$2000?
   (c) What percent less than \$120 is \$100?
   (d) \$975 is what percent more than \$150?
   (e) \$98 is 75% more than what amount?
   (f) After a reduction of 15%, the amount paid for a CD player was \$289. What was the price before the reduction?
   (g) What sum of money increased by 250% will amount to \$490?

8. D, E, and F own a business jointly and share profits and losses in the same proportion as their investments. How much of a profit of \$4500 will each receive if their investments are \$4000, \$6000, and \$5000 respectively?

9. Departments A, B, and C occupy floor space of 80 m², 140 m², and 160 m² respectively. If the total rental cost for the floor space is \$11 400 per month, how much of the rental cost should each department pay?

EXCEL SPREADSHEET

10. Four beneficiaries are to divide an estate of \$189 000 in the ratio $\frac{1}{3} : \frac{1}{4} : \frac{3}{8} : \frac{1}{24}$. How much should each receive?

EXCEL SPREADSHEET

11. Three insurance companies have insured a building in the ratio $\frac{1}{2}$ to $\frac{1}{3}$ to $\frac{2}{5}$. How much of a fire loss of \$185 000 should each company pay?

12. A hot water tank with a capacity of 220 L can be heated in twenty minutes. At the same rate, how many minutes will it take to heat a tank containing 176 L?

13. If the variable cost amounts to \$130 000 when sales are \$250 000, what will the variable cost be when sales are \$350 000?

14. Gross profit for April was two-fifths of net sales, and net income was two-sevenths of gross profit. Net income was $4200.

(a) What was the gross profit for April?

(b) What were net sales for April?

15. In a college, $\frac{4}{9}$ of all employees are faculty and the ratio of the faculty to support staff is 5 : 4. How many people does the college employ if the support staff numbers 192?

16. In the last municipal election, $62\frac{1}{2}\%$ of the population of 94 800 was eligible to vote. Of those eligible, $33\frac{1}{3}\%$ voted.

(a) What was the number of eligible voters?

(b) How many voted?

17. An investment portfolio of $150 000 consists of the following: $37\frac{1}{2}\%$ in bonds, $56\frac{1}{4}\%$ in common stock, and the remainder in preferred shares. How much money is invested in each type of investment security?

18. A sales representative's orders for May were $16\frac{2}{3}\%$ less than her April orders, which amounted to $51 120.

(a) How much were the sales rep's orders in May?

(b) By what amount did her orders decrease?

19. The appraised value of a property has increased $233\frac{1}{3}\%$ since it was purchased by the present owner. The purchase price of the property was $120 000, its appraised value at that time.

(a) How much is the current appraised value?

(b) How much would the owner gain by selling at the appraised value?

20. The direct material cost of manufacturing a product is $103.95, direct labour cost is $46.20, and overhead is $57.75.

(a) What is the percent content of each element of cost in the product?

(b) What is the overhead percent rate based on direct labour?

21. Inspection of a production run of 2400 items showed that 180 items did not meet specifications. Of the 180 that did not pass inspection, 150 could be reworked. The remainder had to be scrapped.

(a) What percent of the production run did not pass inspection?

(b) What percent of the items that did not meet specifications had to be scrapped?

22. The price of a stock a week ago was $56.25 per share. Today the price per share is $51.75.

(a) What is the percent change in price?

(b) What is the new price as a percent of the old price?

23. A wage earner's hourly rate of pay increased from $6.30 to $16.80 during the last decade.

(a) What was the percent change in the hourly rate of pay?

(b) What is the current rate of pay as a percent of the rate a decade ago?

24. A firm's bad debts of $7875 were $2\frac{1}{4}\%$ of sales. What were the firm's sales?

25. A ski shop lists ski boots at 240% of cost. If the ski shop prices the DX2 Model at $396, what was the cost of the ski boots to the shop?

26. A property owner listed his property for 160% more than he paid for it. The owner eventually accepted an offer $12\frac{1}{2}\%$ below his asking price and sold the property for $191 100. How much did the owner pay for the property?

27. A marina listed a yacht at $33\frac{1}{3}\%$ above cost. At the end of the season, the list price was reduced by 22.5% and the yacht was sold for $15 500. What was the cost of the yacht to the marina?

28. A & E Holdings' profit and loss statement showed a net income of $9\frac{3}{4}\%$ of revenue or $29 250. Twenty percent of net income was paid in corporation tax and 75% of the net income after tax was paid out as dividends to Alice and Emile, who hold shares in the ratio 5 to 3.

(a) What was the revenue of A & E Holdings?

(b) How much was the after-tax income?

(c) How much was paid out in dividends?

(d) What percent of net income did Alice receive as a dividend?

29. A farm was offered for sale at 350% above cost. The farm was finally sold for \$330 000, at $8\frac{1}{3}$% below the asking price.

(a) What was the original cost of the farm to the owner?

(b) How much gain did the owner realize?

(c) What percent of the original cost does this gain represent?

30. Suppose it costs C\$260 to purchase US\$245.23.

(a) What is the exchange rate?

(b) How many U.S. dollars will you receive if you convert C\$725 into U.S. dollars?

31. Media Marketing of Atlanta, Georgia, offers a three-day accommodation coupon for a Hilton Head resort in South Carolina at a promotion price of C\$216. If the exchange rate is C\$1.07 per U.S. dollar, what is the value of the coupon in U.S. dollars?

32. Suppose the Consumer Price Index in 2009 is 114.4, with 2002 as the base year.

(a) What is the purchasing power of the dollar in 2009 compared to 2002?

(b) What is the real income, relative to 2002, of a wage earner whose income amounted to \$62 900 in 2009?

33. Abeni calculated her 2010 taxable income to be \$83 450. How much federal income tax should she report?

34. Matt's gross pay had been \$68 000 per year, when he received an increase of \$6000 per year.

(a) What was the annual percent increase in Matt's pay before federal income taxes?

(b) What was the annual percent increase in Matt's pay after federal income taxes were deducted?

Self-Test

1. Compute each of the following.

(a) 125% of \$280

(b) $\frac{3}{8}$% of \$20 280

(c) $83\frac{1}{3}$% of \$174

(d) $1\frac{1}{4}$% of \$1056

2. Solve each of the following proportions.

(a) $65 : 39 = x : 12$

(b) $\frac{7}{6} : \frac{35}{12} = \frac{6}{5} : x$

3. The results of a market survey indicate that 24 respondents preferred Brand X, 36 preferred Brand Y, and 20 had no preference. What percent of the sample preferred Brand Y?

4. Departments A, B, and C occupy floor space of 40 m², 80 m², and 300 m² respectively. If the total rental for the space is \$25 200 per month, how much rent should Department B pay?

5. Past experience shows that the clientele of a restaurant spends \$9.60 on beverages for every \$12 spent on food. If it is expected that food sales will amount to \$12 500 for a month, how much should be budgeted for beverage sales?

6. After a reduction of $16\frac{2}{3}$% off the marked price, a pair of boots sold for \$60. What was the marked price?

EXCEL SPREADSHEET

7. A bonus is to be divided among four employees in the ratio $\frac{1}{2} : \frac{1}{3} : \frac{1}{5} : \frac{1}{6}$. What is each employee's share of a bonus of $40 500?

8. Jorjanna Fawcett's hourly rate of pay was increased from $11 to $12.54. What was the percent raise?

9. A bicycle was sold for $282.50. The selling price included 13% harmonized sales tax. Find the amount of HST on the bike.

10. A microwave oven originally advertised at $220 is reduced to $209 during a sale. By what percent was the price reduced?

11. A special consumer index has increased 100% during the last 10 years. If the index is now 360, what was it 10 years ago?

12. Mr. Braid owned $\frac{3}{8}$ of a store. He sold $\frac{2}{3}$ of his interest in the store for $18 000. What was the value of the store?

13. Suppose it cost C$0.9022 to purchase one Australian dollar.
    (a) How much would it cost in Australian dollars to purchase one Canadian dollar?
    (b) How many Australian dollars would you need to buy 500 Canadian dollars?

14. If one Canadian dollar is equivalent to US$0.9250, how much do you need in Canadian funds to buy US$800.00?

15. What is the purchasing power of the dollar relative to the base year of 2002 if the Consumer Price Index is 113.6?

16. Suppose a taxpayer is in the tax bracket in which federal income tax is calculated as $6145.50 plus 22% of income over $40 970. How much federal income tax must he report if he earns $48 750?

Challenge Problems

1. Two consecutive price reductions of the same percent reduced the price of an item from $25 to $16. By what percent was the price reduced each time?

2. Suppose you own a fast-food outlet and buy 100 kilograms of potatoes that are 99% water. After leaving them outside for a few days, you are told that they are now only 98% water. Assuming that they have simply lost some water, how much do the potatoes now weigh?

3. Luis ordered four pairs of black socks and some additional pairs of blue socks from a clothing catalogue. The price of the black socks per pair was twice that of the blue. When the order was filled, it was found that the number of pairs of the two colours had been interchanged. This increased the bill by 50% (before taxes and delivery charges). Find the ratio of the number of pairs of black socks to the number of pairs of blue socks in Luis's original order.

4. Following a 10% decrease in her annual salary, what percent increase would an employee need to receive in future to get back to her original salary level?

CASE STUDY 3.1 The Business of Taxes

» Camille operates a child care service from her home. Her gross business income for 2010 amounted to $42 350. Her tax-deductible business expenses consisted of the following:

Advertising	$1700
Dues, memberships, subscriptions	520
Motor vehicle expenses	1115
Supplies	582
Meals and entertainment	495
Other expenses	437

Camille can also deduct home expenses, such as utilities, property taxes, house insurance, mortgage interest, and maintenance for the business use of a workspace in her home. The amount that may be deducted is a proportion of the total annual home expenses allocated to the workspace on a reasonable basis, such as area or number of rooms. Camille's eligible home expenses for the year were:

Heat	$3750
Power	2480
Water	610
House insurance	1420
Maintenance	1930
Mortgage interest	6630
Property taxes	3260
Other expenses	690

The house covers 345 square metres and consists of eight rooms. Camille uses one room with an area of 45 square metres as her business office.

QUESTIONS

1. What portion of her eligible home expenses may Camille claim as tax-deductible expenses if the expenses are allocated on the basis of
   (a) area? **(b)** number of rooms?
2. What is her net business income if Camille allocates home expenses on the basis of area?
3. For most individuals, basic federal income tax equals the federal tax calculated according to Table 3.3 less non-refundable tax credits. What is Camille's basic federal income tax if she reports a non-refundable tax credit of $8430?
   Note: Federal tax is reduced by 15.25% of total non-refundable tax credits.
4. What percent of Camille's business income is basic federal income tax?
5. What percent of Camille's taxable income is basic federal income tax?

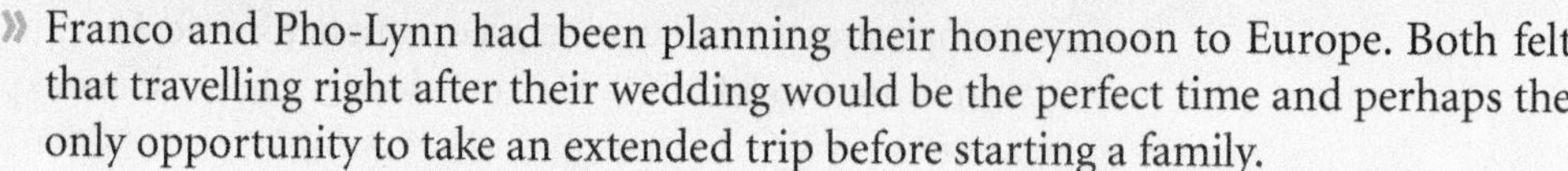

CASE STUDY 3.2 Trip of a Lifetime

» Franco and Pho-Lynn had been planning their honeymoon to Europe. Both felt that travelling right after their wedding would be the perfect time and perhaps the only opportunity to take an extended trip before starting a family.

A major part of their planning focused on the financial costs they would incur over the 21 days of their trip. Their plan was to spend five days in Switzerland, six days in Germany, and ten days in England.

Franco and Pho-Lynn budgeted C$1500 each for the multi-destination round-trip airfare. They would leave Edmonton, land in Zurich, and return from London, England. Research over the Internet indicated that they could each comfortably live on the following amounts in the local currencies (including transportation, food, accommodation, and miscellaneous expenditures):

Switzerland	230 Swiss francs/day
Germany	200 euros/day
England	100 pounds/day

QUESTIONS

1. The currency cross rates in Table 3.2 were in effect when Franco and Pho-Lynn were planning their trip. Using these rates, what is the expected total cost of this trip for each traveller in Canadian dollars?

2. What would be the total cost in U.S. dollars for each traveller if Franco and Pho-Lynn were American citizens planning the same trip? Assume the round-trip airfare from Chicago to London, England, and from Zurich, Switzerland, to Chicago costs each of them US$1050.

SUMMARY OF FORMULAS

Formula 3.1A

$$\text{PERCENTAGE} = \text{RATE} \times \text{BASE}$$

or

$$\text{NEW NUMBER} = \text{RATE} \times \text{ORIGINAL NUMBER}$$

The basic percentage relationship

Formula 3.1B

$$\text{RATE} = \frac{\text{PERCENTAGE}}{\text{BASE}} \text{ or } \frac{\text{NEW NUMBER}}{\text{ORIGINAL NUMBER}}$$

The formula for finding the rate percent when comparing a number (the percentage) to another number (the base or original number)

Formula 3.2

$$\text{ORIGINAL NUMBER} \begin{array}{l} + \text{ INCREASE} \\ - \text{ DECREASE} \end{array} = \begin{array}{c} \text{NEW} \\ \text{NUMBER} \end{array}$$

The relationship to use with problems of increase or decrease (problems of change)

Formula 3.3

$$\text{RATE OF CHANGE} = \frac{\text{AMOUNT OF CHANGE}}{\text{ORIGINAL NUMBER}}$$

The formula for finding the rate of change (rate of increase or decrease)

Formula 3.4

$$\text{REAL INCOME} = \frac{\text{INCOME IN CURRENT DOLLARS}}{\text{CONSUMER PRICE INDEX}}$$

The formula for eliminating the effect of inflation on income

GLOSSARY

Base period in an index, the period of time against which comparisons are made. The base period is arbitrarily selected, but it always has an index number of 100 *(p. 130)*

Consumer Price Index (CPI) the index that shows the price change for a sample of goods and services that is used to indicate the price change for all goods and services *(p. 130)*

Equivalent ratios in higher terms ratios obtained by multiplying each term of a ratio by the same number *(p. 95)*

Exchange rate the value of one nation's currency expressed in terms of another's currency *(p. 125)*

Index number expresses the relative change in the value of an item at different points in time. One of the points in time is a base period, which is always defined to have a value of 100 *(p. 129)*

Marginal tax rate the rate at which your next dollar of earned income is taxed. Marginal tax rates tend to increase as earnings increase *(p. 133)*

Nominal income income stated in current dollars *(p. 131)*

Personal income tax taxes imposed by the federal and provincial governments on the earned income of Canadian residents *(p. 132)*

Proportion a statement of equality between two ratios *(p. 100)*

Purchasing power of the dollar the reciprocal of the Consumer Price Index *(p. 130)*

Ratio a comparison by division of the relative values of numbers or quantities *(p. 94)*

Real income income stated in base-period dollars *(p. 131)*

Terms of a ratio the numbers appearing in a ratio *(p. 94)*

USEFUL INTERNET SITES

www.taxpayer.com

Canadian Taxpayers Federation The Canadian Taxpayers Federation (CTF), a federally incorporated, non-profit, non-partisan organization, acts as a watchdog on government spending and taxation.

money.cnn.com/data/currencies

Foreign Currency Exchange Rates The Cable News Network (CNN) site provides current currency exchange rates on its financial page.

www.globeinvestor.com

The Globe and Mail This Canadian newspaper's site provides price, performance, and index benchmark data on securities trading on North American stock exchanges.

www.statcan.gc.ca

Statistics Canada This government Website for Canadian statistics contains a lengthy and informative discussion of the Consumer Price Index.

CHAPTER 4

Linear Systems

OBJECTIVES

Upon completing this chapter, you will be able to do the following:

1. Solve linear systems consisting of two simultaneous equations in two variables using algebraic elimination.
2. Graph linear equalities in two variables.
3. Graph linear systems consisting of two linear relations in two variables.
4. Solve problems by setting up systems of linear equations in two variables.

Most manufacturing companies produce more than one product. In deciding the quantities of each product to produce, management has to take into account the combination of production levels that will make the most efficient use of labour, materials, and transportation, and produce the highest level of profit. Most companies have so many factors to consider that they need sophisticated methods of evaluation. However, many situations like this can be simplified and solved. Suppose you were in the business of producing children's toys. If you cannot produce all the items because of limited budget or limited manufacturing capacity, you would need to consider the relative profitability of each item to determine which combination of items to produce. You can define the variables, set up a system of linear equations, and solve the system by algebraic or graphical methods to decide how to best allocate your resources.

INTRODUCTION

In many types of problems, the relationship between two or more variables can be represented by setting up linear equations. Algebraic as well as graphic techniques are available to solve such problems.

4.1 ALGEBRAIC SOLUTION OF SYSTEMS OF LINEAR EQUATIONS IN TWO VARIABLES

A. Basic concept

Any linear system that consists of two equations in two variables can be solved algebraically or graphically.

Solving a system of two equations requires finding a pair of values for the two variables that satisfies both of the equations. The value of one of the two variables can be determined by first reducing the system of equations to one equation in one variable and solving this equation. The value of the variable obtained is then substituted into one of the original equations to find the value of the second variable.

Algebraic and graphic solutions of systems of linear equations in two variables are used extensively when doing break-even analysis. Break-even analysis is explored further in Chapter 6.

B. Solving a system of two linear equations by algebraic elimination

If the coefficients of one variable are the same in both equations, the system can be reduced to one equation by addition or subtraction as follows.

(a) If the coefficients of one variable are numerically equal but opposite in sign, addition will eliminate the variable.

(b) If the coefficients of one variable are numerically equal and have the same sign, subtraction can eliminate the variable. Alternatively, one equation can be multiplied by -1; addition can then be used.

EXAMPLE 4.1A

Solve each of the following systems of equations.

(i) $x + y = 1$
$x - y = 7$

(ii) $5x + 4y = 7$
$3x - 4y = 17$

(iii) $x - 3y = 2$
$4x - 3y = -10$

SOLUTION

(i) $x + y = 1$ ——— equation ①

$x - y = 7$ ——— equation ②

$2x = 8$ ——— add ① and ② to eliminate y

$x = 4$ ——— *Note:* The coefficient of y in ① is 1; the coefficient of y in ② is -1. Since the coefficients are the same but opposite in sign, adding the two equations will eliminate the term in y.

$4 + y = 1$ — substitute the value of x in ①

$y = -3$

$\boxed{x = 4, y = -3}$ — solution

Check

in ① LS $= 4 + (-3) = 4 - 3 = 1$

RS $= 1$

in ② LS $= 4 - (-3) = 4 + 3 = 7$

RS $= 7$

(ii) $5x + 4y = 7$ — equation ①

$3x - 4y = 17$ — equation ②

$8x = 24$ — add ① and ② to eliminate y

$x = 3$

$5(3) + 4y = 7$ — substitute 3 for x in ①

$15 + 4y = 7$

$4y = -8$

$y = -2$

$\boxed{x = 3, y = -2}$ — solution

Check

in ① LS $= 5(3) + 4(-2) = 15 - 8 = 7$

RS $= 7$

in ② LS $= 3(3) - 4(-2) = 9 + 8 = 17$

RS $= 17$

(iii) $x - 3y = 2$ — ①

$4x - 3y = -10$ — ②

$x - 3y = 2$ — ①

$-4x + 3y = 10$ — ② multiplied by -1 to set up addition

$-3x = 12$ — add

$x = -4$

$-4 - 3y = 2$ — substitute -4 for x in ①

$-3y = 6$

$y = -2$

$\boxed{x = -4, y = -2}$ — solution

Check

in ① LS $= -4 - 3(-2) = -4 + 6 = 2$

RS $= 2$

in ② LS $= 4(-4) - 3(-2) = -16 + 6 = -10$

RS $= -10$

C. Solving a system of two linear equations when the coefficients are not numerically equal

Sometimes numerical equality of one pair of coefficients must be *created* before addition or subtraction can be used to eliminate a variable. This equality is usually achieved by multiplying one or both equations by a number or numbers that make the coefficients of the variable to be eliminated numerically equal.

EXAMPLE 4.1B

Solve each of the following systems of equations.

(i) $x - 3y = -12$
$3x + y = -6$

(ii) $x + 4y = 18$
$2x + 5y = 24$

(iii) $6x - 5y + 70 = 0$
$4x = 3y - 44$

SOLUTION

(i) $x - 3y = -12$ ——— ①
$3x + y = -6$ ——— ②

To eliminate the term in y, multiply ② by 3.

$x - 3y = -12$ ——— ①
$9x + 3y = -18$ ——— ② multiplied by 3
$10x = -30$ ——— add
$x = -3$
$-3 - 3y = -12$ ——— substitute -3 for x in ①
$-3y = -9$
$y = 3$
$\boxed{x = -3, y = 3}$ ——— solution

(ii) $x + 4y = 18$ ——— ①
$2x + 5y = 24$ ——— ②

To eliminate the term in x, multiply ① by 2.

$2x + 8y = 36$ ——— ① multiplied by 2
$-2x - 5y = -24$ ——— ② multiplied by -1 to set up addition
$3y = 12$ ——— add
$y = 4$
$x + 4(4) = 18$ ——— substitute 4 for y in ①
$x + 16 = 18$
$x = 2$
$\boxed{x = 2, y = 4}$ ——— solution

(iii) $6x - 5y + 70 = 0$ ——— ①
$4x = 3y - 44$ ——— ②

Rearrange the two equations in the same order.

$6x - 5y = -70$ ——— ①
$4x - 3y = -44$ ——— ②

To eliminate the term in y, multiply ① by 3 and ② by -5.

$18x - 15y = -210$ ——— ① multiplied by 3
$-20x + 15y = 220$ ——— ② multiplied by -5
$-2x = 10$ ——— add
$x = -5$
$6(-5) - 5y = -70$ ——— substitute -5 for x in ①
$-30 - 5y = -70$
$-5y = -40$
$y = 8$
$\boxed{x = -5, y = 8}$ ——— solution

D. Solving linear systems in two variables involving fractions

When one or both equations contain decimals or common fractions, it is best to eliminate the decimals or fractions by multiplying; then solve the system as shown in the previous examples.

EXAMPLE 4.1C Solve each of the following systems of equations.

(i) $1.5x + 0.8y = 1.2$
$0.7x + 1.2y = -4.4$

(ii) $\frac{5x}{6} + \frac{3y}{8} = -1$
$\frac{2x}{3} - \frac{3y}{4} = -5$

SOLUTION

(i) $1.5x + 0.8y = 1.2$ ——— ①
$0.7x + 1.2y = -4.4$ ——— ②

To eliminate the decimals, multiply each equation by 10.

$15x + 8y = 12$ ——— ③
$7x + 12y = -44$ ——— ④

To eliminate the term in y, multiply ③ by 3 and ④ by 2.

$45x + 24y = 36$ ——— ③ multiplied by 3
$14x + 24y = -88$ ——— ④ multiplied by 2
$31x = 124$ ——— subtract
$x = 4$
$15(4) + 8y = 12$ ——— substitute 4 for x in ③
$60 + 8y = 12$
$8y = -48$
$y = -6$
$\boxed{x = 4, y = -6}$ ——— solution

(ii) $\frac{5x}{6} + \frac{3y}{8} = -1$ ——— ①
$\frac{2x}{3} + \frac{3y}{4} = -5$ ——— ②

To eliminate the fractions, multiply ① by 24 and ② by 12.

$$\frac{24(5x)}{6} + \frac{24(3y)}{8} = 24(-1) \quad \text{① multiplied by 24}$$
$$4(5x) + 3(3y) = -24$$
$$20x + 9y = -24 \quad \text{③}$$
$$\frac{12(2x)}{3} + \frac{12(3y)}{4} = 12(-5) \quad \text{② multiplied by 12}$$
$$4(2x) - 3(3y) = -60$$
$$8x - 9y = -60 \quad \text{④}$$

To eliminate the term in y, add ③ and ④.

$$20x + 9y = -24 \quad \text{③}$$
$$8x - 9y = -60 \quad \text{④}$$
$$28x = -84$$
$$x = -3$$
$$20(-3) + 9y = -24 \quad \text{substitute } -3 \text{ for } x \text{ in ③}$$
$$-60 + 9y = -24$$
$$9y = 36$$
$$y = 4$$
$$\boxed{x = -3, y = 4} \quad \text{solution}$$

POINTERS AND PITFALLS

When removing decimals or fractions from linear systems in two variables, remember that each equation can, if necessary, be multiplied by a *different quantity.*

For example,

(i) Solve $1.2x + 3.5y = 50$ — multiply by *10* to eliminate decimals
$2.26x - 0.70y = 6.5$ — multiply by *100* to eliminate decimals

(ii) Refer to Example 4.1C(ii). In this example, the first equation is multiplied by a lowest common denominator (LCD) of *24* to eliminate fractions, while the second equation is multiplied by an LCD of *12* to eliminate fractions.

EXERCISE 4.1

A. Solve each of the following systems of equations and check your solutions.

1. $x + y = -9$
$x - y = -7$

2. $x + 5y = 0$
$x + 2y = 6$

3. $5x + 2y = 74$
$7x - 2y = 46$

4. $2x + 9y = -13$
$2x - 3y = 23$

5. $y = 3x + 12$
$x = -y$

6. $3x = 10 - 2y$
$5y = 3x - 38$

B. Solve each of the following systems of equations and check your solutions.

1. $4x + y = -13$
$x - 5y = -19$

2. $6x + 3y = 24$
$2x + 9y = -8$

3. $7x - 5y = -22$
$4x + 3y = 5$

4. $8x + 9y = 129$
$6x + 7y = 99$

5. $12y = 5x + 16$
$6x + 10y - 54 = 0$

6. $3x - 8y + 44 = 0$
$7x = 12y - 56$

C. Solve each of the following systems of equations.

1. $0.4x + 1.5y = 16.8$
$1.1x - 0.9y = 6.0$

2. $6.5x + 3.5y = 128$
$2.5x + 4.5y = 106$

3. $2.4x + 1.6y = 7.60$
$3.8x + 0.6y = 7.20$

4. $2.25x + 0.75y = 2.25$
$1.25x + 1.75y = 2.05$

5. $\frac{3x}{4} - \frac{2y}{3} = \frac{-13}{6}$
$\frac{4x}{5} + \frac{3y}{4} = \frac{123}{10}$

6. $\frac{9x}{5} + \frac{5y}{4} = \frac{47}{10}$
$\frac{2x}{9} + \frac{3y}{8} = \frac{5}{36}$

7. $\frac{x}{3} + \frac{2y}{5} = \frac{7}{15}$
$\frac{3x}{2} - \frac{7y}{3} = -1$

8. $\frac{x}{4} + \frac{3y}{7} = \frac{-2}{21}$
$\frac{2x}{3} + \frac{3y}{2} = \frac{-7}{36}$

4.2 GRAPHING LINEAR EQUATIONS

A. Graphing in a system of rectangular coordinates

A system of rectangular coordinates, as shown in Figure 4.1, consists of two straight lines that intersect at right angles in a plane. The *horizontal* line is called the **X axis** while the *vertical* line is called the **Y axis.** The point of intersection of the two axes is called the **origin.**

FIGURE 4.1 **Rectangular Coordinates**

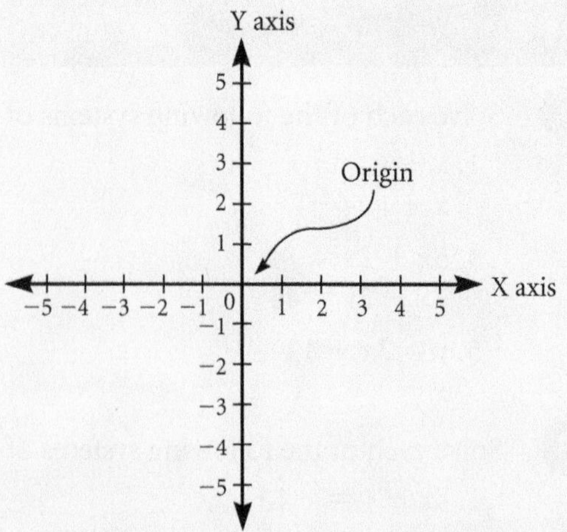

The two axes are used as number lines. By agreement, on the X axis the numbers are positive to the right of the origin and negative to the left. On the Y axis the numbers are positive above the origin and negative below the origin.

The position of any point relative to the pair of axes is defined by an **ordered pair of numbers** (x, y) such that the first number (the x value or ***x* coordinate**) always represents the directed distance of the point from the Y axis. The second number (the y value or ***y* coordinate**) always represents the directed distance of the point from the X axis.

The origin is identified by the ordered pair (0, 0); that is, the coordinates of the origin are (0, 0) since the distance of the point from either axis is zero.

As shown in Figure 4.2, the point marked A is identified by the coordinates (4, 3). That is, the directed distance of the point is four units to the right of the Y axis (its x value or x coordinate is $+4$), and the directed distance of the point is three units above the X axis (its y coordinate is $+3$). Note that the point may be found by counting four units to the right along the X axis and then moving three units up parallel to the Y axis.

FIGURE 4.2 Locating a Point

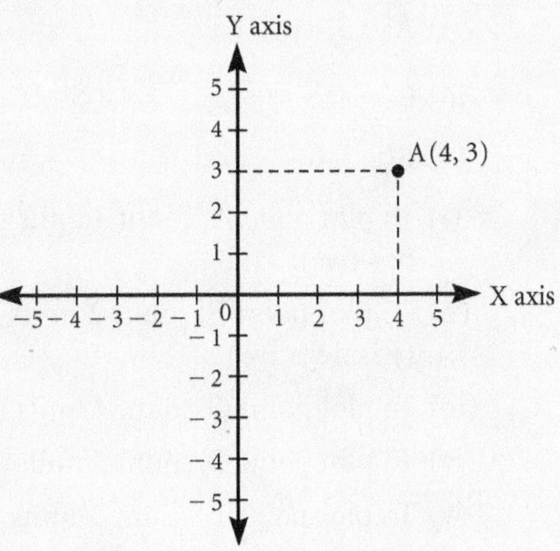

EXAMPLE 4.2A Determine the coordinates of the points A, B, C, D, E, F, G, and H as marked in the following diagram.

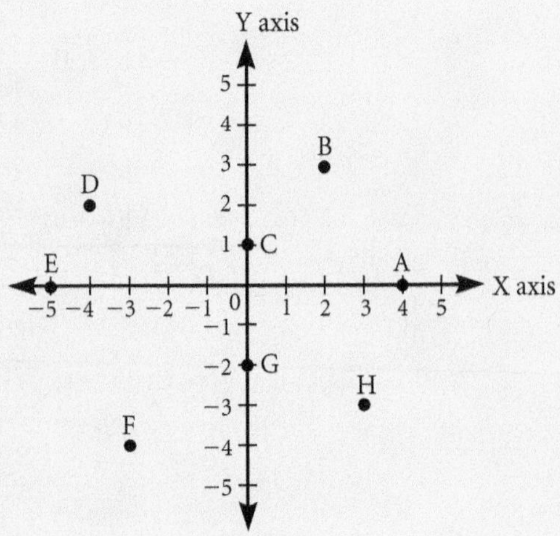

SOLUTION

POINT	COORDINATES	
A	(4, 0)	4 units to the right of the origin ($x = 4$) on the X axis ($y = 0$)
B	(2, 3)	2 units to the right ($x = 2$) and 3 units up ($y = 3$)
C	(0, 1)	on the Y axis ($x = 0$) 1 unit up ($y = 1$)
D	(−4, 2)	4 units to the left ($x = -4$) and 2 units up ($y = 2$)
E	(−5, 0)	5 units to the left ($x = -5$) on the X axis ($y = 0$)
F	(−3, −4)	3 units to the left ($x = -3$) and 4 units down ($y = -4$)
G	(0, −2)	on the Y axis ($x = 0$) 2 units down ($y = -2$)
H	(3, −3)	3 units to the right ($x = 3$) and 3 units down ($y = -3$)

To draw the graphs of linear relations, you must plot two or more points in a set of rectangular axes. To *plot* point (x, y), count the number of units represented by x along the X axis (to the right if x is positive, to the left if x is negative) and then count the number of units represented by y up or down (up if y is positive, down if y is negative).

EXAMPLE 4.2B

Plot the following points in a set of rectangular axes.

(i) A(−3, 4) (ii) B(2, −4)

(iii) C(−4, −4) (iv) D(3, 3)

(v) E(−3, 0) (vi) F(0, −2)

SOLUTION

(i) To plot point A, count 3 units to the left (x is negative) and 4 units up (y is positive).

(ii) To plot point B, count 2 units to the right (x is positive) and 4 units down (y is negative).

(iii) To plot point C, count 4 units to the left and 4 units down.

(iv) To plot point D, count 3 units to the right and 3 units up.

(v) To plot point E, count 3 units to the left and mark the point on the X axis since $y = 0$.

(vi) To plot point F, count 2 units down and mark the point on the Y axis since $x = 0$.

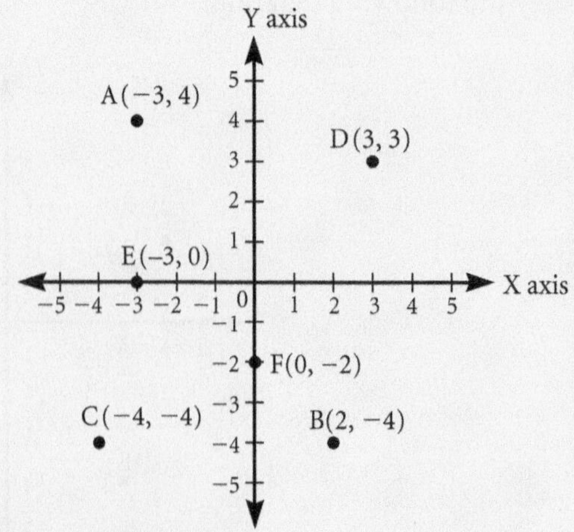

B. Constructing a table of values

To graph linear equations, plot a set of points whose coordinates *satisfy* the equation and then join the points.

A suitable set of points may be obtained by constructing a table of values. Substitute arbitrarily chosen values of x or y in the equation and compute the value of the second variable. The chosen value and the corresponding computed value form an ordered pair (x, y). A listing of such ordered pairs forms a table of values.

EXAMPLE 4.2C

Construct a table of values for

(i) $x = 2y$ for integral values of y from $y = +3$ to $y = -3$;

(ii) $y = 2x - 3$ for integral values of x from $x = -2$ to $x = +4$.

SOLUTION

(i) To obtain the desired ordered pairs, substitute assumed values of y into the equation $x = 2y$.

$y = +3$ $\quad x = 2(3) = 6$
$y = +2$ $\quad x = 2(2) = 4$
$y = +1$ $\quad x = 2(1) = 2$
$y = 0$ $\quad x = 2(0) = 0$
$y = -1$ $\quad x = 2(-1) = -2$
$y = -2$ $\quad x = 2(-2) = -4$
$y = -3$ $\quad x = 2(-3) = -6$

Listing the obtained ordered pairs gives the following table of values.

Table of values

x	6	4	2	0	−2	−4	−6	corresponding computed x values
y	3	2	1	0	−1	−2	−3	chosen y values

(ii) To obtain the desired ordered pairs, substitute assumed values of x into the equation $y = 2x - 3$.

$x = -2$ $\quad y = 2(-2) - 3 = -4 - 3 = -7$
$x = -1$ $\quad y = 2(-1) - 3 = -2 - 3 = -5$
$x = 0$ $\quad y = 2(0) - 3 = 0 - 3 = -3$
$x = 1$ $\quad y = 2(1) - 3 = 2 - 3 = -1$
$x = 2$ $\quad y = 2(2) - 3 = 4 - 3 = +1$
$x = 3$ $\quad y = 2(3) - 3 = 6 - 3 = +3$
$x = 4$ $\quad y = 2(4) - 3 = 8 - 3 = +5$

Table of values

x	−2	−1	0	1	2	3	4
y	−7	−5	−3	−1	1	3	5

chosen x values
corresponding computed y values

Guidelines for constructing a table of values:

(1) Values may be chosen arbitrarily for either x or y.

(2) The values chosen are usually integers.

(3) Integers that yield an integer for the computed value are preferred.

C. Graphing linear equations

To graph a linear equation, you need a minimum of two points. To check for accuracy, a third point should also be plotted. When a line is drawn through the points, the result should be a straight line. To graph linear equations,

(1) *construct* a table of values consisting of at least two (preferably three) ordered pairs (x, y);

(2) *plot* the points in a system of rectangular axes;

(3) *join* the points by a straight line.

EXAMPLE 4.2D

Graph each of the following equations.

(i) $x + y = 4$
(ii) $x - y = 5$
(iii) $x = y$
(iv) $y = -2x$
(v) $y = 2x + 100$ for all values of x from $x = 0$ to $x = 200$

SOLUTION

(i) Equation: $x + y = 4$

Table of values

x	0	4	2
y	4	0	2

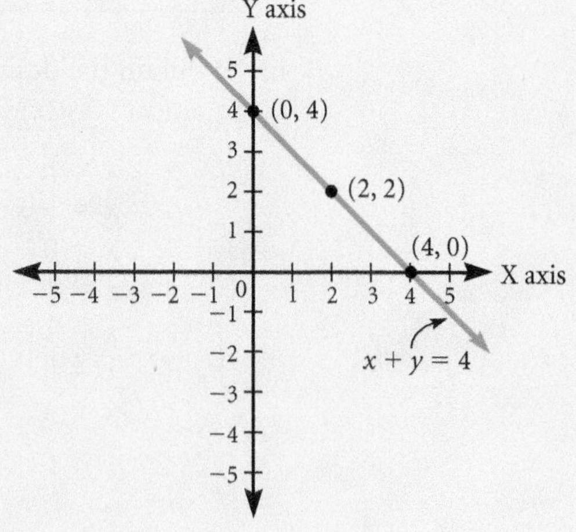

(ii) Equation: $x - y = 5$

Table of values

x	0	5	3
y	−5	0	−2

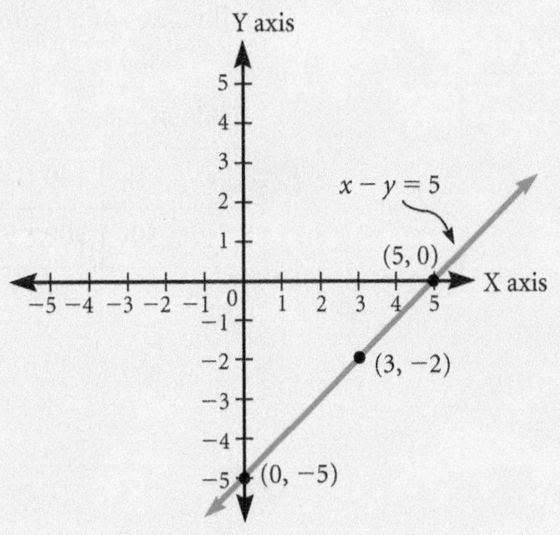

(iii) Equation: $x = y$

Table of values

x	0	3	−3
y	0	3	−3

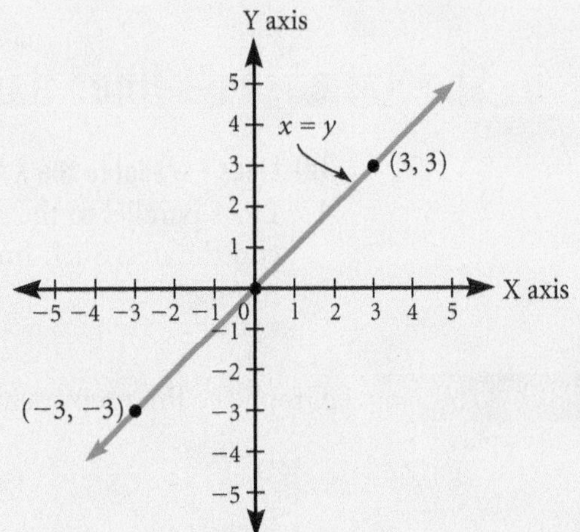

(iv) Equation: $y = -2x$

Table of values

x	0	2	−2
y	0	−4	4

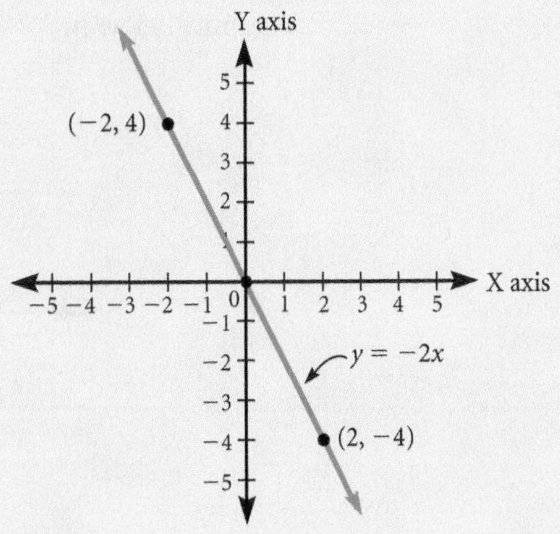

(v) Equation: $y = 2x + 100$ for all values of x from $x = 0$ to $x = 200$

Table of values

x	0	100	200
y	100	300	500

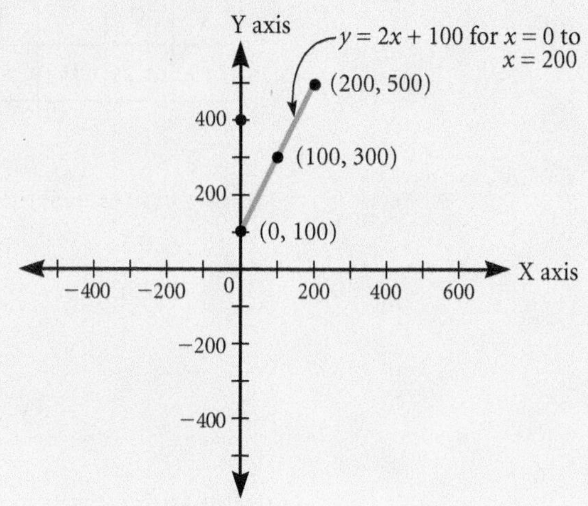

D. Special cases—lines parallel to the axes

(a) Lines Parallel to the X Axis

Lines parallel to the X axis are formed by sets of points that all have the *same* y coordinates. Such lines are defined by the equation $y = b$ where b is any real number.

EXAMPLE 4.2E Graph the lines represented by

(i) $y = 3$ (ii) $y = -3$

SOLUTION

(i) The line represented by $y = 3$ is a line parallel to the X axis and three units above it.

(ii) The line represented by $y = -3$ is a line parallel to the X axis and three units below it.

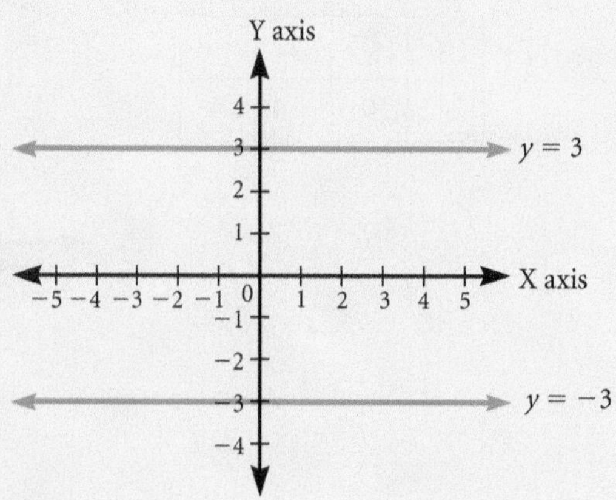

(b) Lines Parallel to the Y Axis

Lines parallel to the Y axis are formed by sets of points that all have the same x coordinates. Such lines are defined by the equation $x = a$ where a is any real number.

EXAMPLE 4.2F

Graph the lines represented by

(i) $x = 3$ (ii) $x = -3$

SOLUTION

(i) The line represented by $x = 3$ is a line parallel to the Y axis and three units to the right of it.

(ii) The line represented by $x = -3$ is a line parallel to the Y axis and three units to the left of it.

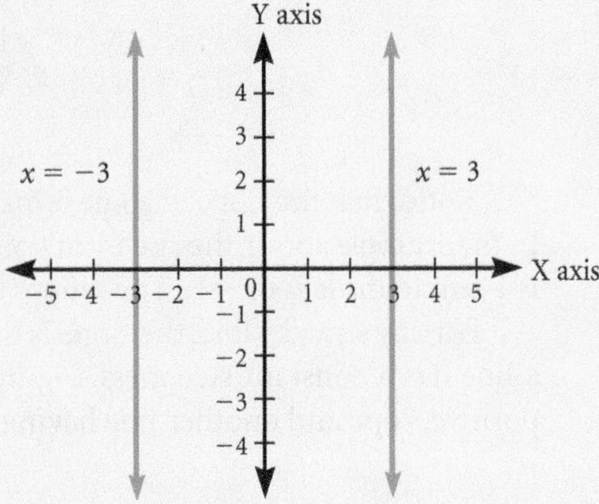

(c) The Axes

X axis The y coordinates of the set of points forming the X axis are zero. Thus the equation $y = 0$ represents the X axis.

Y axis The x coordinates of the set of points forming the Y axis are zero. Thus the equation $x = 0$ represents the Y axis.

E. The slope-y-intercept form of a linear equation

Every line has two important characteristics: its steepness, called the **slope**, and a point where the line intersects with the Y axis, called the **y-intercept**.

In more technical terms, **slope** is the ratio of the *rise* of a line to its *run*. The **rise** of a line is the distance along the Y axis between two points on a line. The **run** of a line is the distance along the X axis between the same two points on the line.

As shown in Figure 4.3, point A(4, 3) and point B(3, 1) lie on the line $2x - y = 4$. The rise between point A and point B is -2, since you must move 2 units down, parallel to the Y axis, when you move from point A to point B. The run between point A and point B is -1, since you must move 1 unit to the left, parallel to the X axis, when you move from point A to point B. The ratio $^{\text{rise}}/_{\text{run}}$ is $^{-2}/_{-1}$, or $+2$.

FIGURE 4.3

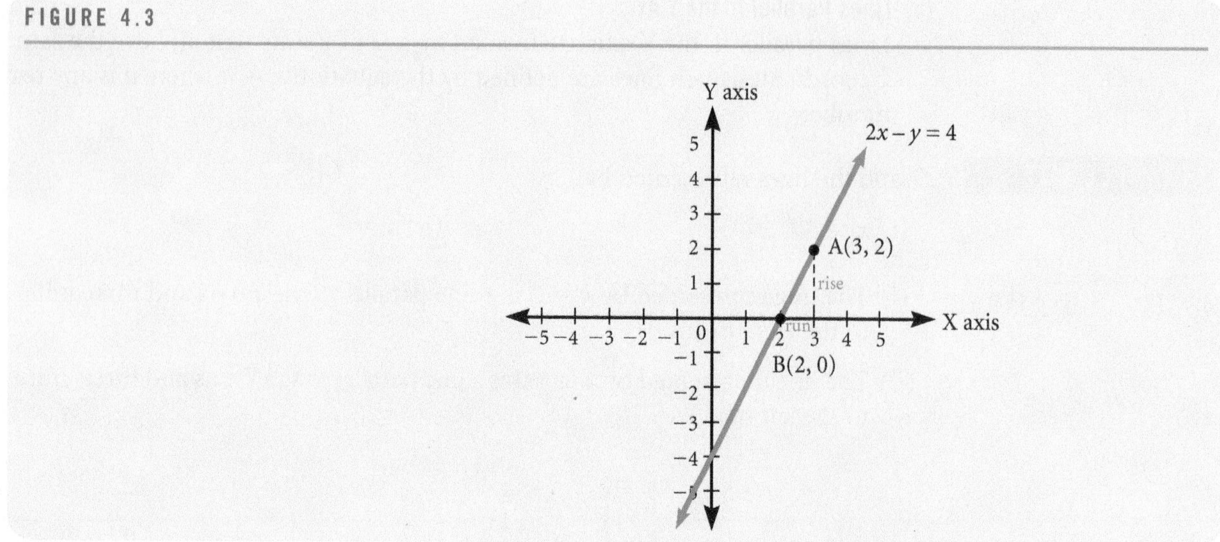

Notice that the slope of a line remains the same if you go from point B to point A. In the example above, the rise from point B to point A is 2 units down, or −2. The run is 1 unit to the left, or −1. The ratio rise/run is −2/−1, or +2, the same as was shown earlier.

For any straight line, the slope is the same for *any* two points on the line because a line has a constant steepness. Figure 4.4 shows an example of one line having a positive slope and another line having a negative slope.

FIGURE 4.4

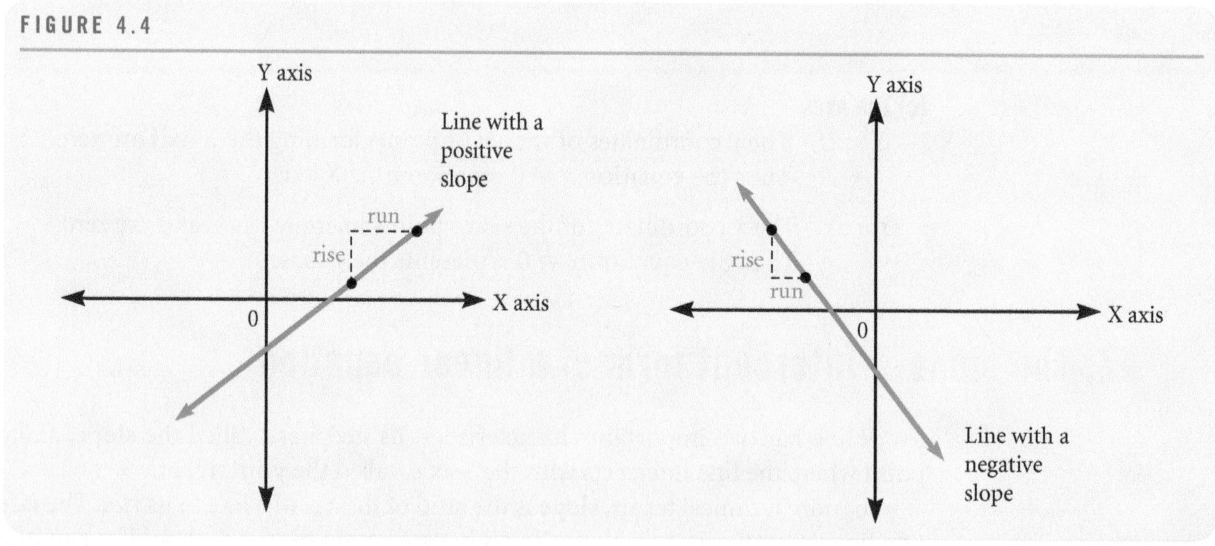

We know from Figure 4.3 that the slope of the line representing $2x - y = 4$ is $+2$. By rearranging the terms of this equation, we see that the equation of this line can be written $y = 2x - 4$. We say the line's equation is in the form $y = mx + b$. When a linear equation is in this form, it is easy to see that m, the coefficient of x, represents the slope of the line, which is $+2$.

By substituting $x = 0$ into $y = 2x - 4$, we find that $y = -4$. You can see that the line $y = 2x - 4$ crosses the Y axis at the point $(0, -4)$ in Figure 4.3. In the linear equation $y = mx + b$, b is the y-intercept of the line.

The **slope-y-intercept form of a linear equation** is a linear equation expressed in the form $y = mx + b$.

$$y = mx + b \qquad \text{Formula 4.1}$$

In any equation in the form $y = mx + b$, m is the slope and b is the y-intercept.

EXAMPLE 4.2G Using algebra, find the slope and y-intercept of each of the following equations.

(i) $y = \frac{2}{3}x - 7$ (ii) $3x + 4y = -2$

SOLUTION (i) $y = \frac{2}{3}x - 7$ is already in the form $y = mx + b$.

Thus, slope $= \frac{2}{3}$, since $m = \frac{2}{3}$ in the equation $y = \frac{2}{3}x - 7$.

The y-intercept $= -7$, since $b = -7$ in the equation $y = \frac{2}{3}x - 7$

(ii)

$$3x + 4y = -2 \text{ must be expressed in the form } y = mx + b.$$
$$-3x + 3x + 4y = -3x - 2 \qquad \text{add } -3x \text{ to each side}$$
$$4y = -3x - 2 \qquad \text{simplify}$$
$$y = -\frac{3}{4}x - \frac{1}{2} \qquad \text{slope-}y\text{-intercept form}$$

Thus, slope $= -\frac{3}{4}$, since $m = -\frac{3}{4}$ in the equation $y = -\frac{3}{4}x - \frac{1}{2}$.

The y-intercept $= -\frac{1}{2}$, since $b = -\frac{1}{2}$ in the equation $y = -\frac{3}{4}x - \frac{1}{2}$.

Once you have found m and b, you can use the slope and y-intercept to graph a linear equation.

1. Graph the y-intercept, which is the point $(0, b)$.
2. Find another point on the line by using the slope. Beginning at the y-intercept, move up (if positive) or down (if negative) by the number of units in the rise (the numerator of the slope). Then move right (if positive) or left (if negative) by the number of units in the run (the denominator of the slope), and mark this point.
3. Draw a line through the point you just marked and the y-intercept to represent the linear equation.

EXAMPLE 4.2H

Given the linear equation $6x + 2y = 8$,

(i) rearrange the equation into the slope-y-intercept form;

(ii) determine the values of m and b;

(iii) graph the equation.

SOLUTION

(i)
$$6x + 2y = 8$$
$$-6x + 6x + 2y = -6x + 8 \quad \text{——— add } -6x \text{ to each side}$$
$$2y = -6x + 8 \quad \text{——— simplify}$$
$$y = -3x + 4 \quad \text{——— slope-}y\text{-intercept form}$$

(ii) $m = -3, b = 4$

(iii) Since $b = 4$, the y-intercept is 4, which is represented by the point (0, 4). Since $m = -3$ (or $-3/1$), plot a second point on the graph by beginning at the point (0, 4) and moving 3 units down and 1 unit to the right. (You could also move 3 units up and 1 unit to the left if you consider $m = -3$ to be $m = 3/-1$.) Draw the line that passes through these two points, as shown below.

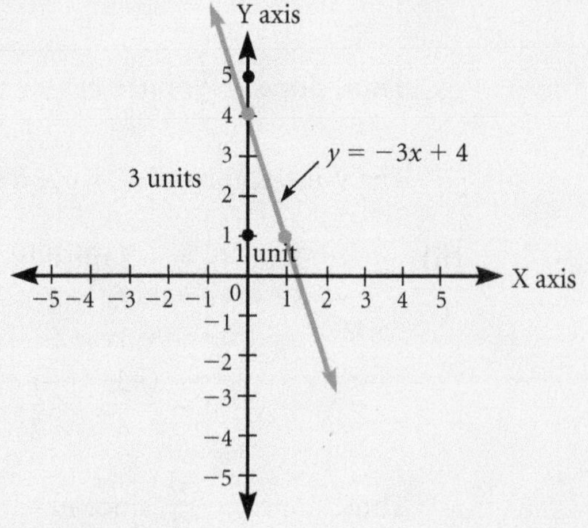

EXAMPLE 4.2I

Graph the equation $x - 2y + 400 = 0$ for all values of x from $x = 0$ to $x = 400$.

SOLUTION

Rearrange the equation into the slope-y-intercept form:

$$-x + x - 2y + 400 - 400 = 0 - x - 400 \quad \text{——— add } -x - 400 \text{ to each side}$$
$$-2y = -x - 400 \quad \text{——— simplify}$$
$$y = \frac{1}{2}x + 200$$
$$m = \frac{1}{2},\ b = 200$$

Since $b = 200$, the y-intercept is 200, which is represented by the point (0, 200). Since $m = 1/2$, the slope is $1/2$. To make plotting points easier, convert $m = 1/2$ to the equivalent slope $m = 100/200$. Plot a second point on the graph by beginning at the point (0, 200) and moving 100 units up and 200 units to the right.

Draw the line through that point starting at (0, 200) and extend the line to the point where $x = 400$. The graph should indicate that for the last point, $x = 400$ and $y = 400$.

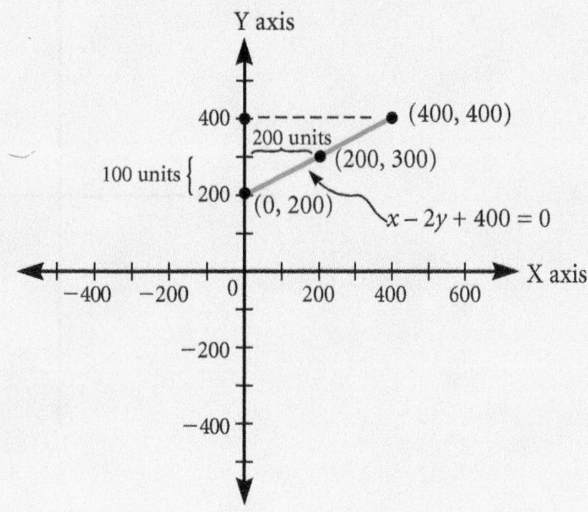

F. Special cases of the slope-y-intercept form of a linear equation

1. Lines Parallel to the X Axis

Recall from Section 4.2D that lines parallel to the X axis are defined by the equation $y = b$, where b is any real number. Since there is no mx in the equation $y = b$, the linear equation $y = b$ represents a line parallel to the X axis that crosses the Y axis at point $(0, b)$ and has a slope of 0.

FIGURE 4.5

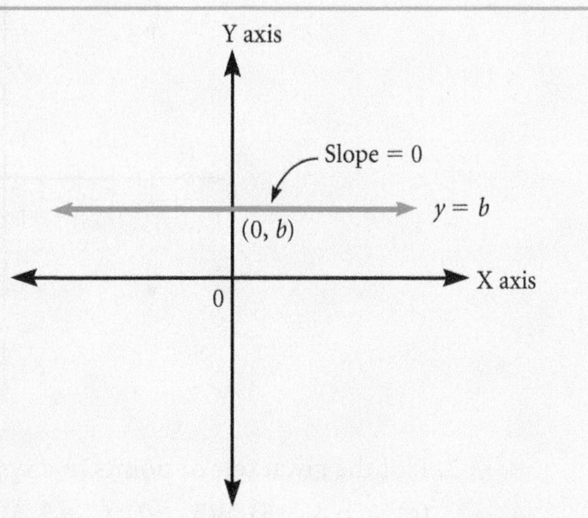

2. Lines Parallel to the Y Axis

Recall from Section 4.2D that lines parallel to the Y axis are defined by the equation $x = a$, where a is any real number. Since there is no y in the equation $x = a$, it cannot be expressed in the form $y = mx + b$. The equation $x = a$ represents a line parallel to the Y axis that crosses the X axis at point $(a, 0)$. Its slope is undefined.

FIGURE 4.6

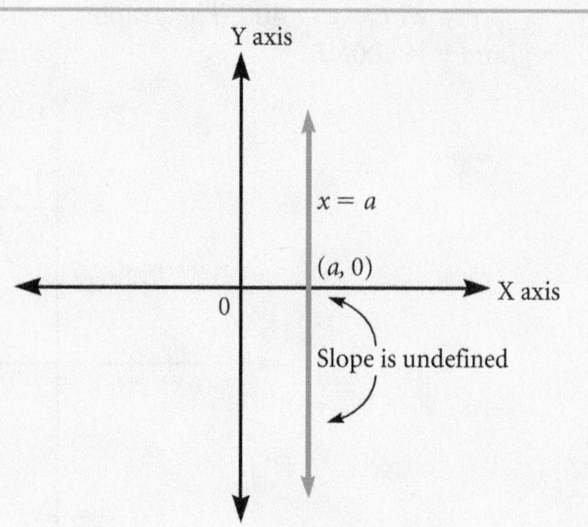

EXERCISE 4.2

Do each of the following.

1. Write the coordinates of the points A, B, C, D, E, F, G, and H marked in the diagram below.

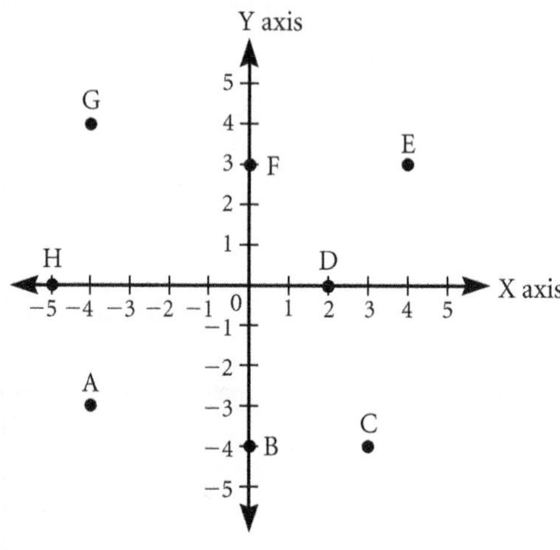

2. Plot the given sets of points in a system of rectangular axes.
   (a) A(−4, −5), B(3, −2), C(−3, 5), D(0, −4), E(4, 1), F(−2, 0)
   (b) K(4, −2), L(−3, 2), M(0, 4), N(−2, −4), P(0, −5), Q(−3, 0)

3. Construct a table of values for each of the following equations as shown.
   (a) $x = y - 2$ for integral values of y from -3 to $+5$
   (b) $y = 2x - 1$ for integral values of x from $+3$ to -2
   (c) $y = 2x$ for integral values of x from $+3$ to -3
   (d) $x = -y$ for integral values of y from $+5$ to -5

4. Using algebra, find the slope and y-intercept of the lines represented by each of the following equations.

(a) $4x + 5y = 11$ **(b)** $2y - 5x = 10$

(c) $1 - \frac{1}{2}y = 2x$ **(d)** $3y + 6 = 0$

(e) $\sqrt{2x - y} = 3$ **(f)** $0.15x + 0.3y - 0.12 = 0$

(g) $2 - \frac{1}{2}x = 0$ **(h)** $(x - 2)(y + 1) - xy = 2$

B. Graph each of the following equations.

1. $x - y = 3$ **2.** $x + 2y = 4$

3. $y = -x$ **4.** $x = 2y$

5. $3x - 4y = 12$ **6.** $2x + 3y = 6$

7. $y = -4$ **8.** $x = 5$

9. $y = 2x - 3$ **10.** $y = -3x + 9$

C. Graph each of the following equations for all of the values of x indicated.

1. $y = 3x + 20$ for $x = 0$ to $x = 40$ **2.** $y = -\frac{2}{5}x + 40$ for $x = 0$ to $x = 100$

3. $3x + 4y = 1200$ for $x = 0$ to $x = 400$ **4.** $3y - 12x - 2400 = 0$ for $x = 0$ to $x = 300$

4.3 GRAPHING LINEAR SYSTEMS OF EQUATIONS IN TWO UNKNOWNS

Systems that consist of two linear equations in two variables may be solved by drawing the graph of each equation. The graph of the system (or solution) is the point where the two lines representing the equations intersect.

EXAMPLE 4.3A Graph the linear system $x + y = 5$ and $x - y = 3$.

SOLUTION For the first equation, rearrange the equations into the slope-y-intercept form:

$$x + y = 5$$
$$y = -x + 5$$

Since $b = 5$, the y-intercept is $+5$, represented by the point $(0, 5)$. Since $m = -1$, the slope is -1. A second point can be determined by moving up by 1 unit and to the left by 1 unit. The point is $(1, 4)$.

Table of values for $x + y = 5$

x	0	1	2	5
y	5	4	3	0

For the second equation, rearrange the equations into the slope-y-intercept form:

$$x - y = 3$$
$$y = x - 3$$

Since $b = -3$, the y-intercept is -3, represented by the point $(0, -3)$. Since $m = 1$, the slope is 1. A second point can be determined by moving up by 1 unit and to the right by 1 unit. The point is $(1, -2)$.

Table of values for $x - y = 3$

x	0	1	2	3
y	−3	−2	−1	0

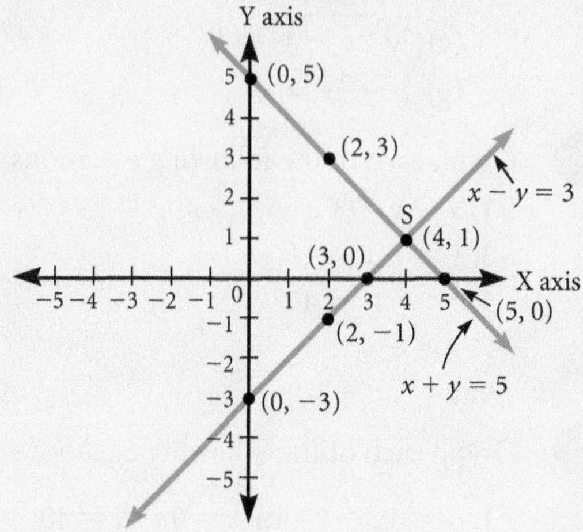

The graph of the system is S, the point of intersection of the two lines, whose coordinates apparently are (4, 1). The coordinates (4, 1) satisfy the equation of either line and are called the *solution* of the system.

EXAMPLE 4.3B Graph the system $x = -2y$ and $y = 3$.

SOLUTION First equation:

$$x = -2y \qquad y = -\frac{1}{2}x$$

Therefore, $b = 0$, the y-intercept is 0. Since $m = -\frac{1}{2}$, the slope is $-\frac{1}{2}$.

Table of values for $x = -2y$

x	0	−2	−4	4
y	0	1	2	−2

Second equation:

$y = 3$

Therefore, b is 3, the y-intercept is 3. Since m is undefined, the slope is flat.

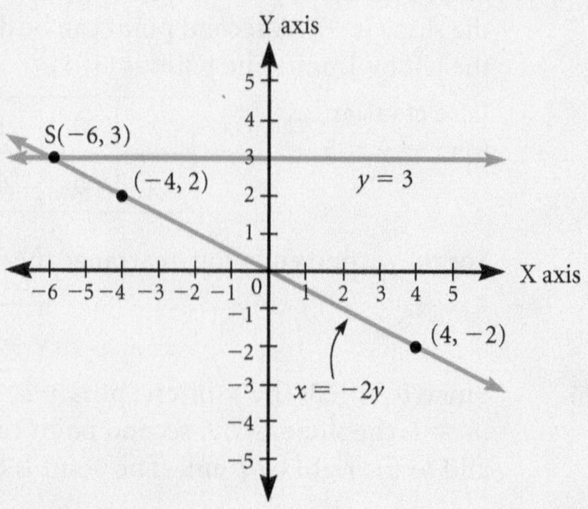

The graph of $y = 3$ is a line parallel to the X axis three units above it. The graph of the system is S, the point of intersection of the two lines. The coordinates of S are apparently $(-6, 3)$ and represent the solution of the system.

EXAMPLE 4.3C

Graph the system $x = y$ and $x - 2y + 2000 = 0$ for all values of x from $x = 0$ to $x = 4000$.

SOLUTION

For the first equation:

$x = y$

Since $b = 0$, the y-intercept is 0. Since $m = 1$, the slope is 1.

Table of values for $x = y$

x	0	1	2000	4000
y	0	1	2000	4000

For the second equation:

$$x - 2y + 2000 = 0$$
$$x - 2y = -2000$$
$$-x + 2y = +2000$$
$$2y = x + 2000$$
$$y = \frac{1}{2}x + 1000$$

Since $b = 1000$, the y-intercept is 1000. Since $m = \frac{1}{2}$, the slope is $\frac{1}{2}$.

Table of values for $x - 2y + 2000 = 0$

x	0	2000	3000	4000
y	1000	2000	2500	3000

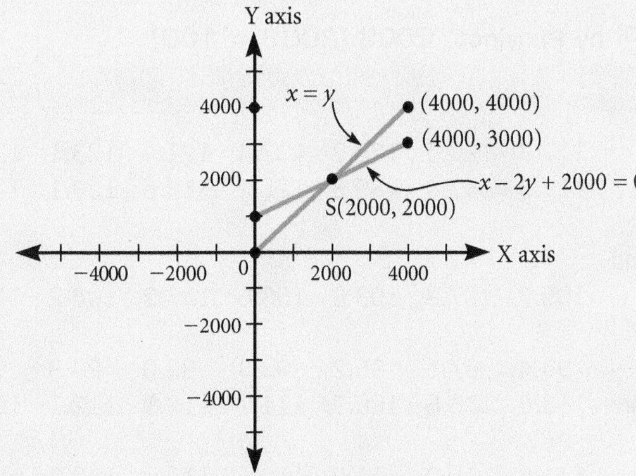

The graph of $x = y$ for all values of x from $x = 0$ to $x = 4000$ is the line joining the points $(0, 0)$ and $(4000, 4000)$. The graph of $x - 2y + 2000 = 0$ for all values of x from $x = 0$ to $x = 4000$ is the line joining the points $(0, 1000)$ and $(4000, 3000)$.

The graph of the system is S, the point of intersection of the two lines. The coordinates of S are apparently $(2000, 2000)$ and represent the solution of the system.

EXERCISE 4.3

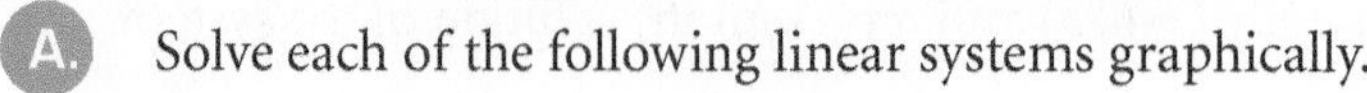

A. Solve each of the following linear systems graphically.

1. $x + y = 4$ and $x - y = -4$

2. $x - y = 3$ and $x + y = 5$

3. $x = 2y - 1$ and $y = 4 - 3x$

4. $2x + 3y = 10$ and $3x - 4y = -2$

5. $3x - 4y = 18$ and $2y = -3x$

6. $4x = -5y$ and $2x + y = 6$

7. $5x - 2y = 20$ and $y = 5$

8. $3y = -5x$ and $x = -3$

B. Graph each of the following systems of equations for all values of x indicated.

1. $y - 4x = 0$ and $y - 2x - 10\,000 = 0$ for $x = 0$ to $x = 10\,000$

2. $4x + 2y = 200$ for $x = 0$ to $x = 50$ and $x + 2y = 80$ for $x = 0$ to $x = 80$

3. $3x + 3y = 2400$ and $x = 500$ for $x = 0$ to $x = 800$

4. $2y = 5x$ and $y = 5000$ for $x = 0$ to $x = 8000$

BUSINESS MATH NEWS BOX

The Consumer Price Index

The Consumer Price Index (CPI) is an indicator of changes in consumer prices experienced by Canadians. It is obtained by comparing the cost of a fixed basket of commodities purchased by consumers through time. Since the basket contains commodities of unchanging or equivalent quantity and quality, the index reflects only pure price movements.

The CPI is widely used as an indicator of the change in the general level of consumer prices or the rate of inflation. Since the purchasing power of money is affected by changes in prices, the CPI is useful to virtually all Canadians. Consumers can compare movements in the CPI to changes in their personal income to monitor and evaluate their financial situation.

Canadian CPI by Province, 2009 (2002 = 100)

Category	BC	AB	SK	MB	ON	PQ	NB	NS	PEI	NL	Nat'l
Food	117.7	120.5	122.2	122.4	121.4	123.1	124.6	125.8	124.6	121.2	121.4
Shelter	112.3	147.4	139.3	122.2	118.6	120.1	120.7	124.0	123.8	128.2	121.6
Household operations and furnishings	105.7	107.8	103.8	108.0	107.2	108.2	107.0	108.4	111.9	105.0	107.3
Clothing and footwear	99.4	97.5	96.2	93.3	92.0	90.3	95.9	90.8	98.5	93.4	93.4
Transportation	113.6	115.6	106.9	111.7	113.9	112.1	107.2	109.1	113.4	113.3	113.1
Health and personal care	111.5	115.9	111.9	110.6	111.9	112.2	108.5	111.1	113.2	111.0	112.1
Recreation, education, and reading	111.0	105.3	103.9	103.2	102.7	96.4	105.4	105.8	104.4	101.6	103.1

Source: Data taken from **www.statcan.ca/101/cst01/cpis01a.htm**, accessed August 1, 2010.

QUESTIONS

1. Which province has the lowest increase in the recreation, education, and reading index?
2. Which two provinces show the greatest decrease in CPI for clothing and footwear? Explain this result.
3. Which category shows the largest range of variation in CPI? Which province shows the largest increase since 2002? By how much over the province showing the lowest?

4.4 PROBLEM SOLVING

A. Problems leading to one equation in two variables

In many problems, the relationship between two or more variables can be represented by setting up linear equations. To find the solution to such problems, there must be as many equations as there are variables.

In the case of problems involving two variables, two equations are needed to obtain a solution. If only one equation can be set up, you can represent the relationship between the two variables graphically.

EXAMPLE 4.4A

A manufacturer processes two types of products through the Finishing Department. Each unit of Product A needs 20 time units in Finishing while each unit of Product B needs 30 time units. Per day, 1200 time units are available. Set up an equation that describes the relationship between the number of units of each product that can be processed daily in Finishing. Graph the relationship.

SOLUTION

Let the number of units of Product A that can be processed daily be represented by x, and let the number of units of Product B be represented by y. Then the number of time units required per day for Product A is $20x$ and the number of time units for Product B is $30y$. The total number of time units per day needed by both products is $20x + 30y$. Since 1200 time units are available,

$$20x + 30y = 1200$$

Table of values

x	60	0	30
y	0	40	20

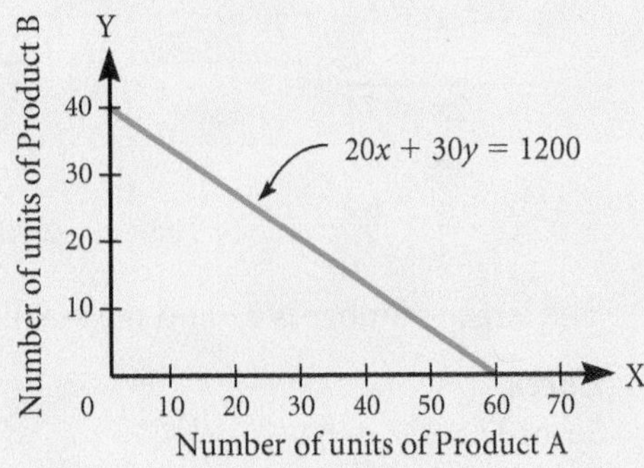

EXAMPLE 4.4B

The Olympic Swim Club rents pool facilities from the city at \$2000 per month. Coaching fees and other expenses amount to \$40 per swimmer per month. Set up an equation that describes the relationship between the number of swimmers and the total monthly cost of operating the swim club. Graph the relationship.

SOLUTION

Let the number of swimmers be represented by x, and let the total monthly cost be represented by $\$y$. Then the monthly coaching fees and expenses are $\$40x$ and total monthly costs amount to $\$(2000 + 40x)$.

$y = 2000 + 40x$

Table of values

x	0	50	100
y	2000	4000	6000

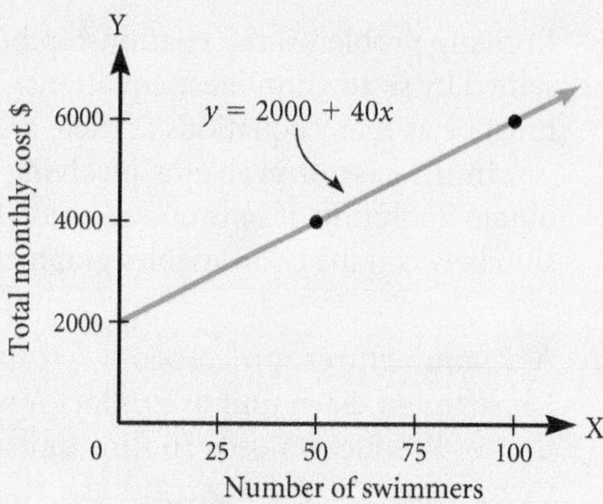

B. Problems leading to systems of equations

The problems in Chapter 2 were solved by using one variable, expressing all the information in terms of that variable, and setting up one equation. To solve many problems, using more than one variable and setting up a system of equations is necessary.

EXAMPLE 4.4C

The total enrolment in two classes is 64 students. One class has 10 more students than the other. How many students are enrolled in each class?

SOLUTION

Let the greater number be x and the smaller number be y. Their sum is $x + y$ and their difference is $x - y$.

$$x + y = 64 \quad \text{①}$$
$$x - y = 10 \quad \text{②}$$
$$2x = 74$$
$$x = 37$$
$$37 + y = 64$$
$$y = 27$$

The larger number is 37 and the smaller number is 27.

Check

Sum: $37 + 27 = 64$

Difference: $37 - 27 = 10$

EXAMPLE 4.4D Kim invested a total of \$24 000 in two mutual funds. Her investment in the Equity Fund is \$4000 less than three times her investment in the Bond Fund. How much did Kim invest in the Equity Fund?

SOLUTION Let the amount invested in the Bond Fund be \$$x$; let the amount invested in the Equity Fund be \$$y$; the total amount invested is

$$x + y = 24\,000 \quad \text{———} \ ①$$

\$4000 less than three times the investment in the Bond Fund is

$$y = 3x - 4000 \quad \text{———} \ ②$$

Substitute ② in ①

$$x + 3x - 4000 = 24\,000$$
$$4x = 28\,000$$
$$x = 7000$$
$$y = 3(7000) - 4000$$
$$y = 17\,000$$

The amount invested in the Equity Fund is \$17 000.

EXAMPLE 4.4E The Clarkson Soccer League has set a budget of \$3840 for soccer balls. High-quality game balls cost \$36 each while lower-quality practice balls cost \$20 each. If 160 balls are to be purchased, how many balls of each type can be purchased to exactly use up the budgeted amount?

SOLUTION Let the number of game balls be x;
let the number of practice balls be y;
then the total number of balls is $x + y$.

$$x + y = 160 \quad \text{———} \ ①$$

The value of the x game balls is \$$36x$;
the value of the y practice balls is \$$20y$;
the total value of the balls is \$$(36x + 20y)$.

$$36x + 20y = 3840 \quad \text{———} \ ②$$
$$-20x - 20y = -3200 \quad \text{———} \ ① \text{ multiplied by } -20$$
$$16x = 640 \quad \text{———} \ \text{add}$$
$$x = 40$$
$$40 + y = 160 \quad \text{———} \ \text{substitute in } ①$$
$$y = 120$$

Forty game balls and 120 practice balls can be bought.

EXAMPLE 4.4F The Dutch Nook sells two brands of coffee—one for \$7.90 per kilogram, and the other for \$9.40 per kilogram. If the store owner mixes 20 kilograms and intends to sell the mixture for \$8.50 per kilogram, how many kilograms of each brand should she use to make the same revenue as she would if the two brands were sold unmixed?

SOLUTION

Let the number of kilograms of coffee sold for \$7.90 be x;
let the number of kilograms of coffee sold for \$9.40 be y;
then the number of kilograms of coffee in the mixture is $x + y$.

$x + y = 20$ ——— ① weight relationship

The value of coffee in the mixture selling for \$7.90 is \$7.90x;
the value of coffee in the mixture selling for \$9.40 is \$9.40y;
the total value of the mixture is \$$(7.90x + 9.40y)$. Since each kilogram of mixture is to be sold at \$8.50, the value is \$8.50(20), or \$170.

$7.90x + 9.40y = 170.00$ ——— ② value relationship

$79x + 94y = 1700.00$ ——— ② multiplied by 10

$79x + 79y = 1580.00$ ——— ① multiplied by 79

$15y = 120.00$ ——— subtract

$y = 8$

$x + 8 = 20$ ——— substitute in ①

$x = 12$

The store owner should mix 12 kilograms of coffee selling for \$7.90 per kilogram with 8 kilograms of coffee selling for \$9.40 per kilogram.

Check

Weight: $12 + 8 = 20$ kg

Value: $12 \times 7.90 + 8 \times 9.40 = 94.80 + 75.20 = \$170.00$

EXERCISE 4.4

A. Set up an equation that describes the relationship between the two variables in each of the following. Graph that relationship.

1. A manufacturer makes two types of products. Profit on Product A is \$30 per unit while profit on Product B is \$40 per unit. Budgeted monthly profit is \$6000.
2. Nakia Company manufactures two products. Product 1 requires three hours of machine time per unit while Product 2 requires four hours of machine time per unit. There are 120 hours of machine time available per week.
3. U-Save-Bucks tax consulting service rents space at \$200 per week and pays the accounting personnel \$4 per completed tax return.
4. Raimi is offered a position as a sales representative. The job pays a salary of \$500 per month plus a commission of 10% on all sales.

B. Set up a system of simultaneous equations to solve each of the following problems.

1. Career Printers Ltd. has two locations with a total of 24 employees. If twice the number of employees at the larger location is three more than three times the number of employees at the smaller location, how many employees are at each location?
2. A restaurant is offering two special meals. The difference between seven times the orders for the first special and four times the orders for the second special is 12. The sum of three-fourths of the orders for the first special and two-thirds of the orders for the second special is 21. Find the number of orders for each special.

3. Loblaws sells two brands of jam. Brand X sells for $2.25 per jar while the No-Name brand sells for $1.75 per jar. If 140 jars were sold for a total of $290, how many jars of each brand were sold?

4. Nancy's sales last week were $140 less than three times Andrea's sales. Together they sold $940. Determine how much each person sold last week.

5. Kaya and Fred agree to form a partnership. The partnership agreement requires that Fred invest $2500 more than two-thirds of what Kaya is to invest. If the total investment in the partnership is to be $55 000, how much should each partner invest?

6. A Brush with Wood has been producing 2320 chairs a day working two shifts. The second shift has produced 60 chairs fewer than four-thirds of the number of chairs produced by the first shift. Determine the number of chairs each shift has produced.

7. An inventory of two types of floodlights showed a total of 60 lights valued at $2580. If Type A cost $40 each and Type B cost $50 each, how many of each type of floodlight were in inventory?

8. A machine requires four hours to make a unit of Product A and three hours to make a unit of Product B. Last month the machine operated for 200 hours producing a total of 60 units. How many units of each type of product did it produce?

9. Marysia has saved $85.75 in quarters and loonies. If she has one quarter more than three-fourths the number of loonies, how many coins of each type does Marysia have?

10. The local amateur football club spent $675 on tickets to a professional football game. If the club bought three fewer fifteen-dollar tickets than four-fifths the number of twelve-dollar tickets, how many tickets of each type did the club buy?

Go to MathXL at www.mathxl.com. You can practise many of this chapter's exercises as often as you want. The guided solutions help you find an answer step by step. You'll find a personalized study plan available to you too!

Review Exercise

1. Using algebra, find the slope and y-intercept of the line represented by each of the following equations.

(a) $7x + 3y = 6$ **(b)** $10y = 5x$

(c) $\frac{2y - 3x}{2} = 4$ **(d)** $1.8x + 0.3y - 3 = 0$

(e) $\frac{1}{3}x = -2$ **(f)** $11x - 33y = 99$

(g) $xy - (x + 4)(y - 1) = 8$

(h) $2.5y - 12.5 = 0$

2. Graph each of the following.

(a) $2x - y = 6$ **(b)** $3x + 4y = 0$

(c) $5x + 2y = 10$ **(d)** $y = -3$

(e) $5y = -3x + 15$ **(f)** $5x - 4y = 0$

(g) $x = -2$ **(h)** $3y = -4x - 12$

3. Graphically solve each of the following.

(a) $3x + y = 6$ and $x - y = 2$

(b) $x + 4y = -8$ and $3x + 4y = 0$

(c) $5x = 3y$ and $y = -5$

(d) $2x + 6y = 8$ and $x = -2$

(e) $y = 3x - 2$ and $y = 3$

(f) $y = -2x$ and $x = 4$

(g) $x = -2$ and $3x + 4y = 12$

(h) $y = -2$ and $5x + 3y = 15$

4. Solve each of the following systems of equations.

(a) $3x + 2y = -1$
$5x + 3y = -2$

(b) $4x - 5y = 25$
$3x + 2y = 13$

(c) $y = -10x$
$3y = 29 - x$

(d) $2y = 3x + 17$
$3x = 11 - 5y$

(e) $2x - 3y = 13$
$3x - 2y = 12$

(f) $2x = 3y - 11$
$y = 13 + 3x$

(g) $2a - 3b - 14 = 0$
$a + b - 2 = 0$

(h) $a + c = -10$
$8a + 4c = 0$

(i) $3b - 3c = -15$
$-2b + 4c = 14$

(j) $48a - 32b = 128$
$16a + 48b = 32$

(k) $0.5m + 0.3n = 54$
$0.3m + 0.7n = 74$

(l) $\frac{3}{4}m + \frac{5}{8}n = \frac{3}{4}$
$\frac{5}{6}n + \frac{2}{3}m = \frac{7}{9}$

5. Write an equation describing the relationship between the two variables in each of the following problems and graph the relationship.

(a) Sun 'N' Ski Travel pays for radio advertising at the fixed rate of \$1000 per week plus \$75 per announcement during the week.

(b) The Bi-Products Company markets two products. Each unit of Product A requires five units of labour while each unit of Product B requires two units of labour. Two hundred units of labour are available per time period.

6. Set up a system of equations to solve each of the following problems.

(a) A tire store sold two types of tires, a sports tire and an all-season tire. The sum of six times the sports tire and five times the all-season tire is 93, and the difference between three-quarters of the sports tire and two-thirds of the all-season tires is zero. For the store manager, find the number of each type of tire sold in one day.

(b) The college theatre collected \$1300 from the sale of 450 tickets. If the tickets were sold for \$2.50 and \$3.50, how many tickets were sold at each price?

(c) A jacket and two pairs of pants together cost \$175. The jacket is valued at three times the price of one pair of pants. What is the value of the jacket?

(d) Three cases of white bordeaux and five cases of red bordeaux together cost \$438. Each case of red bordeaux costs \$6 less than twice the cost of a case of white bordeaux. Determine the cost of a case of each type.

Self-Test

1. Using algebra, find the slope and y-intercept of the line represented by each of the following equations.
   (a) $4y + 11 = y$ (b) $\frac{2}{3}x - \frac{1}{9}y = 1$
   (c) $x + 3y = 0$ (d) $-6y - 18 = 0$
   (e) $13 - \frac{1}{2}x = 0$ (f) $ax + by = c$

2. Graphically solve each of the following systems of equations.
   (a) $y = -x - 2$ and $x - y = 4$ (b) $3x = -2y$ and $x = 2$

3. Graph each of the following systems of equations for all values of x indicated.
   (a) $-x = -55 + y$ and $y = 30$ for $x = 0$ to $x = 55$ (b) $x = 125$ and $3x + 2y + 600 = 0$ for $x = 0$ to $x = 200$

4. Solve each of the following systems of equations.
   (a) $6x + 5y = 9$
   $4x - 3y = 25$
   (b) $12 - 7x = 4y$
   $6 - 2y = 3x$
   (c) $0.2a + 0.3b = 0$
   $0.7a - 0.2b = 250$
   (d) $\frac{4}{3}b - \frac{3}{5}c = -\frac{17}{3}$
   $\frac{5}{6}b + \frac{4}{9}c = \frac{5}{9}$

5. Erica Lottsbriner invests \$12 000 so that part earns interest at 4% per annum and part at 6% per annum. If the total annual interest on the investment is \$560, how much has Erica invested at each rate?

6. Eyad and Rahia divide a profit of \$12 700. If Eyad is to receive \$2200 more than two-fifths of Rahia's share, how much will Rahia receive?

Challenge Problems

1. Terry invested a total of \$4500. A portion was invested at 4% and the rest was invested at 6%. The amount of Terry's annual return on each portion is the same. Find the average rate of interest Terry earned on the \$4500.

2. In September, Polar Bay Wines had a net revenue of \$574.56 from the sale of 3216 new wine bottles less the refund paid for 1824 returned bottles. In October, net revenue was \$944.88 from the sale of 5208 bottles less the refund paid on 2232 returned bottles. How much did Polar Bay Wines charge per new wine bottle and how much was the refund for each returned bottle?

3. Ezhno, the owner of AAA College Painting, pays wages totalling \$29 760 for a 40-hour workweek to a crew consisting of 16 painters and 24 helpers. To keep their jobs, the painters accepted a wage cut of 10% and the helpers a wage cut of 8%. The wage cut reduces Ezhno's weekly payroll by \$2688. What hourly rates of pay does Ezhno pay after the wage cut?

CASE STUDY 4.1 Finding the Right Combination

» Amarjit was preparing his annual tax return when he realized that he had a \$28 500 unused RRSP contribution limit. Through discussion with his financial advisor, Amarjit realized that he had not fully contributed to his RRSP in past years.

The advisor suggested that Amarjit borrow funds through an RRSP loan to take advantage of his unused contribution limit, as she believed that his RRSP's growth rate would be higher than the interest paid on the loan. The advisor knew of a bank making RRSP loans at a simple interest rate of 7% with four end-of-year principal payments required of \$7125 each.

Amarjit agreed to this idea, and contemplated being more aggressive with his investments. He asked his advisor to discuss investments in the stock market.

The advisor suggested to him that while investing in the stock market had the potential for higher gains, there was also the possibility of losing money. Investing in equities (stocks) was riskier than his current conservative portfolio of bank savings accounts, treasury bills, and guaranteed investment certificates (GICs).

Details of several leading Canadian companies were provided to Amarjit to consider investing in:

Company	Latest Selling Price per Share	52-Week High/Low Price
Goldcorp	\$26.36	\$45.99/\$20.57
TELUS	\$62.90	\$64.74/\$42.62
International Forest Products	\$6.65	\$8.11/\$6.01
Bank of Montreal	\$67.60	\$70.24/\$56.00

QUESTIONS

1. What is the cost of borrowing if Amarjit borrows \$28 500 and repays it over a four-year period?
2. How many shares of each stock would he get if he used the \$28 500 and invested equally in all four companies?
3. Suppose Amarjit decided to buy shares in only TELUS and Goldcorp. How many shares of each would he get if he used the \$28 500 and bought three times as many shares of TELUS as he bought of Goldcorp?
4. Suppose Amarjit decided to buy shares in only International Forest Products and the Bank of Montreal. How many shares of each company would he get if he used the \$28 500 and bought two shares of the Bank of Montreal for every three shares of International Forest Products?

CASE STUDY 4.2 What to Produce?

» The Tiny Tikes Toy Company produces play sets and swinging apparatus for children three to eight years of age. The company has developed many different designs, and through experience and testing has decided to produce two designs that were popular with daycare and recreation centres.

Both models consist of prefabricated material and require assembly by the purchaser. The first model, the Jungle Jackie, can be produced for \$260 and sold for \$450. The second model, the Eagle's Nest, can be produced for \$315 and sold for \$510.

The company's senior accountant says, "We used a lot of the budget for this year on design and testing, so we really have to watch what we spend on production. The most we can spend to produce Jungle Jackies and Eagle's Nests is \$650 500 per month. It's up to the sales manager to decide which models to produce and sell."

The sales manager says, "Let's use the full plant capacity to produce as many Jungle Jackies and Eagle's Nests as we can. The kids are screaming for these things! We can sell all we produce. Let's get as many of these items out there as soon as possible!" The plant's capacity is 2100 units per month.

QUESTIONS

1. Which of the two designs has the greater percent gross profit per unit based on cost? (Gross profit is the difference between selling price and cost.)
2. (a) Assume Tiny Tikes Toy Company decides to produce as many Jungle Jackies and Eagle's Nests as possible, given the plant's capacity. How many of each model would be produced in one month if the entire \$650 500 per month were spent on production?
   (b) What gross profit would be earned when these quantities of Jungle Jackies and Eagle's Nests are sold?

SUMMARY OF FORMULAS

Formula 4.1

$y = mx + b$ — Slope-*y*-intercept form of a linear equation

GLOSSARY

Ordered pair of numbers the coordinates of a point (x, y) *(p. 149)*

Origin the point of intersection of the two axes in a system of rectangular coordinates *(p. 148)*

Rise the vertical distance (distance along Y axis) between two points on a line or line segment *(p. 155)*

Run the horizontal distance (distance along X axis) between two points on a line or line segment *(p. 155)*

Slope the measure of the steepness of a line; it is the ratio of the rise of a line to its run *(p. 155)*

Slope-*y*-intercept form of a linear equation a linear equation expressed in the form $y = mx + b$ *(p. 157)*

X axis the horizontal reference line in a system of rectangular coordinates *(p. 148)*

***x* coordinate** the first number in an ordered pair of numbers. It describes the position of a point relative to the axes or the directed distance of a point from the vertical axis (Y axis). *(p. 149)*

Y axis the vertical reference line in a system of rectangular coordinates *(p. 148)*

***y* coordinate** the second number in an ordered pair of numbers. It describes the position of a point relative to the axes or the directed distance of a point from the horizontal axis (X axis). *(p. 149)*

***y*-intercept** the *y* coordinate of the point of intersection of a line and the Y axis *(p. 155)*

USEFUL INTERNET SITES

www.financialpost.com

Financial Post *The Financial Post*, one of Canada's leading business newspapers, provides valuable financial information. Use this site to find information about corporations and their stocks, mutual funds, and articles on the latest financial topics.

www.fpsc.ca

Financial Planning Standards Council This non-profit organization is the certifying body for Canadian financial planning professionals. The FPSC is dedicated to ensuring the financial planning needs of Canadians are well-served by establishing and enforcing standards for financial planners who earn Certified Financial Planner (CFP) certification in Canada.

CHAPTER 5

Trade Discount, Cash Discount, Markup, and Markdown

OBJECTIVES

Upon completing this chapter, you will be able to do the following:

1. Solve problems involving trade discounts.
2. Calculate equivalent single rates of discount for discount series and solve problems involving discount series.
3. Apply methods of cash discount.
4. Solve problems involving markup based on either cost or selling price.
5. Solve problems involving markdown.
6. Solve integrated problems involving discounts, markup, and markdown.

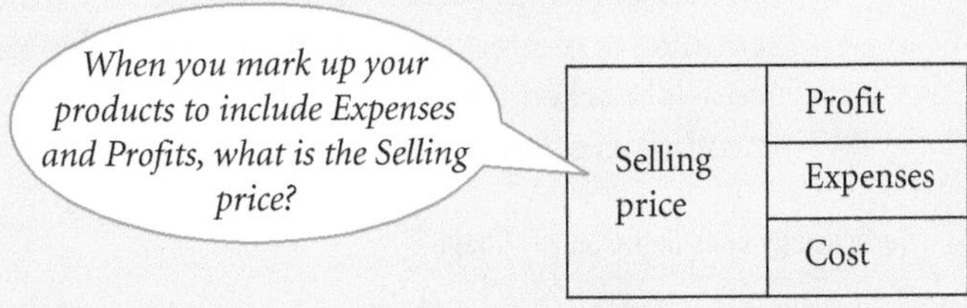

Suppose you are the owner of a bicycle retailer. What is your cost to purchase a bicycle if you have several trade discounts available to you? How much money can you save if you take advantage of a cash discount? If you mark up your product based on its cost, what would be the resulting price? If you mark up your product to include expenses and a targeted profit, what would be the resulting price? If you applied a markdown, what would be the effect on your profit? Regardless of the business that you are in, the answers to all of these questions are important to you in making the best decisions and assuring a profitable business.

INTRODUCTION

The *supply chain* defines the channels or stages that a product passes through as it is converted from a raw material to a finished product purchased by the consumer. Figure 5.1 outlines this process in detail.

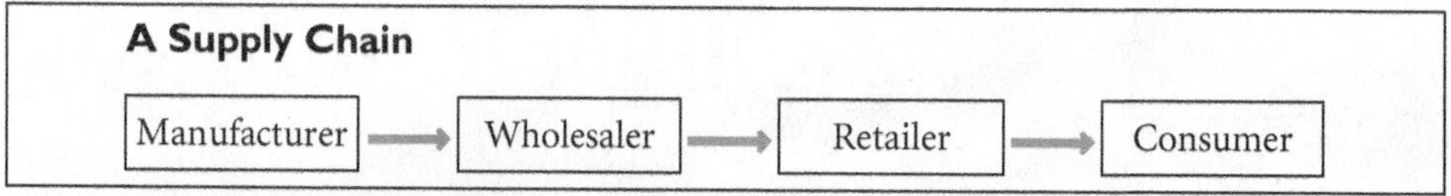

By the time the product is purchased by the consumer, the raw materials have been converted by the manufacturer, distributed through the wholesaler, and offered for sale by the retailer. In some supply chains, the distributor and wholesaler are separated, and in some cases the retailer can also serve as the wholesaler. In other supply chains, the manufacturer also serves as the wholesaler. Within the supply chain, all of the channels must make a profit on the product to remain in business. Each channel applies a *markup* above their cost to buy the merchandise, which increases the price of the product. Sometimes a manufacturer or supplier sets a *list price* and then offers a *trade discount* or a *series of trade discounts* from that price to sell more of their product or to promote the product within the supply chain. Any of the channels within the supply chain may offer a *cash discount* to encourage prompt payment for the product. When the product is sold to the consumer, the regular selling price may be *marked down* or *discounted* to a sale price in response to competitors' prices or other economic conditions.

Cost, price, and expenses of a product determine the profit for that product. Calculation of the relationships between these amounts is crucial in maintaining a successful business. This chapter calculates the cost if trade discounts are offered within the supply chain and calculates the amount of cash to be paid when cash discounts are offered for early payment. It also calculates the price and profit when the cost is marked up and calculates the discounted price and resulting profit when a product is offered "on sale."

FIGURE 5.1 Terminology Used in the Supply Chain

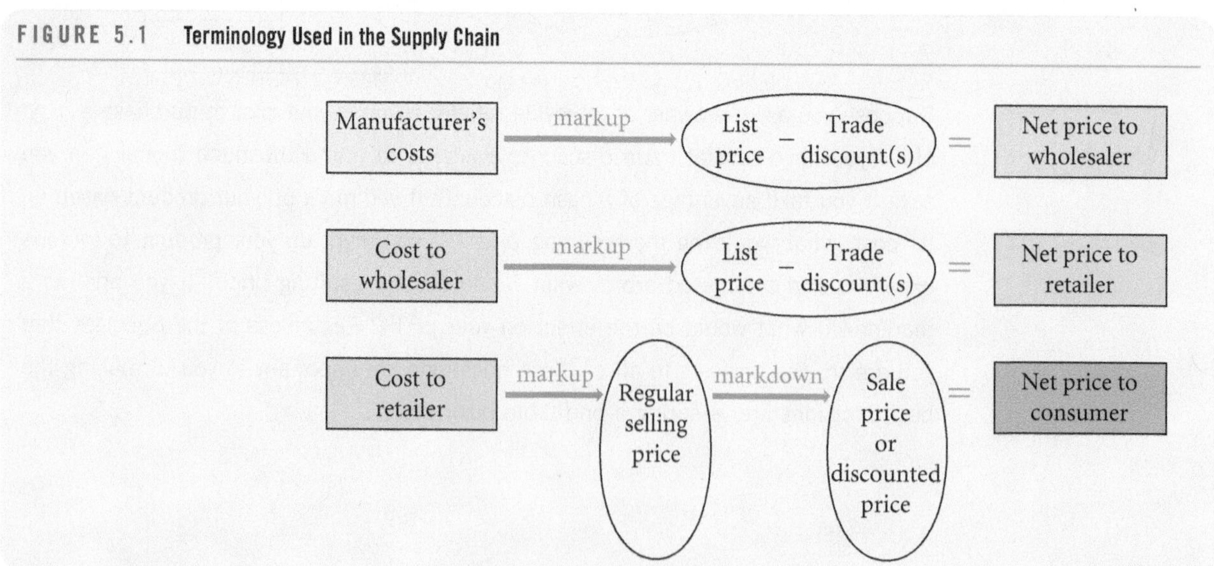

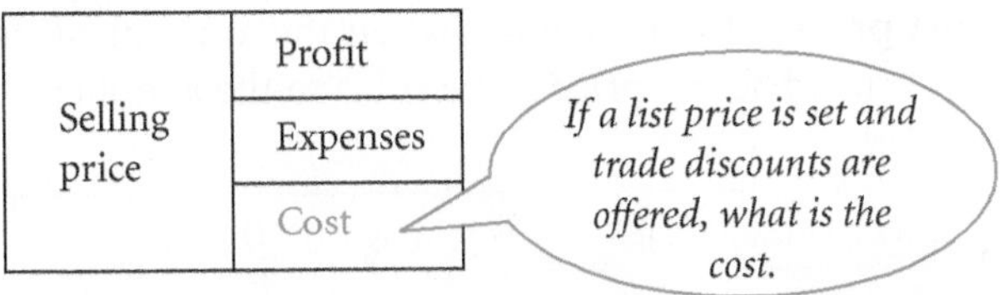

5.1 DETERMINING COST WITH TRADE DISCOUNTS

A. Computing discount amounts, discount rate, net price, and list price

The supply chain is made up of manufacturers, wholesalers, and retailers. Merchandise is usually bought and sold among the members of the chain on credit terms. The prices quoted to other members often involved trade discounts. A **trade discount** is a reduction of a **list price** or **manufacturer's suggested retail price (MSRP)** and is usually stated as a percent of the list price or MSRP.

Trade discounts are used by manufacturers, distributors, and wholesalers as pricing tools for several reasons, such as to

(a) determine different prices for different levels of the supply chain;

(b) communicate changes in prices;

(c) enable changes in prices.

When computing a trade discount, keep in mind that the **rate of discount** is based on the list price.

$$\text{AMOUNT OF DISCOUNT} = \text{LIST PRICE} \times \text{RATE OF DISCOUNT}$$

$$\text{AMOUNT OF DISCOUNT} = \text{L} \times d \qquad \text{Formula 5.1A}$$

When the amount of the discount and the discount rate are known, the list price can be determined. Rearrange Formula 5.1A to determine the list price.

$$\text{LIST PRICE} = \frac{\text{AMOUNT OF DISCOUNT}}{\text{RATE OF DISCOUNT}}$$

$$\text{L} = \frac{\text{AMOUNT OF DISCOUNT}}{d} \qquad \text{Formula 5.1B}$$

Since the rate of trade discount is based on the list price, computing a rate of discount involves comparing the amount of discount to the list price. Rearrange Formula 5.1A to determine the rate of trade discount.

$$\text{RATE OF DISCOUNT} = \frac{\text{AMOUNT OF DISCOUNT}}{\text{LIST PRICE}}$$

$$d = \frac{\text{AMOUNT OF DISCOUNT}}{\text{L}} \qquad \text{Formula 5.1C}$$

The **net price** is the remainder when the amount of discount is subtracted from the list price. The net price is the price to the supplier, and becomes the cost to the purchaser.

NET PRICE = LIST PRICE − AMOUNT OF DISCOUNT

$$N = L - Ld \quad \text{or} \quad N = L(1 - d)$$ ——— **Formula 5.2**

To compute the amount of the discount and the net price when the list price and discount rate are known, apply Formula 5.1A to determine the amount of the trade discount, and then apply Formula 5.2 to calculate the net price.

EXAMPLE 5.1A

An item listed at $80 is subject to a trade discount of 25%. Compute

(i) the amount of discount;
(ii) the net price.

SOLUTION

(i) Amount of trade discount = List price × Rate of discount
= (80.00)(0.25) = $20.00

(ii) Net price = List price − Trade discount
= 80.00 − 20.00 = $60.00

EXAMPLE 5.1B

The 30% discount on a tennis racket amounts to $89.70. Compute

(i) the list price;
(ii) the net price.

SOLUTION

(i) $\text{List price} = \dfrac{\text{Amount of discount}}{\text{Rate of discount}} = \dfrac{89.70}{0.3} = \$299.00$

(ii) Net price = List price − Amount of discount
= 299.00 − 89.70 = $209.30

EXAMPLE 5.1C

Find the rate of discount for

(i) snowboards listed at $280 less a discount of $67.20;
(ii) snow-sport helmets listed at $129.99 whose net price is $84.49;
(iii) goalie pads whose net price is $368.99 after a discount of $81.00.

SOLUTION

(i) $\text{Rate of discount} = \dfrac{\text{Amount of discount}}{\text{List price}} = \dfrac{67.20}{280.00} = 0.24 = 24\%$

(ii) Since Net price = List price − Amount of discount (Formula 5.2),
Amount of discount = List price − Net price = 129.99 − 84.49 = $45.50

$\text{Rate of discount} = \dfrac{\text{Amount of discount}}{\text{List price}} = \dfrac{45.50}{129.99} = 0.35 = 35\%$

(iii) Since Net price = List price − Amount of discount (Formula 5.2),
List price = Net price + Amount of discount = 368.99 + 81.00 = $449.99

$$\text{Rate of discount} = \frac{\text{Amount of discount}}{\text{List price}} = \frac{81.00}{449.99} = 0.18 = 18\%$$

B. The net price factor approach

Instead of computing the amount of discount and then deducting this amount from the list price, the net price can be found by using the more efficient net factor approach developed in the following illustration.

Referring back to Example 5.1A, the solution can be restated as follows:

List price	$80.00
Less trade discount 25% of 80.00	20.00
Net price	$60.00

Since the discount is given as a percent of the list price, the three dollar values may be stated as percents of list price:

List price	$80.00	⟶	100% of list price
Less trade discount	20.00	⟶	25% of list price
Net price	$60.00	⟶	75% of list price

Note: The resulting "75%" is called the **net price factor** or **net factor** (in abbreviated form **NPF**) and is obtained by deducting the 25% discount from 100%.

NET PRICE FACTOR (NPF) = 100% − % DISCOUNT ——— **Formula 5.3A**

The resulting relationship between net price and list price may be stated generally.

NET PRICE = LIST PRICE × NET PRICE FACTOR (NPF) ——— **Formula 5.4A**

The two relationships represented by Formulas 5.3A and 5.4A can be restated in algebraic terms:

Convert the % discount into its decimal equivalent represented by d, and express 100% by its decimal equivalent 1.

NET PRICE FACTOR = $1 - d$ ——— **Formula 5.3B**

Let the list price be represented by L and let the net price be represented by N.

$N = L(1 - d)$ ——— **Formula 5.4B**

EXAMPLE 5.1D Find the net price for

(i) list price $36.00 less 15%;

(ii) list price $86.85 less $33\frac{1}{3}$%.

SOLUTION

(i) Net price = List price × Net price factor — using Formula 5.4A
= (36.00)(100% − 15%) — using Formula 5.3A
= (36.00)(85%) — subtract
= (36.00)(0.85) — convert the percent into a decimal
= \$30.60

(ii) Net price = (86.85)(100% − $33\frac{1}{3}$%) — using Formula 5.3A
= (86.85)($66\frac{2}{3}$%)
= (86.85)($0.\dot{6}$) — use a sufficient number of decimals
= \$57.90

EXAMPLE 5.1E

A manufacturer can cover its cost and make a reasonable profit if it sells an article for \$63.70. At what price should the article be listed so that a discount of 30% can be allowed?

SOLUTION

Let the list price be represented by \$L. The net price factor is $1 - d = 100\% - 30\% = 70\% = 0.7$ and the net price is \$63.70.

63.70 = 0.7L — using Formula 5.4A

$$L = \frac{63.70}{0.7} = \$91.00$$

The article should be listed at \$91.

C. Discount series

A manufacturer may offer two or more **discounts** to different members of the supply chain. If a list price is subject to two or more discounts, these discounts are called a **discount series**. For example, a chain member closest to the consumer might be offered additional discounts, if there are fewer chain members who must make a profit on an item. If the manufacturer wants to encourage large-volume orders or early orders of seasonal items, it may offer additional discounts. For example, a manufacturer might offer a retailer a 5% discount on orders over 1000 items and an additional discount of 6% for ordering Christmas items in April. It may also offer additional discounts to compensate for advertising, promotion, and service costs handled by supply chain members.

When computing the net price, the discounts making up the discount series are applied to the list price successively. The net price resulting from the first discount becomes the list price for the second discount; the net price resulting from the second discount becomes the list price for the third discount; and so on. In fact, finding the net price when a list price is subject to a discount series consists of solving as many discount problems as there are discounts in the discount series.

EXAMPLE 5.1F

An item listed at \$150 is subject to the discount series 20%, 10%, 5%. Determine the net price.

SOLUTION

List price	\$150.00	Problem 1
Less first discount 20% of 150.00	30.00	

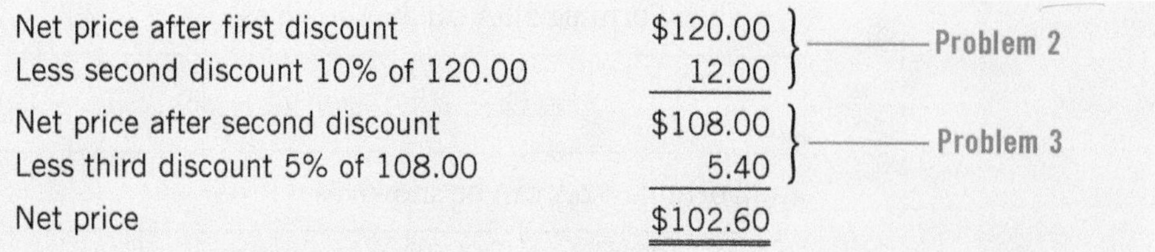

Net price after first discount	\$120.00	Problem 2
Less second discount 10% of 120.00	12.00	
Net price after second discount	\$108.00	Problem 3
Less third discount 5% of 108.00	5.40	
Net price	\$102.60	

Because the solution to Example 5.1F consists of three problems involving a simple discount, the net price factor approach can be used to solve it or any problem involving a series of discounts.

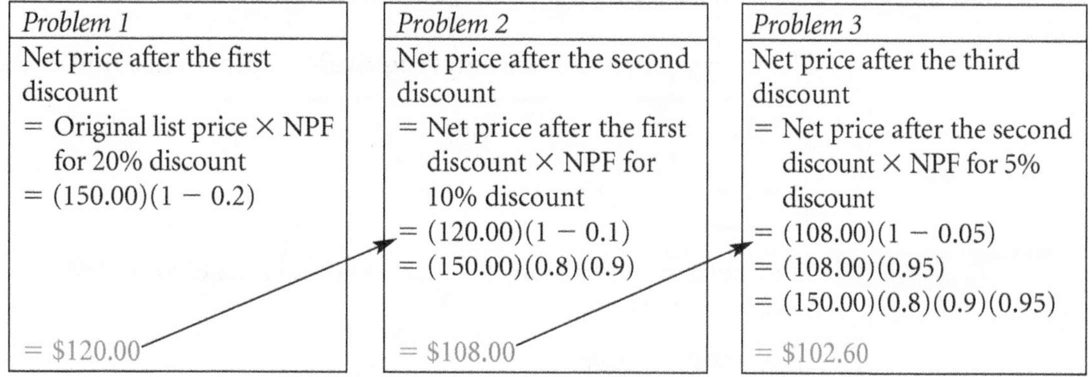

Problem 1	*Problem 2*	*Problem 3*
Net price after the first discount = Original list price × NPF for 20% discount = (150.00)(1 − 0.2) = \$120.00	Net price after the second discount = Net price after the first discount × NPF for 10% discount = (120.00)(1 − 0.1) = (150.00)(0.8)(0.9) = \$108.00	Net price after the third discount = Net price after the second discount × NPF for 5% discount = (108.00)(1 − 0.05) = (108.00)(0.95) = (150.00)(0.8)(0.9)(0.95) = \$102.60

The final net price of \$102.60 is obtained from
(150.00)(0.95)(0.9)(0.8)
= (150.00)(0.8)(0.9)(0.95) ——— the order of the factors may be rearranged
= Original list price × NPF for 20% × NPF for 10% × NPF for 5%
= Original list price × Product of the NPFs for the discounts in the discount series
= Original list price × Net price factor for the discount series

This result may be generalized to find the net price for a list price subject to a discount series.

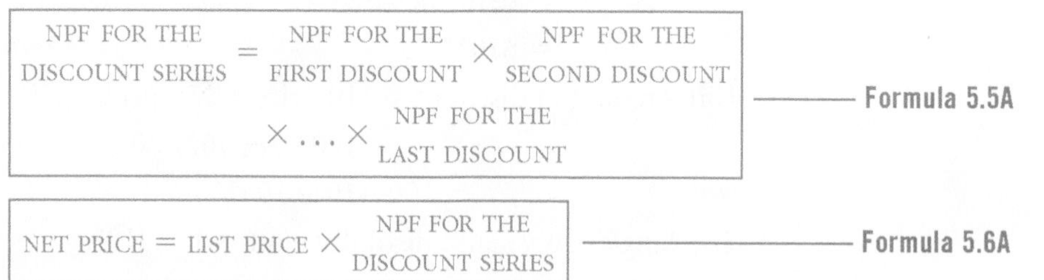

NPF FOR THE DISCOUNT SERIES = NPF FOR THE FIRST DISCOUNT × NPF FOR THE SECOND DISCOUNT × . . . × NPF FOR THE LAST DISCOUNT ——— Formula 5.5A

NET PRICE = LIST PRICE × NPF FOR THE DISCOUNT SERIES ——— Formula 5.6A

The two relationships represented by Formulas 5.5A and 5.6A can be restated in algebraic terms:

Let the net price be represented by N,
the original list price by L,
the first rate of discount by d_1,
the second rate of discount by d_2,
the third rate of discount by d_3, and
the last rate of discount by d_n.

Then Formula 5.5A can be shown as

$$\text{NPF FOR A DISCOUNT SERIES} = (1 - d_1)(1 - d_2)(1 - d_3)\ldots(1 - d_n)$$ —— **Formula 5.5B**

and Formula 5.6A can be shown as

$$\text{NET PRICE} = L(1 - d_1)(1 - d_2)(1 - d_3)\ldots(1 - d_n)$$ —— **Formula 5.6B**

D. Single equivalent rates of discount

For every discount series, a **single equivalent rate of discount** exists.

SINGLE EQUIVALENT RATE OF DISCOUNT FOR A DISCOUNT SERIES

$$= 1 - \text{NPF FOR THE DISCOUNT SERIES}$$

$$= 1 - [(1 - d_1)(1 - d_2)(1 - d_3)\ldots(1 - d_n)]$$ —— **Formula 5.7**

EXAMPLE 5.1G

A manufacturer sells cabinets to dealers at a list price of \$2100 less 40%, 10%, 5%. Determine the

(i) net price factor;
(ii) net price;
(iii) amount of discount;
(iv) single equivalent rate of discount.

SOLUTION

(i) Net price factor (NPF) = (1 − 0.4)(1 − 0.1)(1 − 0.5)
= (0.6)(0.9)(0.95)
= 0.513 = 51.3% —— **using Formula 5.5B**

(ii) Net price = List price × NPF
= (2100.00)(0.513)
= \$1077.30 —— **using Formula 5.6B**

(iii) Amount of discount = List price − Net price
= 2100.00 − 1077.30
= \$1022.70

(iv) Single equivalent rate of discount = 1 − NPF
= 1 − 0.513
= 0.487
= 48.7% —— **using Formula 5.7**

Note: Taking off a single discount of 48.7% has the *same* effect as using the discount series 40%, 10%, 5%. That is, the single discount of 48.7% is equivalent to the discount series 40%, 10%, 5%.

Caution: The sum of the discounts in the series, 40% + 10% + 5% or 55%, is not equivalent to the single discount.

You can find the single equivalent rate of discount by choosing a suitable list price and computing first the amount of discount and then the rate of discount.

EXAMPLE 5.1H

Determine the amount of discount for a \$1000 list price subject to the discount series 40%, 12.5%, 8⅓%, 2%.

SOLUTION

$$\begin{aligned}\text{Net price factor (NPF)} &= (1 - 0.4)(1 - 0.125)(1 - 0.08\dot{3})(1 - 0.2)\\ &= (0.6)(0.875)(0.91\dot{6})(0.98)\\ &= 0.471625 = 47.1625\%\end{aligned}$$

$$\begin{aligned}\text{Single equivalent rate of discount} &= 1 - 0.471625\\ &= 52.8375\%\end{aligned}$$

$$\begin{aligned}\text{Amount of discount} &= \text{List price} \times \text{Single equivalent rate of discount}\\ &= 1000.00(0.528375)\\ &= \$528.375\end{aligned}$$

POINTERS AND PITFALLS

The single equivalent rate of discount is not simply the sum of the individual discounts. Proper application of Formula 5.7 will always result in a single equivalent discount rate that is less than the sum of the individual discounts. You can use this fact to check whether the single equivalent discount rate you calculate is reasonable.

EXAMPLE 5.1I

The local hardware store has listed a power saw for \$136 less 30%. A department store in a nearby shopping mall lists the same model for \$126 less 20%, less an additional 15%. What additional rate of discount must the hardware store give to meet the department store price?

SOLUTION

Hardware store net price = 136.00(0.7)	\$95.20
Department store price = 126.00(0.8)(0.85)	85.68
Additional discount needed	\$ 9.52

$$\text{Additional rate of discount needed} = \frac{9.52}{95.20} = 0.1 = 10\%$$

EXAMPLE 5.1J

Redden Distributors bought a shipment of camcorders at a net price of \$477.36 each, after discounts of 15%, 10%, 4%. What is the list price?

SOLUTION

Let the list price be \$L.

The net price factor is (0.85)(0.9)(0.96) ——— using Formula 5.5A

The net price is \$477.36.

$$477.36 = L(0.85)(0.9)(0.96)$$

$$L = \frac{477.36}{(0.85)(0.9)(0.96)} = \$650.00$$

The camcorders are listed at \$650.

EXERCISE 5.1

A. Find the missing values (represented by question marks) for each of the following questions.

	Rate of Discount	List Price	Amount of Discount	Net Price
1.	45%	$ 24.60	?	?
2.	$16\frac{2}{3}$%	$184.98	?	?
3.	?	$ 76.95	?	$ 51.30
4.	?	$724.80	?	$616.08
5.	?	?	$37.89	$214.71
6.	?	?	$19.93	$976.57
7.	62.5%	?	$83.35	?
8.	1.5%	?	$13.53	?
9.	37.5%	?	?	$ 84.35
10.	22.5%	?	?	$121.29

B. Find the missing values (represented by question marks) for each of the following questions.

	Rate of Discount	List Price	Net Price	Single Equivalent Rate of Discount
1.	25%, 10%	$ 44.80	?	?
2.	$33\frac{1}{3}$%, 5%	$126.90	?	?
3.	40%, 12.5%, 2%	$268.00	?	?
4.	20%, $16\frac{2}{3}$%, 3%	$ 72.78	?	?
5.	35%, $33\frac{1}{3}$%, 10%	?	$617.50	?
6.	20%, 20%, 10%	?	$ 53.28	?

C. Answer each of the following questions.

1. An item with a list price of $125.64 is offered at a discount of 37.5%. What is the net price? Reference Example 5.1A
2. An item with a list price of $49.98 is offered at a discount of $16\frac{2}{3}$%. What is the net price?
3. A 17.5% discount on a flat-screen TV amounts to $560. What is the list price? Reference Example 5.1B
4. Golf World sells a set of golf clubs for $762.50 below the suggested retail price. Golf World claims that this represents a 62.5% discount. What is the suggested retail price (or list price)?
5. A $16\frac{2}{3}$% discount allowed on a silk shirt amounted to $14.82. What was the net price?
6. A store advertises a discount of $44.75 on a screwdriver set. If the discount is 25%, for how much were the sets of screwdrivers sold?
7. The net price of a freezer after a discount of $16\frac{2}{3}$% is $355. What is the list price?

8. The net price of an article is $63.31. What is the suggested retail price (the list price) if a discount of 35% was allowed?

9. A mountain bike listed for $975 is sold for $820. What rate of discount was allowed?

Reference Example 5.1C

10. A washer-dryer combination listed at $1136 has a net price of $760. What is the rate of discount?

11. A tool cabinet was originally listed at $769.99. The price was first discounted to $550.54, followed by a final discounted price of $449.79. What was the single equivalent rate of discount at the final price?

12. In the original online ad, a speciality coffee maker was listed at a price of $399.99. To promote business to a retailer, the appliance was offered at "$120 off" if five or more items were purchased at the same time. If a buyer purchased within three days, a further $42 discount off the price was allowed. Compute the net price and the single equivalent rate of discount if a buyer took advantage of both offers.

13. Compute the equivalent single rate of discount for each of the following discount series.
    (a) 30%, 12.5%
    (b) $33\frac{1}{3}$%, 20%, 3%

14. Determine the equivalent single rate of discount for each of the following series of discounts.
    (a) $16\frac{2}{3}$%, 7.5%
    (b) 25%, $8\frac{1}{3}$%, 2%

15. An outdoor furniture set is listed for $599 less 30%, 20%, 5%.
    (a) What is the net price?
    (b) What is the total amount of discount allowed?
    (c) What is the exact single rate of discount that was allowed?

Reference Example 5.1G

16. A power saw is listed for $174 less $16\frac{2}{3}$%, 10%, 8%.
    (a) What is the net price?
    (b) What is the total amount of discount allowed?
    (c) What is the exact single rate of discount that was allowed?

17. A compressor is listed for $786.20 less 36%, 10%, 2%.
    (a) What is the net price?
    (b) What is the total amount of discount allowed?
    (c) What is the exact single rate of discount that was allowed?

18. A tractor is listed for $1293.44 less $18\frac{1}{3}$%, $9\frac{1}{9}$%, 3%.
    (a) What is the net price?
    (b) What is the total amount of discount allowed?
    (c) What is the exact single rate of discount that was allowed?

19. An item listed by a wholesaler for $750 less 20%, 5%, 2% is reduced at a clearance sale to $474.81. What additional rate of discount was offered?

Reference Example 5.1I

20. An office desk listed at $440 less 25%, 15% is offered at a further reduced price of $274.89. What additional rate of discount was offered?

21. An electronic game listed at \$180 less 30%, 12.5%, 5% is offered at a further reduced price of \$99.50. What additional rate of discount was offered?

22. A computer listed at \$1260 less $33\frac{1}{3}$%, $16\frac{2}{3}$% is offered at a clearance price of \$682.50. What additional rate of discount was offered?

23. Arrow Manufacturing offers discounts of 25%, 12.5%, 4% on a line of products. For how much should an item be listed if it is to be sold for \$113.40?

24. What is the list price of an article that is subject to discounts of $33\frac{1}{3}$%, 10%, 2% if the net price is \$564.48?

25. A distributor lists an item for \$85 less 20%. To improve lagging sales, the net price of the item is reduced to \$57.80. What additional rate of discount does the distributor offer?

26. A hat is listed for \$66 less 40%. The net price of the hat is further reduced to \$35.64. What additional rate of discount is offered?

27. Galaxy Jewellers sells diamond necklaces for \$299 less 25%. Brilliants Jewellers offers the same necklace for \$350 less 35%, 10%. What additional rate of discount must Galaxy offer to meet the competitor's price?

28. Polar Bay Wines advertises California Juice listed at \$125 per bucket at a discount of 24%. A nearby competitor offers the same type of juice for \$87.40 per bucket. What additional rate of discount must Polar Bay Wines give to meet the competitor's price?

5.2 PAYMENT TERMS AND CASH DISCOUNTS

A. Basic concepts

Among each other manufacturers, wholesalers, distributors, and retailers usually sell goods on credit rather than for cash. An invoice for the goods is sent, and the seller specifies **payment terms** on the invoice. These payment terms indicate when the invoice amount is due for payment and how much is to be paid. The business selling the goods can offer a **cash discount** to encourage prompt payment. This discount reduces the amount to be paid, and is based on the original amount of the invoice, the discount rate, and the timing of the payment or payments.

All payment terms have three things in common:

1. The **rate of discount** is stated as a percent of the net amount of the invoice. The net amount of the invoice is the amount after trade discounts are deducted.

2. The **discount period** is stated, indicating the time period when the cash discount can be applied.

3. The **credit period** is stated, indicating the time period when the invoice must be paid.

If payment is not made during the stated discount period, the net amount of the invoice is to be paid by the end of the credit period. The end of the credit period is called the *due date*, and is either stipulated by the payment terms or implied by the prevailing business practice. If payment is not made by the due date, the account is considered to be overdue and may be subject to a late payment fee or interest charges.

Cash discounts are offered in a variety of ways. The most commonly used method is **ordinary dating**, where payment terms are based on the invoice date. Occasionally, **end-of-month dating**, or **E.O.M.** (*end of month*) dating is used. End-of-month payment terms shift the invoice date to the last day of the month, so that a discount period or credit period starts after the end of the current month. When the abbreviation **R.O.G.** (*receipt of goods*) appears in the terms of payment, the discount and credit periods start the day after the merchandise has been received. **Receipt-of-goods dating** is used when the transportation of the goods takes a long time, possibly due to the distance the goods are being shipped.

Regardless of when the discount and credit periods begin, the mathematics of working with cash discounts is similar to that used in working with trade discounts.

B. Ordinary dating

The most frequently used method of offering a cash discount is ordinary dating, and the most commonly used payment terms are *2/10, n/30* (read "two ten, net thirty").

This payment term means that if payment is made *within* ten days of the date of the invoice, a discount of 2% may be deducted from the net amount of the invoice. Otherwise, payment of the net amount of the invoice is due within 30 days. (See Figure 5.2.)

FIGURE 5.2 Interpretation of Payment Terms

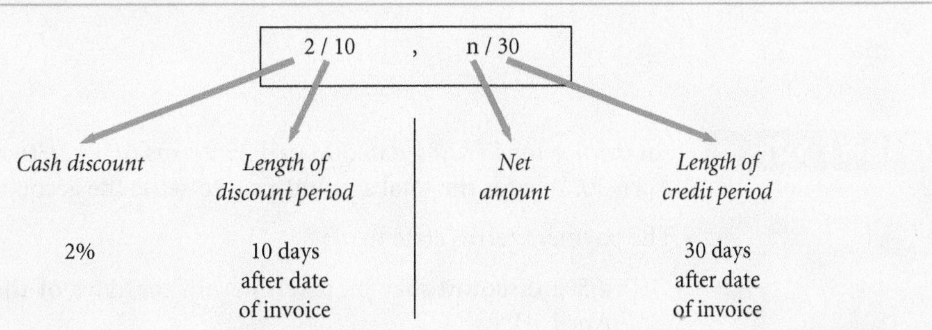

EXAMPLE 5.2A Determine the payment needed to settle an invoice with a net amount of $950 dated September 22, terms 2/10, n/30, if the invoice is paid

(i) on October 10;

(ii) on October 1.

SOLUTION The terms of the invoice indicate a credit period of 30 days and state that a 2% discount may be deducted from the invoice net amount of $950 if the invoice is paid within ten days of the invoice date of September 22. The applicable time periods and dates are shown in Figure 5.3.

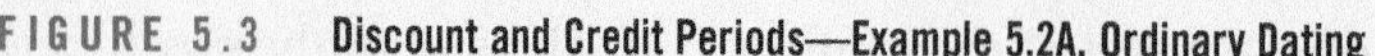

FIGURE 5.3 Discount and Credit Periods—Example 5.2A, Ordinary Dating

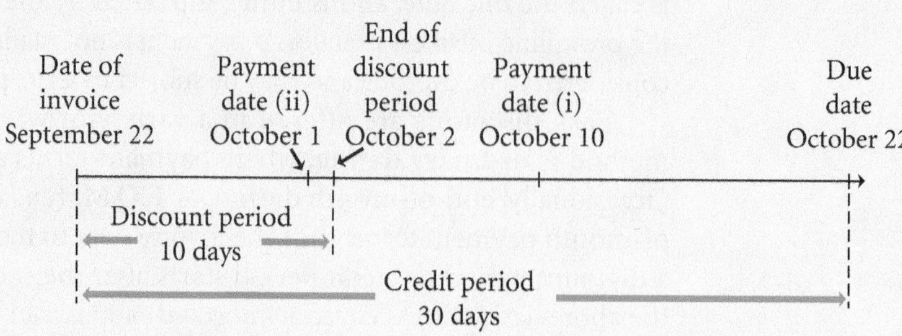

Ten days after September 22 is October 2. The discount period ends October 2.

(i) Payment on October 10 is beyond the last day for taking the discount. The discount cannot be taken. The full amount of the invoice of $950 must be paid.

(ii) October 1 is within the discount period; the 2% discount can be taken.

$$\begin{aligned}\text{Amount paid} &= \text{Net amount} - 2\% \text{ of the net amount}\\ &= 950.00 - 0.02(950.00)\\ &= 950.00 - 19.00\\ &= \$931.00\end{aligned}$$

Alternatively: Using the net price factor approach,

$$\begin{aligned}\text{Amount paid} &= \text{NPF for a 2\% discount} \times \text{Net amount}\\ &= (1 - 0.02)(950.00)\\ &= 0.98(950.00)\\ &= \$931.00\end{aligned}$$

EXAMPLE 5.2B

An invoice for $752.84 dated March 25, terms 5/10, 2/30, n/60, is paid in full on April 20. What is the total amount paid to settle the account?

SOLUTION

The payment terms state that

(i) a 5% discount may be taken within ten days of the invoice date (up to April 4); or

(ii) a 2% discount may be taken within 30 days of the invoice date (after April 4 but no later than April 24); or

(iii) the net amount is due within 60 days of the invoice date if advantage is not taken of the cash discounts offered.

The 5% cash discount is *not* allowed; payment on April 20 is after the end of the discount period for the 5% discount. However, the 2% discount *is* allowed, since payment on April 20 is within the 30 day period for the 2% discount.

Amount paid = 0.98(752.84) = $737.78 (See Figure 5.4.)

FIGURE 5.4 Discount and Credit Periods—Example 5.2B, Ordinary Dating

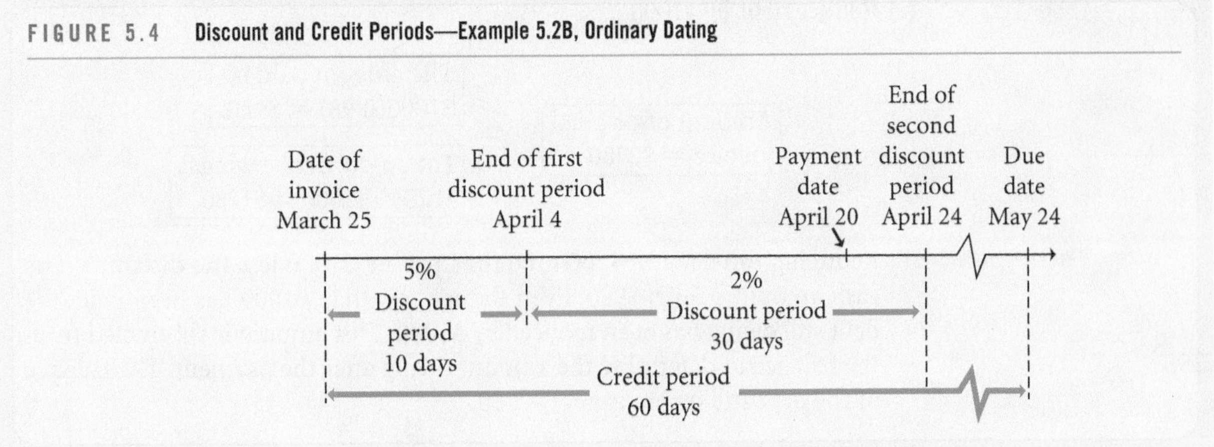

EXAMPLE 5.2C

Three invoices with terms 5/10, 3/20, and n/60 are paid on November 15. The invoices are for $645 dated September 30, $706 dated October 26, and $586 dated November 7. What is the total amount paid?

SOLUTION

Invoice Dated	End of Discount Period For 5%	End of Discount Period For 3%	Discount Allowed		Amount Paid
Sept. 30	Oct. 10	Oct. 20	None		$ 645.00
Oct. 26	Nov. 5	Nov. 15	3%	0.97(706.00)	684.82
Nov. 7	Nov. 17	Nov. 27	5%	0.95(586.00)	556.70
				Amount paid	$1886.52

C. Partial payments and additional problems

The problem of a cash discount for a **partial payment** arises when a business pays *part* of an invoice within the discount period. In such cases, the purchaser is entitled to the cash discount on the partial amount paid. Each time a partial payment is made, separate the invoice into different parts, and then determine whether the discount applies to each individual part.

EXAMPLE 5.2D

George Brown Inc. has received an invoice of $2780 dated August 28, terms 2/10. What payment must be made on September 5 to reduce the debt

(i) by $1000?

(ii) to $1000?

SOLUTION

The last day for taking the cash discount is September 7. Since the payment on September 5 is within the discount period, the discount of 2% may be taken off the partial payment.

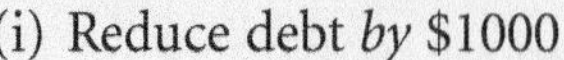

(i) Reduce debt *by* $1000

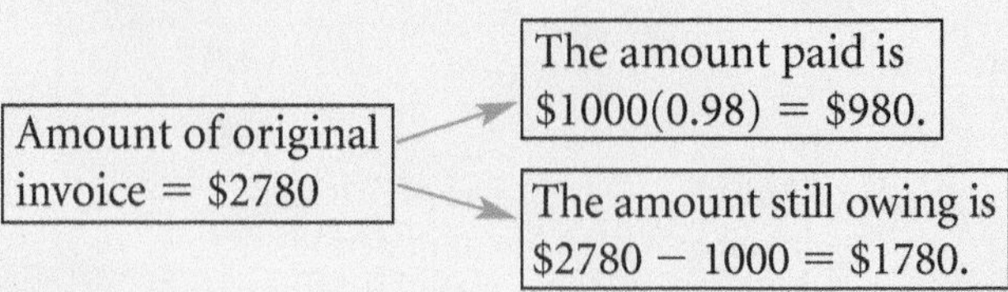

Reducing the debt *by* $1000 requires paying $1000 less the discount. The cash amount paid is $980. Even though less than $1000 has been paid, the debt still owing has been reduced by $1000. This amount is subtracted from the balance to determine the amount owing after the payment. The balance of the debt still owing is now $1780.

(ii) Reduce debt *to* $1000

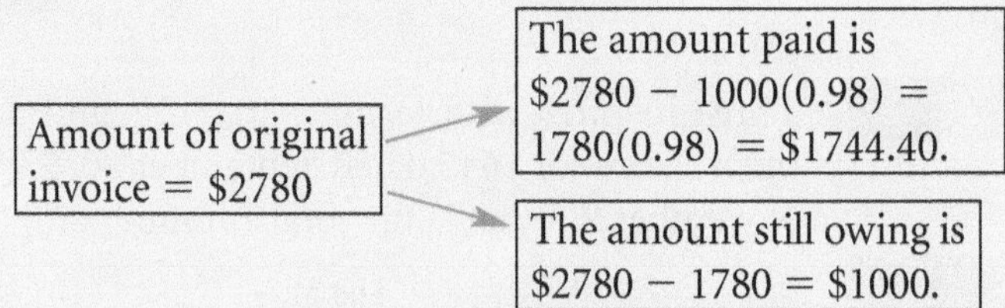

Reducing the debt *to* $1000 requires separating the debt into two parts, the first debt being $1780. The discount is then applied to that amount. The amount paid is $1744.40. The balance of the debt still owing in this case is now $1000.

EXAMPLE 5.2E

Applewood Supplies received a payment of $807.50 from Main Street Service on October 7 on an invoice of $2231.75 dated September 28, terms 5/10.

(i) For how much should Applewood credit Main Street Service's account for the payment?

(ii) How much does Main Street Service still owe on the invoice?

SOLUTION

The payment is within the discount period. Main Street Service is entitled to the 5% discount on the partial payment. The amount of $807.50 represents a partial payment already reduced by 5%.

Let the credit allowed be x.

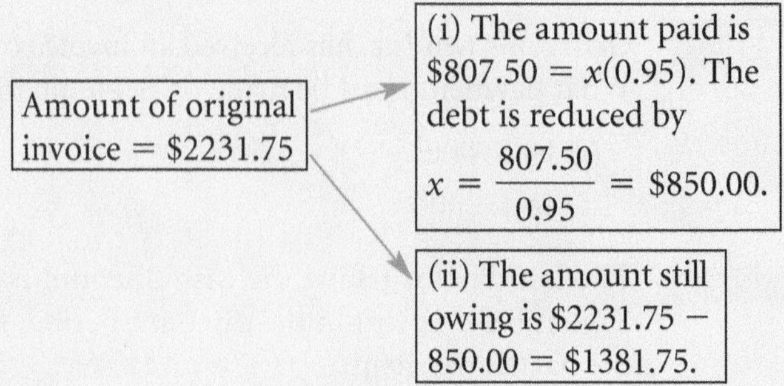

(i) Applewood should credit the account of Main Street Service with \$850.

(ii) Main Street Service still owes (\$2231.75 − 850.00) = \$1381.75.

EXAMPLE 5.2F

Thrifty Furniture sells family room furniture consisting of a couch, loveseat, and two tables for a package price of \$2495 if the purchase is financed. The company also advertises "no payments and no interest for one year." Diana buys the furniture and pays \$2395.20 in cash at the time of the purchase.

(i) How much was the discount for paying cash?

(ii) What was the rate of discount on the cash purchase?

(iii) Is this actually no interest for one year?

SOLUTION

Since the payment was in cash at the time of purchase, Thrifty Furniture did allow a discount.

List price − Amount paid = Discount
\$2495.00 − 2395.20 = \$99.80

(i) Thrifty Furniture allowed a discount of \$99.80.

$$\text{Discount rate} = \frac{99.80}{2495.00} = 4\%$$

(ii) Thrifty Furniture allowed a 4% discount rate for this cash payment.

(iii) No, the advertising is misleading. Since a discount is allowed for early payment, the extra amount paid if the purchase is financed is equivalent to interest on the cash paid at the time of the purchase.

EXERCISE 5.2

A. Determine the amount paid to settle each of the following eight invoices on the date indicated.

	Invoice Amount	Payment Terms	Date of Invoice	Date Paid
1.	\$ 640.00	2/10, n/30	Aug. 10	Sept. 9
2.	\$1520.00	3/15, n/60	Sept. 24	Oct. 8
3.	\$ 783.95	3/10, 1/20, n/60	May 18	June 5
4.	\$1486.25	5/10, 2/30, n/60	June 28	July 8
5.	\$1160.00	2/10, n/45	Mar. 22	April 11
6.	\$ 920.00	3/15, n/60	Oct. 30	Nov. 12
7.	\$4675.00	2/10, n/45	May 28	June 5
8.	\$2899.65	4/20, n/60	Sept. 21	Oct. 10

B. Determine the missing values for each of the following six invoices. Assume that a partial payment was made on each of the invoices by the last day for taking the cash discount.

	Invoice Amount	Payment Terms	Amount of Credit for Payment	Net Payment Received	Invoice Balance Due
1.	$1450.00	3/10, n/30	$ 600.00	?	?
2.	$3126.54	2/10, n/30	$2000.00	?	?
3.	$ 964.50	5/20, n/60	?	?	$400.00
4.	$1789.95	4/15, n/60	?	?	$789.95
5.	$1620.00	3/20, n/90	?	$ 785.70	?
6.	$2338.36	2/10, n/45	?	$1311.59	?

C. Answer the following questions.

1. Canadian Wheel received an invoice dated May 13 with terms 2/10, n/30. The amount stated on the invoice was $2499.
   (a) What is the last day for taking the cash discount?
   (b) What is the amount due if the invoice is paid on the last day for taking the discount? Reference Example 5.2A

2. An invoice was received for $6200 dated June 21 with terms 2/10, n/30.
   (a) What is the last day for taking the cash discount?
   (b) What is the amount due if the invoice is paid on the last day for taking the discount?

3. Triton Company received an invoice for $842 dated March 9 with terms 5/10, 2/20, n/60.
   (a) If the invoice is paid on March 19, how much is to be paid?
   (b) If the invoice is paid on March 27, how much is to be paid?
   (c) If the invoice is paid on April 3, how much is to be paid? Reference Example 5.2B

4. Manual Company received an invoice for $2412 dated January 22 with terms 3/15, 1/30, n/60.
   (a) If the invoice is paid on January 31, how much is to be paid?
   (b) If the invoice is paid on February 20, how much is to be paid?
   (c) If the invoice is paid on March 22, how much is to be paid?

5. What amount must be remitted if invoices dated July 25 for $929, August 10 for $763, and August 29 for $864, all with terms 3/20, n/40, are paid together on August 30?

6. The following invoices, all with terms 5/10, 2/30, n/60, were paid together on May 15. Invoice No. 234 dated March 30 is for $394.45; Invoice No. 356 dated April 15 is for $595.50; and Invoice No. 788 dated May 10 is for $865.20. What amount was remitted?

7. An invoice for $5275 dated November 12, terms 4/10, n/30, was received on November 14. What payment must be made on November 20 to reduce the debt to $3000?

8. What amount will reduce the amount due on an invoice of $1940 by $740 if the terms of the invoice are 5/10, n/30 and the payment was made during the discount period?

9. Santucci Appliances received an invoice dated August 12 with terms 3/10, n/30 for the items listed below:

5 GE refrigerators at $980 each less 25%, 5%;

4 Inglis dishwashers at $696 each less $16\frac{2}{3}$%, 12.5%, 4%.

(a) What is the last day for taking the cash discount?
(b) What is the amount due if the invoice is paid on the last day for taking the discount?
(c) What is the amount of the cash discount if a partial payment is made such that a balance of $2000 remains outstanding on the invoice?

10. Import Exclusives Ltd. received an invoice dated June 28 from Dansk Specialties of Copenhagen with terms 5/20, n/45 for:

100 teak trays at $34.30 each;
25 teak icebuckets at $63.60 each;
40 teak salad bowls at $54.50 each.

All items are subject to trade discounts of $33\frac{1}{3}$%, $7\frac{1}{2}$%, 5%.

(a) What is the last day of the discount period?
(b) What is the amount due if the invoice is paid in full on July 15?
(c) If a partial payment only is made on the last day of the discount period, what amount is due to reduce the outstanding balance to $2500?

11. Sheridan Service received an invoice dated September 25 from Wolfedale Automotive. The invoice amount was $2540.95, and the payment terms were 3/10, 1/20, n/30. Sheridan Service made a payment on October 5 to reduce the balance due by $1200, made a second payment on October 15 to reduce the balance to $600, and paid the remaining balance on October 25.
(a) How much did Sheridan Service pay on October 5?
(b) How much did it pay on October 15?
(c) What was the amount of the final payment on October 25?

Reference Example 5.2D

12. The Ski Shop received an invoice for $9600 dated August 11, terms 5/10, 2/30, n/90, for a shipment of skis. The Ski Shop made two partial payments.
(a) How much was paid on August 20 to reduce the unpaid balance to $7000?
(b) How much was paid on September 10 to reduce the outstanding balance by $3000?
(c) What is the remaining balance on September 10?

13. Jelinek Sports received a cheque for $1867.25 in partial payment of an invoice owed by The Ski Shop. The invoice was for $5325 with terms 3/20, n/60 dated September 30, and the cheque was received on October 18.
(a) By how much should Jelinek Sports credit the account of The Ski Shop?
(b) How much does The Ski Shop still owe Jelinek?

14. Darrigo Grape received an invoice for $13 780 dated October 20, terms 5/20, n/60, from Nappa Vineyards for a carload of grape juice. Darrigo made a partial payment of $5966 on November 8.
(a) By how much did Darrigo reduce the amount due on the invoice?
(b) How much does Darrigo still owe?

15. Highway One Gas sells gas for vehicles at \$1.12 per litre. Louis purchases 50 litres of gas for his car. He pays for the purchase in cash, paying a total of \$54.04.
  (a) How much did he save by paying cash?
  (b) What was the rate of discount on the cash purchase?

16. Deals on Wheels advertises a vehicle at \$26 465. Marina buys the vehicle, paying \$24 877.10 in cash.
  (a) How much did she save by paying cash?
  (b) What was the rate of discount on the cash purchase?

5.3 MARKUP

A. Basic concepts and calculations

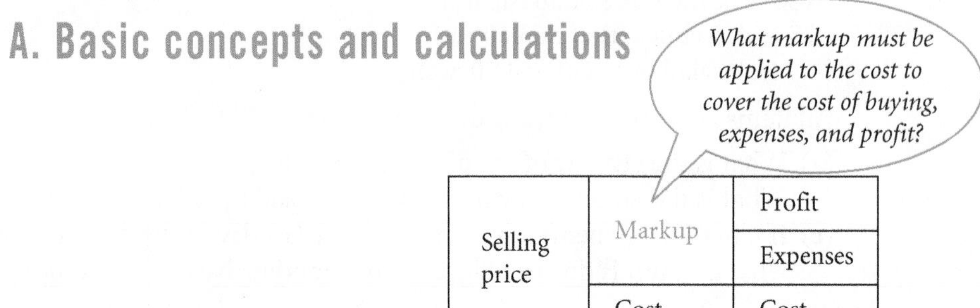

The primary purpose of operating a business is to generate profits. Businesses engaged in merchandising generate profits through their buying and selling activities. The amount of profit depends on many factors, one of which is the pricing of goods. The selling price must cover

1. the cost of buying the goods;
2. the operating expenses (or overhead) of the business;
3. the profit required by the owner to stay in business.

SELLING PRICE = COST OF BUYING + EXPENSES + PROFIT

$$S = C + E + P$$ —— **Formula 5.8A**

EXAMPLE 5.3A Twelfth Street Service buys a certain type of battery at a cost of \$84 each. Operating expenses of the business are 25% of cost and the owner requires a profit of 10% of cost. For how much should Twelfth Street sell this type of battery?

SOLUTION

Selling price = Cost of buying + Expenses + Profit
= 84.00 + 25% of 84.00 + 10% of 84.00
= 84.00 + 0.25(84.00) + 0.1(84.00)
= 84.00 + 21.00 + 8.40
= \$113.40

Twelfth Street should sell the batteries for \$113.40 to cover the cost of buying, the operating expenses, and the required profit.

Formula 5.8A can then be rearranged, so that the selling price less the cost equals expenses plus profit.

SELLING PRICE − COST OF BUYING = EXPENSES + PROFIT

$S - C = E + P$ ——— **Formula 5.8B**

In Example 5.3A, the selling price is $113.40 while the cost is $84. The difference between selling price and cost = 113.40 − 84.00 = $29.40. This difference covers operating expenses of $21 and a profit of $8.40 and is known as the **markup**, **margin**, or **gross profit**.

MARKUP = EXPENSES + PROFIT

$M = E + P$ ——— **Formula 5.9**

Using this relationship between markup, expenses, and profit, the relationship stated in Formula 5.8A becomes

SELLING PRICE = COST OF BUYING + MARKUP

$S = C + M$ ——— **Formula 5.8C**

Figure 5.5 illustrates the relationships among cost of buying (C), markup (M), operating expenses (E), profit (P), and selling price (S) established in Formulas 5.8A, 5.8B, 5.8C, and 5.9.

FIGURE 5.5

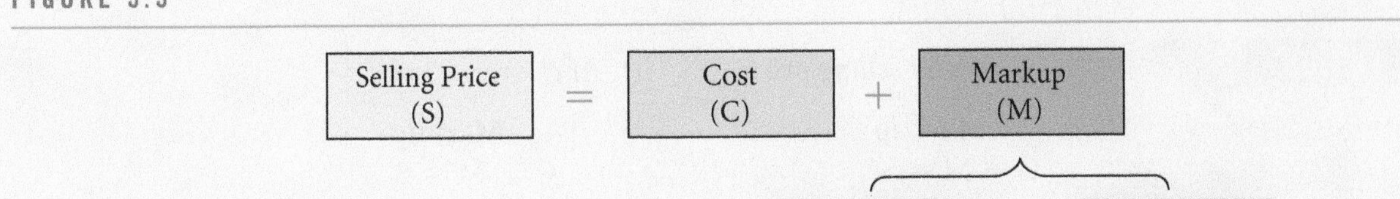

EXAMPLE 5.3B

Island Business bought two types of electronic calculators for resale. Model A costs $42 and sells for $56.50. Model B costs $78 and sells for $95. Business overhead is 24% of cost. For each model, determine

(i) the markup (or gross profit);

(ii) the operating expenses (or overhead);

(iii) the profit.

SOLUTION

	Model A	**Model B**	
(i)	$C + M = S$	$C + M = S$	using Formula 5.8C
	$42.00 + M = 56.50$	$78.00 + M = 95.00$	
	$M = 56.50 - 42.00$	$M = 95.00 - 78.00$	
	$M = 14.50$	$M = 17.00$	
	The markup on Model A is $14.50.	The markup on Model B is $17	

(ii) Expenses (or overhead)

Model A	Model B
Expenses (or overhead)	Expenses (or overhead)
= 24% of 42.00	= 24% of 78.00
= 0.24(42.00)	= 0.24(78.00)
= 10.08	= 18.72
Overhead for Model A is $10.08.	Overhead for Model B is $18.72.

(iii)

Model A	Model B
E + P = M	E + P = M ——— **Formula 5.9**
10.08 + P = 14.50	18.72 + P = 17.00
P = 14.50 − 10.08	P = 17.00 − 18.72
P = 4.42	P = −1.72
Profit on Model A is $4.42.	Profit on Model B is –$1.72, that is, a loss of $1.72.

EXAMPLE 5.3C

A ski shop bought 100 pairs of skis for $105 per pair and sold 60 pairs for the regular selling price of $295 per pair. The remaining skis were sold during a clearance sale for $180 per pair. Overhead is 40% of the regular selling price. Determine

(i) the markup, the overhead, and the profit per pair of skis sold at the regular selling price;

(ii) the markup, the overhead, and the profit per pair of skis sold during the clearance sale;

(iii) the total profit realized.

SOLUTION

(i) *At regular selling price*	(ii) *At clearance price*
Markup	**Markup**
C + M = S	C + M = S
105.00 + M = 295.00	105.00 + M = 180.00
M = $190.00	M = $75.00
Overhead	**Overhead**
E = 40% of regular selling price	E = 40% of regular selling price
= 0.4(295.00)	= 0.4(295.00)
= $118.00	= $118.00
Profit	**Profit**
E + P = M	E + P = M
118.00 + P = 190.00	118.00 + P = 75.00
P = $72.00	P = −$43.00

(iii)

Profit from sale of 60 pairs at regular selling price = 60(72.00)	$4320.00
Profit from sale of 40 pairs during clearance sale = 40(−43.00)	−1720.00
Total profit	$2600.00

B. Rate of markup

A markup may be stated in one of two ways:

1. As a percent of cost; or
2. As a percent of selling price.

The method used is usually determined by the way in which a business keeps its records. Since most manufacturers keep their records in terms of cost, they usually calculate markup as a percent of cost. Since most department stores and other retailers keep their records in terms of selling price, they usually calculate markup as a percent of selling price.

Computing the rate of markup involves comparing the amount of markup to a base amount. Depending on the method used, the base amount is either the cost or the selling price. Since the two methods produce different results, great care must be taken to note whether the markup is based on the cost or on the selling price.

$$\text{RATE OF MARKUP BASED ON COST} = \frac{\text{MARKUP}}{\text{COST}} = \frac{M}{C}$$ —— Formula 5.10

$$\text{RATE OF MARKUP BASED ON SELLING PRICE} = \frac{\text{MARKUP}}{\text{SELLING PRICE}} = \frac{M}{S}$$ —— Formula 5.11

EXAMPLE 5.3D

Compute (a) the missing value (cost, selling price, or markup), (b) the rate of markup based on cost, and (c) the rate of markup based on selling price for each of the following:

(i) cost, \$60; selling price, \$75

(ii) cost, \$48; markup, \$16

(iii) selling price, \$88; markup, \$33

(iv) cost, \$8; markup, \$8

(v) selling price, \$24; markup, \$18

SOLUTION

	(a) Missing Value	(b) Rate of Markup Based on Cost	(c) Rate of Markup Based on Selling Price
(i)	Markup = 75.00 − 60.00 = \$15.00	$\frac{15}{60} = 0.25 = 25\%$	$\frac{15}{75} = 0.2 = 20\%$
(ii)	Selling price = 48.00 + 16.00 = \$64.00	$\frac{16}{48} = \frac{1}{3} = 33\frac{1}{3}\%$	$\frac{16}{64} = 0.25 = 25\%$

(iii)	Cost = 88.00 − 33.00 = \$55.00	$\frac{33}{55} = 0.6 = 60\%$	$\frac{33}{88} = 0.375 = 37.5\%$
(iv)	Selling price = 8.00 + 8.00 = \$16.00	$\frac{8}{8} = 1 = 100\%$	$\frac{8}{16} = 0.5 = 50\%$
(v)	Cost = 24.00 − 18.00 = \$6.00	$\frac{18}{6} = 3 = 300\%$	$\frac{18}{24} = 0.75 = 75\%$

C. Finding the cost or the selling price

When the rate of markup is given and either the cost or the selling price is known, the missing value can be found using Formula 5.8C.

COST + MARKUP = SELLING PRICE $\qquad$ C + M = S

When using this formula, pay special attention to the base of the markup, that is, whether it is based on cost or based on selling price.

EXAMPLE 5.3E What is the selling price of an article costing \$72 if the markup is

(i) 40% of cost?

(ii) 40% of the selling price?

SOLUTION

(i)

$$C + M = S$$ — using Formula 5.8C

$$C + 40\% \text{ of } C = S$$ — replacing M by 40% of C is the crucial step in the solution

$$72.00 + 0.4(72.00) = S$$

$$72.00 + 28.80 = S$$

$$S = 100.80$$

When the markup is 40% based on cost, the selling price is \$100.80.

(ii)

$$C + M = S$$

$$C + 40\% \text{ of } S = S$$

$$72.00 + 0.4S = S$$

$$72.00 = S - 0.4S$$

$$72.00 = 0.6S$$

$$S = \frac{72.00}{0.6}$$

$$S = 120.00$$

When the markup is 40% based on selling price, the selling price is \$120.00.

Note: In problems of this type, replace M by *X*% of C or *X*% of S before using specific numbers. This approach is used in the preceding problem and in the following worked examples.

EXAMPLE 5.3F What is the cost of an article selling for \$65 if the markup is

(i) 30% of selling price?

(ii) 30% of cost?

SOLUTION (i)

$$C + M = S$$

$$C + 30\% \text{ of } S = S \quad \text{———— replace M by 30\% of S}$$

$$C + 0.3(65.00) = 65.00$$

$$C + 19.50 = 65.00$$

$$C = 65.00 - 19.50$$

$$C = 45.50$$

When the markup is 30% based on selling price, the cost is \$45.50.

(ii)

$$C + M = S$$

$$C + 30\% \text{ of } C = S \quad \text{———— replace M by 30\% of C}$$

$$C + 0.3C = 65.00$$

$$1.3C = 65.00$$

$$C = \frac{65.00}{1.3}$$

$$C = 50.00$$

If the markup is 30% based on cost, the cost is \$50.

EXAMPLE 5.3G The Beaver Ski Shop sells ski vests for \$98. The markup based on cost is 75%.

(i) What did the Beaver Ski Shop pay for each vest?

(ii) What is the rate of markup based on the selling price?

SOLUTION (i)

$$C + M = S$$

$$C + 75\% \text{ of } C = S$$

$$C + 0.75C = 98.00$$

$$1.75C = 98.00$$

$$C = 56.00$$

The Beaver Ski Shop paid \$56 for each vest.

(ii)

$$\text{Rate of markup based on selling price} = \frac{\text{Markup}}{\text{Selling price}}$$

$$= \frac{98.00 - 56.00}{98.00}$$

$$= \frac{42.00}{98.00} = 0.428571 = 42.8571\%$$

EXAMPLE 5.3H Main Street Service bought four Michelin tires from a wholesaler for \$343 and sold the tires at a markup of 30% of the selling price.

(i) For how much were the tires sold?

(ii) What is the rate of markup based on cost?

SOLUTION

(i)
$$C + M = S$$
$$C + 30\% \text{ of } S = S$$
$$343.00 + 0.3S = S$$
$$343.00 = 0.7S$$
$$S = 490.00$$

Main Street Service sold the tires for \$490.

(ii) $\text{Rate of markup based on cost} = \dfrac{\text{Markup}}{\text{Cost}}$

$$= \frac{490.00 - 343.00}{343.00}$$

$$= \frac{147.00}{343.00} = 0.428571 = 42.8571\%$$

EXAMPLE 5.3I

The markup, or gross profit, on each of two separate articles is \$25.80. If the rate of markup for Article A is 40% of cost while the rate of markup for Article B is 40% of the selling price, determine the cost and the selling price of each.

SOLUTION

For Article A

Markup (or gross profit) = 40% of cost
$$25.80 = 0.4C$$
$$C = 64.50$$

The cost of Article A is \$64.50.
The selling price is 64.50 + 25.80 = \$90.30.

For Article B

Markup (or gross profit) = 40% of selling price
$$25.80 = 0.4S$$
$$S = 64.50$$

The selling price of Article B is \$64.50.
The cost is 64.50 − 25.80 = \$38.70.

EXERCISE 5.3

For each of the following six questions, determine
(a) the amount of markup;
(b) the amount of overhead;
(c) the profit or loss realized on the sale;
(d) the rate of markup based on cost;
(e) the rate of markup based on selling price.

	Cost	Selling Price	Overhead
1.	$24.00	$30.00	16% of cost
2.	$72.00	$96.00	15% of selling price
3.	$52.50	$87.50	36% of selling price
4.	$42.45	$67.92	60% of cost
5.	$27.00	$37.50	34% of selling price
6.	$36.00	$42.30	21% of cost

B. For each of the following twelve questions, compute the missing values represented by the question marks.

		Selling		Rate of Markup Based On:	
	Cost	Price	Markup	Cost	Selling Price
1.	$25.00	$ 31.25	?	?	?
2.	$63.00	$ 84.00	?	?	?
3.	$64.00	?	$38.40	?	?
4.	?	$162.00	$27.00	?	?
5.	$54.25	?	?	40%	?
6.	?	$ 94.50	?	?	30%
7.	?	$ 66.36	?	50%	?
8.	?	$133.25	?	$66\frac{2}{3}\%$	?
9.	$31.24	?	?	?	60%
10.	$87.74	?	?	?	$33\frac{1}{3}\%$
11.	?	?	$22.26	?	$16\frac{2}{3}\%$
12.	?	?	$90.75	125%	?

C. Answer each of the following questions.

1. Giuseppe's buys supplies to make pizzas for $4. Operating expenses of the business are 110% of the cost and the profit made is 130% of cost. What is the regular selling price of each pizza?
2. Neptune Dive Shop sells snorkelling equipment for $50. Their cost is $25 and their operation expenses are 30% of regular selling price. How much profit will they make on each sale?
3. Mi Casa imports pottery from Mexico. Their operation expenses are 260% of the cost of buying and the profit is 110% of the cost of buying. They sell a vase for $14.10. What is their cost for each piece?
4. Peninsula Hardware buys cabinet doors for $25 less 40%, 10%, 4%. The store's overhead expenses are 35% of cost and the required profit is 15% of cost. For how much should the cabinet doors be sold?
5. A merchant buys an item listed at $96 less $33\frac{1}{3}\%$ from a distributor. Overhead is 32% of cost and profit is 27.5% of cost. For how much should the item be retailed?
6. Tennis racquets were purchased for $55 less 40% (for purchasing more than 100 items), and less a further 25% (for purchasing the racquets in October). They were sold for $54.45.

(a) What is the markup as a percent of cost?
(b) What is the markup as a percent of selling price?

7. A dealer bought computers for \$1240 less 50%, 10%. They were sold for \$1395.
(a) What was the markup as a percent of cost?
(b) What was the markup as a percent of selling price?

8. The Bargain Bookstore marks up books by \$3.42 per book. The store's markup is 15% of cost.
(a) For how much did the bookstore buy each book?
(b) What is the selling price of each book?
(c) What is the rate of markup based on the selling price?

9. An appliance store sells electric kettles at a markup of 18% of the selling price. The store's margin on a particular model is \$6.57.
(a) For how much does the store sell the kettles?
(b) What was the cost of the kettles to the store?
(c) What is the rate of markup based on cost?

10. At Town Lighting, a light fixture is sold at a price of \$382.20, including a markup of 40% of cost.
(a) What is the cost of the item?
(b) What is the rate of markup based on the selling price?

11. Sheridan Service sells oil at a markup of 40% of the selling price. If Sheridan paid \$0.99 per litre of oil,
(a) what is the selling price per litre?
(b) what is the rate of markup based on cost?

12. Skis & Boards purchased gloves for \$20.28 per pair. The gloves are marked up 48% of the selling price.
(a) For how much does Skis & Boards sell a pair of gloves?
(b) What is the rate of markup based on cost?

13. Neal's Photographic Supplies sells a Pentax camera for \$444.98. The markup is 90% of cost.
(a) How much does the store pay for this camera?
(b) What is the rate of markup based on selling price?

14. The Cookery buys sets of cookware for \$45 and marks them up at $33\frac{1}{3}\%$ of cost.
(a) What is the selling price of the cookware sets?
(b) What is the rate of markup based on selling price?

15. The Leather Factory buys bags for \$84 and marks them up at 40% of selling price.
(a) What is the selling price of the bags?
(b) What is the rate of markup based on cost?

16. Boxes of candles are sold for \$3.24. The store's markup based on selling price is $16\frac{2}{3}\%$.
(a) What is the cost of the boxes of candles?
(b) What is the rate of markup based on cost?

17. It's About Time sells clocks for \$23.10. The store's markup based on cost is 37.5%.
 (a) What is the cost of the clocks?
 (b) What is the rate of markup based on selling price?

18. A car accessory is sold for \$42.90. The store's markup based on cost is 50%.
 (a) What is the cost of the car accessory?
 (b) What is the rate of markup based on selling price?

5.4 MARKDOWN

A. Pricing strategies

Pricing strategies can be based on internal or external influences. Setting a price based on the business' "internal" factors involves examining the actual costs and expenses, and a desired profit level. Consideration of the relationship stated in Formula 5.8A, Selling price = Cost + Expense + Profit (or S = C + E + P), is essential in determining how large a markup is needed to cover overhead expenses and a reasonable profit.

The cost of buying an article plus the overhead represents the **total cost** of the article.

COST OF BUYING + EXPENSES = TOTAL COST

If an article is sold at a price that *equals* the total cost, the business makes no profit nor does it suffer a loss. This price is called the break-even point and is discussed in Chapter 6. Any business, of course, prefers to sell at a price that is at least the break-even price. If the price is insufficient to recover the total cost, the business will suffer an operating loss. If the price does not even cover the cost of buying the item, the business suffers an absolute loss.

Often, pricing decisions are determined by actions of competitors or consumers, changes to economic conditions that affect interest rates and income available for purchases, or other "external" market factors. In response to market changes, marking down selling prices may be required to maintain profit levels.

B. Concepts and calculations

After the price to the retailer has been marked up to determine the regular selling price, the retailer may discount the regular selling price to offer the goods to the consumer at a lower sale price. The reduction from the regular selling price is called a **markdown**. The purpose of a markdown may be for promoting sales, matching competitors' prices, or clearing out inventories that are discontinued or seasonal.

In the merchandising industry, a wide variety of terms are used to identify the price to be reduced, such as regular selling price, selling price, list price, marked price, price tag, or ticket price. The reduced price can be referred to as the sale price or clearance price. The many terms can cause confusion. In this text, we use **regular selling price**, S, to describe the price to be reduced and **sale price** to describe the reduced price.

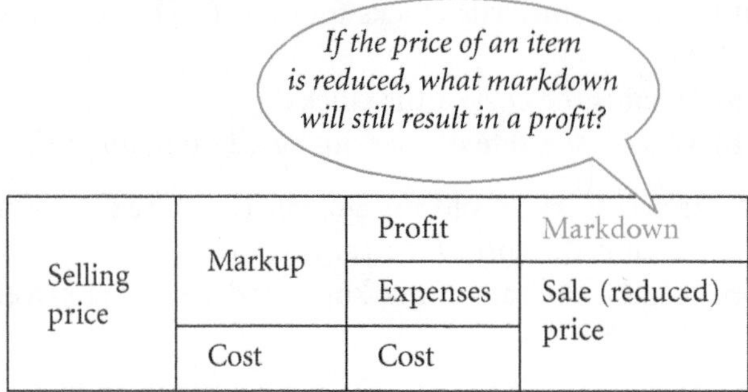

Using these standardized terms, a markdown can be calculated as the difference between the regular selling price and the sale price.

REGULAR SELLING PRICE − MARKDOWN = SALE PRICE

The markdown, or discount, rate is the relationship between the amount of the markdown and the regular selling price, and is stated as a percent of the regular selling price.

$$\text{MARKDOWN RATE} = \frac{\text{MARKDOWN}}{\text{REGULAR SELLING PRICE}} = \frac{MD}{S}$$

Since the markdown is a percent of the regular selling price, the net price factor approach used with discounts is applicable (see Formula 5.4A).

$$\text{SALE PRICE} = \text{REGULAR SELLING PRICE} \times \text{NPF}$$
$$\text{where NPF} = 100\% - \%\text{ markdown}$$

When an article is sold at the sale price, the resulting profit, called the realized profit, can be determined using a variation of Formula 5.8A, $S - C - E = P$. The regular selling price, S, would be replaced with the sale price. If the sale price of an article does not cover the total cost, the cost of buying, and the overhead expense, the result is a loss.

EXAMPLE 5.4A The Cook Nook paid $115.24 for a set of dishes. Expenses are 18% of selling price and the required profit is 15% of selling price. During an inventory sale, the set of dishes was marked down 30%.

(i) What was the regular selling price?
(ii) What was the sale price?
(iii) What was the operating profit or loss?

SOLUTION

(i) Selling price = Cost + Expenses + Profit

$$S = C + 18\% \text{ of } S + 15\% \text{ of } S$$
$$S = C + 0.18S + 0.15S$$
$$S = 115.24 + 0.33S$$
$$0.67S = 115.24$$
$$S = \frac{115.24}{0.67} = \$172.00$$

The regular selling price is \$172.

(ii) Sale price = Regular selling price − Markdown

$$= S - 30\% \text{ of } S$$
$$= S - 0.3S$$
$$= 0.7S$$
$$= 0.7(172.00)$$
$$= \$120.40$$

The sale price is \$120.40.

(iii) Total cost = Cost of buying + Expenses

$$= C + 18\% \text{ of } S$$
$$= 115.24 + 0.18(172.00)$$
$$= 115.24 + 30.96$$
$$= \$146.20$$

Profit = Revenue − Total cost

$$= 120.40 - 146.20$$
$$= -\$25.80$$

The dishes were sold at an operating loss of \$25.80.

EXAMPLE 5.4B

Lund Sporting Goods sold a bicycle regularly priced at \$195 for \$144.30.

(i) What is the amount of markdown?

(ii) What is the rate of markdown?

SOLUTION

The regular selling price, S, is \$195.
The sale price is \$144.30.

(i) Markdown = Regular selling price − Sale price

$$= 195.00 - 144.30$$
$$= \$50.70$$

(ii) $$\text{Rate of markdown} = \frac{\text{Markdown}}{\text{Regular selling price}}$$

$$= \frac{50.70}{195.00} = 0.26 = 26\%$$

EXAMPLE 5.4C

During its annual Midnight Madness Sale, The Ski Shop sold a pair of ski boots, regularly priced at \$245, at a discount of 40%. The boots cost \$96 and expenses are 26% of the regular selling price.

(i) For how much were the ski boots sold?

(ii) What was the total cost of the ski boots?

(iii) What operating profit or loss was made on the sale?

SOLUTION

The regular selling price, S, is \$245.
The net price factor (NPF) is $(1 - 0.40) = 0.60$.

(i) Sale price $= \text{NPF} \times \text{S}$
$= 0.6 \times 245.00 = \$147.00$

(ii) Total cost = Cost of buying + Expenses
$= 96.00 + 0.26(245.00)$
$= 96.00 + 63.70$
$= \$159.70$

(iii) Profit = Sale price − Total cost
$= 147.00 - 159.70$
$= -\$12.70$ (a loss)

Since the total cost was higher than the revenue received from the sale of the ski boots, The Ski Shop had an operating loss of \$12.70.

EXAMPLE 5.4D

The Winemaker sells Okanagan concentrate for \$22.50. The store's overhead expenses are 50% of cost and the owners require a profit of 30% of cost.

(i) For how much does The Winemaker buy the concentrate?

(ii) What is the price needed to cover all of the costs and expenses?

(iii) What is the highest rate of markdown at which the store will still break even?

(iv) What is the highest rate of discount that can be advertised without incurring an absolute loss?

SOLUTION

The regular selling price, S, is \$22.50.

(i)
$$S = C + E + P$$
$$S = C + 50\% \text{ of } C + 30\% \text{ of } C$$
$$S = C + 0.5C + 0.3C$$
$$22.50 = 1.8C$$
$$C = \frac{22.50}{1.80} = \$12.50$$

The Winemaker buys the concentrate for \$12.50.

(ii) Total cost = C + 50% of C
$= 1.5C$
$= 1.5(12.50)$
$= \$18.75$

The price needed to cover costs and expenses is \$18.75.

(iii) To break even, the maximum markdown is 22.50 − 18.75 = \$3.75.

$$\text{Rate of markdown} = \frac{3.75}{22.50} = 0.1\dot{6} = 16.\dot{6}\%$$

The highest rate of markdown to break even is $16.\dot{6}\%$.

(iv) The lowest price at which the concentrate can be offered for sale without incurring an absolute loss is the cost at which the concentrate was purchased, that is, \$12.50. The maximum amount of discount is 22.50 − 12.50 = \$10.00.

$$\text{Rate of discount} = \frac{10.00}{22.50} = 0.\dot{4} = 44.\dot{4}\%$$

The maximum rate of discount that can be advertised without incurring an absolute loss is $44.\dot{4}\%$.

EXERCISE 5.4

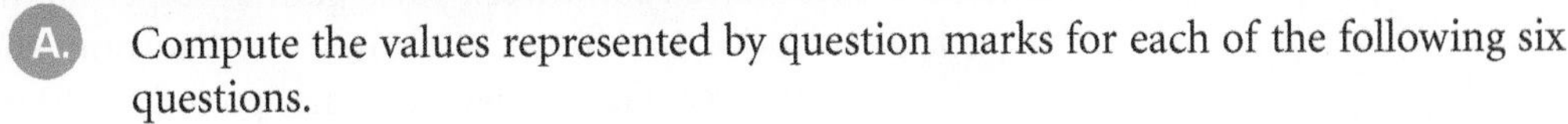

A. Compute the values represented by question marks for each of the following six questions.

	Regular Selling Price	Markdown	Sale Price	Cost (C)	Overhead	Total Cost	Operating Profit (Loss)
1.	\$85.00	40%	?	\$ 42.00	20% of S	?	?
2.	?	$33\frac{1}{3}\%$	\$ 42.00	\$ 34.44	12% of S	?	?
3.	?	35%	\$ 62.66	?	25% of S	\$54.75	?
4.	\$72.80	$12\frac{1}{2}\%$	?	\$ 54.75	20% of C	?	?
5.	?	25%	\$120.00	\$105.00	? of S	?	(\$4.20)
6.	\$92.40	$16\frac{2}{3}\%$	?	?	15% of C	?	\$8.46

B.

1. The Music Store paid \$14.95 for a DVD. Expenses are 21% of regular selling price and the required profit is 11% of regular selling price. During an inventory sale, the DVD was marked down 20%.
(a) What was the regular selling price?
(b) What was the sale price?
(c) What was the operating profit or loss?

Reference Example 5.4A

2. A retail store paid \$44 for a microwave oven. Expenses are 27% of regular selling price and the required profit is 18% of regular selling price. During an inventory sale, the microwave was marked down 40%.
(a) What was the regular selling price?
(b) What was the sale price?
(c) What was the operating profit or loss?

3. A sports drink was offered for sale at \$1.99 at West Store. At East Store, the regular selling price of a similar sports drink was \$2.49. What rate of markdown would East Store have to offer to sell the drink at the same price as West Store?

Reference Example 5.4B

4. An eyeglass company sells frames for $279. If they wanted to offer the lower price of $239, what rate of markdown would they have to offer?

5. A seminar was advertised at a price of $125 per person. If the tickets were purchased at least two weeks in advance, the price would be lowered to $105 per person. What rate of markdown has been offered?

6. A seven-day Mexican cruise was advertised at a price of $1299 per person based on double occupancy. If the cruise was booked two months in advance, the price would be lowered to $935 per person. What rate of markdown has been offered?

7. Luigi's Restaurant offered a "buy one get one half off" sale for the midweek period. The "one half off" referred to the lesser-priced dinner. A customer ordered a steak dinner, with a regular price of $19, and a chicken dinner, with a regular price of $14.

(a) What was the overall markdown at which the dinners were sold?

(b) What was the overall rate of markdown at which the dinners were sold?

8. A lakeside resort offered a midweek package at $199 per night for two people. The package included accommodation in a one-bedroom suite, which regularly sold for $225, breakfast for two, regularly priced at $12 per person, and a 25% discount on spa services, a value of $20 per person.

(a) What was the overall markdown at which the packages were sold?

(b) What was the overall rate of markdown at which the packages were sold?

9. Par Putters Company sells golf balls for $29 per dozen. The store's overhead expenses are 43% of cost and the owners require a profit of 20% of cost.

(a) For how much does Par Putters Company buy the golf balls?

(b) What is the price needed to cover all of the costs and expenses?

(c) What is the highest rate of markdown at which the store will still break even?

(d) What is the highest rate of discount that can be advertised without incurring an absolute loss? Reference Example 5.4D

10. Get-Aways Company sells sightseeing tours of the Ottawa Valley for C$3849 per person. Overhead expenses for the company are 31% of cost and the target profit is 17% of cost.

(a) How much does Get-Aways Company pay for the tours?

(b) What is the lowest price they can offer while still covering all of the costs and expenses?

(c) What is the highest rate of markdown at which the company will still break even?

5.5 INTEGRATED PROBLEMS

Decisions involving discounts, markups, and markdowns are faced by business owners and managers on a regular basis. To achieve desired profits, prices must be set carefully. With each complex situation, a series of calculations are needed, with one calculation often building upon another. To achieve an overall solution, the steps to that solution must be defined and the costs and prices calculated.

EXAMPLE 5.5A

Rocky Sports purchased ski bindings for $57.75 that were marked up 45% of the regular selling price. The store's overhead expenses were 28% of the regular selling price. When the binding was discontinued, it was marked down 40%. What was the sale price of the binding? How much was the operating profit or loss as a result of the sale?

SOLUTION

Consider the given information step by step. First the regular selling price must be calculated. Next, the sale price can be calculated, and finally, the profit or loss can be calculated.

STEP 1

Since the sale price A is based on a markdown from the regular selling price, S, the first step is to determine the regular selling price, S.

$$C + M = S$$
$$C + 45\% \text{ of } S = S$$
$$57.75 + 0.45S = S$$
$$57.75 = 0.55S$$
$$S = \$105.00$$

The regular selling price is $105.00.

STEP 2

Based on the regular selling price, S, determine the sale price.

$$\text{Sale price} = \text{Regular selling price} - \text{Markdown}$$
$$\text{Sale price} = 105.00 - 40\% \text{ of } 105.00$$
$$\text{Sale price} = 105.00 - 42.00$$
$$\text{Sale price} = \$63.00$$

Alternatively:

$$\text{Sale price} = \text{NPF} \times \text{Regular selling price}$$
$$\text{Sale price} = 0.6 \times 105.00$$
$$\text{Sale price} = \$63.00$$

The sale price is $63.00.

STEP 3

Based on the sale price, determine the profit or loss.

$$\text{Profit(loss)} = \text{Sale price} - \text{Cost of buying} - \text{Expenses}$$
$$P = 63.00 - 57.75 - 0.28(105.00)$$
$$P = 63.00 - 57.75 - 29.40$$
$$P = -\$24.15$$

With the sale price, the operating loss was $24.15.

In some industries, businesses incorporate a third price into their pricing strategy. In this case, the marked price or sticker price is set so that an ongoing discount is deducted to determine the regular selling price. Even though the merchandise is marked with a price, it is seldom sold at that price. When a discount is offered on a regular basis, the discounted price becomes the regular selling price. In addition, the business can apply a markdown to the marked price to determine a sale price. The resulting sale price may be higher or lower than the regular selling price.

EXAMPLE 5.5B

The Cheetah, a fast, sporty, and efficient new vehicle, has just been introduced by Canadian Motors. The local dealer, Andretti's, purchased one of the cars at a list price of \$27 685 less 30%. Andretti's sets a marked price on all vehicles so that they can offer a regular advertised discount of 10% and maintain a markup of 45% of the cost. During its annual sale, instead of the usual discount, a different markdown was offered by advertising the car at \$27 995. Determine the cost, the regular selling price, the original marked price, and the sale markdown rate.

SOLUTION

The step-by-step calculations are: determine cost, regular selling price, original marked price, and then the sale markdown rate.

STEP 1 The cost, C, (or purchase price) to the dealer.

$$\text{Cost} = \text{Manufacturer's list price} \times \text{NPF}$$
$$C = (27\,685.00)(0.70) = \$19\,379.50$$

The cost, C, to the business is \$19 379.50.

STEP 2 The regular selling price, S, required to maintain the markup based on cost.

$$S = C + \text{Markup}$$
$$S = C + 45\% \text{ of } C$$
$$S = C + 0.45C$$
$$S = 1.45(19\,379.50)$$
$$S = \$28\,100.28$$

The regular selling price, S, is \$28 100.28.

STEP 3 The original marked price to allow a 10% discount.

Let the marked price be MP.

$$MP - 10\% \text{ of } MP = \text{Regular selling price}$$
$$MP - 0.1MP = 28\,100.28$$
$$0.9MP = 28\,100.28$$
$$MP = \frac{28\,100.28}{0.9} = \$31\,222.53$$

The marked price is \$31 222.53.

STEP 4 The sale markdown rate.

$$\text{Markdown} = \text{Marked price} - \text{Sale price}$$
$$= 31\,222.53 - 25\,995.00$$
$$= \$5\,227.53$$

$$\text{Markdown rate} = \frac{\text{Markdown}}{\text{Marked price}} = \frac{5227.53}{31\,222.53} = 16.74\%$$

The markdown is \$5227.53, which is 16.74% of the marked price.

EXAMPLE 5.5C

Big Sound Electronics purchased equipment from the manufacturer at a cost of \$960 less 30%, 15%. According to Big Sound's pricing strategy, all merchandise is marked at a price that allows an ongoing discount of 20% and maintains a profit of 15% of regular selling price. Overhead is 25% of regular selling price. During its annual Boxing Week sale, the usual discount of 20% was replaced by a markdown of 45% on selected models. What operating profit or loss was made during the Boxing Week sale?

SOLUTION

Step-by-step calculations needed: determine cost, regular selling price, marked price, sale price, then profit or loss.

STEP 1 The cost, C, (or purchase price) to the store.

$$\text{Cost} = \text{Manufacturer's list price} \times \text{NPF}$$
$$C = (960.00)(0.70)(0.85) = \$571.20$$

The cost, C, to the store is $571.20.

STEP 2 Let the regular selling price be S.

$$S = C + E + P$$
$$S = C + 25\% \text{ of } S + 15\% \text{ of } S$$
$$S = C + 0.25S + 0.15S$$
$$S = 571.20 + 0.40S$$
$$0.60S = 571.20$$
$$S = \frac{571.20}{0.6} = \$952.00$$

The regular selling price, S, is $952.00.

STEP 3 The original marked price to allow a 20% discount.
Let the marked price be MP.

$$MP - \text{Discount} = \text{Regular selling price}$$
$$MP - 20\% \text{ of } MP = 952.00$$
$$MP - 0.2MP = 952.00$$
$$0.8MP = 952.00$$
$$MP = \frac{952.00}{0.8} = \$1190.00$$

The marked price is $1190.00.

STEP 4 The Boxing Week sale price.

$$\begin{aligned}\text{Boxing Week sale price} &= \text{Marked price} - \text{Markdown}\\ &= 1190.00 - 45\% \text{ of } 1190.00\\ &= 1190.00 - 0.45(1190.00)\\ &= \$654.50\end{aligned}$$

The sale price is $654.50.

STEP 5 The profit or loss.

$$\begin{aligned}\text{Profit} &= \text{Sale price} - \text{Cost of buying} - \text{Expenses}\\ &= 654.50 - 571.20 - 0.25(952.00)\\ &= 654.50 - 809.20\\ &= (\$154.70)\end{aligned}$$

The merchandise was sold at an operating loss of $154.70.

EXAMPLE 5.5D

Magder's Furniture Emporium bought a dining room suite that must be regularly sold for $5250 to cover the cost, overhead expenses of 50% of the cost, and a normal net profit of 25% of the cost. The suite is marked at a price so that the store can allow a 20% discount and still receive the required regular selling price.

When the suite remained unsold, the store owner decided to mark the suite down for an inventory clearance sale. To arrive at the rate of markdown, the owner decided that the store's profit would have to be no less than 10% of the normal net profit and that part of the markdown would be covered by reducing the commission paid to the salesperson. The normal commission (which accounts for 40% of the overhead) was reduced by $33\frac{1}{3}\%$.

What is the maximum rate of markdown that can be advertised instead of the usual 20%?

The steps required: determine the cost, the normal and required net profits, the normal overhead expense, and the commissions. From these results, the inventory clearance price can be calculated. Determine the marked price and, using the inventory clearance price, calculate the amount of markdown from the marked price. Then calculate the rate of markdown.

SOLUTION

STEP 1 Determine the cost, C.

Let the regular selling price be S.

$$S = C + E + P$$
$$S = C + 50\% \text{ of } C + 25\% \text{ of } C$$
$$S = C + 0.5C + 0.25C$$
$$5250.00 = 1.75C$$
$$C = \frac{5250.00}{1.75} = \$3000.00$$

STEP 2 Determine the required profit.

$$\text{Normal net profit} = 25\% \text{ of cost}$$
$$= 0.25(3000.00)$$
$$= \$750.00$$
$$\text{Required net profit} = 10\% \text{ of normal net profit}$$
$$= 0.1(750.00)$$
$$= \$75.00$$

STEP 3 Determine the amount of overhead expense to be recovered.

$$\text{Normal overhead expense} = 50\% \text{ of cost}$$
$$= 0.5(3000.00)$$
$$= \$1500.00$$
$$\text{Normal commission} = 40\% \text{ of normal overhead expense}$$
$$= 0.4(1500.00)$$
$$= \$600.00$$
$$\text{Reduction in commission} = 33\tfrac{1}{3}\% \text{ of normal commission}$$
$$= 33\tfrac{1}{3}\%(600.00)$$
$$= \$200.00$$
$$\text{Overhead expense to be recovered} = 1500.00 - 200.00 = \$1300.00$$

STEP 4 Determine the inventory clearance price.

$$\text{Inventory clearance price} = \text{Cost} + \text{Overhead} + \text{Profit}$$
$$= 3000.00 + 1300.00 + 75.00$$
$$= \$4375.00$$

STEP 5 Determine the marked price, MP.

Let the marked price be \$MP.

$$\begin{aligned} \text{Marked price} - \text{Discount} &= \text{Regular selling price} \\ MP - 20\% \text{ of } MP &= 5250.00 \\ MP - 0.2MP &= 5250.00 \\ 0.8MP &= 5250.00 \\ MP &= \frac{5250.00}{0.8} = \$6562.50 \end{aligned}$$

STEP 6 Determine the amount of markdown.

$$\begin{aligned} \text{Markdown} &= \text{Marked price} - \text{Inventory clearance price} \\ &= 6562.50 - 4375.00 \\ &= \$2187.50 \end{aligned}$$

STEP 7 Determine the rate of markdown.

$$\begin{aligned} \text{Rate of markdown} &= \frac{\text{Amount of markdown}}{\text{Marked price}} \\ &= \frac{2187.50}{6562.50} \\ &= 0.\dot{3} \\ &= 33.\dot{3}\% \end{aligned}$$

Instead of the usual 20%, the store can advertise a markdown of $33.\dot{3}\%$.

EXERCISE 5.5

Answer each of the following questions.

1. A hand-held telephone set that cost a dealer \$240 less 55%, 25% is marked up 230% of cost. The dealer overhead expenses are 25% of the regular selling price. For a sales promotion, the telephone sets were reduced 40%.
   (a) What is the regular selling price?
   (b) What is the sale price?
   (c) At the sale price, what profit or loss was realized? Reference Example 5.5A

2. A gas barbecue cost a retailer \$420 less 33⅓%, 20%, 5%. It carries a regular selling price on its price tag at a markup of 60% of the regular selling price. During the end-of-season sale, the barbecue is marked down 45%.
   (a) What is the end-of-season sale price?
   (b) What rate of markup based on cost will be realized during the sale?

3. The Stereo Shop sold a radio regularly priced at \$125 for \$75. The cost of the radio was \$120 less 33⅓%, 15%. The store's overhead expense is 12% of the regular selling price.
   (a) What was the rate of markdown at which the radio was sold?
   (b) What was the operating profit or loss?
   (c) What rate of markup based on cost was realized?
   (d) What was the rate of markup based on the sale price?

4. An automatic dishwasher cost a dealer $620 less 37½%, 4%. It is regularly priced at $558. The dealer's overhead expense is 15% of the regular selling price and the dishwasher was cleared out for $432.45.
  (a) What was the rate of markdown at which the dishwasher was sold?
  (b) What is the regular markup based on selling price?
  (c) What was the operating profit or loss?
  (d) What rate of markup based on cost was realized?

5. A hardware store paid $33.45 for a set of cookware. Overhead expense is 15% of the regular selling price and profit is 10% of the regular selling price. During a clearance sale, the set was sold at a markdown of 15%. What was the operating profit or loss on the sale?

6. Aldo's Shoes bought a shipment of 200 pairs of women's shoes for $42 per pair. The store sold 120 pairs at the regular selling price of $125 per pair, 60 pairs at a clearance sale at a discount of 40%, and the remaining pairs during an inventory sale at a price that equals cost plus overhead (i.e., a break-even price). The store's overhead is 50% of cost.
  (a) What was the price at which the shoes were sold during the clearance sale?
  (b) What was the selling price during the inventory sale?
  (c) What was the total profit realized on the shipment?
  (d) What was the average rate of markup based on cost that was realized on the shipment?

Reference Example 5.5B

7. The Pottery bought 600 pans auctioned off for $4950. This means that each pan has the same cost. On inspection, the pans were classified as normal quality, seconds, or substandard. The 360 normal-quality pans were sold at a markup of 80% of cost, the 190 pans classified as seconds were sold at a markup of 20% of cost, and the remaining pans classified as substandard were sold at 20% below their cost.
  (a) What was the unit price at which each of the three classifications was sold?
  (b) If overhead is $33\frac{1}{3}$% of cost, what was the amount of profit realized on the purchase?
  (c) What was the average rate of markup based on the selling price at which the pans were sold?

8. A clothing store buys shorts for $24 less 40% for buying over 50 pairs, and less a further $16\frac{2}{3}$% for buying last season's style. The shorts are marked up to cover overhead expenses of 25% of cost and a profit of 33⅓% of cost.
  (a) What is the regular selling price of the shorts?
  (b) What is the maximum amount of markdown to break even?
  (c) What is the rate of markdown if the shorts are sold at the break-even price?

9. Furniture City bought chairs for $75 less 33⅓%, 20%, 10%. The store's overhead is 75% of cost and net profit is 25% of cost.
  (a) What is the regular selling price of the chairs?

(b) At what price can the chairs be put on sale so that the store incurs an operating loss of no more than 33⅓% of the overhead?

(c) What is the maximum rate of markdown at which the chairs can be offered for sale in part (b)?

10. Bargain City clothing store purchased raincoats for $36.75. The store requires a markup of 30% of the sale price. What regular selling price should be marked on the raincoats if the store wants to offer a 25% discount without reducing its markup?

11. A jewellery store paid $36.40 for a watch. Store expenses are 24% of regular selling price and the normal net profit is 20% of regular selling price. During a Special Bargain Day Sale, the watch was sold at a discount of 30%. What operating profit or loss was realized on the sale?

12. The Outdoor Shop buys tents for $264 less 25% for buying more than 20 tents. The store operates on a markup of 33⅓% of the sale price and advertises that all merchandise is sold at a discount of 20% of the regular selling price. What is the regular selling price of the tents?

13. Sky Sales Inc. purchased portable communication devices listed at $198 less 60%, 16⅚%. Expenses are 45% of the regular selling price and net profit is 25% of the regular selling price. According to the company's pricing strategy, the merchandise is marked with a price so that it could advertise a 37.5% discount while still maintaining its usual markup. During the annual inventory sale, the unsold equipment was marked down 55% of the marked price. What operating profit or loss was realized on the devices sold during the sale?

14. Lund's Pro Shop purchased sets of golf clubs for $500 less 40%, 16⅔%. Expenses are 20% of the regular selling price and the required profit is 17.5% of the regular selling price. The store decided to place a marked price on the clubs so that it could offer a 36% discount without affecting its margin. At the end of the season, the unsold sets were advertised at a discount of 54% of the new regular selling price. What operating profit or loss was realized on the sets sold at the end of the season?

15. Big Boy Appliances bought self-cleaning ovens for $900 less 33⅓%, 5%. Expenses are 15% of the regular selling price and profit is 9% of the regular selling price. For competitive reasons, the store marks all merchandise with a price so that a discount of 25% can be advertised without affecting the margin. To promote sales, the ovens were marked down 40%. What operating profit or loss did the store make on the ovens sold during the sales promotion?

16. Blue Lake Marina sells a make of cruiser for $16 800. This regular selling price covers overhead of 15% of cost and a normal net profit of 10% of cost. The cruisers were marked with a price so that the marina can offer a 20% discount while still maintaining its regular gross profit. At the end of the boating season, the cruiser was marked down. The marina made 25% of its usual profit and reduced the usual commission paid to the sales personnel by 33⅓%. The normal commission accounts for 50% of the normal overhead. What was the rate of markdown?

BUSINESS MATH NEWS BOX

lululemon athletica inc. Announces First Quarter Fiscal 2010 Results

lululemon athletica, a high-end retail chain dedicated to yoga and fitness apparel, has experienced record growth over the past five years, expanding from US$18 million in annual sales in 2003 to an estimated US$600 million in 2010, and tripling its profits in the first quarter 2010.

Founded and headquartered in Vancouver, British Columbia, in 1998 by Chip Wilson, lululemon manufactures and sells technical athletic wear aimed primarily at active men and women who are willing to pay premium prices for workout gear. These high prices have allowed the retailer to maintain a gross margin annually above 50% since 2003, topping at 53.8% in first quarter 2010.

Although the initial goal was to have only one store, lululemon athletica ended the first quarter of 2010 with 128 stores, compared with 114 a year ago. Stores are located mostly in major cities in Canada, the United States, and Australia, and in Hong Kong. lululemon's huge sales growth can be largely attributed to the company's store expansion.

However, to reach even more customers, lululemon launched a successful e-commerce operation on its company Website in 2009. After posting its best-ever first quarter, lululemon said that its priorities were to grow existing stores and to invest more in its thriving online division

The company offers regular-priced in-store products online. Admitting "we're not perfect," it also offers discounted men's and women's athletic wear under its "we made too much" clearance link.

The following items were recently discounted on the lululemon Website:
Women's Wunder Under Pant: $69.00 CAD (was $88.00)
Women's Get Started Jacket: $49 CAD (was $118.00)
Men's Cardio SS Tech Top: $24.00 CAD (was $58.00)
Men's Performance Jacket: $44.00 CAD (was $88.00)

Sources: lululemon athletic inc., "lululemon athletic inc. Announces First Quarter Financial 2010 Results," press release, **www.lululemon.com**, retrieved August 1, 2010; Hollie Shaw, "Lululemon Triples Profits as Sales Soar Past Estimates," *Times Colonist*, June 11, 2010.

QUESTIONS

1. lululemon athletic inc. reported that its net revenue for first quarter 2010 increased 69.3% from US$81.7 million in the first quarter of fiscal 2009. Calculate the net revenue for first quarter 2010 (rounded to the nearest hundred thousand dollars).
2. Revenue from the direct-to-consumer channel, including e-commerce and phone sales, reached US$9.1 million for first quarter 2010. Calculate direct-to-consumer revenue as a percentage of total revenue for the period.
3. Calculate the rate of discount for each of the four clearance items listed under the "we made too much" link.
4. Assuming lululemon's overhead is 30% of the regular selling price, and that the cost of the Women's Wonder Under Pant is $36, determine
   (a) the markup, the overhead, and the profit for this item sold at the regular selling price;
   (b) the markup, the overhead, and the profit for this item sold at the clearance price.

Go to MathXL at www.mathxl.com. You can practise many of this chapter's exercises as often as you want. The guided solutions help you find an answer step by step. You'll find a personalized study plan available to you too!

Review Exercise

1. A toolbox is listed for $56 less 25%, 20%, 5%.

(a) What is the net price of the toolbox?

(b) What is the amount of discount?

(c) What is the single rate of discount that was allowed?

2. Compute the rate of discount allowed on a lawnmower that lists for $168 and is sold for $105.

3. Determine the single rate of discount equivalent to the discount series 35%, 12%, 5%.

4. A 40% discount allowed on an article amounts to $1.44. What is the net price?

5. Baton Construction Supplies has been selling wheelbarrows for $112 less 15%. What additional discount percent must the company offer to meet a competitor's price of $80.92?

6. A freezer was sold during a clearance sale for $387.50. If the freezer was sold at a discount of 16⅔%, what was the list price?

7. The net price of a snow shovel is $20.40 after discounts of 20%, 15%. What is the list price?

8. On May 18, an invoice dated May 17 for $4000 less 20%, 15%, terms 5/10, n/30, was received by Aldo Distributors.

(a) What is the last day of the discount period?

(b) What is the amount due if the invoice is paid within the discount period?

9. Air Yukon received a shipment of plastic trays. The invoice amounting to $25 630 was dated August 15, terms 2/10, n/30. What is the last day for taking the cash discount and how much is to be paid if the discount is taken?

10. What amount must be remitted if the following invoices, all with terms 5/10, 2/30, n/60, are paid together on December 8?
Invoice No. 312 dated November 2 for $923.00
Invoice No. 429 dated November 14 for $784.00
Invoice No. 563 dated November 30 for $873.00

11. Delta Furnishings received an invoice dated June 21 for a shipment of goods. The invoice was for $8400.00 less 33⅓%, 12½% with terms 3/20, n/60. How much must Delta pay on July 9 to reduce its debt

(a) by $2000?

(b) to $2000?

12. The Peel Trading Company received an invoice dated September 20 for $16 000 less 25%, 20%, terms 5/10, 2/30, n/60. Peel made a payment on September 30 to reduce the debt to $5000 and a payment on October 20 to reduce the debt by $3000.

(a) What amount must Peel remit to pay the balance of the debt at the end of the credit period?

(b) What is the total amount paid by Peel?

13. Emco Ltd. received an invoice dated May 5 for $4000 less 15%, 7½%, terms 3/15, n/45. A cheque for $1595.65 was mailed by Emco on May 15 as part payment of the invoice.

(a) By how much did Emco reduce the amount due on the invoice?

(b) How much does Emco still owe?

14. Homeward Hardware buys cat litter for $6 less 20% per bag. The store's overhead is 45% of cost and the owner requires a profit of 20% of cost.

(a) For how much should the bags be sold?

(b) What is the amount of markup included in the selling price?

(c) What is the rate of markup based on selling price?

(d) What is the rate of markup based on cost?

(e) What is the break-even price?

(f) What operating profit or loss is made if a bag is sold for $6?

15. A retail store realizes a markup of $31.50 if it sells an article at a markup of 35% of the selling price.

(a) What is the regular selling price?

(b) What is the cost?

(c) What is the rate of markup based on cost?

(d) If overhead expense is 28% of cost, what is the total cost?

(e) If the article is sold at a markdown of 24%, what is the operating profit or loss?

16. Using a markup of 35% of cost, a store priced a book at $8.91.

(a) What was the cost of the book?

(b) What is the markup as a percent of selling price?

17. A bicycle helmet costing $54.25 was marked up to realize a markup of 30% of the regular selling price.

(a) What was the regular selling price?

(b) What was the markup as a percent of cost?

18. A bedroom suite that cost a dealer $1800 less 37.5%, 18% carries a price tag with a regular selling price at a markup of 120% of cost. For quick sale, the bedroom suite was marked down 40%.

(a) What was the sale price?

(b) What rate of markup based on cost was realized?

19. Gino's purchased men's suits for $195 less 33⅓%. The store operates at a normal markup of 35% of regular selling price. The owner marks all merchandise with prices so that the store can offer a 16⅔% discount while maintaining the same gross profit. What is the marked price?

20. An appliance store sold GE coffeemakers for $22.95 during a promotional sale. The store bought the coffeemakers for $36 less 40%, 15%. Overhead is 25% of the regular selling price.

(a) If the store's markup is 40% of the regular selling price, what was the rate of markdown?

(b) What operating profit or loss was made during the sale?

(c) What rate of markup based on cost was realized?

21. Billington's buys shirts for $21 less 25%, 20%. The shirts are priced at a regular selling price to cover expenses of 20% of regular selling price and a profit of 17% of regular selling price. For a special weekend sale, shirts were marked down 20%.

(a) What was the operating profit or loss on the shirts sold during the weekend sale?

(b) What rate of markup was realized based on cost?

22. A jewellery store paid a unit price of $250 less 40%, 16⅔%, 8% for a shipment of designer watches. The store's overhead is 65% of cost and the normal profit is 55% of cost.

(a) What is the regular selling price of the watches?

(b) What must the sale price be for the store to break even?

(c) What is the rate of markdown to sell the watches at the break-even price?

23. Sight and Sound bought large-screen colour TV sets for $1080.00 less 33⅓%, 8⅓%. Overhead is 18% of regular selling price and required profit is 15⅓% of regular selling price. The TV sets were marked at a price so that the store was able to advertise a discount of 25% while still maintaining its margin. To clear the inventory, the remaining TV sets were marked down 37½%.

(a) What operating profit or loss is realized at the clearance price?

(b) What is the realized rate of markup based on cost?

24. Ward Machinery lists a log splitter at $1860 less 33⅓%, 15%. To meet competition, Ward wants to reduce its net price to $922.25. What additional percent discount must Ward allow?

25. South Side Appliances bought bread makers for $180 less 40%, 16⅚%, 10%. The store's overhead is 45% of regular selling price and the profit required is 21¼% of the regular selling price. During a year-end inventory clearance sale, the store marked down the bread makers by 30%.

(a) What was the regular selling price?

(b) What is the sale price?

(c) What is the profit or loss during the clearance sale?

26. A merchant realizes a markup of $42 by selling an item at a markup of 37.5% of cost. The merchant's overhead expenses are 17.5% of the regular selling price. At a promotional sale, the item was reduced in price to $121.66.
   (a) What is the regular selling price?
   (b) What is the rate of markup based on the regular selling price?
   (c) What is the rate of markdown?
   (d) What is the profit or loss during the promotional sale?

27. The Knit Shoppe bought 250 sweaters for $3100; 50 sweaters were sold at a markup of 150% of cost and 120 sweaters at a markup of 75% of cost; 60 of the sweaters were sold during a clearance sale for $15 each; and the remaining sweaters were disposed of at 20% below cost. Assume all sweaters had the same cost.
   (a) What was the amount of markup realized on the purchase?
   (b) What was the percent markup realized based on cost?
   (c) What was the gross profit realized based on selling price?

Self-Test

1. Determine the net price of an article listed at $590 less 37.5%, 12.5%, 8⅓%.
2. What rate of discount has been allowed if an item that lists for $270 is sold for $168.75?
3. Compute the single discount percent equivalent to the discount series 40%, 10%, 8⅓%.
4. Discount Electronics lists an article for $1020 less 25% and 15%. A competitor carries the same article for $927 less 25%. What further discount (correct to the nearest 1/10 of 1%) must the competitor allow so that its net price is the same as Discount's?
5. What amount must be remitted if the following invoices, all with terms 4/10, 2/30, n/60, are paid on May 10?
   $850 less 20%, 10% dated March 21
   $960 less 30%, 16⅔% dated April 10
   $1040 less 33⅓%, 25%, 5% dated April 30
6. An invoice for $3200, dated March 20, terms 3/10, n/30, was received March 23. What payment must be made on March 29 to reduce the debt to $1200?
7. On January 15, Sheridan Service received an invoice dated January 31, terms 4/10, n/30, for $2592. On February 9, Sheridan Service mailed a cheque for $1392 in partial payment of the invoice. By how much did Sheridan Service reduce its debt?
8. What is the regular selling price of an item purchased for $1270 if the markup is 20% of the regular selling price?
9. The regular selling price of merchandise sold in a store includes a markup of 40% based on the regular selling price. During a sale, an item that cost the store $180 was marked down 20%. For how much was the item sold?

10. The net price of an article is $727.20 after discounts of 20% and 10% have been allowed. What was the list price?

11. An item that cost the dealer $350 less 35%, 12.5% carries a regular selling price on the tag at a markup of 150% of cost. For quick sale, the item was reduced 30%. What was the sale price?

12. Find the cost of an item sold for $1904 to realize a markup of 40% based on cost.

13. An article cost $900 and sold for $2520. What was the percent markup based on cost?

14. A markup of $90 is made on a sale. If the markup was 45% based on selling price, what was the cost?

15. An appliance shop reduces the price of an appliance for quick sale from $1560 to $1195. Compute the markdown correct to the nearest $\frac{1}{100}$ of 1%.

16. An invoice shows a net price of $552.44 after discounts of $33\frac{1}{3}$%, 20%, $8\frac{1}{3}$%. What was the list price?

17. A retailer buys an appliance for $1480 less 25%, 15%. The store prices the merchandise at a regular selling price to cover expenses of 40% of the regular selling price and a net profit of 10% of the regular selling price. During a clearance sale, the appliance was sold at a markdown of 45%. What was the operating profit or loss?

18. Discount Electronics buys stereos for $830 less 37.5%, 12.5%. Expenses are 20% of the regular selling price and the required profit is 15% of the regular selling price. All merchandise is marked with a price so that the store can advertise a discount of 30% while still maintaining its regular markup. During the annual clearance sale, the new regular selling price of unsold items is marked down 50%. What operating profit or loss does the store make on items sold during the sale?

Challenge Problems

1. Rose Bowl Florists buys and sells roses only by the complete dozen. The owner buys 12 dozen fresh roses daily for $117. He knows that 10% of the roses will wilt before they can be sold. What price per dozen must Rose Bowl Florists charge for its saleable roses to realize a 55% markup based on selling price?

2. A merchant bought some goods at a discount of 25% of the list price. She wants to mark them at a regular price so that she can give a discount of 20% of the marked price and still make a markup of 25% of the selling price.

(a) At what percent of the list price should she mark the regular selling price of the goods?

(b) Suppose the merchant decides she must make a markup of 25% of the cost price. At what percent of the regular selling price should she mark the price of the goods?

3. On April 13, a stereo store received a new sound system with a list price of $2500 from the manufacturer. The stereo store received a trade discount of 25%. The invoice, with terms 2/10, n/30, arrived on the same day as the sound system. The owner of the store marked up the sound system by 60% of the invoice amount (before cash discount) to cover overhead and profits. The owner paid the invoice on April 20. How much extra profit will be made on the sale, as a percent of the regular selling price, due to the early payment of the invoice?

CASE STUDY 5.1 Focusing on Prices

» Edward's Electronics is a small electronics store selling a variety of electronics equipment. It has a small but progressive camera department. Since Edward's does not sell very many cameras during the year, it only has a small number in stock. Edward's has just ordered six of the new digital cameras from Nikon. Edward's owner has been told that the cost of each camera will be $170, with terms 2/15, n/30. The manufacturer's suggested retail price (MSRP) of each camera is $400. Edward's owner calculates that the overhead is 15% of the MSRP and that the desired profit is 18% of the MSRP.

Zellers has a large camera shop in its store in the mall in the same town. It has ordered 70 of the same cameras from Nikon. Zellers has been offered both a cash discount and a quantity discount off the list price of $170. The cash discount is 3/20, n/45, while the quantity discount is 3.5%. Zellers estimates its overhead is 25% of the MSRP and it would like to make a profit of 35% of the MSRP.

QUESTIONS

1. What is the cost per camera (ignoring taxes) for Edward's Electronics and for Zellers?

2. For each store, what is the minimum selling price required to cover cost, overhead, and desired profits?

3. If Edward's and Zellers sell the camera at the MSRP, how much extra profit will each store make
   (a) in dollars?
   (b) as a percent of MSRP?

4. What rate of a markdown from MSRP can Edward's offer to cover its overhead and make its originally intended profit?

CASE STUDY 5.2 Putting a Price on Furniture

» Superior Sofa Company manufactures a variety of upscale sofas. Superior has found that there is confusion surrounding the term *list price*. For instance, there is the list price at which Superior offers its product to the furniture retailers. These retailers expect to receive a discount on this list price, because they pay their bills early, they order large quantities, or they offer a prestigious location for selling Superior's sofas. In addition, Superior also has a list price or manufacturer's suggested retail price (MSRP) at which it would like to see its product sold. Superior feels that this MSRP is a fair price in comparison with competing products and will provide a good return to both Superior Sofa and the retailer. Most retailers, of course, would like to advertise the list price (MSRP) less a discount, so that consumers will feel that they are getting a bargain. To resolve this problem, Superior has decided to offer its sofas to retail outlets at the MSRP and offer a larger trade discount.

Putting its new policy into practice, Superior has offered its newest sofa to Johnston's Furniture Store for a list price (MSRP) of $1400, less a trade discount of 35%. Johnston's will now advertise the sofa as $1400 less 15%.

QUESTIONS

1. For how much did Johnston's purchase the sofa?
2. What is Johnston's selling price?
3. If Johnston's sells at the price calculated in Question 2, what will be the rate of markup on the basis of cost?
4. Johnston's discovers that Becker Furniture, across town, is advertising a similar sofa for $1000. By what additional percent must Johnston's mark down its sofa to match this price?
5. If Johnston's marks down its sofa to match the Becker Furniture advertised price, what rate of markup on the basis of cost will Johnston's make?

SUMMARY OF FORMULAS

Formula 5.1A

$$\text{AMOUNT OF DISCOUNT} = \text{LIST PRICE} \times \text{RATE OF DISCOUNT}$$

Finding the amount of discount when the list price is known

Formula 5.1B

$$\text{LIST PRICE} = \frac{\text{AMOUNT OF DISCOUNT}}{\text{RATE OF DISCOUNT}}$$

Finding the list price when the amount of discount is known

Formula 5.1C

$$\text{RATE OF DISCOUNT} = \frac{\text{AMOUNT OF DISCOUNT}}{\text{LIST PRICE}}$$

Finding the rate of discount when the amount of discount is known

Formula 5.2

$$\text{NET PRICE} = \text{LIST PRICE} - \text{AMOUNT OF DISCOUNT}$$

Finding the net amount when the amount of discount is known

Formula 5.3A

$$\text{NET PRICE FACTOR (NPF)} = 100\% - \%\ \text{DISCOUNT}$$

Finding the net price factor (NPF)

Formula 5.3B

$$\text{NET PRICE FACTOR (NPF)} = (1 - d)$$

where d = rate of discount in decimal form

Restatement of Formula 5.3A in algebraic terms

Formula 5.4A

$$\text{NET PRICE} = \text{LIST PRICE} \times \text{NET PRICE FACTOR (NPF)}$$

Finding the net amount directly without computing the amount of discount

Formula 5.4B

$$\text{N} = \text{L}(1 - d)$$

Restatement of Formula 5.4A in algebraic terms

Formula 5.5A

$$\text{NET PRICE FACTOR (NPF) FOR THE DISCOUNT SERIES} = \text{NPF FOR THE FIRST DISCOUNT} \times \text{NPF FOR THE SECOND DISCOUNT} \times \ldots \times \text{NPF FOR THE LAST DISCOUNT}$$

Formula 5.5B

$$\text{NPF FOR A DISCOUNT SERIES} = (1 - d_1)(1 - d_2)(1 - d_3)\ldots(1 - d_n)$$

Restatement of Formula 5.5A in algebraic terms

Formula 5.6A

$$\text{NET PRICE} = \text{LIST PRICE} \times \text{NET PRICE FACTOR FOR THE DISCOUNT SERIES}$$

Finding the net amount directly when a list price is subject to a series of discounts

Formula 5.6B

$$\text{NET PRICE} = \text{L}(1 - d_1)(1 - d_2)(1 - d_3)\ldots(1 - d_n)$$

Restatement of Formula 5.6A in algebraic terms

Formula 5.7

SINGLE EQUIVALENT RATE OF DISCOUNT FOR A DISCOUNT SERIES

$$= 1 - \text{NPF FOR THE DISCOUNT SERIES}$$

$$= 1 - [(1 - d_1)(1 - d_2)(1 - d_3)\ldots(1 - d_n)]$$

Finding the single rate of discount that has the same effect as a given series of discounts

Formula 5.8A

$$\text{SELLING PRICE} = \text{COST OF BUYING} + \text{EXPENSES} + \text{PROFIT}$$

or

$$\text{S} = \text{C} + \text{E} + \text{P}$$

Basic relationship between selling price, cost of buying, operating expenses (or overhead), and profit

Formula 5.8B

$$\text{SELLING PRICE} - \text{COST} = \text{EXPENSES} + \text{PROFIT}$$

$$\text{S} - \text{C} = \text{E} + \text{P}$$

Basic relationship between selling price, cost of buying, operating expenses (or overhead), and profit

Formula 5.8C

$$\text{SELLING PRICE} = \text{COST OF BUYING} + \text{MARKUP}$$

or

$$S = C + M$$

Formula 5.9

$$\text{MARKUP} = \text{EXPENSES} + \text{PROFIT}$$

or

$$M = E + P$$

Basic relationship between markup, cost of buying, operating expenses (or overhead), and profit

Formula 5.10

$$\frac{\text{RATE OF MARKUP}}{\text{BASED ON COST}} = \frac{\text{MARKUP}}{\text{COST}} = \frac{M}{C}$$

Finding the rate of markup as a percent of cost

Formula 5.11

$$\text{RATE OF MARKUP BASED ON SELLING PRICE} = \frac{\text{MARKUP}}{\text{SELLING PRICE}} = \frac{M}{S}$$

Finding the rate of markup as a percent of selling price

GLOSSARY

Cash discount a reduction in the amount of an invoice, usually to encourage prompt payment of the invoice *(p. 186)*

Credit period the time period at the end of which an invoice has to be paid *(p. 186)*

Discount a reduction from the original price *(p. 180)*

Discount period the time period during which a cash discount applies *(p. 186)*

Discount series two or more discounts taken off a list price in succession *(p. 180)*

End-of-month dating (E.O.M.) payment terms based on the last day of the month in which the invoice is dated *(p. 187)*

Gross profit *see* **Markup**

List price price printed in a catalogue or in a list of prices *(p. 177)*

Manufacturer's suggested retail price (MSRP) catalogue or list price that is reduced by a trade discount *(p. 177)*

Margin *see* **Markup**

Markdown a reduction in the price of an article sold to the consumer *(p. 203)*

Markup the difference between the cost of merchandise and the selling price *(p. 195)*

Net factor *see* **Net price factor (NPF)**

Net price the difference between a list price and the amount of discount *(p. 178)*

Net price factor (NPF) the difference between 100% and a percent discount—the net price expressed as a fraction of the list price *(p. 179)*

Ordinary dating payment terms based on the date of an invoice *(p. 187)*

Partial payment part payment of an invoice *(p. 189)*

Payment terms a statement of the conditions under which a cash discount may be taken *(p. 186)*

Rate of discount a reduction in price expressed as a percent of the original price *(pp. 177, 186)*

Receipt-of-goods dating (R.O.G.) payment terms based on the date the merchandise is received *(p. 187)*

Regular selling price the price of an article sold to the consumer before any markdown is applied *(p. 203)*

Sale price the price of an article sold to the consumer after a markdown has been applied *(p. 203)*

Single equivalent rate of discount the single rate of discount that has the same effect as a specific series of discounts *(p. 182)*

Total cost the cost at which merchandise is purchased plus the overhead *(p. 203)*

Trade discount a reduction of a catalogue or list price *(p. 177)*

USEFUL INTERNET SITES

www.pwc.com

PricewaterhouseCoopers From the PricewaterhouseCoopers home page, click on "Industry Sectors," then "Consumer." This Website provides insight into markdown effectiveness, competitive strategy, and customer relationship management.

www.retailcouncil.org

Retail Council of Canada The Retail Council of Canada (RCC) Website offers discussion and learning opportunities on retail finance, operations, loss prevention, and marketing.

CHAPTER 7

Simple Interest

OBJECTIVES

Upon completing this chapter, you will be able to do the following:

1. Compute the amount of simple interest using the formula $I = Prt$.
2. Compute the principal, interest rate, or time using variations of the formula $I = Prt$.
3. Compute the maturity value (future value) using the formula $S = P(1 + rt)$.
4. Compute the principal (present value) using the formula $P = \frac{S}{1 + rt}$.
5. Compute equivalent or dated values for specified focal dates.

Every day in business, money is borrowed for short periods of time. Businesses lend money when they extend credit to customers or clients, or when they make short-term investments. Businesses borrow money when they purchase on credit from vendors, use a line of credit from a financial institution, or utilize credit cards to make a purchase. With these loans, interest must be considered.

INTRODUCTION

Transactions in business often involve the daily borrowing or lending of money. To compensate the lenders for the use of their money, interest is paid. The amount of interest paid is based on three factors: the amount of money borrowed, the rate of interest at which it is borrowed, and the time period for which it is borrowed.

7.1 FINDING THE AMOUNT OF SIMPLE INTEREST

A. Basic concepts and formula

Interest is the rent charged for the use of money. The amount of **simple interest** is determined by the relationship

Interest = Principal × Rate × Time

$$I = Prt$$ —— Formula 7.1A

where I is the amount of interest earned, measured in dollars and cents;
P is the principal sum of money earning the interest, measured in dollars and cents;
r is the simple annual (yearly or **nominal) rate** of interest, expressed as a percent, which can be converted into a decimal;
t is the **interest period** in years.

Simple interest is often used in business, through short-term loans to and from financial institutions, vendors, and customers.

POINTERS AND PITFALLS

To use the TI BAII Plus financial calculator to determine the number of days between two dates, choose the DATE worksheet by pressing 2nd DATE. The first date, DT1, is usually the earlier date. The date format can be set to show the U.S. format, mm/dd/yy, or the European format, dd/mm/yy. When the U.S. format is used, enter the date by choosing the one- or two-digit number representing the month, followed by a period, and then enter two digits for the day and the last two digits for the year. Only one period is entered, between the month and the day. Press Enter to save the data. To move to the next label, press the down arrow. The second date, DT2, is usually the later date. Enter the second date in the same manner as the first date, with one or two digits for the number of the month, a period, two digits for the day, and two digits for the year. Following the second date is the "days between dates" (DBD) calculation. Press the down arrow to access this part of the worksheet. To show the exact days, press CPT (Compute) to instruct the calculator to perform the calculation. When the first date precedes the second date, the days between dates will appear as a positive number. If the second date is entered as the earlier date, the days between dates will appear as a negative number. The fourth label within the worksheet sets the calculator to show the actual number of days between the dates indicated, including adjustments for leap years. Set this label to ACT by pressing 2nd SET.

For example, to determine the number of days between April 23, 2012, and July 21, 2012, press

2nd	DATE	DT1	04.2312	Enter	↓
		DT2	07.2112	Enter	↓
CPT		DBD			Result is 89

Note that the month is entered first, with one or two digits, followed by a period; the day is entered using two digits; and then the year is entered using two digits.

If only one of the dates and the desired days between the dates are entered, it is possible to determine the second date.

EXCEL NOTES If you choose, you can use Excel's Coupon Days, or days between dates (COUPDAYSNC) function, to find the number of days between two dates. Refer to COUPDAYSNC on MathXL to learn how.

You can also use Excel's Accrued Interest (ACCRINT) function to compute the amount of interest when the time is given in days. Refer to ACCRINT on MathXL to learn how.

B. Matching *r* and *t*

While the time may be stated in days, months, or years, the rate of interest is generally stated as a yearly charge, often followed by "per annum" or "p.a." In using the simple interest formula, it is imperative that the time t correspond to the interest rate r. Time expressed in months or days often needs to be converted into years. The number of days between two dates can be determined manually or by using the DATE function on a financial calculator. Manual techniques are outlined in a section on MathXL accompanying the text.

EXAMPLE 7.1A State r and t for each of the following:

(i) rate 6.5% p.a. (per annum); time 6 months;

(ii) rate 5.25% p.a.; time 243 days.

SOLUTION (i) The annual rate $r = 6.5\% = 0.065$

The time in years $t = \frac{6}{12} = 0.5$

Note: To convert months into years, divide by 12.

(ii) The annual rate $r = 5.25\% = 0.0525$

The time in years $t = \frac{243}{365} = 0.67$

Note: To convert days into years, divide by 365.

C. Computing the amount of interest

When the principal, rate, and time are known, the amount of interest can be determined by Formula 7.1A, where I = P*rt*.

EXAMPLE 7.1B

Compute the amount of interest for

(i) \$3600 at 6.25% p.a. (per annum) for 1 year;

(ii) \$5240 at 4.5% p.a. for 9 months;

(iii) \$1923.60 at 3% p.a. for 215 days.

SOLUTION

(i) $P = \$3600.00; \quad r = 6.25\% = 0.0625; \quad t = 1$

$I = Prt = (3600.00)(0.0625)(1) = \$225.00$

(ii) $P = \$5240.00; \quad r = 4.5\% = 0.045; \quad t = 9 \text{ months} = \frac{9}{12}$

$$I = Prt = (5240.00)(0.045)\left(\frac{9}{12}\right) = \$176.85$$

(iii) $P = \$1923.60; \quad r = 3\% = 0.03; \quad t = 215 \text{ days} = \frac{215}{365}$

$$I = Prt = (1923.60)(0.03)\left(\frac{215}{365}\right) = \$33.99$$

EXAMPLE 7.1C

Compute the amount of interest on \$785.95 borrowed at 8% p.a. from January 30, 2013, until March 21, 2013.

SOLUTION

Number of days = 50

$$P = \$785.95; \quad r = 8\% = 0.08; \quad t = \frac{50}{365}$$

$$I = (785.95)(0.08)\left(\frac{50}{365}\right) = \$8.61$$

EXAMPLE 7.1D

Compute the amount of interest on \$1240 earning 6% p.a. from September 30, 2012, to May 16, 2013.

SOLUTION

The starting date is September 30, 2012 (DT1). The ending date is May 16, 2013 (DT2).

Days between dates (DBD) = 228

$$P = \$1240.00; \quad r = 6\% = 0.06; \quad t = \frac{228}{365}$$

$$I = (1240.00)(0.06)\left(\frac{228}{365}\right) = \$46.47$$

EXERCISE 7.1

A. State r and t for each of the following:

1. rate is $3\frac{1}{2}\%$; time is 7 months
2. rate is $9\frac{3}{4}\%$; time is 11 months
3. rate is 8.25%; time is 183 days
4. rate is $5\frac{1}{2}\%$; time is 332 days

EXCEL SPREADSHEET

B. Compute the amount of interest for each of the following:

1. \$5000 at $9\frac{3}{4}\%$ for 10 months
2. \$645 at $6\frac{1}{4}\%$ for 4 months
3. \$1755 at 4.65% for 6 months
4. \$1651.43 at 4.9% for 9 months
5. \$980 at 11.5% for 244 days
6. \$1697.23 at 3.4% for 163 days
7. \$275 at 9.25% from November 30, 2012, to May 5, 2013
8. \$1090.60 at 7.8% from October 12, 2013, to April 24, 2014
9. \$424.23 at $8\frac{3}{4}\%$ from April 4, 2012, to November 4, 2012
10. \$1713.09 at 4.4% from August 30, 2013, to March 30, 2014
11. \$629.99 at 6.9% from June 16, 2012, to January 24, 2013
12. \$17 000 at 15.6% from November 12, 2012, to July 31, 2013

C.

1. On April 1, 2011, Faircloud Variety Company deposited \$24 000 into a savings account earning simple interest of 1.5%. Interest is paid to the account at the end of every calendar quarter. How much interest was paid to Faircloud's account on June 30, 2011?
2. On July 17, 2012, Leah deposited \$1500 into a savings account that earned simple interest of 1.05%. How much interest was earned and paid into Leah's account on December 1, 2012?
3. Kenneth borrowed \$8100 to buy a car. If interest was charged on the loan at 7.7%, how much interest would he have to pay in 90 days?
4. Lin Yan borrowed \$1800 from her parents to finance a vacation. If interest was charged on the loan at 5.2%, how much interest would she have to pay in 220 days?

7.2 FINDING THE PRINCIPAL, RATE, OR TIME

A. Formulas derived from the simple interest formula

The simple interest formula I = Prt contains the four variables I, P, r, and t. If any three of the four are given, the value of the unknown variable can be computed by substituting the known values in the formula or by solving for the unknown variable first and then substituting in the resulting derived formula.

The three derived formulas are

(i) To find the principal P,

$$P = \frac{I}{rt} \qquad \text{Formula 7.1B}$$

(ii) To find the rate of interest r,

$$r = \frac{I}{Pt} \qquad \text{Formula 7.1C}$$

(iii) To find the time period t,

$$t = \frac{I}{Pr} \qquad \text{Formula 7.1D}$$

Note:

(a) In Formula 7.1C, if the time period t is expressed in years, the value of r represents an annual rate of interest in decimal form.

(b) In Formula 7.1D, if the rate of interest r is an annual rate, the value of t represents years in decimal form.

POINTERS AND PITFALLS

This diagram is a useful aid in remembering the various forms of the simple interest formula I = Prt. Anything on the same line is multiplied together. Anything on different lines is divided.

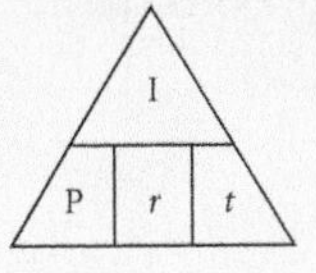

For example, in solving for P, note that I is above the r and t. Also note that r and t are on the same line.

Therefore, $P = \frac{I}{rt}$.

B. Finding the principal

When the amount of interest, the rate of interest, and the time period are known, the principal can be determined.

EXAMPLE 7.2A What principal will earn interest of $18.20 at 3.25% in 8 months?

SOLUTION

$I = 18.20; \quad r = 3.25\%; \quad t = \frac{8}{12}$

(i) Using the formula I = Prt,

$$18.20 = (P)(0.0325)\left(\frac{8}{12}\right) \qquad \text{by substitution}$$

$$18.20 = (P)(0.021\dot{6}) \quad \text{——— } (0.0325)\left(\frac{8}{12}\right)$$

$$P = \frac{18.20}{0.021\dot{6}} \quad \text{——— divide 18.20 by the coefficient of P}$$

$$= \$840.00$$

(ii) Using the derived formula $P = \frac{I}{rt}$,

$$P = \frac{18.20}{(0.0325)\left(\frac{8}{12}\right)} \quad \text{——— by substitution}$$

$$= \frac{18.20}{0.021\dot{6}} = \$840.00$$

EXAMPLE 7.2B

Determine the amount of money that must be invested for 245 days at 5.75% to earn $42.46.

SOLUTION

$I = 42.46$; $r = 5.75\% = 0.0575$; $t = \frac{245}{365}$

(i) Using the formula $I = Prt$,

$$42.46 = (P)(0.0575)\left(\frac{245}{365}\right)$$

$$42.46 = (P)(0.038596)$$

$$P = \frac{42.46}{0.038596} = \$1100.12$$

(ii) Using the derived formula $P = \frac{I}{rt}$,

$$P = \frac{42.46}{(0.0575)\left(\frac{245}{365}\right)} = \$1100.12$$

C. Finding the rate

When the amount of interest, the principal, and the time period are known, the rate of interest can be determined.

EXAMPLE 7.2C

Find the annual rate of interest required for $744 to earn $54.25 in 10 months.

SOLUTION

$I = 54.25$; $P = 744.00$; $t = \frac{10}{12}$

(i) Using the formula $I = Prt$,

$$54.25 = (744)(r)\left(\frac{10}{12}\right)$$

$$54.25 = (620)(r)$$

$$r = \frac{54.25}{620} = 0.0875 = 8.75\% \quad \text{——— convert to a percent}$$

(ii) Using the derived formula $r = \frac{I}{Pt}$,

$$r = \frac{54.25}{(744.00)\left(\frac{10}{12}\right)}$$

$$= \frac{54.25}{620} = 0.0875 = 8.75\%$$

D. Finding the time

When the amount of interest, the principal, and the rate of interest are known, the time period can be determined.

EXAMPLE 7.2D

Find the number of years required for $745 to earn $59.60 simple interest at 8% p.a.

SOLUTION

I = 59.60; P = 745.00; $r = 8\% = 0.08$

(i) Using the formula I = Prt,

$$59.60 = (745.00)(0.08)(t)$$
$$59.60 = (59.60)(t)$$
$$t = \frac{59.60}{59.60}$$
$$= 1 \text{ (year)}$$

(ii) Using the derived formula $t = \frac{I}{Pr}$,

$$t = \frac{59.60}{(745.00)(0.08)}$$
$$= 1 \text{ (year)}$$

Note: The value of t in the formula I = Prt will be in years. If the time period is to be stated in months or in days, it is necessary to multiply the initial value of t by 12 for months or 365 for days.

EXAMPLE 7.2E

Determine the number of months required for a deposit of $1320 to earn $16.50 interest at 3.75%.

SOLUTION

I = 16.50; P = 1320.00; $r = 3.75\% = 0.0375$

(i) Using the formula I = Prt,

$$16.50 = (1320.00)(0.0375)(t)$$
$$16.50 = (49.50)(t)$$
$$t = \frac{16.50}{49.50}$$
$$= 0.\dot{3} \text{ years}$$
$$= (0.\dot{3})(12) \text{ months}$$
$$= 4 \text{ months}$$

(ii) Using the derived formula $t = \dfrac{I}{Pr}$,

$$t = \frac{16.50}{(1320.00)(0.0375)} \text{ years}$$
$$= \frac{16.50}{49.50} \text{ years} = \frac{1}{3} \text{ years}$$
$$= \left(\frac{1}{3}\right)(12) \text{ months} = 4 \text{ months}$$

EXAMPLE 7.2F For how many days would a loan of $1500 be outstanding to earn interest of $36.16 at 5.5% p.a.?

SOLUTION $I = 36.16; \quad P = 1500.00; \quad r = 5.5\% = 0.055$

(i) Using the formula $I = Prt$,

$$36.16 = (1500.00)(0.055)(t)$$
$$36.16 = (82.50)(t)$$
$$t = \frac{36.16}{82.50}$$
$$= 0.4383\dot{0}\dot{3} \text{ years}$$
$$= (0.4383\dot{0}\dot{3})(365) \text{ days}$$
$$= 159.98\dot{0}\dot{6} \text{ days} = 160 \text{ days}$$

(ii) Using the derived formula $t = \dfrac{I}{Pr}$,

$$t = \frac{36.16}{(1500.00)(0.055)} \text{ years}$$
$$= \frac{36.16}{82.50} \text{ years}$$
$$= 0.4383\dot{0}\dot{3} \text{ years}$$
$$= (0.4383\dot{0}\dot{3})(365) \text{ days} = 159.98\dot{0}\dot{6} \text{ days}$$
$$= 160 \text{ days}$$

EXERCISE 7.2

EXCEL SPREADSHEET

 Determine the missing value for each of the following.

	Interest	Principal	Rate	Time
1.	$ 67.83	?	9.5%	7 months
2.	$106.25	?	4.25%	250 days
3.	$215.00	$2400.00	?	10 months
4.	$ 53.40	$ 750.00	?	315 days
5.	$ 36.17	$ 954.00	3.25%	? (months)
6.	$ 52.64	$1295.80	9.75%	? (months)
7.	$ 7.14	$ 344.75	5.25%	? (days)
8.	$ 68.96	$ 830.30	10.75%	? (days)

EXCEL SPREADSHEET

B. Find the value indicated for each of the following:

1. Find the principal that will earn $148.32 at 6.75% in eight months.
2. Determine the deposit that must be made to earn $39.27 in 225 days at 2.75%.
3. A loan of $880 can be repaid in 15 months by paying the principal sum borrowed plus $104.50 interest. What was the rate of interest charged?
4. Joan borrowed $650 and is to repay the balance plus interest of $23.70 in seven months. What was the rate of interest charged?
5. At what rate of interest will $1387 earn $63.84 in 200 days?
6. A deposit of $2400 will earn $22.74 in 91 days at what rate of interest?
7. In how many months will $1290 earn $100.51 interest at $8\frac{1}{2}$%?
8. Interest of $20.95 is earned at 3.15% on a deposit of $2660 in how many months?
9. Determine the number of days it will take $564 to earn $15.09 at $7\frac{3}{4}$%.
10. How many days will it take $1200 to earn $12.22 interest at 16.9%?
11. What principal will earn $39.96 from June 18, 2012, to December 15, 2012, at 9.25%?
12. What rate of interest is required for $740.48 to earn $42.49 interest from September 10, 2013, to March 4, 2014?
13. Philip wants to supplement his pension by $2000 per month with income from his investments. His investments pay him monthly and earn 6% p.a. What value of investments must Philip have in his portfolio to generate enough interest to give him his desired income?
14. Bunny's Antiques received $88.47 interest on a 120-day term deposit of $7800. At what rate of interest was the term deposit invested?
15. Anne's Dress Shop borrowed $3200 to buy material. The loan was paid off seven months later by a lump-sum payment that included $168 of interest. What was the simple rate of interest at which the money was borrowed?
16. Mac's credit card statement included $360 in cash advances and $3.20 in interest charges. The interest rate on the statement was 13.5%. For how many days was Mac charged interest?
17. Bill filed his income tax return with the Canada Revenue Agency (CRA) after the April 30 deadline. He calculated that he owed the CRA $3448, but did not include a payment for this amount when he sent in his tax return. The CRA's Notice of Assessment indicated agreement with Bill's tax calculation. It also showed that the balance due was $3827.66, which included a 10% late-filing penalty and interest at 9% p.a. For how many days was Bill charged interest?
18. On August 15, 2013, Low Rider Automotive established a line of credit at its bank, with interest at 8.75% p.a. This line of credit was used to purchase

$5000 of inventory and supplies. Low Rider paid $5113.87 to satisfy the incurred debt. On what date did Low Rider Automotive honour the line of credit?

7.3 COMPUTING FUTURE VALUE (MATURITY VALUE)

A. Basic concept

When you borrow money, you are obligated to repay, at some point in the future, both the sum borrowed (the principal) and any interest due. Therefore, the **future value of a sum of money** (or **maturity value**) is the value obtained by adding the original principal and the interest due.

FUTURE VALUE (OR MATURITY VALUE) = PRINCIPAL + INTEREST
$$S = P + I$$
Formula 7.2

EXAMPLE 7.3A

Determine the future value (maturity value), principal, or interest as indicated.

(i) The principal is $2200 and the interest is $240. Find the future value (maturity value).

SOLUTION

$P = 2200.00; \quad I = 240.00$

$$\begin{aligned} S &= P + I \\ &= 2200.00 + 240.00 \\ &= \$2440.00 \end{aligned}$$

The future value is $2440.

(ii) The principal is $850 and the future value (maturity value) is $920. Compute the amount of interest.

SOLUTION

$P = 850.00; \quad S = 920.00$

$$\begin{aligned} S &= P + I \\ I &= S - P \\ I &= 920.00 - 850.00 \\ I &= \$70.00 \end{aligned}$$

The amount of interest is $70.

(iii) The future value (maturity value) is $430 and the interest is $40. Compute the principal.

SOLUTION

$S = 430.00; \quad I = 40.00$

$$\begin{aligned} S &= P + I \\ P &= S - I \\ P &= 430.00 - 40.00 \\ P &= \$390.00 \end{aligned}$$

The principal is $390.

B. The future value formula $S = P(1 + rt)$

To obtain the future value (maturity value) formula for simple interest, the formulas $I = Prt$ and $S = P + I$ are combined.

$S = P + I$

$S = P + Prt$ ——— substitute Prt for I

$S = P(1 + rt)$ ——— take out the common factor P

$$\boxed{S = P(1 + rt)}$$ ——— Formula 7.3A

EXAMPLE 7.3B

Find the future value (maturity value) of an investment of $720 earning 4% p.a. for 146 days.

SOLUTION

$P = 720.00; \quad r = 4\% = 0.04; \quad t = \frac{146}{365}$

$$\begin{aligned} S &= P(1 + rt) \\ &= (720.00)\left[1 + (0.04)\left(\frac{146}{365}\right)\right] \\ &= (720.00)\ (1 + 0.016) \\ &= (720.00)\ (1.016) \\ &= \$731.52 \end{aligned}$$

The future value of the investment is $731.52.

EXAMPLE 7.3C

Find the maturity value of a deposit of $1250 invested at 2.75% p.a. from October 15, 2012, to May 1, 2013.

SOLUTION

The time period in days = 198

$P = 1250.00; \quad r = 2.75\% = 0.0275; \quad t = \frac{198}{365}$

$$\begin{aligned} S &= P(1 + rt) \\ &= (1250.00)\left[1 + (0.0275)\left(\frac{198}{365}\right)\right] \\ &= (1250.00)\ (1 + 0.014918) \\ &= (1250.00)\ (1.014918) \\ &= \$1268.65 \end{aligned}$$

The maturity value of the deposit is $1268.65.

EXERCISE 7.3

Use the future value (maturity value) formula to answer each of the following.

1. Find the future value of \$480 at 3½% for 220 days.
2. Find the future value of \$1100 invested at 6.75% for 360 days.
3. EXCEL SPREADSHEET Find the maturity value of \$732 invested at 9.8% from May 20, 2013, to November 23, 2013.
4. EXCEL SPREADSHEET Find the maturity value of \$775 invested at 6.25% from March 1, 2012, to October 20, 2012.
5. Compute the future value of \$820 over nine months at 4¾%.
6. Compute the future value of \$570 over seven months at 5½%.

1. Paul invested \$2500 in a 180-day term deposit at 3.45% p.a. What is the maturity value of the deposit?
2. Suzette invested \$800 in a 210-day term deposit at 2.75% p.a. What is the maturity value of the deposit?
3. EXCEL SPREADSHEET On September 30, 2012, Red Flag Inn invested \$26 750 in a short-term investment of 215 days. An investment of this length earns 1.3% p.a. How much will the investment be worth at maturity?
4. Speedy Courier invested \$13 500 in a 270-day term deposit. What is the maturity value if the rate of interest is 3.65%?
5. Mishu wants to invest an inheritance of \$50 000 for one year. His credit union offers 3.95% for a one-year term or 3.85% for a six-month term.
   (a) How much will Mishu receive after one year if he invests at the one-year rate?
   (b) How much will Mishu receive after one year if he invested for six months at a time at 3.85% each time?
   (c) What would the one-year rate have to be to yield the same amount of interest as the investment described in part (b)?
6. Prairie Grains Cooperative wants to invest \$45 000 in a short-term deposit. The bank offers 1.3% interest for a one-year term and 1.1% for a six-month term.
   (a) How much would Prairie Grains receive if the \$45 000 is invested for one year?
   (b) How much would Prairie Grains receive at the end of one year if the \$45 000 is invested for six months and then the principal and interest earned is reinvested for another six months?
   (c) What would the one-year rate have to be to yield the same amount of interest as the investment described in part (b)?

7.4 FINDING THE PRINCIPAL (PRESENT VALUE)

A. Finding the principal when the maturity value (future value) is known

When the maturity value, the rate, and the time are given, calculation of the principal utilizes the formula $S = P(1 + rt)$.

When interest is paid for the use of money, the value of any sum of money subject to interest changes with time. This change is called the **time value of money**. The **present value** of an amount at any given time is the principal needed to grow to that amount at a given rate of interest over a given period of time.

Since the problem of finding the present value is equivalent to finding the principal when the future value, rate, and time are given, the future value formula $S = P(1 + rt)$ applies. However, because the problem of finding the present value of an amount is one of the frequently recurring problems in financial analysis, it is useful to solve the future value formula for P to obtain the present value formula.

$$S = P(1 + rt)$$ ——— starting with the future value formula

$$\frac{S}{(1 + rt)} = \frac{P(1 + rt)}{(1 + rt)}$$ ——— divide both sides by $(1 + rt)$

$$\frac{S}{(1 + rt)} = P$$ ——— reduce the fraction $\frac{(1 + rt)}{(1 + rt)}$ to 1

This is the present value formula for simple interest.

$$\boxed{P = \frac{S}{(1 + rt)}}$$ ——— Formula 7.3B

EXAMPLE 7.4A Compute the value of an investment eight months before the maturity date that earns interest at 6% p.a. and has a maturity value of \$884 (see Figure 7.1).

FIGURE 7.1 Time Graph for Example 7.4A

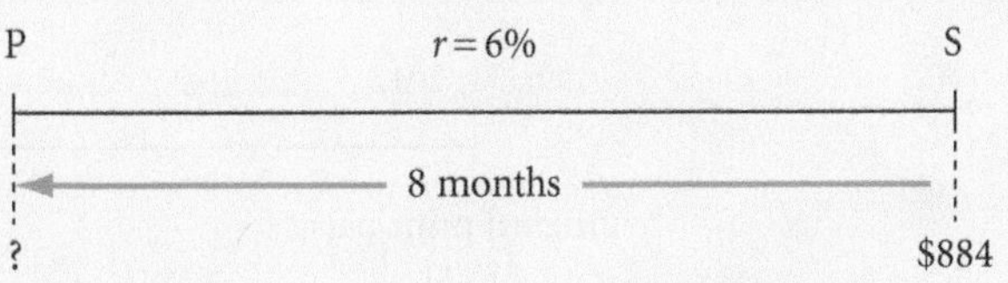

SOLUTION

$S = 884.00; \quad r = 6\% = 0.06; \quad t = \frac{8}{12}$

$$P = \frac{S}{(1 + rt)}$$ ——— use the present value formula when S is known

$$P = \frac{884.00}{1 + (0.06)\left(\frac{8}{12}\right)}$$ ——— using Formula 7.3B

$$P = \frac{884.00}{1.04}$$

$$= \$850.00$$

The present value of the investment is $850.00

EXAMPLE 7.4B

What sum of money must be invested on January 31, 2012, to amount to $7500 on August 18, 2012, at 5% p.a.?

SOLUTION

Since 2012 is a leap year, the time period in days = 200.

$$P = \frac{S}{(1 + rt)}$$ ——— use the present value formula when S is known

$S = 7500.00; \quad r = 5\% = 0.05; \quad t = \frac{200}{365}$

$$P = \frac{7500.00}{1 + (0.05)\left(\frac{200}{365}\right)}$$

$$P = \frac{7500.00}{1.027397}$$

$$= \$7300.00$$

On January 31, 2012, the sum of $7300.00 should be invested.

To illustrate the concept of the time value of money, Example 7.4B is represented on the time graph shown in Figure 7.2.

FIGURE 7.2 Time Graph for Example 7.4B

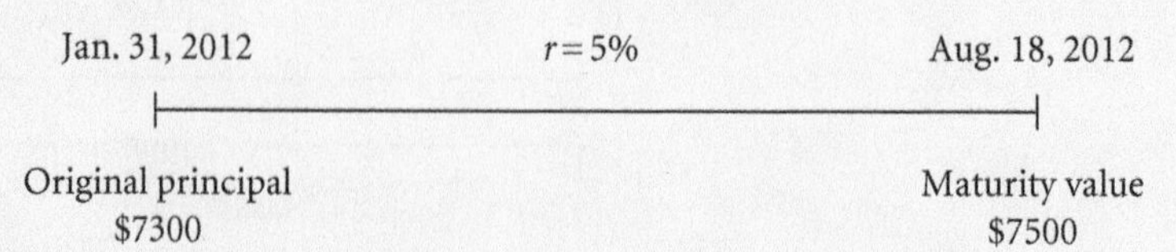

The original principal of \$7300 will grow to \$7500 at 5% in 200 days. Interest of \$200 will be earned in those 200 days, indicating that the original principal will grow by \$1 each day. The value of the investment changes day by day. On January 31, 2012, the \$7300 principal is known as the present value of the August 18, 2012, \$7500.

EXERCISE 7.4

Find the principal and the missing value in each of the following.

	Present Value (Principal)	Interest Amount	Future Value (Maturity Value)	Interest Rate	Time
1.	?	?	\$ 279.30	4%	15 months
2.	?	\$117.30	\$ 729.30	?	20 months
3.	?	\$ 29.67	?	8.6%	8 months
4.	?	\$ 27.11	?	9.5%	240 days
5.	?	\$ 84.24	\$2109.24	5.2%	?
6.	?	?	\$1035.38	7.5%	275 days

Solve each of the following.

1. What principal will have a future value of \$1241.86 at 3.9% in five months?
2. What amount of money will accumulate to \$480.57 in 93 days at 4.6%?
3. Determine the present value of a debt of \$1760 due in four months if interest at $9\frac{3}{4}\%$ is allowed.
4. Compute the present value of a debt of \$708.13 eighty days before it is due if money is worth 5.3%.
5. Compute the amount of money that, deposited in an account on April 1, 2013, will grow to \$657.58 by September 10, 2013, at 4.75% p.a.
6. The annual Deerfield Golf Club membership fees of \$1750 are due on March 1, 2012. Club management offers a reduction of membership fees of 18.9% p.a. to members who pay the dues by September 1, 2011. How much must a member pay on September 1 if she chooses to take advantage of the club management's offer?
7. You are the accountant for Peel Credit Union. The lawyer for a member has sent a cheque for \$7345.64 in full settlement of the member's loan balance including interest at 6.25% for 11 months. How much of the payment is interest?
8. On March 15, 2012, Ben bought a government-guaranteed short-term investment maturing on September 12, 2012. How much did Ben pay

for the investment if he will receive $10 000 on September 12, 2012, and interest is 2.06%?

9. On October 29, 2013, Toddlers' Toys borrowed money with a promise to pay $23 520.18 on March 5, 2014. This loan included interest at 6.5%. How much money did Toddlers' Toys borrow on October 29?

10. On May 28, 2012, Ling purchased a government-guaranteed short-term investment maturing on August 4, 2012. How much did Ling pay for the investment if $10 000 will be received on August 4, 2012, and interest is 1.35% p.a.?

BUSINESS MATH NEWS BOX

Save for Your Dream

The Canada Savings Bonds Payroll Savings Program is an easy and effortless way to save for your dreams. You can do this by following three "rules." The first "rule" is to pay yourself first. The Payroll Savings Program allows your employer to deduct weekly, bi-weekly, or monthly amounts specified by you and transfer the amounts into an account set up by the Bank of Canada. These funds are then used to purchase Canada Savings Bonds. Once you have signed up, you are eligible once a year, at campaign time, to increase your bond purchase or start a new plan with a new application. In addition, after the first three months you can redeem all or part of your savings at any time and have the money deposited into your bank account or sent to you as a cheque.

The second "rule" is to start right away. The minimum purchase amounts for each regular payroll deduction are as follows: $2 if you are paid once a week, $4 if you are paid every two weeks, and $8 if you are paid once a month. Regardless of how often you are paid, the maximum purchase amount for each regular payroll deduction is $9999.00.

The third "rule" is to stick with your plan. Redeem your Canada Savings Bonds only if you must.

QUESTIONS

1. Patricia and Louie have dreamed of a European vacation for years at a cost between $10 000 and $12 000. They plan to leave on April 4, 2011, for a month of backpacking. They decided that the Canada Savings Bonds Payroll Savings Program was the most convenient and painless way of saving for the vacation. Both of their employers offer the program, so Patricia and Louie signed up for deductions starting on April 1, 2010, at $500 and $550 respectively, to be deposited at the beginning of each month. The April 2010, Canada Savings Bonds pay 0.40% simple interest for the first year, calculated on the highest balance for each month. How much can they save toward their vacation if they both redeem their saving bonds on March 31, 2011?

2. Alex is just out of school and has started working. He is looking forward to buying his first car. Although Canada Savings Bonds are offering low rates, Alex is looking for a disciplined approach and security to achieve his financial goal. At current rates, how much could Alex save toward a down payment in one year if he saves $100 per month through the Canada Savings Bonds Payroll Savings Program?

3. Twenty years ago, Canada Savings Bonds earned 7.5% annually. If that rate existed today, how much more interest would Alex earn in his 12th month by following the same steps?

Sources: Canada Savings Bond Program Information site, **csb.gc.ca/payroll-savings-program/employees/** and **csb.gc.ca/about/rates/**, accessed August 25, 2010.

7.5 COMPUTING EQUIVALENT VALUES

A. Dated values

If an amount of money is subject to a rate of interest, it will grow over time. Thus, the value of the amount of money changes with time. This change is known as the time value of money. For example, if you invested \$1000 today at 4% p.a. simple interest, your investment has a value of \$1000 today, \$1010 in three months, \$1020 in six months, and \$1040 in one year.

The value of the original amount at any particular time is a **dated value**, or **equivalent value**, of that amount. The dated value combines the original sum with the interest earned up to the dated value date. Each dated value at a different time is equivalent to the original amount of money. The table below shows four dated values for \$1000 invested at 4% p.a. The longer the time is from today, the greater is the dated value. This is so because interest has been earned on the principal over a longer time period.

Time	Dated Value
Today	\$1000.00
3 months from today	\$1010.00
6 months from today	\$1020.00
1 year from today	\$1040.00

Timberwest Company owes Abco Inc. \$500 and payment is due today. Timberwest asks for an extension of four months to pay off the obligation. How much should they expect to pay in four months' time if money is worth 6%?

Since Abco could invest the \$500 at 6% p.a., Timberwest should be prepared to pay the dated value. This dated value includes interest for the additional four-month time period. It represents the amount to which the \$500 will grow in four months (the future value) and is found using Formula 7.3A.

$$S = P(1 + rt)$$

$$= 500.00\left[1 + (0.06)\left(\frac{4}{12}\right)\right]$$

$$= 500.00\ (1 + 0.02)$$

$$= \$510.00$$

In addition, Red Rock Construction owes Abco Inc. \$824, due to be paid six months from now. Suppose Red Rock Construction offers to pay the debt today. How much should Red Rock Construction pay Abco Inc. if money is worth 6%?

Since Abco Inc. could invest the payment at 6%, the payment should be the sum of money that will grow to \$824 in six months earning 6% p.a. interest. By definition, this amount of money is the present value of the \$824. The present value represents today's dated value of the \$824 and is found using Formula 7.3B.

$$\begin{aligned} P &= \frac{S}{1 + rt} \\ &= \frac{824.00}{1 + (0.06)\left(\frac{6}{12}\right)} \\ &= \frac{824.00}{1 + 0.03} \\ &= \$800.00 \end{aligned}$$

Because of the time value of money, sums of money given at different times are not directly comparable. For example, imagine you are given a choice between \$2000 today and \$2200 one year from now. It does not automatically follow, from the point of view of investing money, that either the larger amount of money or the chronologically earlier amount of money is preferable.

To make a rational choice, we must allow for the rate of interest money can earn and choose a comparison date or **focal date** to obtain the dated values of the amounts of money at a specific time.

Equivalent values on the same date are directly comparable and may be obtained for simple interest by using either the maturity value (future value) formula, Formula 7.3A, $S = P(1 + rt)$, or the present value formula, Formula 7.3B, $P = \frac{S}{1 + rt}$.

B. Choosing the appropriate formula

The choice of which formula to use for computing dated values depends on the due date of the sum of money relative to the selected focal (or comparison) date.

(a) If the due date falls before the focal date, use the future value (maturity value) formula.

FIGURE 7.3 **When to Use the Future Value (or Maturity Value) Formula**

Due date		Focal date
\$1000		?
(Known amount)	————→	(Find S)
	Use $S = P(1 + rt)$	

Explanation of Figure 7.3: We are looking for a future value relative to the given value. This future value will be higher than the known value by the interest that accumulates on the known value from the due date to the focal date. Because this is a future value problem (note that the arrow points to the right), the future value (or maturity value) formula $S = P(1 + rt)$ applies.

(b) If the due date falls after the focal date, use the present value formula.

FIGURE 7.4 **When to Use the Present Value Formula**

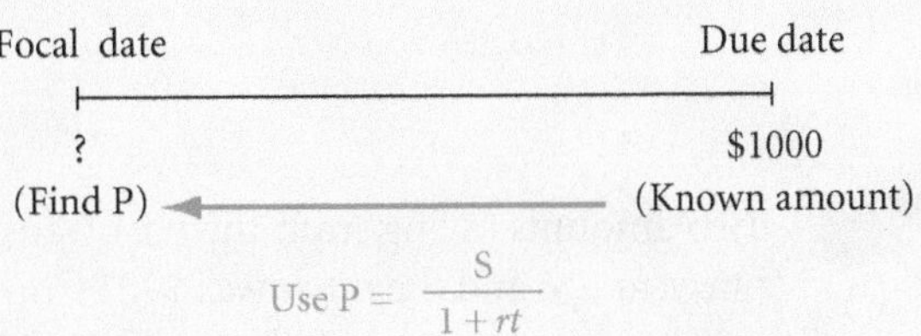

Explanation of Figure 7.4: We are looking for an earlier value relative to the given value. This earlier value will be less than the given value by the interest that would accumulate on the unknown earlier value from the focal date to the due date. We are, in fact, looking for the principal that will grow to the given value. Because this is a present value problem (note that the arrow points to the left), the present value formula $P = \frac{S}{1 + rt}$ is appropriate.

C. Finding the equivalent single payment

EXAMPLE 7.5A A debt can be paid off by payments of $872 one year from now and $1180 two years from now. Determine the single payment now that would fully repay the debt. Allow for simple interest at 9% p.a.

SOLUTION See Figure 7.5 for the graphic representation of the dated values. Refer to Figures 7.3 and 7.4 to determine which formula is appropriate.

FIGURE 7.5 **Graphical Representation of the Dated Values**

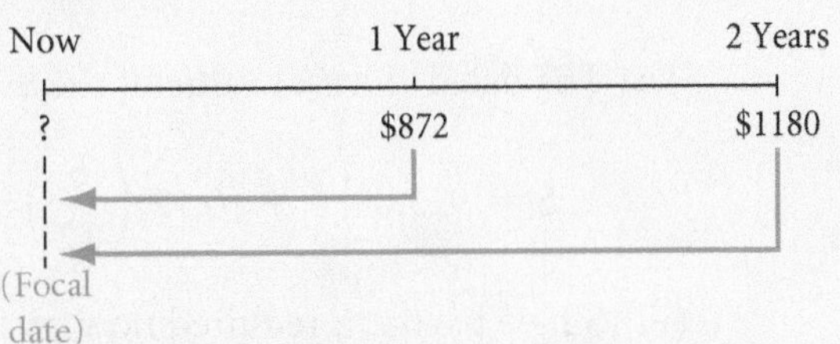

Since the focal date is *earlier* relative to the dates for the given sums of money (the arrows point to the left), the present value formula $P = \frac{S}{1 + rt}$ is appropriate.

(i) The dated (present) value of the $872.00 at the focal date:

$$P = \frac{872.00}{1 + (0.09)(1)} = \frac{872.00}{1.09} = \$800.00$$

(ii) The dated (present) value of the \$1180.00 at the focal date:

$$P = \frac{1180.00}{1 + (0.09)(2)} = \frac{1180.00}{1.18} = \$1000.00$$

(iii) Single payment required now = 800.00 + 1000.00 = \$1800.00

EXAMPLE 7.5B

Two amounts owing from the past were to be paid today. One debt was \$620 from one year ago and the other was \$925 from six months ago. Determine the single payment today that would fully repay the debts. Allow for simple interest at 12% p.a.

SOLUTION

See Figure 7.6 for the graphical representation of the dated values. Refer to Figures 7.3 and 7.4 to determine which formula is appropriate.

FIGURE 7.6 Graphical Representation of the Dated Values

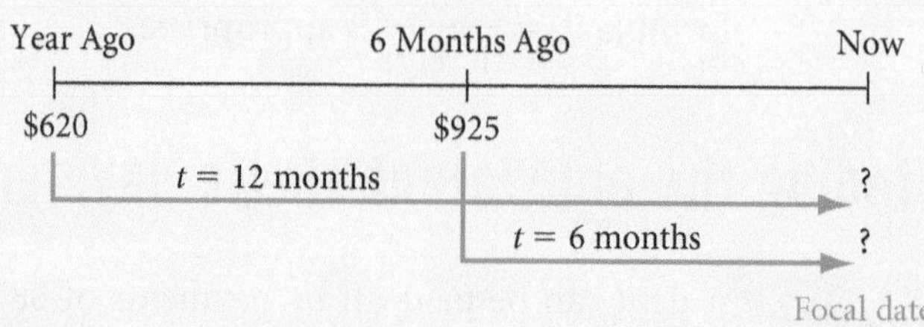

Since the focal date is *future* relative to the dates for the given sums of money (the arrows point to the right), the future value formula $S = P(1 + rt)$ is appropriate.

(i) The dated (future) value of the \$620 at the focal date:

$$S = 620.00\left[1 + (0.12)(1)\right] = \$694.40$$

(ii) The dated (future) value of the \$925 at the focal date:

$$S = 925.00\left[1 + (0.12)\left(\frac{6}{12}\right)\right] = \$980.50$$

(iii) Single payment required now = 694.40 + 980.50 = \$1674.90

EXAMPLE 7.5C

You are owed payments of \$400 due today, \$500 due in five months, and \$618 due in one year. You have been approached to accept a single payment nine months from now with interest allowed at 12% p.a. How much will the single payment be? (See Figure 7.7.)

SOLUTION

FIGURE 7.7 Graphical Representation of the Dated Values

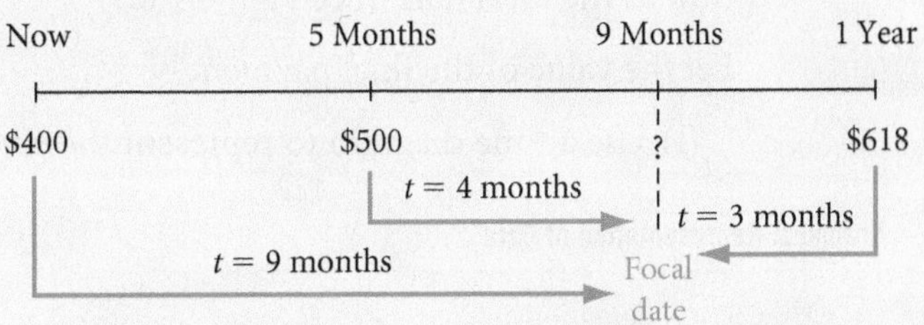

Since the focal date is in the *future* relative to the $400 now and the $500 five months from now (the arrows point to the right), the future value formula $S = P(1 + rt)$ is appropriate for these two amounts. However, since the focal date is *earlier* relative to the $618 one year from now (the arrow points to the left), the present value formula $P = \frac{S}{1 + rt}$ is appropriate for this amount.

(i) The dated (future) value of $400 at the focal date:

$$P = 400.00; \quad r = 12\% = 0.12; \quad t = \frac{9}{12}$$

$$S = 400\left[1 + (0.12)\left(\frac{9}{12}\right)\right] = 400(1 + 0.09) = 400(1.09) = \$436.00$$

(ii) The dated (future) value of $500 at the focal date:

$$P = 500.00; \quad r = 12\% = 0.12; \quad t = \frac{4}{12}$$

$$S = 500\left[1 + (0.12)\left(\frac{4}{12}\right)\right] = 500(1 + 0.04) = 500(1.04) = \$520.00$$

(iii) The dated (present) value of $618 at the focal date:

$$S = 618.00; \quad r = 12\% = 0.12; \quad t = \frac{3}{12}$$

$$P = \frac{618.00}{1 + (0.12)\left(\frac{3}{12}\right)}$$

$$= \frac{618.00}{1 + 0.03}$$

$$= \frac{618.00}{1.03} = \$600.00$$

(iv) The single payment to be made nine months from now will be = 436.00 + 520.00 + 600.00 = $1556.00.

EXAMPLE 7.5D Scheduled payments of \$400 due now and \$700 due in five months are to be settled by a payment of \$500 in three months and a final payment in eight months. Determine the amount of the final payment at 6% p.a., using eight months from now as the focal date. (See Figure 7.8.)

SOLUTION Let the value of the final payment be \$x.

(i) Use a time diagram to represent the given data.

FIGURE 7.8 Graphical Representation of Data

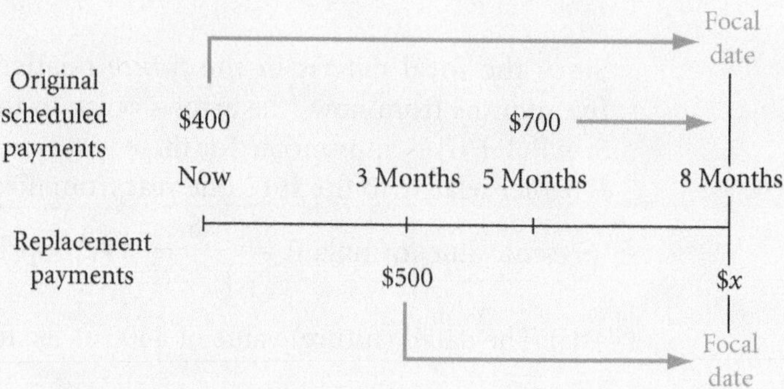

(ii) Dated value of the original scheduled payments:

(a) The value at the focal date of the \$400 payment due eight months before the focal date is found by using the future value formula.

$$S = 400\left[1 + (0.06)\left(\frac{8}{12}\right)\right] = 400(1 + 0.04) = 400(1.04) = \$416.00$$

(b) The value at the focal date of the \$700 payment due three months before the focal date is found by using the future value formula.

$$S = 700\left[1 + (0.06)\left(\frac{3}{12}\right)\right]$$

$$= 700(1 + 0.015)$$

$$= 700(1.015)$$

$$= \$710.50$$

(iii) Dated value of the replacement payments:

(a) The value at the focal date of the \$500 payment made five months before the focal date is found by using the future value formula.

$$S = 500\left[1 + (0.06)\left(\frac{5}{12}\right)\right]$$

$$= 500(1 + 0.025)$$

$$= 500(1.025)$$

$$= \$512.50$$

(b) The value at the focal date of the final payment is $x (no adjustment for interest is necessary for an amount of money located at the focal date).

(iv) The **equation of values** at the focal date is now set up by matching the dated values of the original debts to the dated values of the replacement payments.

THE SUM OF THE DATED VALUES OF THE REPLACEMENT PAYMENTS = THE SUM OF THE DATED VALUES OF THE ORIGINAL SCHEDULED PAYMENTS

$$500\left[1 + (0.06)\left(\frac{5}{12}\right)\right] + x = 400\left[1 + (0.06)\left(\frac{8}{12}\right)\right] + 700\left[1 + (0.06)\left(\frac{3}{12}\right)\right]$$

$$512.50 + x = 416.00 + 710.50$$

$$512.50 + x = 1126.50$$

$$x = 1126.50 - 512.50$$

$$x = 614.00$$

The final payment to be made in eight months is $614.

D. Finding the value of two or more equivalent payments

Sometimes you might be interested in changing a schedule of payments of irregular amounts to equivalent values at a single date. The equation of values will be used to determine the equivalent values, but to carry out your calculations you need to determine a focal date and the dates of the equivalent values. To make your calculations easier, choose as your focal date the date of one of the equivalent values.

EXAMPLE 7.5E Jeremy had two equal outstanding loans, one from 63 days ago and one from 105 days ago. He repaid both loans today with the single amount of $3700. If interest is 9% on the loans, what was the size of the equal amounts borrowed? (See Figure 7.9.)

SOLUTION Let the value of each of the equal loans be $x.

(i) Use a time diagram to represent the given data.

FIGURE 7.9 Graphical Representation of Data

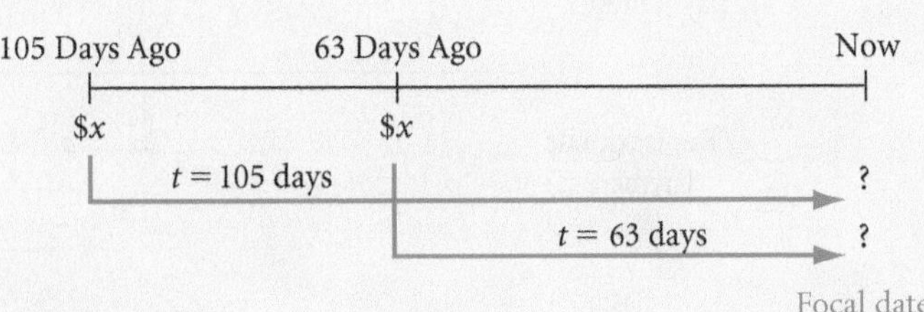

(ii) Dated value of the original scheduled payments:

(a) The value at the focal date of the first $x payment due 105 days before the focal date is found by using the future value formula.

$$S = x\left[1 + (0.09)\left(\frac{105}{365}\right)\right] = x(1 + 0.025890) = 1.025890x$$

(b) The value at the focal date of the second $x payment due 63 days before the focal date is found by using the future value formula.

$$S = x\left[1 + (0.09)\left(\frac{63}{365}\right)\right] = x(1 + 0.015534) = 1.015534x$$

(iii) Dated value of the replacement payments:

(a) The value at the focal date of the repayment is $3700 on the focal date.

(b) The value at the focal date of the two equal loans is

$$1.025890x + 1.015534x = 2.041425x$$

(iv) The equation of values at the focal date is now set up by matching the dated values of the original debts to the dated values of the replacement payment.

$$3700 = 2.041425x$$

$$x = \frac{3700.00}{2.041425}$$

$$x = 1812.46$$

Each of the two equal loans had been $1812.46.

EXAMPLE 7.5F

Clarkson Developments was supposed to pay Majestic Flooring $2000 sixty days ago and $1800 in thirty days. Majestic Flooring agreed to accept three equal payments due today, 60 days from today, and 120 days from today. Compute the size of the equal payments at 10% p.a. Use today as the focal date. (See Figure 7.10.)

SOLUTION

Let the size of the equal payments be $x.

(i) Graphical representation of data:

FIGURE 7.10 Graphical Representation of Data

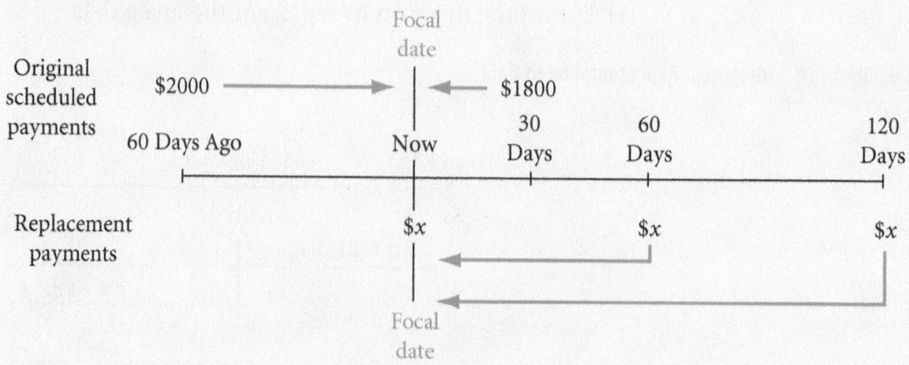

(ii) Dated value of the original scheduled payments at the focal date:

(a) Because the \$2000 payment is due 60 days before the focal date, the future value formula is appropriate.

$$S = 2000\left[1 + (0.10)\left(\frac{60}{365}\right)\right] = 2000(1 + 0.016438) = \$2032.88$$

(b) Because the \$1800 payment is due 30 days after the focal date, the present value formula is appropriate.

$$P = \frac{1800.00}{1 + (0.10)\left(\frac{30}{365}\right)} = \frac{1800.00}{1 + 0.008219} = \$1785.33$$

(iii) Dated value of the replacement payments at the focal date:

(a) Since the first payment is to be made at the focal date, its value is $\$x$.

(b) Because the second payment is to be made 60 days after the focal date, the present value formula is appropriate.

$$P = \frac{x}{1 + (0.10)\left(\frac{60}{365}\right)} = \frac{x}{1 + 0.016438} = \frac{1(x)}{1.016438} = \$0.983827x$$

(c) Because the third payment is to be made 120 days after the focal date, the present value formula is appropriate.

$$P = \frac{x}{1 + (0.10)\left(\frac{120}{365}\right)} = \frac{x}{1 + 0.032877}$$

$$= \frac{1(x)}{1.032877} = \$0.968170x$$

(iv) The equation of values (dated value of the replacement payments = dated value of the original scheduled payments):

$$x + 0.983827x + 0.968170x = 2032.88 + 1785.33$$

$$2.951997x = 3818.21$$

$$x = \frac{3818.21}{2.951997}$$

$$x = \$1293.43$$

The size of each of the three equal payments is \$1293.43.

E. Loan repayments

Loans by financial institutions to individuals are usually repaid by **blended payments**, which are equal periodic payments that include payment of interest and repayment of principal. To repay the loan, the sum of the present values of the periodic payments must equal the original principal. The concept of equivalent values is used to determine the size of the blended payments.

EXAMPLE 7.5G A loan of \$2000 made at 8.5% p.a. is to be repaid in four equal payments due at the end of the next four quarters respectively. Determine the size of the quarterly payments if the agreed focal date is the date of the loan. (See Figure 7.11.)

SOLUTION Let the size of the equal quarterly payments be represented by \$x.

(i) Graphical representation of data:

FIGURE 7.11 Graphical Representation of Data

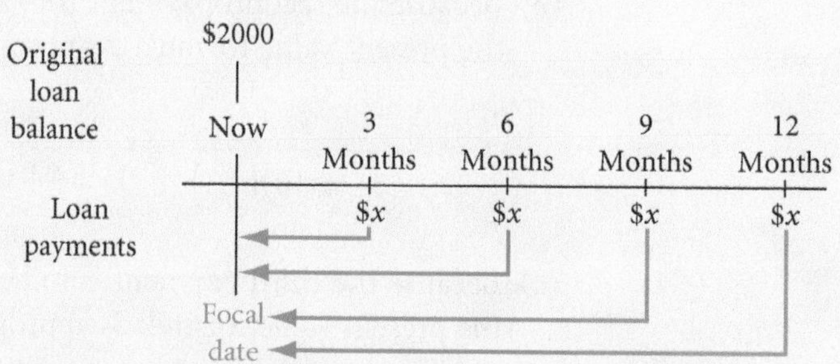

(ii) Dated value of the loan balance at the focal date is \$2000.

(iii) Dated value of the loan payments at the focal date:
The payments are due three, six, nine, and twelve months after the focal date respectively. Their values are

(a) $$P_1 = \frac{x}{1 + (0.085)\left(\frac{3}{12}\right)} = \frac{x}{1 + 0.02125} = \frac{1(x)}{1.02125} = 0.979192x$$

(b) $$P_2 = \frac{x}{1 + (0.085)\left(\frac{6}{12}\right)} = \frac{x}{1 + 0.0425} = \frac{1(x)}{1.0425} = 0.959233x$$

(c) $$P_3 = \frac{x}{1 + (0.085)\left(\frac{9}{12}\right)} = \frac{x}{1 + 0.06375} = \frac{1(x)}{1.06375} = 0.940071x$$

(d) $$P_4 = \frac{x}{1 + (0.085)\left(\frac{12}{12}\right)} = \frac{x}{1 + 0.085} = \frac{1(x)}{1.085} = 0.921659x$$

(iv) $$0.979192x + 0.959233x + 0.940071x + 0.921659x = 2000.00$$
$$3.800154x = 2000.00$$
$$x = 526.29$$

The size of the quarterly payment is \$526.29.

EXERCISE 7.5

Find the equivalent replacement payments indicated for each of the following scheduled payments.

	Original Scheduled Payments	Replacement Payments	Focal Date	Rate
1.	$800 due today	In full	4 months from today	11%
2.	$1200 due 4 months ago	In full	Today	6%
3.	$600 due in 2 months	In full	7 months from today	7%
4.	$1000 due in 8 months	In full	2 months from today	10%
5.	$500 due 4 months ago, $600 due in 2 months	In full	Today	5%
6.	$800 due today, $700 due in 2 months	In full	4 months from today	9%
7.	$2000 due today	$1200 in 4 months and the balance in 8 months	Today	6%
8.	$400 due 1 month ago, $600 due in 3 months	$500 today and the balance in 6 months	Today	8%
9.	$1500 due today	Two equal payments due in 2 and 7 months	Today	10%
10.	$1800 due 30 days ago	Three equal payments due today, in 30 days, and in 60 days	Today	9%
11.	$1500 due 4 months ago, $1200 due in 8 months with interest at 10%	$700 due now and two equal payments due in 6 months and in 12 months	Today	5%
12.	$2000 due in 6 months with interest at 8%, $1600 due in 2 years with interest at 7%	Three equal payments due in 6, 12, and 18 months	1 year from today	11%

Solve each of the following problems.

1. Scheduled debt payments of $600 each are due three months and six months from now. If interest at 10% is allowed, what single payment today is required to settle the two scheduled payments? Reference Example 7.5A

2. Debt payments are due of $700 in two months and $800 in five months. If interest at 8.3% is allowed, what single payment today is required to settle the two scheduled payments?

3. A loan payment of $1000 was due 60 days ago and another payment of $1200 is due 30 days from now. What single payment 90 days from now will pay off the two obligations if interest is to be 8% and the agreed focal date is 90 days from now? Reference Example 7.5B

4. A loan payment of $2200 was due 91 days ago and another payment of $1800 is due 45 days from now. What single payment 75 days from now will pay off

the two obligations if interest is to be 9% and the agreed focal date is 75 days from now?

5. Jay was due to make loan payments of $500 four months ago, $800 today, and $400 in three months. He has agreed instead to make a single payment one month from today. If money is worth 10.5% and the agreed focal date is one month from today, what is the size of the replacement payment? Reference Example 7.5C

6. Jane was due to make loan payments of $1200 six months ago, $1500 one month ago, and $700 in two months. Instead, she is to make a single payment today. If money is worth 9.8% and the agreed focal date is today, what is the size of the replacement payment?

7. Loan payments of $400 due 95 days ago and $700 due today are to be repaid by a payment of $600 30 days from today and the balance in 125 days. If money is worth 6% and the agreed focal date is 125 days from today, what is the size of the final payment? Reference Example 7.5D

8. Loan payments of $4000 due 200 days ago and $6000 due 63 days ago are to be replaced by a payment of $5000 today and the balance 92 days from today. If money is worth 8.3% and the agreed focal date is 92 days from today, what is the size of the final payment?

9. Dan borrowed $1100 today and is to repay the loan in two equal payments, one in four months and one in six months. If interest is 8.5% on the loan, what is the size of the equal payments if a focal date of today is used? Reference Example 7.5E

10. When Ruby borrowed $2300, she agreed to repay the loan in two equal payments, to be made 90 days and 135 days from the day the money was borrowed. If interest is 9.25% on the loan, what is the size of the equal payments if a focal date of today is used?

11. Ruben repaid $800, paying back two equal outstanding loans from seven months ago and five months ago. If interest is 11% on the loans, and the agreed focal date is today, what was the size of the equal amounts borrowed?

12. Judy received a payment of $2950 and used it to pay back two equal outstanding loans from 45 days ago and 190 days ago. If interest is 12.5% on the loans, and the agreed focal date is today, what was the size of the equal amounts borrowed?

13. Jessica should have made two payments of $800 each. The first was due 60 days ago and the second payment was due 30 days ago. The two original scheduled payments are to be settled by two equal payments to be made today and 60 days from now. If interest allowed is 7.25% and the agreed focal date is today, what is the size of the equal payments?

14. Krista borrowed $14 000. The loan is to be repaid by three equal payments due in 120, 240, and 260 days from now. Determine the size of the equal payments at 7% with a focal date of today. Reference Example 7.5F

15. Jerry borrowed $4000. The loan is to be repaid by three equal payments due in four, eight, and twelve months from now. Determine the size of the equal payments at 8.5% with a focal date of today.

16. On March 1, Bear Mountain Tours borrowed $1500. Three equal payments are required, on April 30, June 20, and August 10, as well as a final payment of $400 on September 30 of the same year. If the focal date is September 30, what is the amount of the equal payments at 6.75%?

Go to MathXL at www.mathxl.com. You can practise many of this chapter's exercises as often as you want. The guided solutions help you find an answer step by step. You'll find a personalized study plan available to you too!

Review Exercise

1. How much interest is owed on a loan of $1975 borrowed at 5.5% for 215 days?
2. What principal will earn $34.44 interest at 8.25% from May 30, 2012, to January 4, 2013?
3. What was the rate of interest if the interest on a loan of $675 for 284 days was $39.39?
4. If $680 is worth $698.70 after three months, what interest rate was charged?
5. How many days will it take for $2075 to earn $124.29 interest at 8.25% p.a.?
6. What principal will earn $24.87 at 4.75% in 156 days?
7. What sum of money will earn $148.57 from September 1, 2012, to April 30, 2013, at 7.5%?
8. At what rate of interest must a principal of $1545 be invested to earn interest of $58.93 in 150 days?
9. At what rate of interest will $1500 grow to $1562.04 from June 1, 2013, to December 1, 2013?
10. In how many months will $2500 earn $51.04 interest at 3.5%?
11. In how many days will $3100 grow to $3195.72 at 5.75%?
12. Compute the accumulated value of $4200 at 4.5% after 11 months.
13. What is the amount to which $1550 will grow from June 10, 2012, to December 15, 2012, at 6.5%?
14. What amount of money will accumulate to $1516.80 in eight months at 8%?
15. What principal will amount to $3367.28 if invested at 9% from November 1, 2011, to May 31, 2012?
16. What is the present value of $3780 due in nine months if interest is 5%?
17. Compute the present value on June 1, 2014, of $1785 due on October 15, 2014, if interest is 7.5%.
18. Payments of $1750 and $1600 are due four months from now and nine months from now respectively. What single payment is required to pay off the two scheduled payments today if interest is 9% and the focal date is today?
19. A loan payment of $1450 was due 45 days ago and a payment of $1200 is due in 60 days. What single payment made 30 days from now is required to settle the two payments if interest is 7% and the focal date is 30 days from now?
20. Scheduled payments of $800 due two months ago and $1200 due in one month are to be repaid by a payment of $1000 today and the balance in three months. What is the amount of the final payment if interest is 7.75% and the focal date is one month from now?
21. An obligation of $10 000 is to be repaid by equal payments due in 90 days and 180 days. What is the amount of the equal payments if money is worth 6.5% and the focal date is today?
22. Payments of $4000 each due in four, nine, and eleven months from now are to be settled by two equal payments due today and twelve months from now. What is the amount of the equal payments if interest is 7.35% and the agreed focal date is today?
23. Three debts, the first for $1000 due two months ago, the second for $1200 due in two months, and the third for $1400 due in four months, are to be paid by a single payment today. How much is the single payment if money is worth 8.25% p.a. and the focal date is today?
24. Loan payments of $700 due three months ago and of $1000 due today are to be paid by a payment of $800 in two months and a final payment in five months. If 9% interest is

allowed, and the focal date is five months from now, what is the amount of the final payment?

25. A loan of $5000 due in one year is to be repaid by three equal payments due today, six months from now, and one year from now. What is the amount of the equal payments if interest is 6.5% and the focal date is today?

26. A loan of $5000 is to be repaid in three equal installments due 60, 120, and 180 days after the date of the loan. If the focal date is the date of the loan and interest is 6.9% p.a., compute the amount of the installments.

Self-Test

EXCEL SPREADSHEET

1. Compute the amount of interest earned by $1290 at 3.5% p.a. in 173 days.

2. In how many months will $8500 grow to $8818.75 at 5% p.a.?

3. What interest rate is paid if the interest on a loan of $2500 for six months is $81.25?

4. What principal will have a maturity value of $10 000 at 8.25% p.a. in three months?

5. What is the amount to which $6000 will grow at 3.75% p.a. in ten months?

6. What principal will earn $67.14 interest at 6.25% for 82 days?

7. What is the present value of $4400 due at 3.25% p.a. in 243 days?

8. What rate of interest is paid if the interest on a loan of $2500 is $96.06 from November 14, 2011, to May 20, 2012?

9. How many days will it take for $8500 to earn $689.72 at 8.25% p.a.?

10. What principal will earn $55.99 interest at 9.75% p.a. from February 4, 2012, to July 6, 2012?

11. What amount invested will accumulate to $7500 at 3.75% p.a. in 88 days?

12. Compute the amount of interest on $835 at 7.5% p.a. from October 8, 2011, to August 4, 2012.

13. Loan payments of $1725 due today, $510 due in 75 days, and $655 due in 323 days are to be combined into a single payment to be made 115 days from now. What is that single payment if money is worth 8.5% p.a. and the focal date is 115 days from now?

14. Scheduled payments of $1010 due five months ago and $1280 due today are to be repaid by a payment of $615 in four months and the balance in seven months. If money is worth 7.75% p.a. and the focal date is in seven months, what is the amount of the final payment?

15. A loan of $3320 is to be repaid by three equal payments due in 92 days, 235 days, and 326 days. Determine the amount of the equal payments at 8.75% p.a. with a focal date of today.

Challenge Problems

1. Nora borrows \$37 500 on September 28, 2011, at 7% p.a. simple interest, to be repaid on October 31, 2012. She has the option of making payments toward the loan before the due date. Nora pays \$6350 on February 17, 2012, \$8250 on July 2, 2012, and \$7500 on October 1, 2012. Compute the payment required to pay off the debt on the focal date of October 31, 2012.

2. A supplier will give Shark Unibase Company a discount of 2% if an invoice is paid 60 days before its due date. Suppose Shark wants to take advantage of this discount but needs to borrow the money. It plans to pay back the loan in 60 days. What is the highest annual simple interest rate at which Shark Unibase can borrow the money and still save by paying the invoice 60 days before its due date?

CASE STUDY 7.1 Short-Term Loans

» Skyline Sports stocked and sold seasonal sporting equipment for hiking and skiing. Due to a spell of warm weather during the ski season, sales of skiing and snowboarding equipment had not been as high as expected. Since Skyline Sports had already purchased the equipment from their suppliers, payment was due. Aaron Baxter, the manager, was trying to borrow the cash to make the payment of \$14 600. At the company's bank, he would be able to obtain a one-month loan for the full amount, at 6.95% per annum simple interest. At a second bank, he would have three months to pay, with interest at 7.3%.

Later that same day, in talking with his suppliers, Aaron learned that they were willing to finance the purchases at 8.15% per annum if he signed a promissory note. Three equal payments would then be due, two months, four months, and six months from now.

QUESTIONS

1. What are the maturity values of the two different bank loans?
2. What equal payments would have to be made to the supplier?
3. As of today's date, compute the equivalent values of each of the three options. Which option should Aaron choose?

CASE STUDY 7.2 Cost of Financing Pay Now or Pay Later

» Along with licensing, the purchase of auto insurance for vehicles is required in Canada. Benefits of auto insurance are as follows:

- Safeguards the investment in the automobile.
- Pays for medical expenses in case of an accident.

- Covers losses caused by uninsured or underinsured drivers.
- Compensates for damage due to theft, vandalism, or natural disasters.

Quick Courier Service is about to purchase insurance on its new delivery van. Taylor, the manager, has the company's insurance agent outline three payment plans to provide coverage for the next 12 months.

Plan One requires that the full year's premium of $4000 be paid at the beginning of the year.

Plan Two allows payment of the annual premium in two installments. The first installment would have to be paid immediately and would amount to one-half of the annual premium, plus a $60 service charge. The second installment would be paid in six months' time, and would amount to the remaining half of the premium.

Plan Three allows for twelve equal monthly payments of $355 each. These payments would be made on the same date within each month, starting immediately.

Quick Courier Service pays its insurance using Plan One. However, the company realizes that it is missing out on interest it could have earned on this money when it pays the full year's premium at the beginning of the policy term. Taylor considers this to be the "cost" of paying its bill in one lump sum. Taylor is interested in knowing the cost of its insurance payment options.

QUESTIONS

1. Suppose Quick Courier Service could earn 4% p.a. simple interest on its money over the next year. Assume the first premium payment is due today (the first day of the insurance policy term) and the focal date is today. Ignoring all taxes, compute the cost to Quick Courier Service of paying the insurance using each of the three payment plans.
2. Suppose Quick Courier Service expects to earn 2.5% p.a. simple interest on any money it invests in the first three months of this year, and 1.8% p.a. simple interest on any money it invests during the rest of this year. Assume the focal date is today. Which option—Plan One, Plan Two, or Plan Three—will have the least cost for the company?
3. Examine a vehicle insurance policy of your own or of a family member. Calculate what you could earn on your money at today's rates of interest. What is the cost of this insurance policy if you pay the annual premium at the beginning of the policy term? Make the focal date the first day of the policy term.

SUMMARY OF FORMULAS

Formula 7.1A

$I = Prt$

Finding the amount of interest when the principal, the rate, and the time are known

Formula 7.1B

$$P = \frac{I}{rt}$$

Finding the principal directly when the amount of interest, the rate of interest, and the time are known

Formula 7.1C

$$r = \frac{I}{Pt}$$

Finding the rate of interest directly when the amount of interest, the principal, and the time are known

Formula 7.1D

$$t = \frac{I}{Pr}$$

Finding the time directly when the amount of interest, the principal, and the rate of interest are known

Formula 7.2

$S = P + I$

Finding the future value (maturity value) when the principal and the amount of interest are known

Formula 7.3A

$S = P(1 + rt)$

Finding the future value (maturity value) at simple interest directly when the principal, rate of interest, and time are known

Formula 7.3B

$$P = \frac{S}{1 + rt}$$

Finding the present value at simple interest when the future value (maturity value), the rate of interest, and the time are known

GLOSSARY

Blended payments equal periodic payments that include payment of interest and repayment of principal, usually paid by individuals to financial institutions *(p. 286)*

Dated value the value of a sum of money at a specific time relative to its due date, including interest *(p. 277)*

Equation of values the equation obtained when matching the dated values of the original payments at an agreed focal date to the dated values of the replacement payments at the same focal date *(p. 283)*

Equivalent value see **Dated value**

Focal date a specific time chosen to compare the time value of one or more dated sums of money *(p. 278)*

Future value of a sum of money the value obtained when the amount of interest is added to the original principal *(p. 270)*

Interest rent paid for the use of money *(p. 261)*

Interest period the time period for which interest is charged *(p. 261)*

Maturity value see **Future value of a sum of money**

Nominal rate the yearly or annual rate of interest charged on the principal of a loan *(p. 261)*

Present value the principal that grows to a given future value (maturity value) over a given period of time at a given rate of interest *(p. 273)*

Simple interest the interest calculated on the original principal by the formula $I = Prt$, and paid only when the principal is repaid *(p. 261)*

Time value of money a concept of money value that allows for a change in the value of a sum of money over time if the sum of money is subject to a rate of interest *(p. 273)*

USEFUL INTERNET SITES

www.fin.gc.ca

Department of Finance Canada The Department of Finance Canada Website is the source for government publications on financial issues such as debt management, economic leadership, budgets, and legislation. Available are news releases on topics such as harmonized sales taxes, tax-free savings accounts, and codes of conduct for the credit card industry.

www.tmx.com

TMX Group The Toronto Stock Exchange and TSX Venture Exchange are owned and operated by the TMX Group. Search this site to access members and participating organizations, equity trading, and market data.

www.standardandpoors.com

Standard & Poor's Standard & Poor's research services provide data, analysis, and economic forecasts, and analyze economic events and trends in business and government around the globe to help people make informed business decisions.

CHAPTER 8 Simple Interest Applications

OBJECTIVES

Upon completing this chapter, you will be able to do the following:

1. Compute maturity value and present value for promissory notes.
2. Compute present values for treasury bills.
3. Compute interest and balances for demand loans.
4. Compute interest and balances for lines of credit and credit card loans.
5. Construct repayment schedules for loans using blended payments.

A business often needs to borrow money for a short period of time, a period of less than one year. Payments for products purchased or for work done by employees need to be made now, but collections from customers may not take place until a few days or months in the future. A higher-interest-rate loan, such as a credit card debt, may need to be replaced with a lower-interest-rate loan, such as a demand loan or line of credit. Also, cash in excess of current requirements needs to be invested in a short-term investment, such as a treasury bill. Financial institutions are making it easier for businesses and individuals to borrow and invest money, and are making it more convenient to repay what is borrowed or redeem what is invested.

INTRODUCTION

Businesses often encounter situations that involve the application of simple interest. Simple interest calculation is usually restricted to financial instruments subject to time periods of less than one year. In this chapter we apply simple interest to short-term promissory notes, treasury bills, lines of credit, credit card loans, and demand loans.

8.1 PROMISSORY NOTES

A. Promissory notes and related terms

A **promissory note** is a written promise by one party to pay a certain sum of money, with or without interest, at a specific date or on demand, to another party. (See Figure 8.1.)

FIGURE 8.1 **Promissory Note**

$650.00 MISSISSAUGA, ONTARIO OCTOBER 30, 2012

FOUR MONTHS after date I promise to pay to the order of

VALLEY NURSERY

SIX-HUNDRED-FIFTY and 00/100 ································ Dollars

at SHERIDAN CREDIT UNION LIMITED for value received

with interest at 7.25% per annum.

Signed D. Peel

This is an **interest-bearing promissory note** because it is a note subject to the rate of interest stated on the face of the note.

The following information is directly available in the promissory note (see items (a) through (f)) or can be determined (see items (g) through (j)).

(a) The **maker** of the note is the party making the promise to pay. —— (D. Peel)

(b) The **payee** of the note is the party to whom the promise to pay is made. —— (Valley Nursery)

(c) The **face value** of the note is the sum of money (principal) specified. —— ($650.00)

(d) The **rate of interest** is stated as a simple annual rate based on the face value. —— (7.25%)

(e) The **date of issue** or **issue date** is the date on which the note was made. —— (October 30, 2012)

(f) The **term** of the promissory note is the length of time before the note matures (becomes payable). ——— (four months)

(g) The **due date** or **date of maturity** is the date on which the note is to be paid. ——— (See Subsection C)

(h) The **interest period** is the time period from the date of issue to the legal due date. ——— (See Subsection C)

(i) The **amount of interest** is payable together with the face value on the legal due date. ——— (See Subsection C)

(j) The **maturity value** is the amount payable on the due date (face value plus interest). ——— (See Subsection C)

The Canadian law relating to promissory notes adds **three days of grace** to the term of the note to obtain the **legal due date** (Bills of Exchange Act, Section 41). This is to allow for the situation of the repayment date falling on a statutory holiday. In this case, without three days of grace, you would either have to pay the note early, or take a penalty for paying three days late. Therefore, three days are added to the due date of a promissory note. Interest must be paid for those three days of grace, but there is no late payment penalty and your credit rating remains good. Today, with electronic banking, you can arrange to pay your note at any time, even on the weekend, so you may not need the three days of grace. If you decide not to include the three days of grace, write "No Grace Days" on the note when you negotiate the loan.

EXAMPLE 8.1A

For the promissory note illustrated in Figure 8.1, determine

(i) the due date;

(ii) the interest period;

(iii) the amount of interest;

(iv) the maturity value.

SOLUTION

(i) *Finding the due date*

Add three days of grace to the term of the note to obtain the legal due date. Since calendar months vary in length, the month in which the term ends does not necessarily have a date that corresponds to the date of issue. In such cases, the last day of the month is used as the end of the term of the note. Three days of grace are added to that date to determine the legal due date. (Throughout this chapter, we have included three days of grace in the exercises. However, as we pointed out earlier, electronic banking has reduced the need for three days of grace.)

With reference to the promissory note in Figure 8.1,

- the date of issue is October 30, 2012;
- the term of the note is four months;
- the month in which the term ends is February 2013;
- the end of the term is February 28 (since February has no day corresponding to day 30, the last day of the month is used to establish the end of the term of the note);
- the legal due date (adding three days) is March 3.

(ii) *Determining the interest period*
If the note bears interest, the interest period covers the number of days from the date of issue of the note to the legal due date.

October 30 to March 3 = 124 days

(iii) *Computing the amount of interest*
The interest payable on the note is the simple interest based on the face value of the note for the interest period at the stated rate. It is found using the simple interest formula:

$$I = Prt$$ ——— Formula 7.1A

$$I = (650.00)(0.0725)\left(\frac{124}{365}\right) = \$16.01$$

(iv) *Finding the maturity value of the note*
The maturity value of the promissory note is the total amount payable at the legal due date.
Face value + Interest = 650.00 + 16.01 = $666.01

EXCEL NOTES

In Excel, use the following functions to do these calculations:

COUPDAYSNC	Days between dates
ACCRINTM	Accrued interest
YIELDDISC	Simple interest yields
ACCRINTM	Accrued interest to maturity

B. Maturity value of interest-bearing promissory notes

Since the maturity value of a promissory note is the principal (face value) plus the interest accumulated to the legal due date, the future value formula for simple interest will determine the maturity value directly.

$$S = P(1 + rt)$$ ——— Formula 7.3A

S = maturity value of the promissory note;
P = the face value of the note;
r = the rate of interest on the note;
t = the interest period (the number of days between the *date of issue* and the *legal due date*).

EXAMPLE 8.1B

Find the maturity value of an $800, six-month note with interest at 7.5% dated May 31, 2012.

SOLUTION

The date of issue is May 31, 2012;
the term of the note is six months;
the term ends November 30, 2012;
the legal due date is December 3, 2012;

the interest period (May 31 to December 3) has 186 days.

$$P = 800.00; \quad r = 0.075; \quad t = \frac{186}{365}$$

$$S = 800.00\left[1 + (0.075)\left(\frac{186}{365}\right)\right] = 800.00(1 + 0.038219) = \$830.58$$

C. Present value of promissory notes

The present value of a promissory note is its value any time before the due date, allowing for the maturity value, the prevailing interest rate, and the time between the present date and its date of maturity. The prevailing interest rate is called the **rate money is worth.**

The first step in determining the present value is to ascertain whether the note is an interest-bearing or a non-interest-bearing note.

1. Interest-bearing promissory notes: When the rate of interest is stated on the note, it is an interest-bearing promissory note. The face value of the note is the principal amount borrowed. The promise or obligation is to repay the principal amount borrowed, plus interest based on the rate of interest *stated* on the face of the note.

   To determine the present value of an interest-bearing note, two steps are required:
   Step 1: Calculate the maturity value of the note, using the *stated interest rate,* then
   Step 2: Calculate the present value of the note, using the *rate money is worth.*

2. Non-interest-bearing promissory notes: When there is no rate of interest stated, the promissory note is a **non-interest-bearing note**. Interest on money borrowed may be implied, but is not stated. The face value of the note is the amount to be repaid at maturity.

   To determine the present value of a non-interest-bearing note, only one step is required:
   Calculate the present value of the non-interest-bearing note, using the *rate money is worth.*

The face value (or principal) of promissory notes can be obtained by solving the future value formula $S = P(1 + rt)$ for P, that is, by using the present value formula

$$P = \frac{S}{1 + rt}$$ — Formula 7.3B

P = the face value (or present value) of the note at the date of issue;
S = the maturity value;
r = the rate of interest;
t = the interest period.

EXAMPLE 8.1C A five-month note dated January 31, 2013, and bearing interest at 8% p.a. (per annum, i.e., per year) has a maturity value of $558.11. Find the face value of the note.

SOLUTION See Figure 8.2.

FIGURE 8.2 Graphical Representation of Data

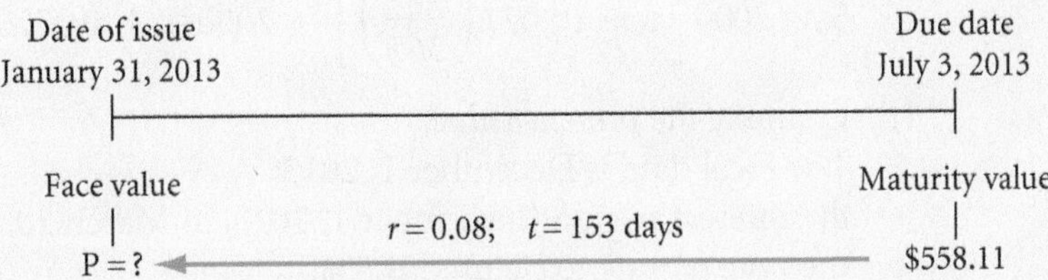

The term of the note ends June 30;
the legal due date is July 3;
the interest period (January 31 to July 3) has 153 days.

$$S = 558.11; \quad r = 0.08; \quad t = \frac{153}{365}$$

$$P = \frac{558.11}{1 + (0.08)\left(\frac{153}{365}\right)} = \frac{558.11}{1 + 0.033534} = \$540.00$$

EXAMPLE 8.1D A 180-day note for $2000 with interest at 7% is dated September 18, 2013. Compute the value of the note on December 1, 2013, if money is worth 5%.

SOLUTION Since the note bears interest at 7%, it is identified as an interest-bearing note. To calculate the present value of the note, two steps are required. Compute the maturity value of the note based on the stated interest rate, 7%. Based on the result, compute the present value of the note based on the rate money is worth, 5% (see Figure 8.3).

FIGURE 8.3 Graphical Representation of Data

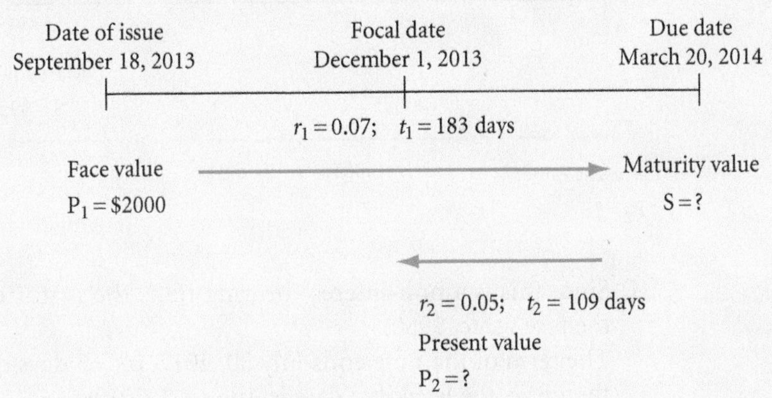

(i) *Compute the maturity value of the note.*
The term of the note is 180 days plus 3 days of grace;
therefore, the term ends March 20, 2014;
the interest rate to be used is 7%.

$$P_1 = 2000; \quad r_1 = 0.07; \quad t_1 = \frac{183}{365}$$

$$S = 2000\left[1 + (0.07)\left(\frac{183}{365}\right)\right] = 2000(1 + 0.035096) = \$2070.19$$

(ii) *Compute the present value.*
The focal date is December 1, 2013;
the interest period (December 1, 2013, to March 20, 2014) has 109 days:
the interest rate to be used is 5%.

$$S = 2070.19; \quad r_2 = 0.05; \quad t_2 = \frac{109}{365}$$

$$P_2 = \frac{2070.19}{\left[1 + (0.05)\left(\frac{109}{365}\right)\right]} = \frac{2070.19}{(1 + 0.014932)} = \$2039.73$$

EXAMPLE 8.1E

Compute the present value on the date of issue of a non-interest-bearing, \$950, three-month promissory note dated April 30, 2012, if money is worth 6.5%.

SOLUTION

This non-interest-bearing note does not state an interest rate. The present value of the note is calculated in one step (see Figure 8.4.).

FIGURE 8.4 Graphical Representation of Data

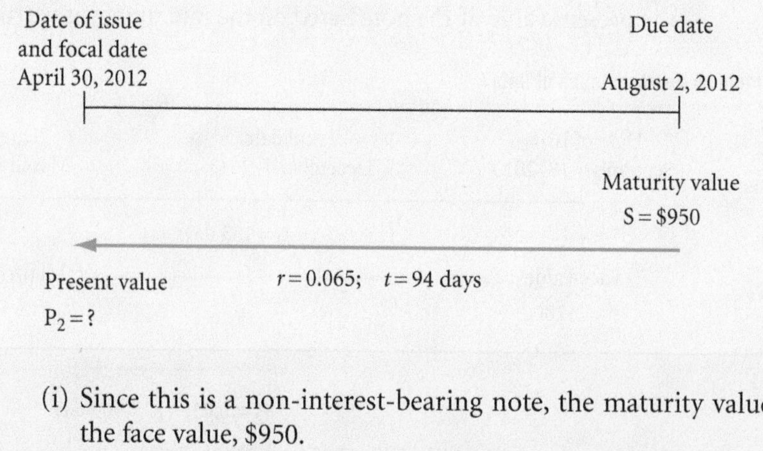

(i) Since this is a non-interest-bearing note, the maturity value of the note is the face value, \$950.
The term of the note ends July 30, 2012, plus 3 days of grace;
therefore, the legal due date is August 2, 2012;
the interest period (April 30 to August 2) has 94 days;

the interest rate to be used is 6.5%.

$$S = 950; \quad r = 0.065; \quad t = \frac{94}{365}$$

$$P = \frac{950}{\left[1 + (0.065)\left(\frac{94}{365}\right)\right]} = \frac{950}{(1 + 0.016740)} = \$934.36$$

EXAMPLE 8.1F

Henry purchased a large-screen TV at a local store that had advertised, "No payment until 2012." He signed the contract on March 14, 2011, agreeing to pay $1995 on January 2, 2012. If money is worth 11%, what is the value of the note on the day of signing?

SOLUTION

The contract serves as a non-interest-bearing promissory note because no interest rate is stated. The maturity value of the contract is its face value, $1995. The present value of the note is calculated in one step. There are 294 days between March 14, 2011, and January 2, 2012. (See Figure 8.5.)

FIGURE 8.5 **Graphical Representation of Data**

March 14, 2011 — January 2, 2012

$1832.62 ← t = 294 days — $1995

Focal date

$$S = 1995.00; \quad r = 0.11; \quad t = \frac{294}{365}$$

$$P = \frac{1995.00}{\left[1 + (0.11)\left(\frac{294}{365}\right)\right]} = \frac{1995.00}{(1 + 0.088603)} = \$1832.62$$

EXERCISE 8.1

Determine each of the items listed from the information provided in the promissory note below.

$530.00 OAKVILLE, ONTARIO DECEMBER 30, 2012

FIVE MONTHS after date I promise to pay

to the order of JANE WELTON

FIVE-HUNDRED-THIRTY and 00/100 .... Dollars

at SHERIDAN CENTRAL BANK for value received

with interest at 6.5% per annum.

Signed *E. Salt*

1. Date issued
2. Legal due date
3. Face value
4. Interest rate
5. Interest period (days)
6. Amount of interest
7. Maturity value

EXCEL SPREADSHEET

B. For each of the following notes, determine

EXCEL SPREADSHEET

(a) the legal due date
(b) the interest period (in days)
(c) the amount of interest
(d) the maturity value

1. The face value of a five-month, 6% note dated September 30, 2011, is $840.
2. A four-month, 5.25% note for $2000 is issued July 31, 2014.

Use the future value formula to compute the maturity value of each of the following promissory notes.

EXCEL SPREADSHEET

1. A four-month, 5.25% note for $620 is issued May 25, 2013.
2. A $350 note is issued on October 30, 2011, at 4.5% for 90 days.
3. A 150-day note for $820 with interest at 5% is dated June 28, 2012.
4. A seven-month, $575 note dated November 1, 2011, earns interest at 7.5%.
5. A five-month, 6.18% note for $835 is issued January 24, 2014.
6. A $230 note is issued on July 18, 2013, at 7.5% for 101 days.
7. A 92-day note for $10 200 with interest at 8.05% is dated August 22, 2012.
8. A ten-month, $5650 note dated September 1, 2013, earns interest at 3.8%.

D. Find the present value, on the date indicated, of each of the following promissory notes.

1. A non-interest-bearing note for $2500 issued June 10, 2013, for four months if money is worth 6.15%, on July 20, 2013.
2. A non-interest-bearing note for $7200 issued February 20, 2012, for 183 days if money is worth 5.63%, on June 1, 2012.
3. A 95-day, 5.81% note for $3600 issued October 28, 2011, if money is worth 6.27%, on November 30, 2011.
4. A six-month note for $1930 dated April 1, 2014, with interest at 6.5% if money is worth 7.2%, on June 20, 2014.

8.2 TREASURY BILLS—PRESENT VALUE

Treasury bills (or **T-bills**) are promissory notes issued by the federal government and most provincial governments to meet short-term financing requirements.

Government of Canada T-bills are for terms of 91 days, 182 days, and 364 days. There are no days of grace with T-bills. T-bills are auctioned by the Bank of Canada on behalf of the federal government. They are available in denominations of $1000,

\$5000, \$25 000, \$100 000, and \$1 000 000. T-bills are bought at the auction mainly by chartered banks and investment dealers for resale to other investors, such as smaller financial institutions, corporations, mutual funds, and individuals.

T-bills are promissory notes that do not carry an interest rate. The issuing government guarantees payment of the face value at maturity. The investor purchases T-bills at a discounted price reflecting a rate of return that is determined by current market conditions. The discounted price is determined by computing the present value of the T-bills.

EXAMPLE 8.2A

An investment dealer bought a 91-day Canada T-bill to yield an annual rate of return of 4.21%.

(i) What was the price paid by the investment dealer for a T-bill with a face value of \$100 000?

(ii) The investment dealer resold the \$100 000 T-bill the same day to an investor to yield 4.06%. What was the investment dealer's profit on the transaction?

SOLUTION

(i) Find the purchase price, P_1.
The maturity value is the face value of the T-bill, \$100 000.00; the discount period has 91 days (no days of grace are allowed on T-bills).

$$S = 100\,000.00; \quad r_1 = 0.0421; \quad t_1 = \frac{91}{365}$$

$$P_1 = \frac{S}{1 + r_1t_1} = \frac{100\,000.00}{1 + 0.0421\left(\frac{91}{365}\right)} = \frac{100\,000.00}{1 + 0.010496} = \$98\,961.29$$

The investment dealer paid \$98 961.29 for a \$100 000 T-bill.

(ii) Find the resale price, P_2.

$$S = 100\,000.00; \quad r_2 = 0.0406; \quad t_2 = \frac{91}{365}$$

$$P_2 = \frac{100\,000.00}{1 + 0.0406\left(\frac{91}{365}\right)} = \frac{100\,000.00}{1 + 0.010122} = \$98\,997.92$$

Investment dealer's profit = Resale price – Price paid by dealer
$= P_2 - P_1$
$= 98\,997.92 - 98\,961.29 = \$36.63$

The investment dealer's profit on the transaction was \$36.63.

EXAMPLE 8.2B

An investor purchased \$250 000 in 364-day T-bills 315 days before maturity to yield 3.38%. He sold the T-bills 120 days later to yield 3.72%.

(i) How much did the investor pay for the T-bills?

(ii) For how much did the investor sell the T-bills?

(iii) What rate of return did the investor realize on the investment?

SOLUTION

(i) Find the purchase price of the T-bills, P_1.

$$S = 250\,000.00; \quad r_1 = 0.0338; \quad t_1 = \frac{315}{365}$$

$$P_1 = \frac{250\,000.00}{1 + 0.0338\left(\frac{315}{365}\right)} = \frac{250\,000.00}{1 + 0.029170} = \$242\,914.23$$

The investor purchased the T-bills for \$242 914.23.

(ii) Find the selling price of the T-bills, P_2.
The time to maturity at the date of sale is 195 days (315−120).

$$S = 250\,000.00; \quad r_2 = 0.0372; \quad t_2 = \frac{195}{365}$$

$$P_2 = \frac{250\,000.00}{1 + 0.0372\left(\frac{195}{365}\right)} = \frac{250\,000.00}{1 + 0.019874} = \$245\,128.33$$

The investor sold the T-bills for \$245 128.33.

(iii) The investment of \$242 914.23 grew to \$245 128.33 in 120 days.
To compute the rate of return, use the future value formula (Formula 7.3A).

$$P = 242\,914.23; \quad S = 245\,128.33; \quad t = \frac{120}{365}$$

$$S = P(1 + rt)$$

$$245\,128.33 = 242\,914.23\left[1 + r\left(\frac{120}{365}\right)\right]$$

$$\frac{245\,128.33}{242\,914.23} = 1 + \left(\frac{120}{365}\right)r$$

$$1.009115 = 1 + 0.328767r$$

$$0.009115 = 0.328767r$$

$$\frac{0.009115}{0.328767} = r$$

$$r = 0.027724 = 2.7724\%$$

The investor realized a rate of return of 2.7724%.

Alternatively:

The gain realized represents the interest.
$I = 245\,128.33 - 242\,914.23 = \$2214.10$

Using the formula $r = \frac{I}{Pt}$,

$$r = \frac{2214.10}{242\,914.23\left(\frac{120}{365}\right)} = \frac{2214.10}{79\,862.21} = 0.027724 = 2.7724\%.$$

EXERCISE 8.2

EXCEL SPREADSHEET

A. Answer each of the following questions.

1. What is the price of a one-year, $50 000 Province of British Columbia treasury bill that yields 1.36% per annum?

2. What is the price of a 91-day, $100 000 Government of Canada treasury bill that yields 0.53% per annum?

3. An investment dealer acquired a $5000, 91-day Province of Alberta treasury bill on its date of issue at a price of $4966.20. What was the annual rate of return?

4. An investment dealer acquired a $10 000, 183-day Province of Quebec treasury bill on its date of issue at a price of $9822.00. What was the annual rate of return?

5. An investor purchased a 91-day, $100 000 T-bill on its issue date for $99 326.85. After holding it for 42 days, she sold the T-bill for a yield of 2.72%.
  (a) What was the original yield of the T-bill?
  (b) For what price was the T-bill sold?
  (c) What rate of return (per annum) did the investor realize while holding this T-bill?

6. On April 1, $25 000 364-day treasury bills were auctioned off to yield 2.92%.
  (a) What is the price of each $25 000 T-bill on April 1?
  (b) What is the yield rate on August 15 if the market price is $24 377.64?
  (c) Calculate the market value of each $25 000 T-bill on October 1 if the rate of return on that date is 4.545%.
  (d) What is the rate of return realized if a $25 000 T-bill purchased on April 1 is sold on November 20 at a market rate of 4.625%?

8.3 DEMAND LOANS

A. Nature of demand loans

A **demand loan** is a loan for which repayment, in full or in part, may be required at any time, or made at any time. The financial instrument representing a demand loan is called a **demand note.**

When borrowing on a demand note, the borrower receives the full face value of the note. The lender may demand payment of the loan in full or in part at any time. Conversely, the borrower may repay all of the loan or any part at any time without notice and without interest penalty. Interest, based on the unpaid balance, is usually payable monthly. The interest rate on such loans is normally not fixed for the duration of the loan but fluctuates with market conditions. Thus the total interest cost cannot be predicted with certainty. Note that the method of counting days is to count the first day but not the last.

Demand loans and similar debts are sometimes paid off by a series of **partial payments.** The commonly used approach to dealing with this type of loan repayment is the **declining balance approach**, requiring that each partial payment be applied first to the accumulated interest. Any remainder is then used to reduce the outstanding principal. Thus, interest is always calculated on the unpaid balance and the new unpaid balance is determined after each partial payment.

The following step-by-step procedure is useful in dealing with such problems:

(a) Compute the interest due to the date of the partial payment.

(b) Compare the interest due computed in part (a) with the partial payment received, and do part (c) if the partial payment is *greater than* the interest due or do part (d) if the partial payment is *less than* the interest due.

(c) *Partial payment greater than interest due:*
   (i) Deduct the interest due from the partial payment.
   (ii) Deduct the remainder in part (i) from the principal balance to obtain the new unpaid balance.

(d) *Partial payment less than interest due:*
   In this case, the partial payment is not large enough to cover the interest due.
   (i) Deduct the partial payment from the interest due to determine the unpaid interest due at the date of the principal payment.
   (ii) Keep a record of this balance and apply any future partial payments to this unpaid interest first.

EXAMPLE 8.3A

On April 20, 2011, Bruce borrowed $4000 at 5% on a note requiring payment of principal and interest on demand. Bruce paid $600 on May 10 and $1200 on July 15. What payment is required on September 30 to pay the note in full?

SOLUTION

April 20

Original loan balance		$4000.00	
May 10			
Deduct			
First partial payment	$ 600.00		
Less interest			
April 20–May 10	10.96		$(4000)(0.05)\left(\frac{20}{365}\right)$
		589.04	
Unpaid balance		$3410.96	
July 15			
Deduct			
Second partial payment	$1200.00		
Less interest			
May 10–July 15	30.84		$(3410.96)(0.05)\left(\frac{66}{365}\right)$
		1169.16	
Unpaid balance		$2241.80	

September 30

Add

Interest

July 15–Sept. 30 → 23.65 $(2241.80)(0.05)\left(\frac{77}{365}\right)$

Payment required to pay the note in full → $2265.45

POINTERS AND PITFALLS

When determining the number of days in any given time period between interest rate changes or between two partial payments, remember to always count the first day and omit the last day. As well, keep in mind that

(a) The date on which there is a change in the interest rate is counted as the first day at the new interest rate.

(b) The date on which a partial payment is made is counted as the first day at the new outstanding principal balance.

EXAMPLE 8.3B

The Provincial Bank lent $20 000 to the owner of the Purple Pelican on April 1, 2012, for commercial improvements. The loan was secured by a demand note subject to a variable rate of interest. This rate was 7% on April 1. The rate of interest was raised to 9% effective August 1 and reduced to 8% effective November 1. Partial payments, applied to the loan by the declining balance method, were made as follows: June 10, $1000; September 20, $400; November 15, $1200. How much interest is due to the Provincial Bank on December 31?

SOLUTION

April 1

Original loan balance → $20 000.00

June 10

Deduct

First partial payment → $1000.00

Less interest

April 1–June 10 → 268.49 — $(20\,000)(0.07)\left(\frac{70}{365}\right)$

731.51

Unpaid loan balance → $19 268.49

September 20

Deduct

Second partial payment $ 400.00

Less interest

June 10–Sept. 20:

June 10–July 31 (inclusive) $192.16 — $(19\,268.49)(0.07)\left(\frac{52}{365}\right)$

Aug. 1–Sept. 20	237.56	429.72		$(19\,268.49)(0.09)\left(\frac{50}{365}\right)$
Unpaid interest to				
Sept. 20 →		$ 29.72		
Unpaid loan balance →			$19 268.49	
November 15				
Deduct				
Third partial payment →		$1200.00		
Less interest				
Unpaid interest to				
Sept. 20 →	$ 29.72			(see above)
Sept. 20–Oct. 31 → (inclusive)	199.55			$(19\,268.49)(0.09)\left(\frac{42}{365}\right)$
Nov. 1–Nov. 15 →	59.13			$(19\,268.49)(0.08)\left(\frac{14}{365}\right)$
		288.40		
			911.60	
Unpaid loan balance →			$18 356.89	
December 31				
Interest due				
Nov. 15–Dec. 31 →			$ 185.08	$(18\,356.89)(0.08)\left(\frac{46}{365}\right)$

EXERCISE 8.3

Answer each of the following.

EXCEL SPREADSHEET

1. Erindale Automotive borrowed $8000 from the Bank of Montreal on a demand note on May 10. Interest on the loan, calculated on the daily balance, is charged to Erindale's current account on the 10th of each month. Erindale made a payment of $2000 on July 20, a payment of $3000 on October 1, and repaid the balance on December 1. The rate of interest on the loan on May 10 was 8% per annum. The rate was changed to 9.5% on August 1 and to 8.5% on October 1. What was the total interest cost for the loan?

EXCEL SPREADSHEET

2. The Tomac Swim Club arranged short-term financing of $12 500 on July 20 with the Bank of Commerce and secured the loan with a demand note. The club repaid the loan by payments of $6000 on September 15, $3000 on November 10, and the balance on December 30. Interest, calculated on the daily balance and charged to the club's current account on the last day of each month, was at 9.5% per annum on July 20. The rate was changed to 8.5% effective September 1 and to 9% effective December 1. How much interest was paid on the loan?

EXCEL SPREADSHEET

3. On March 10, Fat Tires Ltd. borrowed $10 000 with an interest rate of 5.5%. The loan was repaid in full on November 15, with payments of $2500 on June 30 and $4000 on September 4. What was the final payment?

4. Automotive Excellence Inc. borrowed $20 000 on August 12 with an interest rate of 6.75% per annum. On November 1, $7500 was repaid, and on December 15, $9000 was repaid. Automotive Excellence paid the balance of the loan on February 20. What was the final payment?

5. A loan of $6000 made at 11% per annum on March 10 is repaid in full on November 15. Payments were made of $2000 on June 30 and $2500 on September 5. What was the final payment?

6. D. Slipp borrowed $15 000 on August 12. She paid $6000 on November 1, $5000 on December 15, and the balance on February 20. The rate of interest on the loan was 10.5%. How much did she pay on February 20?

7. The Continental Bank made a loan of $20 000 on March 25 to Dr. Hirsch to purchase equipment for her office. The loan was secured by a demand loan subject to a variable rate of interest that was 7% on March 25. The rate of interest was raised to 8.5% effective July 1 and to 9.5% effective September 1. Dr. Hirsch made partial payments on the loan as follows: $600 on May 15; $800 on June 30; and $400 on October 10. The terms of the note require payment of any accrued interest on October 31. How much must Dr. Hirsch pay on October 31?

8. Dirk Ward borrowed $12 000 for investment purposes on May 10 on a demand note providing for a variable rate of interest and payment of any accrued interest on December 31. He paid $300 on June 25, $150 on September 20, and $200 on November 5. How much is the accrued interest on December 31 if the rate of interest was 7.5% on May 10, 6% effective August 1, and 5% effective November 1?

8.4 LINES OF CREDIT AND CREDIT CARD LOANS

A **line of credit** is a pre-approved loan agreement between a financial institution and a borrower. The borrower may withdraw money, up to an agreed maximum, at any time. Interest is charged only on the amount withdrawn from the line of credit. A minimum repayment may be required each month. The borrower may repay any additional amount at any time without further penalty. The rate of interest charged for money borrowed on a line of credit is often lower than the rate of interest charged on most credit cards. The interest rate can change over time.

A **credit card** is a plastic card entitling the bearer to a revolving line of credit with a pre-established credit limit. Interest rates are set by the credit card issuers, vary considerably, and can be changed at any time. Generally, interest rates charged on credit cards are higher than rates charged on loans made by financial institutions. Some credit card issuers require an annual fee to be paid by the user. When the bearer withdraws cash by presenting the credit card, a cash advance fee is usually charged. Depending on the issuer of the credit card, the cash advance fee may be deducted directly from the cash advance at the time the money is received or it may be posted to the account on the day the cash is received. Interest on the cash advance is calculated starting from the day the money is withdrawn. The bearer of the credit card, with an authorizing signature, may make purchases instead of using cash to pay.

An **unsecured line of credit** is a line of credit with no assets promised to the lender to cover non-payment of the loan. Since no security is offered to the lender, the limit of an unsecured line of credit depends on the individual's credit rating and past relationship with the lender.

A **secured line of credit** is a line of credit with assets promised to the lender to cover non-payment of the loan. For example, homeowners might pledge the value of their home, that is, their home equity, to secure a line of credit. In general, the limit of a secured line of credit is higher than the limit of an unsecured one. Furthermore, the interest rate of a secured line of credit is lower than the interest rate of an unsecured one.

Lines of credit secured by home equity are used by some borrowers as an alternative to other types of loans. Home equity lines of credit (HELOC) provide access to larger credit limits.

EXAMPLE 8.4A

Deb has secured a line of credit for her business and received the following statement of account for the month of February.

Date	Transaction Description	Deposit	Withdrawal	Balance
Feb. 01	Balance			−600.00
04	Cheque 262		500.00	−1100.00
10	Deposit	2050.00		950.00
16	Cheque 263		240.00	710.00
20	Cheque 264		1000.00	−290.00
22	Cheque 265		80.00	−370.00
27	Cheque 266		150.00	−520.00
28	Interest earned	?		
	Line of credit interest		?	
	Overdraft interest		?	
	Service charge		?	

Note: "−" indicates a negative balance.

The limit on her line of credit is $1000. She receives daily interest of 1.5% p.a. on positive balances and pays daily interest of 7% p.a. on *negative (line of credit) balances.* Overdraft interest is 18% p.a. on the daily amount exceeding her line of credit limit. There is a service charge of $5 for each transaction causing an overdraft or adding to an overdraft.

Determine

(i) the amount of interest earned;

(ii) the amount of interest charged on the line of credit;

(iii) the amount of interest charged on overdrafts;

(iv) the amount of the service charge;

(v) the account balance on February 28.

SOLUTION

(i) Interest earned (on positive balances):
February 10 to February 15 inclusive: 6 days at 1.5% on \$950.00

$$I = 950.00(0.015)\left(\frac{6}{365}\right) = \$0.23$$

February 16 to February 19 inclusive: 4 days at 1.5% on \$710.00

$$I = 710.00(0.015)\left(\frac{4}{365}\right) = \$0.12$$

Total interest earned = 0.23 + 0.12 = \$0.35

(ii) Line of credit interest charged (on negative balances up to \$1000.00):
February 1 to February 3 inclusive: 3 days at 7% on \$600.00

$$I = 600.00(0.07)\left(\frac{3}{365}\right) = \$0.35$$

February 4 to February 9 inclusive: 6 days at 7% on \$1000.00

$$I = 1000.00(0.07)\left(\frac{6}{365}\right) = \$1.15$$

February 20 to February 21 inclusive: 2 days at 7% on \$290.00

$$I = 290.00(0.07)\left(\frac{2}{365}\right) = \$0.11$$

February 22 to February 26 inclusive: 5 days at 7% on \$370.00

$$I = 370.00(0.07)\left(\frac{5}{365}\right) = \$0.35$$

February 27 to February 28 inclusive: 2 days at 7% on \$520.00

$$I = 520.00(0.07)\left(\frac{2}{365}\right) = \$0.20$$

Total line of credit interest charged
= 0.35 + 1.15 + 0.11 + 0.35 + 0.20 = \$2.16

(iii) Since the line of credit limit is \$1000.00, overdraft interest is charged on the amount in excess of a negative balance of \$1000.00. The account was in overdraft from February 4 to February 9 inclusive in the amount of \$100.00.

$$\text{Overdraft interest} = 100.00\,(0.18)\left(\frac{6}{365}\right) = \$0.30$$

(iv) There was one transaction causing an overdraft or adding to an overdraft.
Service charge = 1(5.00) = \$5.00

(v) The account balance on February 28
= −520.00 + 0.35 − 2.16 − 0.30 − 5.00 = −\$527.11

EXAMPLE 8.4B

You have applied for and received a credit card. The interest rate charged is 18.9% per annum. You note the following transactions for the month of September.

September 6	Purchased textbooks and supplies for a total of \$250.
September 10	Withdrew \$100 as a cash advance through your credit card.
September 30	Received the credit card statement, showing a minimum balance owing of \$25. A payment date of October 10 is stated on the statement.

(i) Compute the amount of interest charged on the cash advance from September 10 until September 30.

(ii) You decide to pay the amount owing, in full, on October 1. How much must you pay?

(iii) Instead of paying the full amount, you decide to pay the minimum, \$25, on October 1. What is the balance owing after the payment?

(iv) If there are no further transactions during October, how much is owing at the end of October?

SOLUTION

(i) Interest charged (on cash advance):
September 10 to September 30 inclusive: \$100 at 18.9% for 21 days.

$$I = 100.00(0.189)\left(\frac{21}{365}\right) = \$1.09$$

(ii) \$250.00 + 100.00 + 1.09 = \$351.09

(iii) \$351.09 − 25.00 = \$326.09

(iv) $I = 326.09(0.189)\left(\frac{31}{365}\right) = \$5.23$

\$326.09 + 5.23 = \$331.32
At the end of October \$331.32 is owing.

EXERCISE 8.4

Determine the missing information for each of the following lines of credit.

1. Suppose you have a line of credit and receive the following statement for the month of March.

Date	Transaction Description	Deposit	Withdrawal	Balance
Feb. 28	Balance			−527.71
Mar. 02	Cheque 264		600.00	−1127.71
05	Cheque 265		300.00	−1427.71
10	Deposit	2000.00		572.29
16	Cheque 266		265.00	307.29

20	Cheque 267		1000.00	−692.71
22	Cheque 268		83.50	−776.21
27	Cheque 269		165.00	−941.21
31	Interest earned	?		
	Line of credit interest		?	
	Overdraft interest		?	
	Service charge		?	?

Note: "−" indicates a negative balance.

The limit on the line of credit is $1000. Daily interest of 1.25% p.a. is received on positive balances and daily interest of 8% p.a. is paid on negative (line of credit) balances. Overdraft interest is 18% p.a. on the daily amount exceeding the line of credit limit. There is a service charge of $5 for each transaction causing an overdraft or adding to an overdraft.

(a) Calculate the amount of interest earned.
(b) Calculate the amount of interest charged on the line of credit.
(c) Calculate the amount of interest charged on overdrafts.
(d) Calculate the amount of the service charge.
(e) What is the account balance on March 31?

2. Exotic Furnishings Ltd. has a line of credit secured by the equity in the business. The limit on the line of credit is $45 000. Transactions for the period April 1 to September 30 are shown below. Exotic owed $25 960.06 on its line of credit on April 1.

Date	Principal Withdrawal	Principal Payment	Interest Payment	Balance
Apr. 01				−25 960.06
30		200.00	?	
May 23	5 000.00			
31		200.00	?	
June 30		200.00	?	
July 19	5 000.00			
31		200.00	?	
Aug. 05	10 500.00			
31		200.00	?	
Sept. 30		200.00	?	?

Note: "−" indicates a negative balance.

The line of credit agreement requires a regular payment of $200 on the principal plus interest (including overdraft interest) by electronic transfer after closing on the last day of each month. Overdraft interest is 17% p.a. The line of credit interest is variable. It was 6.00% on April 1, 5.50% effective June 20, and 5.00% effective September 10.

(a) Calculate the interest payments on April 30, May 31, June 30, July 31, August 31, and September 30.
(b) What is the account balance on September 30?

8.5 LOAN REPAYMENT SCHEDULES

A. Purpose

In the case of loans repaid in fixed installments (often called **blended payments**), the constant periodic payment is first applied to pay the accumulated interest. The remainder of the payment is then used to reduce the unpaid balance of the principal.

While lenders are obliged to disclose to the borrower the total cost of borrowing as well as the interest rate (see Figure 8.6), a detailed statement of the cost of borrowing as well as the effect of the periodic payments on the principal may be obtained by constructing a **loan repayment schedule**, or an **amortization schedule.**

FIGURE 8.6 **Statement of Disclosure**

STATEMENT OF DISCLOSURE

(COST OF LOAN AND ANNUAL INTEREST RATE) PURSUANT TO THE CONSUMER PROTECTION ACT

Name of Credit Union *SHERIDAN* Account No. 13465–274

1) Balance of existing loan (if any) $ *2000.00*

2) Add new amount loaned $ *4000.00*

3) Full amount of loan $ *6000.00*

4) Cost of Borrowing expressed in dollars and cents (Interest calculated on full amount of loan (Item 3)) $ *1473.00*

5) Annual Interest Rate charged (calculated in accordance with the Consumer Protection Act) *9* %

6) If any charge is made to the borrower in addition to interest herein noted, it must be disclosed here. $ ________
(Description) ....
Frequency of installments *60 MONTHS* Amount of installments $ *124.55* First instalment due ________ 20 __

I, the undersigned, acknowledge receipt of this statement of cost of loan and annual interest rate, prior to the advance of the credit.

DATE ________ X ....

SIGNATURE OF BORROWER

COMPLETE IN DUPLICATE Original to Borrower NOTE: Where more than one maker or co-maker, separate Disclosure Forms should be signed for individually.

The information usually contained in such a schedule includes

(a) the payment number or payment date;
(b) the amount paid at each payment date;
(c) the interest paid by each payment;
(d) the principal repaid by each payment;
(e) the unpaid loan balance after each payment.

Figure 8.7 provides a possible design for such schedules, and the same design is used in the solution to Example 8.5A.

FIGURE 8.7 **Basic Design of a Loan Repayment Schedule**

① Payment Number	② Balance Before Payment	③ Amount Paid	④ Interest Paid	⑤ Principal Repaid	⑥ Balance After Payment

B. Construction of loan repayment schedules illustrated

EXAMPLE 8.5A Great Lakes Marina borrowed $1600 from Sheridan Credit Union at 9% p.a. and agreed to repay the loan in monthly installments of $300 each, such payments to cover interest due and repayment of principal. Use the design shown in Figure 8.7 to construct a complete repayment schedule, including the totalling of columns ③, ④, and ⑤ ("Amount Paid," "Interest Paid," and "Principal Repaid").

SOLUTION See Figure 8.8 and the explanatory notes that follow.

FIGURE 8.8 **Loan Repayment Schedule for Example 8.5A**

① Payment Number	② Balance Before Payment	③ Amount Paid (1)		④ Interest Paid (2)		⑤ Principal Repaid (3)		⑥ Balance After Payment (4)	
0								1600.00	(5)
1	1600.00	300.00		12.00	(6)	288.00	(7)	1312.00	(8)
2	1312.00	300.00		9.84	(9)	290.16	(10)	1021.84	(11)
3	1021.84	300.00		7.66		292.34		729.50	
4	729.50	300.00		5.47		294.53		434.97	
5	434.97	300.00		3.26		296.74		138.23	(12)
6	138.23	139.27	(15)	1.04	(14)	138.23	(13)	0.00	
Totals (16)		1639.27	(18)	39.27	(19)	1600.00	(17)		

Notes:

(1) The Amount Paid shown in column ③ is the agreed-upon monthly payment of $300.

(2) The Interest Paid shown in column ④ is at 9% per annum. This figure is converted into a periodic (monthly) rate of $\frac{9\%}{12}$ (0.75% per month) to facilitate the computation of the monthly amount of interest paid. (See notes (6) and (9).)

(3) The amount of Principal Repaid each month shown in column ⑤ is found by subtracting the Interest Paid for the month (column ④) from the Amount Paid for the month (column ③). (See notes (7) and (10).)

(4) The Balance After Payment for a month shown in column ⑥ is found by subtracting the Principal Repaid for the month (column ⑤) from the Balance Before Payment for the month (column ②) *or* from the previous Balance After Payment figure (column ⑥). (See notes (8) and (11).)

(5) The original loan balance of $1600 is introduced as the starting amount for the schedule and is the only amount shown in Line 0.

(6) Interest paid in Payment Number 1
= 0.75% of 1600.00 = (0.0075)(1600.00) = $12.00

(7) Principal repaid by Payment Number 1
= 300.00 − 12.00 = $288.00

(8) Balance after Payment Number 1
= 1600.00 − 288.00 = $1312.00

(9) Interest paid in Payment Number 2
= 0.75% of 1312.00 = (0.0075)(1312.00) = $9.84

(10) Principal repaid by Payment Number 2
= 300.00 − 9.84 = $290.16

(11) Balance after Payment Number 2
= 1312.00 − 290.16 = $1021.84

(12) The Balance after Payment Number 5 of $138.23 is smaller than the regular monthly payment of $300. The next payment need only be sufficient to pay the outstanding balance of $138.23 plus the interest due. (See notes (13), (14), and (15).)

(13) Principal repaid in Payment Number 6 must be $138.23 to pay off the outstanding loan balance.

(14) Interest paid in Payment Number 6 is the interest due on $138.23
= 0.75% of 138.23 = (0.0075)(138.23) = $1.04.

(15) Amount paid in Payment Number 6
= 138.23 + 1.04 = $139.27.

(16) The Totals of columns ③, ④, and ⑤ serve as a check of the arithmetic accuracy of the payment schedule. (See notes (17), (18), and (19).)

(17) Principal Repaid, the total of column 5, must equal the original loan balance of $1600.

(18) Amount Paid, the total of column ③, must equal the total of all the payments made (five payments of $300 each plus the final payment of $139.27).

(19) Interest paid, the total of column ④, must be the difference between the totals of columns ④ and ⑤ = 1639.27 − 1600.00 = $39.27.

C. Computer application—loan repayment schedule

This exercise assumes a basic understanding of spreadsheet applications; however, an individual who has no previous experience with spreadsheets can complete this task.

EXCEL NOTES

Microsoft Excel and other spreadsheet programs allow the user to easily create a flexible loan repayment schedule. The finished repayment schedule will reflect any changes made to the loan amount, the interest rate, or the schedule of payments. (The following example was created in Excel, but most programs work similarly.)

The following Excel application is based on Example 8.5A, which uses six months to repay the loan. An additional row of formulas similar to row 3 would be added for each additional month required to repay the loan.

STEP 1 Enter the labels shown in Figure 8.9 in row 1 and in column A.

STEP 2 Enter the numbers shown in row 2.

STEP 3 Enter only the formulas shown in rows 3, 8, and 9. Make sure that the entry includes the dollar sign ($) as shown in the figure.

FIGURE 8.9

Workbook 1

	A	B	C	D	E	F	G
1	Payment	Balance before payment	Amount paid	Interest paid	Principal repaid	Balance	
2	0					1600.00	300.00
3	1	= F2	= G2	= G4*B3	= C3–D3	= B3–E3	
4	2	= F3	= G2	= G4*B4	= C4–D4	= B4–E4	= 0.09/12
5	3	= F4	= G2	= G4*B5	= C5–D5	= B5–E5	
6	4	= F5	= G2	= G4*B6	= C6–D6	= B6–E6	
7	5	= F6	= G2	= G4*B7	= C7–D7	= B7–E7	
8	6	= F7	= D8+E8	= G4*B8	= B8	= B8–E8	
9	Totals		= SUM(C3:C8)	= SUM(D3:D8)	= SUM(E3:E8)		

STEP 4 The formulas that are entered in row 3 can be copied through the remaining rows.
(a) Select cells B3 to F3, and select Copy.
(b) Select cells B4 to F7, and select Paste.
(c) The formulas are now active in all the cells.

STEP 5 To ensure readability of the spreadsheet, format the numbers to display as two decimal places, and widen the columns to display the full labels.

This spreadsheet can now be used to reflect changes in aspects of the loan and display the effects quickly. Put a new principal amount in cell F2 and a new interest rate in cell G4. The interest rate must be divided by 12 to convert the annual interest rate to a monthly rate. For example, new annual interest rate of 5% would be entered as $\frac{0.05}{12}$.

EXCEL NOTES A copy of this spreadsheet, called Template 2, appears on MathXL.

EXERCISE 8.5

Use the design shown in Figure 8.7 to construct a complete repayment schedule including the totalling of the Amount Paid, Interest Paid, and Principal Repaid columns for each of the following loans.

1. Carla borrowed $1200 from the Royal Bank at 8.5% per annum calculated on the monthly unpaid balance. She agreed to repay the loan in blended payments of $180 per month.

2. Blended payments on a $3400 loan were $800 per month. Interest was charged at 7.75% per annum calculated on the monthly unpaid balance.

3. On March 15, Julio borrowed $900 from Sheridan Credit Union at 7.5% per annum calculated on the daily balance. He gave the Credit Union six cheques

for $135 dated the 15th of each of the next six months starting April 15 and a cheque dated October 15 for the remaining balance to cover payment of interest and repayment of principal.

4. On February 8, Manuel borrowed $700 from his uncle at 6% per annum calculated on the daily balance. He gave his uncle seven cheques for $100 dated the 8th of each of the next seven months starting March 8 and a cheque dated September 8 for the remaining balance to cover payment of interest and repayment of principal.

BUSINESS MATH NEWS BOX

Exploring Personal Lines of Credit

Your local bank branch recently distributed the information shown below.

Consolidate high-interest credit cards with our convenient Line of Credit

A line of credit is a great way to consolidate balances from your credit cards and loans to create one easy-to-manage monthly payment. These examples show you how much your unsecured line of credit can help you save in just six months:

Your Balance	Some Department Store Cards 28.8%	Other Credit Cards 19.50%	Unsecured Line of Credit 7%	In Six Months You Can Save Up To
$8000	$1152	$780	$280	$872
$5000	$720	$488	$175	$545
$2500	$360	$244	$88	$272

(The savings above are based on the rates remaining the same for six months. Calculations have been rounded down to the nearest dollar. Unsecured line of credit rates are subject to change without notice.)

QUESTIONS

1. Suppose you had a balance of $5000 on a credit card charging interest at a rate of 19.97%. How much interest would you save in six months with the unsecured line of credit?
2. Look at the situation in Question 1 again, this time make the rate 9.5% after the first two months. Now what are your savings at the end of six months?

Sources: **http://money.canoe.ca/rates/credit.html** and **www.canadianbusiness.com/my_money/rates.**

Go to MathXL at www.mathXL.com. You can practise many of this chapter's exercises as often as you want. The guided solutions help you find an answer step by step. You'll find a personalized study plan available to you too!

Review Exercise

1. A four-month promissory note for $1600 dated June 30 bears interest at 6.5%.

(a) What is the due date of the note?

(b) What is the amount of interest payable at the due date?

(c) What is the maturity value of the note?

2. Determine the maturity value of a 120-day note for $1250 dated May 23 and bearing interest at 5.75%.

3. Compute the face value of a 120-day note dated September 10 bearing interest at 6.75% whose maturity value is $1534.12.

4. The maturity value of a seven-month promissory note issued July 31, 2012, is $3275. What is the present value of the note on the date of issue if interest is 7.75%?

5. Compute the maturity value of a 150-day, 6% promissory note with a face value of $5000 dated August 5.

6. What is the face value of a three-month promissory note dated November 30, 2011, with interest at 4.5 percent, if its maturity value is $950.89?

7. A 90-day, $800 promissory note was issued July 31 with interest at 8%. What is the value of the note on October 20?

8. On June 1, 2012, a four-month promissory note for $1850 with interest at 5% was issued. Compute the proceeds of the note on August 28, 2012, if money is worth 6.5%.

9. Determine the value of a $1300 non-interest-bearing note four months before its maturity date of July 13, 2013, if money is worth 7%.

10. Compute the proceeds of a five-month, $7000 promissory note dated September 6, 2012, with interest at 5.5% if the note is paid on November 28, 2012, when money is worth 6.5%.

11. An investment dealer paid $24 256.25 to acquire a $25 000, 182-day Government of Canada treasury bill at the weekly auction. What was the rate of return on this T-bill?

12. Government of Alberta 364-day T-bills with a face value of $1 000 000 were purchased on April 7 for $971 578. The T-bills were sold on May 16 for $983 500.

(a) What was the market yield rate on April 7?

(b) What was the yield rate on May 16?

(c) What was the rate of return realized?

13. Mel's Photography borrowed $15 000 on March 10 on a demand note. The loan was repaid by payments of $4000 on June 20, $3000 on September 1, and the balance on November 15. Interest, calculated on the daily balance and charged to Mel's Photography current account on the last day of each month, was at 5.5% on March 10 but was changed to 6.25% effective June 1 and to 6% effective October 1. How much did the loan cost?

14. Quick Print Press borrowed $20 000 from the Provincial Bank on May 25 at 7.5% and secured the loan by signing a promissory note subject to a variable rate of interest. Quick Print made partial payments of $5000 on July 10 and $8000 on September 15. The rate of interest was increased to 8% effective August 1 and to 8.5% effective October 1. What payment must Quick Print make on October 31 if, under the terms of the loan agreement, any interest accrued as of October 31 is to be paid on October 31?

15. Muriel has a line of credit with a limit of $10 000. She owed $8195 on July 1. Principal withdrawals for the period July 1 to November 30 were $3000 on August 20 and $600 on October 25. The line of credit agreement requires regular payments of $300 on the 15th day of each month. Muriel has made all required payments. Interest (including overdraft interest) is charged to the account on the last day of each month. The interest rate was 8% on July 1, but was changed to 7.5% effective September 15. Overdraft interest is 16% for any balance in excess of $10 000.

(a) Calculate the interest charges on July 31, August 31, September 30, October 31, and November 30.

(b) Calculate the account balance on November 30.

16. You borrowed $3000 at 9% per annum calculated on the unpaid monthly balance and agreed to repay the principal together with interest in monthly payments of $500 each. Construct a complete repayment schedule.

Self-Test

EXCEL SPREADSHEET

1. The owner of the Wilson Lumber Company signed a promissory note on January 10, 2013, stating that the company was due to pay $565.00 with interest at 8.25% per annum in five months. How much interest is due at maturity of the note?

2. Find the maturity value of a $1140, 7.75%, 120-day note dated February 19, 2012.

3. Determine the face value of a four-month promissory note dated May 20, 2011, with interest at 7.5% p.a. if the maturity value of the note is $1190.03.

4. Find the present value of a non-interest-bearing seven-month promissory note for $1800 dated August 7, 2013, on December 20, 2013, if money is then worth 6%.

5. A 180-day note dated September 14, 2014, is made at 5.25% for $1665. What is the present value of the note on October 18, 2014, if money is worth 6.5%?

6. What is the price of a 91-day, $25 000 Government of Canada treasury bill that yields 3.28% per annum?

7. An investor purchased a 182-day, $100 000 T-bill on its issue date. It yielded 3.85%. The investor held the T-bill for 67 days, then sold it for $98 853.84.

(a) What was the original price of the T-bill?

(b) When the T-bill was sold, what was its yield?

8. The owner of Jane's Boutique borrowed $6000 from Halton Community Credit Union on June 5, 2012. The loan was secured by a demand note with interest calculated on the daily balance and charged to the store's account on the 5th day of each month. The loan was repaid by payments of $1500 on July 15, $2000 on October 10, and $2500 on December 30. The rate of interest charged by the credit union was 8.5% on June 5. The rate was changed to 9.5% effective July 1 and to 10% effective October 1. Determine the total interest cost on the loan.

9. Herb's Restaurant borrowed $24 000 on March 1 on a demand note providing for a variable rate of interest. While repayment of principal is open, any accrued interest is to be paid on November 30. Payments on the loan were made as follows: $600 on April 15, $400 on July 20, and $400 on October 10.

The rate of interest was 7% on March 1 but was changed to 8.5% effective August 1 and to 7.5% effective November 1. Using the declining balance method to record the partial payments, determine the accrued interest on November 30.

10. Jing has a line of credit from her local bank with a limit of $10 000. On March 1 she owed $7265. From March 1 to June 30, she withdrew principal amounts of $3000 on April 10 and $500 on June 20. According to the line of credit agreement, Jing must make a regular payment of $200 on the 15th of each month. She has made these payments. Interest (including overdraft interest) is charged to the account on the last day of each month. On March 1, the interest rate was 9%, but it was changed to 8.5% effective May 15. Overdraft interest is 18% for any balance in excess of $10 000.

(a) Calculate the interest charges on March 31, April 30, May 31, and June 30.

(b) What is the account balance on June 30?

11. Use the design shown in Figure 8.7 to construct a complete repayment schedule, including the totalling of the "Amount Paid," "Interest Paid," and "Principal Repaid" columns, for a loan of $4000 repaid in monthly installments of $750 each including interest of 6.5% per annum calculated on the unpaid balance.

Challenge Problems

1. Mike Kornas signed a 12-month, 11% p.a. simple interest promissory note for $12 000 with MacDonald's Furniture. After 100 days, MacDonald's Furniture sold the note to the Royal Bank at a rate of 13% p.a. Royal Bank resold the note to Friendly Finance Company 25 days later at a rate of 9% p.a. Find the gain or loss on this note for each company and bank involved.

2. A father wanted to show his son what it might be like to borrow money from a financial institution. When his son asked if he could borrow $120, the father lent him the money and set up the following arrangements. He charged his son $6 for the loan of $120. The son therefore received $114 and agreed to pay his father 12 installments of $10 a month, beginning one month from today, until the loan was repaid. Find the approximate rate of simple interest the father charged on this loan.

CASE STUDY 8.1 The Business of Borrowing

» Bits and Bytes Computer Store agrees to purchase some new computer monitors costing $3500 plus 5% GST. Farid Kamlani, the store's owner, was informed that if he paid cash on receipt of the goods he could take a cash discount of 4.5% of the invoice price before GST. GST would then be added to the new invoice price. Farid would like to take advantage of this discount, but his store is short of cash right now. A number of customers are expected to pay their invoices in the next 30 to 60 days.

Farid went to his bank manager to negotiate a short-term loan to pay for the monitors when they arrive and take advantage of the cash discount. The bank manager suggested a 60-day promissory note bearing interest at 6.5%. Farid agreed to the note and suggested that the three days of grace should be added to provide him more repayment flexibility.

QUESTIONS

1. What is the maturity value of the 60-day promissory note using three days of grace for the goods, including GST?
2. Suppose Farid decides he does not need the three days of grace. What effect would this have on the maturity value of the note?
3. Farid later discussed his situation with a friend, who suggested that Farid could have negotiated a short-term loan for 60 days instead of using a promissory note. What is the highest annual simple interest rate at which Farid could have borrowed the money and still saved by taking the cash discount?

CASE STUDY 8.2 Debt Consolidation

» Shannon and Duncan Fisher were concerned about their level of debt. They had borrowed from their bank to purchase their house, car, and computer. For these three loans, the Fishers must make regular monthly payments. The couple also owe $6000 to MasterCard and $2500 to Visa. Shannon and Duncan decided to meet with a consumer credit counsellor to gain control of their debts.

The counsellor explained to them the details of their loans and credit card debts. Shannon and Duncan were shocked to discover that whereas their computer and car loans had an interest rate of 10.5% p.a., their credit cards had an interest rate of 19.5% p.a. The counsellor pointed out that the interest rate on their three loans was reasonable. However, because the interest rate on the credit cards was so high, she advised Shannon and Duncan to borrow money at a lower interest rate and pay off the credit card debts.

The credit counsellor suggested that they should consider obtaining a line of credit. She explained that the rate of interest on the line of credit would likely be a few percentage points higher than the prime rate, but much lower than the rate of interest charged on credit card balances. Shannon and Duncan would have to make a minimum payment every month, similar to that of a credit card. The payment would then be applied to pay all the interest and a portion of the principal balance owing on the line of credit. The line of credit would allow them to make monthly payments higher than the minimum so that they could pay as much toward the principal balance as they could afford. Due to the much lower interest rate on a line of credit as compared to a typical credit card, the money they would save on interest each month could be paid toward the principal. A line of credit appealed to Shannon and Duncan, as it helped them feel more in control of their finances and gave them the resolve to pay off their credit card debts.

Shannon and Duncan then met with their bank manager and were approved for a \$15 000 line of credit. Immediately, they paid off the \$6000 owed to MasterCard and the \$2500 owed to Visa with money from the line of credit. They then decided to pay off the line of credit over the next ten months by making monthly payments equal to one-tenth of the original line of credit balance plus the simple interest owed on the remaining line of credit balance. The simple interest rate on the line of credit is expected to be 6.25% over the next ten months. Shannon and Duncan agreed to cut up their credit cards and not charge any more purchases until they had paid off their line of credit.

QUESTIONS

1. Suppose Shannon and Duncan pay off their credit cards with their line of credit on April 20. They will make their monthly payments on the 20th of each month, beginning in May. Create a schedule showing their monthly payments for the next ten months. How much interest will they pay using this repayment plan?
2. Suppose Shannon and Duncan had not gotten a line of credit but kept their credit cards. They decided not to make any more credit card purchases. Instead, they made monthly payments equal to one-tenth of the original credit card balance plus the simple interest owed on the remaining credit card balance. They will make their monthly payments on the 20th of each month, beginning in May. Create a schedule showing their monthly payments for the next ten months. How much interest would they have paid using this repayment plan?
3. How much money did Shannon and Duncan save on interest by getting the line of credit?
4. What are the requirements for obtaining a line of credit from your financial institution?

SUMMARY OF FORMULAS

Formula 7.1A

$I = Prt$ **Finding the amount of interest on promissory notes**

Formula 7.3A

$S = P(1 + rt)$ **Finding the maturity value of promissory notes directly**

Formula 7.3B

$P = \frac{S}{1 + rt}$ **Finding the present value of promissory notes or treasury bills given the maturity value**

GLOSSARY

Amortization schedule see **Loan repayment schedule**

Amount of interest the interest, in dollars and cents, payable to the payee on the legal due date *(p. 298)*

Blended payment the usual method of repaying a personal consumer loan by a fixed periodic (monthly) payment that covers payment of interest and repayment of principal *(p. 316)*

Credit card a card entitling the bearer to a revolving line of credit with a pre-approved credit limit *(p. 311)*

Date of issue the date on which a promissory note is made *(p. 297)*

Date of maturity *see* **Legal due date**

Declining balance approach the commonly used approach to applying partial payments to demand loans whereby each partial payment is first applied to pay the interest due and then applied to the outstanding principal *(p. 308)*

Demand loan a loan for which repayment in full or in part may be required at any time or made at any time *(p. 307)*

Demand note the financial instrument representing a demand loan *(p. 307)*

Due date *see* **Legal due date**

Face value the sum of money specified on the promissory note *(p. 297)*

Interest-bearing promissory note a note subject to the rate of interest stated on the note *(p. 297)*

Interest period the time, in days, from the date of issue to the legal due date for promissory notes *(p. 298)*

Issue date *see* **Date of issue**

Legal due date the date on which the promissory note is to be paid; it includes three days of grace unless "No Grace Days" is written on the promissory note *(p. 298)*

Line of credit a pre-approved loan amount issued by a financial institution for use by an individual or business at any time for any purpose; interest is charged only for the time money is borrowed on the line of credit; a minimum monthly payment is required (similar to a credit card); the interest rate can change over time *(p. 311)*

Loan repayment schedule a detailed statement of installment payments, interest cost, repayment of principal, and outstanding balance of principal for an installment plan *(p. 316)*

Maker the party making the promise to pay by signing the promissory note *(p. 297)*

Maturity value the amount (face value plus interest) that must be paid on the legal due date to honour the note *(p. 298)*

Non-interest-bearing promissory note a note in which no interest rate is stated *(p. 300)*

Partial payments a series of payments on a debt *(p. 308)*

Payee the party to whom the promise to pay is made *(p. 297)*

Promissory note a written promise to pay a specified sum of money after a specified period of time or on demand, with or without interest as specified *(p. 297)*

Rate money is worth the prevailing rate of interest *(p. 300)*

Rate of interest the simple annual rate of interest based on the face value *(p. 297)*

Secured line of credit a line of credit with assets pledged as security *(p. 312)*

T-bills *see* **Treasury bills**

Term (of a promissory note) the time period for which the note was written (in days or months) *(p. 298)*

Three days of grace the number of days added to the term of a note in Canada to determine its legal due date *(p. 298)*

Treasury bills promissory notes issued at a discount from their face values by the federal government and most provincial governments to meet short-term financing requirements (the maturity value of treasury bills is the same as their face value) *(p. 304)*

Unsecured line of credit a line of credit in which no assets are pledged by the borrower to the lender to cover non-payment of the line of credit *(p. 312)*

USEFUL INTERNET SITES

www.royalbank.com

Royal Bank Visit the "Daily Numbers" area of this site for current interest rates on investment products. This site also provides links to detailed rate schedules for mortgages, T-bills, personal accounts, and RRSPs.

www.bankofcanada.ca/en/rates/tbill.html

Bank of Canada Current T-bill rates are posted on this section of the Bank of Canada site. A link to selected historical interest rates is also provided.

www.equifax.ca

Equifax Consumer Services Canada This organization will help you to monitor your credit rating with a credit report, learn about credit scores and consumer privacy, and protect yourself from identity theft.

CHAPTER 9

Compound Interest—Future Value and Present Value

OBJECTIVES

Upon completing this chapter, you will be able to do the following:

1. Calculate interest rates and the number of compounding periods.
2. Compute future (maturity) values of investments.
3. Compute present values of future sums of money.
4. Discount long-term promissory notes.
5. Solve problems involving equivalent values.

The world of computerized banking and investing uses compound interest extensively. With compound interest, you earn interest on a principal, and the interest is then added to form a new principal. You then earn interest on this new higher principal. This is what is meant by the expression "earning interest on interest."

Understanding how compound interest works, calculating interest, and deciding which interest terms are best are essential in operating businesses. To calculate compound interest amounts, an understanding of exponents is required to use the formulas. Preprogrammed financial calculators and computers aid in determining compound interest amounts for all sorts of interest rates and time periods.

INTRODUCTION

Under the compound interest method, interest is added periodically to the principal. As we did with simple interest, we use compound interest calculations to determine future values and present values. The compound interest formulas contain the compounding factor $(1 + i)^n$. The calculations are not difficult if you use electronic calculators equipped with an exponential function, especially if they are financial calculators preprogrammed with the ability to calculate future value and present value for compound interest.

9.1 BASIC CONCEPTS AND COMPUTATIONS

A. Basic procedure for computing compound interest

The term **compound interest** refers to a procedure for computing interest whereby the interest for a specified time period is added to the original principal. The resulting amount becomes the new principal for the next time period. The interest earned in earlier periods earns interest in future periods.

The compound interest method is generally used to calculate interest for long-term investments. The amount of compound interest for the first interest period is the same as the amount of simple interest, but for further interest periods the amount of compound interest becomes increasingly greater than the amount of simple interest.

The basic procedure for computing compound interest and the effect of compounding is illustrated in Table 9.1. The table also provides a comparison of

Table 9.1 **Compound Interest Versus Simple Interest for a Principal of $10 000 Invested at 10% per Annum for 6 Years**

		At Compound Interest		At Simple Interest	
Year		Interest Computation	Amount	Interest Computation	Amount
	Original principal		$10 000.00		$10 000.00
1	Add interest	(0.10)(10 000.00)	1 000.00	(0.10)(10 000.00)	1 000.00
	Amount end Year 1		11 000.00		11 000.00
2	Add interest	(0.10)(11 000.00)	1 100.00	(0.10)(10 000.00)	1 000.00
	Amount end Year 2		12 100.00		12 000.00
3	Add interest	(0.10)(12 100.00)	1 210.00	(0.10)(10 000.00)	1 000.00
	Amount end Year 3		13 310.00		13 000.00
4	Add interest	(0.10)(13 310.00)	1 331.00	(0.10)(10 000.00)	1 000.00
	Amount end Year 4		14 641.00		14 000.00
5	Add interest	(0.10)(14 641.00)	1 464.10	(0.10)(10 000.00)	1 000.00
	Amount end Year 5		16 105.10		15 000.00
6	Add interest	(0.10)(16 105.10)	1 610.51	(0.10)(10 000.00)	1 000.00
	Amount end Year 6		$17 715.61		$16 000.00

compound interest and simple interest for an original principal of \$10 000 invested at 10% per annum for six years.

The method of computation used in Table 9.1 represents the step-by-step approach used in maintaining a compound interest record, such as a savings account. Note that the amount of interest is determined for each interest period on the basis of the previous balance and is then added to that balance.

Note the following about the end results after six years:

	At compound interest	*At simple interest*
Amount after six years	\$17 715.61	\$16 000.00
Less original principal	10 000.00	10 000.00
Amount of interest	\$ 7715.61	\$ 6 000.00

In this case, the compound interest exceeds the simple interest by \$1715.61. This difference represents the amount of interest earned by interest added to the principal at the end of each compounding period.

B. The future value formula for compound interest

Creating a compound interest table without using a computer application is useful, and serves many purposes, but can be time-consuming. As in calculating simple interest, the **future value** or **maturity value** of a loan or investment can be found by using the future value formula.

For *simple interest*, the future value formula is $S = P(1 + rt)$, Formula 7.3A.

For *compound interest*, the formula for the future value is

$$S = P(1 + i)^n$$ restated as:

$$FV = PV(1 + i)^n$$ **Formula 9.1A**

S or FV = the future or maturity value;
P or PV = the original principal;
i = the periodic rate of interest;
n = the number of compounding periods for the term of the loan or investment.

The results of Table 9.1 could have been obtained by using the two future value formulas.

For simple interest: $P = 10\,000.00$; $r = 0.1$; $t = 6$

$$\begin{aligned} S = P(1 + rt) &= 10\,000.00[1 + (0.1)(6)] \\ &= 10\,000.00(1 + 0.6) \\ &= 10\,000.00(1.6) \\ &= \$16\,000.00 \end{aligned}$$

For compound interest: PV = 10 000.00; $i = 0.1$; $n = 6$

$$\begin{aligned} FV = PV(1+i)^n &= 10\,000.00(1+0.1)^6 \\ &= 10\,000.00(1.1)^6 \\ &= 10\,000.00(1.1)(1.1)(1.1)(1.1)(1.1)(1.1) \\ &= 10\,000.00(1.771561) \\ &= \$17\,715.61 \end{aligned}$$

When using the compound interest formula, determining the factor $(1 + i)^n$ is the main computational problem. The value of this factor, called the **compounding factor** or **accumulation factor**, depends on the values of i and n.

C. Determining the periodic rate of interest

The value of i, the **periodic rate of interest**, is determined from the stated rate of interest to be used in the compounding situation. The stated rate is called the **nominal rate of interest**. Since the nominal rate of interest is usually stated as an annual rate, the value of i depends on the **compounding** (or **conversion**) **frequency** per year. The value of i is obtained by dividing the nominal annual rate by the number of **compounding** (or **conversion**) **periods** per year.

The compounding (conversion) periods commonly used in business and finance cover a number of months, usually an exact divisor of 12, and are listed in Table 9.2.

The relationship between the periodic rate of interest and the nominal annual rate of interest can be stated in the form of a formula.

$$\text{PERIODIC RATE OF INTEREST, } i = \frac{\text{NOMINAL (ANNUAL) RATE}}{\text{NUMBER OF COMPOUNDING (CONVERSION) PERIODS PER YEAR}}$$

Therefore,

$$i = \frac{j}{m} \qquad \text{Formula 9.2}$$

where i = periodic rate of interest
j = nominal annual rate of interest
m = number of compounding (conversion) periods per year

Table 9.2 **Commonly Used Compounding Frequencies and Conversion Periods**

Compounding (Conversion) Frequency	Length of Compounding (Conversion) Period	Number of Compounding (Conversion) Periods per Year
Annual	12 months (1 year)	1
Semi-annual	6 months	2
Quarterly	3 months	4
Monthly	1 month	12

EXAMPLE 9.1A Determine the periodic rate of interest i for

(i) 5% p.a. compounded annually;

(ii) 7% p.a. compounded semi-annually;

(iii) 12% p.a. compounded quarterly;

(iv) 10.5% p.a. compounded monthly;

(v) 28% p.a. compounded daily

SOLUTION

	Nominal Annual Rate j	Compounding Frequency	Length of Compounding Period	Number of Compounding Periods per Year m	Periodic Rate of Interest $i = \frac{j}{m}$
(i)	5%	Annually	12 months	1	$\frac{5\%}{1} = 5.0\%$
(ii)	7%	Semi-annually	6 months	2	$\frac{7\%}{2} = 3.5\%$
(iii)	12%	Quarterly	3 months	4	$\frac{12\%}{4} = 3.0\%$
(iv)	10.5%	Monthly	1 month	12	$\frac{10.5\%}{12} = 0.875\%$
(v)	28%	Daily	1 day	365	$\frac{28\%}{365} = 0.0767\%$

D. Determining the number of compounding (conversion) periods in the term of an investment or loan

To find the number of compounding (conversion) periods in the term of an investment or a loan, multiply the number of years in the term by the number of compounding periods per year.

The value n in the compounding factor $(1 + i)^n$ is not restricted to integral values; n may take any fractional value. The future value can be determined by means of the formula $FV = PV(1 + i)^n$ whether the time period contains an integral number of conversion periods or not.

EXAMPLE 9.1B Determine the number of compounding periods when

(i) compounding annually for 14 years;

(ii) compounding semi-annually for 15 years;

(iii) compounding quarterly for 12.5 years;

(iv) compounding monthly for 10.75 years;

(v) compounding quarterly for 32 months;

(vi) compounding semi-annually for 40 months.

SOLUTION

	Term (in years)	Compounding Frequency	Number of Compounding Periods per Year, m	Number of Compounding Periods in Term, n
(i)	14	annually	1	14(1) = 14
(ii)	15	semi-annually	2	15(2) = 30
(iii)	12.5	quarterly	4	12.5(4) = 50
(iv)	10.75	monthly	12	10.75(12) = 129
(v)	$\frac{32}{12} = 2.6\dot{6}$	quarterly	4	$2.6\dot{6}(4) = 10.6\dot{6}$
(vi)	$\frac{40}{12} = 3.3\dot{3}$	semi-annually	2	$3.3\dot{3}(2) = 6.6\dot{6}$

POINTERS AND PITFALLS

Many students have difficulty determining the value of m when compounding is stated as "quarterly." This term means that interest is compounded every quarter of a year. Since there are four quarters in a year, m then becomes 4, each quarter of a year being 3 months in length. The value of m is never 3.

E. Setting up the compounding factor $(1 + i)^n$

The *compounding (accumulation) factor* $(1 + i)^n$ can be set up by first determining i and n and then substituting i and n in the general form of the factor, $(1 + i)^n$.

EXAMPLE 9.1C

Set up the compounding factor $(1 + i)^n$ for

(i) 5% p.a. compounded annually for 14 years;
(ii) 7% p.a. compounded semi-annually for 15 years;
(iii) 12% p.a. compounded quarterly for 12.5 years;
(iv) 10.5% p.a. compounded monthly for 10.75 years;
(v) 8% p.a. compounded quarterly for 30 months;
(vi) 9.5% p.a. compounded semi-annually for 42 months.

SOLUTION

	i	m	n	$(1 + i)^n$
(i)	5% = 0.05	1	14(1) = 14	$(1 + 0.05)^{14} = 1.05^{14}$
(ii)	3.5% = 0.035	2	15(2) = 30	$(1 + 0.035)^{30} = 1.035^{30}$
(iii)	3.0% = 0.03	4	12.5(4) = 50	$(1 + 0.03)^{50} = 1.03^{50}$
(iv)	0.875% = 0.00875	12	10.75(12) = 129	$(1 + 0.00875)^{129} = 1.00875^{129}$
(v)	2% = 0.02	4	30/12(4) = 10	$(1 + 0.02)^{10} = 1.02^{10}$
(vi)	4.75% = 0.0475	2	42/12(2) = 7	$(1 + 0.0475)^{7} = 1.0475^{7}$

F. Computing the numerical value of the compounding factor $(1 + i)^n$

The numerical value of the compounding factor can now be computed using an electronic calculator. For calculators equipped with the exponential function feature y^x, the numerical value of the compounding factor can be computed directly.

STEP 1 Enter the numerical value of $(1 + i)$ in the keyboard.

STEP 2 Press the exponential function key y^x.

STEP 3 Enter the numerical value of n in the keyboard.

STEP 4 Press =.

STEP 5 Read the answer in the display.

The numerical value of the compounding factors in Example 9.1C are obtained as follows.

		(i)	(ii)	(iii)	(iv)	(v)	(vi)
STEP 1	Enter	1.05	1.035	1.03	1.00875	1.02	1.0475
STEP 2	Press	y^x	y^x	y^x	y^x	y^x	y^x
STEP 3	Enter	14	30	50	129	10	7
STEP 4	Press	=	=	=	=	=	=
STEP 5	Read	1.979932	2.806794	4.383906	3.076647	1.218994	1.383816

Note: Do not be concerned if your calculator shows a difference in the last decimal. There is no error. It reflects the precision of the calculator and the number of decimal places formatted to show on the display of the calculator.

For example, if your calculator has been set to show only two decimal places, it will automatically round the answer to (i) above to 1.98. If you were to continue calculating without clearing your calculator, it would use the non-rounding number in the further calculations.

With the increasing availability of inexpensive electronic calculators, the two traditional methods of determining the compounding factor $(1 + i)^n$—logarithms and tables—are rapidly falling into disuse. Neither method is used in this text.

EXERCISE 9.1

A. Determine m, i, and n for each of the following.

1. 12% compounded annually for 5 years
2. 7.4% compounded semi-annually for 8 years

3. 5.5% compounded quarterly for 9 years
4. 7% compounded monthly for 4 years
5. 11.5% compounded semi-annually for 13.5 years
6. 4.8% compounded quarterly for $5\frac{3}{4}$ years
7. 8% compounded monthly for 12.5 years
8. 10.75% compounded quarterly for 3 years, 9 months
9. 12.25% compounded semi-annually for 54 months
10. 8.1% compounded monthly for 15.5 years

B. Set up and compute the compounding factor $(1 + i)^n$ for each of the questions in Part A.

C. Answer each of the following questions.

1. For a sum of money invested at 10% compounded quarterly for 12 years, state
   (a) the number of compounding periods;
   (b) the periodic rate of interest;
   (c) the compounding factor $(1 + i)^n$;
   (d) the numerical value of the compounding factor.
2. For each of the following periodic rates of interest, determine the nominal annual compounding rate.
   (a) $i = 2\%$; compounding is quarterly
   (b) $i = 0.75\%$; compounding is monthly
   (c) $i = 5.5\%$; compounding is semi-annually
   (d) $i = 9.75\%$; compounding is annually

9.2 USING THE FUTURE VALUE FORMULA OF A COMPOUND AMOUNT $FV = PV(1 + i)^n$

A. Finding the future value (maturity value) of an investment

EXAMPLE 9.2A Find the amount to which $6000 will grow if invested at 4% per annum compounded quarterly for five years.

SOLUTION The original principal PV = 6000.00;
the nominal annual rate $j = 4\%$;
the number of compounding periods per year $m = 4$;

the quarterly rate of interest $i = \frac{4\%}{4} = 1.0\% = 0.01$

the number of compounding periods (quarters) $n = (5)(4) = 20$.

$$
\begin{aligned}
FV &= PV(1+i)^n && \text{using Formula 9.1A} \\
&= 6000.00(1+0.01)^{20} && \text{substituting for P, } i, n \\
&= 6000.00(1.01)^{20} && \text{exponential form of factor} \\
&= 6000.00(1.220190) && \text{using a calculator*} \\
&= \$7321.14
\end{aligned}
$$

*Note that, when recording the result of the calculation, the number has been rounded to six decimal places. To complete the calculations, continue with the number stored in the calculator. If the rounded number is used to complete the calculations, the end result may be different by a small amount.

EXAMPLE 9.2B

What is the future value after 78 months of \$2500 invested at 5.25% p.a. compounded semi-annually?

SOLUTION

The original principal PV = 2500.00;
the nominal annual rate $j = 5.25$;
the number of compounding periods per year $m = 2$;
the semi-annual rate of interest $i = \frac{5.25\%}{2} = 2.625\% = 0.02625$;
the number of compounding periods (each period is six months)
$n = \left(\frac{78}{12}\right)(2) = (6.5)(2) = 13.$

$$
\begin{aligned}
FV &= PV(1+i)^n \\
&= 2500.00(1+0.02625)^{13} \\
&= 2500.00(1.02625)^{13} \\
&= 2500.00(1.400526) \\
&= \$3501.32
\end{aligned}
$$

EXAMPLE 9.2C

What will be the worth of a deposit of \$1750 made into a registered retirement savings plan from March 1, 1995, to December 1, 2015, at 4.4% p.a. compounded quarterly?

SOLUTION

The original principal PV = 1750.00; $j = 4.4\%$; $m = 4$;
the quarterly rate of interest $i = \frac{4.4\%}{4} = 1.1\% = 0.011$;
the time period from March 1, 1995, to December 1, 2015, contains 20 years and 9 months, or 20.75 years: $n = (20.75)(4) = 83$.

$$
\begin{aligned}
FV &= PV(1+i)^n \\
&= 1750.00(1+0.011)^{83} \\
&= 1750.00(1.011)^{83} \\
&= 1750.00(2.479396) \\
&= \$4338.94
\end{aligned}
$$

B. Using preprogrammed financial calculators

Compound interest calculations, which can become complex, are performed frequently and repeatedly. Doing the calculations algebraically can enhance your understanding and appreciation of the theory, but it can also be time-consuming, laborious, and subject to mechanical errors. Using preprogrammed financial calculators can save time and reduce or eliminate mechanical errors, assuming they are set up properly and numerical sign conventions are observed when entering data and interpreting results.

Different models of financial calculators vary in their operation and labelling of the function keys and faceplate. Appendix II, entitled "Instructions and Tips for Three Preprogrammed Financial Calculator Models," highlights the relevant variations for students using Texas Instruments' BAII Plus, Sharp's EL-733A, and Hewlett-Packard's 10B calculators. (Note that Appendix II is intended to help you use one of these three calculators, and merely supplements the instruction booklet that came with your calculator. Refer to the instruction booklet for your particular model to become familiar with your calculator.)

Specific function keys on preprogrammed financial calculators correspond to the five variables used in compound interest calculations. Function keys used for the calculator models presented in Appendix II are shown in Table 9.3.

The function keys are used to enter the numerical values of the known variables into the appropriate preprogrammed calculator registers. The data may be entered in any order. The answer is then displayed by using a computation key or by

Table 9.3 **Financial Calculator Function Keys that Correspond to Variables Used in Compound Interest Calculations**

Variable	Algebraic Symbol	Function Key: TI BAII+	Function Key: Sharp EL-733A	Function Key: HP 10B
The number of compounding periods	n	N	n	N
The rate of interest[1]	i	I/Y C/Y	i	I/YR
The periodic annuity payment[2]	R	PMT	PMT	PMT
The present value or principal	P	PV	PV	PV
The future value or maturity value	S	FV	FV	FV

Notes: 1. The periodic rate of interest is entered as a percent and not as a decimal equivalent (as it is when using the algebraic method to solve compound interest problems). For example, 8% is entered as "8" not ".08". With some calculators, the rate of interest is the periodic rate. In the case of the BAII Plus, the rate of interest entered is the rate per year (nominal rate).

2. The periodic annuity payment function key PMT is used only for annuity calculations, which are introduced in Chapter 11.

depressing the key representing the unknown variable, depending on the calculator model.

Before entering the numerical data to complete compound interest calculations, it is important to verify that your calculator has been set up correctly to ensure error-free operation. There are a number of items to check during this "pre-calculation" phase. Specifically, does the calculator require a mode change within a register to match the text presentation? Does the calculator have to be in the financial mode? Are the decimal places set to the correct number to ensure the required accuracy?

Further checks must be made when entering data during the "calculation" phase. For example, have the function key registers been cleared? What numerical data require a minus sign to avoid errors in operation and incorrect answers? How can the data entered be confirmed? Responses to these queries in the "pre-calculation" and "calculation" phases for three preprogrammed financial calculators are given in Appendix II, along with general information.

Instructions in this text are given for the Texas Instruments BAII Plus calculator. Refer to Appendix II for instructions for setting up and using the Sharp EL-733A and Hewlett-Packard 10B calculators.

Using the Texas Instruments BAII Plus to Solve Compound Interest Problems

Follow the steps below to compute the future value of a sum of money using the formula FV = PV$(1 + i)^n$ and a Texas Instruments BAII Plus calculator. Compare your result with Example 9.2A.

Pre-calculation Phase (Initial Setup)

STEP 1 The P/Y register, and behind it, the C/Y register, must be set to match the calculator's performance to the text presentation. The P/Y register is used to represent the number of regular payments per year. If the text of the question does not discuss regular payments per year, this should be set to equal the C/Y in the calculator. The C/Y register is used to represent the number of compounding periods per year, that is, the compounding frequency. The description of the compounding frequency is usually contained within the phrase that describes the nominal interest rate. An example would be "8% p.a. compounded quarterly." This means that the nominal, or annual, interest rate of 8% is compounded four times each year at 8%/4, or 2%, each period. The compounding frequency of 4 is entered into the C/Y register within the calculator.

Key in	*Press*	*Display shows*	
	2nd (P/Y)	P/Y = 12	checks the P/Y register
4	ENTER	P/Y = 4	changes the value to "4"
	↓	C/Y = 4	changed automatically to match the P/Y
	2nd (QUIT)	0	returns to the standard calculation mode

STEP 2 Verify that the decimal format is set to the number you require. A setting of "9" represents a floating decimal point format. The default setting is "2."

Key in	*Press*	*Display shows*
	2nd (Format)	DEC = 2 — checks the decimal format
6	ENTER	DEC = 6 — changes to "6"
	2nd (QUIT)	0 — returns to the standard calculation mode

This calculator is ready for financial calculations in its standard mode.

Calculation Phase

STEP 3 Always clear the function key registers before beginning compound interest calculations. This action resets all values to their default values.

Key in	*Press*	*Display shows*
	2nd (CLR TVM)	0 — clears the function key registers

STEP 4 To solve Example 9.2A, in which P = 6000, i = 1.0%, and n = 20, use the following procedure. Remember that i represents the interest rate per compounding period, and n represents the number of times that interest is compounded. To enter the accurate information into the calculator, you must determine the nominal interest rate for the year, and enter this information into the I/Y register. In this example, the interest rate per year is 4%. The compounding frequency, denoted by the phrase "compounded quarterly," is four times per year. This must be entered into the C/Y register. Also, notice that 6000 is entered as a negative number since it is cash paid out for an investment. This "cash flow sign convention" is explained below.

If you follow this convention, your calculation will be error-free, and the answer will be accurate and interpreted consistently.

Key in	*Press*	*Display shows*
	2nd (P/Y)	P/Y = 12 — checks the P/Y register
4	ENTER	P/Y = 4 — changes the value to "4"
	↓	C/Y = 4 — changed automatically to match the P/Y
	2nd (QUIT)	0 — returns to the standard calculation mode

6000	[±] [PV]	PV = −6000	this enters the present value P (principal) with the correct sign convention
4	[I/Y]	I/Y = 4	this enters the nominal interest rate as a percent
20	[N]	N = 20	this enters the number of compounding periods *n*
	[CPT] [FV]	FV = 7321.140240	this computes and displays the unknown future value S

The future value is $7321.14.

Cash Flow Sign Convention for Entering Numerical Data

The Texas Instruments BAII Plus calculator follows the established convention of treating cash inflows (cash received) as positive numbers and cash outflows (cash paid out) as negative numbers. In the calculation above, the present value was considered to be cash paid out for an investment, and so the present value of 6000 was entered as a negative number. The resulting future value was considered to be cash received from the investment and so had a positive value. Note that if the present value had been entered as a positive value, then the future value would have been displayed as a negative number. The *numerical* value would have been correct but the result would have been a negative number. "Error 5" is displayed when calculating I/Y or n if both the present value and future value are entered using the same sign. Therefore, to avoid errors, always enter the present value as a negative number for compound interest calculations. Enter all other values as positive numbers. This topic is discussed further in Appendix II and throughout this text as required.

EXCEL NOTES

Excel has a Future Value (FV) function you can use to calculate the future value of an investment subject to compound interest. Refer to FV on MathXL to learn how to use this Excel function.

EXAMPLE 9.2D

Find the accumulated value of $1000 invested for two years and nine months at 10% p.a. compounded annually.

SOLUTION

The entire time period is 2 years and 9 months; the number of whole conversion periods is 2; the fractional conversion period is $\frac{9}{12}$ of a year.

$$PV = 1000.00;\ I/Y = 10;\ C/Y = 1;\ i = 10\% = 0.10;\ n = 2\frac{9}{12} = 2.75$$

$$FV = 1000.00(1.10)^{2.75} = 1000.00(1.299660) = \$1299.66$$

Programmed Solution

(Set P/Y, C/Y = 1) [2nd] (CLR TVM) 1000 [±] [PV] 10 [I/Y]

2.75 [N] [CPT] [FV] [1299.660393]

EXAMPLE 9.2E

Determine the future value amount of \$400 invested at 6% p.a. compounded quarterly for three years and five months.

SOLUTION

PV = 400.00; i = 1.5% = 0.015

$$n = \left(3\frac{5}{12}\right)(4) = \left(\frac{41}{12}\right)(4) = \frac{41}{3} = 13\frac{2}{3} = 13.\dot{6}$$

$$FV = 400.00(1.015)^{13.\dot{6}} = 400.00(1.225658) = \$490.26$$

Programmed Solution

(Set P/Y, C/Y = 4) [2nd] (CLR TVM) 400 [±] [PV] 6 [I/Y]

13.6̇ [N] [CPT] [FV] [490.263132]

EXAMPLE 9.2F

A debt of \$3500 dated August 31, 2012, is payable together with interest at 9% p.a. compounded quarterly on June 30, 2015. Determine the amount to be paid.

SOLUTION

PV = 3500.00; I/Y = 9; C/Y = 4; $i = \frac{9\%}{4} = 2.25\% = 0.0225$; the time period August 31, 2012, to June 30, 2015, contains 2 years and 10 months; the number of quarters $n = 11.\dot{3}$.

$$\begin{aligned} FV &= 3500.00(1.0225)^{11.\dot{3}} \\ &= 3500.00(1.286819) \\ &= \$4503.87 \end{aligned}$$

Programmed Solution

(Set P/Y, C/Y = 4) [2nd] (CLR TVM) 3500 [±] [PV] 9 [I/Y]

11.3̇ [N] [CPT] [FV] [4503.867790]

C. Applications involving changes in interest rate of principal

EXAMPLE 9.2G

A deposit of \$2000 earns interest at 6% p.a. compounded monthly for four years. At that time, the interest rate changes to 7% p.a. compounded quarterly. What is the value of the deposit three years after the change in the rate of interest?

SOLUTION

The data given can be represented on a time diagram as shown in Figure 9.1.

Separate the entire problem into the time periods during which different interest rates apply.

FIGURE 9.1 **Graphical Representation of Data**

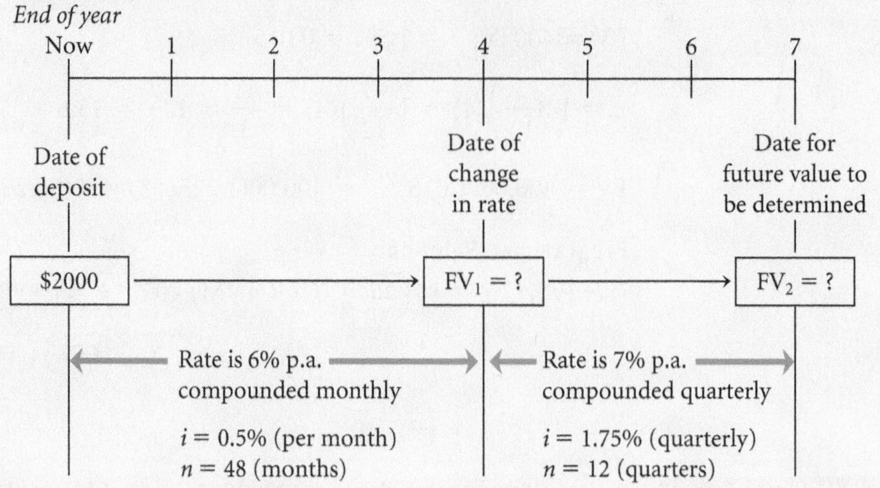

STEP 1 Determine the accumulated value of the original deposit at the time the interest rate changes, that is, after four years.

$$PV = 2000.00; I/Y = 6; C/Y = 12; i = \frac{6\%}{12} = 0.5\% = 0.005; n = 48$$

$$FV_1 = 2000.00(1 + 0.005)^{48} = 2000.00(1.270489) = \$2540.978322$$

STEP 2 Use the accumulated value after four years as the new principal and calculate its accumulated value three years later using the new rate of interest.

$$PV = 2540.978322; I/Y = 7; C/Y = 4; i = \frac{7\%}{4} = 1.75\% = 0.0175; n = 12$$

$$FV_2 = 2540.978322(1 + 0.0175)^{12} = 2540.978322(1.231439) = \$3129.06$$

Solution by Preprogrammed Calculator

Keys are applicable to the Texas Instruments BAII Plus calculator (this is the case throughout the rest of this chapter).

STEP 1

Key in	*Press*	*Display shows*
	2nd (P/Y)	
12	ENTER	P/Y = 12
	↓	C/Y = 12
	2nd (QUIT)	0
	2nd (CLR TVM)	0
2000	± PV	–2000
6	I/Y	6
48	N	48
	CPT FV	2540.978322 —— **answer to Step 1 (FV_1 = 2540.978322)**

Do *not* clear your display. Proceed to Step 2.

STEP 2

Key in	*Press*	*Display shows*	
	± PV	−2540.978322	— this step enters the new principal and the proper sign convention, since this amount is reinvested (a cash outflow)
	2nd (P/Y)	P/Y = 12	
4	ENTER	P/Y = 4	
	↓	C/Y = 4	
	2nd (QUIT)	0	
7	I/Y	7	
12	N	12	
	CPT FV	3129.060604	— final answer (FV_2 = \$3129.06)

EXAMPLE 9.2H

A debt of \$500 accumulates interest at 8% p.a. compounded quarterly from April 1, 2012, to July 1, 2013, and 9% p.a. compounded monthly thereafter. Determine the accumulated value of the debt on December 1, 2014.

SOLUTION

STEP 1

Determine the accumulated value of the debt on July 1, 2013.

$PV_1 = 500.00$; I/Y = 8; C/Y = 4; $i = \frac{8\%}{4} = 2\% = 0.02$;

the period April 1, 2012, to July 1, 2013, contains 15 months: $n = 5$

$FV_1 = 500.00(1.02)^5 = 500.00(1.104081) = \$552.040402$

STEP 2

Use the result of Step 1 as new principal and find its accumulated value on December 1, 2014.

$PV_2 = 552.040402$; I/Y = 9; P/Y = 12; $i = \frac{9\%}{12} = 0.75\% = 0.0075$;

the period July 1, 2013, to December 1, 2014, contains 17 months: $n = 17$

$FV_2 = 552.040402(1.0075)^{17} = 552.040402(1.135445) = \$626.81$

Programmed Solution

STEP 1

(Set P/Y, C/Y= 4) 2nd (CLR TVM) 500 ± PV 8 I/Y 5 N CPT FV

Result: 552.040402

STEP 2

552.040402 ± PV (Set P/Y, C/Y= 12) 9 I/Y 17 N CPT FV

Result: 626.811268

EXAMPLE 9.2I

Jay opened a registered retirement savings plan with his credit union on February 1, 2007, with a deposit of \$2000. He added \$1900 on February 1, 2008, and another \$1700 on February 1, 2011. What will his account amount to on August 1, 2017, if the plan earns a fixed rate of interest of 7% p.a. compounded semi-annually?

SOLUTION

See Figure 9.2.

FIGURE 9.2 Graphical Representation of Data

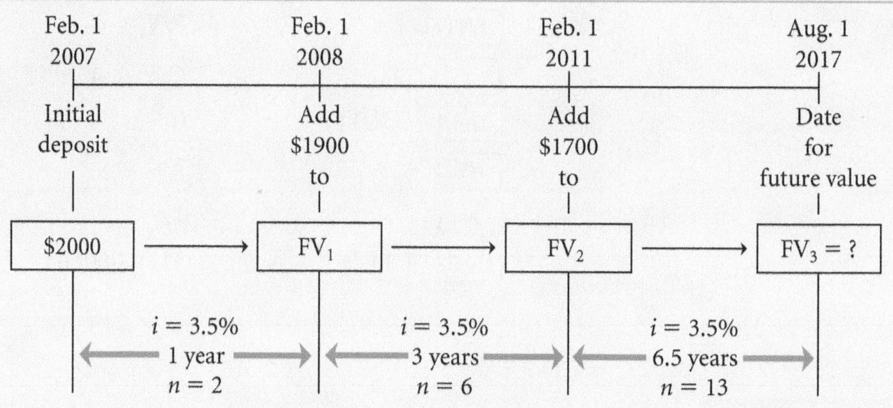

STEP 1 Determine the future value, FV_1, of the initial deposit on February 1, 2008.

$PV_1 = 2000.00$; I/Y = 7; C/Y = 2; $i = \frac{7\%}{2} = 3.5\% = 0.035$;

the period February 1, 2007, to February 1, 2008, contains 1 year: $n = 2$
$FV_1 = 2000.00(1.035)^2 = 2000.00(1.071225) = \$2142.45$

STEP 2 Add the deposit of \$1900 to the amount of \$2142.45 to obtain the new principal as of February 1, 2008, and determine its future value, FV_2, on February 1, 2011.

$PV_2 = 2142.45 + 1900.00 = 4042.45$; $i = 0.035$;

the period February 1, 2008, to February 1, 2011, contains 3 years: $n = 6$
$FV_2 = 4042.45(1.035)^6 = 4042.45(1.229255) = \$4969.203194$

STEP 3 Add the deposit of \$1700 to the amount of \$4969.203194 to obtain the new principal as of February 1, 2011, and determine its future value, FV_3, on August 1, 2017.

$PV_3 = 4969.203194 + 1700.00 = 6669.203194$; $i = 0.035$;
the period February 1, 2011, to August 1, 2017, contains 6.5 years: $n = 13$
$FV_3 = 6669.203194(1.035)^{13} = 6669.203194(1.563956) = \$10\,430.34$

Programmed Solution

STEP 1 (Set P/Y, C/Y=2) [2nd] (CLRTVM)2000 [±] [PV] 7 [I/Y] 2 [N] [CPT] [FV]

Result: [2142.45]

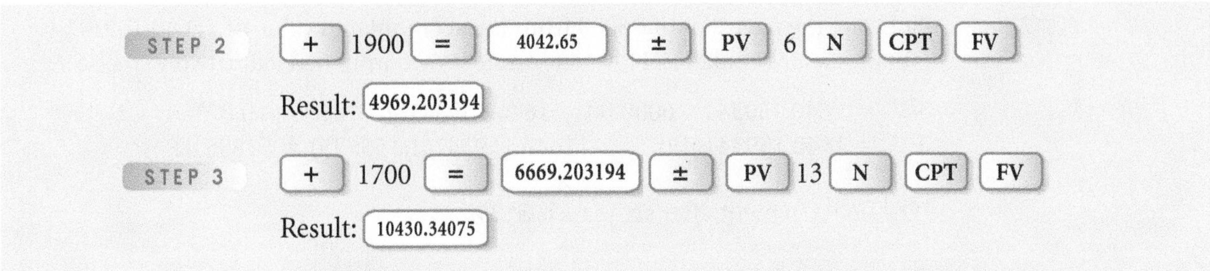

Note: Since the numbers are not being cleared after each step, there is no need to re-enter the interest rate in Steps 2 and 3—it has not changed and is already programmed from Step 1.

EXAMPLE 9.2J

A demand loan of $10 000 is repaid by payments of $5000 in one year, $6000 in four years, and a final payment in six years. Interest on the loan is 10% p.a. compounded quarterly during the first year, 8% p.a. compounded semi-annually for the next three years, and 7.5% p.a. compounded annually for the remaining years. Determine the final payment.

SOLUTION

See Figure 9.3.

STEP 1 Determine the accumulated value of the debt at the time of the first payment.

$PV_1 = 10\,000.00$; I/Y = 10; C/Y = 4; $i = \frac{10\%}{4} = 2.5\% = 0.025$; $n = 4$

$FV_1 = 10\,000.00(1.025)^4 = 10\,000.00(1.103813) = \$11\,038.12891$

STEP 2 Subtract the payment of $5000 from the accumulated value of $11 038.12891 to obtain the debt balance. Now determine its accumulated value at the time of the second payment three years later.

FIGURE 9.3 Graphical Representation of Data

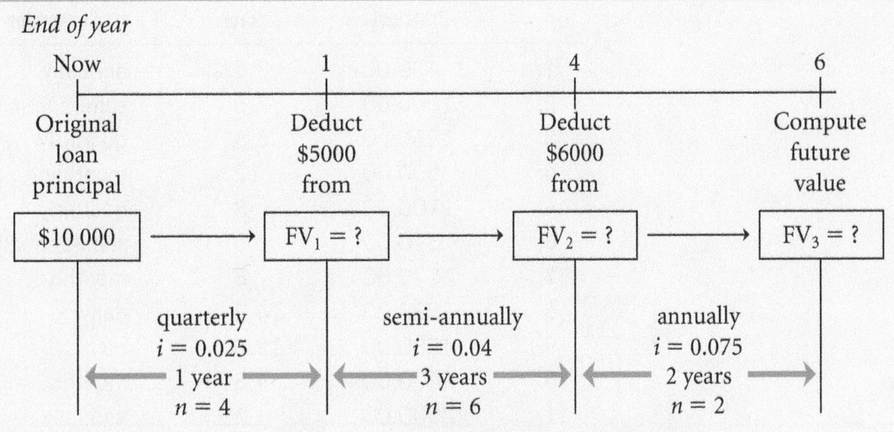

$PV_2 = 11\,038.12891 - 5000.00 = 6038.12891$; $i = 4\% = 0.04$; $n = 6$

$FV_2 = 6038.12891(1.04)^6 = 6038.12891(1.265319) = \$7640.159341$

STEP 3 Subtract the payment of \$6000 from the accumulated value of \$7640.159341 to obtain the debt balance. Now determine its accumulated value two years later.

$PV_3 = 7640.159341 - 6000.00 = 1640.159341; i = 7.5\% = 0.075; n = 2$
$FV_3 = 1640.159341(1.075)^2 = 1640.159341(1.155625) = \$1895.41$

The final payment after six years is \$1895.41.

Programmed Solution

STEP 1 (Set P/Y, C/Y = 4) 2nd (CLR TVM) 10 000 ± PV 10 I/Y 4 N CPT FV Result: 11038.12891

STEP 2 − 5000 = 6038.128906 ± PV (Set P/Y, C/Y = 2) 8 I/Y 6 N CPT FV Result: 7640.159341

STEP 3 − 6000 = 1640.159341 ± PV (Set P/Y, C/Y = 1) 7.5 I/Y 2 N CPT FV Result: 1895.4092139

EXERCISE 9.2

EXCEL NOTES If you choose, you can use Excel's Future Value (FV) function to calculate the future value of an investment subject to compound interest. Refer to **FV** on the MathXL to learn how to use this Excel function.

EXCEL SPREADSHEET  A. Find the future value for each of the investments in the table below.

	Principal	Nominal Rate	Frequency of Conversion	Time
1.	\$ 400.00	7.5%	annually	8 years
2.	1000.00	3.5	semi-annually	12 years
3.	1250.00	6.5	quarterly	9 years
4.	500.00	12	monthly	3 years
5.	1700.00	8	quarterly	14.75 years
6.	840.00	5.5	semi-annually	8.5 years
7.	2500.00	8	monthly	12.25 years
8.	1598.00	14.2	daily	180 days
9.	4230.00	19.6	daily	2 years
10.	1400.00	4.8	monthly	18.75 years
11.	2500.00	7	annually	7 years, 6 months
12.	400.00	9	quarterly	3 years, 8 months
13.	1300.00	5	semi-annually	9 years, 3 months
14.	\$ 4500.00	3.5	monthly	7.5 months

EXCEL SPREADSHEET

B. Answer each of the following questions.

1. What is the maturity value of a five-year term deposit of $5000 at 3.5% compounded semi-annually? How much interest did the deposit earn?
2. How much will a registered retirement savings deposit of $1500 be worth in 15 years at 3.45% compounded quarterly? How much of the amount is interest?
3. You made a registered retirement savings plan deposit of $1000 on December 1, 2008, at a fixed rate of 3% compounded monthly. If you withdraw the deposit on August 1, 2015, how much will you receive?
4. Ray's parents made a trust deposit of $500 on October 31, 1990, to be withdrawn on Ray's twenty-fifth birthday on July 31, 2015. What will be the amount of the deposit on that date at 7% compounded quarterly?
5. What is the accumulated value of $100 invested for twenty years at 3% p.a. compounded

   (a) annually? (b) semi-annually? (c) quarterly? (d) monthly?
6. To what future value will a principal of $500.00 amount in five years at 7.5% p.a. compounded

   (a) annually? (b) semi-annually? (c) quarterly? (d) monthly?
7. What is the future value of and the amount of compound interest for $100 invested at 4.4% compounded quarterly for

   (a) 5 years? (b) 10 years? (c) 20 years?
8. Find the future value of and the compound interest on $500 invested at 4.5% compounded monthly for

   (a) 3.5 years; (b) 6 years; (c) 11.5 years.
9. A demand loan for $5000 with interest at 7.75% compounded semi-annually is repaid after five years, ten months. What is the amount of interest paid?
10. Suppose $4000 is invested for four years, eight months at 3.83% compounded annually. What is the compounded amount?
11. Determine the maturity value of a $600 promissory note dated August 1, 2012, and due on June 1, 2017, if interest is 5% p.a. compounded semi-annually.
12. Find the maturity value of a promissory note for $3200 dated March 31, 2010, and due on August 31, 2016, if interest is 7% compounded quarterly.
13. A debt of $8000 is payable in seven years, five months. Determine the accumulated value of the debt at 10.8% p.a. compounded annually.
14. A $6000 investment matures in three years, eleven months. Find the maturity value if interest is 9% p.a. compounded quarterly.
15. The Canadian Consumer Price Index was approximately 98.5 (base year 1992) at the beginning of 1991. If inflation continued at an average annual rate of 3%, what would the index have been at the beginning of 2012?

16. Peel Credit Union expects an average annual growth rate of 8% for the next five years. If the assets of the credit union currently amount to $2.5 million, what will the forecasted assets be in five years?

17. A local bank offers $5000 five-year certificates at 1.75% compounded semi-annually. Your credit union makes the same type of deposit available at 1.62% compounded monthly.

    (a) Which investment gives more interest over the five years?

    (b) What is the difference in the amount of interest?

18. The Continental Bank advertises capital savings at 4.25% compounded semi-annually while TD Canada Trust offers premium savings at 4% compounded monthly. Suppose you have $1000 to invest for two years.

    (a) Which deposit will earn more interest?

    (b) What is the difference in the amount of interest?

EXCEL SPREADSHEET

C. Answer each of the following questions.

1. A deposit of $2000 earns interest at 3% p.a. compounded quarterly. After two-and-a-half years, the interest rate is changed to 2.75% compounded monthly. How much is the account worth after six years?

2. An investment of $2500 earns interest at 4.5% p.a. compounded monthly for three years. At that time the interest rate is changed to 5% compounded quarterly. How much will the accumulated value be one-and-a-half years after the change?

3. A debt of $800 accumulates interest at 10% compounded semi-annually from February 1, 2013, to August 1, 2015, and 11% compounded quarterly thereafter. Determine the accumulated value of the debt on November 1, 2018.

4. Accumulate $1300 at 8.5% p.a. compounded monthly from March 1, 2012, to July 1, 2014, and thereafter at 8% p.a. compounded quarterly. What is the amount on April 1, 2017?

5. Patrice opened an RRSP deposit account on December 1, 2008, with a deposit of $1000. He added $1000 on July 1, 2010, and $1000 on November 1, 2012. How much is in his account on January 1, 2016, if the deposit earns 6% p.a. compounded monthly?

6. Terri started an RRSP on March 1, 2010, with a deposit of $2000. She added $1800 on December 1, 2012, and $1700 on September 1, 2014. What is the accumulated value of her account on December 1, 2021, if interest is 7.5% compounded quarterly?

7. A debt of $4000 is repaid by payments of $1500 in nine months, $2000 in 18 months, and a final payment in 27 months. If interest was 10% compounded quarterly, what was the amount of the final payment?

8. Sheridan Service has a line of credit loan with the bank. The initial loan balance was $6000. Payments of $2000 and $3000 were made after four months and nine months respectively. At the end of one year, Sheridan Service borrowed an additional $4000. Six months later, the line of credit loan was converted into a

collateral mortgage loan. What was the amount of the mortgage loan if the line of credit interest was 9% compounded monthly?

9. A demand loan of $3000 is repaid by payments of $1500 after two years, $1500 after four years, and a final payment after seven years. Interest is 9% compounded quarterly for the first year, 10% compounded semi-annually for the next three years, and 10% compounded monthly thereafter. What is the size of the final payment?

10. A variable rate demand loan showed an initial balance of $12 000, payments of $5000 after eighteen months, $4000 after thirty months, and a final payment after five years. Interest was 11% compounded semi-annually for the first two years and 12% compounded monthly for the remaining time. What was the size of the final payment?

11. Joan borrowed $15 000 to buy a car. She repaid $2000 two months later and $5000 seven months later. After twelve months, she borrowed an additional $4000, and repaid $3000 after 16 months. She paid the entire balance, including the interest, after 24 months. Interest was 7% compounded monthly for the first year and 7.5% compounded monthly for the remaining time. What was the size of the final payment?

12. A variable rate demand loan showed an initial balance of $9000, payments of $2500 after six months, $2500 after 21 months, and a final payment after four years. Interest was 8% compounded quarterly for the first 21 months and 7.75% compounded monthly for the remaining time. What was the size of the final payment?

9.3 PRESENT VALUE AND COMPOUND DISCOUNT

A. The present value concept and related terms

EXAMPLE 9.3A Find the principal that will amount in six years to $17 715.61 at 10% p.a. compounded annually.

SOLUTION The problem may be graphically represented as shown in Figure 9.4.

FIGURE 9.4 **Graphical Representation of Data**

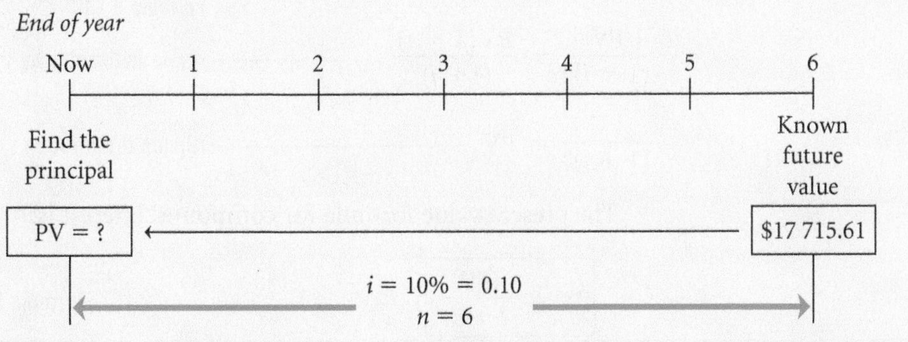

This problem is the inverse of the problem used to illustrate the meaning of compound interest. Instead of knowing the value of the principal and finding its future value, we know that the future value is $17 715.61. What we want to determine is the value of the principal.

To solve the problem, we use the future value formula FV = PV$(1 + i)^n$ and substitute the known values.

$$FV = 17\,715.61; I/Y = 10; C/Y = 1; i = \frac{10\%}{1} = 10\% = 0.1; n = 6$$

$17\,715.61 = PV(1.1)^6$ ——— by substituting in $FV = PV(1 + i)^n$

$17\,715.61 = PV(1.771561)$ ——— computing $(1.10)^6$

$PV = \frac{17\,715.61}{1.771561}$ ——— solve for PV by dividing both sides by 1.771561

$PV = \$10\,000.00$

The principal that will grow to $17 715.61 in six years at 10% p.a. compounded annually is $10 000.

This principal is called the **present value** or **discounted value** or **proceeds** of the known future amount.

The difference between the known future amount of $17 715.61 and the computed present value (principal) of $10 000 is the **compound discount** and represents the compound interest accumulating on the computed present value.

The process of computing the present value or discounted value or proceeds is called **discounting.**

B. The present value formula

With compound interest, the present value of an amount at a given time is defined as the principal that will grow to the given amount if compounded at a given periodic rate of interest over a given number of conversion periods.

Since the problem of finding the present value is equivalent to finding the principal when the future value, the periodic rate of interest, and the number of conversion periods are given, the formula for the future value formula, FV = PV$(1 + i)^n$, applies.

However, because the problem of finding the present value of an amount is frequently encountered in financial analysis, it is useful to solve the future value formula for PV to obtain the present value formula.

$FV = PV(1 + i)^n$ ——— start with the future value formula, Formula 9.1A

$\frac{FV}{(1 + i)^n} = \frac{PV(1 + i)^n}{(1+ i)^n}$ ——— divide both sides by the compounding factor $(1 + i)^n$

$\frac{FV}{(1 + i)^n} = PV$ ——— reduce the fraction $\frac{(1 + i)^n}{(1 + i)^n}$ to 1

The present value formula for compound interest is:

$$PV = \frac{FV}{(1 + i)^n}$$ ——— Formula 9.1B

EXAMPLE 9.3B Find the present value of \$6836.56 due in nine years at 6% p.a. compounded quarterly.

SOLUTION FV = 6836.56; I/Y = 6; P/Y = 4; $i = \frac{6\%}{4} = 1.5\% = 0.015$; $n = 36$

$$PV = \frac{FV}{(1+i)^n} \quad \text{—— using the present value formula}$$

$$= \frac{6836.56}{(1+0.015)^{36}} \quad \text{—— by substitution}$$

$$= \frac{6836.56}{1.709140}$$

$$= \$4000.00$$

Note: The division of 6836.56 by 1.709140, like any division, may be changed to a multiplication by using the reciprocal of the divisor.

$$\frac{6386.56}{1.709140} \quad \text{—— the division to be changed into a multiplication}$$

$$= 6836.56\left(\frac{1}{1.709140}\right) \quad \text{—— the reciprocal of the divisor 1.709140 is found by dividing 1 by 1.709140}$$

$$= 6836.56(0.585090) \quad \text{—— computed value of the reciprocal}$$

$$= \$4000.00$$

For calculators equipped with the reciprocal function key [1/x], converting the division into a multiplication is easily accomplished by first computing the compounding factor and then using the [1/x] key to obtain the reciprocal.

EXAMPLE 9.3C What principal will amount to \$5000 seven years from today if interest is 4.88% p.a. compounded monthly?

SOLUTION Finding the principal that amounts to a future sum of money is equivalent to finding the present value.

FV = 5000.00; I/Y = 9; C/Y = 12; $i = \frac{4.88\%}{12} = 0.406\dot{6}\% = 0.00406\dot{6}$; $n = 84$

$$PV = \frac{500.00}{(1.00406\dot{6})^{84}} \quad \text{—— using Formula 9.1B}$$

$$= \frac{5000.00}{1.406223} \quad \text{—— computing the factor } (1.00406\dot{6})^{84}$$

$$= 5000.00(0.711125) \quad \text{—— using the reciprocal function key}$$

$$= \$3555.62$$

Using the reciprocal of the divisor to change division into multiplication is reflected in the practice of stating the present value formula with a negative exponent.

$$\frac{1}{a^n} = a^{-n}$$ ——— negative exponent rule

$$\frac{1}{(1+i)^n} = (1+i)^{-n}$$

$$\frac{\text{FV}}{(1+i)^n} = \text{FV}(1+i)^{-n}$$

Formula 9.1B, the present value formula, can be restated in multiplication form using a negative exponent.

$$\boxed{\text{PV} = \text{FV}(1+i)^{-n}}$$ ——— Formula 9.1C

The factor $(1 + i)^{-n}$ is called the **discount factor** and is the reciprocal of the compounding factor $(1 + i)^n$.

C. Using preprogrammed financial calculators to find present value

As explained in Section 9.2B, preprogrammed calculators provide quick solutions to compound interest calculations. Three of the four variables are entered and the value of the fourth variable is retrieved.

To solve Example 9.3C, in which FV = 5000, $i = 0.406\dot{6}\%$, $n = 84$, and PV is to be determined, use the following procedure. (Remember that the interest rate for the year, 4.88%, must be entered into the calculator as I/Y.)

Key in	*Press*	*Display shows*	
	2nd (CLR TVM)	0	clears the function key registers
	2nd (P/Y)		opens the P/Y register
12	ENTER	P/Y = 12	changes the value to "12"
	↓	C/Y = 12	changed automatically to match the P/Y
	2nd (QUIT)	0	returns to the standard calculation mode

5000	FV	5000	enters the future value amount, FV
4.88	I/Y	4.88	enters the nominal interest rate
84	N	84	enters the number of compounding periods, n
	CPT PV	−3555.624165	retrieves the unknown principal (present value) PV, an investment or cash outflow as indicated by the negative sign

The principal is \$3555.62.

EXCEL NOTES

Excel has a Present Value (PV) function you can use to calculate the present value of an investment subject to compound interest. Refer to PV on MathXL to learn how to use this Excel function.

EXAMPLE 9.3D

Find the present value of \$2000 due in three years and eight months if money is worth 8% p.a. compounded quarterly.

SOLUTION

$\text{FV} = 2000.00;\ \text{I/Y} = 8;\ \text{P/Y} = 4;\ i = \frac{8\%}{4} = 2\% = 0.02;$

$n = \left(3\frac{8}{12}\right)(4) = 14\frac{2}{3} = 14.\dot{6}$

$$\text{PV} = \frac{\text{FV}}{(1+i)^n}$$ — using Formula 9.1B

$$= \frac{2000.00}{(1+0.02)^{14.\dot{6}}}$$ — use as many decimals as are available in your calculator

$$= 2000.00(0.747936)$$ — multiply by the reciprocal

$$= \$1495.87$$

Programmed Solution

(Set P/Y, C/Y = 4) 2nd (CLR TVM) 2000 FV 8 I/Y

$14.\dot{6}$ N CPT PV -1495.871001

EXAMPLE 9.3E

Determine the principal that will accumulate to \$2387.18 from September 1, 2012, to April 1, 2016, at 5% p.a. compounded semi-annually.

SOLUTION

Finding the principal that will grow to the given amount of \$2387.18 is equivalent to finding the present value or discounted value of this amount.

The time period September 1, 2012, to April 1, 2016, contains three years and seven months; that is, it consists of seven whole conversion periods of six months each and a fractional conversion period of one month.

Use $PV = \dfrac{FV}{(1 + i)^n}$

$FV = 2387.18$; $I/Y = 5$; $P/Y = 2$; $i = \dfrac{5\%}{2} = 2.5\% = 0.025$;

$n = \left(3\tfrac{7}{12}\right)(2) = 7\tfrac{1}{6} = 7.1\dot{6}$

$$PV = \frac{2387.18}{(1.025)^{216}}$$
$$= \frac{2387.18}{1.193588}$$
$$= 2387.18(0.837810)$$
$$= \$2000.33$$

Programmed Solution

(Set P/Y = 2) [2nd] (CLR TVM) 2387.18 [FV] 5 [I/Y]

$7.1\dot{6}$ [N] [CPT] [PV] [-2000.003698]

EXERCISE 9.3

EXCEL NOTES

If you choose, you can use Excel's Present Value (PV) function to calculate the present value of an investment subject to compound interest. Refer to PV on MathXL to learn how to use this Excel function.

EXCEL SPREADSHEET

A. Find the present value of each of the following amounts.

	Amount	Nominal Rate	Frequency of Conversion	Time
1.	$1000.00	8%	quarterly	7 years
2.	1500.00	6.5	semi-annually	10 years
3.	600.00	8	monthly	6 years
4.	350.00	7.5	annually	8 years
5.	1200.00	9	monthly	12 years
6.	3000.00	12.25	semi-annually	5 years, 6 months
7.	900.00	6.4	quarterly	9 years, 3 months
8.	500.00	8.4	monthly	15 years
9.	1500.00	4.5	annually	15 years, 9 months
10.	900.00	5.5	semi-annually	8 years, 10 months
11.	6400.00	7	quarterly	5 years, 7 months
12.	7200.00	6	monthly	21.5 months

EXCEL SPREADSHEET

B. Answer each of the following questions.

1. Find the present value and the compound discount of \$1600 due four-and-a-half years from now if money is worth 4% compounded semi-annually.
2. Find the present value and the compound discount of \$2500 due in six years, three months, if interest is 6% compounded quarterly.
3. Find the principal that will amount to \$1250 in five years at 10% p.a. compounded quarterly.
4. What sum of money will grow to \$2000 in seven years at 9% compounded monthly?
5. A debt of \$5000 is due November 1, 2017. What is the value of the obligation on February 1, 2011, if money is worth 7% compounded quarterly?
6. How much would you have to deposit in an account today to have \$3000 in a five-year term deposit at maturity if interest is 7.75% compounded annually?
7. What is the principal that will grow to \$3000 in eight years, eight months at 9% compounded semi-annually?
8. Find the sum of money that accumulates to \$1600 at 5% compounded quarterly in six years, four months.
9. You have the choice of receiving \$100 000 now or \$60 000 now and another \$60 000 five years from now. In terms of today's dollar, which choice is better and by how much? Money is worth 6% compounded annually.
10. In winning the lottery you have the choice of receiving \$50 000 now or \$20 000 now and \$35 000 three years from now. In terms of today's dollar, which choice is better and by how much? Money is worth 4.25% compounded annually.
11. Joe is negotiating the purchase of a sound system. He can either pay \$2000 now or pay \$100 now and \$2200 in eighteen months. Which option is better if money is worth 8% compounded monthly?
12. Jane is purchasing a membership in a fitness centre. She can pay either \$350 now or pay \$130 now, \$150 in twelve months, and \$170 in fifteen months. Which option is better if money is worth 7.5% compounded monthly?

9.4 APPLICATION—DISCOUNTING NEGOTIABLE FINANCIAL INSTRUMENTS AT COMPOUND INTEREST

A. Discounting long-term promissory notes

Long-term promissory notes (written for a term longer than one year) are usually subject to compound interest. Long-term promissory notes are negotiable and can be bought and sold (*discounted*) at any time before maturity. The principles involved in discounting long-term promissory notes are similar to those used in discounting short-term promissory notes by the simple discount method *except* that no requirement exists to add three days of grace in determining the legal due date of a long-term promissory note.

The discounted value (or proceeds) of a long-term promissory note is the present value at the date of discount of the maturity value of the note. It is found using the present value formula $PV = \frac{FV}{(1+i)^n}$ or $PV = FV(1+i)^{-n}$.

For non-interest-bearing notes, the maturity value is the face value. However, for interest-bearing promissory notes, the maturity value must be determined first by using the future value formula $FV = PV(1+i)^n$.

Like promissory notes, long-term bonds promise to pay a specific face value at a specified future point in time. In addition, there is a promise to periodically pay a specified amount of interest. Long-term bonds will be covered in detail in Chapter 15.

B. Discounting non-interest-bearing promissory notes

Since the face value of a non-interest-bearing note is also its maturity value, the proceeds of a non-interest-bearing note are the present value of its face value at the date of discount.

EXAMPLE 9.4A

Determine the proceeds of a non-interest-bearing note for $1500 discounted two-and-a-quarter years before its due date at 9% p.a. compounded monthly.

SOLUTION

The maturity value FV = 1500.00;

the rate of discount I/Y = 9; P/Y, C/Y = 12; $i = \frac{9\%}{12} = 0.75\% = 0.0075$;

the number of conversion periods $n = (2.25)(12) = 27$.

$PV = FV(1+i)^{-n}$ ——————— using restated Formula 9.1C

$$= 1500.00(1 + 0.0075)^{-27}$$

$$= 1500.00\left(\frac{1}{1.223535}\right)$$

$$= 1500.00(0.817304)$$

$$= \$1225.96$$

Programmed Solution

(Set P/Y, C/Y = 12) [2nd] (CLR TVM) 1500 [FV] 9 [I/Y] 27 [N] [CPT] [PV]

[-1225.955705]

EXAMPLE 9.4B

A four-year, non-interest-bearing promissory note for $6000 was dated August 31, 2011, and earned interest at 6% p.a. compounded quarterly. Determine the proceeds of the note if it was discounted on October 31, 2012.

SOLUTION

The due date of the note is August 31, 2015; the discount period October 31, 2012, to August 31, 2015, contains 2 years and 10 months.

$$\text{FV} = 6000.00;\ \text{I/Y} = 6;\ \text{C/Y} = 4;\ i = \frac{6\%}{4} = 1.5\% = 0.015;$$

$$n = \left(2\frac{10}{12}\right)(4) = 11\frac{1}{3} = 11.\dot{3}$$

$$\begin{aligned} \text{PV} &= \text{FV}(1 + i)^{-n} \\ &= 6000.00(1 + 0.015)^{-11.\dot{3}} \\ &= 6000.00(0.844731) \\ &= \$5068.39 \end{aligned}$$

Programmed Solution

(Set P/Y, C/Y = 4) [2nd] (CLR TVM) 6000 [FV] 6 [I/Y] $11.\dot{3}$ [N] [CPT] [PV] [-5068.383148]

C. Discounting interest-bearing promissory notes

The proceeds of an interest-bearing note are equal to the present value at the date of discount of the value of the note at maturity. Two steps are required:

STEP 1 Determine the maturity value of the note. The calculation of future value is required, using the note's stated interest rate and the entire length of the note.

STEP 2 Determine the proceeds by discounting the maturity value. The calculation of present value is required, using the prevailing interest rate and the time between the discount date and the maturity date.

EXAMPLE 9.4C

Determine the proceeds of a promissory note for $3600 with interest at 6% p.a. compounded quarterly, issued September 1, 2010, due on June 1, 2016, and discounted on December 1, 2012, at 8% p.a. compounded semi-annually.

SOLUTION

STEP 1 Find the maturity value of the note using Formula 9.1A, $\text{FV} = \text{PV}(1 + i)^n$.

$\text{PV}_1 = 3600.00$; I/Y = 6; P/Y, C/Y = 4; $i = \frac{6\%}{4} = 1.5\% = 0.015$; the interest period,

September 1, 2010, to June 1, 2016, contains 5 years and 9 months:

$n = (5\tfrac{9}{12})(4) = 23$

$$FV_1 = 3600.00(1 + 0.015)^{23}$$
$$= 3600.00(1.408377)$$
$$= \$5070.157757$$

STEP 2 Find the present value at the date of discount of the maturity value found in Step 1 using $PV = FV(1 + i)^{-n}$.

$FV_1 = 5070.157757$; I/Y = 8; P/Y, C/Y = 2; $i = \frac{8\%}{2} = 4\% = 0.04$;

the discount period, December 1, 2012, to June 1, 2016, contains 3 years and 6 months: $n = (3\tfrac{6}{12})(2) = 7$.

$$PV_2 = 5070.157757(1 + 0.04)^{-7}$$
$$= 5070.157757(0.759918)$$
$$= \$3852.90$$

The proceeds of the note on December 1, 2012, are \$3852.90. The method and the data are represented graphically in Figure 9.5.

FIGURE 9.5 Graphical Representation of Method and Data

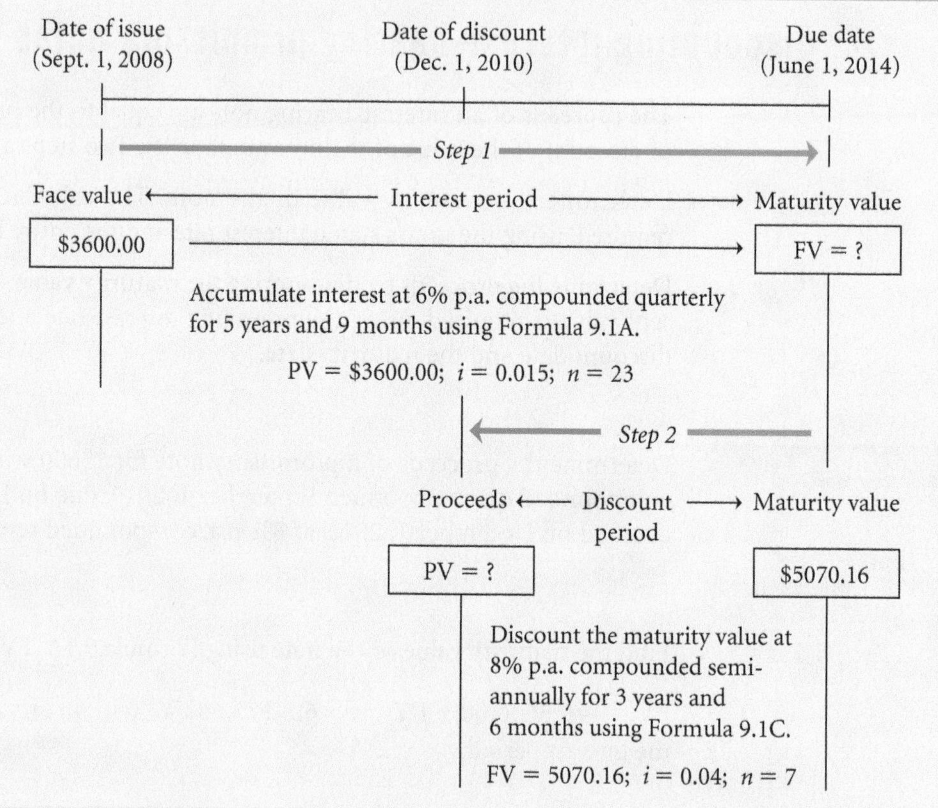

Programmed Solution

STEP 1 (Set P/Y, C/Y = 4) 2nd (CLR TVM) 3600 ± PV 6 I/Y 23 N CPT FV 5070.157757

The answer to Step 1 is now programmed as FV for Step 2.

STEP 2 (Set P/Y, C/Y = 2) 5070.157757 FV 8 I/Y 7 N CPT PV -3852.9049

EXAMPLE 9.4D

A five-year note for \$8000 bearing interest at 6% p.a. compounded monthly is discounted two years and five months before the due date at 5% p.a. compounded semi-annually. Determine the proceeds of the note.

SOLUTION

STEP 1 Find the maturity value using $FV = PV(1 + i)^n$.

$PV_1 = 8000.00$; I/Y = 6; P/Y, C/Y = 12; $i = \frac{6\%}{12} = 0.5\% = 0.005$; $n = 60$

$$\begin{aligned} FV_1 &= 8000.00(1.005)^{60} \\ &= 8000.00(1.348850) \\ &= \$10\,790.80122 \end{aligned}$$

STEP 2 Find the present value of the maturity value found in Step 1 using

$PV_2 = FV(1 + i)^{-n}$.

$FV_2 = 10\,790.80122$; I/Y = 5; P/Y = 2; $i = \frac{5\%}{2} = 2.5\% = 0.025$;

$$n = \left(\frac{29}{12}\right)(2) = 4.8\dot{3}$$

$$\begin{aligned} PV &= 10\,790.80122(1.025)^{-4.8\dot{3}} \\ &= 10\,790.80122(0.887499) \\ &= \$9575.25 \end{aligned}$$

Programmed Solution

STEP 1 (Set P/Y, C/Y = 12) 2nd (CLR TVM) 8000 ± PV 6 I/Y 60 N CPT FV 10790.80122

STEP 2 (Set P/Y, C/Y = 2) 10790.80122 FV 5 I/Y 4.8$\dot{3}$ N CPT PV -9576.826669

EXERCISE 9.4

EXCEL NOTES If you choose, you can use Excel's Future Value (FV) or Present Value (PV) functions to answer the questions below. Refer to FV and PV on MathXL to learn how to use these Excel functions.

A. Find the proceeds and the compound discount for each of the long-term promissory notes shown in the table below. Note that the first six are non-interest-bearing promissory notes.

	Face Value	Date of Issue	Term	Int. Rate	Frequency of Conversion	Date of Discount	Discount Rate	Frequency of Conversion
1.	$2000.00	30-06-2010	5 years	—	—	31-12-2014	5%	semi-annually
2.	700.00	01-04-2008	10 years	—	—	01-07-2015	10	quarterly
3.	5000.00	01-04-2008	10 years	—	—	01-08-2017	5	annually
4.	900.00	31-08-2009	8 years	—	—	30-06-2016	4	quarterly
5.	3200.00	31-03-2010	6 years	—	—	31-10-2013	8	quarterly
6.	1450.00	01-10-2011	9 years	—	—	01-12-2016	6	semi-annually
7.	780.00	30-09-2007	10 years	8%	annually	30-04-2015	8	quarterly
8.	2100.00	01-02-2006	12 years	6	monthly	01-07-2017	7	semi-annually
9.	1850.00	01-11-2012	5 years	10	quarterly	01-10-2014	9	semi-annually
10.	3400.00	31-01-2009	7 years	9	monthly	31-12-2015	7.5	quarterly
11.	1500.00	31-05-2012	8 years	7	annually	31-05-2017	8	semi-annually
12.	4000.00	30-09-2011	4 years	5	semi-annually	31-03-2013	4	quarterly
13.	800.00	01-02-2010	7.75 years	9	quarterly	01-11-2015	9	monthly
14.	$2200.00	31-10-2009	8.25 years	6	monthly	31-01-2016	7	quarterly

EXCEL SPREADSHEET

B. Find the proceeds of each of the following promissory notes.

1. A non-interest-bearing promissory note for $6000, discounted 54 months before its due date at 6% compounded quarterly.
2. A $4200, non-interest-bearing note due August 1, 2018, discounted on March 1, 2014, at 7.5% compounded monthly.
3. A promissory note with a maturity value of $1800 due on September 30, 2015, discounted at 8.5% compounded semi-annually on March 31, 2012.
4. A fifteen-year promissory note discounted after six years at 9% compounded quarterly with a maturity value of $7500.
5. A five-year promissory note for $3000 with interest at 8% compounded semi-annually, discounted 21 months before maturity at 9% compounded quarterly.

6. A $5000, seven-year note bearing interest at 8% compounded quarterly, discounted two-and-a-half years after the date of issue at 6% compounded monthly.

7. A six-year, $900 note bearing interest at 10% compounded quarterly, issued June 1, 2013, discounted on December 1, 2018, to yield 8.5% compounded semi-annually.

8. A ten-year promissory note dated April 1, 2013, with a face value of $1300 bearing interest at 7% compounded semi-annually, discounted seven years later when money was worth 9% compounded quarterly.

EXCEL SPREADSHEET

C. Solve each of the following problems.

1. Determine the proceeds of an investment with a maturity value of $10 000 if discounted at 9% compounded monthly 22.5 months before the date of maturity.

2. Compute the discounted value of $7000 due in three years, five months if money is worth 8% compounded quarterly.

3. Find the discounted value of $3800 due in six years, eight months if interest is 7.5% compounded annually.

4. Calculate the proceeds of $5500 due in seven years, eight months discounted at 4.5% compounded semi-annually.

5. A four-year non-interest-bearing promissory note for $3750 is discounted 32 months after the date of issue at 5.5% compounded semi-annually. Find the proceeds of the note.

6. A seven-year non-interest-bearing note for $5200 is discounted three years, eight months before its due date at 9% compounded quarterly. Find the proceeds of the note.

7. A non-interest-bearing eight-year note for $4500 issued August 1, 2012, is discounted April 1, 2016, at 6.5% compounded annually. Find the compound discount.

8. A $2800 promissory note issued without interest for five years on September 30, 2014, is discounted on July 31, 2017, at 8% compounded quarterly. Find the compound discount.

9. A six-year note for $1750 issued on December 1, 2012, with interest at 6.5% compounded annually, is discounted on March 1, 2015, at 7% compounded semi-annually. What are the proceeds of the note?

10. A ten-year note for $1200 bearing interest at 6% compounded monthly is discounted at 8% compounded quarterly three years, ten months after the date of issue. Find the proceeds of the note.

11. Four years, seven months before its due date, a seven-year note for $2650 bearing interest at 9% compounded quarterly is discounted at 8% compounded semi-annually. Find the compound discount.

12. On April 15, 2019, a ten-year note dated June 15, 2014, is discounted at 10% compounded quarterly. If the face value of the note is $4000 and interest is 8% compounded quarterly, find the compound discount.

BUSINESS MATH NEWS BOX

Starting Early—The Power of Compound Growth

One of the costly mistakes Canadians make with their registered retirement savings plans (RRSPs) is not starting them early enough. According to a 2008 report by Statistics Canada, only 56% of major income earners between the ages of 25 and 44 even have an RRSP, and only 68% of those who are between 45 and 54 years of age have one.

The longer you wait, the more you miss out on one of the key benefits of your registered plan: the incredible power of long-term tax-deferred compound growth. Even with a small deposit, the more years you have to invest, and the higher your investment return, the more dramatic this growth potential will be (see table).

Watch Your Savings Grow

This table illustrates the effect of compound growth on a single investment of $1000, assuming that you cash it in at age 60*. The higher the rate of return, and the longer you invest, the more powerful the effect.

Rate of Return	Years Invested		
	20	25	30
6%	$3 207	$ 4 292	$ 5 743
8%	$4 661	$ 6 848	$10 063
10%	$6 727	$10 835	$17 449

* The effect of taxation is not taken into account in these examples.

Source: Investor's Group. Used with permission; Wendy Pyper, "RRSP investments," **www.statcan.ca/english/freepub/75-001-XIE/2008102/pdf/10520-en.pdf**, accessed August 26, 2010.

QUESTIONS

1. What principal is used to calculate the figures in the table?
2. Suppose you were 25 years old when you made your first $1000 RRSP contribution. What would be the value of your investment when you reach age 60 given each of the following rates of return?

   (a) 6% (b) 8% (c) 10%

3. Compare the values of the investment you calculated in Question 2 with the values of the investment made at age 30 given in the table. For each interest rate, what is the difference in the values of the investment at age 60?
4. Suppose you were 30 years old when you made your first $1000 RRSP contribution and that your investment would earn 6% for the first ten years and 8% for the next twenty years. What would be the value of your contribution when you turned 60?

9.5 EQUIVALENT VALUES

A. Equations of value

Because of the time value of money, amounts of money have different values at different times, as explained in Chapter 7. When sums of money fall due or are payable at different times, they are not directly comparable. To make such sums of money comparable, a point in time—the **comparison date** or **focal date**—must be chosen. Allowance must be made for interest from the due dates of the sums of money to the selected focal date; that is, the dated values of the sums of money must be determined.

Any point in time may be chosen as the focal date; the choice does not affect the final answers. It is advisable, however, to choose a date on which an amount is unknown but desired to be known. The choice of date determines which formula is to be used. For compound interest, equations of value need to be set up.

Which formula is appropriate depends on the position of the due dates relative to the focal date. The following rules apply:

(a) If an amount in the future of, or after, the due date is to be determined, use the future value formula, $FV = PV(1 + i)^n$ (see Figure 9.7).

(b) If an amount in the past of, or before, the due date is to be determined, use the present value formula, $PV = FV(1 + i)^{-n}$ (see Figure 9.8).

B. Finding the equivalent single payment

Equivalent values are the dated values of an original sum of money.

EXAMPLE 9.5A

A sum of $4000 is due for payment three years from now. If money is worth 9% p.a. compounded semi-annually, determine the equivalent value

(i) seven years from now; (ii) now.

SOLUTION

(i) Using "seven years from now" as the focal date, the method and the data can be represented graphically as shown in Figure 9.6.

FIGURE 9.6 Graphical Representation of Method and Data

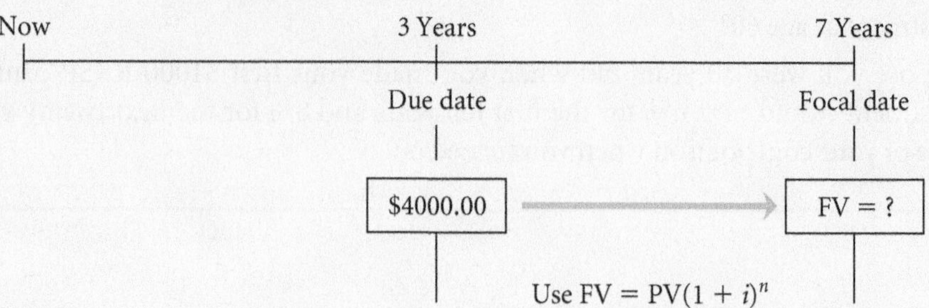

Since the focal date falls *after* the due date, use the future value formula.

$$PV = 4000.00; I/Y = 9; P/Y, C/Y = 2; i = \frac{9\%}{2} = 0.045; n = 4(2) = 8$$

$$FV = 4000.00(1 + 0.045)^8 = 4000.00(1.422101) = \$5688.40$$

The equivalent value of the $4000 seven years from now is $5688.40.

(ii) Using "now" as the focal date, the method and the data can be represented graphically as shown in Figure 9.7.

FIGURE 9.7 Graphical Representation of Method and Data

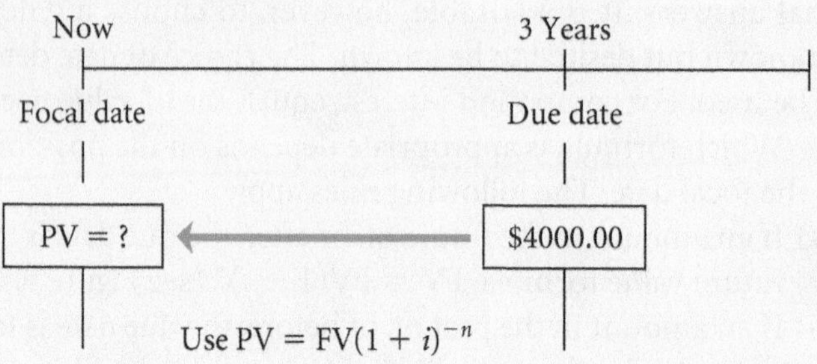

Since the focal date falls *before* the due date, use the present value formula.

$$FV = 4000.00; i = \frac{9\%}{2} = 0.045; n = 3(2) = 6$$

$$PV = 4000.00(1 + 0.045)^{-6} = 4000.00(0.767896) = \$3071.58$$

The equivalent value of the $4000.00 now is $3071.58.

Programmed Solution

(i) (Set P/Y, C/Y = 2) [2nd] (CLR TVM) 4000 [±] [PV] 9 [I/Y]

8 [N] [CPT] [FV] [5688.402451]

(ii) [2nd] (CLR TVM) 4000 [FV] 9 [I/Y] 6 [N] [CPT] [PV] [-3071.582953]

EXAMPLE 9.5B Joanna plans to pay off a debt by payments of \$1600 one year from now, \$1800 eighteen months from now, and \$2000 thirty months from now. Determine the single payment now that would settle the debt if money is worth 8% p.a. compounded quarterly.

SOLUTION While any date may be selected as the focal date, a logical choice for the focal date is the time designated "now," since the single payment "now" is wanted. As is shown in Figure 9.8, for the three scheduled payments, the chosen focal date falls before each of the due dates. Therefore, the present value formula $PV = FV(1 + i)^{-n}$ is appropriate for finding the equivalent values of each of the three scheduled payments.

The equivalents of the three scheduled payments at the selected focal date are

$$PV_1 = 1600.00(1 + 0.02)^{-4} = 1600.00(0.923845) = \$1478.15$$
$$PV_2 = 1800.00(1 + 0.02)^{-6} = 1800.00(0.887971) = \$1598.35$$
$$PV_3 = 2000.00(1 + 0.02)^{-10} = 2000.00(0.820348) = \$1640.70$$

The equivalent single payment to settle the debt now is \$4717.20.

FIGURE 9.8 **Graphical Representation of Method and Data**

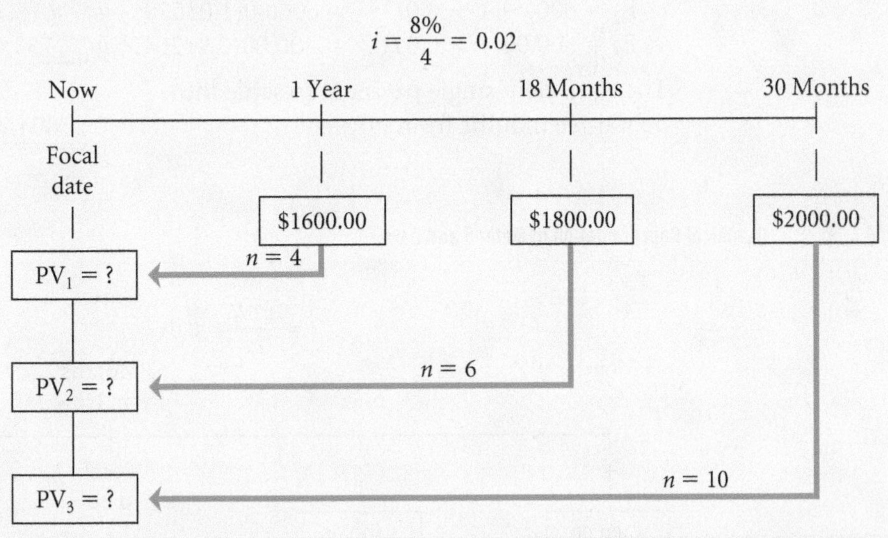

Programmed Solution

PV_1 (Set P/Y, C/Y = 4) [2nd] (CLR TVM) 1600 [FV] 8 [I/Y] 4 [N] [CPT] [PV] [-1478.152682]

PV_2 [2nd] (CLR TVM) 1800 [FV] 8 [I/Y] 6 [N] [CPT] [PV] [-1598.348488]

PV_3 [2nd] (CLR TVM) 2000 [FV] 8 [I/Y] 10 [N] [CPT] [PV] [-1640.6966]

Note: Remember that the negative sign indicates a cash payment or outflow. Disregard the negative signs when finding equivalent single payments.

$1478.15 + 1598.35 + 1640.70 = \$4717.20$

EXAMPLE 9.5C

Debt payments of \$400 due five months ago, \$600 due today, and \$800 due in nine months are to be combined into one payment due three months from today at 12% p.a. compounded monthly.

SOLUTION

The logical choice for the focal date is "3 months from now," the date when the equivalent single payment is to be made.

As shown in Figure 9.9, the focal date is after the first two scheduled payments, and therefore, the future value formula $FV = PV(1 + i)^n$ should be used. However, the focal date is before the due date for the third scheduled payment, which means that, for that payment, the present value formula $PV = FV(1 + i)^{-n}$ applies.

The equivalent values (designated E_1, E_2, E_3) of the scheduled debt payments at the selected focal date are

$$E_1 = 400.00(1 + 0.01)^8 = 400.00(1.082857) = \$\ 433.14$$
$$E_2 = 600.00(1 + 0.01)^3 = 600.00(1.030301) = 618.18$$
$$E_3 = 800.00(1 + 0.01)^{-6} = 800.00(0.942045) = \underline{753.64}$$

The equivalent single payment to settle the debt three months from now is $\underline{\underline{\$1804.96}}$

FIGURE 9.9 Graphical Representation of Method and Data

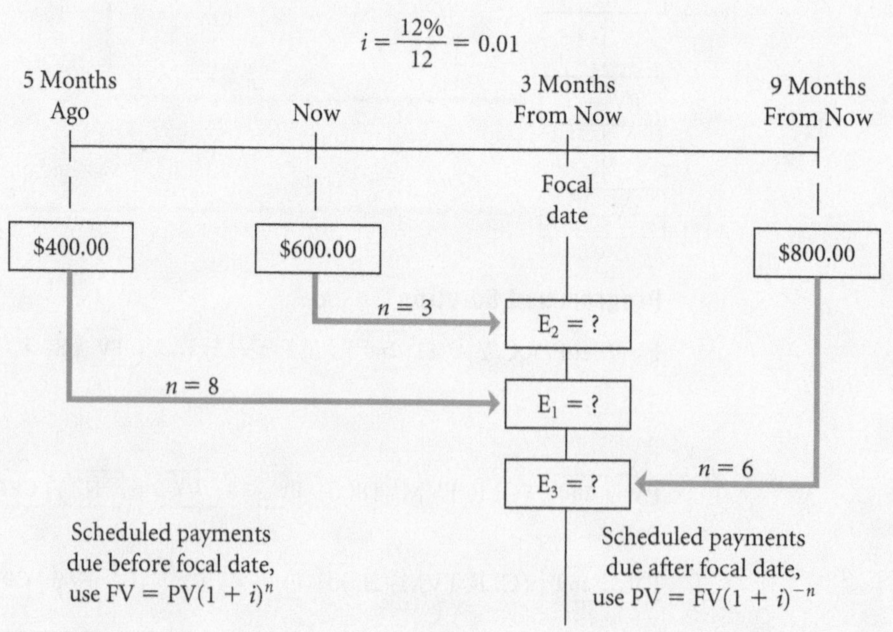

Programmed Solution

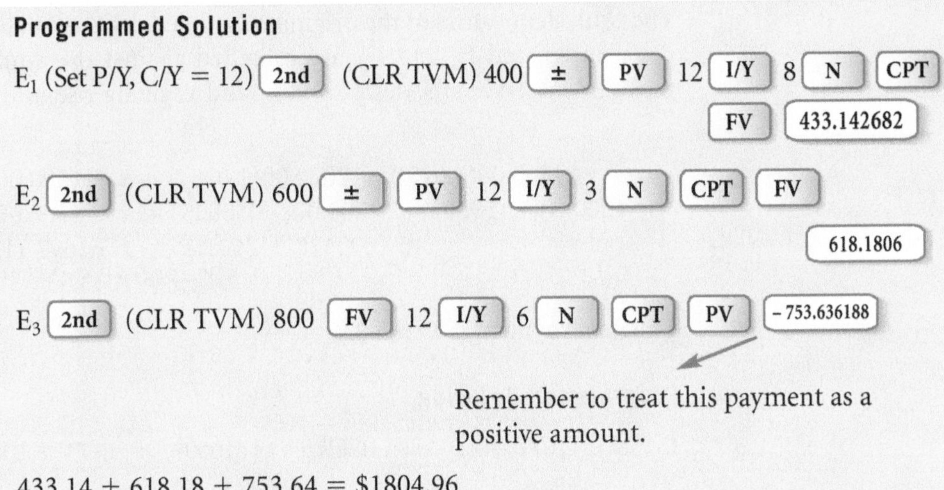

$433.14 + 618.18 + 753.64 = \$1804.96$

EXAMPLE 9.5D

Scheduled debt payments of \$1000 due today and \$2000 due one year from now are to be settled by a payment of \$1500 three months from now and a final payment eighteen months from now. Determine the size of the final payment if interest is 10% p.a. compounded quarterly.

SOLUTION

Let the size of the final payment be $\$x$. The logical focal date is the date of the final payment, which is eighteen months from now.

As shown in Figure 9.10, the focal date is after the two original scheduled payments and the first replacement payment. The future value formula $FV = PV(1 + i)^n$ applies. Because the final payment is dated on the focal date, its dated value is $\$x$.

FIGURE 9.10 Graphical Representation of Method and Data

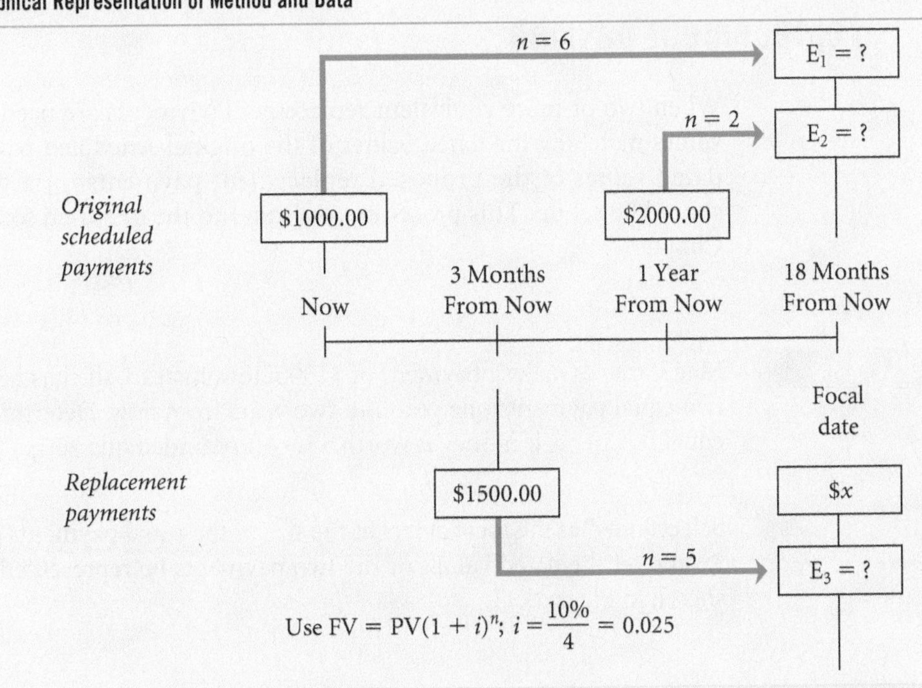

The equivalent values of the original scheduled debt payments at the selected focal date, designated E_1 and E_2, are matched against the equivalent values of the replacement payments, designated E_3 and x, giving rise to the equation of values.

$$E_1 + E_2 = x + E_3$$
$$1000.00(1.025)^6 + 2000.00(1.025)^2 = x + 1500.00(1.025)^5$$
$$1000.00(1.159693) + 2000.00(1.050625) = x + 1500.00(1.131408)$$
$$1159.693418 + 2101.25 = x + 1697.112319$$
$$x = 1563.83$$

The final payment is $1563.83.

Programmed Solution

E_1 (Set P/Y, C/Y = 4) [2nd] (CLR TVM) 1000 [±] [PV] 10 [I/Y] 6 [N] [CPT] [FV] [1159.693418]

E_2 2000 [±] [PV] 2 [N] [CPT] [FV] [2101.25]

E_3 1500 [±] [PV] 5 [N] [CPT] [FV] [1697.112319]

$$1159.69 + 2101.25 = x + 1697.11$$
$$x = 1563.83$$

C. Finding the value of two or more equivalent replacement payments

When two or more equivalent replacement payments are needed, an equation of values matching the dated values of the original scheduled payments against the dated values of the proposed replacement payments on a selected focal date should be set up. This procedure is similar to the one used for simple interest in Chapter 7.

EXAMPLE 9.5E

Mae is due to make a payment of $1000 now. Instead, she has negotiated to make two equal payments one year and two years from now. Determine the size of the equal payments if money is worth 8% compounded quarterly.

SOLUTION

Select "now" as the focal date. Let the size of the equal payments be represented as $$x$ and let the dated values of the two payments be represented by E_1 and E_2, as shown in Figure 9.11.

FIGURE 9.11 Graphical Representation of Method and Data

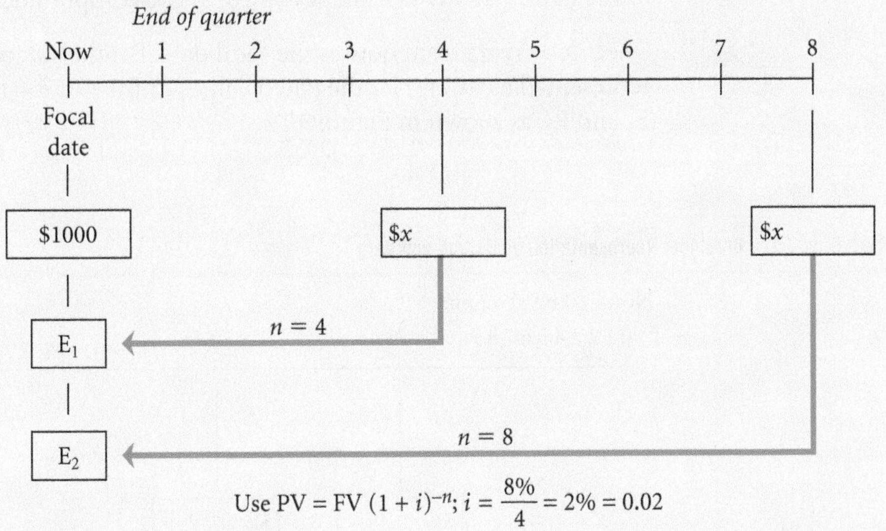

Then the equation of values can be set up.

$1000.00 = E_1 + E_2$

$1000.00 = x(1.02)^{-4} + x(1.02)^{-8}$

$1000.00 = x(0.923845 + 0.853490)$

$1000.00 = 1.777336x$

$x = \$562.64$

The size of the equal payments is $562.64.

Programmed Solution

E_1 (Set P/Y = 4) [2nd] (CLR TVM) 1 [FV] 8 [I/Y] 4 [N] [CPT] [PV]

[-0.923845] [±] [STO] 1

E_2 (Set P/Y = 4) [2nd] (CLR TVM) 1 [FV] 8 [I/Y] 8 [N] [CPT] [PV]

[-0.853490] [±] [STO] 2

Remember to treat these payments as positive amounts.

[RCL] 1 + [RCL] 2 = 1.777336 [STO] 3

$0.923845x + 0.853490x = \$1000.00$

$1.777336x = \$1000.00$

$x = \$562.64$ (1000 ÷ [RCL] 3 =)

EXAMPLE 9.5F Olympia owes \$4000 in four years. She wants to repay the debt earlier and plans to make two equal payments in 16 months and in 28 months. Determine the size of the equal payments if money is worth 6% compounded monthly.

SOLUTION Select four years from now as the focal date. Let the size of the equal payments be represented as \$x and let the dated values of the two payments be represented by E_1 and E_2, as shown in Figure 9.12.

FIGURE 9.12 **Graphical Representation of Method and Data**

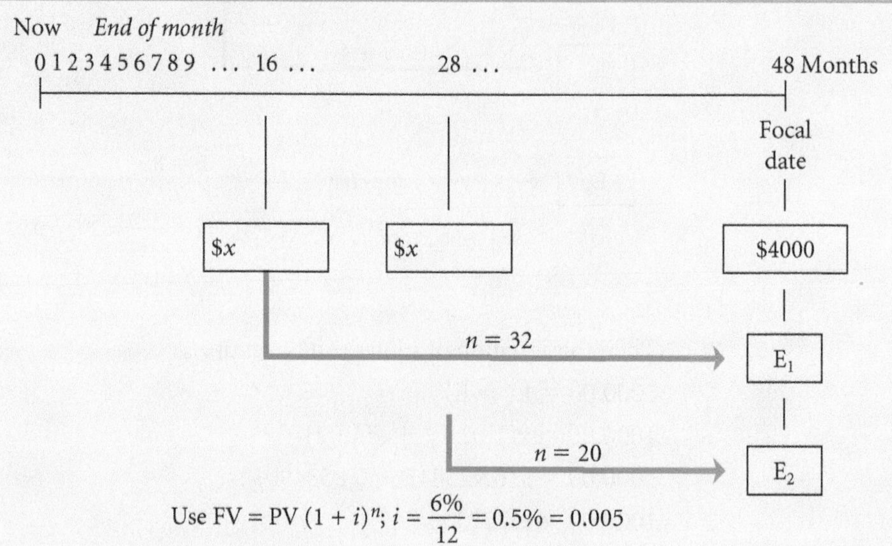

The equation of values may be set up.

$$4000.00 = E_1 + E_2$$
$$4000.00 = x(1.005)^{32} + x(1.005)^{20}$$
$$4000.00 = x(1.173043 + 1.104896)$$
$$4000.00 = 2.277939x$$
$$x = \$1755.97$$

The size of the equal payments is \$1755.97.

Programmed Solution

E_1 (Set P/Y = 12) [2nd] (CLR TVM) 1 [±] [PV] 6 [I/Y]
32 [N] [CPT] [FV] [1.173043] [STO] 1

E_2 (Set P/Y = 12) [2nd] (CLR TVM) 1 [±] [PV] 6 [I/Y]
20 [N] [CPT] [FV] [1.104896] [STO] 2

Remember to enter these values as negative amounts.

RCL 1 + RCL 2 = 2.277939 STO 3

$1.173043x + 1.104896x = \$4000.00$

$2.277939x = \$4000.00$

$x = \$1755.97$ (4000 ÷ RCL 3 =)

EXAMPLE 9.5G

What is the size of the equal payments that must be made at the end of each of the next five years to settle a debt of \$5000 due in five years if money is worth 9% p.a. compounded annually?

SOLUTION

Select as the focal date "five years from now." Let the equal payments be represented by \$$x$ and let the dated values of the first four payments be represented by E_1, E_2, E_3, and E_4 respectively, as shown in Figure 9.13.

Then the equation of values may be set up.

$$5000.00 = x + E_4 + E_3 + E_2 + E_1$$
$$5000.00 = x + x(1.09) + x(1.09)^2 + x(1.09)^3 + x(1.09)^4$$
$$5000.00 = x[1 + (1.09) + (1.09)^2 + (1.09)^3 + (1.09)^4]$$
$$5000.00 = x(1 + 1.09 + 1.1881 + 1.295029 + 1.411582)$$
$$5000.00 = 5.984711x$$
$$x = \$835.46$$

The size of the equal payments is \$835.46.

FIGURE 9.13 Graphical Representation of Method and Data

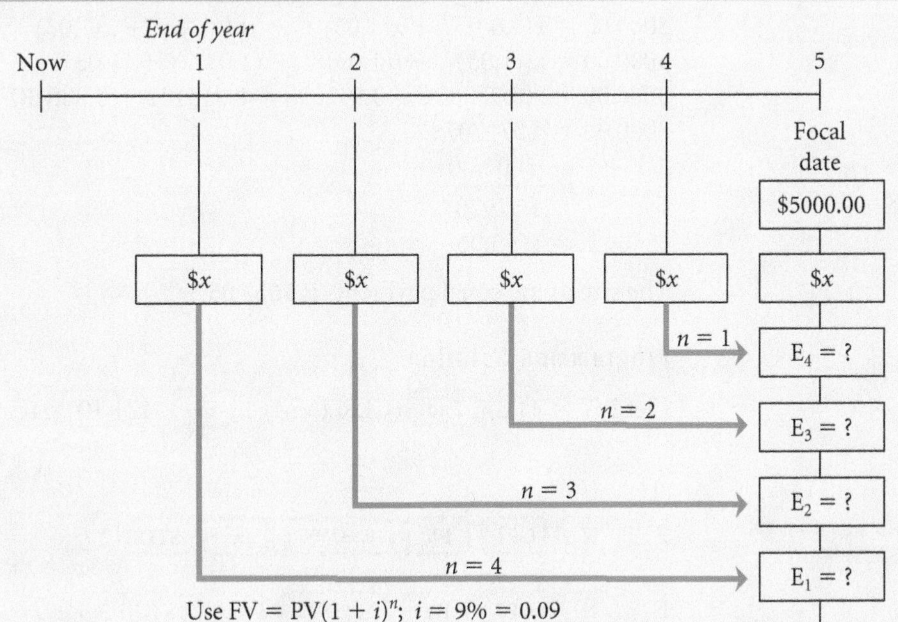

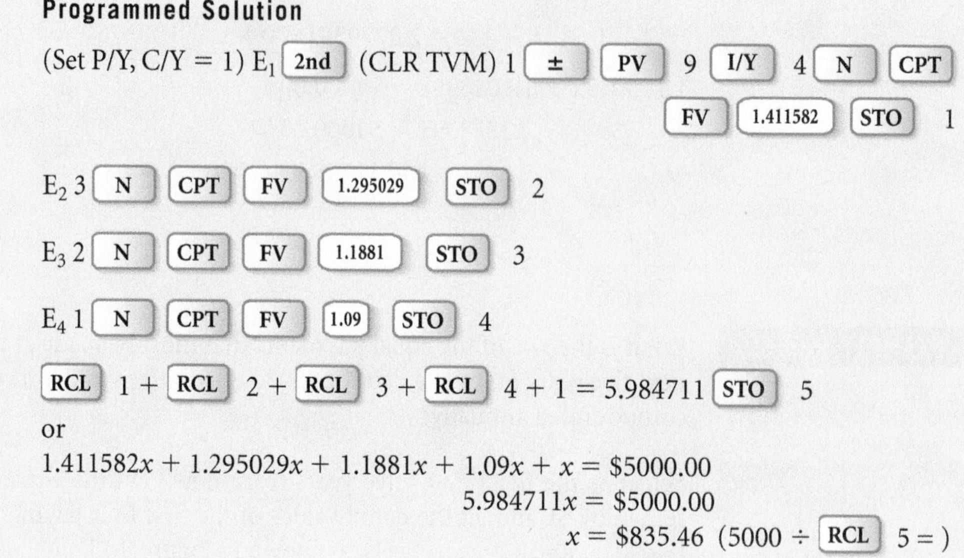

EXAMPLE 9.5H

What is the size of the equal payments that must be made at the end of each of the next five quarters to settle a debt of \$3000 due now if money is worth 12% p.a. compounded quarterly?

SOLUTION

Select as the focal date "now." Let the size of the equal payments be represented by $\$x$ and let the dated values of the five payments be represented by E_1, E_2, E_3, E_4, and E_5 respectively, as shown in Figure 9.14.

Then the equation of values may be set up.

$$3000.00 = E_1 + E_2 + E_3 + E_4 + E_5$$
$$3000.00 = x(1.03)^{-1} + x(1.03)^{-2} + x(1.03)^{-3} + x(1.03)^{-4} + x(1.03)^{-5}$$
$$3000.00 = x[(1.03)^{-1} + (1.03)^{-2} + (1.03)^{-3} + (1.03)^{-4} + (1.03)^{-5}]$$
$$3000.00 = x(0.970874 + 0.942596 + 0.915142 + 0.888487 + 0.862609)$$
$$3000.00 = 4.579707x$$
$$x = \frac{3000.00}{4.579707}$$
$$x = \$655.06$$

The size of the equal payments is \$655.06.

Programmed Solution

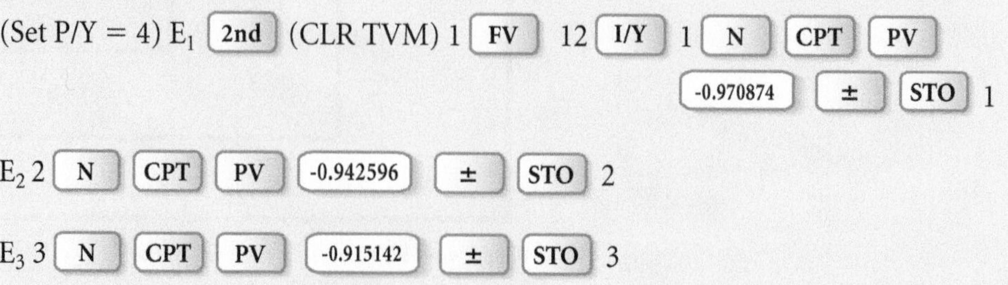

FIGURE 9.14 Graphical Representation of Method and Data

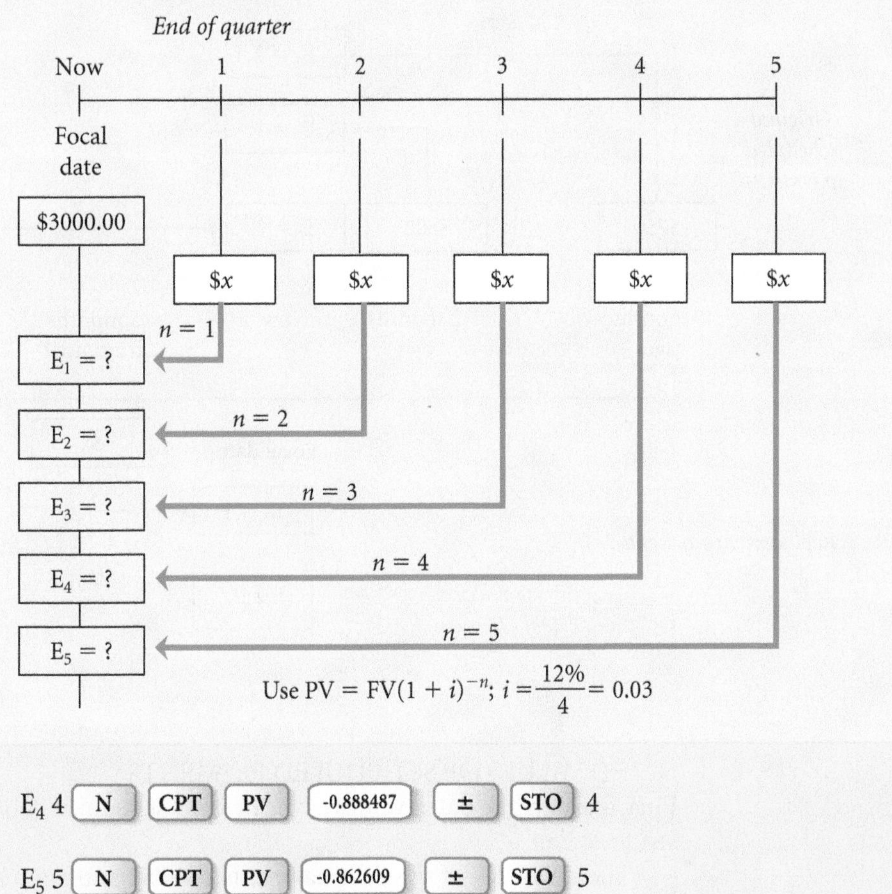

E_4 4 N CPT PV -0.888487 ± STO 4

E_5 5 N CPT PV -0.862609 ± STO 5

Remember to treat these payments as positive amounts.

RCL 1 + RCL 2 + RCL 3 + RCL 4 + RCL 5 = 4.594707 STO 6

$$0.970874x + 0.942596x + 0.915142x + 0.888487x + 0.862609x = \$3000.00$$
$$4.579707x = \$3000.00$$
$$x = \$655.06 \ (3000 \div \text{RCL } 6 =)$$

EXAMPLE 9.5I

Scheduled debt payments of $750 due seven months ago, $600 due two months ago, and $900 due in five months are to be settled by two equal replacement payments due now and three months from now. Determine the size of the equal replacement payments at 9% p.a. compounded monthly.

SOLUTION

Let the size of the equal replacement payments be represented by $x and choose "now" as the focal date.

$$I/Y = 9; \ P/Y, C/Y = 12; \ i = \frac{9\%}{12} = 0.0075$$

Figure 9.15 shows the method and data.

FIGURE 9.15 Graphical Representation of Method and Data

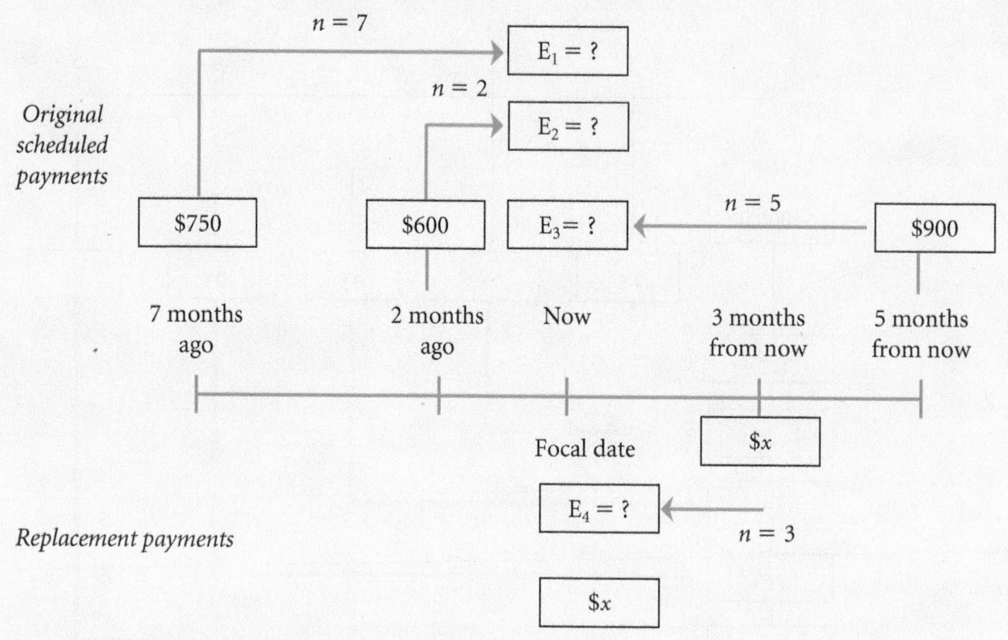

STEP 1 DATED VALUES OF SCHEDULED PAYMENTS

First, consider the dated values of the original scheduled debt payments at the chosen focal date.

The due dates of the debt payments of $750 and $600 are seven months and two months respectively before the focal date. Their dated values at the focal date are $750.00(1.0075)^7$ and $600.00(1.0075)^2$, represented by E_1 and E_2 respectively.

The due date of the scheduled payment of $900 is five months after the focal date. Its dated value is $900.00(1.0075)^{-5}$, shown as E_3.

STEP 2 DATED VALUES OF REPLACEMENT PAYMENTS

Second, consider the dated values of the replacement payments at the selected focal date.

The first replacement payment due at the focal date is $x. The second replacement payment is due three months after the focal date. Its dated value is $x(1.0075)^{-3}$, shown as E_4.

STEP 3 EQUATION OF DATED VALUES

Now equate the dated values of the replacement payments with the dated values of the original scheduled debt payments to set up the equation of values.

$$x + x(1.0075)^{-3} = 750.00(1.0075)^7 + 600.00(1.0075)^2 + 900.00(1.0075)^{-5}$$

$$x + 0.977833x = 750.00(1.053696) + 600.00(1.015056) + 900.00(0.963329)$$

$$1.977833x = 790.272095 + 609.03375 + 866.996283$$

$$1.977833x = 2266.302128$$

$$x = \frac{2266.302128}{1.977833}$$

$$x = \$1145.85$$

The size of the two equal payments is \$1145.85.

For E_1 and E_2, use $FV = PV(1 + i)^n$; $i = \frac{9\%}{12} = 0.0075$

For E_3 and E_4, use or $PV = FV(1 + i)^{-n}$; $i = \frac{9\%}{12} = 0.0075$

Programmed Solution

$x + x(1.0075)^{-3}$

(Set P/Y, C/Y = 12) [2nd] (CLR TVM) 1 [FV] 9 [I/Y] 3 [N] [CPT] [PV] [-0.977833] [±]

$x + 0.977833x$

$750(1.0075)^7$

750 [±] [PV] 7 [N] [CPT] [FV] [790.272095] (E_1)

$600(1.0075)^2$

600 [±] [PV] 2 [N] [CPT] [FV] [609.03375] (E_2)

$900(1.0075)^{-5}$

900 [FV] 5 [N] [CPT] [PV] [-866.996283] [±] (E_3)

$x + (E_4) = (E_1) + (E_2) + (E_3)$

$x + 0.977833x = 790.272095 + 609.03375 + 866.996283$

$$1.977833x = 2266.302128$$

$$x = 1145.85$$

Note: In $x(1.0075)^{-3}$, [FV] is not known. To obtain the factor $(1.0075)^{-3}$, use [FV] = 1.

EXAMPLE 9.5J Two scheduled payments, one of \$4000 due in three months with interest at 9% compounded quarterly and the other of \$3000 due in eighteen months with interest at 8.5% compounded semi-annually, are to be discharged by making two equal replacement payments. What is the size of the equal replacement payments if the first is due one year from now, the second two years from now, and money is now worth 10% compounded monthly?

SOLUTION Let the size of the equal replacement payments be represented by \$$x$. Choose "one year from now" as the focal date.

Figure 9.16 illustrates the problem.

FIGURE 9.16 Graphical Representation of Method and Data

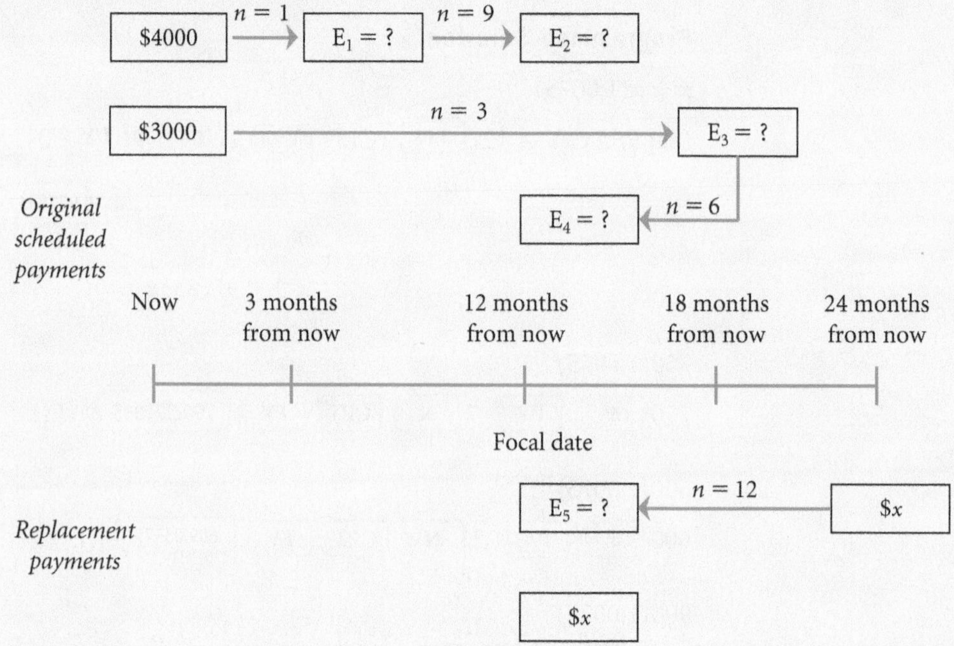

STEP 1 MATURITY VALUES OF SCHEDULED PAYMENTS

Since the two scheduled payments are interest-bearing, first determine their maturity value.

The maturity value of \$4000 due in three months at 9% compounded quarterly $= 4000(1.0225)^1 = \$4090.00$, shown as E_1.

The maturity value of \$3000 due in eighteen months at 8.5% compounded semi-annually $= 3000(1.0425)^3 = 3000(1.132996) = \$3398.98655$, shown as E_3.

STEP 2 DATED VALUES OF SCHEDULED PAYMENTS

Now determine the dated values of the two maturity values at the selected focal date subject to 10% compounded monthly.

The first scheduled payment matures nine months *before* the selected focal date. Its dated value $= 4090.00(1.008\dot{3})^9 = 4090.00(1.077549) = \$4407.176326$, shown as E_2.

The second scheduled payment matures six months *after* the selected focal date. Its dated value = $3398.99(1.008\dot{3})^{-6} = 3398.99(0.951427) = \$3233.889239$, shown as E_4.

STEP 3 DATED VALUES OF REPLACEMENTS PAYMENTS

The dated values of the two replacement payments at the selected focal date are $\$x$ and $\$x(1.008\dot{3})^{-12}$, shown as E_5.

STEP 4 EQUATION OF VALUES

Therefore, the equation of values is

$$x + x(1.008333)^{-12} = 4407.176326 + 3233.889239$$

$$x + 0.905212x = 7641.065565$$

$$x = \frac{7641.065565}{1.905212}$$

$$x = \$4010.611714$$

The size of the two equal replacement payments is \$4010.61.

For E_1 use $FV = PV(1 + i)^n$; $i = \frac{9\%}{4} = 0.0225$

For E_3 use $FV = PV(1 + i)^n$; $i = \frac{8.5\%}{2} = 0.0425$

For E_2 use $FV = PV(1 + i)^n$; $i = \frac{10\%}{12} = 0.008\dot{3}$

For E_4 and E_5, use $PV = \frac{FV}{(1 + i)^n}$ or $PV = FV(1 + i)^{-n}$; $i = \frac{10\%}{12} = 0.008\dot{3}$

Programmed Solution

Maturity value of \$4000

(Set P/Y, C/Y = 4) [2nd] (CLR TVM) 4000 [±] [PV] 9 [I/Y] 1 [N] [CPT] [FV] [4090] [STO] 1

Maturity value of \$3000

(Set P/Y, C/Y = 2) [2nd] (CLR TVM)3000 [±] [PV] 8.5 [I/Y] 3 [N] [CPT] [FV] [3398.98655]

$x + x(1.008333)^{-12}$

(Set P/Y, C/Y = 12) [2nd] (CLR TVM) 1 [FV] 10 [I/Y] 12 [N] [CPT] [PV] [-0.905212] [±] [STO] 2

This gives $x + 0.905212x$.

[RCL] 1 [±] [PV] 9 [N] [CPT] [FV] [4407.176326]

3398.98655 FV 6 N CPT PV -3233.889239

1 + RCL 2 = STO 3

4407.176326 + 3233.889239 = STO 4

$$x + 0.905212x = 4407.176326 + 3233.889239$$
$$1.905212x = 7641.065565$$
$$x = 4010.611714$$ (RCL 4 ÷ RCL 3 =)

EXERCISE 9.5

EXCEL NOTES

If you choose, you can use Excel's Future Value (FV) or Present Value (PV) functions to answer the questions below. Refer to FV and PV on MathXL to learn how to use these Excel functions.

EXCEL SPREADSHEET

Find the equivalent single replacement payment on the given focal date for each of the following eight situations.

	Scheduled Payments	Int. Rate	Frequency of Conversion	Focal Date
1.	$5000.00 due in 2 years	6%	monthly	5 years from now
2.	$1600.00 due in 18 months	8%	quarterly	42 months from now
3.	$3400.00 due in 4 years	10%	semi-annually	1 year from now
4.	$2700.00 due in 60 months	7%	quarterly	6 months from now
5.	$800.00 due in 6 months and $700.00 due in 15 months	9.5%	monthly	2 years from now
6.	$1000.00 due in 9 months and $1200.00 due in 18 months	8.8%	quarterly	3 years from now
7.	$400.00 due in 3 years and $600.00 due in 5 years	11%	semi-annually	now
8.	$2000.00 due in 20 months and $1500.00 due in 40 months	10.5%	monthly	9 months from now

EXCEL SPREADSHEET

Solve each of the following problems.

1. A loan of $4000 is due in five years. If money is worth 7% compounded annually, find the equivalent payment that would settle the debt
(a) now; (b) in 2 years; (c) in 5 years; (d) in 10 years. Reference Example 9.5A

2. A debt payment of $5500 is due in 27 months. If money is worth 8.4% p.a. compounded quarterly, what is the equivalent payment
   (a) now?
   (b) 15 months from now?
   (c) 27 months from now?
   (d) 36 months from now?

3. A debt can be paid by payments of $2000 scheduled today, $2000 scheduled in three years, and $2000 scheduled in six years. What single payment would settle the debt four years from now if money is worth 10% compounded semi-annually? Reference Example 9.5C

4. Scheduled payments of $600, $800, and $1200 are due in one year, three years, and six years respectively. What is the equivalent single replacement payment two-and-a-half years from now if interest is 7.5% compounded monthly?

5. Scheduled payments of $400 due today and $700 due with interest at 4.5% compounded monthly in eight months are to be settled by a payment of $500 six months from now and a final payment in fifteen months. Determine the size of the final payment if money is worth 6% compounded monthly.

6. Scheduled payments of $1200 due one year ago and $1000 due six months ago are to be replaced by a payment of $800 now, a second payment of $1000 nine months from now, and a final payment eighteen months from now. What is the size of the final payment if interest is 10.8% compounded quarterly?

7. Two debts—the first of $800 due six months ago and the second of $1400 borrowed one year ago for a term of three years at 6.5% compounded annually—are to be replaced by a single payment one year from now. Determine the size of the replacement payment if interest is 7.5% compounded quarterly and the focal date is one year from now.

8. Scheduled payments of $2000 due now and $2000 due in four years are to be replaced by a payment of $2000 due in two years and a second payment due in seven years. Determine the size of the second payment if interest is 10.5% compounded annually and the focal date is seven years from now.

9. Scheduled loan payments of $1500 due in six months and $1900 due in 21 months are rescheduled as a payment of $2000 due in three years and a second payment due in 45 months. Determine the size of the second payment if interest is 7% compounded quarterly and the focal date is 45 months from now. Reference Example 9.5D

10. A loan of $3000 borrowed today is to be repaid in three equal installments due in one year, three years, and five years respectively. What is the size of the equal installments if money is worth 7.2% compounded monthly? Reference Example 9.5E

11. Savona borrowed $7500 from her aunt today and has agreed to repay the loan in two equal payments to be made in one year and three years from now. What is the size of the equal payments if money is worth 8% compounded quarterly?

12. What is the size of the equal payments that must be made at the end of each of the next four years to settle a debt of $3000 due four years from now and subject to interest at 10% compounded annually?

13. Karina is due to pay $9000 in five years. If she makes three equal payments, in twenty months, thirty months, and five years from today, what is the size of the equal payments if money is worth 5.16% compounded monthly?

14. Scheduled payments of $800 due two years ago and $1000 due in five years are to be replaced by two equal payments. The first replacement payment is due in four years and the second payment is due in eight years. Determine the size of the two replacement payments if interest is 12% compounded semi-annually and the focal date is four years from now.

15. Loan payments of $3000 due one year ago and $2500 due in four years are to be replaced by two equal payments. The first replacement payment is due now and the second payment is due in six years. Determine the size of the two replacement payments if interest is 6.9% compounded monthly and the focal date is now. Reference Example 9.5I

16. A payment of $500 is due in six months with interest at 12% compounded quarterly. A second payment of $800 is due in 18 months with interest at 10% compounded semi-annually. These two payments are to be replaced by a single payment nine months from now. Determine the size of the replacement payment if interest is 9% compounded monthly and the focal date is nine months from now.

17. Scheduled payments of $900 due in three months with interest at 11% compounded quarterly and $800 due in thirty months with interest at 11% compounded quarterly are to be replaced by two equal payments. The first replacement payment is due today and the second payment is due in three years. Determine the size of the two replacement payments if interest is 9% compounded monthly and the focal date is today. Reference Example 9.5J

18. Scheduled payments of $1400 due today and $1600 due with interest at 11.5% compounded annually in five years are to be replaced by two equal payments. The first replacement payment is due in 18 months and the second payment is due in four years. Determine the size of the two replacement payments if interest is 11% compounded quarterly and the focal date is 18 months from now.

Go to MathXL at www.mathXL.com. You can practise many of this chapter's exercises as often as you want. The guided solutions help you find an answer step by step. You'll find a personalized study plan available to you too!

Review Exercise

1. What is the accumulated value of \$500 in fifteen years at 6% compounded
   (a) annually? (b) quarterly? (c) monthly?

2. What is the amount of \$10 000 at 10.5% compounded monthly
   (a) in four years?
   (b) in eight-and-a-half years?
   (c) in twenty years?

3. Landmark Trust offers five-year investment certificates at 3.5% compounded semi-annually.
   (a) What is the value of a \$2000 certificate at maturity?
   (b) How much of the maturity value is interest?

4. Western Savings offers three-year term deposits at 2.25% compounded annually while your credit union offers such deposits at 2.0% compounded quarterly. If you have \$5000 to invest, what is the maturity value of your deposit
   (a) at Western Savings?
   (b) at your credit union?

5. Find the future value and the compound interest of
   (a) \$1800 invested at 3.7% compounded quarterly for 15.5 years;
   (b) \$1250 invested at 2.6% compounded monthly for 15 years.

6. If \$6000 is invested for six years and seven months at 6% compounded semi-annually, what is the interest that the investment earns?

7. Compute the maturity value of a \$5000 promissory note dated November 15, 2010, and due on June 15, 2020, if interest is 8% compounded quarterly.

8. An investment of \$2000 is made for three years, four months at 4.5% compounded semi-annually. What is the amount of interest?

9. Determine the sum of money that will grow to \$14 000 in four years, eight months at 5% compounded quarterly.

10. Determine the proceeds of a non-interest-bearing note with a maturity value of \$9000 three years and ten months before the due date if the interest rate is 7% compounded semi-annually.

11. Determine the discounted value now of \$5200 due in forty months if money is worth 6.5% compounded quarterly.

12. Find the present value and the compound discount of
    (a) \$3600 due in 9 years if interest is 8% compounded semi-annually;
    (b) \$9000 due in 5 years if money is worth 6.8% compounded quarterly.

13. The Ram Company borrowed \$20 000 at 10% compounded semi-annually and made payments toward the loan of \$8000 after two years and \$10 000 after three-and-a-half years. How much is required to pay off the loan one year after the second payment?

14. Ted deposited \$1750 in an RRSP on March 1, 2014, at 3% compounded quarterly. Subsequently the interest rate was changed to 4% compounded monthly on September 1, 2016, and to 4.5% compounded semi-annually on June 1, 2018. What was the value of the RRSP deposit on December 1, 2020, if no further changes in interest were made?

15. An investment of \$2500 is accumulated at 5% compounded quarterly for two-and-a-half years. At that time the interest rate is changed to 6% compounded monthly. How much is the investment worth two years after the change in interest rate?

16. To ensure that funds are available to repay the principal at maturity, a borrower deposits \$2000 each year for three years. If interest is 6% compounded quarterly, how much will the borrower have on deposit four years after the first deposit was made?

17. Cindy started a registered retirement savings plan on February 1, 2012, with a deposit of \$2500. She

added $2000 on February 1, 2013, and $1500 on February 1, 2018. What is the accumulated value of her RRSP account on August 1, 2022, if interest is 5% compounded quarterly?

18. A demand loan of $8000 is repaid by payments of $3000 after fifteen months, $4000 after thirty months, and a final payment after four years. If interest was 8% for the first two years and 9% for the remaining time, and compounding is quarterly, what is the size of the final payment?

19. A non-interest-bearing note for $1500 is due on June 30, 2016. The note is discounted at 10% compounded quarterly on September 30, 2012. What are the proceeds of the note?

20. Find the present value and the compound discount of $4000 due in seven years and six months if interest is 8.8% compounded quarterly.

21. Find the principal that will accumulate to $6000 in fifteen years at 5% compounded monthly.

22. Find the proceeds of a non-interest-bearing promissory note for $75 000 discounted 42 months before maturity at 6.5% compounded semi-annually.

23. A ten-year promissory note for $1750 dated May 1, 2013, bearing interest at 4% compounded semi-annually is discounted on August 1, 2019, to yield 6% compounded quarterly. Determine the proceeds of the note.

24. A seven-year, $10 000 promissory note bearing interest at 8% compounded quarterly is discounted four years after the date of issue at 7% compounded semi-annually. What are the proceeds of the note?

25. A $40 000, 15-year promissory note dated June 1, 2010, bearing interest at 12% compounded semi-annually is discounted on September 1, 2018, at 11% compounded quarterly. What are the proceeds of the note?

26. A fifteen-year promissory note for $16 500 bearing interest at 12% compounded semi-annually is discounted at 9% compounded monthly three years and four months after the date of issue. Compute the proceeds of the note.

27. An eight-year promissory note for $20 000 dated May 2, 2011, bearing interest at 10% compounded quarterly, is discounted on September 2, 2013, at 9.5% compounded semi-annually. Determine the proceeds of the note.

28. Three years and five months after its date of issue, a six-year promissory note for $3300 bearing interest at 7.5% compounded monthly is discounted at 7% compounded semi-annually. Find the proceeds of the note.

29. A sum of money has a value of $3000 eighteen months from now. If money is worth 6% compounded monthly, what is its equivalent value

(a) now?

(b) one year from now?

(c) three years from now?

30. Payments of $1000, $1200, and $1500 are due in six months, eighteen months, and thirty months from now, respectively. What is the equivalent single payment two years from now if money is worth 9.6% compounded quarterly?

31. An obligation of $10 000 is due one year from now with interest at 10% compounded semi-annually. The obligation is to be settled by a payment of $6000 in six months and a final payment in fifteen months. What is the size of the second payment if interest is now 9% compounded monthly?

32. Waldon Toys owes $3000 due in two years with interest at 11% compounded semi-annually and $2500 due in fifteen months at 9% compounded quarterly. If the company wants to discharge these debts by making two equal payments, the first now and the second eighteen months from now, what is the size of the two payments if money is now worth 8.4% compounded monthly?

33. Debt payments of $400 due today, $500 due in eighteen months, and $900 due in three years are to be combined into a single payment due two years from now. What is the size of the single payment if interest is 8% p.a. compounded quarterly?

34. Debt payments of $2600 due one year ago and $2400 due two years from now are to be replaced by two equal payments due one year from now and four years from now. What is the size of the equal payments if money is worth 9.6% p.a. compounded semi-annually?

35. A loan of $7000 taken out two years ago is to be repaid by three equal installments due now, two years from now, and three years from now. What is the size of the equal installments if interest on the debt is 12% p.a. compounded monthly?

Self-Test

EXCEL SPREADSHEET

1. What sum of money invested at 4% compounded quarterly will grow to $3300 in 11 years?

2. Find the compound interest earned by $1300 invested at 7.5% compounded monthly for seven years.

3. Determine the compounding factor for a sum of money invested for 14.5 years at 7% compounded semi-annually.

4. Determine the maturity value of $1400 due in 71 months compounded annually at 7.75%.

5. Five years after Anne deposited $3600 in a savings account that earned interest at 4.8% compounded monthly, the rate of interest was changed to 6% compounded semi-annually. How much was in the account twelve years after the deposit was made?

6. A debt can be repaid by payments of $4000 today, $4000 in five years, and $3000 in six years. What single payment would settle the debt one year from now if money is worth 7% compounded semi-annually?

7. A $10 200 debt will accumulate for five years at 11.6% compounded semi-annually. For how much will the debt sell three years after it was incurred if the buyer of the debt charges 10% compounded quarterly?

8. What is the present value of $5900 payable in 15 years if the current interest rate is 7.5% compounded semi-annually?

9. Determine the compound discount on $8800 due in 7.5 years if interest is 9.6% compounded monthly.

10. Two debt payments, the first for $800 due today and the second for $600 due in nine months with interest at 10.5% compounded monthly, are to be settled by a payment of $800 six months from now and a final payment in 24 months. Determine the size of the final payment if money is now worth 9.5% compounded quarterly.

11. A note dated July 1, 2008, promises to pay $8000 with interest at 7% compounded quarterly on January 1, 2017. Find the proceeds from the sale of the note on July 1, 2012, if money is then worth 8% compounded semi-annually.

12. Adam borrowed $5000 at 10% compounded semi-annually. He repaid $2000 after two years and $2500 after three years. How much will he owe after five years?

13. A debt of \$7000 due today is to be settled by three equal payments due three months from now, 15 months from now, and 27 months from now. What is the size of the equal payments at 11% compounded quarterly?

14. Seven years and two months after its date of issue, an eleven-year promissory note for \$8200 bearing interest at 13.5% compounded monthly is discounted at 10.5% compounded semi-annually. Find the proceeds of the note.

15. Compute the proceeds of a non-interest-bearing note for \$1100 three years and seven months before the due date if money is worth 7.5% compounded annually.

Challenge Problems

1. Jean-Guy Renoir wanted to leave some money to his grandchildren in his will. He decided that they should each receive the same amount of money when they each turn 21. When he died, his grandchildren were 19, 16, and 13 years old. How much will they each receive when they turn 21 if Jean-Guy left a lump sum of \$50 000 to be shared among them equally? Assume the interest rate will remain at 7.75% p.a. compounded semi-annually from the time of Jean-Guy's death until the youngest grandchild turns 21.

2. Miranda has \$1000 to invest. She has narrowed her options to two four-year certificates, A and B. Certificate A pays interest at 8% p.a. compounded semi-annually the first year, 8% p.a. compounded quarterly the second year, 8% p.a. compounded monthly the third year, and 8% p.a. compounded daily the fourth year. Certificate B pays 8% p.a. compounded daily the first year, 8% p.a. compounded monthly the second year, 8% p.a. compounded quarterly the third year, and 8% p.a. compounded semi-annually the fourth year.

(a) What is the value of each certificate at the end of the four years?

(b) How do the values of certificates A and B compare with the value of a third certificate that pays interest at 7% compounded daily for the full four-year term?

CASE STUDY 9.1 Savings Options

» Erin's grandmother gave her some money as a gift, with the instructions that Erin was to invest the money to save for her education. At her bank, Erin explored the investment possibilities for the money, finding that there were three options that she could consider. All of them pay compound interest.

Option 1: The Daily Interest Savings Account pays annual interest of 0.050%, calculated on the minimum balance in the account each day and paid monthly.

Option 2: The Investment Savings Account pays annual interest of 0.050% if the balance is between \$25 000 and \$59 999, 0.050% if the balance is between \$10 000 and $24 999, 0.025% if the balance is between $5000 and $9999, and 0.010% if the balance is under $5000. The interest is calculated on the minimum balance each month and is paid monthly.

Option 3: The Smart Saver Account pays annual interest of 1.250% if the balance is $5000 or more, or 0.000% if the balance is under $5000. The interest is calculated on the minimum balance each day and is paid monthly.

While exploring her options at her bank, Erin was advised that she should also consider the number and type of transactions made in the account each month or year when choosing an account.

QUESTIONS

1. Suppose Erin's gift was $9000 and she invested the money immediately in a bank account for a one-year period. Assume that the bank's interest rates remain the same throughout the year.
   (a) For each of the three options, how much interest would Erin earn in one year's time?
   (b) Which option would pay the most interest?
2. Suppose Erin's gift was $12 000 and she invested the money immediately in a bank account for a one-year period. Assume that the bank's interest rates remain the same throughout the year.
   (a) For each of the three options, how much interest would Erin earn in one year's time?
   (b) Which option would pay the most interest?
   (c) If Erin knew she would have to withdraw $3500 after ten months, which savings option would pay the most interest?
3. Suppose Erin's gift was $12 000, and she planned to leave the money in the account for one year and then withdraw $5000. She would then leave the remaining balance in the account for one more year. Which option would pay the most interest over the two-year period? Assume that the bank's interest rates will stay the same over the next two years.
4. For the savings accounts at your bank, credit union, or trust company, find the features and interest rates offered for each. If you had $3500 to deposit for one year, which option would you choose?

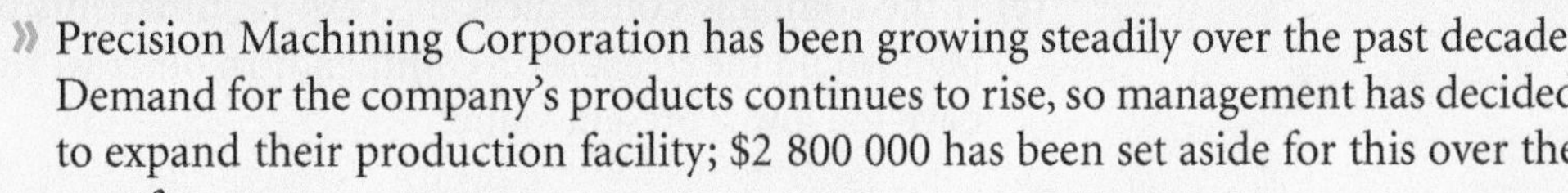

CASE STUDY 9.2 Planning Ahead

» Precision Machining Corporation has been growing steadily over the past decade. Demand for the company's products continues to rise, so management has decided to expand their production facility; $2 800 000 has been set aside for this over the next four years.

Management has developed two different plans for expanding over the next four years, Plan A and Plan B. Plan A would require equal amounts of $750 000 one year from now, two years from now, three years from now, and four years from now. Plan B would require \$300 000 now, \$700 000 one year from now, \$900 000 two years from now, and \$975 000 four years from now.

The company has decided to fund the expansion with only the \$2 800 000 and any interest it can earn on it. Before deciding which plan to use, the company asks its treasurer to predict the rates of interest it can earn on the \$2 800 000. The treasurer expects that Precision Machining Corporation can invest the \$2 800 000 and earn interest at a rate of 4.5% p.a. compounded semi-annually during Year 1, 5.0% p.a. compounded semi-annually during Years 2 and 3, and 5.5% p.a. compounded semi-annually during Year 4. The company can withdraw part of the money from this investment at any time without penalty.

QUESTIONS

1. **(a)** Could Precision Machining Corporation meet the cash requirement of Plan A by investing the \$2 800 000 as described above? (Use "now" as the focal date.)

   (b) What is the exact difference between the cash required and the cash available from the investment?

2. **(a)** Could Precision Machining Corporation meet the cash requirements of Plan B by investing the \$2 800 000 as described above? (Use "now" as the focal date.)

   (b) What is the difference between the cash required and the cash available from the investment?

3. **(a)** Suppose Plan A was changed so that it required equal amounts of \$750 000 now, one year from now, two years from now, and four years from now. Could Precision Machining Corporation meet the cash requirements of the new Plan A by investing the \$2 800 000 as described above? (Use "now" as the focal date.)

   (b) What is the difference between the cash required and the cash available from the investment?

4. Suppose the treasurer found another way to invest the \$2 800 000 that earned interest at a rate of 4.9% compounded quarterly for the next five years.
   (a) Could the company meet the cash requirements of the original Plan A with this new investment? (Show all your calculations.)
   (b) Could the company meet the cash requirements of Plan B with this new investment? (Show all your calculations.)
   (c) If the company could meet the cash requirements of both plans, which plan would the treasurer recommend? In other words, which plan would have the lower present value?

SUMMARY OF FORMULAS

Formula 9.1A

$S = P(1 + i)^n$ — **Finding the future value (or maturity value) when the original principal, the rate of interest, and the time period are known**

restated as

$FV = PV(1 + i)^n$

Formula 9.1B

$$P = \frac{S}{(1 + i)^n}$$

Finding the present value (or principal, or proceeds, or discounted value) when the future value, the rate of interest, and the time period are known

restated as

$$PV = \frac{FV}{(1 + i)^n}$$

Formula 9.1C

$P = S(1 + i)^{-n}$ — **Finding the present value by means of the discount factor (the reciprocal of the compounding factor)**

restated as

$PV = FV(1 + i)^{-n}$

Formula 9.2

$$i = \frac{j}{m}$$

Finding the periodic rate of interest

GLOSSARY

Accumulation factor *see* **Compounding factor**

Comparison date *see* **Focal date**

Compound discount the difference between a given future amount and its present value (or proceeds or discounted value) at a specified time *(p. 350)*

Compound interest a procedure for computing interest whereby interest earned during an interest period is added onto the principal at the end of the interest period *(p. 329)*

Compounding factor the factor $(1 + i)^n$ found in compound interest formulas *(p. 331)*

Compounding frequency the number of times interest is compounded during a given time period (usually one year) *(p. 331)*

Compounding period the time between two successive interest dates *(p. 331)*

Conversion frequency *see* **Compounding frequency**

Conversion period *see* **Compounding period**

Discount factor the factor $(1 + i)^{-n}$; the reciprocal of the compounding factor *(p. 352)*

Discounted value *see* **Present value**

Discounting the process of computing the present value (or proceeds or discounted value) of a future sum of money *(p. 350)*

Equivalent values the dated values of an original sum of money *(p. 363)*

Focal date a specific date chosen to compare the time values of one or more dated sums of money *(p. 363)*

Future value the sum of money to which a principal will grow at compound interest in a specific number of compounding or conversion periods at a specified periodic rate of interest *(p. 330)*

Maturity value *see* **Future value**

Nominal rate of interest the stated rate at which the compounding is done one or more times per year; usually stated as an annual rate *(p. 331)*

Periodic rate of interest the value of interest is obtained by dividing the nominal annual rate by the number of compounding periods per year *(p. 331)*

Present value the principal at any time that will grow at compound interest to a given future value over a given number of compounding periods at a given rate of interest *(p. 350)*

Proceeds *see* **Present value**

USEFUL INTERNET SITES

www.globefund.com

Globefund.com This popular site for mutual fund information and analysis is hosted by the *Globe and Mail* Website.

www.fin.gc.ca/fin-eng.html

Department of Finance This site has information on the preparation of the federal government's budget that shows what is happening to taxes, as well as information related to interest rates and the economy.

www.cannex.com

CANNEX This site has a large list of comparative interest rates for GICs and term deposits offered by financial institutions in Canada and the United States.

CHAPTER 10

Compound Interest—Further Topics

OBJECTIVES

Upon completing this chapter, you will be able to do the following:

1. Determine the number of conversion periods and find equated dates.
2. Compute periodic and nominal rates of interest.
3. Compute effective and equivalent rates of interest.

When you see ads for merchandise, such as computers or furniture, the all-cash price and the monthly financed price are often given. Would you be paying the same amount for the item if you financed the purchase with a loan as you would if you purchased it for cash? Do you know what interest rate is being charged, or whether the interest is simple or compound? Do you know whether the rates of interest are the same for each type of loan? Do you know the number of payments you would have to make? These details are often omitted.

We should read such ads critically before making decisions on purchases. It is important to know all of the information needed to compare the offer with loans available from other sources.

INTRODUCTION

In the previous chapter, we considered future value and present value when using compound interest. In this chapter, we will look at other aspects of compound interest, including finding the number of conversion periods, and computing equated dates and equivalent and effective rates of interest.

For these calculations we can either manipulate the formulas or use electronic calculators. In this and the following chapters, we will use calculators.

We can save time on our calculations by using the memory of the calculator when working with these functions. Of course, we might get slightly different results if we use memory rather than rekeying the displayed digits, because the number of digits retained in memory is almost always greater than the number of digits displayed. However, the differences are so small that we can ignore them. For the worked examples in this text, we have used the memory in the calculator whenever it was convenient to do so.

10.1 FINDING *n* AND RELATED PROBLEMS

A. Finding the number of conversion periods

If the principal PV, the future value FV, and the periodic rate of interest i are known, the number of conversion periods n can be determined by substituting the known values in Formula 9.1A and solving for n.

$$FV = PV(1 + i)^n \qquad \text{Formula 9.1A}$$

This method involves the use of logarithms. You can solve the problem using an electronic calculator as long as the calculator is equipped with the natural logarithm function (LN key).

You may also use a financial calculator, such as the TI BAII Plus, that is preprogrammed with the time value of money (TVM) worksheet. After entering all of the relevant data into the calculator, press CPT N. Note that the units of n relate to the payment periods. For example, if you have quarterly payment periods, your answer for n indicates the number of quarterly periods.

EXCEL NOTES

You can use Excel's Number of Compounding Periods (NPER) function to find the number of conversion periods. Refer to NPER on MathXL to learn how to use this Excel function.

EXAMPLE 10.1A In how many years will \$2000.00 grow to \$2440.38 at 4% compounded quarterly?

SOLUTION

$PV = 2000.00$; $FV = 2440.38$; $I/Y = 4$; $P/Y = 4$; $i = \frac{4\%}{4} = 1\% = 0.01$

$$2440.38 = 2000.00(1.01)^n \qquad \text{substituting in Formula 9.1A}$$

$$(1.01)^n = 1.22019$$

$$n \ln 1.01 = \ln 1.22019 \qquad \text{solve for } n \text{ using the natural logarithm}$$

$0.009950n = 0.199007$ ——— **obtain the numerical values using the LN key**

$$n = \frac{0.199007}{0.009950}$$
$$= 19.999997 = 20 \text{ (quarters)}$$

$$\text{Number of years} = \frac{20}{4} = 5$$

Programmed Solution

You can use preprogrammed financial calculators to find n by the same procedure previously used to find FV and PV.

(Set P/Y, C/Y = 4) 2nd (CLR TVM) 2000 ± PV

2440.38 FV 4 I/Y CPT N 19.999997

At 4% compounded quarterly, \$2000 will grow to \$2440.38 in 20 quarters or five years.

Note: Another way to solve Example 10.1A is first to rearrange Formula 9.1A to solve for n:

$$FV = PV(1 + i)^n$$

$$(1 + i)^n = \frac{FV}{PV}$$

$$n \ln(1 + i) = \ln\left(\frac{FV}{PV}\right)$$

$$n = \frac{\ln\left(\frac{FV}{PV}\right)}{\ln(1 + i)}$$

Recall that the total number of conversion periods is n. To convert to years if compounding semi-annually, divide n by 2; if compounding quarterly, divide by 4; if compounding monthly, divide by 12; and if compounding daily, divide by 365. Remember, you do not have to memorize this equation if you understand the principles of formula rearrangement.

EXAMPLE 10.1B

How long does it take for money to double

(i) at 5% compounded annually?

(ii) at 10% compounded annually?

SOLUTION

While neither PV nor FV is given, any sum of money may be used as principal. For this calculation, a convenient value for the principal is \$1.00.

PV = 1.00; FV = 2.00; I/Y = 5; P/Y = 1

(i) At 5% compounded annually, $i = 5\% = 0.05$

$$\begin{aligned} 2 &= 1(1.05)^n \\ 1.05^n &= 2 \\ n \ln 1.05 &= \ln 2 \\ 0.048790n &= 0.693147 \\ n &= 14.206699 \text{ (years)} \end{aligned}$$

Programmed Solution

(Set P/Y, C/Y = 1) **2nd** (CLR TVM) 1 **±** **PV** 2 **FV** 5 **I/Y**

CPT **N** 14.206699 (years)

At 5% compounded annually, money doubles in approximately 14.21 years.

(ii) At 10% compounded annually, I/Y = 10; P/Y = 1; $i = 10\% = 0.10$

$$\begin{aligned} 2 &= 1(1 + 0.10)^n \\ 1.10^n &= 2 \\ n \ln 1.10 &= \ln 2 \\ 0.095310n &= 0.693147 \\ n &= 7.272541 \text{ (years)} \end{aligned}$$

Programmed Solution

2nd (CLR TVM)1 **±** **PV** 2 **FV**

10 **I/Y** **CPT** **N** 7.272541 (years)

At 10% compounded annually, money doubles in approximately 7.27 years.

EXAMPLE 10.1C

How many years will it take for $5000, invested at 6% compounded monthly, to grow to $15 000?

SOLUTION

Let PV = 5000; then FV = 15 000; I/Y = 6; P/Y = 12; $i = \frac{6\%}{12} = 0.5\% = 0.005$

$$n = \frac{\ln\left(\frac{FV}{PV}\right)}{\ln(1 + i)}$$

$$n = \frac{\ln\left(\frac{15\,000}{5000}\right)}{\ln(1.005)}$$

$$n = \frac{\ln(3)}{\ln(1.005)}$$

$$n = \frac{1.098612}{0.004988} = 220.271307 \text{ months}$$

Programmed Solution

(Set P/Y, C/Y = 12) [2nd] (CLR TVM) 5000 [±] [PV] 15 000 [FV]

6 [I/Y] [CPT] [N] [220.271307] (months)

At 6% compounded monthly, the desired amount will be achieved in approximately 220.27 months or $\frac{220.57}{12} = 18.36$ years.

B. Equated date

The concept of *equivalence* of values when using the compound interest method was discussed in Chapter 9, Section 9.5. In solving problems of equivalence, the unknown value was the size of a payment at the selected focal date. While we often need to find the size of the payment, occasionally we need to find the interest rate on the focal date instead. To find a specific date to solve your problem, solve for n, and then use the [DATE] worksheet within the calculator.

The **equated date** is the date on which a single sum of money is equal to the sum of two or more dated sums of money. An equation of values can be set up by the same technique used in Section 9.5. The method can also be applied to problems in which the single sum of money does not equal the sum of the dated sums of money considered.

EXAMPLE 10.1D

An existing financial agreement requires three payments: \$2000 in 6 months, \$3000 in 15 months, and \$5000 in 24 months. Alternatively, a single payment equal to the sum of the required payments could be made. If money is worth 9% compounded monthly, when would the single payment have to be made?

SOLUTION

The single payment equal to the sum of the required payments is \$2000 plus \$3000 plus \$5000, or \$10 000. Select as the focal date "now." Let the number of compounding periods from the focal date to the equated date be represented by n. Since the compounding is done monthly, n will be a number of months, I/Y = 9, P/Y = 12, and $i = \frac{9}{12}\% = 0.75\% = 0.0075$. The method and data are shown graphically in Figure 10.1.

Let E_1, E_2, and E_3 represent the equivalent values of the original payments at the focal date, as shown in Figure 10.1.

Let E_4 represent the equivalent value of the single payment of \$10 000 at the focal date.

The equation of values can now be set up.

$$E_4 = E_1 + E_2 + E_3$$

$$10\,000.00(1.0075)^{-n} = 2000.00(1.0075)^{-6} + 3000.00(1.0075)^{-15} + 5000.00(1.0075)^{-24}$$

$$10\,000.00(1.0075)^{-n} = 2000.00(0.956158) + 3000.00(0.893973) + 5000.00(0.835831)$$
$$10\,000.00(1.0075)^{-n} = 1912.316036 + 2681.917614 + 4179.157020$$
$$10\,000.00(1.0075)^{-n} = 8773.39067$$
$$(1.0075)^{-n} = \frac{8773.39067}{10\,000.00}$$
$$(1.0075)^{-n} = 0.877339$$
$$-n(\ln 1.0075) = \ln 0.87734$$
$$-n(0.007472) = -0.130861$$
$$n = \frac{-0.130861}{-0.007472}$$
$$n = 17.513439$$

The equated date is about 17.5 months from now.

FIGURE 10.1 Graphical Representation of Method and Data

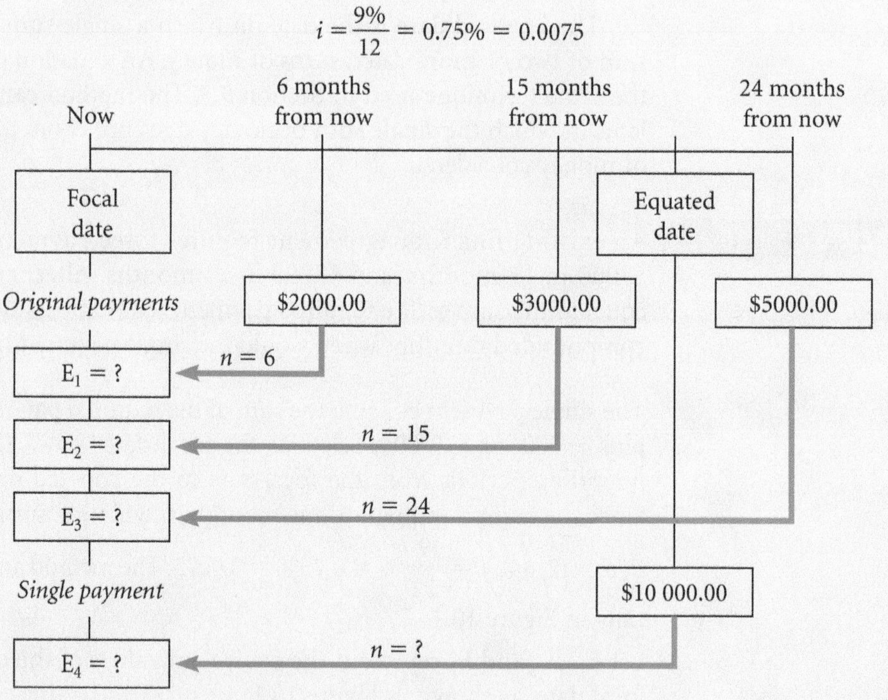

Programmed Solution

First simplify the equation $E_4 = E_1 + E_2 + E_3$.

$$10\,000(1.0075)^{-n} = 2000.00(1.0075)^{-6} + 3000(1.0075)^{-15} + 5000(1.0075)^{-24}$$

$2000(1.0075)^{-6}$

(Set P/Y, C/Y = 12) 2nd (CLR TVM) 2000 FV

9 I/Y 6 N CPT PV -1912.316036

$3000(1.0075)^{-15}$

3000 [FV] 15 [N] [CPT] [PV] -2681.917614

$5000(1.0075)^{-24}$

5000 [FV] 24 [N] [CPT] [PV] -4179.157020

$10\,000(1.0075)^{-n} = 1912.316036 + 2681.917614 + 4179.157020$

Remember to remove the negative (cash outflow) signs.

$10\,000(1.0075)^{-n} = 8773.39067$

Now solve the simplified equation:

$10\,000(1.0075)^{-n} = 8773.39067$

in which FV = 10 000; PV = 8773.39067; $i = 0.75\%$

[2nd] (CLR TVM) 10 000 [FV] 8773.39067

[±] [PV] 9 [I/Y] [CPT] [N] 17.513581

The equated date is approximately 17.5 months from now.

EXAMPLE 10.1E

When Josh borrowed money, he originally agreed to repay the loan by making three equal payments of \$1500, with a payment due now, another payment due two years from now, and the final payment due four years from now. Instead of the original payments, he plans to pay off the loan by making a single payment of \$5010. If interest is 10% compounded annually, when will he make the single payment?

SOLUTION

Select as the focal date "now." Let the number of compounding periods from the focal date to the equated date be represented by n. Since the compounding is done annually, n will be a number of years, I/Y = 10, P/Y = 1, and $i = 10\% = 0.10$.

Let E_1, E_2, and E_3 represent the equivalent values of the original payments at the focal date.

$$E_1 = 1500.00 = 1500.00$$
$$E_2 = 1500.00(1.10)^{-2} = 1500.00(0.826446) = 1239.669421$$
$$E_3 = 1500.00(1.10)^{-4} = 1500.00(0.683013) = 1024.520183$$
$$E_1 + E_2 + E_3 = 3764.189605$$

Let E_4 represent the equivalent value of the single payment of \$5010 at the focal date.

$$E_4 = 5010.00(1.10)^{-n}$$
$$E_4 = E_1 + E_2 + E_3$$
$$5010.00(1.10)^{-n} = 3764.189605$$
$$(1.10)^{-n} = 0.751335$$
$$-n(\ln 1.10) = \ln 0.751335$$
$$-0.095310n = -0.285903$$
$$n = 2.999713 \text{ (years)}$$

The equated date is approximately three years from now.

Programmed Solution

$E_4 = E_1 + E_2 + E_3$
$5010.00(1.10)^{-n} = 1500.00 + 1500(1.10)^{-2} + 1500(1.10)^{-4}$
$1500(1.10)^{-2}$
(Set P/Y, C/Y = 1) 2nd (CLR TVM) 1500 FV 10 I/Y
2 N CPT PV -1239.669421
$1500(1.10)^{-4}$
4 N CPT PV -1024.520183

$5010.00(1.10)^{-n} = 1500.00 + 1239.669421 + 1024.520183$
$5010.00(1.10)^{-n} = 3764.189605$
2nd (CLR TVM) 5010 FV 3764.189605 ± PV
10 I/Y CPT N 2.999713

The single payment should be made three years from now.

EXAMPLE 10.1F

A loan of \$2000 taken out today is to be repaid by a payment of \$1200 in six months and a final payment of \$1000.00. If interest is 12% compounded monthly, when should the final payment be made?

SOLUTION

Let the focal point be "now"; I/Y = 12; P/Y = 12; $i = \frac{12\%}{12} = 1.0\% = 0.01$.

$$\begin{aligned}
2000.00 &= 1200.00(1.01)^{-6} + 1000.00(1.01)^{-n} \\
2000.00 &= 1200.00(0.942045) + 1000.00(1.01)^{-n} \\
2000.00 &= 1130.454282 + 1000.00(1.01)^{-n} \\
869.545718 &= 1000.00(1.01)^{-n} \\
(1.01)^{-n} &= 0.869546 \\
-n(\ln 1.01) &= \ln 0.869546 \\
-0.009950n &= -0.139784 \\
n &= 14.048213 \text{ (months)}
\end{aligned}$$

Programmed Solution

$2000.00 = 1200.00(1.01)^{-6} + 1000(1.01)^{-n}$
$1200.00(1.01)^{-6}$
(Set P/Y, C/Y = 12) 2nd (CLR TVM) 1200 FV 12 I/Y
6 N CPT PV -1130.454282

$2000.00 = 1130.454282 + 1000(1.01)^{-n}$
$869.545718 = 1000(1.01)^{-n}$
869.545718 ± PV 1000 FV 12 I/Y
CPT N 14.048213 (months)

$n = 427$ days ———— $\left(\frac{14.047718}{12}\right)(365) = 427.299812$

The final payment should be made in 427 days.

EXERCISE 10.1

EXCEL NOTES If you choose, you can use Excel's Number of Compounding Periods (NPER) function to answer the questions indicated below. Refer to NPER on MathXL to learn how to use this Excel function.

1. Determine the number of compounding periods for each of the following six investments.

EXCEL SPREADSHEET

	Principal	Future Value	Interest Rate	Frequency of Conversion
(a)	$2600.00	$6437.50	7%	annually
(b)	1240.00	1638.40	4	quarterly
(c)	560.00	1350.00	9	monthly
(d)	3480.00	4762.60	8	semi-annually
(e)	950.00	1900.00	7.5	quarterly
(f)	$1300.00	$3900.00	6	semi-annually

2. Find the equated date at which the original payments are equivalent to the single payment for each of the following four sets of payments.

	Original Payments	Interest Rate	Frequency of Conversion	Single Payment
(a)	$400 due in 9 months and $700 due in 21 months	12%	quarterly	$1256.86
(b)	$1200 due today and $2000 due in 5 years	8	semi-annually	3808.70
(c)	$1000 due 8 months ago, $1200 due in 6 months, and $1500 due in 16 months	9	monthly	3600.00
(d)	$600 due in 2 years, $800 due in 3.5 years, and $900 due in 5 years	10	quarterly	$1800.00

Answer each of the following questions.

EXCEL SPREADSHEET

1. How long will it take $400 to accumulate to $760 at 7% p.a. compounded semi-annually?
2. In how many days will $580 grow to $600 at 4.5% p.a. compounded monthly?
3. In how many years will money quadruple at 8% compounded quarterly?
4. In how many months will money triple at 9% compounded semi-annually?
5. If an investment of $800 earned interest of $320 at 6% compounded monthly, for how many years was the money invested?
6. A loan of $2000 was repaid together with interest of $604.35. If interest was 8% compounded quarterly, for how many months was the loan taken out?

7. If you borrowed \$1000 on May 1, 2009, at 10% compounded semi-annually and interest on the loan amounts to \$157.63, on what date is the loan due?

8. A promissory note for \$600 dated May 15, 2008, requires an interest payment of \$150 at maturity. If interest is at 9% compounded monthly, determine the due date of the note.

9. A non-interest-bearing promissory note for \$1500 was discounted at 5% p.a. compounded quarterly. If the proceeds of the note were \$1375.07, how many months before the due date was the note discounted?

10. A five-year, \$1000 note bearing interest at 9% compounded annually was discounted at 12% compounded semi-annually yielding proceeds of \$1416.56. How many months before the due date was the discount date?

11. A contract requires payments of \$4000 today, \$5000 in three years, and \$6000 in five years. When can the contract be fulfilled by a single payment equal to the sum of the required payments if money is worth 9% p.a. compounded monthly?

12. A financial agreement requires the payment of \$1200 in 9 months, \$1400 in 18 months, and \$1600 in 30 months. When would an alternative single payment of \$4000 have to be made if money is worth 7% compounded quarterly?

13. Graham purchased a business by agreeing to make three payments of \$12 000 each in one year, two years, and four years. Because of cash flow difficulties in the first year, he renegotiated the payment schedule so that he would pay \$16 000 in 18 months, \$10 000 in 30 months, and a third payment of \$10 000. In how many years should he make the third payment if interest is 7.2% compounded semi-annually?

14. Henrik, a Canadian hockey player, agreed to a contract where he was to receive \$40 000 in 6 months, \$60 000 in 8 months, and \$100 000 in 18 months. The deal was renegotiated after 4 months when he received a payment of \$30 000. He agreed to accept a payment of \$172 000 at a later date. When should Henrik receive the payment if money is worth 8% compounded monthly?

10.2 FINDING i AND RELATED PROBLEMS

A. Finding the periodic rate i and the nominal annual rate of interest j

If the original principal PV, the future value FV, and the number of conversion periods n are known, the periodic rate of interest (conversion rate) i can be determined by substituting in Formula 9.1A, $FV = PV(1 + i)^n$, and solving for i. The nominal annual rate of interest j can then be found by multiplying i by the number of conversion periods per year m.

EXAMPLE 10.2A What is the annually compounded rate if \$200 accumulates to \$318.77 in eight years?

SOLUTION PV = 200.00; FV = 318.77; C/Y(m) = 1; $n = 8$

$$318.77 = 200.00(1 + i)^8 \quad \text{——— } i \text{ is an } annual \text{ rate}$$
$$(1 + i)^8 = 1.59385$$
$$[(1 + i)^8]^{\frac{1}{8}} = 1.59385^{0.125} \quad \text{——— raise each side to the power } \frac{1}{8}$$
$$1 + i = 1.59385^{0.125}$$
$$1 + i = 1.060000$$
$$i = 0.060000$$
$$i = 6.0\% \quad \text{——— the desired annual rate}$$

The annually compounded rate is 6.0%.

Programmed Solution

You can use preprogrammed financial calculators to find i by the same procedure used previously to determine FV or PV. That is, select the compound interest mode, enter the given variables FV, PV, and N, and retrieve the fourth variable I/Y.

(Set P/Y, C/Y = 1) [2nd] (CLR TVM) 200 [±] [PV] 318.77 [FV]

8 [N] [CPT] [I/Y] [6.000016] (annual)

Note: As we emphasized in Chapter 2, it is important to know how to rearrange the terms of an equation. For instance, another way to solve Example 10.2A is first to rearrange Formula 9.1A to solve for i:

$$\text{FV} = \text{PV}(1 + \text{i})^n$$
$$(1 + i)^n = \frac{\text{FV}}{\text{PV}}$$
$$1 + i = \left(\frac{\text{FV}}{\text{PV}}\right)^{\frac{1}{n}}$$
$$i = \left(\frac{\text{FV}}{\text{PV}}\right)^{\frac{1}{n}} - 1$$

Recall that i is the periodic rate of interest. If interest is calculated m times per year, then the nominal annual rate of interest $j = m(i)$.

Remember, you do not have to memorize this equation if you understand the principles of formula rearrangement.

Note: In the financial calculator that you use, you must determine whether the interest rate to be entered represents i, the periodic rate of interest, or j, the nominal rate of interest. In the TI BAII Plus calculator the [I/Y] to be used equates to j in the formula. Thus, the variables in the formula $i = j/m$ can be translated into i = [I/Y] / [C/Y] for use in the calculator. The value of I/Y obtained from the calculator is to be expressed as the nominal rate. For example, if C/Y = 4, or quarterly, and the calculator determines that I/Y = 8.5, then the rate is expressed as 8.5% p.a. compounded quarterly.

EXAMPLE 10.2B

Find the nominal annual rate of interest compounded monthly if $1200 accumulates to $1618.62 in five years.

SOLUTION

PV = 1200.00; FV = 1618.62; C/Y(m) = 12; n = 60

$1618.62 = 1200.00(1 + i)^{60}$ ——— i is a *monthly* (periodic) rate

$(1 + i)^{60} = 1.348850$

$1 + i = 1.348850^{0.016667}$ ——— raise both sides to the power $\frac{1}{60}$, that is, 0.016667

$1 + i = 1.005$

$i = 0.005$

$i = 0.5\%$

The monthly compounded periodic rate is 0.5%.

The nominal rate is 0.5% × 12 = 6% compounded monthly.

Programmed Solution

(Set P/Y, C/Y = 12) [2nd] (CLR TVM) 1200 [±] [PV]

1618.62 [FV] 60 [N] [CPT] [I/Y] 6.0

The nominal annual rate of interest is 6% per annum compounded monthly.

The periodic rate of interest would be $i = j/m$ = 6%/12 = 0.5% per month.

EXAMPLE 10.2C

At what nominal rate of interest compounded quarterly will money double in ten years?

SOLUTION

While neither PV nor FV are given, any sum of money may be used as principal. For this calculation, a convenient value for the principal is $1.00.

PV = 1; FV = 2; C/Y(m) = 4; n = 40; m = 4

$2 = 1(1 + i)^{40}$ ——— i is a *quarterly* rate

$(1 + i)^{40} = 2$

$1 + i = 2^{\frac{1}{40}}$

$1 + i = 2^{0.025}$

$1 + i = 1.017480$

$i = 0.017480$

$i = 1.7480\%$

Nominal rate = 1.7480% × 4 = 6.9919% compounded quarterly.

Programmed Solution

(Set P/Y, C/Y = 4) [2nd] (CLR TVM) 1 [±] [PV] 2 [FV] 40 [N]

[CPT] [I/Y] [6.991877]

The nominal annual rate is 6.99% per annum compounded quarterly. The quarterly rate is 6.99%/4 = 1.748%.

EXAMPLE 10.2D

Suppose $1000 earns interest of $93.81 in one year.

(i) What is the nominal annual rate of interest compounded annually?

(ii) What is the nominal annual rate of interest compounded monthly?

SOLUTION

(i) PV = 1000.00; I = 93.81; FV = PV + I = 1093.81; C/Y(m) = 1; $n = 1$

$$1093.81 = 1000.00(1 + i)^1 \quad \text{———— } i \text{ is an } \textit{annual} \text{ rate } (m = 1)$$
$$1 + i = 1.09381$$
$$i = 0.09381$$
$$i = 9.381\%$$

Programmed Solution

(Set P/Y, C/Y = 1) [2nd] (CLR TVM) 1000 [±] [PV]

1093.81 [FV] 1 [N] [CPT] [I/Y] [9.381]

The annual rate of interest is 9.381%.

Notice that both the nominal rate and the periodic rate of interest are 9.381%, since interest is compounded annually.

(ii) P/Y = 12

$$1093.81 = 1000.00\ (1 + i)^{12} \quad \text{———— } i \text{ is a } \textit{monthly} \text{ rate } (m = 12)$$
$$(1 + i)^{12} = 1.09381$$
$$1 + i = 1.09381^{\frac{1}{12}}$$
$$1 + i = 1.09381^{0.08\dot{3}}$$
$$1 + i = 1.007500$$
$$i = 0.007500$$
$$i = 0.7500\%$$

Nominal rate = 0.7500% × 12 = 9.0003% compounded monthly

Programmed Solution

(Set P/Y, C/Y = 12) [2nd] (CLR TVM) 1000 [±] [PV]

1093.81 [FV] 12 [N] [CPT] [I/Y] [9.0003]

The nominal annual rate of interest compounded monthly is 9.0003% p.a. The periodic rate of interest is 9.0003%/12 = 0.7500% per month.

EXCEL NOTES

You can use Excel's Compound Interest Rate per Period (RATE) function to find the periodic rate of interest i. Refer to RATE on MathXL to learn how to use this Excel function.

EXERCISE 10.2

Answer each of the following.

EXCEL SPREADSHEET

Find the nominal annual rate of interest for each of the following investments.

	Principal	Future Value	Time Due	Frequency of Conversion
1.	$1400.00	$1905.21	7 years	annually
2.	2350.00	3850.00	5 years	quarterly
3.	690.00	1225.00	6 years	monthly
4.	1240.00	2595.12	12 years	semi-annually
5.	3160.00	5000.00	4 years, 9 months	quarterly
6.	$ 900.00	$1200.00	3 years, 8 months	monthly

Solve each of the following.

EXCEL SPREADSHEET

1. What is the nominal annual rate of interest compounded quarterly at which $420 will accumulate to $1000 in nine years and six months?

2. A principal of $2000 compounded monthly amounts to $2800 in 7.25 years. What is the nominal annual rate of interest?

3. At what nominal annual rate of interest will money double itself in
   (a) six years, nine months if compounded quarterly?
   (b) nine years, two months if compounded monthly?

4. What is the nominal annual rate of interest at which money will triple itself in 12 years
   (a) if compounded annually?
   (b) if compounded semi-annually?

5. Yin Li deposited $800 into a savings account that compounded interest monthly. What nominal annual rate compounded monthly was earned on the investment if the balance was $952.75 in five years?

6. An investment of $4000 earned interest semi-annually. If the balance after 6½ years was $6000, what nominal annual rate compounded semi-annually was charged?

7. Surinder borrowed $1200 and agreed to pay $1400 in settlement of the debt in three years, three months. What annual nominal rate compounded quarterly was charged on the debt?

8. A debt of $600 was to be repaid in 15 months. If $705.25 was repaid, what was the nominal rate compounded monthly that was charged?

10.3 EFFECTIVE AND EQUIVALENT INTEREST RATES

A. Effective rate of interest

In Example 10.2D, compounding at an annual rate of interest of 9.381% has the same effect as compounding at 9.0% p.a. compounded monthly since, in both cases, the interest amounts to $93.81.

The annually compounded rate of 9.381% is called the **effective rate of interest.** This rate is defined as the rate of interest compounded annually that yields the same amount of interest as a nominal annual rate of interest compounded a number of times per year other than one.

Converting nominal rates of interest to effective rates is the method used for comparing nominal rates of interest. Since the effective rates of interest are the equivalent rates of interest compounded annually, they may be obtained for any set of nominal rates by computing the accumulated value of $1 after one year for each of the nominal rates under consideration.

Effective Rates Using the BAII Plus: Interest Rate Conversion

The BAII Plus is programmed in the **2nd** function to quickly and efficiently calculate effective interest rates by inputting the nominal rate and the number of compounds. You can also calculate the nominal rate if you know the effective rate.

To go from nominal to effective the process is:

1. **2nd** (ICONV) (2-key).
2. Enter the nominal rate, NOM = and press **Enter**.
3. Arrow down to C/Y = and enter the number of times interest compounds in a year. Press **Enter**.
4. Arrow up to EFF = and press **CPT**.

To go from effective to nominal the process is:

1. **2nd** (ICONV).
2. Arrow down to EFF = and enter the effective rate. Press **Enter**.
3. Arrow down to C/Y = and enter the compounding number relating to the nominal rate you are converting to. Press **Enter**.
4. Arrow down to NOM = and press **CPT**.

Equivalent Rates Using the BAII Plus

The BAII Plus can be used to calculate equivalent interest rates by using the effective rate as a constant to make equivalent calculations.

The process is:

1. 2nd (ICONV).
2. Enter any nominal rate, NOM = Press Enter.
3. Arrow down to C/Y = and enter the compounds relating to the nominal rate entered in Step 2. Press Enter.
4. Arrow up to EFF = and press CPT.
5. Arrow down and change C/Y = to the compounds you want to convert to.
6. Arrow down to NOM = and press CPT. Press Enter.
7. Repeat the process as many times as required to calculate all equivalent rates you are interested in.

EXAMPLE 10.3A

Assume you are given a choice of a term deposit paying 7.2% compounded monthly or an investment certificate paying 7.25% compounded semi-annually. Which rate offers the higher rate of return?

SOLUTION

The investment certificate offers the higher nominal rate of return while the term deposit offers the higher compounding frequency. Because of the different compounding frequencies, the two nominal rates are not directly comparable. To determine which nominal rate offers the higher rate of return, we need to determine the effective rates for the two given rates.

For the term deposit
I/Y = 7.2; P/Y = 12; $i = 0.6\% = 0.006$; $m = 12$;
the accumulated value of $1 after one year,
$FV = 1(1.006)^{12} = 1.074424$

The decimal fraction 0.074424 is the interest earned in one year and represents the effective rate of interest = 7.4424%.

For the investment certificate
I/Y = 7.25; P/Y = 2; $i = 3.625\% = 0.03625$; $m = 2$;
the accumulated value of $1 after one year,
$FV = 1(1.03625)^2 = 1.073814$

The decimal fraction 0.073814 represents the effective rate of interest = 7.3814%.

Since the term deposit has the higher effective rate, it offers the higher rate of return.

Programmed Solution

For the term deposit
$(1 + i)^{12} = (1.006)^{12} = 1.074424$
(Set P/Y, C/Y = 12) 2nd (CLR TVM) 1 ± PV 7.2 I/Y

12 N CPT FV 1.074424

Alternatively:

[2nd] (IConv) Nom = 7.2; C/Y = 12; Eff = [CPT] 7.4424

For the investment certificate

$(1 + i)^2 = (1.03625)^2 = 1.073814$

(Set P/Y, C/Y = 2) [2nd] (CLR TVM) 1 [±] [PV] 7.25 [I/Y]

2 [N] [CPT] [FV] [1.073814]

Alternatively:

[2nd] (IConv) Nom = 7.25; C/Y = 2; Eff = [CPT] 7.3814

The nominal annual rate is 7.4424% for the term deposit and 7.3814% for the investment certificate.

EXAMPLE 10.3B

Ariel has $1000 to investment and must make a choice between 3.6% compounded monthly and 3.6% compounded semi-annually. Which investment is better and by how much?

SOLUTION

Investment	3.6% Compounded Monthly	3.6% Compounded Semi-annually
I/Y	3.6	3.6
P/Y	12	2
i	0.003 = 0.3%	0.18 = 1.8%
m	12	2
FV after one year	$FV = 1000([1.003])^{12} = 1036.600$	$FV = 1000([1.018])^2 = 1036.324$
Effective rate	3.66%	3.6324%

The amount exceeding the original investment is the interest earned in one year and represents the effective rate of interest.

The investment compounded monthly earns more interest than the investment compounded semi-annually. The difference in the effective rate is 3.66% − 3.6324% = 0.0276%. With the investment of $1000, after one year the difference is $1036.60 − $1036.32 = $0.28.

Alternatively:

For 3.6% compounded monthly

[2nd] (IConv) Nom = 3.6; C/Y = 12; Eff = [CPT] 3.66

For 3.6% compounded semi-annually

[2nd] (IConv) Nom = 3.6; C/Y = 2; Eff = [CPT] 3.6324

The effective rates of interest can also be determined by using Formula 10.1 obtained from the method of calculation used in Examples 10.3A and 10.3B.

The formula is obtained as follows:

Let the nominal annual rate of interest be compounded m times per year, and let the interest rate per conversion period be i.

Then the accumulated amount after one year is $FV_1 = PV(1 + i)^m$.
Let the corresponding effective annual rate of interest be f.

Then the accumulated amount after one year is $FV_1 = PV(1 + f)^1$.

$PV(1 + f)^1 = PV(1 + i)^m$ ———— the amounts are equal by definition

$1 + f = (1 + i)^m$ ———— divide both sides by PV

$f = (1 + i)^m - 1$ ———— Formula 10.1

EXAMPLE 10.3C

Determine the effective rate of interest corresponding to 9% p.a. compounded

(i) annually;

(ii) semi-annually;

(iii) quarterly;

(iv) monthly.

SOLUTION

Calculate the effective rate f using Formula 10.1.

Steps	Annually	Semi-annually	Quarterly	Monthly
I/Y	9.0	9.0	9.0	9.0
P/Y	1	2	4	12
i	0.09 = 9.0%	0.09/2 = 4.5%	0.09/4 = 2.25%	0.09/12 = 0.75%
m	1	2	4	12
f	$f = (1 + .09)^1 - 1$	$f = (1 + .045)^2 - 1$	$f = (1 + .0225)^4 - 1$	$f = (1 + .0075)^{12} - 1$
	= 1.09 − 1	= 1.092025 − 1	= 1.093083 − 1	= 1.093807 − 1
	= 9%	= 9.2025%	= 9.3083%	= 9.3807%

Programmed Solution: ***Find Future Value***

Steps	Annually	Semi-annually	Quarterly	Monthly
P/Y C/Y	1	2	4	12
I/Y	9.0	9.0	9.0	9.0
PV	1 ±	1 ±	1 ±	1 ±
n	1	2	4	12
CPT FV	1.09	1.092025	1.093083	1.93807

Alternatively: Use Interest Conversion

Steps	Annually	Semi-annually	Quarterly	Monthly
2nd IConv				
Nom =	9.0	9.0	9.0	9.0
C/Y =	1	2	4	12
Eff = CPT	9.0	9.2025	9.3083	9.3807

POINTERS AND PITFALLS

For nominal annual interest rates and effective rates, the following two points are always true:

1. The nominal annual rate is the effective rate of interest *only* if the number of conversion periods per year is 1, that is, if compounding annually.
2. For a given nominal annual rate, the effective rate of interest increases as the number of conversion periods per year increases.

EXAMPLE 10.3D

You have money to invest in interest-earning deposits. Deposits at your bank pay 3.5% compounded semi-annually. Deposits at a local trust company pay 3.625% compounded annually, and deposits at a credit union pay 3.45% compounded monthly. What institution offers the best rate of interest for your deposit?

SOLUTION

The interest rates given are not directly comparable. To make the rates comparable, determine the effective rates of interest corresponding to the nominal annual rates.

Calculate the effective rate f using Formula 10.1.

Steps	Bank	Trust Company	Credit Union
i	3.5%/2 = 1.75%	3.625%/1 = 3.625%	3.45%/12 = 0.2875%
m	2	1	12
f	$f = (1 + .0175)^2 - 1$	$f = (1 + .03625)^1 - 1$	$f = (1 + .002875)^{12} - 1$
	= 1.035306	= 1.03625 − 1	= 1.035051 − 1
	= 3.5306%	= 3.625%	= 3.5051%

Programmed Solution: ***Use Interest Conversion***

Steps	Bank	Trust Company	Credit Union
2nd IConv			
Nom =	3.5	3.625	3.45
C/Y =	2	1	12
Eff = CPT	3.5306	3.625	3.5051

The rate offered by the trust company is best.

B. Equivalent rates

Notice that in Example 10.2D, two different nominal annual rates of interest (9.381% compounded annually and 9% compounded monthly) produced the same future value ($1093.81) for a given principal ($1000.00) after one year. Interest rates that increase a given principal to the same future value over the same period of time are called **equivalent rates**—9.381% compounded annually and 9% compounded monthly are equivalent rates.

EXAMPLE 10.3E

Find the future value after one year of a debt of $100 accumulated at

(i) 12.55% compounded annually;

(ii) 12.18% compounded semi-annually;

(iii) 12.00% compounded quarterly;

(iv) 11.88% compounded monthly.

SOLUTION

	(i)	(ii)	(iii)	(iv)
Principal (PV)	100.00	100.00	100.00	100.00
Nominal rate	12.55%	12.18%	12.00%	11.88%
i	0.1255	0.0609	0.03	0.0099
n	1	2	4	12
Future value (FV)	$100.00(1.1255)^1$ $= 100.00(1.1255)$ $= \$112.55$	$100.00(1.0609)^2$ $= 100.00(1.125509)$ $= \$112.55$	$100.00(1.03)^4$ $= 100.00(1.125509)$ $= \$112.55$	$100.00(1.0099)^{12}$ $= 100.00(1.125487)$ $= \$112.55$

Note: The four different nominal annual rates produce the same future value of $112.55 for the same principal of $100 over the same time period of one year. By definition, the four nominal rates are equivalent rates.

We can find equivalent rates by equating the accumulated values of $1 for the rates under consideration based on a selected time period, usually one year.

EXAMPLE 10.3F

Find the nominal annual rate compounded semi-annually that is equivalent to an annual rate of 6% compounded annually.

SOLUTION

Let the semi-annual rate of interest be represented by i; P/Y = 2.
For PV = 1, $n = 2$, the accumulated value $FV_1 = (1 + i)^2$.
For the given nominal rate compounded annually the accumulated value $FV_2 = (1 + 0.06)^1$.
By definition, to be equivalent, $FV_1 = FV_2$.

$$(1 + i)^2 = 1.06$$
$$1 + i = 1.06^{0.5}$$
$$1 + i = 1.029563$$
$$i = 0.029563 \quad \text{semi-annual rate}$$

Nominal rate = 2.9563% × 2 = 5.9126% compounded semi-annually.

Programmed Solution

$1\,(1 + i)^2 = 1.06$ (1 → PV, 1.06 → FV)

(Set P/Y, C/Y = 2) [2nd] (CLR TVM) 1 [±] [PV] 1.06 [FV]

2 [N] [CPT] [I/Y] [5.912603]

Alternatively:

[2nd] (IConv) Eff = 6.0; C/Y = 2; Nom = [CPT] 5.9126

The nominal annual rate compounded semi-annually is 5.9126%.

The periodic rate is 5.9126%/2 = 2.9563% per semi-annual period.

EXAMPLE 10.3G

What nominal annual rate compounded quarterly is equivalent to 8.4% p.a. compounded monthly?

SOLUTION

Let the quarterly rate be i; PV = 1; $n = 4$.
The accumulated value of \$1 after one year $FV_1 = (1 + i)^4$.

For the given rate I/Y = 8.4; P/Y = 12; $i = \frac{8.4\%}{12} = 0.7\% = 0.007$; $n = 12$.

The accumulated value of \$1 after one year $FV_2 = (1.007)^{12}$.
To be equivalent, $FV_1 = FV_2$.

$$
\begin{aligned}
(1 + i)^4 &= (1.007)^{12} \\
1 + i &= (1.007)^3 \\
1 + i &= 1.021147 \\
i &= 0.021147 \quad \text{—— quarterly rate}
\end{aligned}
$$

Programmed Solution

(Set P/Y, C/Y = 12) [2nd] (CLR TVM) 1 [±] [PV] 8.4 [I/Y]

12 [N] [CPT] [FV] [1.087311] [STO] 1

(Set P/Y, C/Y = 4) [2nd] (CLR TVM) 1 [±] [PV] [RCL] 1 [FV]

4 [N] [CPT] [I/Y] 8.458937%

Alternatively:

[2nd] (IConv) Nom = 8.4; C/Y = 12; Eff = [CPT] 8.7311

C/Y = 4; Nom = [CPT] 8.4589

The nominal annual rate compounded quarterly is 8.4589%. The periodic rate is 2.1147% per quarterly period.

EXAMPLE 10.3H

Roy's bank currently offers 2.4% compounded semi-annually on premium savings deposits. His friend has told him that he would earn more interest if his savings compounded more frequently. What is the nominal annual rate compounded monthly that would be equivalent to his semi-annual rate?

SOLUTION

Let the monthly rate be i; P/Y = 12; $n = 12$; PV = 1.
The accumulated value of \$1 after one year $FV_1 = (1 + i)^{12}$.

For the existing rate, P/Y = 2; $n = 2$; $i = 0.012$.
The accumulated value of \$1 in one year $FV_2 = (1.012)^2$.
To maintain the same yield the two rates must be equivalent.

$$(1 + i)^{12} = (1.012)^2$$
$$1 + i = (1.012)^{\frac{1}{6}}$$
$$1 + i = 1.001990$$
$$i = 0.001990 \text{ ——— monthly rate}$$

Nominal rate = 0.1990% × 12 = 2.3881% compounded monthly.

Programmed Solution

$$(1 + i)^{12} = (1.012)^2$$
$$1(1 + i)^{12} = 1.024144$$

(Set P/Y, C/Y = 2) [2nd] (CLR TVM) 1 [±] [PV] 2.4 [I/Y]

2 [N] [CPT] [FV] [1.024144] [STO] 1

(Set P/Y, C/Y = 12) [2nd] (CLR TVM) 1 [±] [PV] [RCL] 1 [FV]

12 [N] [CPT] [I/Y] [2.388087]

Alternatively:

[2nd] (IConv) Nom = 2.4; C/Y = 2; Eff = [CPT] 2.4144

C/Y = 12; Nom = [CPT] 2.388087

The nominal rate compounded monthly is 2.388087%. The periodic rate is 2.388087%/12 = 0.199007% per monthly period.

EXERCISE 10.3

EXCEL NOTES If you choose, you can use Excel's Effective Annual Interest Rate (EFFECT) or RATE functions to answer the questions indicated below. Refer to EFFECT or RATE on MathXL to learn how to use these functions.

Answer each of the following.

EXCEL SPREADSHEET

1. Find the nominal rate of interest compounded annually equivalent to each of the following.
   (a) 12.5% compounded semi-annually
   (b) 6% compounded monthly
   (c) 7.2% compounded quarterly
   (d) 10.2% compounded monthly

2. Compute the effective annual rate of interest for each of the following.
   (a) 9.5% compounded semi-annually
   (b) 10.5% compounded quarterly
   (c) 5.0% compounded monthly
   (d) 7.2% compounded monthly
   (e) 3.6% compounded quarterly
   (f) 8.2% compounded semi-annually

3. Find the nominal annual rate compounded
   (a) quarterly that is equivalent to 9% compounded semi-annually
   (b) monthly that is equivalent to 6.5% compounded quarterly
   (c) monthly that is equivalent to 7.5% compounded semi-annually
   (d) semi-annually that is equivalent to 4.25% compounded quarterly

B. Solve each of the following.

EXCEL SPREADSHEET

1. What is the effective annual rate of interest if $100 grows to $150 in six years compounded quarterly?

2. What is the effective annual rate of interest if $450 grows to $750 in three years, five months compounded monthly?

3. If $1100 accumulates to $1350 in four years, six months compounded semi-annually, what is the effective annual rate of interest?

4. An amount of $2300 earns $500 interest in three years, two months. What is the effective annual rate if interest compounds monthly?

5. Find the nominal annual rate of interest compounded quarterly that is equal to an effective rate of 9.25%.

6. What nominal annual rate of interest compounded semi-annually is equivalent to an effective rate of 6.37%?

7. If the effective rate of interest on an investment is 6.4%, what is the nominal rate of interest compounded monthly?

8. What is the nominal rate of interest compounded quarterly if the effective rate of interest on an investment is 5.3%?

9. The Central Bank pays 7.5% compounded semi-annually on certain types of deposits. If interest is compounded monthly, what nominal rate of interest will maintain the same effective rate of interest?

10. The treasurer of National Credit Union proposes changing the method of compounding interest on premium savings accounts to daily compounding. If the current rate is 6% compounded quarterly, what nominal rate should the treasurer suggest to the board of directors to maintain the same effective rate of interest?

11. Sofia made a deposit of $600 into a bank account that earns interest at 3.5% compounded monthly. The deposit earns interest at that rate for five years.
    (a) Find the balance of the account at the end of the period.
    (b) How much interest is earned?
    (c) What is the effective rate of interest?

12. Ying invested $5000 into an account earning 2.75% interest compounding daily for two years.
    (a) Find the balance of the account at the end of the period.
    (b) How much interest is earned?
    (c) What is the effective rate of interest?

13. An RRSP earns interest at 4.25% compounded quarterly. An amount of $1200 is invested into the RRSP and earns interest for ten years.
    (a) Find the balance of the account at the end of the period.
    (b) How much interest is earned?
    (c) What is the effective rate of interest?

14. Josef invested $1750 into an RRSP that earned interest at 5% compounded semi-annually for eight years.
    (a) Find the balance of the account at the end of the period.
    (b) How much interest is earned?
    (c) What is the effective rate of interest?

BUSINESS MATH NEWS BOX

High Interest Rates "Hammering" Canadians

One of the biggest consumer complaints about credit cards is persistently high interest rates.

Many factors go into setting credit card interest rates, including the provision of an interest-free grace period, the risks of providing unsecured credit, transaction processing costs, technology support, statement costs, rewards programs, fraud losses, and consumer defaults.

But why are credit card interest rates staying high at a time when other interest rates are at historic lows?

According to the Canadian Bankers Association, "Credit card rates tend to be higher than other loans because there is no collateral involved so there is a higher risk for the issuer." Unpaid credit card balances are essentially unsecured loans, whose risks rise during economic downturns. So while other borrowing rates have been decreasing in the last few years, credit card interest rates haven't experienced the same relief.

Today, debt has become a way of life, and easy access to credit cards, loans, and deferred financing has left thousands of Canadians in a perilous financial position. A recent survey conducted by the Certified General Accountants Association and the Saskatchewan Chamber of Commerce found that 87% of Saskatchewan residents have some type of debt, compared to 84% for the rest of Canada, with credit card debt by far the most common.

Many young people raised on instant gratification see credit cards as free money. The Financial Consumer Agency of Canada reports that as many Canadian youths have a credit card (72%) as have a savings account (74%), and that credit cards are increasingly being used to pay for day-to-day items, rather than for larger one-off purchases. Moreover, many young people don't understand the amount of interest they are paying, or the potential credit trouble for parents who cosign a credit card for their children.

How to avoid the trap? Make sure you read the fine print. Pay the balance in full each month so that the interest rate is completely immaterial. Better yet, stick to cash.

A Comparison—Current Credit Card Rates

Institution	Annual Interest Rate
TD Canada Trust (TD Green card)	19.99%
Bank of Nova Scotia (No-fee Money Back card)	19.50%
Canadian Imperial Bank of Commerce (CIBC Classic card)	19.50%
President's Choice (PC MasterCard)	19.97%
Sears Club Card	29.90%

Sources: "Mortgaging Our Future: A Generation in Debt," *Regina Leader Post*, May 6, 2010; "High Interest Rates 'Hammering' Canadians, MP Says," *Toronto Star*, December 12, 2009; Credit card rates retrieved from **www.money.canoe.ca/rates/credit.html** August 25, 2010; the Financial Consumer Agency of Canada, *Youth Financial Literacy Study*, **www.fcac-acfc.gc.ca/eng/publications/SurveyStudy/YouthFinLit2008/YouthFinLit2008_04-eng.asp**.

QUESTIONS

1. Paul recently purchased a new loveseat and flat-screen TV for his first apartment on his Sears department store credit card. Its annual interest rate is 29.90% compounded monthly.
   a. Calculate how many payments it will take him to pay off a $1000 balance if he makes a regular monthly payment of $200. How much interest will he pay during this time?
   b. How much interest would he have saved during the same time period if he had used his CIBC credit card (which carries an annual interest rate of 19.5% compounded monthly) instead?
2. Many young people don't understand the amount of interest they are actually paying on their credit cards. What is the effective rate of interest corresponding to a credit card that is advertised at 2% per month?

Go to MathXL at www.mathXL.com. You can practise many of this chapter's exercises as often as you want. The guided solutions help you find an answer step by step. You'll find a personalized study plan available to you too!

Review Exercise

1. At what nominal rate of interest compounded monthly will $400 earn $100 interest in four years?

2. At what nominal rate of interest compounded quarterly will $300 earn $80 interest in six years?

3. Find the equated date at which payments of $500 due six months ago and $600 due today could be settled by a payment of $1300 if interest is 9% compounded monthly.

4. Find the equated date at which two payments of $600 due four months ago and $400 due today could be settled by a payment of $1100 if interest is 7.25% compounded semi-annually.

5. In what period of time will money triple at 10% compounded semi-annually?

6. In how many years will money double at 8% compounded monthly?

7. What nominal rate of interest compounded monthly is equivalent to an effective rate of 6.2%?

8. What nominal rate of interest compounded quarterly is equivalent to an effective rate of 5.99%?

9. Find the nominal annual rate of interest

(a) at which $2500 will grow to $4000 in eight years compounded quarterly;

(b) at which money will double in five years compounded semi-annually;

(c) if the effective annual rate of interest is 9.2% and compounding is done monthly;

(d) that is equivalent to 8% compounded quarterly.

10. Find the nominal annual rate of interest

(a) at which $1500 will grow to $1800 in four years compounded monthly;

(b) at which money will double in seven years compounded quarterly;

(c) if the effective annual rate of interest is 7.75% and compounding is done monthly;

(d) that is equivalent to 6% compounded quarterly.

11. Compute the effective annual rate of interest

(a) for 4.5% compounded monthly;

(b) at which $2000 will grow to $3000 in seven years compounded quarterly.

12. Compute the effective annual rate of interest

(a) for 6% compounded monthly;

(b) at which $1100 will grow to $2000 in seven years compounded monthly.

13. What is the nominal annual rate of interest compounded monthly that is equivalent to 8.5% compounded quarterly?

14. What is the nominal annual rate of interest compounded quarterly that is equivalent to an effective annual rate of 5%?

15. Patrick had $2000 to invest. Which of the following options should he choose?

(a) 4% compounded annually

(b) 3.75% compounded semi-annually

(c) 3.5% compounded quarterly

(d) 3.25% compounded monthly

16. (a) How many years will it take for $7500 to accumulate to $9517.39 at 3% compounded semi-annually?

(b) Over what period of time will money triple at 9% compounded quarterly?

(c) How many years will it take for a loan of $10 000 to amount to $13 684 at 10.5% compounded monthly?

17. Matt had agreed to make two payments—a payment of $2000 due in nine months and a payment of $1500 in a year. If Matt makes a payment of $1800 now, when should he make a second payment of $1700 if money is worth 8% compounded quarterly?

18. A $4000 debt due in four years was paid with $3885.35 cash. If money is worth 7% compounded monthly, how many months before the due date was the debt paid?

19. A financial obligation requires the payment of $2000 now, $2500 in six months, and $4000 in one year. When will a single payment of $9000 discharge the obligation if interest is 6% compounded monthly?

20. Girard owes two debt payments—a payment of $5000 due in six months and a payment of $6000 due in fifteen months. If Girard makes a payment of $5000 now, when should he make a second payment of $6000 if money is worth 11% compounded semi-annually?

21. A debt of $12 000 was replaced with two payments. If $7500 was paid in two years, when should a second payment of $7500 be made if interest compounds at 8% quarterly?

22. Sasha promised to pay $3000 in 2½ years and $5000 in five years. If she replaces those payments with a payment of $4000 in four years and three months, and money is worth 10% compounded quarterly, when should she make the second payment of $6000?

Self-Test

EXCEL SPREADSHEET

1. An investment with an original value of $11 000 is sold for proceeds of $12 950.00. If the investment yield was 5% compounded semi-annually, for how many years was the money invested?

2. An amount of $1400 was invested for 71 months, maturing to $2177.36. What annually compounded rate was earned?

3. Determine the effective annual rate of interest equivalent to 5.4% compounded monthly.

4. How many months from now can a payment of $1000 due twelve months ago and a payment of $400 due six months from now be settled by a payment of $1746.56 if interest is 10.2% compounded monthly?

5. At what nominal rate of interest compounded semi-annually will $6900 earn $3000 interest in five years?

6. In how many years will money double at 7.2% compounded quarterly?

7. What is the nominal rate of interest compounded semi-annually that is equivalent to an effective rate of 10.25%?

8. A financial obligation requires the payment of $1000 in two months, $3000 in eight months, and $4000 in fourteen months. Instead, if a payment of $2000 is made now, when should a second payment of $6000 be made if interest is 9% compounded monthly?

9. Sean needs to decide how to invest his savings. He can choose between 3.95% compounded semi-annually, 3.92% compounded quarterly, or 3.90% compounded monthly. Which choice will maximize his return?

Challenge Problems

1. Olga deposited $800 in an investment certificate paying 9% compounded semi-annually. On the same day, her sister Ursula deposited $600 in an account paying 7% compounded semi-annually. To the nearest day, when will the future value of Olga's investment be equal to twice the future value of Ursula's investment?
2. A financial institution is advertising a new three-year investment certificate. The interest rate is 7.5% compounded quarterly the first year, 6.5% compounded monthly the second year, and 6% compounded daily the third year. What nominal rate of interest compounded semi-annually for three years would a competing institution have to offer to match the interest produced by this investment certificate?

CASE STUDY 10.1 Choosing a Credit Card

» Jane Zhao is deciding which credit card to apply for. She has just received advertising from several large credit card companies, some of which feature low introductory rates. She has estimated that, based on her good credit rating, she could successfully apply for any of the credit cards being offered.

Credit card A has a $33 annual fee and advertises the relatively low interest rate of 9.5%. A $5 fee is charged for each cash advance, plus the applicable interest charges.

Credit card B has no annual fee and advertises a 17.5% interest rate on purchases and cash advances.

Credit card C advertises an introductory promotional interest rate of 3.9% on cash advances and balance transfers for the first six months, if you make your minimum monthly payments on time. The regular annual interest rate is 18.50% on purchases and cash advances.

For all three credit cards, interest will not be assessed if the monthly statement amount is paid in full by the payment due date and no cash advances have been taken during the billing period. If the new balance is not paid in full, interest will be charged (1) on the outstanding balance from the statement closing date and (2) on future purchases from the day the purchases are posted to the account. On cash advance transactions, interest is always charged from the date the cash advance is taken.

Currently, Jane has a credit card with a major Canadian department store. For this card, D, there is an outstanding balance of $1000. Its annual interest rate is 27.5%. If she receives one of the other three cards, she would transfer the department store credit card balance to the new card.

QUESTIONS

1. Jane maintains an average daily balance of $1500 for the first year, based solely on purchases and balance transfers. For each of the four credit cards,
   (a) calculate the interest charge and fees that she would have to pay over a twelve-month period;

(b) determine the effective annual rate of interest over the first twelve-month period;
(c) decide which credit card she should choose.

2. If the introductory interest rate fell to 2.5% for credit card C, and the regular annual interest rate rose to 19.5% on purchases, what would be the effective annual rate of interest over the twelve-month period?

3. If you have a credit card, how do its rates and conditions compare with those of the cards described above?

CASE STUDY 10.2 Comparing Car Loans

» After reading consumer car guides and receiving advice from family and friends, Aysha has chosen the new car she wants to purchase. She now wants to research her financing options to choose the best way to pay for the car.

Aysha knows that with taxes, licence, delivery, and dealer preparation fees, her car will cost $17 650. She has saved $7500 toward the purchase price but must borrow the rest. She has narrowed her financing choices to three options: dealer financing, credit union financing, and bank financing.

(i) The car dealer has offered 48-month financing at 8.5% compounded monthly.
(ii) The credit union has offered 36-month financing at 9% compounded quarterly. It has also offered 48-month financing at 9.3% compounded quarterly.
(iii) The bank has offered 36-month financing at 8.8% compounded semi-annually. It has also offered 48-month financing at 9.1% compounded semi-annually.

Aysha desires the financing option that offers the best interest rate. However, she also wants to explore the financing options that allow her to pay off her car loan more quickly.

QUESTIONS

1. Aysha wants to compare the 48-month car loan options offered by the car dealer, the credit union, and the bank.
   (a) What is the effective annual rate of interest for each 48-month option?
   (b) How much interest will Aysha save by choosing the best option as against the worst option?

2. Suppose Aysha wants to try to pay off her car loan within three years.
   (a) What is the effective annual rate of interest for both of the 36-month options?
   (b) How much interest will Aysha save by choosing the better option?

3. If you wanted to get a car loan today, what are the rates of interest for 36-month and 48-month terms? Are car dealers currently offering better interest rates than the banks or credit unions? If so, why?

SUMMARY OF FORMULAS

Formula 9.1A

$FV = PV(1 + i)^n$ — **Finding the future value of a sum of money when *n* is a fractional value using the exact method**

Formula 9.1B

$PV = \frac{FV}{(1 + i)^n}$ — **Finding the present value (discounted value or proceeds) when *n* is a fractional value using the exact method**

Formula 9.1C

$PV = FV(1 + i)^{-n}$

Formula 10.1

$f = (1 + i)^m - 1$ — **Finding the effective rate of interest, *f*, for a nominal annual rate compounded *m* times per year**

GLOSSARY

Effective rate of interest the annual rate of interest that yields the same amount of interest per year as a nominal rate compounded a number of times per year *(p. 403)*

Equated date the date on which a single sum of money is equal to the sum of two or more dated sums of money *(p. 393)*

Equivalent rates interest rates that accumulate a given principal to the same future value over the same period of time *(p. 407)*

USEFUL INTERNET SITES

www.money.canoe.ca

Credit Card Rates Compare credit card rates and terms for major Canadian financial institutions and department stores.

www.ratedexpro.com

American Bankers Association The site analyzes interest rate performance and financial stability of numerous financial institutions and markets.

www.ruleof72.net

The Rule of 72 Albert Einstein, calling it the eighth wonder of the world, was credited with discovering the compound interest rule of 72. Learn about compound interest and financial success with this mathematical discovery.

CHAPTER 11

Ordinary Simple Annuities

OBJECTIVES

Upon completing this chapter, you will be able to do the following:

1. Distinguish between types of annuities based on term, payment date, and conversion period.
2. Compute the future value (or accumulated value) for ordinary simple annuities.
3. Compute the present value (or discounted value) for ordinary simple annuities.
4. Compute the payment for ordinary simple annuities.
5. Compute the number of periods for ordinary simple annuities.
6. Compute the interest rate for ordinary simple annuities.

"After five years of depositing $100 each month, how much money will be in a savings account?" "How long will it take to repay a loan if regular payments are made?" These questions represent common business situations involving compound interest calculations. Often businesses need to calculate the present value or the future value, the payment amount, the interest rate, or the term when making payments for rent, insurance, loans, or pensions. With regular equal payments, these are all examples of annuities. Annuity formulas and calculations enable us to answer these questions.

INTRODUCTION

An annuity is a series of payments, usually of equal size, made at periodic time intervals. The term *annuity* applies to all periodic payment plans, the most frequent of which require annual, semi-annual, quarterly, or monthly payments. Practical applications of annuities are widely encountered in the finances of both businesses and individuals. Various types of annuities are identified based on the term of an annuity, the date of payment, and the length of the conversion period. In this chapter, we will deal with ordinary simple annuities, and calculate the future value, present value, payment amount, number of periods, and the interest rate.

11.1 INTRODUCTION TO ANNUITIES

A. Basic concepts

An **annuity** is a series of payments, usually of equal size, made at periodic intervals. The length of time between the successive payments is called the **payment interval** or **payment period**. The length of time from the beginning of the first payment interval to the end of the last payment interval is called the **term of an annuity**. The size of each of the regular payments is the **periodic rent**.

When performing annuity calculations, the timing of payments must be considered. Depending on the frequency and regularity of payments, different formulas will be used in annuity calculations. When a payment is made only once, it is treated as either the present value, PV, or the future value, FV, of a calculation. When there are a series of payments, it must be determined if the payments are equal amounts and are paid at the same time within each payment interval of the term. If the payment is equal and periodic, it is treated as the periodic payment, PMT, of an annuity calculation. The types of annuities are described in Section B below.

B. Types of annuities

1. *Simple and general annuities*
   Annuities are classified by the length of the conversion period relative to the payment period (Section 9.1). With a **simple annuity,** the conversion period is the same length as the payment interval. An example is when there are monthly payments on a loan for which the interest is compounded monthly. Since the interest compounding period (C/Y: compounding periods per year) is equal to the payment period (P/Y: payment periods per year), this is a simple annuity.

   With a **general annuity,** the conversion period and the payment interval are not equal. For a residential mortgage, interest is compounded semi-annually but payments may be made monthly, semi-monthly, bi-weekly, or weekly. The conversion period, C/Y, does not equal the payment period, P/Y.

2. *Ordinary annuities and annuities due*
   Annuities are classified by the date of payment. In an **ordinary annuity**, payments are made at the end of each payment period. In an **annuity due**,

payments are made at the beginning of each payment period. Loan payments, mortgage payments, and interest payments on bonds are all examples of ordinary annuities. Examples of annuities due include lease rental payments on real estate or equipment.

3. *Deferred annuities*
   A **deferred annuity** occurs when the first payment is delayed for a period of time. For example, a severance amount may be deposited into a fund that earns interest, and then later converted into another fund that pays out a series of payments until the fund is exhausted.

4. *Perpetuities*
   A **perpetuity** is an annuity for which the payments continue forever. When the size of the periodic payment from a fund is equal to or less than the periodic interest earned by the fund, such as an endowment fund to a university or a continuous benefit from a capital investment, a perpetuity is the result.

5. *Annuities certain and contingent annuities*
   If both the beginning date and ending date of an annuity are known, indicating a fixed term, the classification is an **annuity certain**. Typical examples of annuities certain include lease payments on equipment, instalment payments on loans, and interest payments on bonds.
   If the beginning date, the ending date, or both, are unknown, the classification is a **contingent annuity**. Life insurance premiums or pension payments are typical examples of contingent annuities. The ending date is unknown for these annuities since they terminate with the death of the recipient.

Ordinary simple annuities will be discussed in the current chapter. Ordinary general annuities will be discussed in Chapter 12. Other annuities, such as annuities due, deferred annuities, and perpetuities, will be discussed in Chapter 13.

The classification of annuities and the choice of formulas can be clarified if the following questions are asked. For each question, refer to the chapters that are identified for further references to those concepts.

Annuity Questions

Question	If the answer is YES:	If the answer is NO:
Is there a series of equal periodic payments?	This is an annuity Ch 11–13	This is not an annuity. The amount is either the PV or FV. Ch 9–10
Is the conversion period C/Y equal to the payment interval P/Y?	Simple annuity Ch 11	General annuity Ch 12
Is the payment made at the end of the payment period?	Ordinary annuity Ch 11–12	Annuity due Ch 13
Does the payment start in the first payment period?	Not deferred Ch 11–12	Deferred annuity Ch 13
Are the beginning and ending dates known?	Annuity certain Ch 11–13	Perpetuity if term is continuous; contingent annuity if dates are not known Ch 13

EXAMPLE 11.1A Classify each of the following annuities by

(i) term;

(ii) date of payment;

(iii) conversion period.

(a) Deposits of $150 earning interest at 4% compounded quarterly are made at the beginning of each quarter for four years.

(b) Payments of $200 are made at the end of each month for five years. Interest is 7% compounded semi-annually.

(c) A fund of $10 000 is deposited in a trust account earning interest compounded annually. Starting five years from the date of deposit, the interest earned for the year is to be paid out as a scholarship.

(d) In his will, Dr. Chu directed that part of his estate be invested in a trust fund earning interest compounded quarterly. His surviving wife was to be paid, for the remainder of her life, $2000 at the end of every three months starting three months after his death.

SOLUTION Question (a)

(i) annuity certain (the term is fixed: four years)

(ii) annuity due (payments are made at the beginning of each quarter)

(iii) simple annuity (the quarterly conversion period equals the quarterly payment period)

SOLUTION Question (b)

(i) annuity certain (the term is fixed: five years)

(ii) ordinary annuity (payments are made at the end of each month)

(iii) general annuity (semi-annual conversion period does not match the monthly payment period)

SOLUTION Question (c)

(i) perpetuity (the payments can go on forever)

(ii) deferred annuity (the first payment is deferred for five years)

(iii) simple annuity (the annual conversion period equals the annual interest period)

SOLUTION Question (d)

(i) contingent annuity (both the starting date and the ending date are uncertain)

(ii) ordinary annuity (payments at the end of every three months)

(iii) simple annuity (the quarterly conversion period equals the quarterly payment period)

EXERCISE 11.1

Classify each of the following by (a) term; (b) date of payment; (c) conversion period.

1. Payments of $50 are made at the beginning of each month for five years at 5% compounded semi-annually.
2. Deposits of $500 are made at the end of each quarter for nine years earning interest at 7% compounded quarterly.
3. A fund with an initial deposit of $50 000 is set up to provide annual scholarships to eligible business students in an amount not exceeding the annual interest earned by the fund. Scholarship payments are to begin three years from the date of deposit. Interest earned by the fund is compounded semi-annually.
4. The Saskatoon Board of Education introduced a long-term disability plan for its employees. The plan provides for monthly payments equal to 90% of regular salary starting one month after the beginning of the disability. Assume that the plan is subject to monthly compounding.
5. Gary invested $10 000 in an account paying interest compounded monthly with the provision that equal monthly payments be made to him from the account for fifteen years at the beginning of each month starting ten years from the date of deposit.
6. Ms. Baka set up a trust fund earning interest compounded semi-annually to provide equal monthly support payments for her surviving husband starting one month after her death.

11.2 ORDINARY SIMPLE ANNUITY—FINDING FUTURE VALUE FV

A. Future value of a series of payments—basic computation

EXAMPLE 11.2A Deposits of $2000, $4000, $5000, $1000, and $3000 were made at the end of each of five consecutive years respectively at 6% compounded annually. Find the future value just after the last deposit was made.

SOLUTION The series of deposits can be represented on a time graph as shown:

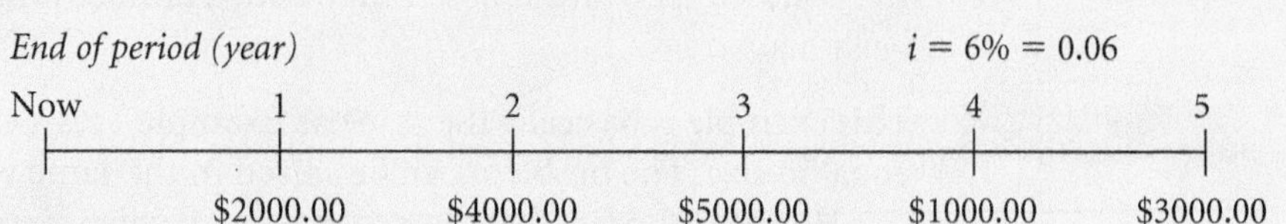

To find the future value of a series of unequal deposits, we first need to determine the future value of each of the deposits, including interest, at the focal point five years from now. We choose the focal point as five years from now because we need to calculate the equated value of all deposits at that time. The combined future value is the sum of the individual equivalent future values at the focal date. These calculations can be done using Formula 9.1A, $FV = PV(1 + i)^n$. A graphical representation of the method and data is shown in Figure 11.1 below.

By the focal date, the deposit of $1000 has earned interest for a period of one year ($n = 1$). Interest has been earned by the $5000 deposit for two years ($n = 2$), by the $4000 deposit for three years ($n = 3$), and by the $2000 for four years ($n = 4$). The $3000 deposit has just been made and has a value of $3000 at the focal date. The future values are calculated, and then added.

FIGURE 11.1 Graphical Representation of Method and Data

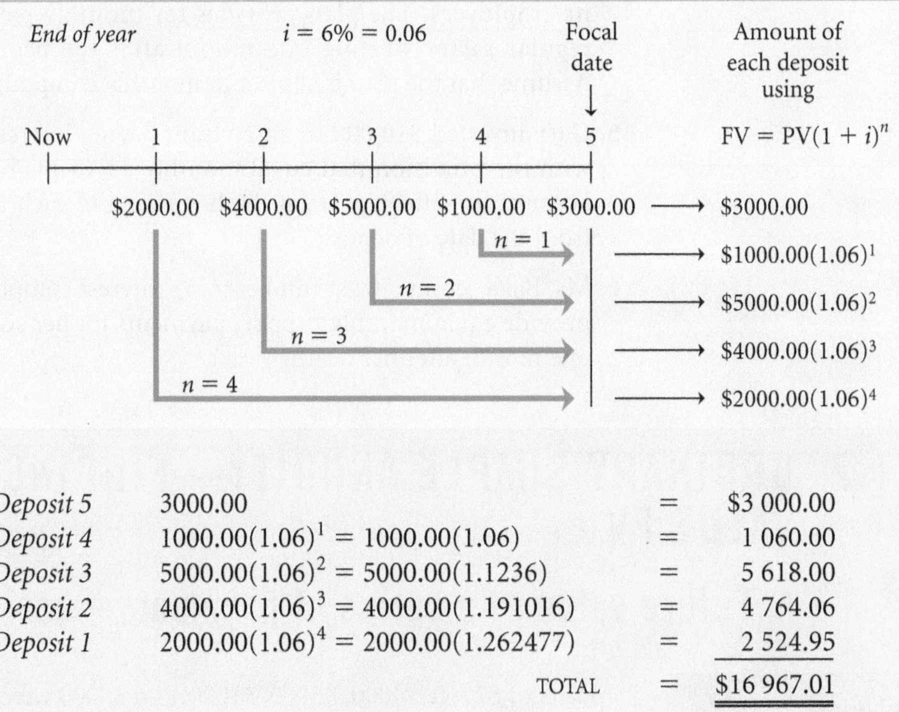

Deposit 5	3000.00	=	$3 000.00
Deposit 4	$1000.00(1.06)^1 = 1000.00(1.06)$	=	1 060.00
Deposit 3	$5000.00(1.06)^2 = 5000.00(1.1236)$	=	5 618.00
Deposit 2	$4000.00(1.06)^3 = 4000.00(1.191016)$	=	4 764.06
Deposit 1	$2000.00(1.06)^4 = 2000.00(1.262477)$	=	2 524.95
	TOTAL	=	$16 967.01

EXAMPLE 11.2B

Find the future value of five equal deposits of $3000 made at the end of each of five consecutive years at 6% compounded annually, just after the last deposit has been made.

SOLUTION

This example is basically the same as Example 11.2A except that all deposits are equal in size. The problem can be solved in the same way.

However, the fact that the deposits are *equal in size* permits a useful mathematical simplification (see Figure 11.2). The equal deposit of $3000 can be taken out as a common factor and the individual compounding factors can be combined.

FIGURE 11.2 Graphical Representation of Method and Data

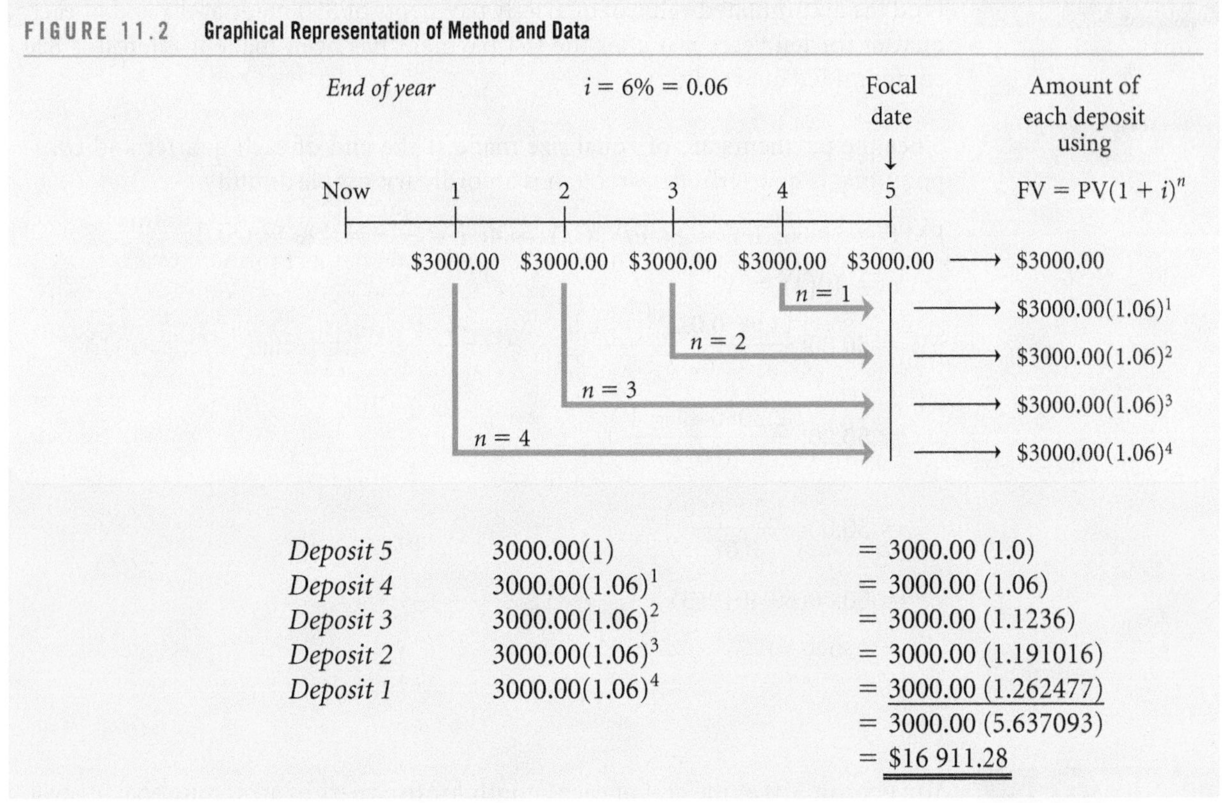

B. Formula for finding the future value of an ordinary simple annuity

In Example 11.2B, the payments are of equal size and are made periodically (at the end of each year) within the term of five years. By identifying payments as equal and periodic, the future value of an annuity can be found.

The following formula has been developed for finding the accumulated value of ordinary simple annuities.

$$FV_n = PMT\left[\frac{(1+i)^n - 1}{i}\right] \qquad \text{——— Formula 11.1}$$

where FV_n = the future value (accumulated value) of an ordinary simple annuity;
PMT = the size of the periodic payment (rent);
i = the interest rate per conversion period;
n = the number of periodic payments (which for simple annuities is also the number of conversion periods).

The factor $\frac{(1+i)^n - 1}{i}$ is called the **compounding** or **accumulation factor for annuities** or the **accumulated value of one dollar per period.**

EXAMPLE 11.2C Find the accumulated value of quarterly payments of $50 made at the end of each quarter for ten years just after the last payment has been made if interest is 8% compounded quarterly.

SOLUTION Since the payments are of equal size made at the end of each quarter and compounding is quarterly, the problem is an ordinary simple annuity.

PMT = 50.00; I/Y = 8; P/Y, C/Y = 4; $i = \frac{8\%}{4} = 2\% = 0.02$;
$n = 10(4) = 40$

$$FV = 50.00\left[\frac{(1 + 0.02)^{40} - 1}{0.02}\right]$$ ——— substituting in Formula 11.1

$$= 50.00\left(\frac{2.208040 - 1}{0.02}\right)$$

$$= 50.00\left(\frac{1.208040}{0.02}\right)$$

$$= 50.00(60.401983)$$

$$= \$3020.10$$

EXAMPLE 11.2D You deposit $10 at the end of each month for five years in an account paying 6% compounded monthly.

(i) What will be the balance in your account at the end of the five-year term?

(ii) How much of the balance will you have contributed?

(iii) How much is interest?

SOLUTION (i) PMT = 10.00; I/Y = 6; P/Y = 12; $i = \frac{6\%}{12} = 0.5\% = 0.005$; $n = 12(5) = 60$

$$FV = 10.00\left[\frac{(1 + i)^n - 1}{i}\right]$$

$$= 10.00\left[\frac{1.005^{60} - 1}{0.005}\right]$$

$$= 10.00\left[\frac{(1.348850 - 1)}{0.005}\right]$$

$$= 10.00(69.770031)$$

$$= \$697.70$$

(ii) Your contribution is $10 per month for 60 months, or 10.00(60) = $600.

(iii) Since your contribution is $600, the interest earned is 697.70 – 600.00 = $97.70.

C. Using preprogrammed financial calculators

Preprogrammed financial calculators can be used to perform compound interest calculations involving annuities. As outlined in Section 9.2, function keys correspond to the variables used in annuity calculations. The use of three models of calculators is outlined in Appendix II, "Instructions and Tips for Three Preprogrammed Financial Calculator Models." Relevant highlights are shown in Table 11.1. Instructions in this text are given for the Texas Instruments BAII Plus calculator.

Table 11.1 **Financial Calculator Function Keys That Correspond to Variables Used in Ordinary Simple Annuity Calculations**

		Function Key		
Variable	**Algebraic Symbol**	**TI BAII+**	**Sharp EL-733A**	**HP 10B**
The periodic rate of interest*	i	I/Y and C/Y	I	I/YR and P/YR
The number of payment intervals per year	None	P/Y	None	P/YR
The number of payment periods in the term	n	N	N	N
The periodic annuity payment	PMT	PMT	PMT	PMT
The present value or principal	PV	PV	PV	PV
The future value or maturity value	FV	FV	FV	FV

*Note: The periodic rate of interest is entered into the calculator as a percent and not as a decimal equivalent. For example, for I/Y, 8% is entered as "8" not ".08".

To perform calculations for an ordinary simple annuity:

STEP 1 Clear all previous data: Reset all entries to the default values for each field: [2nd] [CLR TVM]

STEP 2 Determine the number of payments per year and enter as the [P/Y]: If the number of payments per year is specified as "monthly," follow the sequence [2nd] [P/Y] 12 [ENTER] [2nd] [QUIT]. Substitute the number for the appropriate number of payments per year in each case. The most common frequencies are monthly, quarterly, semi-annually, and annually.

STEP 3 Enter the other given values in any order. Remember that the value is entered first, then the appropriate button is pressed without the use of the [ENTER] button.

STEP 4 Compute the unknown number: press [CPT] followed by the key representing the unknown variable.

Note: This assumes that the calculator is in the END mode, indicating payment is made at the end of the payment interval. This is the default. To check, look at the upper right corner of the display screen. If no letters are shown in that corner above the numbers, the calculator is in the END mode. If the letters BGN are showing, you must switch modes:

[2nd] [BGN] ([PMT] Key)

[2nd] [SET] (END will now appear.)

[2nd] [QUIT] (Back to standard calculator—upper-right corner is now blank.)

When performing an annuity calculation, usually only one of either the present value PV *or* the future value FV is involved. To avoid incorrect answers, the present value **PV** should be set to zero when determining the future value **FV** and vice versa. In addition, recall that the Texas Instruments BAII Plus calculator follows the established convention of treating cash inflows (cash received) as positive numbers and cash outflows (cash paid out) as negative numbers. Since periodic annuity payments are considered to be cash outflows, always enter the periodic payment as a negative number. Also, continue to always enter the present value as a negative number (if the present value is other than 0) to ensure your result has a positive value.

To solve Example 11.2D, in which PMT = 10.00, I/Y = 6, P/Y = 12, and n = 60, use the following procedure.

	Key in	*Press*	*Display shows*	
(Set P/Y, C/Y = 12)	0	PV	0	a precaution to avoid incorrect answers
	10	± PMT	−10	this enters the periodic payment, PMT
	6.0	I/Y	6.0	this enters the interest rate per year
	60	N	60	this enters the number of payments, n
	CPT	FV	697.700305	this retrieves the wanted amount, FV

The future value is $697.70.

D. Applications

EXAMPLE 11.2E

Jim set up a savings plan with TD Canada Trust whereby he deposits $300 at the end of each quarter for eight years. The amount in his account at that time will become a term deposit withdrawable after a further five years. Interest throughout the total time period is 5% compounded quarterly.

(i) How much will be in Jim's account just after he makes his last deposit?

(ii) What will be the balance of his account when he can withdraw the deposit?

(iii) How much of the total at the time of withdrawal did Jim contribute?

(iv) How much is the interest earned?

SOLUTION

As Figure 11.3 shows, problems of this type may be solved in stages. The first stage involves finding the future value of an *ordinary annuity*. This amount becomes the principal or present value for the second stage, which involves finding the future value of a *single* sum of money invested for five years.

STEP 1 Find the accumulated value, FV_1, of the annuity at the end of the 8-year annuity period.

(i) PMT = 300.00; I/Y = 5; P/Y, C/Y = 4; $i = \frac{5\%}{4} = 1.25\% = 0.0125$;
$n = 8(4) = 32$

$$FV_1 = 300.00\left[\frac{(1.0125^{32} - 1)}{0.0125}\right]$$ ——— Formula 11.1

$$= 300.00\left[\frac{(1.488131 - 1)}{0.0125}\right]$$
$$= 300.00(39.050441)$$
$$= \$11\,715.13$$

STEP 2 Enter the result of Step 1, FV_1, as the present value (deposit), PV_2, for the 5-year term, and compute the accumulated value, FV_2, at the end of the 5-year term. Note that there is no payment amount in this second step.

(ii) $PV_2 = FV_1 = 11\,715.13;\ PMT = 0;\ i = 0.0125;\ n = 5(4) = 20$

$$FV_2 = 11\,715.13(1.0125)^{20} \quad \text{——— Formula 9.1A}$$
$$= 11\,715.13(1.282037)$$
$$= \$15\,019.23$$

FIGURE 11.3 Graphical Representation of Method and Data

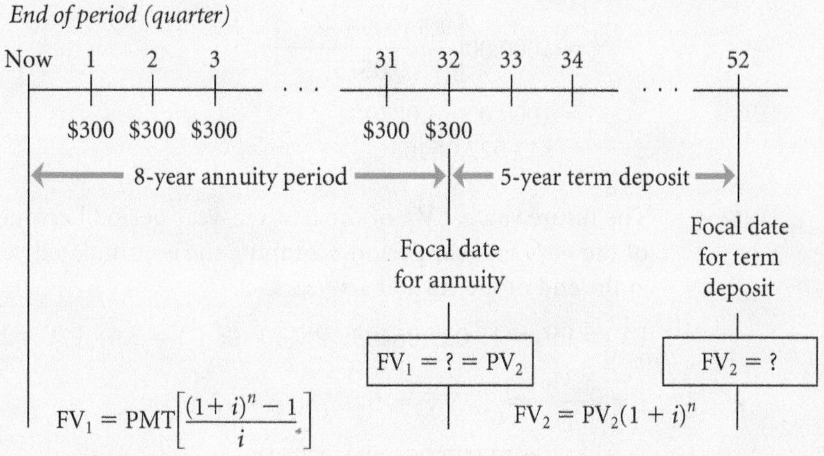

STEP 3 Calculate the total contribution as the payment, PMT, amount made during the 8-year annuity period multiplied by the number of times, n, a contribution was made during that period.

(iii) Jim's contribution = 32(300.00) = \$9600.00.

STEP 4 Calculate the amount of interest earned by subtracting the total contribution from Step 3 from the final future value in Step 2.

(iv) The amount of interest earned = 15 019.23 – 9600.00 = \$5419.23.

Programmed Solution for Parts (i) and (ii)

(i) (Set P/Y, C/Y = 4) 0 [PV] 300 [±] [PMT]

5 [I/Y] 32 [N] [CPT] [FV] [11715.132206]

(ii) 11 715.13 [±] [PV] 0 [PMT]

5 [I/Y] 20 [N] [CPT] [FV] [15019.235663]

EXAMPLE 11.2F

The Gordons saved for the purchase of their dream home by making deposits of \$1000 at the end of each year for ten consecutive years in an account with Cooperative Trust in Saskatoon. The account earned interest at 5.75% compounded annually. At the end of the ten-year contribution period, the deposit was left for a further six years earning interest at 5.5% compounded semi-annually.

(i) What down payment were the Gordons able to make on their house?

(ii) How much of the down payment was interest?

SOLUTION

STEP 1

(i) Find the accumulated value, FV_1, of the contributions of the ordinary annuity at the end of the 10 years of yearly deposits.

$$PMT = 1000.00;\ I/Y = 5.75;\ P/Y = 1;\ i = 5.75\% = 0.0575;\ n = 10$$

$$\begin{aligned} FV_1 &= 1000.00\left[\frac{(1.0575^{10} - 1)}{0.0575}\right] \\ &= 1000.00\left[\frac{1.749056 - 1}{0.0575}\right] \\ &= 1000.00(13.027064) \\ &= \$13\,027.06408 \end{aligned}$$

STEP 2

The future value, FV_1, of the first ten-year period becomes the present value, PV_2, of the next six-year period. Compute the accumulated value of the savings, FV_2, at the end of the further six years.

$$PV_2 = FV_1 = 13\,027.06408;\ PMT = 0;\ I/Y = 5.5;\ P/Y = 2;$$

$$i = \frac{5.5\%}{2} = 2.75\% = 0.0275;\ n = 12$$

$$\begin{aligned} FV_2 &= 13\,027.06408(1.0275)^{12} \\ &= 13\,027.06408(1.384784) \\ &= \$18\,039.67 \end{aligned}$$

The Gordons made a down payment of \$18 039.67.

(ii) Calculate the amount of interest earned by subtracting the total contribution from the accumulated value at the end of the six years. Since the Gordons contributed (1000.00)(10) = \$10 000.00, the amount of interest in the down payment is \$8039.67.

Programmed Solution for Part (i)

(Set P/Y, C/Y = 1) 0 [PV] 1000 [±] [PMT]

5.75 [I/Y] 10 [N] [CPT] [FV] 13027.06408

(Set P/Y, C/Y = 2) 13 027.06408 [±] [PV]

0 [PMT] 5.5 [I/Y] 12 [N] [CPT] [FV] 18039.66698

EXAMPLE 11.2G

Heather contributed \$1500 at the end of each year for twelve years into a savings account. Interest earned on the savings account was 4.5% compounded annually for the first eight years, then increased to 5.5% compounded annually. How much was the balance in the account five years after her last contribution?

SOLUTION

As Figure 11.4 shows, the problem may be divided into three terms. The first term covers the annuity for the first eight years; the second term covers the annuity for the next four years. These are separated into different calculations because of the differing interest rates. The final term covers the five years where no further payments are made, but interest continues to increase the balance.

STEP 1

The focal date for the first annuity is at the end of Year 8 (focal date 1). The accumulated value (future value) of this simple annuity is computed by using Formula 11.1.

$$
\begin{aligned}
FV_1 &= 1500.00\left[\frac{(1.045^8 - 1)}{0.045}\right] \\
&= 1500.00\left[\frac{(1.422101 - 1)}{0.045}\right] \\
&= 1500.00(9.380014) \\
&= \$14\,070.02043
\end{aligned}
$$

STEP 2

FV_1 then accumulates for four years at 5.5% compounded annually. Focal date 2 is at the end of Year 12.

$$
\begin{aligned}
FV_2 &= 14\,070.02043[(1.055)^4] \\
&= 14\,070.02043(1.238825) \\
&= 17\,430.288141
\end{aligned}
$$

STEP 3

The focal date for the second annuity is at the end of Year 12 (focal date 3). This part of the annuity earns interest at 5.5% compounded annually. The accumulated value (future value) of this four-year annuity is computed.

$$
\begin{aligned}
FV_3 &= 1500.00\left[\frac{(1.055^4 - 1)}{0.055}\right] \\
&= 1500.00\left[\frac{(1.238825 - 1)}{0.055}\right] \\
&= 1500.00(4.342266) \\
&= \$6513.399562
\end{aligned}
$$

STEP 4

For the final five years of accumulating interest, the beginning balance is determined by adding the future values of Steps 2 and 3. Then, the future value after the five years is computed.

$$FV_2 + FV_3 = PV_4$$

$$17430.288141 + 6513.399562 = 23\,943.687703$$

$$
\begin{aligned}
FV_4 &= 23\,943.68770[(1.055)^5] \\
&= 23\,943.68770(1.306960) \\
&= \$31\,293.44234
\end{aligned}
$$

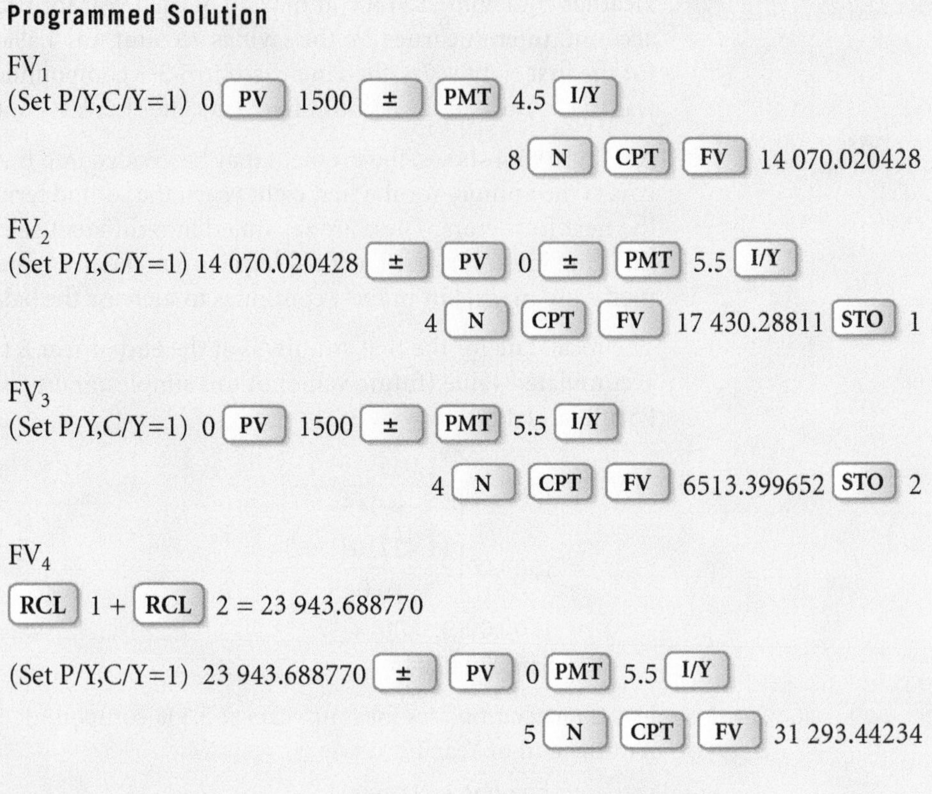

FIGURE 11.4 Graphical Representation of Method and Data

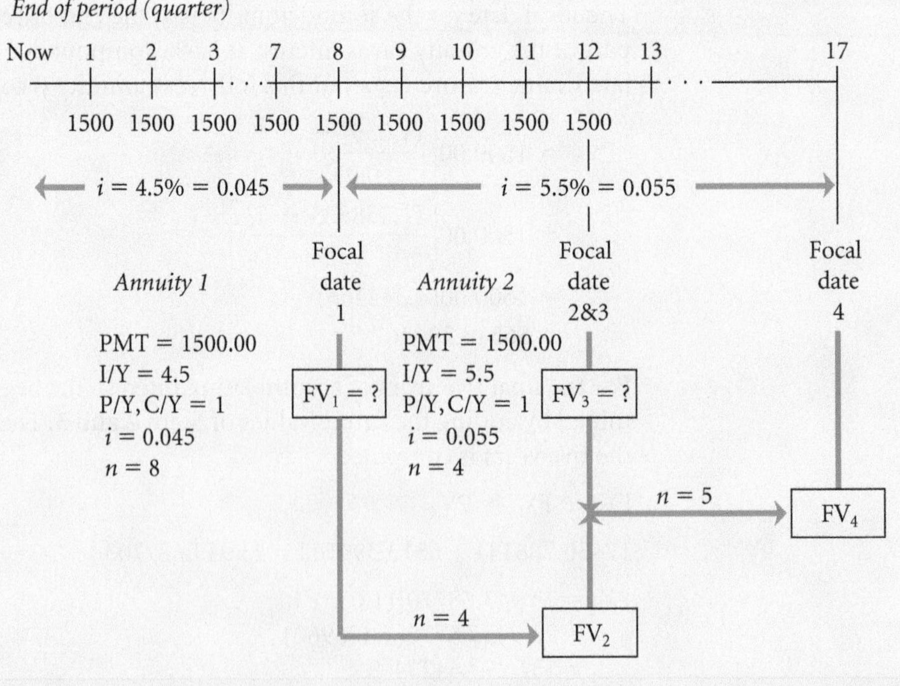

EXERCISE 11.2

EXCEL NOTES

If you choose, you can use Excel's Future Value (FV) function to answer the questions indicated below. Refer to FV on MathXL to learn how to use this Excel function.

EXCEL SPREADSHEET

A. Find the future value of the ordinary simple annuity for each of the following six series of payments.

	Periodic Payment	Payment Interval	Term	Interest Rate	Conversion Period
1.	\$1500	1 quarter	$7\frac{1}{2}$ years	5%	quarterly
2.	20	1 month	6.75 years	6	monthly
3.	700	6 months	20 years	7	semi-annually
4.	10	1 month	15 years	9	monthly
5.	320	3 months	8 years, 9 months	10.4	quarterly
6.	\$2000	$\frac{1}{2}$ year	11 years, 6 months	8.8	semi-annually

EXCEL SPREADSHEET

B. Answer each of the following questions.

1. Find the accumulated value of payments of \$200 made at the end of every three months for twelve years if money is worth 5% compounded quarterly.

Reference Example 11.2C

2. What will deposits of \$60 made at the end of each month amount to after six years if interest is 4.8% compounded monthly?

3. How much interest is included in the future value of an ordinary simple annuity of \$1500 paid every six months at 7% compounded semi-annually if the term of the annuity is fifteen years?

Reference Example 11.2D

4. Jane Allison made ordinary annuity payments of \$15 per month for sixteen years earning 4.5% compounded monthly. How much interest is included in the future value of the annuity?

5. Saving for his retirement 25 years from now, Jimmy Olsen set up a savings plan whereby he will deposit \$25 at the end of each month for the next 15 years. Interest is 3.6% compounded monthly.
(a) How much money will be in Mr. Olsen's account on the date of his retirement?
(b) How much will Mr. Olsen contribute?
(c) How much will be interest?

Reference Example 11.2E

6. Aisha contributed \$2000 per year for the last ten years into an RRSP account earning 3.8% compounded annually. Suppose she leaves the accumulated contributions for another five years in the RRSP at the same rate of interest.
(a) How much will Aisha have in total in her RRSP account?
(b) How much did Aisha contribute?
(c) How much interest will have been earned?

7. Cam saved \$250 each month for the last five years while he was working. Since he has now gone back to school, his income is lower and he cannot continue to save this amount during the time he is studying. He plans to

continue with his studies for four years and not withdraw any money from his savings account. Money is worth 4.5% compounded monthly.
(a) How much will Cam have in total in his savings account when he finishes his studies?
(b) How much did he contribute?
(c) How much will be interest? Reference Example 11.2F

8. Scott has saved $560 per quarter for the last three years in a savings account earning 5.2% compounded quarterly. He plans to leave the accumulated savings for seven years in the savings account at the same rate of interest.
(a) How much will Scott have in total in his savings account?
(b) How much did he contribute?
(c) How much will be interest?

9. To purchase a specialty guitar for his band, for the last two years JJ Morrison has made payments of $92 at the end of each month into a savings account earning interest at 4.03% compounded monthly. If he leaves the accumulated money in the savings account for another two years at 5.03% compounded quarterly, how much will he have saved to buy the guitar? Reference Example 11.2G

10. For the last six years Joe Borelli has made deposits of $300 at the end of every six months earning interest at 5% compounded semi-annually. If he leaves the accumulated balance in an account earning 6% compounded quarterly, what will the balance be in Joe's account at the end of another ten years?

11.3 ORDINARY SIMPLE ANNUITY—FINDING PRESENT VALUE PV

A. Present value of series of payments—basic computation

EXAMPLE 11.3A Find the single sum of money whose value now is equivalent to payments of $2000, $4000, $5000, $1000, and $3000 made at the end of each of five consecutive years respectively at 6% compounded annually.

SOLUTION The series of payments can be represented on a time graph.

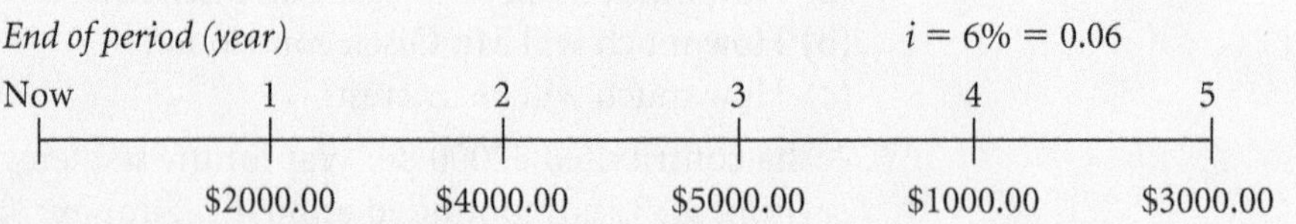

To find the present value of the series of payments, we need to determine the combined present value of the five payments at the focal point "now." This can be done using Formula 9.1C, $PV = FV(1 + i)^{-n}$. A graphical representation of the method and data is shown in Figure 11.5.

In this problem, the payments are examined to determine if they are equal and periodic. They are not of equal size, even though they are periodic. The present value of each individual payment must be computed separately, and then added together.

FIGURE 11.5 Graphical Representation of Method and Data

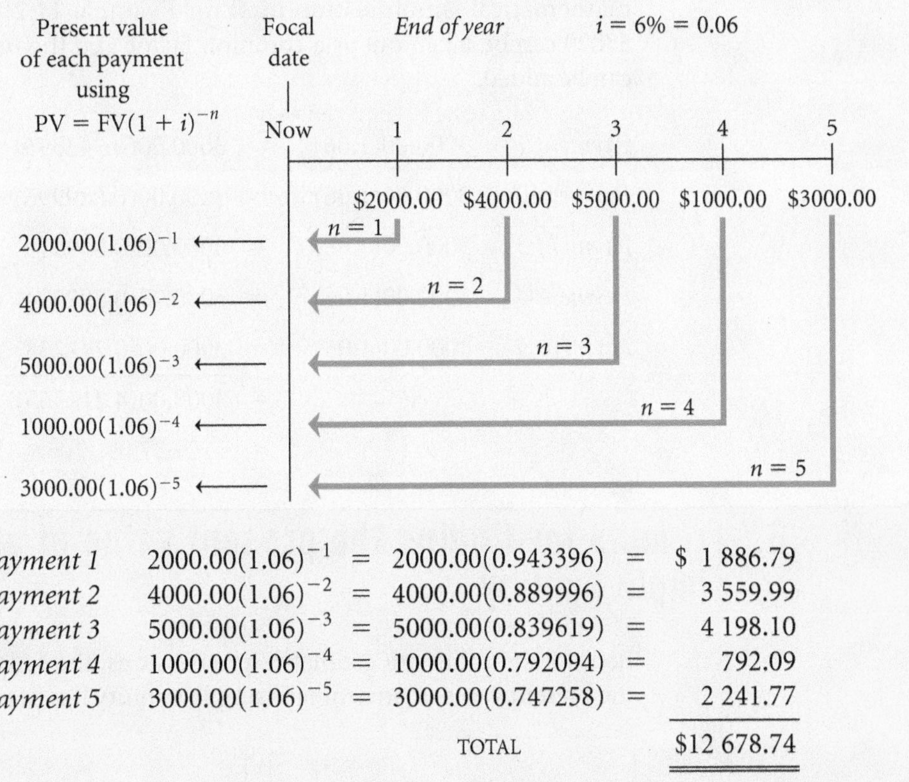

Payment 1	$2000.00(1.06)^{-1}$	=	2000.00(0.943396)	=	$ 1 886.79
Payment 2	$4000.00(1.06)^{-2}$	=	4000.00(0.889996)	=	3 559.99
Payment 3	$5000.00(1.06)^{-3}$	=	5000.00(0.839619)	=	4 198.10
Payment 4	$1000.00(1.06)^{-4}$	=	1000.00(0.792094)	=	792.09
Payment 5	$3000.00(1.06)^{-5}$	=	3000.00(0.747258)	=	2 241.77
			TOTAL		$12 678.74

EXAMPLE 11.3B Find the present value of five payments of $3000 made at the end of each of five consecutive years respectively if money is worth 6% compounded annually.

SOLUTION As shown in Figure 11.6, example is basically the same as Example 11.3A except that all payments are equal in size.

FIGURE 11.6 Graphical Representation of Method and Data

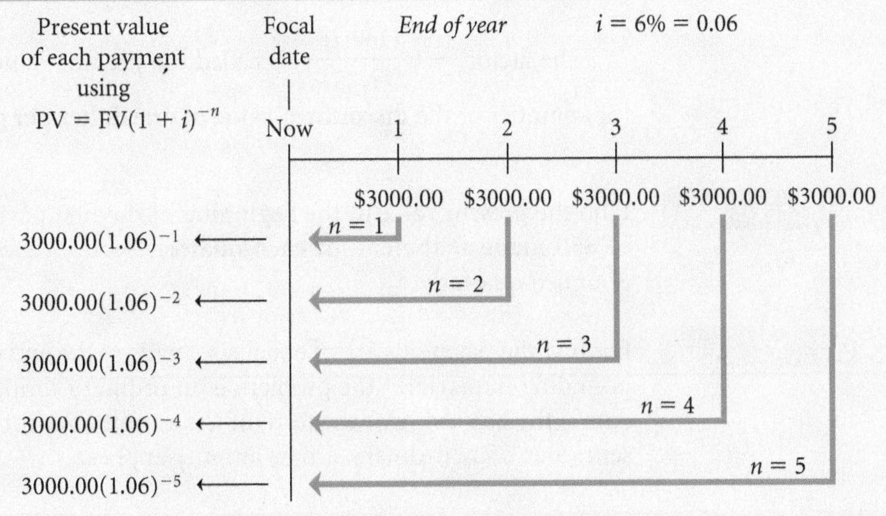

While the approach to solving the problem is fundamentally the same as in Example 11.3A, the fact that the payments are equal in size permits the same mathematical simplification used for Example 11.2B. The equal payment of $3000 can be taken out as a common factor and the individual discount factors can be added.

Payment 1	$3000.00(1.06)^{-1}$	=	3000.00(0.943396)
Payment 2	$3000.00(1.06)^{-2}$	=	3000.00(0.889996)
Payment 3	$3000.00(1.06)^{-3}$	=	3000.00(0.839619)
Payment 4	$3000.00(1.06)^{-4}$	=	3000.00(0.792094)
Payment 5	$3000.00(1.06)^{-5}$	=	3000.00(0.747258)
		=	3000.00(4.212363)
		=	$12 637.09

B. Formula for finding the present value of an ordinary simple annuity

Because annuities are geometric progressions, the following formula for finding the present value of an ordinary simple annuity has been developed.

$$PV_n = PMT\left[\frac{1-(1+i)^{-n}}{i}\right]$$ ——— **Formula 11.2**

where PV_n = the present value (discounted value) of an ordinary simple annuity;
PMT = the size of the periodic payment (rent);
i = the interest rate per conversion period;
n = the number of periodic payments (which for simple annuities equals the number of conversion periods).

The factor $\frac{1-(1+i)^{-n}}{i}$ is called the present value factor or **discount factor** for annuities or the **discounted value of one dollar per period.**

EXAMPLE 11.3C

Find the present value at the beginning of the first payment period of payments of $50 made at the end of each quarter for ten years, if interest is 8% compounded quarterly.

SOLUTION

Because the payments are of equal size made at the end of each quarter and compounding is quarterly, the problem is an ordinary simple annuity. Since the focal date is the beginning of the term of the annuity, the formula for finding the present value of an ordinary simple annuity applies.

$$\text{PMT} = 50.00;\ \text{I/Y} = 8;\ \text{P/Y, C/Y} = 4;\ i = \frac{8\%}{4} = 0.02;\ n = 10(4) = 40$$

$$\text{PV} = 50.00\left[\frac{1 - (1 + 0.02)^{-40}}{0.02}\right] \quad \text{——— substituting in Formula 11.2}$$

$$= 50.00\left[\frac{1 - 0.452890}{0.02}\right]$$

$$= 50.00\left[\frac{0.547110}{0.02}\right]$$

$$= 50.00(27.355480)$$

$$= \$1367.77$$

EXAMPLE 11.3D

Suppose you want to withdraw \$100 at the end of each month for five years from an account paying 4.5% compounded monthly.

(i) How much must you have on deposit at the beginning of the month in which the first withdrawal is made at the end of the month?

(ii) How much will you receive in total?

(iii) How much of what you will receive is interest?

SOLUTION

(i) $\text{PMT} = 100.00;\ \text{I/Y} = 4.5;\ \text{P/Y, C/Y} = 12;\ i = \frac{4.5\%}{12} = 0.375\% = 0.00375;$

$n = 12(5) = 60$

$$\text{PV} = \text{PMT}\left[\frac{1 - (1 + i)^{-n}}{i}\right]$$

$$= 100.00\left[\frac{1 - (1.00375)^{-60}}{0.00375}\right]$$

$$= 100.00\left[\frac{(1 - 0.798852)}{0.00375}\right]$$

$$= 100.00\left(\frac{0.201148}{0.00375}\right)$$

$$= 100(53.639381)$$

$$= \$5363.94$$

(ii) Total receipts will be \$100 per month for 60 months or \$6000.

(iii) Since the initial balance must be \$5363.94, the interest received will be 6000.00 – 5363.94 = \$636.06.

C. Present value using preprogrammed financial calculators

To find the present value of the ordinary simple annuity in Example 11.3D, in which PMT = 100.00, I/Y = 4.5, P/Y, C/Y = 12, and n = 60, proceed as follows.

	Key in	*Press*	*Display shows*	
(Set P/Y, C/Y = 12)	0	FV	0	a precaution
	100	± PMT	−100	
	4.5	I/Y	4.5	
	60	N	60	
	CPT	PV	5363.938035	pressing the PV key retrieves the unknown present value PV_n

You must have \$5363.94 on deposit.

D. Applications

When buying a home or vehicle, most people do not have enough money saved to pay the entire price. However, a small initial payment, called a **down payment**, is often accepted in the meantime. A mortgage loan from a financial institution is needed to supply the balance of the purchase price. The larger the down payment, the smaller the amount that needs to be borrowed. Based on the amount borrowed, the rate of interest, and the time to repay, the payments are determined. The amount of the loan is the *present value of the future periodic payments*.

The *cash value* is the price of the property at the date of purchase and represents the dated value of all payments at that date.

CASH VALUE = DOWN PAYMENT + PRESENT VALUE OF THE PERIODIC PAYMENTS

Analysis of mortgages and amortization of loans is covered in further depth in Chapter 14.

EXAMPLE 11.3E

Mr. and Mrs. Hong bought a vacation property, paying \$3000 as a down payment and making further payments of \$1000 every six months for twelve years. If interest is 7% compounded semi-annually, what was the cash value of the property?

SOLUTION

Since the first ongoing payment is due at the end of the first six-month period and compounding is semi-annual, the present value of an ordinary simple annuity is calculated.

$\text{PMT} = 1000.00$; $\text{I/Y} = 7$; $\text{P/Y, C/Y} = 2$; $i = \dfrac{7\%}{2} = 3.5\% = 0.035$;

$n = 12(2) = 24$

$$PV = 1000.00\left[\frac{(1 - 1.035^{-24})}{0.035}\right]$$
$$= 1000.00\left[\frac{(1 - 0.437957)}{0.035}\right]$$
$$= 1000.00\left(\frac{0.562043}{0.035}\right)$$
$$= 1000.00(16.058368)$$
$$= \$16\,058.37$$

Programmed Solution

(Set P/Y, C/Y = 2) 0 [FV] 1000 [±] [PMT] 7 [I/Y]

24 [N] [CPT] [PV] [16058.367603]

The cash value = 3000.00 + 16 058.37 = $19 058.37.

EXAMPLE 11.3F

Marcello renovated the kitchen in his house to take advantage of a tax rebate program. To pay for the renovations, he arranged a loan where he made payments of $288 at the end of every three months for three years. The bank charged interest on the loan at 8.4% compounded quarterly.

(i) How much money was borrowed?

(ii) If the loan was repaid over the three years, how much interest was paid?

(iii) If Marcello made the same payments, but the interest rate was reduced to 7.4% compounded quarterly, by how much would the amount borrowed be increased or decreased?

SOLUTION

Since the first ongoing payment was due at the end of the first three-month period and compounding was quarterly, the present value of the ordinary simple annuity is calculated.

PMT = 288.00; I/Y = 8.4; P/Y,C/Y = 4; $i = 8.4\%/4 = 2.1\% = 0.021$; $n = 3(4) = 12$

(i) $PV = 288.00\left[\frac{1 - 1.021^{-12}}{0.021}\right] = 288.00(10.510684) = \$3027.08$

Programmed Solution

(Set P/Y,C/Y = 4) 288 [±] [PMT] 8.4 [I/Y]

12 [N] [CPT] [PV] 3027.077073

The amount borrowed was $3027.08.

(ii) The interest is the difference between the amount borrowed and the total payments made.

Interest = 288.00(12) − 3027.08 = 3456.00 − 3027.08 = 428.92

The amount of interest paid was $428.92.

(iii) Calculate the new present value using the new interest rate.

$I/Y = 7.4;\ i = 7.4\%/4 = 1.85\% = 0.0185$

$$PV = 288.00\left[\frac{1 - 1.0185^{-12}}{0.0185}\right] = 288.00(10.673422) = \$3073.95$$

Programmed Solution

(Set P/Y, C/Y = 4) 288 [±] [PMT] 7.4 [I/Y]

12 [N] [CPT] [PV] 3073.945646

The amount borrowed would be $3073.95.

The loan amount would be increased by $3073.95 – 3027.08 = $46.87.

EXAMPLE 11.3G

Sheila Davidson borrowed money from her credit union and agreed to repay the loan in blended monthly payments of $161.75 over a four-year period. Interest on the loan was 9% compounded monthly.

(i) How much did she borrow?

(ii) If Sheila did not make the payments in the first year, and if the credit union demanded payment in full, how much money would she need?

(iii) Assuming the situation in part (ii) occurs, what would have been the total cost of the loan?

(iv) If she missed the first eleven payments, how much would she have to pay at the end of the first year to bring her payments up to date?

(v) How much of the total loan cost is additional interest paid on the missed payments?

SOLUTION

(i) The amount borrowed is the present value (or discounted value) of the 48 payments as in the original agreement, as the time diagram shows.

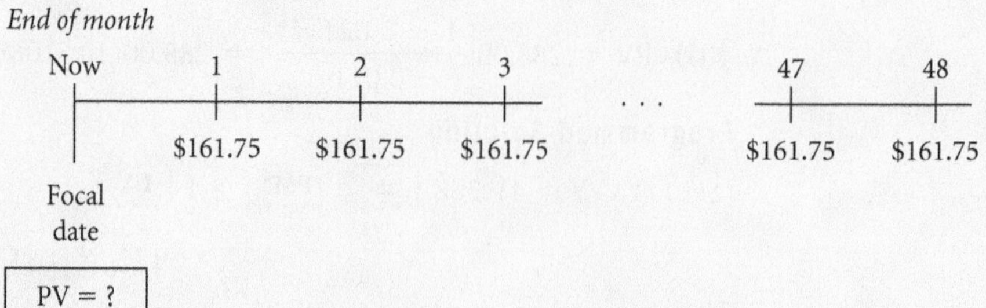

End of month

Now	1	2	3	. . .	47	48
	$161.75	$161.75	$161.75		$161.75	$161.75

Focal date

PV = ?

$PMT = 161.75;\ I/Y = 9;\ P/Y, C/Y = 12;\ i = \frac{9\%}{12} = 0.75\% = 0.0075;$

$n = 4(12) = 48$

$$PV = 161.75\left[\frac{(1 - 1.0075^{-48})}{0.0075}\right] \quad \text{—— using Formula 11.2}$$

$$= 161.75\left[\frac{1 - 0.698614}{0.0075}\right]$$

$$= 161.75(40.184782)$$

$$= \$6499.89$$

Programmed Solution

(Set P/Y, C/Y = 12) 0 [FV] 161.75 [±] [PMT]

9 [I/Y] 48 [N] [CPT] [PV] [6499.898847]

Sheila borrowed $6499.89.

(ii) The sum of money required to pay off the loan in full is the balance owing on the loan after one year. Calculate the future value of the original loan amount, twelve months in the future.

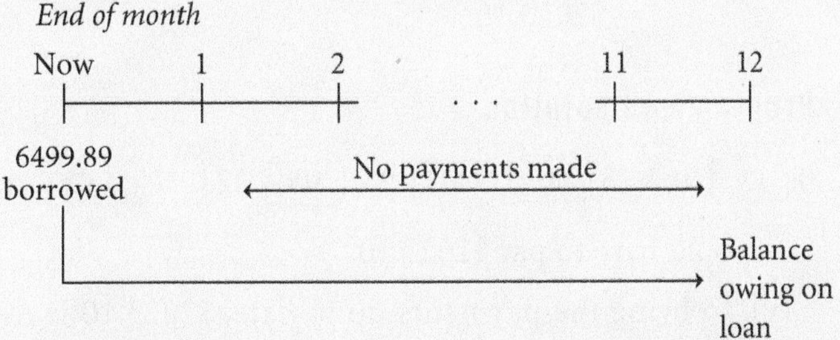

The balance owing can be found through using Formula 9.1A.

$$PV = 6499.89; \quad i = 0.0075; \quad n = 12$$

$$FV = 6499.89(1 + 0.0075)^{12}$$

$$= 6499.89(1.0075)^{12}$$

$$= 6499.89(1.093807)$$

$$= \$7109.62$$

Programmed Solution

(Set P/Y, C/Y = 12) 6499.89 [PV] 0 [PMT] 9 [I/Y]

12 [N] [CPT] [FV] [7109.622842]

The amount of money needed is $7109.62.

(iii) The total cost of the loan if paid off after one year is the difference between the value of the loan after one year and the original loan balance: 7109.62 – 6499.89 = $609.73.

(iv) As the following diagram shows, Sheila Davidson must pay the accumulated value of the first twelve payments to bring her payments up to date after one year. Calculate the future value of the first twelve payments.

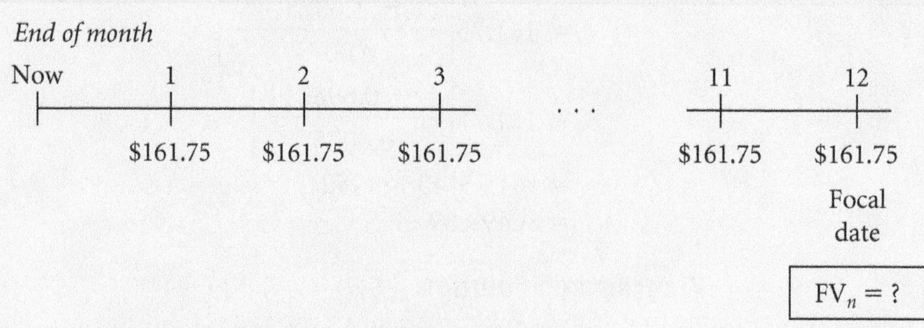

$\text{PMT} = 161.75; \quad i = 0.0075; \quad n = 12$

$$\text{FV} = 161.75\left[\frac{(1.0075^{12} - 1)}{0.0075}\right] \text{ ——— using Formula 11.1}$$

$$= 161.75\left[\frac{1.093807 - 1}{0.0075}\right]$$

$$= 161.75(12.507586)$$

$$= \$2023.10$$

Programmed Solution

0 [PV] 161.75 [±] [PMT] 9.0 [I/Y] 12 [N] [CPT] [FV] [2023.102093]

She would have to pay $2023.10.

(v) To bring the payments up to date, $2023.10 is needed. Since the normal amount paid during the first year would have been 161.75(12) = $1941.00, the additional interest paid is 2023.10 – 1941.00 = $82.10.

EXERCISE 11.3

EXCEL NOTES If you choose, you can use Excel's Present Value (PV) function to answer the questions indicated below. Refer to PV on MathXL to learn how to use this Excel function.

EXCEL SPREADSHEET

A. Determine the present value of the ordinary simple annuity for each of the following series of payments.

	Periodic Payment	Payment Interval	Term	Interest Rate	Compounding Period
1.	$1600	6 months	$3\frac{1}{2}$ years	8.5%	semi-annually
2.	700	1 quarter	4 years, 9 months	5	quarterly
3.	4000	1 year	12 years	7.5	annually
4.	45	1 month	18 years	6.6	monthly
5.	250	3 months	14 years, 3 months	4.4	quarterly
6.	$80	1 month	9.25 years	7.2	monthly

EXCEL SPREADSHEET

B. Answer each of the following questions.

1. Find the present value of payments of $375 made at the end of every six months for fifteen years if money is worth 7% compounded semi-annually.

Reference Example 11.3C

2. What is the discounted value of payments of $60 made at the end of each month for nine years if interest is 4.5% compounded monthly?

3. You want to receive $600 at the end of every three months for five years. Interest is 7.6% compounded quarterly.
   (a) How much would you have to deposit at the beginning of the five-year period?
   (b) How much of what you receive will be interest?

Reference Example 11.3D

4. An installment contract for the purchase of a car requires payments of $252.17 at the end of each month for the next three years. Suppose interest is 8.4% p.a. compounded monthly.
   (a) What is the amount financed?
   (b) How much is the interest cost?

5. For home entertainment equipment, Ted paid $400 down and signed an installment contract that required payments of $69.33 at the end of each month for three years. Suppose interest is 10.8% compounded monthly.
   (a) What was the cash price of the equipment?
   (b) How much was the cost of financing?

Reference Example 11.3E

6. Jeffery purchased a new car by making a down payment of $2000 and agreeing to make payments of $458 at the end of each month for five years. Interest is 9.2% compounded monthly.
   (a) What was the purchase price of the car?
   (b) How much interest will Jeffery pay?

7. Having earned a bonus at his work, Rick placed the money in an investment earning 4.18% compounded monthly. He withdrew $343 at the end of every month for the next eight years.
   (a) What was the amount of the bonus?
   (b) If he made all of the withdrawals as planned, how much interest was paid?
   (c) If Rick made the same withdrawals, but the interest rate was 4.31% compounded monthly, by how much was the new investment amount increased or decreased?

8. Luisa borrowed to buy a piano, paying $135 at the end of each month for five years. The bank charges interest on the loan at 8.8% compounded monthly.
   (a) What was the cash price of the piano?
   (b) How much is the cost of financing?
   (c) By how much would the cash price change if the bank charged interest at 7.7% compounded monthly?

Reference Example 11.3F

9. Wayne borrowed to purchase his son's hockey equipment. He made month-end loan payments of $74 for two years on a loan that charges interest at

8.4% compounded monthly. Roberto also borrowed to purchase his daughter's hockey equipment. He made loan payments of $244 at the end of each quarter for two years on a loan that charges interest at 6.4% compounded quarterly. What was the cash price of each of the sets of hockey equipment, and which parent paid less?

10. Helena and George are planning to purchase a new plasma TV. If they finance the purchase through the store's promotional financing option, they would pay $97 at the end of each month for three years, starting with the first month.

(a) With the store's promotional financing option, what is the cash price of the TV if the interest rate on the loan is 12.9% compounded monthly?

(b) If they borrow from the bank at 13.5% compounded monthly, the payments would be $93 per month for three years. Which option results in the lower purchase price, and by how much?

11. Kimiko signed a mortgage requiring payments of $234.60 at the end of every month for six years at 7.2% compounded monthly.

(a) How much was the original mortgage balance?

(b) If Kimiko missed the first five payments, how much would she have to pay after six months to bring the mortgage payments up to date?

(c) How much would Kimiko have to pay after six months to pay off the mortgage (assuming she missed all the payments)?

(d) If the mortgage were paid off after six months, what would the total interest cost be?

(e) How much of the total interest cost is additional interest because of the missed payments? Reference Example 11.3G

12. Field Construction agreed to lease payments of $642.79 on construction equipment to be made at the end of each month for three years. Financing is at 9% compounded monthly.

(a) What is the value of the original lease contract?

(b) If, due to delays, the first eight payments were deferred, how much money would be needed after nine months to bring the lease payments up to date?

(c) How much money would be required to pay off the lease after nine months (assuming no payments were made)?

(d) If the lease were paid off after nine months, what would the total interest be?

(e) How much of the total interest would be due to deferring the first eight payments?

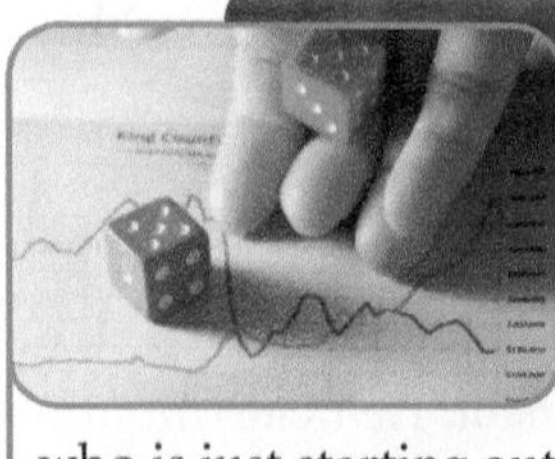

BUSINESS MATH NEWS BOX

Get Rich, DRIP by DRIP

One of the best ways to make safe, small investments is through Dividend Reinvestment Plans (DRIPs). DRIPs are ideal for a thirty-something investor who is just starting out.

DRIPs, currently offered by more than 1000 companies in North America, allow current shareholders to reinvest their dividend income to purchase additional stock directly from the company, free of brokerage and commission fees. Instead of receiving dividends, the proceeds are immediately used to buy shares in the company so that your investment continues to grow.

For Canadian DRIPs, you usually need only one share of a company stock to join. Purchase the initial share in the open market; you will incur an initial transaction fee. However, once enrolled in a DRIP, the process is completely automated and your subsequent purchases and reinvested dividends will result in no commissions.

By purchasing shares at regular intervals over time, you can take advantage of "dollar-cost averaging." Regular investments at the same dollar amount ensure that more shares are purchased when the share price is low and fewer are purchased when the share price is high. This approach effectively lowers the average price paid for shares.

Lou Caci, an investment executive at ScotiaMcLeod in Winnipeg, says some companies will allow you to buy their shares through a DRIP at a discount of between 3% and 5% off the current market price. If, for example, your dividend comes in and the stock is trading at $20, you may be able to purchase shares for as little as $19 each.

Dividends tend to average between 1% and 3% per year of the value of a stock, with blue-chip companies typically sitting at the upper end of the range. It might not seem like much in the short term, but over the long run the financial benefits can be substantial.

Source: CIBC Mellon, "Benefits of DRIPs," **www.cibcmellon.com/Contents/en_CA/English/InvestorCentre/DividendOptions/DividendReinvestmentPlans/Benefits.html.**

QUESTIONS

1. You purchase 1000 shares of a stock each year for five years. Assume that in the first year the stock price is $20 per share and the shares increase in price by 1% per year.
   - (a) What is the value of your investment in five years?
   - (b) If the same company provides annual dividends equal to 3% of stock price, calculate the amount of dividends that an investor will attain over this five-year period.
   - (c) If a company provides a DRIP that allows investors to acquire stocks with the annual dividend of 3% at a discounted price of 5% below market price, calculate the value of the investment after five years.
2. Using dollar-cost averaging will help you reduce your risk over time by ensuring that you do not try to time the market. An investor regularly contributes $20 000 to his DRIP account for five years. The share price fluctuates over time as follows:

Year 1	Year 2	Year 3	Year 4	Year 5
$22.00	$25.00	$21.50	$31.20	$36.70

   - (a) Calculate the investor's average cost per share.
   - (b) Calculate the value of the investment after five years.
   - (c) Calculate the yield of the investments.

11.4 ORDINARY SIMPLE ANNUITIES—FINDING THE PERIODIC PAYMENT PMT

A. Finding the periodic payment PMT when the future value of an annuity is known

If the future value of an annuity, FV_n, the number of conversion periods, n, and the conversion rate, i, are known, you can find the periodic payment, PMT, by substituting the given values in the appropriate future value formula.

For ordinary simple annuities, use Formula 11.1.

$$FV_n = PMT\left[\frac{(1+i)^n - 1}{i}\right] \qquad \text{Formula 11.1}$$

When using a preprogrammed financial calculator, you can find PMT by entering the five known values (FV, N, I/Y, P/Y, and C/Y) and pressing **CPT** **PMT**.

Recall that the PMT amount will be negative since payments are considered to be cash outflows.

EXAMPLE 11.4A

What deposit made at the end of each quarter will accumulate to \$10 000 in four years at 4% compounded quarterly?

SOLUTION

FV = 10 000.00; I/Y = 4; P/Y, C/Y = 4; $i = \frac{4\%}{4} = 1.0\% = 0.01$; $n = 4(4) = 16$

$$10\,000.00 = PMT\left(\frac{1.01^{16} - 1}{0.01}\right) \qquad \text{substituting in Formula 11.1}$$

$$10\,000.00 = PMT\left(\frac{1.172579 - 1}{0.01}\right)$$

$$10\,000.00 = PMT(17.25786)$$

$$PMT = \frac{10\,000.00}{17.25786}$$

$$PMT = \$579.45$$

As we have emphasized throughout this book, understanding how to rearrange terms in a formula is a very important skill. By knowing how to do this, you avoid having to memorize equivalent forms of the same formula.

You can find PMT by first rearranging the terms of the future value formulas as shown below. Then substitute the three known values (FV, n, and i) into the rearranged formula and use the calculator to solve for PMT.

$$FV_n = PMT\left[\frac{(1+i)^n - 1}{i}\right] \qquad \text{Formula 11.1}$$

$$PMT = \frac{FV_n}{\left[\frac{(1+i)^n - 1}{i}\right]} \qquad \text{divide both sides by } \left[\frac{(1+i)^n - 1}{i}\right]$$

$$\text{PMT} = \frac{\text{FV}_n i}{(1 + i)^n - 1}$$ ——— dividing by a fraction is the same as inverting the fraction and multiplying

$\text{FV} = 10\,000.00; \quad i = 0.01; \quad n = 16$

$$\text{PMT} = \frac{10\,000.00(0.01)}{1.01^{16} - 1}$$ ——— substituting in rearranged Formula 11.1

$\text{PMT} = \$579.45$

EXAMPLE 11.4B If you want to have a \$5000 balance in your bank account in three years, how much must you deposit at the end of each month if interest is 4.5% compounded monthly?

SOLUTION $\text{FV} = 5000.00; \quad \text{I/Y} = 4.5; \quad \text{P/Y, C/Y} = 12; \quad i = \frac{4.5}{12} = 0.375\%; \quad n = 3(12) = 36$

(Set P/Y = 12) [2nd] (CLR TVM) 0 [PV] 5000 [FV]

4.5 [I/Y] 36 [N] [CPT] [PMT] [-129.984622]

The monthly deposit required is \$129.98.

B. Finding the periodic payment PMT when the present value of an annuity is known

If the present value of an annuity, PV_n, the number of conversion periods, n, and the conversion rate, i, are known, you can find the periodic payment PMT by substituting the given values in the appropriate present value formula.

For ordinary simple annuities, use Formula 11.2.

$$\text{PV}_n = \text{PMT}\left[\frac{1 - (1 + i)^{-n}}{i}\right]$$ ——— Formula 11.2

When using a preprogrammed financial calculator, you can find PMT by entering the five known values (PV, N, P/Y, C/Y, and I/Y) and pressing [CPT] [PMT].

EXAMPLE 11.4C What semi-annual payment at the end of each six-month period is required to pay off a loan of \$8000 in ten years if interest is 10% compounded semi-annually?

SOLUTION $\text{PV} = 8000.00; \; \text{I/Y} = 10; \; \text{P/Y, C/Y} = 2; \; i = \frac{10\%}{2} = 5\% = 0.05; \; n = 10(2) = 20$

$$8000.00 = \text{PMT}\left(\frac{1 - 1.05^{-20}}{0.05}\right)$$ ——— substituting in Formula 11.2

$$8000.00 = \text{PMT}\left(\frac{1 - 0.376889}{0.05}\right)$$

$$8000.00 = \text{PMT}(12.462210)$$

$$\text{PMT} = \frac{8000.00}{12.462210}$$

$$\text{PMT} = \$641.94$$

Alternatively:

You can first rearrange the terms of Formula 11.2 to solve for PMT.

$$\text{PV} = \text{PMT}\left[\frac{1-(1+i)^{-n}}{i}\right]$$ ——— Formula 11.2

$$\text{PMT} = \frac{\text{PV}_n}{\left[\frac{1-(1+i)^{-n}}{i}\right]}$$ ——— divide both sides by $\left[\frac{1-(1+i)^{-n}}{i}\right]$

$$\text{PMT} = \frac{\text{PV}_n\, i}{1-(1+i)^{-n}}$$ ——— dividing by a fraction is the same as inverting the fraction and multiplying

$$\text{PV} = 8000.00; \quad i = 0.05; \quad n = 20$$

$$\text{PMT} = \frac{8000.00(0.05)}{1-1.05^{-20}}$$

$$\text{PMT} = \$641.94$$

Programmed Solution

(Set P/Y = 2) 8000 [±] [PV] 0 [FV] 10 [I/Y]

20 [N] [CPT] [FV] 641.940698

EXAMPLE 11.4D

Derek bought a new car valued at $9500.00. He paid $2000 down and financed the remainder over five years at 9% compounded monthly. How much must Derek pay at the end of each month?

SOLUTION

PV = 9500.00 − 2000.00 = 7500.00; I/Y = 9; P/Y, C/Y = 12; $i = \frac{9\%}{12} = 0.75\%$; $n = 60$

(Set P/Y = 12) 0 [FV] 7500 [±] [PV]

9 [I/Y] 60 [N] [CPT] [PMT] 155.687664

Derek's monthly payment is $155.69.

EXAMPLE 11.4E

Taylor Marche, now age 37, expects to retire at age 62. To plan for her retirement, she intends to deposit $1500.00 at the end of each of the next 25 years in a savings plan. After her last contribution, she intends to convert the existing balance into a fund from which she expects to make 20 equal annual withdrawals. If she makes the first withdrawal one year after her last contribution and interest is 6.5% compounded annually, how much is the size of the annual retirement withdrawal?

SOLUTION

As the following time diagram shows, the problem must be broken down into two steps.

STEP 1 Compute the *accumulated* value FV_1 of the 25 annual deposits of \$1500.00.

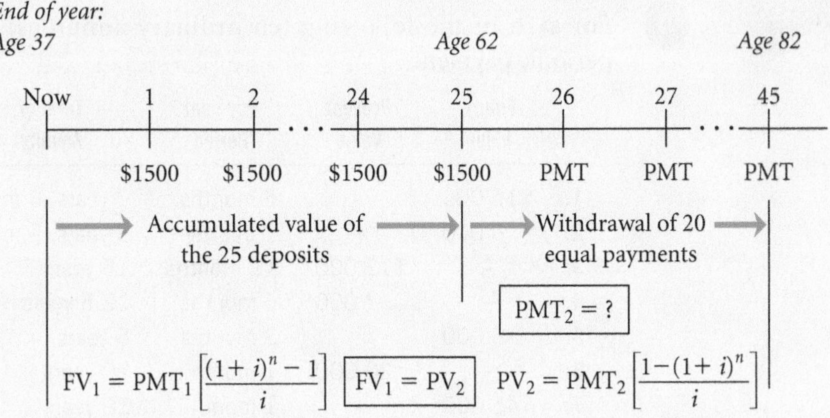

$PMT_1 = 1500.00$; $I/Y = 6.5$; $P/Y = 1$; $i = 6.5\% = 0.065$; $n = 25$

$$FV_1 = 1500.00\left(\frac{1.065^{25} - 1}{0.065}\right)$$ substituting in Formula 11.1

$$= 1500.00(58.887679)$$
$$= \$88\,331.52$$

STEP 2 The future value, FV_1, of the deposit period becomes the present value, PV_2, of the withdrawal period. Compute the annual payment PMT_2 that can be withdrawn from the fund that has an initial balance of \$88 331.52.

$FV_1 = PV_2 = 88\,331.52$; $i = 0.065$; $n = 20$

$$88\,331.52 = PMT_2\left(\frac{1 - 1.065^{-20}}{0.065}\right)$$ using Formula 11.2

$$88\,331.52 = PMT_2\,(11.018507)$$
$$PMT_2 = \$8016.65$$

Programmed Solution

STEP 1 (Set P/Y, C/Y = 1) 0 [PV] 1500 [±] [PMT] 6.5 [I/Y]
25 [N] [CPT] [FV] [88331.51788]

STEP 2 88 331.52 [±] [PV] 0 [FV] 6.5 [I/Y] 20 [N] [CPT] [PMT] [8016.650159]

The amount of money that Taylor can withdraw each year is \$8016.65.

EXERCISE 11.4

EXCEL NOTES If you choose, you can use Excel's Payment (PMT) function to answer all of the questions below. Refer to PMT on MathXL to learn how to use this Excel function.

EXCEL SPREADSHEET

A. For each of the following ten ordinary annuities, determine the size of the periodic payment.

	Future Value	Present Value	Payment Period	Term of Annuity	Interest Rate	Conversion Period
1.	$15 000	–	6 months	7 years, 6 mos.	5.5%	semi-annually
2.	6 000	–	1 quarter	9 years, 9 mos.	8	quarterly
3.	–	$12 000	12 months	15 years	4.5	annually
4.	–	7 000	6 months	12.5 years	7.5	semi-annually
5.	8 000	–	3 months	6 years	6.8	quarterly
6.	–	20 000	1 month	20 years	12	monthly
7.	45 000	–	1 month	10 years	9	monthly
8.	–	35 000	1 quarter	15 years	4	quarterly
9.	–	20 000	6 months	8 years	7	semi-annually
10.	$16 500	–	3 months	15 years	5.75	quarterly

EXCEL SPREADSHEET

B. Answer each of the following questions.

1. What deposit made at the end of each quarter for fifteen years will accumulate to $20 000 at 6% compounded quarterly? Reference Example 11.4B
2. What payment is required at the end of each month for five years to repay a loan of $8000 at 8.4% compounded monthly?
3. A contract can be fulfilled by making an immediate payment of $7500 or equal payments at the end of every six months for ten years. What is the size of the semi-annual payments at 9.6% compounded semi-annually?
4. What payment is required at the end of each month for twelve years to repay a $32 000 mortgage if interest is 6.5% compounded monthly?
5. How much must be deposited at the end of each quarter for nine years to accumulate to $11 000 at 4% compounded quarterly?
6. What payment made at the end of every six months for fifteen years will accumulate to $18 000 at 5% compounded semi-annually?
7. How much does a depositor have to save at the end of every three months for seven years to accumulate $3500 if interest is 3.75% compounded quarterly?
8. How much would you have to pay into an account at the end of every six months to accumulate $10 000 in eight years if interest is 3% compounded semi-annually?

9. Ontario Credit Union entered a lease contract valued at $7200. The contract provides for payments at the end of each quarter for three years. If interest is 6.5% compounded quarterly, what is the size of the quarterly payment?

10. Hunan bought a used car priced at $15 300 for 15% down and equal monthly payments for four years. If interest is 8% compounded monthly, what is the size of the monthly payment? Reference Example 11.4D

11. Ruben bought a boat valued at $16 500 on the installment plan requiring a $2000 down payment and equal monthly payments for five years. If the first payment is due one month after the date of purchase and interest is 7.5% compounded monthly, what is the size of the monthly payment?

12. Olivia bought a used car priced at $10 600 for 10% down and the balance in equal monthly payments over four years at 7.2% compounded monthly. How much does Olivia have to pay at the end of each month?

13. The Watsons bought a rental property valued at $50 000 by paying 20% down and mortgaging the balance over twenty-five years through equal payments at the end of each quarter at 10% compounded quarterly. What was the size of the quarterly payments?

14. Jie purchased a computer priced at $949.99, financing it by paying $75.12 on the date of purchase, and signing a contract to pay equal monthly payments over the next fifteen months. If the terms of the contract state that interest is calculated at 10.8% compounded monthly, how much does Jie have to pay at the end of each month?

15. George plans to deposit $1200 at the end of every six months for fifteen years into an RRSP account. After the last deposit, he intends to convert the existing balance into an RRIF and withdraw equal amounts at the end of every six months for twenty years. If interest is expected to be 7.5% compounded semi-annually, how much will George be able to collect every six months? Reference Example 11.4E

16. Starting three months after her grandson Robin's birth, Mrs. Devine made deposits of $60 into a trust fund every three months until Robin was twenty-one years old. The trust fund provides for equal withdrawals at the end of each quarter for four years, beginning three months after the last deposit. If interest is 4.75% compounded quarterly, how much will Robin receive every three months?

17. When his daughter was born, Mr. Dodd started depositing $200 every three months into a trust fund earning 3% compounded quarterly. Following her eighteenth birthday, Mr. Dodd's daughter is to receive equal payments at the end of each month for four years while she is at university. If interest is to be 3.9% compounded monthly after the daughter's eighteenth birthday, how much will she receive every month?

18. Mei Li invested $350 at the end of each quarter at 3.2% compounded quarterly. At the end of five years, she was able to withdraw equal amounts at the end of each quarter for nine years. How much is the size of each withdrawal?

19. Mr. Talbot deposits $1500 at the end of every six months into his RRSP. He intends to leave the money for fourteen years, then transfer the balance into a RRIF and make equal withdrawals at the end of every six months for twenty years. If interest is 2.8% compounded semi-annually, what will be the size of each withdrawal?

20. When his aunt died, Ariel inherited an annuity paying $10 000 per year into a savings account for eight years. The terms of the will state that he cannot withdraw any money for the first eight years, and then he can withdraw equal amounts at the end of each year for ten years. If interest is 4.15% compounded annually, what will be the size of each withdrawal?

11.5 FINDING THE TERM *n* OF AN ANNUITY

A. Finding the term *n* when the future value of an annuity is known

If the future value of an annuity, FV_n, the periodic payment, PMT, and the conversion rate, i, are known, you can find the term of the annuity, n, by substituting the given values in the appropriate future value formula.

For ordinary simple annuities, use Formula 11.1.

$$FV_n = PMT\left[\frac{(1+i)^n - 1}{i}\right]$$ — Formula 11.1

EXAMPLE 11.5A How long will it take for $200 deposited at the end of each quarter to amount to $5726.70 at 6% compounded quarterly?

SOLUTION FV = 5726.70; I/Y = 6; P/Y, C/Y = 4; $i = \frac{6\%}{4} = 1.5\% = 0.015$; PMT = 200.00

$$5726.70 = 200.00\left(\frac{1.015^n - 1}{0.015}\right)$$ — substituting in Formula 11.1

$$28.6335 = \frac{1.015^n - 1}{0.015}$$ — divide both sides by 200.00

$$0.429503 = 1.015^n - 1$$ — multiply both sides by 0.015

$$1.015^n = 1.429503$$ — add 1 to both sides

$$n \ln 1.015 = \ln 1.429503$$ — solve for *n* using natural logarithms

$$0.014889n = 0.357326$$

$$n = \frac{0.357326}{0.014889} = 23.999985$$

$$n = 24 \text{ (quarters)}$$

It will take 24 quarters or six years for $200 per quarter to grow to $5726.70.

Alternatively:

You can first rearrange the terms of Formula 11.1 to solve for n.

$$FV_n = PMT\left[\frac{(1+i)^n - 1}{i}\right] \quad \text{——— Formula 11.1}$$

$$\frac{FV_n}{PMT} = \frac{(1+i)^n - 1}{i} \quad \text{——— divide both sides by PMT}$$

$$(1+i)^n = \left(\frac{FV_n\, i}{PMT}\right) + 1 \quad \text{——— multiply both sides by } i \text{ and add 1 to both sides}$$

$$n \ln(1+i) = \ln[(FV_n i/PMT) + 1] \quad \text{——— solve for } n \text{ using natural logarithms}$$

$$n = \frac{\ln[(FV_n i/PMT) + 1]}{\ln(1+i)} \quad \text{——— divide both sides by } \ln(1+i)$$

$FV = 5726.70$; $i = 0.015$; $PMT = 200.00$

$$n = \frac{\ln\left[\frac{5726.70 \times 0.015}{200.00} + 1\right]}{\ln 1.015}$$

$$n = \frac{0.357326}{0.014889} = 23.999985$$

$$n = 24 \text{ (quarters)}$$

POINTERS AND PITFALLS

For annuity problems in which the period of investment or loan repayment must be determined, once n has been calculated, simply divide n by m to calculate the period of investment or loan repayment in years. To illustrate, the solution in Example 11.5A is $n = 24$. Since $m = 4$ (the question states "at the end of each quarter"), the period of investment is n/m, or $24/4 = 6$ years.

EXAMPLE 11.5B In how many payments will your bank account grow to $3000 if you deposit $150 at the end of each month and the account earns 9% compounded monthly?

SOLUTION $FV = 3000.00$; $PMT = 150.00$; $I/Y = 9$; $P/Y, C/Y = 12$; $i = \frac{9\%}{12} = 0.75\%$

(Set P/Y, C/Y = 12) 0 [PV] 3000 [FV]

150 [±] [PMT] 9 [I/Y] [CPT] [N] [18.704720]

It will take about 19 months to accumulate $3000.00.

Interpretation of Result

When FV_n, PMT, and i are known, it is unlikely that n will be a whole number. The fractional time period of 0.7 month indicates that the accumulated value of 18 deposits of \$150 will be less than \$3000, while the accumulated value of 19 deposits will be more than \$3000. This point can be verified by computing FV_{18} and FV_{19}.

$$FV_{18} = 150.00\left(\frac{1.0075^{18} - 1}{0.0075}\right) = 150.00(19.194718) = \$2879.21$$

$$FV_{19} = 150.00\left(\frac{1.0075^{19} - 1}{0.0075}\right) = 150.00(20.338679) = \$3050.80$$

The definition of an annuity does not provide for making payments at unequal time intervals. The appropriate answer to problems in which n is a fractional value is a whole number. The usual approach is to round upward, so in this case $n = 19$.

Rounding upward implies that the deposit made at the end of the nineteenth month is smaller than the usual deposit of \$150.00. The method of computing the size of the final deposit or payment when the term of the annuity is a fractional value rounded upward is considered in Chapter 14.

B. Finding the term *n* when the present value of an annuity is known

If the present value, PV_n, the periodic payment, PMT, and the conversion rate, i, are known, you can find the term of the annuity, n, by substituting the given values in the present value formula.

$$PV_n = PMT\left[\frac{1 - (1 + i)^{-n}}{i}\right] \qquad \text{Formula 11.2}$$

You can find n by first rearranging the terms of the present value formula above. Then substitute the three known values (PV, PMT, and i) into the rearranged formula and solve for n.

When using a preprogrammed financial calculator, you can find n by entering the five known values (PV, PMT, P/Y, C/Y, and I/Y) and pressing CPT N.

Note: When using the Texas Instruments BAII Plus financial calculator, you *must* enter *either* the PV or PMT as a negative amount, *but not both.* Due to the sign conventions used by this calculator, entering *both* PV and PMT as negative amounts or as positive amounts will lead to an *incorrect* final answer. The calculator does *not* indicate that the answer is incorrect or that an entry error was made. (This has not been an issue until now because either PV or PMT was 0 in all the examples we discussed.) To avoid incorrect answers, *always* enter the PV amount as a negative number and the PMT amount as a positive number when FV = 0 and you are calculating n. However, if PV = 0, enter PMT as a negative number and FV as a positive number. The examples in this text follow these rules. Refer to Appendix II to check whether this step is necessary if you use the Sharp EL-733A or the Hewlett-Packard 10B calculator.

EXAMPLE 11.5C How many quarterly payments of $600 are required to repay a loan of $5400 at 6% compounded quarterly?

SOLUTION PV = 5400.00; PMT = 600.00; I/Y = 6; P/Y, C/Y = 4; $i = \frac{6\%}{4} = 1.5\% = 0.015$

$$5400.00 = 600.00\left(\frac{1 - 1.015^{-n}}{0.015}\right) \text{ — substituting in Formula 11.2}$$

$$9.00 = \frac{1 - 1.015^{-n}}{0.015} \text{ — divide both sides by 600.00}$$

$$0.135 = 1 - 1.015^{-n} \text{ — multiply both sides by 0.015}$$

$$1.015^{-n} = 0.865$$

$$-n \ln 1.015 = \ln 0.865 \text{ — solve for } n \text{ using natural logarithms}$$

$$-0.014889n = -0.145026$$

$$n = \frac{-0.145026}{-0.014889}$$

$$n = 9.740718$$

$$n = 10 \text{ quarters}$$

To repay the loan, 10 quarterly payments are required.

Alternatively:

You can first rearrange the terms of Formula 11.2 to solve for n.

$$PV_n = PMT\left[\frac{1 - (1 + i)^{-n}}{i}\right] \text{ — Formula 11.2}$$

$$\frac{PV_n}{PMT} = \frac{1 - (1 + i)^{-n}}{i} \text{ — divide both sides by PMT}$$

$$\left(\frac{PV_n i}{PMT}\right) - 1 = -(1 + i)^{-n} \text{ — multiply both sides by } i \text{ and subtract 1 from both sides}$$

$$(1 + i)^{-n} = 1 - \left(\frac{PV_n i}{PMT}\right) \text{ — multiply both sides by } -1$$

$$-n \ln(1 + i) = \ln\left[1 - \left(\frac{PV_n i}{PMT}\right)\right] \text{ — solve for } n \text{ using natural logarithms}$$

$$n = \frac{\ln\left[1 - \left(\frac{PV_n i}{PMT}\right)\right]}{-\ln(1 + i)} \text{ — divide both sides by } -\ln(1+i)$$

PV = 5400.00; PMT = 600.00; $i = 0.015$

$$n = \frac{\ln\left[1 - \frac{(5400.00)(0.015)}{600.00}\right]}{-\ln(1.015)} \text{ — substituting in rearranged Formula 11.2}$$

$$n = \frac{-0.145026}{-0.014889}$$

$$n = 9.740718$$

$$n = 10 \text{ quarters}$$

EXAMPLE 11.5D

On his retirement, Art received a bonus of \$8000 from his employer. Taking advantage of the existing tax legislation, he invested the money in an annuity that provides for semi-annual payments of \$1200 at the end of every six months. If interest is 6.25% compounded semi-annually, how long will the annuity exist?

SOLUTION

$PV = 8000.00$; $PMT = 1200.00$; $I/Y = 6.25$; $P/Y, C/Y = 2$; $i = \frac{6.25\%}{2} = 3.125\%$

(Set P/Y, C/Y = 2) 0 [FV] 8000 [±] [PV]

1200 [PMT] 6.25 [I/Y] [CPT] [N] [7.591884]

$n = 7.591884 = 8$ half-years $\div 2 = 4$ years

half-year periods

The annuity will be in existence for four years. Art will receive seven half-yearly payments of \$1200 and a final payment that will be less than \$1200.

EXERCISE 11.5

EXCEL NOTES

If you choose, you can use Excel's Number of Compounding Periods (NPER) function to answer all of the questions below. Refer to NPER on MathXL to learn how to use this Excel function.

EXCEL SPREADSHEET

A. Find the term of each of the following ten ordinary annuities. (State your answer in years and months.)

	Future Value	Present Value	Periodic Rent	Payment Interval	Interest Rate	Conversion Period
1.	\$20 000	–	\$ 800	1 year	7.5%	annually
2.	17 000	–	35	1 month	9	monthly
3.	–	\$14 500	190	1 month	5.25	monthly
4.	–	5 000	300	3 months	4	quarterly
5.	3 600	–	175	6 months	7.4	semi-annually
6.	–	9 500	740	1 quarter	5.2	quarterly
7.	–	21 400	1660	6 months	4.5	semi-annually
8.	13 600	–	140	3 months	8	quarterly
9.	\$7 200	–	90	1 month	3.75	monthly
10.	–	\$9 700	\$315	3 months	11	quarterly

EXCEL SPREADSHEET

B. Answer each of the following questions.

1. How many months would it take you to save \$4500 by making deposits of \$50 at the end of every month into a savings account earning 6% compounded monthly? Reference Example 11.5A

2. How many months will it take to save \$5000 by making deposits of \$60 at the end of every month into an account earning interest at 6% monthly?

3. Suppose \$646.56 is deposited at the end of every six months into an account earning 6.5% compounded semi-annually. If the balance in the account four years after the last deposit is to be \$20 000, how many deposits are needed?

4. How long does \$1000 have to be deposited into a savings account at the end of each month to accumulate to \$36 000 if interest is 6.4% compounded monthly?

5. Through a payroll savings plan, Brooke saved \$96 at the end of each month. If the account earns interest at 3.6% compounded monthly, how long will it take to save \$3600?

6. For how long will Amir need to make payments of \$400 at the end of every three months to save a total of \$5000 if interest is 1.7% compounded quarterly?

7. Josie borrowed \$8000 compounded monthly to help finance her education. She contracted to repay the loan in monthly payments of \$300 each. If the payments are due at the end of each month and interest is 4% compounded monthly, how long will Josie have to make monthly payments?

8. A mortgage of \$26 500 is to be repaid by making payments of \$1560 at the end of every six months. If interest is 7% compounded semi-annually, what is the term of the mortgage?

9. A car loan of \$12 000 is to be repaid with end-of-month payments of \$292.96. If interest is 8% compounded monthly, how long is the term of the loan?

10. A deposit of \$4000 is made today. For how long can \$500 be withdrawn from the account at the end of every three months starting three months from now if interest is 4% compounded quarterly? Reference Example 11.5D

11. Lauren deposited \$12 000 today. He plans to withdraw \$1100 every six months. For how long can he withdraw from the account starting six months from now if interest is 3.9% compounded semi-annually?

12. Cathy placed \$7000 into a savings account. For how long can \$800 be withdrawn from the account at the end of every month starting one month from now if interest is 4.58% compounded monthly?

13. Rae deposited \$5741, the earnings from her part-time job, into a savings account. If she withdraws \$650 at the end of each month, how long will the money last if interest is 5.15% compounded monthly?

14. Kaye deposited \$6000 into a savings account today. For how long can \$730 be withdrawn from the account at the end of every three months starting three months from now if interest is 3.9% compounded quarterly?

11.6 FINDING THE PERIODIC RATE OF INTEREST *i* USING PREPROGRAMMED FINANCIAL CALCULATORS

A. Finding the periodic rate of interest *i* for simple annuities

Preprogrammed financial calculators are especially helpful when solving for the conversion rate i. Determining i without a financial calculator is extremely time-consuming. However, it *can* be done by hand, as illustrated in Appendix II on the MathXL.

When the future value, FV, or present value, PV, the periodic payment, PMT, and the term, n, of an annuity are known, the periodic rate of interest, i, can be found by entering the three known values into a preprogrammed financial calculator. (Remember, if both PV and PMT are non-zero, enter PV only as a negative amount.) For ordinary simple annuities, retrieve the answer by pressing CPT I/Y . This represents the nominal annual rate of interest, j. By dividing j by the number of compounding periods per year, m or C/Y, you can obtain the periodic interest rate, i.

EXAMPLE 11.6A

Compute the nominal annual rate of interest at which \$100 deposited at the end of each month for ten years will amount to \$15 000.

SOLUTION

$FV_n = 15\,000.00$; PMT = 100.00; P/Y, C/Y = 12; $n = 120$; $m = 12$

(Set P/Y, C/Y = 12) 0 PV 15 000 FV 100 ± PMT

120 N CPT I/Y 4.350057

Allow several seconds for the computation.

The nominal annual rate of interest is 4.3501% compounded monthly. The monthly conversion rate is approximately 4.3501/12 = 0.362505%.

EXAMPLE 11.6B

A loan of \$6000 is paid off over five years by monthly payments of \$120.23. What is the nominal annual rate of interest on the loan?

SOLUTION

$PV_n = 6000.00$; PMT = 120.23; P/Y, C/Y = 12; $n = 60$; $m = 12$

(Set P/Y, C/Y = 12) 0 FV 6000 ± PV 120.23 PMT

60 N CPT I/Y 7.50081

Allow several seconds for the computation.

The nominal annual rate of interest is 7.50081% compounded monthly. The monthly compounding rate is approximately 7.50081/12 = 0.625067%.

EXERCISE 11.6

EXCEL SPREADSHEET

Compute the nominal annual rate of interest for each of the following eight ordinary simple annuities.

	Future Value	Present Value	Periodic Payment	Payment Interval	Term	Conversion Period
1.	$ 9 000	–	$ 230.47	3 months	8 years	quarterly
2.	4 800	–	68.36	1 month	5 years	monthly
3.	–	$ 7 400	119.06	1 month	7 years	monthly
4.	–	6 980	800.00	6 months	5 years	semi-annually
5.	70 000	–	1014.73	1 year	25 years	annually
6.	–	42 000	528.00	1 month	10 years	monthly
7.	–	$28 700	2015.00	6 months	15 years	semi-annually
8.	$36 000	–	584.10	3 months	12 years	quarterly

EXCEL SPREADSHEET

Answer each of the following questions.

1. Compute the nominal annual rate of interest at which $350 paid at the end of every three months for six years accumulates to $12 239.76. Reference Example 11.6A

2. Katrina contributed $2500 at the end of every year into an RRSP for ten years. What nominal annual rate of interest will the RRSP earn if the balance in Katrina's account just after she made her last contribution was $33 600?

3. What nominal annual rate of interest compounded monthly was paid if contributions of $250 made into an RRSP at the end of every month amounted to $35 000 after ten years?

4. Compute the nominal annual rate of interest compounded monthly at which $400 paid at the end of the month for eight years accumulates to $45 000.

5. What is the nominal annual rate of interest if a four-year loan of $6000 is repaid by end-of-month payments of $144.23? Reference Example 11.6B

6. Rita converted an RRSP balance of $119 875.67 into a RRIF that will pay her $1800 at the end of every month for nine years. What is the nominal annual rate of interest?

7. What is the nominal annual rate of interest compounded quarterly if a loan of $21 500 is repaid in seven years by payments of $1000 made at the end of every three months?

8. A car valued at $11 400 can be purchased for 10% down and end-of-month payments of $286.21 for three-and-a-half years. What is the nominal annual rate of interest?

9. Property worth $50 000 can be purchased for 20% down and mortgage payments of $1000 at the end of each quarter for 25 years. What nominal annual rate of interest is charged?

10. A property worth $35 000 is purchased for 10% down and payments of $2100 at the end of every six months for twelve years. What is the nominal annual rate of interest?

Go to MathXL at www.mathXL.com. You can practise many of this chapter's exercises as often as you want. The guided solutions help you find an answer step by step. You'll find a personalized study plan available to you too!

Review Exercise

1. Payments of $360 are made into a fund at the end of every three months for twelve years. The fund earns interest at 7% compounded quarterly.
   (a) What will be the balance in the fund after twelve years?
   (b) How much of the balance is deposits?
   (c) How much of the balance is interest?
2. Pearson sets up a fund to pay $1000 at the end of each month for 9.5 years. Interest on the fund is 3.9% compounded monthly.
   (a) How much money must be deposited into the fund?
   (b) How much will be paid out of the fund?
   (c) How much interest is earned by the fund?
3. If a loan was repaid by payments of $320 at the end of each quarter in five years at 8% compounded quarterly, how much money had been borrowed?
4. How much interest is included in the accumulated value of $75.90 paid at the end of each month for four years if interest is 9% compounded monthly?
5. How long will it take to build up a fund of $10 000 by saving $300 at the end of every six months at 4.5% compounded semi-annually?
6. A car loan of $25 000 is repaid by end-of-month payments of $463.43. If interest is 7.5% compounded monthly, for how long are the payments made?
7. Maria has set a goal to save $10 000 in a savings account that earns 2.4% compounded annually. How much must she deposit each year for five years if the deposits are made at the end of each year?
8. A fund of $30 000 has been set up to pay for Edwin's music lessons over the next twelve years. If interest is 6.21% compounded monthly, what is the size of each month-end withdrawal from the fund?
9. If you contribute $1500 into a vacation account at the end of every six months for four years and interest on the deposits is 4.26% compounded semi-annually, how much would the balance in the account be six years after the last contribution?
10. Doris purchased a piano with $300 down and end-of-month payments of $124 for two-and-a-half years at 9% compounded monthly. What was the purchase price of the piano?
11. A contract valued at $11 500 requires payment of $1450 at the end of every six months. If interest is 10.5% compounded semi-annually, what is the term of the contract?
12. What nominal annual rate of interest is paid on RRSP contributions of $1100 made at the end of each quarter for fifteen years if the balance just after the last contribution is $106 000?
13. What nominal annual rate of interest was charged on a loan of $5600 repaid in end-of-month installments of $121.85 in four-and-a-half years?
14. Glenn has made contributions of $250 at the end of every three months into an RRSP for ten years. Interest for the first four years was 4% compounded quarterly. Since then the interest rate has been 5% compounded quarterly. How much will Glenn have in his RRSP three years after the last contribution?
15. Avi expects to retire in twelve years. Beginning one month after his retirement he would like to receive $500 per month for twenty years. How much must he deposit into a fund today to be able to do so if the rate of interest on the deposit is 6% compounded monthly?
16. A contract is signed requiring payments of $750 at the end of every three months for eight years. How much is the cash value of the contract if money is worth 9% compounded quarterly?
17. The amount of $10 000 is put into a four-year term deposit paying 3.5% compounded semi-annually. After four years the deposit is converted into an ordinary annuity of equal

semi-annual payments of $932 each. If the interest rate remains the same, what is the term of the annuity?

18. Harleen has deposited $125 at the end of each month for 13 years at 4.68% compounded monthly. After her last deposit she converted the balance into an ordinary annuity paying $890 every three months for nine years. What is the nominal annual rate of interest compounded quarterly paid by the annuity?

19. A contract is signed requiring payments of $2750 at the end of every year for six years. How much is the cash value of the contract if money is worth 6.82% compounded annually?

20. Over fourteen years, Casey has saved $7200 by authorizing $30 to be deduced at the end of every month through a payroll deduction plan at his work. The money was sent to his savings account to be invested.
    (a) What is the nominal annual rate of interest compounded monthly on the savings plan?
    (b) If, after the fourteen years, he withdraws $135 at the end of each month, what is the term of the annuity?

Self-Test

EXCEL SPREADSHEET

1. You won $100 000 in a lottery and you want to set some of that sum aside for ten years. After ten years, you would like to receive $2400 at the end of every three months for eight years. How much of your winnings must you set aside if interest is 5.5% compounded quarterly?

2. A sum of money is deposited at the end of every month for ten years at 7.5% compounded monthly. After the last deposit, interest for the account is to be 6% compounded quarterly and the account is to be paid out by quarterly payments of $4800 over six years. What is the size of the monthly deposit?

3. Compute the nominal annual rate of interest compounded semi-annually on a loan of $48 000 repaid in installments of $4000 at the end of every six months in ten years.

4. A loan of $14 400 is to be repaid in end-of-the-quarter payments of $600. How many payments are required to repay the loan at 10.5% compounded quarterly?

5. The amount of $574 is invested monthly at 6% compounded monthly for six years. The balance in the fund is then converted into an annuity paying $3600 at the end of every three months. If interest on the annuity is 5.9% compounded quarterly, for how many months is the term of the annuity?

6. A loan was repaid in seven years by end-of-month payments of $450. If interest was 12% compounded monthly, how much interest was paid?

7. Ms. Simms made deposits of $540 at the end of every three months into a savings account. For the first five years interest was 5% compounded quarterly. Since then the rate of interest has been 5.5% compounded quarterly. How much is the account balance after thirteen years?

8. How much interest is included in the accumulated value of $3200 paid at the end of every six months for four years if the interest rate is 6.5% compounded semi-annually?

9. What is the size of deposits made at the end of each period that will accumulate to $67 200 after eight years at 6.5% compounded semi-annually?

Challenge Problem

1. On March 1, 2012, Yves decided to save for a new truck. He deposited \$500 at the end of every three months in a bank account earning interest at 5% compounded quarterly. He made his first deposit on June 1, 2012. On June 1, 2014, Yves decided that he needed the money to go to college, so on September 1, 2014, he stopped making deposits and started withdrawing \$300 at the end of each quarter until December 1, 2015. How much is left in his account after the last withdrawal if his bank account interest rate changed to 6.5% compounded quarterly on March 1, 2015?

CASE STUDY 11.1 Saving for Your Dream

» Andrea Shertov dreams of spending an extended holiday in Thailand. If she can save enough money, she wants to have six months to travel with friends. She has done some research and determined that she would need approximately \$1800 in Canadian currency per month to achieve her dream.

At her current salary, she plans to save \$150 at the end of each month, investing it at 2.8% interest compounded monthly. She hopes to be able to take this trip three years from now.

QUESTIONS

1. If Andrea saves \$150 per month for three years, will she have enough to pay for her trip?

2. If Andrea saves the \$150 per month, and earns an interest rate of 4.6% compounded monthly, will she have enough to pay for her trip?

3. If Andrea saves \$300 per month for three years, with interest at 5.5% compounded monthly, how much will she have in her vacation investment account?

CASE STUDY 11.2 Getting the Picture

» Suzanne had a summer job working in the business office of Blast-It TV and Stereo, a local chain of home electronics stores. When Michael Jacobssen, the owner of the chain, heard she had completed one year of business courses, he asked Suzanne to calculate the profitability of two new large-screen TVs. He plans to offer a special payment plan for the two new models to attract customers to his stores. He wants to heavily promote the more profitable TV.

When Michael gave Suzanne the information about the two TVs, he told her to ignore all taxes when making her calculations. The cost of TV A to the company is $1950 and the cost of TV B to the company is $2160, after all trade discounts have been taken. The company plans to sell TV A for a $500 down payment and $230 per month for twelve months, beginning one month from the date of the purchase. The company plans to sell TV B for a $100 down payment and $260 per month for eighteen months, beginning one month from the date of purchase. The monthly payments for both TVs reflect an interest rate of 15.5% compounded monthly.

Michael wants Suzanne to calculate the profit of TV A and TV B as a percent of the TV's cost to the company. To calculate profit, Michael deducts overhead (which he calculates as 15% of cost) and the cost of the item from the selling price of the item. When he sells items that are paid for at a later time, he calculates the selling price as the *cash value* of the item. (Remember that cash value equals the down payment plus the present value of the periodic payments.)

Suzanne realized that she could calculate the profitability of each TV by using her knowledge of ordinary annuities. She went to work on her assignment to provide Michael with the information he requested.

QUESTIONS

1. **(a)** What is the cash value of TV A? Round your answer to the nearest dollar.

(b) What is the cash value of TV B? Round your answer to the nearest dollar.

2. **(a)** Given Michael's system of calculations, how much overhead should be assigned to TV A?

(b) How much overhead should be assigned to TV B?

3. **(a)** According to Michael's system of calculations, what is the profit of TV A as a percent of its cost?

(b) What is the profit of TV B as a percent of its cost?

(c) Which TV should Suzanne recommend be more heavily promoted?

4. Three months later, due to Blast-It's successful sales of TV A and TV B, the suppliers of each model gave the company new volume discounts. For TV A, Blast-It received a discount of 9% off its current cost, and for TV B one of 6%. The special payment plans for TV A and TV B will stay the same. Under these new conditions, which TV should Suzanne recommend be more heavily promoted?

SUMMARY OF FORMULAS

Formula 9.1A

$FV = PV(1 + i)^n$ — **Finding the future value of a compound amount (maturity value) when the original principal, the rate of interest, and the time period are known**

Formula 9.1C

$PV = FV(1 + i)^{-n}$ — **Finding the present value by means of the discount factor (the reciprocal of the compounding factor)**

Formula 11.1

$$FV_n = PMT\left[\frac{(1 + i)^n - 1}{i}\right]$$

Finding the future value (accumulated value) of an ordinary simple annuity

Formula 11.2

$$PV_n = PMT\left[\frac{1 - (1 + i)^{-n}}{i}\right]$$

Finding the present value (discounted value) of an ordinary simple annuity

GLOSSARY

Accumulated value of one dollar per period *see* **Accumulation factor for annuities**

Accumulation factor for annuities the factor $\frac{(1 + i)^n - 1}{i}$ *(p. 425)*

Annuity a series of payments, usually equal in size, made at equal periodic time intervals *(p. 420)*

Annuity certain an annuity for which the term is fixed *(p. 421)*

Annuity due an annuity in which the periodic payments are made at the beginning of each payment interval *(p. 420)*

Compounding factor for annuities *see* **Accumulation factor for annuities**

Contingent annuity an annuity in which the term is uncertain; that is, either the beginning date of the term or the ending date of the term or both are unknown *(p. 421)*

Deferred annuity an annuity in which the first payment is delayed for a number of payment periods *(p. 421)*

Discount factor the factor $\frac{1 - (1 + i)^{-n}}{i}$ *(p. 436)*

Discounted value of one dollar per period *see* **Discount factor**

Down payment the portion of the purchase price that is supplied by the purchaser as an initial payment *(p. 438)*

General annuity an annuity in which the conversion (or compounding) period is different from the payment interval *(p. 420)*

Ordinary annuity an annuity in which the payments are made at the end of each payment interval *(p. 420)*

Payment interval the length of time between successive payments *(p. 420)*

Payment period *see* **Payment interval**

Periodic rent the size of the regular periodic payment *(p. 420)*

Perpetuity an annuity for which the payments continue forever *(p. 421)*

Simple annuity an annuity in which the conversion period is the same as the payment interval *(p. 420)*

Term of an annuity the length of time from the beginning of the first payment interval to the end of the last payment interval *(p. 420)*

USEFUL INTERNET SITES

www.canadianbusiness.com

Annuity Rates Based on several Canadian financial publications, this site provides discussion and figures for annuities, mutual funds, and estate planning.

www.nmfn.com/tn/learnctr-lifeevents-longevity

The Longevity Game Click on "Learning Centre/The Longevity Game" to predict your life expectancy with this game on Northwestern Mutual Financial Network's site. Life expectancy is used to calculate life insurance rates.

finance.sympatico.msn.ca

RRSP This site provides information on advantages and disadvantages of RRSPs, including a calculator to determine tax savings. Some U.S. news is included.

CHAPTER 12

Ordinary General Annuities

OBJECTIVES

Upon completing this chapter, you will be able to do the following:

1. Compute the future value (or accumulated value) for ordinary general annuities.
2. Compute the present value (or discounted value) for ordinary general annuities.
3. Compute the payment for ordinary general annuities.
4. Compute the number of periods for ordinary general annuities.
5. Compute the interest rate for ordinary general annuities.

We often encounter situations when the frequency of interest compounding is not the same as the frequency of the payment in an annuity. In these cases, we are dealing with a general annuity. The interest rate will have to be adjusted to reflect the rate per payment period. When the payment is made at the end of the period, we have an ordinary general annuity. To make informed decisions about different payment options, we need to understand these annuities.

INTRODUCTION

In Chapter 11, we calculated values for ordinary simple annuities. In this chapter, we will calculate the future value, present value, payment, term, and interest rate for ordinary general annuities. The relationship between the payment interval and the interest conversion period will be analyzed. New formulas for ordinary general annuities will be introduced, and rearranged. Alternatively, preprogrammed calculators will be used to determine results.

12.1 ORDINARY GENERAL ANNUITIES—FINDING THE FUTURE VALUE FV

A. Basic concepts and computation

With ordinary simple annuities, as in Chapter 11, the payment interval and the interest conversion period are the same length. Often, however, interest is compounded more or less frequently than payments are made. For example, payments may be made weekly or monthly, whereas interest may be compounded less frequently, such as annually.

When the length of the interest conversion period is different from the length of the payment interval, these annuities are called *general annuities.*

To solve compound interest problems, the basic method uses equivalent sets of financial obligations at a selected focal date. The essential tool when dealing with any kind of annuity is the equation of value. This approach is used to make basic computations and develop useful formulas.

EXAMPLE 12.1A

What is the accumulated value of $100 deposited at the end of every six months for three years if interest is 4% compounded annually?

SOLUTION

Since the payments are made semi-annually while the compounding is done annually, this annuity is classified as a general annuity. Furthermore, since the payments are at the end of each payment interval, the annuity is an ordinary general annuity. While the difference in the length of the payment period compared to the length of the compounding period introduces a mathematical complication, the basic approach to finding the amount of the ordinary general annuity is the same as that used in finding the amount of an ordinary simple annuity.

The basic solution and data for the problem are shown graphically in Figure 12.1. Since deposits are made at the end of every six months for three years, there are six deposits of $100 at the times indicated. Because interest is compounded annually, I/Y = 4%, P/Y = 2, C/Y = 1, $i = 4\% = 0.04$, and there are three conversion periods.

FIGURE 12.1 **Graphical Representation of Method and Data**

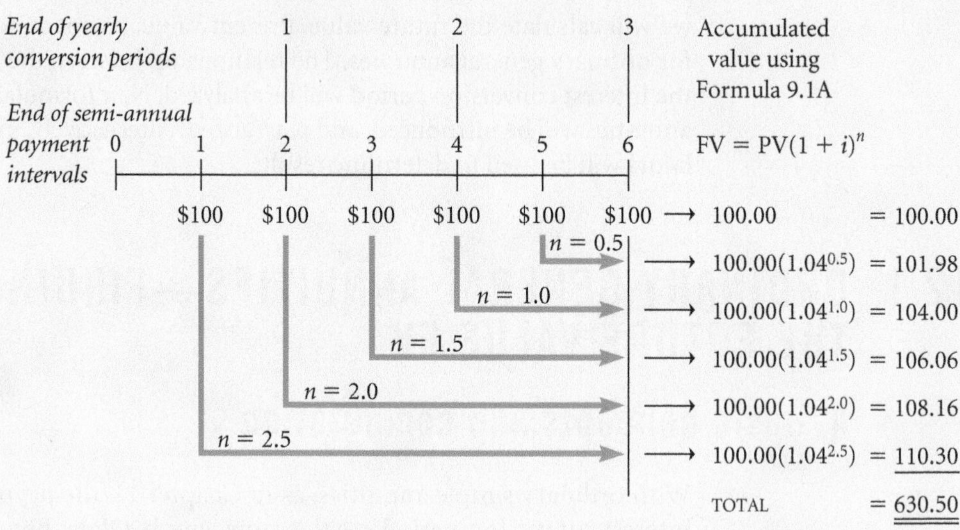

The focal point is at the end of Year 3. The last deposit is made at the focal date and has a value of $100 on that date. The fifth deposit is made after 2.5 years and, in terms of conversion periods, has accumulated for a half conversion period ($n = 0.5$); its accumulated value is $100.00(1.04^{0.5}) = \$101.98$ at the focal date.

The fourth deposit made after two years has accumulated for one conversion period ($n = 1.0$); its accumulated value at the focal date is $100.00(1.04^{1.0}) = \$104.00$. Similarly, the accumulated value of the third deposit is $100.00(1.04^{1.5}) = \$106.06$, while the accumulated value of the second deposit is $100.00(1.04^{2.0}) = \$108.16$. Finally, the accumulated value of the first deposit is $100.00(1.04^{2.5}) = \$110.30$. The total accumulated value after three years is $630.50.

EXAMPLE 12.1B What is the accumulated value of deposits of $100 made at the end of each year for four years if interest is 4% compounded quarterly?

SOLUTION Since the deposits are made at the end of every year for four years, there are four payments of $100.00 at the times shown in Figure 12.2. Since interest is compounded quarterly, I/Y = 4, P/Y, C/Y = 4, $i = \frac{4}{4}\% = 1\% = 0.01\%$, and there are $4(4) = 16$ conversion periods.

The focal point is the end of Year 4. The last payment is made at the focal point and has a value of $100 at that date. The third payment is made after three years and, in terms of conversion periods, has accumulated for four conversion periods ($n = 4$); its accumulated value is $100.00(1.01^4) = \$104.06$. The second deposit has accumulated for 8 conversion periods ($n = 8$); its accumulated value

FIGURE 12.2 **Graphical Representation of Method and Data**

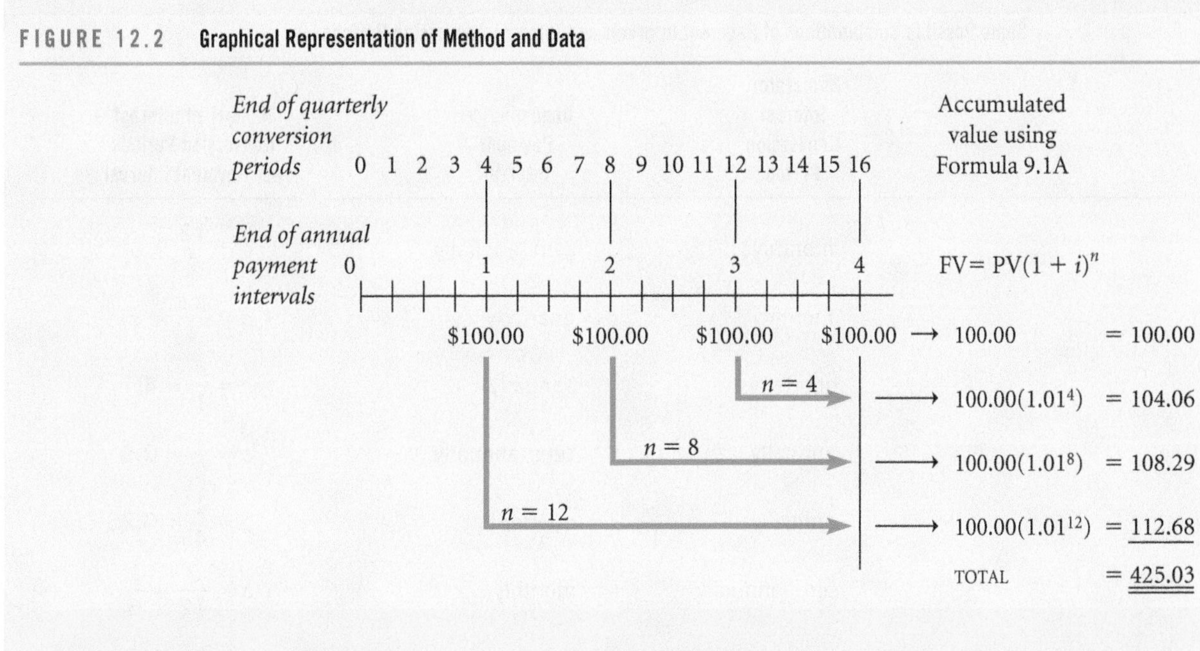

is 100.00(1.018) = \$108.29. The first deposit has accumulated for 12 conversion periods ($n = 12$); its accumulated value is 100.00(1.0112) = \$112.68. The total accumulated value of the deposits after four years is \$425.03.

B. Relationship between payment interval and interest conversion period

It is important to understand the relationship between the *payment interval* and the number of *interest conversion periods* per payment interval.

As defined in Chapter 11, the length of time between the successive payments is called the payment interval or payment period. The number of interest conversion periods per payment interval, designated by the letter c, can be determined from the following ratio:

$$c = \frac{\text{THE NUMBER OF INTEREST CONVERSION PERIODS PER YEAR}}{\text{THE NUMBER OF PAYMENT PERIODS PER YEAR}}$$

If the interest conversion period is longer than the payment period, each payment interval contains only a fraction of one conversion period. In this case, c has a fractional value.

If the interest conversion period is shorter than the payment period, each payment interval contains more than one conversion period. In this case, c has a value greater than 1.

Table 12.1 provides a sampling of possible combinations of payment intervals and interest conversion periods you might encounter when dealing with general annuities. One of the most important is the monthly payment interval combined with semi-annual compounding since this combination is usually encountered with residential mortgages in Canada.

Table 12.1 **Some Possible Combinations of Payment Intervals and Interest Conversion Periods**

Numerator: Interest Conversion Period	Denominator: Payment Interval	Number of Interest Conversion Periods per Payment Interval
monthly	semi-annually	$c = \frac{12}{2} = 6$
monthly	quarterly	$c = \frac{12}{4} = 3$
quarterly	annually	$c = \frac{4}{1} = 4$
annually	semi-annually	$c = \frac{1}{2} = 0.5$
annually	quarterly	$c = \frac{1}{4} = 0.25$
semi-annually	monthly	$c = \frac{2}{12} = \frac{1}{6}$
quarterly	monthly	$c = \frac{4}{12} = \frac{1}{3}$
annually	monthly	$c = \frac{1}{12}$

C. Computing the effective rate of interest per payment period

In Chapter 10 you were introduced to the concept of the effective rate of interest. It was defined as the nominal rate of interest compounded annually and represented by the symbol f. It can readily be determined from the periodic rate of interest i by means of Formula 10.1, $f = (1 + i)^m - 1$, where m is the number of compounding periods per year.

When dealing with general annuities, it is useful to utilize the **equivalent rate of interest per payment period.** Depending on the length of the payment interval, the equivalent interest rate per payment period may be a monthly, quarterly, semi-annual, or annual rate. It can be obtained from the periodic rate of interest i by a formula identical in nature to Formula 10.1.

We distinguish the equivalent rate of interest per payment period from the effective annual rate of interest, f, by using the symbol p for the equivalent rate of interest per payment period. It can be determined by means of Formula 12.1 that

$$p = (1 + i)^c - 1 \qquad \text{Formula 12.1}$$

$$\text{where } c = \frac{\text{THE NUMBER OF INTEREST CONVERSION PERIODS PER YEAR}}{\text{THE NUMBER OF PAYMENT PERIODS PER YEAR}}$$

EXAMPLE 12.1C

Jean receives annuity payments at the end of every six months. If she deposits these payments in an account earning interest at 9% compounded monthly, what is the equivalent semi-annually compounded rate of interest?

SOLUTION

Since the payments are made at the end of every six months while interest is compounded monthly,

$$c = \frac{\text{THE NUMBER OF INTEREST CONVERSION PERIODS PER YEAR}}{\text{THE NUMBER OF PAYMENT PERIODS PER YEAR}} = \frac{12}{2} = 6$$

$$i = \frac{9\%}{12} = 0.75\% = 0.0075$$

$$p = (1 + i)^c - 1$$

$$p = 1.0075^6 - 1$$ ——— substituting in Formula 12.1

$$p = 1.045852 - 1$$

$$p = 0.045852 = 4.5852\%$$

The rate of interest is 4.5852% per semi-annual period.

EXAMPLE 12.1D

Peel Credit Union pays 6% compounded quarterly on its Premium Savings Accounts. If Ray Ketch deposits $25 in his account at the end of every month, what is the monthly equivalent compounded rate of interest?

SOLUTION

Since the payments are made at the end of every month while interest is compounded quarterly,

$$c = \frac{4}{12} = \frac{1}{3}; \qquad i = \frac{6\%}{4} = 1.5\% = 0.015$$

$$p = 1.015^{\frac{1}{3}} - 1$$ ——— substituting in Formula 12.1

$$p = 1.004975 - 1$$

$$p = 0.004975 = 0.4975\%$$

The rate of interest is 0.4975% per month.

D. Future value of an ordinary general annuity

Determining the equivalent rate per payment period, p, allows us to treat the ordinary general annuity problem in a similar way to an ordinary simple annuity problem. The following notation will be used for an ordinary general annuity:

FV_g = the future value (or accumulated value) of an ordinary general annuity;
PMT = the size of the periodic payment;
n = the number of periodic payments;
c = the number of interest conversion periods per payment interval;
i = the interest rate per interest conversion period;
p = the equivalent rate of interest per payment period.

Substituting p for i in Formula 11.1, we obtain

$$FV_g = PMT\left[\frac{(1+p)^n - 1}{p}\right] \text{ where } p = (1+i)^c - 1$$ ——— Formula 12.2

As in Chapter 11, note the meaning of the word "payments." To determine if the payment qualifies as a periodic payment, PMT, it must fit the equal and periodic criteria. The payments must be equal amounts paid at the same time within each payment interval. If there is a single payment only, this amount would be identified as either the present value, PV, or the future value, FV.

EXAMPLE 12.1E

Determine the accumulated value after ten years of payments of $2000 made at the end of each year if interest is 6% compounded monthly.

SOLUTION

The problem is an ordinary general annuity. The payments are of equal size, $2000, and are made periodically (at the end of each year). Therefore, they are regular, periodic payments. Since there is one payment per year, over the ten years, the number of periodic payments n is 10.

$$PMT = 2000.00; \quad n = 10; \quad c = \frac{12}{1} = 12; \quad i = \frac{6\%}{12} = 0.5\% = 0.005$$

The equivalent annual rate of interest

$$p = 1.005^{12} - 1 = 1.061678 - 1 = 0.061678 = 6.1678\%$$

$$PMT = 2000.00; \quad n = 10; \quad p = 0.061678$$

$$FV = 2000.00\left(\frac{1.061678^{10} - 1}{0.061678}\right)$$ ——— substituting in Formula 12.2

$$= 2000.00(13.285114)$$

$$= \$26\,570.23$$

The accumulated value after ten years is $26 570.23.

EXAMPLE 12.1F

Crestview Farms set aside $1250 at the end of each month for the purchase of a combine. How much money will be available after five years if interest is 6.0% compounded semi-annually?

SOLUTION

This problem involves an ordinary general annuity.

$$PMT = 1250.00; \quad n = 5(12) = 60; \quad c = \frac{2}{12} = \frac{1}{6}; \quad i = \frac{6.0\%}{2} = 3.0\% = 0.03$$

The equivalent monthly rate of interest

$$p = 1.03^{\frac{1}{6}} - 1 = 1.004939 - 1 = 0.004939 = 0.4939\%$$

$$FV = 1250.00\left(\frac{1.004939^{60} - 1}{0.004939}\right)$$ ——— substituting in Formula 12.2

$$= 1250(69.5553)$$

$$= \$87\,048.66$$

After five years, the amount available is $87 048.66.

E. Using preprogrammed financial calculators to find the future value of an ordinary general annuity

When using formulas, the use of p rather than i as the rate of interest is the only difference in the solutions for the general annuity compared to the solution for a simple annuity.

When using preprogrammed financial calculators, such as the Texas Instruments BAII Plus, we must identify the following:

P/Y : the number of payment periods per year

N : the number of payments made during the term of the annuity. Remember that the N is determined by multiplying the number of years in the term by the number of payment periods per year (years × P/Y).

I/Y : the annual nominal rate of interest per year

C/Y : the number of interest compounding periods per year

In Example 12.1E, the number of payments each year is 2 and there are 20 payments (10 × 2), the annual nominal rate of interest per year is 6% and interest is compounded 4 times per year.

To set the calculator for Example 12.1E, follow these steps:

2nd P/Y 2 Enter ↓ C/Y 4 Enter 2nd QUIT

Note that each time the P/Y is changed, the C/Y automatically changes to match the P/Y. To make the C/Y different from the P/Y, it must be re-entered separately, after the changes to the P/Y have been made.

EXAMPLE 12.1G Find the future value of \$2500 deposited at the end of every six months for ten years if interest is 6% compounded quarterly.

SOLUTION PMT = 2500.00; $n = 2(10) = 20$; P/Y = 2; C/Y = 4; $c = \frac{4}{2} = 2$;

I/Y = 6; $i = \frac{6\%}{4} = 1.5\% = 0.015$

(Set P/Y = 2; C/Y = 4)

Key in	*Press*	*Display shows*
6	I/Y	6
0	PV	0
2500	± PMT	−2500
20	N	20 ——— the number of payments (number of years × P/Y)
CPT	FV	67329.89319

The amount on deposit after ten years will be \$67 329.89.

EXAMPLE 12.1H Determine the accumulated value of payments of $1250 made at the end of each quarter for eight years if interest is 5.5% compounded annually.

SOLUTION PMT = 1250.00; $n = 8(4) = 32$; P/Y = 4; C/Y = 1; $c = \frac{1}{4} = 0.25$;
I/Y = 5.5; $i = 5.5\% = 0.055$

(Set P/Y = 4; C/Y = 1) 5.5 [I/Y] 0 [PV]

1250 [±] [PMT] 32 [N] [CPT] [FV] [49599.22016]

The accumulated value of the payments is $49 599.22.

EXERCISE 12.1

EXCEL NOTES If you choose, you can use Excel's Future Value (FV) function to answer the questions indicated below. Refer to FV on MathXL to learn how to use this Excel function.

EXCEL SPREADSHEET

A. Find the future value of each of the following eight ordinary annuities.

	Periodic Payment	Payment Interval	Term	Interest Rate	Conversion Period
1.	$2500	6 months	7 years	8%	quarterly
2.	900	3 months	5 years	6	monthly
3.	72	1 month	15 years	3	semi-annually
4.	225	3 months	10 years	5	annually
5.	1750	6 months	12 years	7	annually
6.	680	1 month	3 years	9	annually
7.	7500	1 year	4 years	6	quarterly
8.	$143	1 month	9 years	4	quarterly

EXCEL SPREADSHEET

B. Answer each of the following questions.

1. Aisha saved $300 at the end of every three months. If interest is 4.10% compounded monthly, how much would she have saved after three years?
Reference Example 12.1A

2. To attend school, Sam deposits $1500 at the end of every six months for four and one-half years. What is the accumulated value of the deposits if interest is 6% compounded quarterly?

3. How much will deposits of $25 made at the end of each month amount to after ten years if interest is 5% compounded quarterly? Reference Example 12.1B

4. Rex dreams of owning a $18 500 Kawasaki Nomad motorcycle. If he saves $270 at the end of each month for five years and earns interest at 6.2% compounded quarterly, will he have saved enough money, and by how much is he over or short?

5. Mr. Tomas has contributed $1000 at the end of each year into an RRSP paying 6% compounded quarterly.
   (a) How much will Mr. Tomas have in the RRSP after ten years?
   (b) After ten years, how much of the amount is interest?

6. Kristina saves $20 at the end of each week and deposits the money in an account paying 4% compounded monthly.
   (a) How much will she accumulate in 10 years?
   (b) How much of the accumulated amount is interest?

7. Edwin Ng has made deposits of $500 into his savings account at the end of every three months for ten years. If interest is 4.5% compounded semi-annually and if he leaves the accumulated balance for another five years, what will be the balance in his account then?

8. Mrs. Cook has made deposits of $950 at the end of every six months for fifteen years. If interest is 3% compounded monthly, how much will Mrs. Cook have accumulated ten years after the last deposit?

9. For the last four years, Joely has authorized the payroll department at her work to deduct $30 per week to be placed into an RRSP account. If interest is 5.17% compounded monthly, how much has Joely accumulated in her RRSP?

10. Clark's younger brother has saved $18 per month from his paper route for the last two years. If interest is 4% compounded quarterly, how much will he have accumulated in his savings account?

12.2 ORDINARY GENERAL ANNUITIES—FINDING THE PRESENT VALUE PV

A. Present value of an ordinary general annuity using the equivalent rate of interest per payment period

As with the future value of an ordinary general annuity, we can convert the given periodic rate of interest i into the effective rate of interest per payment period.

$$p = (1 + i)^c - 1$$

The use of p converts the ordinary general annuity problem into an ordinary simple annuity problem.

Substituting p for i in Formula 11.2, we obtain

$$PV_g = PMT\left[\frac{1 - (1 + p)^{-n}}{p}\right]$$ —— **Formula 12.3**

EXAMPLE 12.2A A loan is repaid by making payments of \$2000 at the end of every six months for twelve years. If interest on the loan is 8% compounded quarterly, what was the principal of the loan?

SOLUTION

$\text{PMT} = 2000.00;\quad n = 12(2) = 24;\quad \text{P/Y} = 2;\quad \text{C/Y} = 4;\quad c = \frac{4}{2} = 2;$

$\text{I/Y} = 8;\quad i = \frac{8\%}{4} = 2\% = 0.02$

The equivalent semi-annual rate of interest

$p = 1.02^2 - 1 = 1.0404 - 1 = 0.0404 = 4.04\%$

$$\text{PV} = 2000.00\left(\frac{1 - 1.0404^{-24}}{0.0404}\right)$$ ——— substituting in Formula 12.3

$$= 2000.00(15.184713)$$
$$= \$30\,369.43$$

The loan principal was \$30 369.43.

EXAMPLE 12.2B A second mortgage requires payments of \$370 at the end of each month for fifteen years. If interest is 8% compounded semi-annually, what was the amount borrowed?

SOLUTION

$\text{PMT} = 370.00;\quad n = 15(12) = 180;\quad \text{P/Y} = 12;\quad \text{C/Y} = 2;\quad c = \frac{2}{12} = \frac{1}{6};$

$\text{I/Y} = 8;\quad i = \frac{8\%}{2} = 4\% = 0.04$

The equivalent monthly rate of interest

$p = 1.04^{\frac{1}{6}} - 1 = 1.006558 - 1 = 0.006558 = 0.6558\%$

$$\text{PV} = 370.00\left(\frac{1 - 1.006558^{-180}}{0.006558}\right)$$ ——— substituting in Formula 12.3

$$= 370.00(105.468216)$$
$$= \$39\,023.24$$

The amount borrowed was \$39 023.24.

B. Using preprogrammed financial calculators to find the present value of an ordinary general annuity

STEP 1 Set P/Y as the number of payment periods per year.

STEP 2 Set C/Y as the number of interest compounding periods per year.

STEP 3 Determine the number of payments made during the term of the annuity by multiplying the number of years in the term by the number of payment periods per year (years × P/Y).

STEP 4 Set I/Y as the annual nominal rate of interest per year.

EXAMPLE 12.2C

A contract is fulfilled by making payments of \$8500 at the end of every year for fifteen years. If interest is 7% compounded quarterly, what is the cash price of the contract?

SOLUTION

PMT = 8500.00; $n = 15$; P/Y = 1; C/Y = 4; $c = 4$; I/Y = 7;

$$i = \frac{7\%}{4} = 1.75\% = 0.0175$$

(Set P/Y = 1; C/Y = 4) 7 [I/Y] 0 [FV] 8500 [±] [PMT]

15 [N] [CPT] [PV] 76516.37862

The cash price of the contract is \$76 516.38.

EXAMPLE 12.2D

A 25-year mortgage on a house requires payments of \$915.60 at the end of each month. If interest is 5.5% compounded semi-annually, what was the mortgage principal?

SOLUTION

PMT = 915.60; $n = 25(12) = 300$; P/Y = 12; C/Y = 2; $c = \frac{2}{12} = \frac{1}{6}$;

I/Y = 5.5; $i = \frac{5.5\%}{2} = 2.75\% = 0.0275$

(Set P/Y = 12; C/Y = 2) 5.5 [I/Y] 0 [FV] 915.60 [±] [PMT]

300 [N] [CPT] [PV] 150002.09

The mortgage principal was \$150 002.09.

EXERCISE 12.2

EXCEL NOTES If you choose, you can use Excel's Present Value (PV) function to answer the questions indicated below. Refer to PV on MathXL to learn how to use this Excel function.

EXCEL SPREADSHEET 

A. Find the present value of the following eight ordinary annuities.

	Periodic Payment	Payment Interval	Term	Interest Rate	Conversion Period
1.	\$1400	3 months	12 years	6%	monthly
2.	6000	1 year	9 years	10	quarterly
3.	3000	3 months	4 years	6	annually
4.	200	1 month	2 years	5	semi-annually
5.	95	1 month	5 years	4.5	annually
6.	975	6 months	8 years	8	annually
7.	1890	6 months	15 years	7	quarterly
8.	\$155	1 month	10 years	8	quarterly

EXCEL SPREADSHEET

B. Answer each of the following questions.

1. Find the present value of payments of $250 made at the end of every three months for twelve years if money is worth 3% compounded monthly.

Reference Example 12.2A

2. What is the discounted value of $1560 paid at the end of each year for nine years if interest is 6% compounded quarterly?

3. What cash payment is equivalent to making payments of $825 at the end of every three months for 16 years if interest is 7% compounded semi-annually?

Reference Example 12.2B

4. What is the principal from which $175 can be withdrawn at the end of each month for twenty years if interest is 5% compounded quarterly?

5. A property was purchased for $5000 down and payments of $2500 at the end of every six months for six years. Interest is 6% compounded monthly.
   (a) What was the purchase price of the property?
   (b) How much is the cost of financing?

6. A car was purchased for $1500 down and payments of $265 at the end of each month for four years. Interest is 9% compounded quarterly.
   (a) What was the purchase price of the car?
   (b) How much interest will be paid?

7. Corey makes payments of $715.59 at the end of each month to repay a 25-year mortgage. If interest is 5.6% compounded semi-annually, what was the original mortgage principal?

8. Langara Woodcraft borrowed money to purchase equipment. The loan is repaid by making payments of $924.37 at the end of every three months over seven years. If interest is 7.3% compounded annually, what was the original loan balance?

9. Dale purchased a retirement annuity paying $1800 every six months for twenty years. If interest is 4.6% compounded monthly, how much did Dale invest in the annuity?

10. For her daughter's education, Georgina Harcourt has invested an inheritance in a fund paying 5.2% compounded quarterly. If ordinary annuity payments of $178 per month are to be made out of the fund for eight years, how much was the inheritance?

11. As a settlement for an insurance claim, Craig was offered one of two choices. He could either accept a lump-sum amount of $5000 now, or accept quarterly payments of $145 for the next ten years. If the money is placed into a trust fund earning 3.95% compounded semi-annually, which is the better option and by how much?

12. Carl Hightop, a popular basketball player, has been offered a two-year salary deal. He can either accept $2 000 000 now or accept monthly amounts of $100 000 payable at the end of each month. If money can be invested at 5.7% compounded quarterly, which option is the better option for Carl and by how much?

12.3 ORDINARY GENERAL ANNUITIES—FINDING THE PERIODIC PAYMENT PMT

A. Finding the periodic payment PMT when the future value of a general annuity is known

If the future value of a general annuity FV_g, the number of conversion periods n, and the conversion rate i are known, you can find the periodic payment PMT by substituting the given values in the future value Formula 12.2.

$$FV_g = PMT\left[\frac{(1+p)^n - 1}{p}\right] \text{ where } p = (1+i)^c - 1$$ ——— Formula 12.2

To find PMT, rearrange the terms of the future value formulas as shown below. Then substitute the three known values (FV, n, and i) into the rearranged formula and use the calculator to solve for PMT.

$$FV_g = PMT\left[\frac{(1+p)^n - 1}{p}\right]$$ ——— Formula 12.2

$$PMT = \frac{FV_g}{\left[\frac{(1+p)^n - 1}{p}\right]}$$ ——— divide both sides by $\left[\frac{(1+p)^n - 1}{p}\right]$

$$PMT = \frac{FV_g p}{(1+p)^n - 1}$$ ——— Formula 12.2A: dividing by a fraction is the same as inverting the fraction and multiplying

When using a preprogrammed financial calculator, you can find PMT by entering the five known values (FV, N, I/Y, P/Y, and C/Y) and pressing CPT PMT.

Recall that the PMT amount will be negative since payments are considered to be cash outflows.

EXAMPLE 12.3A What sum of money must be deposited at the end of every three months into an account paying 6% compounded monthly to accumulate to \$25 000 in ten years?

SOLUTION FV = 25 000.00; $n = 10(4) = 40$; P/Y = 4; C/Y = 12; $c = \frac{12}{4} = 3$;

I/Y = 6; $i = 0.5\% = 0.005$

The equivalent quarterly rate of interest

$$p = 1.005^3 - 1 = 1.015075 - 1 = 0.015075 = 1.5075\%$$

$$25\,000.00 = PMT\left(\frac{1.015075^{40} - 1}{0.015075}\right)$$ ——— substituting in Formula 12.2

$$25\,000.00 = PMT(54.354225)$$

$$PMT = \frac{25\,000.00}{54.354225}$$

$$PMT = \$459.95$$

Using Formula 12.2A, which is Formula 12.2 rearranged,

$$\text{PMT} = \frac{\text{FV}_g p}{(1 + p)^n - 1}$$

$$\text{PMT} = \frac{25\,000.00(0.015075)}{1.015075^{40} - 1}$$ ——— substituting in Formula 12.2A

$$\text{PMT} = \$459.95$$

Programmed Solution

(Set P/Y = 4; C/Y = 12) [2nd] (CLR TVM) 6 [I/Y] 0 [PV]

25 000 [FV] 40 [N] [CPT] [PMT] [-459.945847]

The required quarterly deposit is $459.95.

B. Finding the periodic payment PMT when the present value of a general annuity is known

If the present value of a general annuity PV_g, the number of conversion periods n, and the conversion rate i are known, you can find the periodic payment PMT by substituting the given values in the present value Formula 12.3.

$$\text{PV}_g = \text{PMT}\left[\frac{1 - (1 + p)^{-n}}{p}\right]$$ ——— Formula 12.3

To find PMT rearrange the terms of the present value formulas. Then substitute the three known values (PV, n, and i) into the rearranged formula and solve for PMT.

$$\text{PV}_g = \text{PMT}\left[\frac{1 - (1 + p)^{-n}}{p}\right]$$ ——— Formula 12.3

$$\text{PMT} = \frac{\text{PV}_g}{\left[\frac{1 - (1 + p)^{-n}}{p}\right]}$$ ——— divide both sides by $\left[\frac{1 - (1 + p)^{-n}}{p}\right]$

$$\text{PMT} = \frac{\text{PV}_g p}{1 - (1 + p)^{-n}}$$ ——— Formula 12.3A: dividing by a fraction is the same as inverting the fraction and multiplying

When using a preprogrammed financial calculator, you can find PMT by entering the five known values (PV, N, I/Y, P/Y, and C/Y) and pressing [CPT] [PMT].

EXAMPLE 12.3B

Mr. and Mrs. White applied to their credit union for a first mortgage of $190 000 to buy a house. The mortgage is to be amortized over 25 years and interest on the mortgage is 4.9% compounded semi-annually. What is the size of the monthly payment if payments are made at the end of each month?

SOLUTION

$PV = 190\,000.00;\quad n = 25(12) = 300;\quad P/Y = 12;\quad C/Y = 2;\quad c = \frac{2}{12} = \frac{1}{6};$

$I/Y = 4.9;\quad i = \frac{4.9\%}{2} = 2.45\% = 0.0245$

The equivalent monthly rate of interest

$p = 1.0245^{\frac{1}{6}} - 1 = 1.004042 - 1 = 0.004042 = 0.4042\%$

$$190\,000.00 = PMT\left(\frac{1 - 1.004042^{-300}}{0.004042}\right) \quad \text{substituting in Formula 12.3}$$

$$190\,000.00 = PMT(173.633596)$$

$$PMT = \frac{190\,000.00}{173.633596}$$

$$PMT = \$1094.26$$

Programmed Solution

(Set P/Y = 12; C/Y = 2) 4.9 [I/Y] 0 [FV] 190 000 [±] [PV]

300 [N] [CPT] [PMT] [1094.258282]

The monthly payment due at the end of each month is $1094.26.

EXERCISE 12.3

EXCEL NOTES If you choose, you can use Excel's Payment (PMT) function to answer all of the questions below. Refer to PMT on MathXL to learn how to use this Excel function.

EXCEL SPREADSHEET

For each of the following ten ordinary general annuities, determine the size of the periodic rent.

	Future Value	Present Value	Payment Period	Term of Annuity	Interest Rate	Conversion Period
1.	$15 000		6 months	7 years, 6 mos	5.5%	annually
2.	6 000		1 quarter	9 years, 9 mos	8	monthly
3.		$12 000	12 months	15 years	4.5	semi-annually
4.		7 000	6 months	12.5 years	7.5	quarterly
5.	8 000		3 months	6 years	6.8	semi-annually
6.		$20 000	3 months	20 years	12	monthly
7.	45 000		6 months	10 years	9	quarterly
8.	35 000		1 year	15 years	4	quarterly
9.	20 000		1 month	8 years	7	semi-annually
10.	$16 500		3 months	15 years	5.75	annually

EXCEL SPREADSHEET

B. Answer each of the following questions.

1. What payment made at the end of each quarter for fifteen years will accumulate to \$12 000 at 6% compounded monthly? Reference Example 12.3A
2. What payment is required at the end of each month for five years to repay a loan of \$6000 at 7% compounded semi-annually?
3. A contract can be fulfilled by making an immediate payment of \$9500 or equal payments at the end of every six months for eight years. What is the size of the semi-annual payments at 7.4% compounded quarterly?
4. What payment made at the end of each year for eighteen years will amount to \$16 000 at 4.2% compounded monthly?
5. What payment is required at the end of each month for eighteen years to amortize a \$110 000 mortgage if interest is 5.1% compounded semi-annually? Reference Example 12.3B
6. How much must be deposited at the end of each quarter for ten years to accumulate to \$12 000 at 6% compounded monthly?
7. What payment made at the end of every three months for twenty years will accumulate to \$20 000 at 7% compounded semi-annually?
8. Derrick bought a car priced at \$9300 for 15% down and equal monthly payments for four years. If interest is 8% compounded semi-annually, what is the size of the monthly payment?
9. Harlan made equal payments at the end of each month into his RRSP. If interest in his account is 3.7% compounded annually, and the balance after fifteen years is \$10 000.28, what is the size of the monthly payment?
10. To finance the development of a new product, a company borrowed \$30 000 at 7% compounded monthly. If the loan is to be repaid in equal quarterly payments over seven years and the first payment is due three months after the date of the loan, what is the size of the quarterly payment?

12.4 ORDINARY GENERAL ANNUITIES—FINDING THE TERM *n*

A. Finding the term *n* when the future value of a general annuity is known

If the future value of a general annuity FV_g, the periodic payment PMT, and the conversion rate i are known, you can find the term of the annuity by substituting the given values in the future value Formula 12.2.

$$FV_g = PMT\left[\frac{(1+p)^n - 1}{p}\right] \text{ where } p = (1+i)^c - 1$$

Formula 12.2

To find n, rearrange the terms of the future value Formula 12.2. Then substitute the three known values (FV, PMT, and p) into the rearranged formula and solve for n.

$$FV_g = PMT\left[\frac{(1+p)^n - 1}{p}\right] \quad \text{———— Formula 12.2}$$

$$\frac{FV_g}{PMT} = \frac{(1+p)^n - 1}{p} \quad \text{———— divide both sides by PMT}$$

$$(1+p)^n = \left(\frac{FV_g p}{PMT}\right) + 1 \quad \text{———— multiply both sides by } p \text{ and add 1 to both sides}$$

$$n \ln(1+p) = \ln[(FV_g p/PMT) + 1] \quad \text{———— solve for } n \text{ using natural logarithms}$$

$$\boxed{n = \frac{\ln[FV_g p/PMT + 1]}{\ln(1+p)}} \quad \text{———— Formula 12.2B: divide both sides by } \ln(1+p)$$

When using a preprogrammed financial calculator, find n by entering the five known values (FV, PMT, I/Y, P/Y, and C/Y) and press CPT N.

Note: You must enter either the FV or PMT as a negative amount, but not *both*. Due to the sign convention programmed into the calculator, entering both FV and PMT as negative amounts or as positive amounts will lead to an incorrect result when calculating PV, N, or I/Y. The calculator may not indicate that the result is incorrect or that an entry error was made.

EXAMPLE 12.4A What period of time is required for $125 deposited at the end of each month at 11% compounded quarterly to grow to $15 000?

SOLUTION FV = 15 000.00; PMT = 125.00; P/Y = 12; C/Y = 4;

$c = \frac{4}{12} = \frac{1}{3}$; I/Y = 11; $i = \frac{11\%}{4} = 2.75\% = 0.0275$

The equivalent monthly rate of interest

$$p = 1.0275^{\frac{1}{3}} - 1 = 1.009084 - 1 = 0.009084 = 0.9084\%$$

$$15\,000.00 = 125.00\left(\frac{1.009084^n - 1}{0.009084}\right) \quad \text{———— using Formula 12.2}$$

$$120.00 = \frac{(1.009084^n - 1)}{0.009084}$$

$$1.090068 = 1.009084^n - 1$$

$$1.009084^n = 2.090068$$

$$n \ln 1.009084 = \ln 2.090068$$

$$n(0.009043) = 0.737197$$

$$n = \frac{0.737197}{0.009043}$$

$n = 81.522240$
$n = 82$ months

With a preprogrammed calculator, the procedure is

(Set P/Y = 12; C/Y = 4) 11 I/Y 0 PV 15 000 FV

125 ± PMT CPT N 81.522240

It will take 82 months to accumulate $15 000. For the first 81 months, the payment is $125. A smaller amount would be needed for the 82nd payment.

B. Finding the term *n* when the present value of a general annuity is known

If the present value of a general annuity PV_g, the periodic payment PMT, and the conversion rate i are known, you can find the term of the annuity n by substituting the given values in the present value Formula 12.3.

$$PV_g = PMT\left[\frac{1-(1+p)^{-n}}{p}\right]$$ ——— **Formula 12.3**

Alternatively, you can first rearrange the terms of Formula 12.3 to solve for n.

$$\frac{PV_g}{PMT} = \frac{1-(1+p)^{-n}}{p}$$ ——— divide both sides by PMT

$$\left(\frac{PV_g p}{PMT}\right) = 1-(1+p)^{-n}$$ ——— multiply both sides by p and subtract 1 from both sides

$$(1+p)^{-n} = 1-\left(\frac{PV_g p}{PMT}\right)$$ ——— multiply both sides by −1

$$-n\ln(1+p) = \ln\left[1-\left(\frac{PV_g p}{PMT}\right)\right]$$ ——— solve for n using natural logarithms

$$n = \frac{\ln\left[1-\left(\frac{PV_g p}{PMT}\right)\right]}{-\ln(1+p)}$$ ——— Formula 12.3B: divide both sides by $-\ln(1+p)$

To find n, rearrange the terms of the present value formulas. Then substitute the three known values (PV, PMT, and i) into the rearranged formula and solve for n.

When using a preprogrammed financial calculator, find n by entering the five known values (PV, PMT, I/Y, P/Y, and C/Y) and press CPT N.

EXAMPLE 12.4B

A business valued at $96 000 is bought for a down payment of 25% and payments of $4000 at the end of every three months. If interest is 9% compounded monthly, for how long will payments have to be made?

SOLUTION

$\text{PV} = 96\,000.00(0.75) = 72\,000.00$; $\quad \text{PMT} = 4000.00$;

$\text{P/Y} = 4$; $\quad \text{C/Y} = 12$; $\quad c = \dfrac{12}{4} = 3$; $\quad \text{I/Y} = 9$; $\quad i = \dfrac{9\%}{12} = 0.75\% = 0.0075$

The equivalent quarterly rate of interest

$p = 1.0075^3 - 1 = 1.022669 - 1 = 0.022669 = 2.2669\%$

$$72\,000.00 = 4000.00\left(\frac{1 - 1.022669^{-n}}{0.022669}\right) \quad \text{—— using Formula 12.3}$$

$$0.408045 = 1 - 1.022669^{-n}$$
$$1.022669^{-n} = 0.591954$$
$$-n \ln 1.022669 = \ln 0.591954$$
$$-n(0.022416) = -0.524325$$
$$n = 23.390604 \text{ (quarters)}$$
$$n = 24 \text{ quarters}$$

Programmed Solution

(Set P/Y = 4; C/Y = 12) 9 [I/Y] 0 [FV] 72 000

[±] [PV] 4000 [PMT] [CPT] [N] [23.390604]

Payments will have to be made for 24 quarters or six years. The payment for the last quarter would be a smaller amount.

EXERCISE 12.4

EXCEL NOTES If you choose, you can use Excel's Number of Compounding Periods (NPER) function to answer all of the questions below. Refer to NPER on MathXL to learn how to use this Excel function.

EXCEL SPREADSHEET

A. Find the term of each of the following ten ordinary general annuities. (State your answer in years and months.)

	Future Value	Present Value	Periodic Rent	Payment Interval	Interest Rate	Compounding Period
1.	$20 000		$ 800	1 year	7.5%	semi-annually
2.	17 000		35	3 months	9	monthly
3.		$14 500	190	1 month	5.25	quarterly
4.		5 000	300	3 months	4	semi-annually
5.	36 000		175	6 months	7.4	annually
6.		9 500	740	1 quarter	5.2	monthly
7.		21 400	1660	6 months	4.5	monthly
8.	13 600		140	6 months	8	quarterly
9.	$72 000		90	1 month	3.75	semi-annually
10.		$11 700	315	3 months	11	annually

EXCEL SPREADSHEET

B. Answer each of the following questions.

1. How long would it take you to save \$5000 by making deposits of \$100 at the end of every month into a savings account earning 6% compounded quarterly?

Reference Example 12.4A

2. How long will it take to save \$15 000 by making deposits of \$90 at the end of every month into an account earning interest at 4% compounded quarterly?
3. In what period of time could you pay back a loan of \$3000 by making monthly payments of \$90 if interest is 10.5% compounded semi-annually?

Reference Example 12.4B

4. For how many years will Prasad make payments on the \$28 000 he borrowed to start his machine shop if he makes payments of \$3400 at the end of every three months and interest is 8.08% compounded semi-annually?
5. Mirsad is saving \$500 at the end of each month. How soon can he retire if he wants to have a retirement fund of \$120 000 and interest is 5.4% compounded quarterly?
6. For how long must contributions of \$2000 be made at the end of each year to accumulate to \$100 000 at 6% compounded quarterly?
7. For how long can \$800 be withdrawn at the end of each month from an account originally containing \$16 000, if interest is 6.8% compounded semi-annually?
8. A mortgage of \$120 000 is to be repaid by making payments of \$751 at the end of each month. If interest is 5.75% compounded semi-annually, what is the term of the mortgage?
9. Suppose \$370.37 is deposited at the end of every three months into an account earning 6.5% compounded semi-annually. If the balance in the account is to be \$20 000, how many deposits are needed?
10. Mr. Deneau accumulated \$100 000 in an RRSP. He converted the RRSP into a RRIF and started to withdraw \$4500 at the end of every three months from the fund. If interest is 6.75% compounded monthly, for how long can Mr. Deneau make withdrawals?

12.5 ORDINARY GENERAL ANNUITIES—FINDING THE PERIODIC INTEREST RATE *i*

A. Finding the periodic rate of interest *i* using preprogrammed financial calculators

EXCEL NOTES

Preprogrammed financial calculators are especially helpful when solving for the conversion rate *i*. Determining *i* without a financial calculator is extremely time-consuming. However, it *can* be done by hand, as illustrated in Appendix B on the MathXL.

When the future value or present value, the periodic payment, PMT, and the term *n* of a general annuity are known, retrieve the value of I/Y by pressing CPT I/Y.

BUSINESS MATH NEWS BOX

Tax-smart Investing

In the investment world, things aren't always what they seem. For example, because you pay income tax, earning interest at 5% doesn't mean that you'll keep all the $5 you make on every $100 you invest. In fact, if your taxable income is about $40 000, only $3 goes into your pocket. The other $2 goes to the government.

So how do you improve your returns on investments held outside your RRSP? By keeping more, after-tax, of what your investments earn. Choose your investments wisely. Not all investment income is taxed in the same manner. Every dollar of interest income is fully taxable. That means it is taxed just like your salary. Capital gains and Canadian dividends, however, are taxed more lightly.

Capital gains tax generally applies when you sell a capital asset for more than your purchase price plus commissions and expenses incurred in the sale. Only half of the gain is subject to tax. So, if your marginal tax rate—the amount of federal and provincial tax rates combined—is 40%, the effective rate on capital gains is half of that, or 20%.

Dividends from Canadian corporations also get special treatment. Dividends are first "grossed up" by 45% and claimed as taxable income. So, if your dividend was $100, your "taxable income" would be $100 + $100 × 45% = $145. To ensure there is not double taxation (for the company declaring the dividend and the holder of the stock), a federal tax credit of 18.97% is applied plus a provincial tax credit. For example, the provincial tax credit in Manitoba is 3.5% on the "grossed up" amount. To calculate the tax credit, take the "grossed up" amount ($145) and reduce your taxes payable by (18.97% + 3.5%) × $145 = $32.58. If your marginal tax rate was 40% in 2009, Canadian dividends were effectively taxed at about 25% as a result of the dividend tax credit.

What $500 of investment income is really worth (2009 tax figures)

Here's where $500 of investment income goes:

Investment Income	Interest	Capital Gains	Dividends
To Canada Revenue Agency	$200.00	$100.00	$127.09
In your pocket	$300.00	$400.00	$372.91

* Assumes federal tax bracket of 26% and provincial tax bracket of 14%.

QUESTIONS

1. Using the numbers given in the table, calculate (to two decimal places) the percent of the $500.00 investment income that the investor receives after taxes if the investment income is

   (a) interest;
   (b) capital gains;
   (c) dividends.

2. Suppose you had to make a choice. You could receive $1500.00 in dividends every six months for five years, starting today. Or, you could receive $1500.00 in interest every six months for five years, starting today. Assume that income tax is deducted before you reinvest your investment income. Assume a 40% marginal tax rate that will be the same for five years and that money will be worth 5% compounded semi-annually for the next five years. In five years, how much more after-tax investment income would you have if you chose the dividends?

3. Suppose you had a different choice. You could receive \$1500.00 in capital gains every six months for five years, starting today. Or, you could receive either of the interest income options described in Question 2. How much more after-tax investment income would you have if you chose the capital gains rather than the dividends? The interest income? (Use the same assumptions as in Question 2.)

Sources: Canada Revenue Agency Website, **www.cra-arc.gc.ca/tax/individuals/topics/income-tax/return/completing/reporting-income/lines101-170/127/gains/calculate/menu-e.html** and **www.cra-arc.gc.ca/tax/individuals/topics/income-tax/return/completing/reporting-income/lines101-170/120/menu-e.html**; Manitoba Tax Tips website, **www.taxtips.ca/mbtax/dividendtaxcredit.htm**, all accessed August 29, 2010.

EXAMPLE 12.5A

Irina deposited \$150 in a savings account at the end of each month for 60 months. If the accumulated value of the deposits was \$10 000 and interest was compounded semi-annually, what was the nominal annual rate of interest?

SOLUTION

$FV = 10\,000.00$; $PMT = 150.00$; $n = 60$; $P/Y = 12$; $C/Y = 2$; $c = \frac{2}{12} = \frac{1}{6}$

(Set P/Y = 12; C/Y = 2) 0 [PV] 10 000 [FV]

150 [±] [PMT] 60 [N] [CPT] [I/Y] 4.25541

The nominal annual rate of interest is 4.2554% p.a. compounded semi-annually.

EXAMPLE 12.5B

Compute the nominal annual rate of interest compounded monthly at which \$500 paid at the end of every three months for ten years will eliminate a debt of \$16 000.

SOLUTION

$PV = 16\,000.00$; $PMT = 500.00$; $n = 40$; $P/Y = 4$; $C/Y = 12$; $c = \frac{12}{4} = 3$

(Set P/Y = 4; C/Y = 12) 0 [FV] 16 000 [PV]

500 [±] [PMT] 40 [N] [CPT] [I/Y] 4.528237

The nominal annual rate is 4.5282% p.a. compounded monthly.

EXERCISE 12.5

EXCEL SPREADSHEET

For each of the following eight ordinary general annuities, determine the nominal annual rate of interest.

	Future Value	Present Value	Periodic Payment	Payment Interval	Term	Conversion Period
1.	\$39 200		\$2300	1 year	12 years	monthly
2.		\$ 9 600	1220	6 months	5 years	monthly
3.		62 400	2600	6 months	25 years	annually
4.	55 500		75	1 month	20 years	semi-annually

(continued)

	Future Value	Present Value	Periodic Payment	Payment Interval	Term	Conversion Period
5.	6 400		200	6 months	9 years	monthly
6.	$25 000		790	1 year	15 years	quarterly
7.		7 500	420	3 months	5 years	monthly
8.		$60 000	$450	1 month	25 years	semi-annually

EXCEL SPREADSHEET

B. Answer each of the following questions.

1. What is the nominal annual rate of interest compounded quarterly if deposits of $253 made each month for 3½ years accumulate to $11 600?

Reference Example 12.5A

2. Victoria saved $416 every six months for eight years. What nominal rate of interest compounded annually is earned if the savings account amounts to $7720 in eight years?

3. What is the nominal annual rate of interest compounded semi-annually if a four-year loan of $6000 is repaid by monthly payments of $144.23?

Reference Example 12.5B

4. A car valued at $11 400 can be purchased for 10% down and monthly payments of $286.21 for three-and-a-half years. What is the nominal rate of interest compounded annually?

5. A property worth $50 000 can be purchased for 20% down and quarterly mortgage payments of $1000 for 25 years. What nominal rate of interest compounded monthly is charged?

6. A vacation property valued at $25 000 was bought for fifteen payments of $2200 due at the end of every six months. What nominal annual rate of interest compounded annually was charged?

7. Compute the nominal annual rate of interest compounded monthly at which $400 paid at the end of every three months for eight years accumulates to $20 000.

8. What is the nominal annual rate of interest compounded quarterly if a loan of $21 500 is repaid in seven years by payments of $2000 made at the end of every six months?

9. If Paige has accumulated $4850 by saving $120 every month for 3 years, what nominal annual rate of interest compounded quarterly has been earned?

10. Deanna wants to save $3500 in two years by depositing $420 every three months into a savings account. What nominal rate of interest compounded annually does her savings have to earn?

11. A mortgage of $35 500 is repaid by making payments of $570 at the end of each month for fifteen years. What is the nominal annual rate of interest compounded semi-annually?

12. A property worth $35 000 is purchased for 10% down and semi-annual payments of $2100 for twelve years. What is the nominal annual rate of interest if interest is compounded quarterly?

12.6 CONSTANT-GROWTH ANNUITIES

The annuities we have considered so far have the common feature of periodic payments that are equal in size. **Constant-growth annuities** differ from these fixed-payment-size annuities in that the periodic payments change (usually grow) at a constant rate. The assumption of constant growth is often used in sales forecasting and long-term financial planning. It is consistent with the indexing of pensions or annuities.

The types of constant-growth annuities parallel the types of fixed payment annuities considered in Chapter 11 and the previous sections of Chapter 12. However, we will deal only with ordinary simple constant-growth annuities.

With ordinary simple constant-growth annuities, the computations may involve determining the size of any periodic payment, the total amount of the periodic payments, the future value and present value of the stream of periodic payments, the amount of interest earned by the periodic payments, and the size of the first payment if either the present value or the future value is known. We will also consider in this section the special case when the constant growth rate equals the periodic rate of interest.

A. Future value of an ordinary simple constant-growth annuity

To compute the future value of a series of payments growing at a constant rate, the approach is similar to that used in Example 11.2B.

In general, if the first payment is represented by PMT and the constant rate of growth by k, the constant growth factor for the annuity payments is $(1 + k)$ and the size of the successive payments is as follows:

1st payment $= \text{PMT}$
2nd payment $= \text{PMT}(1 + k)$
3rd payment $= \text{PMT}(1 + k)^2$
4th payment $= \text{PMT}(1 + k)^3$
↓ ↓
↓ ↓
10th payment $= \text{PMT}(1 + k)^9$

$$\text{SIZE OF THE } n\text{TH PAYMENT} = \text{PMT}(1 + k)^{n-1}$$ —— **Formula 12.4**

The periodic constant-growth payments form an ordinary simple annuity in which PMT is the size of the first payment, k is the periodic compounding rate, and n is the number of payments.

$$\text{SUM OF THE PERIODIC CONSTANT-GROWTH PAYMENTS} = \text{PMT}\frac{(1 + k)^n - 1}{k}$$ —— **Formula 12.5**

Note: Formula 12.5 is the same as Formula 11.1 except that i has been replaced by k.

The formula for finding the future value of an ordinary simple constant-growth annuity is similar in structure to future value Formula 11.1.

$$FV = PMT\frac{(1+i)^n - (1+k)^n}{i-k}$$ —— **Formula 12.6**

where FV = the future (accumulated) value of an ordinary simple constant-growth annuity;

PMT = the size of the first annuity payment;
i = the interest rate per conversion period;
k = the constant growth rate of the annuity payments;
n = the number of conversion periods.

The factor $\frac{(1+i)^n - (1+k)^n}{i-k}$ is the compounding factor for constant-growth annuities. If $k = 0$, which means there is no growth in the periodic payments, the factor becomes the compounding factor used in Formula 11.1. Formula 11.1 is, in fact, a special case of Formula 12.6—the "zero-growth case."

EXAMPLE 12.6A Five deposits increasing at a constant rate of 2% are made at the end of each of four successive years. The size of the first deposit is \$3000 and the fund earns interest at 6% compounded annually.

(i) What is the size of the last deposit?

(ii) How much was deposited in total?

(iii) What is the accumulated value of the deposits?

(iv) What is the interest earned by the deposits?

SOLUTION The situation is pictured in Figure 12.3.

FIGURE 12.3 **End of period (year) $i = 6\% = 0.06$**

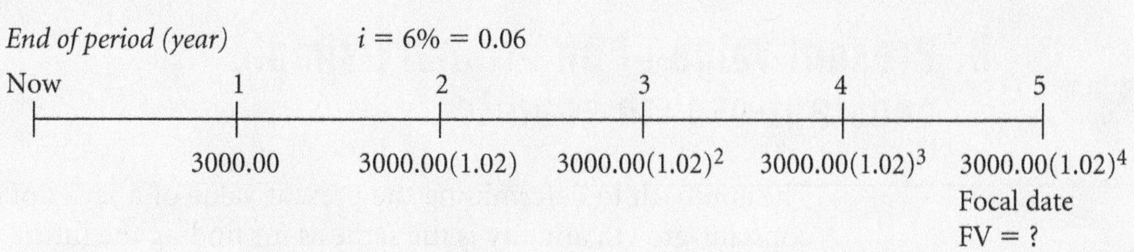

(i) PMT = 3000.00; $k = 2\% = 0.02$; $n = 5$

Size of the 5th payment

$= \text{PMT}(1 + k)^{n-1}$ —— using Formula 12.4

$= 3000.00(1.02)^4$

$= 3000.00(1.082432)$

$= \$3247.30$

(ii) PMT = 3000.00; $k = 2\% = 0.02$; $n = 5$

Sum of the constant-growth deposits

$$= \text{PMT}\left[\frac{(1 + k)^n - 1}{k}\right]$$ —— using Formula 12.5

$$= 3000.00\left[\frac{(1.02)^5 - 1}{0.02}\right]$$

$$= 3000.00\left[\frac{1.010408 - 1}{0.02}\right]$$

$= 3000.00(5.20404)$

$= \$15\,612.12$

(iii) PMT = 3000.00; $k = 2\% = 0.02$; $n = 5$; $i = 6\% = 0.06$

Future value of the combined constant growth deposits

$$\text{FV} = \text{PMT}\left[\frac{(1 + i)^n - (1 + k)^n}{i - k}\right]$$ —— using Formula 12.6

$$= 3000.00\left[\frac{(1.06)^5 - (1.02)^5}{0.06 - 0.02}\right]$$

$$= 3000.00\left[\frac{1.338226 - 1.104081}{0.04}\right]$$

$= 3000.00(5.853619)$

$= \$17\,560.86$

(iv) The interest earned by the deposits

$= 17\,560.86 - 15\,612.12 = \$1948.74.$

B. Present value of an ordinary simple constant-growth annuity

The approach to determining the present value of a series of payments forming a constant-growth annuity is the same as for finding the future value of the series of payments except that each payment must be discounted using Formula 9.1C, $PV = FV(1+i)^{-n}$.

$$PV = PMT\left[\frac{1-(1+k)^n(1+i)^{-n}}{i-k}\right]$$ Formula 12.7

where PV = the present (discounted) value of an ordinary simple constant-growth annuity;

PMT = the size of the first annuity payment;
i = the interest rate per conversion period;
k = the constant growth rate of the annuity payments;
n = the number of conversion periods.

The factor $\left[\frac{(1-(1+k)^n(1+i)^{-n}}{i-k}\right]$ is the discount factor for constant-growth annuities. If $k = 0$, which means there is no growth in the periodic payments, the factor becomes the discount factor used in Formula 11.2. Formula 11.2 is, in fact, a special case of Formula 12.7—the "zero-growth case."

Constant-growth annuity formulas are not part of the programming of most financial calculators. Problems involving constant-growth annuities can be solved by substituting in the appropriate formulas, as shown in Examples 12.6A and 12.6B.

EXAMPLE 12.6B Use Formula 12.7 to calculate the present value of the deposits in Example 12.6A.

SOLUTION PMT = 3000.00; $k = 2\% = 0.02$; $n = 5$; $i = 6\% = 0.06$;

$$PV = 3000.00\left[\frac{1-(1.02)^5(1.06)^{-5}}{0.06-0.02}\right]$$ using Formula 12.7

$$PV = 3000.00\left[\frac{1-(1.104081)(0.747258)}{0.04}\right]$$

$$PV = 3000.00(4.374165)$$

$$PV = \$13\,122.49$$

When the constant-growth rate of the annuity payments (k) and the periodic interest rate (i) are the same, Formula 12.8 is used to calculate future value of an ordinary simple constant-growth annuity.

$$FV = n(PMT)(1+i)^{n-1}$$ Formula 12.8

When the constant-growth rate of the annuity payments (k) and the periodic interest rate (i) are the same, Formula 12.9 is used to calculate present value of an ordinary simple constant-growth annuity.

$$PV = n(PMT)(1 + i)^{-1}$$ Formula 12.9

EXERCISE 12.6

A. Answer each of the following questions.

1. You plan to make twenty-five annual deposits into your RRSP starting with $500 and increasing thereafter by 3%.
   (a) What will be the size of the twenty-fifth deposit?
   (b) What will be the total amount deposited?

2. Sally has accumulated a sizeable balance in her investment fund. She wants to make annual withdrawals for fifteen years starting with $5000 and decreasing (negative growth) by 5% thereafter.
   (a) What will be the size of the fifteenth withdrawal? (***Hint:*** Let $k = -5\%$.)
   (b) What will be the total amount withdrawn?

3. Twenty semi-annual deposits are made earning interest of 5% compounded semi-annually. The size of the first deposit is $1200 and the deposits increase at 1.5% thereafter.
   (a) Determine the total amount deposited.
   (b) How much was the accumulated value of the deposits just after the last deposit was made?
   (c) What is the size of the twelfth deposit?
   (d) What is the amount of interest included in the accumulated value?

4. Withdrawals increasing at a constant rate of 4% are made quarterly for six years from an account earning 6% compounded quarterly.
   (a) What must be the balance in the account to permit the withdrawals if the first withdrawal is $1500?
   (b) What is the size of the last withdrawal?
   (c) What is the total amount withdrawn?
   (d) How much interest is included in the withdrawals?

B. Solve each of the following.

1. Lucy won a large sum in the lottery. She invested part of her winnings into a fund earning 6% compounded monthly. She has arranged a systematic withdrawal plan that provides for 120 monthly payments increasing at a constant rate of 0.5% per payment. The first payment of $400 is due one month after she set up the fund. How much interest is included in the payments? Reference Example 12.6A

2. Trent has opened an RRSP account by making an initial deposit of $1500. He intends to make semi-annual deposits for 30 years increasing at a constant rate of 3.5%. How much of the accumulated value just after the last deposit was made is interest if interest is 7% compounded semi-annually? Reference Example 12.6B

3. Shelby paid $150 000 for a 10-year indexed annuity in which the monthly payments received at the end of each month diminish by 0.6% per payment. What is the total amount received by Shelby if interest is 7.2% compounded monthly?

4. Cecile intends to make end-of-the-year payments growing by 8% per payment for 12 years. If the payments earn 7% compounded annually, what is the size of the last payment if the accumulated value of the payments is $250 000?

Go to MathXL at www.mathxl.com. You can practise many of this chapter's exercises as often as you want. The guided solutions help you find an answer step by step. You'll find a personalized study plan available to you too!

Review Exercise

1. At the end of every three months, Sheila invested $375 into an account earning interest at 3% compounded monthly. What is the accumulated value in the account after eight years?

2. What is the accumulated value after twelve years of monthly deposits of $145 earning interest at 5% compounded semi-annually if the deposits are made at the end of each month?

3. What single cash payment made now is equivalent to eleven years of payments of $4800 made at the end of every six months with interest at 4.4% compounded quarterly?

4. What is the principal invested at 6.5% compounded semi-annually from which monthly withdrawals of $240 can be made at the end of each month for twenty-five years?

5. Contributions of $500 are made at the end of every three months into an RRSP. What is the accumulated balance after twenty years if interest is 6% compounded semi-annually?

6. Kirstie's mortgage is repaid over 20 years by payments of $1055.00 made at the end of each month. If interest is 5.2% compounded semi-annually, what is the mortgage principal?

7. Neena wants to accumulate $18 000 in a fund earning 3.6% compounded semi-annually. How much must she deposit at the end of each year for eight years?

8. What sum of money can be withdrawn from a fund of $15 750 invested at 4.25% compounded semi-annually

(a) at the end of every month for twelve years?

(b) at the end of each year for fifteen years?

9. How long will it take for payments of $350 to accumulate to $12 000 at 3% compounded monthly if made

(a) at the end of every three months?

(b) at the end of every six months?

10. A $92 000 mortgage with a 25-year term is repaid by making payments at the end of each month. If interest is 5.8% compounded semi-annually, how much are the payments?

11. A debt of $14 000 is repaid by making payments of $1500. If interest is 9% compounded monthly, for how long will payments have to be made

(a) at the end of every six months?

(b) at the end of each year?

12. What is the nominal rate of interest compounded monthly at which payments of $200 made at the end of every three months accumulate to $9200 in eight years?

13. A debt of $2290 is repaid by making payments of $198. If interest is 16.95% compounded monthly, for how long will quarterly payments have to be made?

14. A $265 000 mortgage is repaid over 25 years by making monthly payments of $1672. What is the nominal annual rate of interest compounded semi-annually on the mortgage?

15. The balance in Marc's RRSPs was $148 000 when he converted to an RRIF. The RRIF pays $5000 at the end of each quarter. If interest on the RRIF is 4.3% compounded monthly, for how long will Marc receive quarterly payments?

16. Satwinder deposited $145 at the end of each month for fifteen years at 7.5% compounded monthly. After her last deposit she converted the balance into an ordinary annuity paying $1200 every three months for twelve years.

If interest on the annuity is compounded semi-annually, what is the nominal rate of interest paid by the annuity?

17. Fred Larsen contributes $345 at the end of every three months into an RRSP. Interest on the account is 6% compounded monthly.
   (a) What will be the balance after nine years?
   (b) How much of the balance will be interest?
   (c) If Fred converts the balance after nine years into an RRIF earning 5% compounded monthly and makes equal withdrawals at the end of every three months for eight years, what is the size of the withdrawal?
   (d) What is the combined interest earned by the RRSP and the RRIF?

18. How much must be contributed into an RRSP at the end of each year for twenty-five years to accumulate to $100 000 if interest is 8% compounded quarterly?

19. For how long must $75 be deposited at the end of each month to accumulate to $9500 at 6.5% compounded quarterly?

20. A $135 000 mortgage is amortized by making monthly payments of $974.37. If interest is 4.92% compounded semi-annually, for how many years is the term of the mortgage?

21. Toby has opened an RRSP account by making an initial deposit of $1200. She intends to make quarterly deposits for twenty years increasing at a constant rate of 1.5%. How much of the accumulated value just after the last deposit was made is interest if interest is 7% compounded quarterly?

22. Harry paid $250 000 for a fifteen-year indexed annuity in which the monthly payments received at the end of each month increase by 0.7% per payment. What is the total amount received by Harry if interest is 8.4% compounded monthly?

Self-Test

EXCEL SPREADSHEET

1. Monthly deposits of $480 were made at the end of each month for eight years. If interest is 4.5% compounded semi-annually, what amount can be withdrawn immediately after the last deposit?

2. A loan was repaid in five years by end-of-quarter payments of $1200 at 9.5% compounded semi-annually. How much interest was paid?

3. A loan of $6000 was repaid by quarterly payments of $450. If interest was 12% compounded monthly, how long did it take to pay back the loan?

4. A mortgage of $95 000 is to be amortized by monthly payments over twenty-five years. If the payments are made at the end of each month and interest is 8.5% compounded semi-annually, what is the size of the monthly payments?

5. Leo invested $ 67 250 into an annuity earning 4.4% compounded semi-annually. How much is he is able to withdraw from the annuity at the end of every three months for seven years?

6. A $45 000 mortgage is repaid in twenty years by making monthly payments of $387.72. What is the nominal annual rate of interest compounded semi-annually?

7. For how long would you have to deposit $491 at the end of every three months to accumulate $20 000 at 6.0% compounded monthly?

8. What is the size of monthly deposits that will accumulate to $67 200 after eight years at 6.5% compounded semi-annually?

9. Sigrid contributed $200 every month for nine years into an RRSP earning 4.3% compounded annually. She then converted the RRSP into an annuity that pays her monthly for twenty years. If the first payment is due one month after the conversion and interest on the annuity is 5.4% compounded semi-annually, how much will Sigrid receive at the end of every month?

10. Joy would like to receive $6000 at the end of every three months for ten years after her retirement. If she retires now and interest is 6.5% compounded semi-annually, how much must she deposit into an account?

11. Mira has opened a registered retirement income fund (RRIF) with a starting balance of $250 000. Beginning six months later, she plans to make semi-annual withdrawals from the RRIF for twenty years. The withdrawals will increase at a constant rate of 1.75%. If the RRIF earns 8% compounded semi-annually, how much is the amount of interest included in the total withdrawals?

Challenge Problems

1. After winning some money at a casino, Tony is considering purchasing an annuity that promises to pay him $300 at the end of each month for 12 months, then $350 at the end of each month for 24 months, and then $375 at the end of each month for 36 months. If the first payment is due at the end of the first month and interest is 7.5% compounded annually over the life of the annuity, find Tony's purchase price.

2. A loan of $5600 is to be repaid at 9% compounded annually by making ten payments at the end of each quarter. Each of the last six payments is two times the amount of each of the first four payments. What is the size of each payment?

CASE STUDY 12.1 Vehicle Cash-Back Incentives

» Karim Soltan is shopping for a new vehicle, and has noticed that many vehicle manufacturers are offering special deals to sell off the current year's vehicles before the new models arrive. Karim's local Ford dealership is advertising 3.9% financing for a full 48 months (i.e., 3.9% compounded monthly) or up to $4000 cash back on selected vehicles.

The vehicle that Karim wants to purchase costs $24 600 including taxes, delivery, licence, and dealer preparation. This vehicle qualifies for $1800 cash back if Karim pays cash for the vehicle. Karim has a good credit rating and knows that he could arrange a vehicle loan at his bank for the full price of any vehicle he chooses. His other option is to take the dealer financing offered at 3.9% for 48 months.

Karim wants to know which option requires the lower monthly payment. He knows he can use annuity formulas to calculate the monthly payments.

QUESTIONS

1. Suppose Karim buys the vehicle on July 1. What monthly payment must Karim make if he chooses the dealer's 3.9% financing option and pays off the loan over 48 months? (Assume he makes each monthly payment at the end of the month and his first payment is due on July 31.)

2. Suppose the bank offers Karim a 48-month loan with the interest compounded monthly and the payments due at the end of each month. If Karim accepts the bank loan, he can get $1800 cash back on this vehicle.

   Karim works out a method to calculate the bank rate of interest required to make bank financing the same cost as dealer financing. First, calculate the monthly rate of interest that would make the monthly bank payments equal to the monthly dealer payments. Then calculate the effective rate of interest represented by the monthly compounded rate. If the financing from the bank is at a lower rate of interest compounded monthly, choose the bank financing. The reason is that the monthly payments for the bank's financing would be lower than the monthly payments for the dealer's 3.9% financing.

   (a) How much money would Karim have to borrow from the bank to pay cash for this vehicle?

   (b) Using the method above, calculate the effective annual rate of interest and the nominal annual rate of interest required to make the monthly payments for bank financing exactly the same as for dealer financing.

3. Suppose Karim decides to explore the costs of financing a more expensive vehicle. The more expensive vehicle costs $34 900 in total and qualifies for the 3.9% dealer financing for 48 months or $2500 cash back. What is the highest effective annual rate of interest at which Karim should borrow from the bank instead of using the dealer's 3.9% financing?

CASE STUDY 12.2 Fiscal Fitness

» Rosalinda is planning to open Fitness Quest, a new health and fitness club. She must decide what to charge for each type of membership and what payment options to offer.

Rosalinda plans to offer two types of memberships. General membership allows members to use all facilities, and it provides a simple locker room. Premium membership allows members to use all facilities, and it provides towels, shower supplies, and a sauna. When members pay for their annual membership when they join, the fee is $550 for the General membership and $700 for the Premium membership.

QUESTIONS

1. Rosalinda wants to offer members the option of paying their annual membership fees in twelve equal monthly installments. The first installment would be due on the day of joining.
   - **(a)** To the nearest dollar, how much should Rosalinda charge General members monthly if she wants to make interest of 17.5% compounded monthly?
   - **(b)** To the nearest dollar, how much should she charge Premium members monthly if she wants to make interest of 21% compounded monthly?
2. Rosalinda knows that many of the Premium members will be executives whose companies will pay for their memberships. Many companies prefer to make quarterly payments for annual memberships. For this reason, Rosalinda decides to offer a quarterly payment option. The first installment would be due on the day of joining. To the nearest dollar, how much should Rosalinda charge Premium members quarterly if she wants to make interest of 21% compounded monthly?
3. As an opening special, Rosalinda wants to offer all members who join during the opening week three free months of membership. To calculate the nominal rate of interest she would earn on these opening special memberships, Rosalinda will add the payments made for the year for a membership, then spread the total payments equally over fifteen months as if the payment period were fifteen months. She would then calculate the nominal rate of interest earned on these new monthly payments over the fifteen-month membership period.
   - **(a)** What is the nominal rate of interest earned on the opening special for the General membership with the monthly payment option?
   - **(b)** What is the nominal rate of interest earned on the opening special for the Premium membership with the monthly payment option?
   - **(c)** What is the nominal rate of interest earned on the opening special for the Premium membership with the quarterly payment option?

SUMMARY OF FORMULAS

Formula 12.1

$$p = (1 + i)^c - 1$$

Finding the equivalent rate of interest per payment period *p* for a nominal annual rate of interest compounded *c* times per payment interval

Formula 12.2

$$FV_g = PMT\left[\frac{(1 + p)^n - 1}{p}\right]$$

where $p = (1 + i)^c - 1$

Finding the future value of an ordinary general annuity using the effective rate of interest per payment period

Formula 12.2A

$$PMT = \frac{FV_g p}{(1 + p)^n - 1}$$

Finding the payment of an ordinary general annuity using the effective rate of interest per payment period when the future value is known

Formula 12.2B

$$n = \frac{\ln[\mathrm{FV}_g p/\mathrm{PMT} + 1]}{\ln(1 + p)}$$

Finding the number of payments of an ordinary general annuity using the effective rate of interest per payment period when the future value is known

Formula 12.3

$$\mathrm{PV}_g = \mathrm{PMT}\left[\frac{1 - (1 + p)^{-n}}{p}\right]$$

Finding the present value of an ordinary general annuity using the effective rate of interest per payment period

Formula 12.3A

$$\mathrm{PMT} = \frac{\mathrm{PV}_g p}{1 - (1 + p)^{-n}}$$

Finding the payment of an ordinary general annuity using the effective rate of interest per payment period when the present value is known

Formula 12.3B

$$n = \frac{\ln[1 - (\mathrm{PV}_g p/\mathrm{PMT})]}{-\ln(1 + p)}$$

Finding the number of payments of an ordinary general annuity using the effective rate of interest per payment period when the present value is known

Formula 12.4

$$\text{SIZE OF THE } n\text{TH PAYMENT} = \mathrm{PMT}(1 + k)^{n-1}$$

Finding the size of the nth payment of a constant-growth annuity

Formula 12.5

$$\text{SUM OF THE PERIODIC CONSTANT-GROWTH PAYMENTS} = \frac{\mathrm{PMT}\ (1 + k)^{n-1}}{k}$$

Finding the sum of the periodic payments of a constant-growth annuity.

Formula 12.6

$$\mathrm{FV} = \mathrm{PMT}\frac{(1 + i)^n - (1 + k)^n}{i - k}$$

Finding the future value of an ordinary simple constant-growth annuity

Formula 12.7

$$\mathrm{PV} = \mathrm{PMT}\left[\frac{1 - (1 + k)^n (1 + i)^{-n}}{i - k}\right]$$

Finding the present value of a series of payments forming a constant-growth annuity

Formula 12.8

$$\mathrm{FV} = n\ (\mathrm{PMT})(1 + i)^{n-1}$$

Finding the future value of an ordinary simple constant-growth annuity when the constant-growth rate and the periodic interest rate are the same

Formula 12.9

$$\mathrm{PV} = n\ (\mathrm{PMT})(1 + i)^{-1}$$

Finding the present value of an ordinary simple constant-growth annuity when the constant-growth rate and the periodic interest rate are the same

GLOSSARY

Constant-growth annuity an annuity in which the payments change by the same percentage from one period to the next *(p. 490)*

Equivalent rate of interest per payment period the rate of interest earned during the payment period that yields the same amount of interest as a nominal annual rate compounded *c* times per year, where *c* is the number of payment periods per year *(p. 470)*

USEFUL INTERNET SITES

www.money.canoe.ca

RRIF: Savings Find current information and rates of return on RRIFs from several financial institutions and financial services providers on the Canoe Money site.

www.fidelity.ca

Growth Calculator Click on "Education and Planning," and then "Growth Calculator" in the Calculators section. This interactive chart on the Fidelity Investments site allows you to calculate both simple and compound earnings on investment capital by entering values for a series of variables.

CHAPTER 13

Annuities Due, Deferred Annuities, and Perpetuities

OBJECTIVES

Upon completing this chapter, you will be able to do the following:

1. Compute the future value, present value, periodic payment, term, and interest rate for simple annuities due.
2. Compute the future value, present value, periodic payment, term, and interest rate for general annuities due.
3. Compute the future value, present value, periodic payment, term, and interest rate for ordinary deferred annuities.
4. Compute the future value, present value, periodic payment, term, and interest rate for deferred annuities due.
5. Compute the present value, periodic payment, and interest rate for ordinary perpetuities, perpetuities due, and deferred perpetuities.

When you pay rent on an apartment, a house, or a commercial space, your rent is due at the beginning of the month. This series of regular, equal payments paid at the beginning of the period represents a type of annuity called an annuity due. The payment schedule for an annuity due differs from that of an ordinary annuity (which we discussed in Chapters 11 and 12), where payments are due at the end of each period.

In some situations, a series of regular, equal payments may not begin until some future time. These payment situations are known as deferred annuities. For example, if you won a large amount of money today and you wanted a series of regular, equal payments to begin five years from now, you would set up a deferred annuity. Both ordinary annuities and annuities due can be deferred.

INTRODUCTION

In the previous chapters, we considered ordinary annuities, both simple and general, in which the payments are made at the end of each payment period.

In this chapter we will consider other annuities resulting from variations in the payment dates and the length of time that the payments continue. These include annuities due (in which payments are made at the beginning of the period), deferred annuities (in which the first payment is made after the first or several payment intervals have been completed), and perpetuities (in which payments continue indefinitely).

13.1 SIMPLE ANNUITIES DUE

A. Future value of a simple annuity due

When analyzing an annuity, there are several questions that need to be answered. First, how often is a payment made? This determines the payment interval. Next, is the payment made at the beginning or at the end of each payment interval?

If the periodic payment is made at the end of each payment interval, as discussed in Chapters 11 and 12, the annuity is an ordinary annuity. If the periodic payment is made at the beginning of each payment interval, the annuity is an **annuity due.** To determine the future value of an annuity due, we start with the formula to calculate the future value of an ordinary annuity, and adjust it to accommodate the difference in the timing of the payment. The two formulas to calculate future value have a close relationship.

The future value of an ordinary simple annuity is calculated using Formula 11.1. To calculate the future value of a simple annuity due, the result from Formula 11.1 is then multiplied by $(1 + i)$ to include the additional interest earned for the payment made at the beginning of the first period.

$$\text{FUTURE VALUE OF A SIMPLE ANNUITY DUE} = \text{FUTURE VALUE OF AN ORDINARY SIMPLE ANNUITY} \times (1 \times i)$$

The general notation for simple annuities due is the same as for ordinary simple annuities except that the accumulated value (future value) or the annuity due is represented by the symbol FV_n(due).

Thus, the formula for the future value of a simple annuity due is:

$$FV_n(\text{due}) = PMT\left[\frac{(1 + i)^n - 1}{i}\right](1 + i) \qquad \textbf{Formula 13.1}$$

The relationship between an annuity due and the corresponding ordinary annuity is graphically illustrated in the comparison of the line diagrams.

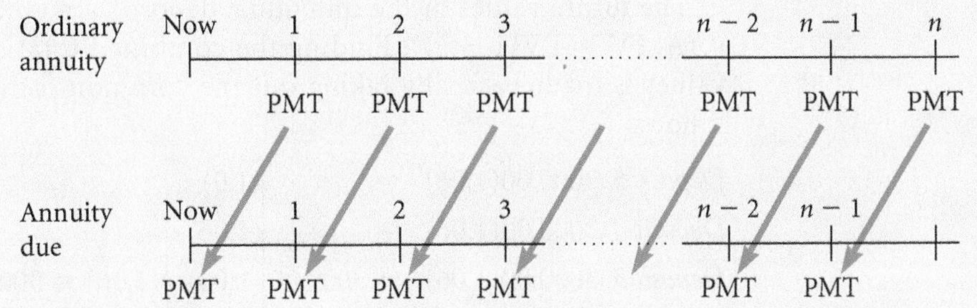

The two line graphs show the shift of the payments by one period. In an annuity due, every payment earns interest for one more period than in an ordinary annuity, and this explains the factor $(1 + i)$.

EXAMPLE 13.1A Find the future value at the end date of the last payment period of deposits of \$3000 each made at the beginning of five consecutive years with interest at 6% compounded annually.

SOLUTION As for any problem involving a series of payments, the method of solution and the data can be shown on a time diagram.

FIGURE 13.1 Graphical Representation of Method and Data

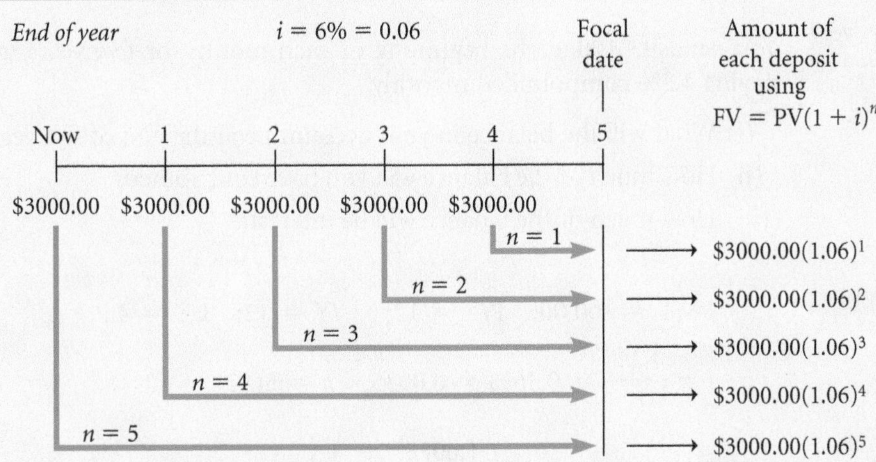

As shown in Figure 13.1, the first deposit is located at the beginning of Year 1, which is the same as "now"; the second deposit is located at the beginning of Year 2, which is the same as the end of Year 1; the third at the beginning of Year 3; the fourth at the beginning of Year 4; and the fifth and last deposit at the beginning of Year 5, which is also the beginning of the last payment period. The focal date, however, is located at the *end* of the last payment period.

The future values of the individual deposits are obtained by using Formula 9.1A, $FV = PV(1 + i)^n$. Finding the combined total of the five accumulated values is made easier by taking out the common factors 3000.00 and 1.06 as follows:

$$\begin{aligned}
&\textit{Deposit 5}\ \ 3000.00(1.06)^1 = \\
&\textit{Deposit 4}\ \ 3000.00(1.06)^2 = \\
&\textit{Deposit 3}\ \ 3000.00(1.06)^3 = \\
&\textit{Deposit 2}\ \ 3000.00(1.06)^4 = \\
&\textit{Deposit 1}\ \ 3000.00(1.06)^5 =
\end{aligned}
\; 3000.00\begin{bmatrix}(1.0)\\(1.06)\\(1.06)^2\\(1.06)^3\\(1.06)^4\end{bmatrix}(1.06) = 3000.00\begin{bmatrix}(1.0)\\(1.06)\\(1.1236)\\(1.191016)\\(1.262477)\end{bmatrix}(1.06)$$

$$\begin{aligned}
&= 3000.00(5.637093)(1.06)\\
&= 16\,911.28(1.06)\\
&= \$17\,925.96
\end{aligned}$$

Note: This example is the same as Example 11.2B except that the deposits are made at the beginning of each payment period rather than at the end. The answer to Example 11.2B was \$16 911.28. We could have obtained the answer to Example 13.1A simply by multiplying \$16 911.28 by 1.06. The future value of the annuity due can be obtained by multiplying the future value of the ordinary annuity by the factor $(1 + i)$.

EXAMPLE 13.1B

You deposit \$100 at the beginning of each month for five years in an account paying 4.2% compounded monthly.

(i) What will the balance in your account be at the end of five years?

(ii) How much of the balance will you have contributed?

(iii) How much of the balance will be interest?

SOLUTION

(i) PMT = 100.00; P/Y = 12; C/Y = 12; I/Y = 4.2;

$$i = \frac{4.2\%}{12} = 0.35\% = 0.0035; \quad n = 5(12) = 60$$

$$\begin{aligned}
\text{FV(due)} &= 100.00\left(\frac{1.0035^{60} - 1}{0.0035}\right)(1.0035)\\
&= 100.00(66.635949)(1.0035)\\
&= 6663.5949(1.0035)\\
&= \$6686.92
\end{aligned}$$

(ii) Your contribution is the amount of the payment, PMT, multiplied by the number of times you made that payment, N = (100.00)(60) = \$6000.00.

(iii) The interest earned is the difference between the accumulated value and the total contribution 6686.92 − 6000.00 = \$686.92.

POINTERS AND PITFALLS

To distinguish between problems dealing with ordinary annuities and annuities due, look for key words or phrases that signal one type of annuity or the other.

Ordinary annuities:	"payments (or deposits) made at the *end* of each (or every) . . ."
	"monthly payments, starting one month from today . . ."
	"interest payments"
Annuities due:	"payments (or deposits) made at the *beginning* of each (or every) . . ."
	"first payment is due on the date of sale (or signing)"
	"payable in advance"
	"monthly payments, starting today . . ."
	"lease or rent payments"

B. Present value of a simple annuity due

The two formulas to calculate present value for ordinary annuities and annuities due also have a close relationship.

We start with the present value formula for an ordinary annuity, Formula 11.2. The formula is then adjusted to accommodate the difference in the timing of the payment by multiplying by the factor $(1 + i)$.

$$\text{PRESENT VALUE OF A SIMPLE ANNUITY DUE} = \text{PRESENT VALUE OF AN ORDINARY SIMPLE ANNUITY} \times (1 + i)$$

The present value of an annuity due is represented by the symbol $\text{PV}_n(\text{due})$. The formula for the present value of a simple annuity due is:

$$\text{PV}_n(\text{due}) = \text{PMT}\left[\frac{1 - (1 + i)^{-n}}{i}\right](1 + i) \qquad \text{Formula 13.2}$$

EXAMPLE 13.1C Find the present value of five payments of \$3000 each made at the beginning of each of five consecutive years if money is worth 6% compounded annually.

SOLUTION As Figure 13.2 shows, the present value of the individual payments is obtained using Formula 9.1C, $\text{PV} = \text{FV}(1 + i)^{-n}$. The sum of the individual present values is easier to find when the common factor 3000.00 is taken out.

$$\begin{array}{ll} \textit{Payment 1} & 3000.00(1.06)^{0} \\ \textit{Payment 2} & 3000.00(1.06)^{-1} \\ \textit{Payment 3} & 3000.00(1.06)^{-2} \\ \textit{Payment 4} & 3000.00(1.06)^{-3} \\ \textit{Payment 5} & 3000.00(1.06)^{-4} \end{array} = 3000.00\begin{bmatrix} (1.0) \\ (1.06)^{-1} \\ (1.06)^{-2} \\ (1.06)^{-3} \\ (1.06)^{-4} \end{bmatrix} = 3000.00\begin{bmatrix} (1.000000) \\ (0.943396) \\ (0.889996) \\ (0.839619) \\ (0.792094) \end{bmatrix}$$

$$= 3000.00(4.465105)$$

$$= \$13\,395.32$$

FIGURE 13.2 Graphical Representation of Method and Data

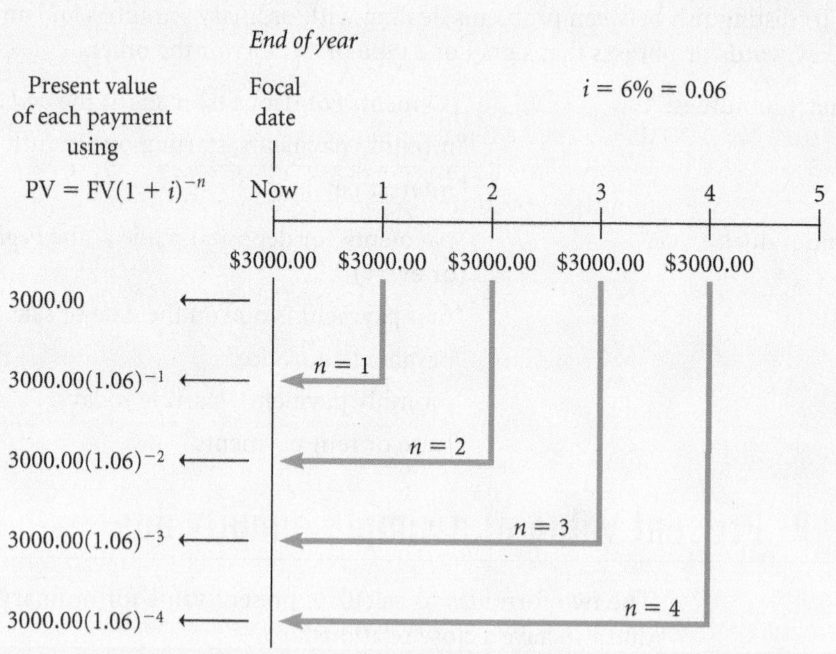

Example 13.1C is the same as Example 11.3B, except that the payments are made at the beginning of each payment period. The answer to Example 11.3B was \$12 637.09. If this amount is multiplied by 1.06, the result is \$13 395.32, the answer to Example 13.1C.

This result implies that we could have obtained the present value of the annuity due in Example 13.1C by multiplying the present value of the ordinary annuity in Example 11.3B by the factor 1.06, which is the factor $(1 + i)$.

EXAMPLE 13.1D

What is the cash value of a three-year lease of office facilities renting for \$536.50 payable at the beginning of each month if money is worth 9% compounded monthly?

SOLUTION

Since the payments for the lease are at the beginning of each payment period, the problem involves an annuity due, and since we want the cash value, the present value of the annuity due is required.

$$\text{PMT} = 536.50; \quad i = \frac{9\%}{12} = 0.75\% = 0.0075; \quad n = 3(12) = 36$$

$$\begin{aligned}\text{PV(due)} &= 536.50\left[\frac{1 - (1.0075)^{-36}}{0.0075}\right](1.0075)\\ &= 536.50(31.446805)(1.0075)\\ &= 16\,871.21(1.0075)\\ &= \$16\,997.75\end{aligned}$$

The cash value of the lease is \$16 997.75.

C. Using preprogrammed financial calculators

The future value or the present value of an annuity due can easily be determined by using a preprogrammed financial calculator. One method is to begin by finding the corresponding value for an ordinary simple annuity and multiply it by $(1 + i)$. If you are using the Texas Instruments BAII Plus, set the calculator in "BGN" mode (since annuity due payments are made at the beginning of each payment period), then solve for the unknown variable the same way as you do for ordinary simple annuities. Follow this key sequence to set the calculator in "BGN" mode:

Key in	*Press*	*Display shows*	
2nd	(BGN)	END *or* BGN	checks the mode
2nd	(SET)	BGN	if previously in "END" mode. BGN will appear in the upper-right corner of the display.
		or END	if previously in "BGN" mode. The display will be blank. Press 2nd (SET) again so that BGN appears in the display.
2nd	(QUIT)		returns to the standard calculation mode

Refer to MathXL for instructions for annuity due calculations if you are using the Sharp EL-733A or a Hewlett-Packard 10B calculator.

EXAMPLE 13.1E

Payments of $425 are to be made at the beginning of each quarter for 10 years. If money is worth 6% compounded quarterly, determine

(i) the accumulated value of the payments;

(ii) the present value of the payments.

SOLUTION

(i) PMT = 425; I/Y = 6; P/Y, C/Y = 4; $i = \frac{6\%}{4} = 1.5\%$; $n = 40$

Ensure the calculator is in "BGN" mode, and then follow this key sequence to retrieve the *future value* of an annuity due.

(Set P/Y, C/Y = 4) 0 [PV] 425 [±] [PMT] 6.0 [I/Y]

40 [N] [CPT] [FV] [23409.81274]

The accumulated value of the annuity due is $23 409.81.

(ii) Ensure the calculator is in "BGN" mode, and then follow this key sequence to retrieve the *present value* of an annuity due.

0 [FV] 425 [±] [PMT] 6.0 [I/Y] 40 [N] [CPT] [PV] [12904.947725]

The present value of the annuity due is $12 904.95.

EXAMPLE 13.1F Frank deposited \$250 at the beginning of each month for four years into a savings account. For the next eight years he made no further deposits but left the money in the account. The savings account paid interest at 4.5% compounded monthly.

(i) What will the balance be after the first four years?

(ii) What will the balance be after the twelve years?

(iii) How much in total was deposited?

(iv) How much interest will have been earned?

SOLUTION This problem involves two time periods, which must be separated and calculated individually. The time periods are the four years when deposits are being made on a regular basis, and the remaining time period of eight years when no further deposits are being made but the balance is earning interest.

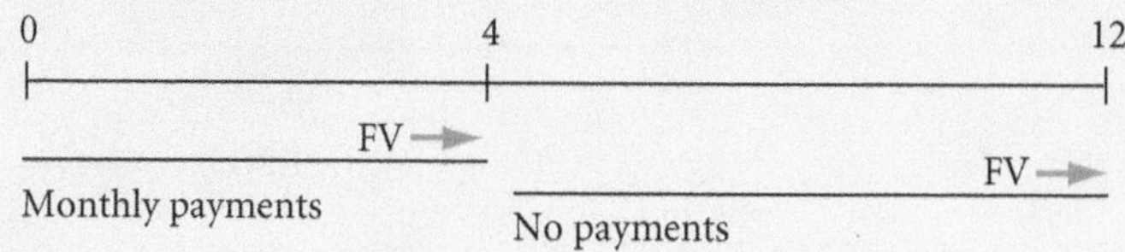

(i) Determine the balance at the end of four years. This problem involves finding the future value of a simple annuity due.

$$\text{PMT} = 250.00;\ \text{I/Y} = 4.5;\ \text{P/Y, C/Y} = 12;\ i = \frac{4.5\%}{12} = 0.375\%;\ n = 48$$

$$\begin{aligned}\text{FV(due)} &= 250.00\left(\frac{1.00375^{48} - 1}{0.00375}\right)(1.00375)\\ &= 250.00(52.483834)(1.00375)\\ &= 13\ 120.96(1.00375)\\ &= \$13\ 170.16\end{aligned}$$

(ii) Accumulate \$13 170.16 for another eight years. Note that the payment is "0" during this period.

$$\text{PV} = 13\ 170.16;\ \text{PMT} = 0;\ i = 0.00375;\quad n = 8(12) = 96$$

$$\begin{aligned}\text{FV} &= 13\ 170.16(1.00375)^{96} \quad \text{substituting in Formula 9.1A}\\ &= 13\ 170.16(1.432365)\\ &= \$18\ 864.47\end{aligned}$$

Programmed Solution

("BGN" mode) (Set P/Y, C/Y = 12) 0 [PV] 250 [±] [PMT]

4.5 [I/Y] 48 [N] [CPT] [FV] [13170.162089]

13 170.16209 [±] [PV] 0 [PMT] 4.5 [I/Y]

96 [N] [CPT] [FV] [18864.474664]

The balance in the account after twelve years is \$18 864.47.

(iii) The total deposited is 250.00(48) = \$12 000.00.

(iv) Interest in the balance is 18 864.47 − 12 000.00 = \$6864.47.

D. Finding the periodic payment PMT of a simple annuity due

If the future value of an annuity, FV_n(due) is known, you can find the periodic payment, PMT, by substituting into the future value Formula 13.1.

$$FV_n(\text{due}) = PMT\left[\frac{(1+i)^n - 1}{i}\right](1+i) \qquad \text{Formula 13.1}$$

If the present value of an annuity PV_n(due) is known, you can find the periodic payment PMT by substituting into the present value Formula 13.2.

$$PV_n(\text{due}) = PMT\left[\frac{1-(1+i)^{-n}}{i}\right](1+i) \qquad \text{Formula 13.2}$$

To find PMT, rearrange the terms of the formula. Then substitute the three known values (FV(due) or PV(due), n, and i) into the appropriate rearranged formula and solve for PMT.

When using a preprogrammed financial calculator, you can find PMT by entering the five known values (FV(due) or PV(due), N, I/Y, P/Y, and C/Y) and pressing CPT PMT.

EXAMPLE 13.1G What semi-annual payment must be made into a fund at the beginning of every six months to accumulate to \$9600 in ten years at 7% compounded semi-annually?

SOLUTION FV(due) = 9600.00; $i = \frac{7\%}{2} = 3.5\% = 0.035\%$; P/Y, C/Y = 2; I/Y = 7

$n = 10(2) = 20$

$$9600.00 = PMT\left(\frac{1.035^{20} - 1}{0.035}\right)(1.035) \qquad \text{substituting in Formula 13.1}$$

$$9600.00 = PMT(28.279682)(1.035)$$

$$9600.00 = PMT(29.269471)$$

$$PMT = \frac{9600.00}{29.269471}$$

$$PMT = \$327.99$$

Programmed Solution

("BGN" mode) (Set P/Y, C/Y = 2) 0 [PV] 9600 [FV] 7 [I/Y] 20 [N] [CPT]

[PMT] [-327.986799]

The semi-annual payment is $327.99.

EXAMPLE 13.1H

What monthly rent payment at the beginning of each month for four years is required to fulfill a lease contract worth $7000 if money is worth 7.5% compounded monthly?

SOLUTION

PV(due) = 7000.00; P/Y = 12; C/Y = 12; I/Y = 7.5;

$$i = \frac{7.5\%}{12} = 0.625\% = 0.00625; \quad n = 4(12) = 48$$

$$7000.00 = \text{PMT}\left(\frac{1 - 1.00625^{-48}}{0.00625}\right)(1.00625)$$ —— substituting in Formula 13.2

$$7000.00 = \text{PMT}(41.358371)(1.00625)$$

$$7000.00 = \text{PMT}(41.616861)$$

$$\text{PMT} = \frac{7000.00}{41.616861}$$

$$\text{PMT} = \$168.20$$

Programmed Solution

("BGN" mode) (Set P/Y = 12; C/Y = 12) 0 [FV] 7000 [±] [PV]

7.5 [I/Y] 48 [N] [CPT] [PMT] [168.201057]

The monthly rent payment due at the beginning of each month is $168.20.

EXAMPLE 13.1I

How much will you have to deposit into an account at the beginning of every three months for twelve years if you want to have a balance of $100 000 twenty years from now and interest is 8% compounded quarterly?

SOLUTION

There are two time periods, the term when no payments are made, the final (20 − 12 =) 8 years, and the initial twelve-year term of annuity payments.

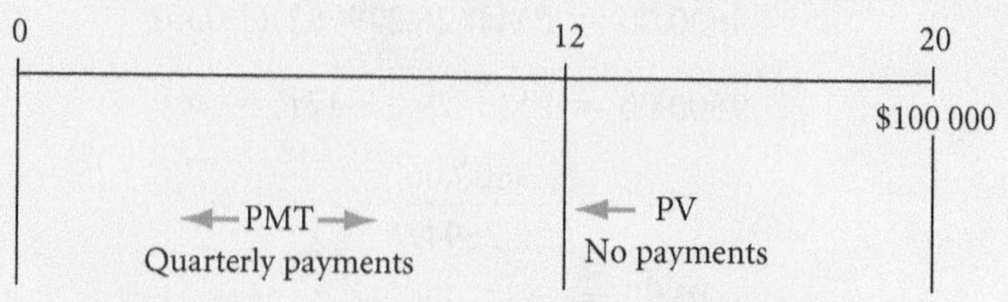

First, find the balance (PV) at the beginning of the eight-year period. This value is needed to calculate the payments during the initial twelve years.

$$\text{FV} = 100\,000.00; \quad \text{P/Y} = 4; \quad \text{C/Y} = 4; \quad \text{I/Y} = 8; \quad i = \frac{8\%}{4} = 2\% = 0.02;$$

$$n = 8(4) = 32$$

$$\text{PV} = 100\,000.00(1.02)^{-32}$$

$$= 100\,000.00(0.530633)$$

$$= \$53\,063.33$$

Next, for the initial twelve-year annuity period, find the quarterly payment needed to accumulate to $53 063.33.

$$\text{FV(due)} = 53\,063.33; \quad \text{P/Y} = 4; \quad \text{C/Y} = 4; \quad \text{I/Y} = 8; \quad i = \frac{8\%}{4} = 0.02;$$

$$n = 12(4) = 48$$

$$53\,063.33 = \text{PMT}\left(\frac{1.02^{48} - 1}{0.02}\right)(1.02)$$

$$53\,063.33 = \text{PMT}(79.353519)(1.02)$$

$$53\,063.33 = \text{PMT}(80.940590)$$

$$\text{PMT} = \frac{53\,063.33}{80.940590}$$

$$\text{PMT} = \$655.58$$

Programmed Solution

(Set P/Y = 4; C/Y = 4) 0 [PMT] 100 000 [FV]

8 [I/Y] 32 [N] [CPT] [PV] [-53063.33035]

("BGN" mode) [±] 53 063.33035 [FV] 0 [PV]

8 [I/Y] 48 [N] [CPT] [PMT] [-655.583689]

The quarterly deposit at the beginning of each payment period is $655.58.

E. Finding the term *n* of a simple annuity due

If the future value of a simple annuity FV_n(due) is known, the term of the annuity n can be found by substituting and then rearranging the terms of Formula 13.1

If the present value of a simple annuity PV_n(due) is known, the term of the annuity n can be found by substituting and then rearranging the terms of Formula 13.2.

When using a preprogrammed financial calculator, you can find n by entering the five known values (PV, PMT, I/Y, P/Y, and C/Y) and pressing [CPT] [N].

EXAMPLE 13.1J

Atlantic Credit Union intends to accumulate a building fund of \$150 000 by depositing \$4125 at the beginning of every three months at 7% compounded quarterly. How long will it take for the fund to reach the desired amount?

SOLUTION

FV(due) = 150 000.00; PMT = 4125.00; P/Y = 4; C/Y = 4; I/Y = 7;

$$i = \frac{7\%}{4} = 1.75\%$$

Programmed Solution

("BGN" mode) (Set P/Y = 4; C/Y = 4) 150 000 [FV]

4125 [±] [PMT] 7 [I/Y] [CPT] [N] 28.000210

It will take 28 quarters or seven years to build up the fund.

EXAMPLE 13.1K

For how long can you withdraw \$480 at the beginning of every three months from a fund of \$9000 if interest is 10% compounded quarterly?

SOLUTION

PV(due) = 9000.00; PMT = 480.00; P/Y = 4; C/Y = 4; I/Y = 10;

$$i = \frac{10\%}{4} = 2.5\% = 0.025$$

$$9000.00 = 480.00\left(\frac{1 - 1.025^{-n}}{0.025}\right)(1.025) \quad \text{—— substituting in Formula 13.2}$$

$$9000.00 = 19\,680.00(1 - 1.025^{-n})$$

$$\frac{9000.00}{19\,680.00} = 1 - 1.025^{-n}$$

$$0.457317 = 1 - 1.025^{-n}$$

$$1.025^{-n} = 1 - 0.457317$$

$$1.025^{-n} = 0.542683$$

$$-n \ln 1.025 = \ln 0.542683$$

$$-n(0.024693) = -0.611230$$

$$n = \frac{0.611230}{0.024693}$$

$$n = 24.753560$$

$$n = 25 \text{ (quarterly withdrawals)}$$

Programmed Solution

(Set P/Y = 4; C/Y = 4) ("BGN" mode) 9000 [±] [PV]

0 [FV] 480 [PMT] 10 [I/Y] [CPT] [N] 24.753560

There will be 24 quarterly withdrawals of \$480. The 25th withdrawal will be less than \$480.

EXAMPLE 13.1L

A lease contract valued at \$7800 is to be fulfilled by rental payments of \$180.00 due at the beginning of each month. If money is worth 9% compounded monthly, what should the term of the lease be?

SOLUTION

PV(due) = 7800.00; PMT = 180.00; P/Y = 12; C/Y = 12; I/Y = 9;

$$i = \frac{9\%}{12} = 0.75\%$$

Programmed Solution

("BGN" mode) (Set P/Y = 12; C/Y = 12) 0 [FV] 7800 [±] [PV]

180.00 [PMT] 9 [I/Y] [CPT] [N] [52.123125]

The term of the lease should be 53 months.

F. Finding the periodic rate of interest of a simple annuity due

Preprogrammed financial calculators are especially helpful when solving for the conversion rate i. Determining i without a financial calculator is extremely time-consuming. However, it *can* be done by hand, as illustrated in MathXL.

When the future value or present value, the periodic payment PMT, and the term of an annuity due are known, the periodic rate of interest i can be found by entering the five known values into a preprogrammed financial calculator. (Remember, if both PV and PMT are non-zero, enter PV *only* as a negative amount.) For simple annuities due, retrieve the answer by being in "BGN" mode and pressing [CPT] [I/Y]. This is the nominal annual rate of interest.

EXAMPLE 13.1M

Compute the nominal annual rate of interest at which \$100 deposited at the beginning of each month for ten years will amount to \$15 000.

SOLUTION

FV(due) = 15 000; PMT = 100.00; P/Y = 12; C/Y = 12; n = 120; m = 12

("BGN" mode) (Set P/Y = 12; C/Y = 12) 0 [PV] 15 000 [FV]

100 [±] [PMT] 120 [N] [CPT] [I/Y] [4.282801]

Allow several seconds for the computation.

The nominal annual rate of interest is 4.2828% compounded monthly.
The monthly conversion rate is 4.2828/12 = 0.3569%.

EXAMPLE 13.1N

A lease agreement valued at $7500 requires payment of $450 at the beginning of every quarter for five years. What is the nominal annual rate of interest charged?

SOLUTION

PV(due) = 7500.00; PMT = 450.00; P/Y = 4; C/Y = 4; $n = 20$; $m = 4$

("BGN" mode) (Set P/Y = 4; C/Y = 4) 0 [FV] 7500 [±] [PV]

450 [PMT] 20 [N] [CPT] [I/Y] [8.0326]

Allow several seconds for the computation.

The nominal annual rate of interest is 8.0326% compounded quarterly.
The quarterly compounding rate is 8.0326/4 = 2.0082%.

EXERCISE 13.1

EXCEL NOTES If you choose, you can use Excel's Present Value (PV) function or Future Value (FV) function to answer the questions indicated below. Refer to PV and FV on MathXL to learn how to use these Excel functions.

EXCEL SPREADSHEET

A. Find the future value and the present value of each of the following six simple annuities due.

	Periodic Payment	Payment Interval	Term	Interest Rate	Conversion Period
1.	$3000	3 months	8 years	8%	quarterly
2.	750	1 month	5 years	7.2	monthly
3.	2000	6 months	12 years	5.6	semi-annually
4.	450	3 months	15 years	4.4	quarterly
5.	65	1 month	20 years	9	monthly
6.	$ 160	1 month	15 years	6	monthly

EXCEL SPREADSHEET

B. Find the periodic payment for each of the following four simple annuities due.

	Future Value	Present Value	Payment Period	Term	Interest Rate	Conversion Period
1.	$20 000		3 months	15 years	6%	quarterly
2.		$12 000	1 year	8 years	7	annually
3.		$18 500	6 months	12 years	3	semi-annually
4.	$ 9 400		1 month	5 years	12	monthly

EXCEL SPREADSHEET

C. Find the length of the term for each of the following four simple annuities due.

	Future Value	Present Value	Periodic Payment	Payment Period	Interest Rate	Conversion Period
1.	$ 5 300		$ 35	1 month	6%	monthly
2.		$8 400	440	3 months	7	quarterly
3.		6 450	1 120	1 year	10	annually
4.	$15 400		396	6 months	5	semi-annually

EXCEL SPREADSHEET

D. Compute the nominal annual rate of interest for each of the following four simple annuities due.

	Future Value	Present Value	Periodic Rent	Payment Interval	Term	Compounding Period
1.	$70 000		$1 014.73	1 year	25 years	annually
2.		$42 000	528.00	1 month	10 years	monthly
3.		$28 700	2 015.00	6 months	15 years	semi-annually
4.	$36 000		$ 584.10	3 months	12 years	quarterly

EXCEL SPREADSHEET

E. Answer each of the following questions.

1. Find the accumulated value of an annuity due of $300 payable at the beginning of every month for seven years at 6% compounded monthly.

Reference Example 13.1A

2. Determine the accumulated value after twelve years of deposits of $360 made at the beginning of every three months and earning interest at 7% compounded quarterly.

3. To finance a vacation in four years, Elsie saves $530 at the beginning of every three months in an account paying interest at 3.92% compounded quarterly.
   (a) What will be the balance in her account when she takes the vacation?
   (b) How much of the balance will be interest?
   (c) If she waits an additional year to start her vacation, and continues to save the same amount of money, how much more money does she have to spend?

4. To save for his post secondary education starting in eighteen years, Harman's family deposits $1200 at the beginning of every year into an education fund earning interest at 4.15% compounded annually.
   (a) What will be the balance in the fund after eighteen years?
   (b) How much of the balance will be interest?
   (c) If the interest rate increases to 4.65% compounded annually, how much more interest is earned?

5. On an annual renewable lease, the quarterly lease payment on office space is $1600 payable in advance. What equivalent yearly payment made in advance would satisfy the lease if interest is 6.6% compounded quarterly?

6. A washer-dryer combination can be purchased from a department store by making monthly credit card payments of $52.50 for two-and-a-half years. The

first payment is due on the date of sale and interest is 21% compounded monthly.

(a) What is the purchase price?
(b) How much will be paid in installments?
(c) How much is the cost of financing?
(d) If an additional $8 per month is added to cover a service contract, what is the value of the service contract on the date of sale?

7. Diane Wallace bought a living-room suite on credit, signing an installment contract with a finance company that requires monthly payments of $62.25 for three years. The first payment is made on the date of signing and interest is 24% compounded monthly.
(a) What was the cash price?
(b) How much will Diane pay in total?
(c) How much of what she pays will be interest?
(d) Based on the cash price calculated in part (a), if the interest rate is changed to 19.9% compounded monthly, what is the new monthly payment?

8. Claude made semi-annual deposits of $3100 at the beginning of a six-month period into a fund earning 6.8% compounded semi-annually for nine years. No further deposits were made.
(a) How much will be in the account fifteen years after the first deposit?
(b) How much in total was deposited?
(c) How much interest will have been earned? Reference Example 13.1F

9. If Gary accumulated $5700 in his savings account over five years, how much did he deposit at the beginning of every month if interest is 4.32% compounded monthly?

10. Elspeth McNab purchased a boat valued at $12 500 on the installment plan requiring equal monthly payments for four years. If the first payment is due on the date of purchase and interest is 7.5% compounded monthly, what is the size of the monthly payment? Reference Example 13.1H

11. Payments on a five-year lease valued at $37 750 are to be made at the beginning of every six months. If interest is 9% compounded semi-annually, what is the size of the semi-annual payments?

12. Mr. Clark makes a deposit at the beginning of every three months into a savings account that earns interest at 5.25% compounded quarterly. He saves for twenty-five years, then converts his savings into an annuity that pays him $900 at the beginning of every three months for twenty years. What is the size of the deposit he makes while he is saving?

13. Joey's family wants to save $5000 to finance a vacation trip to a popular amusement park. If they save $240 at the beginning of each month and the fund is invested to earn 5% compounded monthly, how long will it take them to save enough money to take the trip?

14. Ali deposits $450 at the beginning of every three months. He wants to build up his account so that he can withdraw $1000 every three months starting three months after the last deposit. If he wants to make the withdrawals for

fifteen years and interest is 10% compounded quarterly, for how long must Ali make the quarterly deposits?

15. If you save \$75 at the beginning of every month for ten years, for how long can you withdraw \$260 at the beginning of each month starting ten years from now, assuming that interest is 6% compounded monthly?

16. Quarterly payments of \$1445 are to be made at the beginning of every three months on a lease valued at \$25 000. What should the term of the lease be if money is worth 8% compounded quarterly?

17. What nominal annual rate of interest compounded quarterly was paid if contributions of \$250 made into an RRSP at the beginning of every three months amounted to \$14 559 after ten years? Reference Example 13.1N

18. An insurance policy provides a benefit of \$250 000 twenty years from now. Alternatively, the policy pays \$4220 at the beginning of each year for twenty years. What is the effective annual rate of interest paid?

19. A vacation property valued at \$25 000 was bought for fifteen payments of \$2200 due at the beginning of every six months. What nominal annual rate of interest was charged?

20. A vehicle can be purchased by paying \$27 000 now, or it can be leased by paying \$725 per month for the next four years, with the first payment due on the day of signing the lease. What nominal annual rate of interest is charged on the lease?

13.2 GENERAL ANNUITIES DUE

A. Future value of a general annuity due

As with a simple annuity due, the future value of a **general annuity due** is greater than the future value of the corresponding ordinary general annuity by the interest on it for one payment period.

We start with the future value formula for an ordinary general annuity, Formula 12.2. The future value formula for a general annuity due is then adjusted to accommodate the difference in the timing of the payment. Since the interest on a general annuity for one payment period is $(1 + i)^c$, or $(1 + p)$,

$$\text{FUTURE VALUE OF A GENERAL ANNUITY DUE} = \text{FUTURE VALUE OF AN ORDINARY GENERAL ANNUITY} \times (1 + p)$$

Thus, for the future value of a general annuity due use Formula 13.3:

$$FV_g(\text{due}) = PMT\left[\frac{(1 + p)^n - 1}{p}\right](1 + p)$$

where $p = (1 + i)^c - 1$

——— Formula 13.3

EXAMPLE 13.2A What is the accumulated value after five years of payments of \$20 000 made at the beginning of each year if interest is 7% compounded quarterly?

SOLUTION PMT = 20 000.00; $n = 5$; $c = 4$; P/Y = 1; C/Y = 4; I/Y = 7

$$i = \frac{7\%}{4} = 1.75\% = 0.0175$$

The equivalent annual rate of interest

$$p = 1.0175^4 - 1 = 1.071859 - 1 = 0.071859 = 7.1859\%$$

$$\text{FV(due)} = 20\,000.00\left(\frac{1.071859^5 - 1}{0.071859}\right)(1.071859)$$ ——— substituting in Formula 13.3

$$= 20\,000.00(5.772109)(1.071859)$$

$$= 115\,442.1869(1.071859)$$

$$= \$123\,737.75$$

Programmed Solution

("BGN" mode) (Set P/Y = 1; C/Y = 4) 7 [I/Y] 0 [PV]

20 000 [±] [PMT] 5 [N] [CPT] [FV] [123737.7535]

The accumulated value after five years is \$123 737.75.

B. Present value of a general annuity due

For a general annuity due, the present value is greater than the present value of the corresponding ordinary general annuity by the interest on it for one payment period.

The present value formula for an ordinary general annuity, Formula 12.3, is adjusted to determine the present value formula for a general annuity due.

PRESENT VALUE OF A GENERAL ANNUITY DUE = PRESENT VALUE OF AN ORDINARY GENERAL ANNUITY × $(1 + p)$

Thus, for the present value of a general annuity due use Formula 13.4.

$$\text{PV}_g(\text{due}) = \text{PMT}\left[\frac{1 - (1 + p)^{-n}}{p}\right](1 + p)$$ ——— Formula 13.4

where $p = (1 + i)^c - 1$

EXAMPLE 13.2B A three-year lease requires payments of \$1600 at the beginning of every three months. If money is worth 9.0% compounded monthly, what is the cash value of the lease?

SOLUTION PMT = 1600.00; $n = 3(4) = 12$; P/Y = 4; C/Y = 12; $c = \frac{12}{4} = 3$; I/Y = 9;

$$i = \frac{9.0\%}{12} = 0.75\% = 0.0075$$

The equivalent quarterly rate of interest

$$p = 1.0075^3 - 1 = 1.022669 - 1 = 0.022669 = 2.2669\%$$

$$PV(due) = 1600.00\left(\frac{1 - 1.022669^{-12}}{0.022669}\right)(1.022669)$$ ——— substituting in Formula 13.4

$$= 1600.00(10.404043)(1.022669)$$
$$= 16\,646.46883(1.022669)$$
$$= \$17\,023.83$$

Programmed Solution

("BGN" mode)(Set P/Y = 4; C/Y = 12) 9 [I/Y] 0 [FV]

1600.00 [±] [PMT] 12 [N] [CPT] [PV] [17023.83049]

The cash value of the lease is \$17 023.83.

C. Finding the periodic payment PMT of a general annuity due

If the future value of a general annuity, FV_g(due), is known, the periodic payment PMT can be found by substituting and then rearranging the terms of Formula 13.3.

If the present value of an general annuity PV_g(due) is known, the periodic payment PMT can be found by substituting and then rearranging the terms of Formula 13.4.

When using a preprogrammed financial calculator, you can find PMT by entering the five known values (FV_{nc}(due) or PV_{nc}(due), N, I/Y, P/Y, and C/Y) and pressing [CPT] [PMT].

EXAMPLE 13.2C What deposit made at the beginning of each month will accumulate to \$18 000 at 5% compounded quarterly at the end of eight years?

SOLUTION FV(due) = 18 000.00; $n = 8(12) = 96$; P/Y = 12; C/Y = 4; $c = \frac{4}{12} = \frac{1}{3}$

I/Y = 5; $i = \frac{5\%}{4} = 1.25\% = 0.0125\%$

The equivalent monthly rate of interest

$p = 1.0125^{\frac{1}{3}} - 1 = 1.004149 - 1 = 0.004149 = 0.4149\%$

$18\,000.00 = \text{PMT}\left(\frac{1.004149^{96} - 1}{0.004149}\right)(1.004149)$ —— substituting in Formula 13.3

$18\,000.00 = \text{PMT}(117.638106)(1.004149)$

$18\,000.00 = \text{PMT}(118.126236)$

$\text{PMT} = \frac{18\,000.00}{118.126236}$

$\text{PMT} = \$152.38$

Programmed Solution

("BGN" mode)(Set P/Y = 12; C/Y = 4) 5 [I/Y] 0 [PV]

18 000 [FV] 96 [N] [CPT] [PMT] [-152.379359]

The monthly deposit is $152.38.

EXAMPLE 13.2D What monthly payment must be made at the beginning of each month on a five-year lease valued at $100 000 if interest is 10% compounded semi-annually?

SOLUTION PV(due) = 100 000.00; $n = 5(12) = 60$; P/Y = 12; C/Y = 2; $c = \frac{2}{12} = \frac{1}{6}$;

I/Y = 10; $i = \frac{10\%}{2} = 5\% = 0.05$

The equivalent monthly rate of interest

$p = 1.05^{\frac{1}{6}} - 1 = 1.008165 - 1 = 0.008165 = 0.8165\%$

$100\,000.00 = \text{PMT}\left(\frac{1 - 1.008165^{-60}}{0.008165}\right)(1.008165)$ —— substituting in Formula 13.4

$100\,000.00 = \text{PMT}(47.286470)(1.008165)$

$100\,000.00 = \text{PMT}(47.672557)$

$\text{PMT} = \frac{100\,000.00}{47.672557}$

$\text{PMT} = \$2097.64$

Programmed Solution

("BGN" mode)(Set P/Y = 12; C/Y = 2) 10 [I/Y] 0 [FV]

100 000 [±] [PV] 60 [N] [CPT] [PMT] [2097.642904]

The monthly payment due at the beginning of each month is $2097.64.

D. Finding the term *n* of a general annuity due

If the future value of an general annuity FV_g(due) is known, the term of the annuity n can be found by substituting and then rearranging the terms of Formula 13.3.

If the present value of a general annuity PV_g(due) is known, the term of the annuity n can be found by substituting and then rearranging the terms of Formula 13.4.

When using a preprogrammed financial calculator, you can find n by entering the five known values (FV_{nc}(due) or PV_{nc}(due), PMT, I/Y, P/Y, and C/Y) and pressing CPT N.

EXAMPLE 13.2E

Ted Davis wants to accumulate $140 000 in an RRSP by making annual contributions of $5500 at the beginning of each year. If interest on the RRSP is 11% compounded quarterly, for how long will Ted have to make contributions?

SOLUTION

FV(due) = 140 000.00; PMT = 5500.00; P/Y = 1; C/Y = 4; $c = 4$;

I/Y = 11; $i = \frac{11\%}{4} = 2.75\% = 0.0275$

The equivalent annual rate of interest

$$p = 1.0275^4 - 1 = 1.114621 - 1 = 0.114621 = 11.4621\%$$

$$140\,000.000 = 5500.00\left(\frac{1.114621^n - 1}{0.114621}\right)(1.114621) \quad \text{—— using Formula 13.3}$$

$$140\,000.00 = 53\,484.118(1.114621^n - 1)$$

$$2.617600 = 1.114621^n - 1$$

$$1.114621^n = 3.617600$$

$$n \ln 1.114621 = \ln 3.617600$$

$$n(0.108515) = 1.285811$$

$$n = \frac{1.285811}{0.108515}$$

$$n = 11.849188$$

$$n = 12 \text{ years}$$

Programmed Solution

("BGN" mode)(Set P/Y = 1; C/Y = 4) 11 I/Y 0 PV

5500 ± PMT 140 000 FV CPT N 11.849188

Ted will have to contribute for twelve years.

EXAMPLE 13.2F

Ted Davis, having reached his goal of a $140 000 balance in his RRSP, immediately converts it into an RRIF and withdraws from it $1650 at the beginning of each month. If interest continues at 5.75% compounded quarterly, for how long can he make withdrawals?

SOLUTION

PV(due) = 140 000.00; PMT = 1650.00; P/Y = 12; C/Y = 4; $c = \frac{4}{12} = \frac{1}{3}$;

I/Y = 5.75; $i = \frac{5.75\%}{4} = 1.4375\% = 0.014375$

The equivalent monthly rate of interest

$$p = 1.014375^{\frac{1}{3}} - 1 = 1.004769 - 1 = 0.004769 = 0.4769\%$$

$$140\,000.00 = 1650.00\left(\frac{1 - 1.004769^{-n}}{0.004769}\right)(1.004769) \quad \text{— using Formula 13.4}$$

$$140\,000.00 = 347\,642.59(1 - 1.004769^{-n})$$

$$0.402712 = 1 - 1.004769^{-n}$$

$$1.004769^{-n} = 0.597288$$

$$-n \ln 1.004769 = \ln 0.597288$$

$$-n(0.004758) = -0.515357$$

$$n = 108.32388$$

$$n = 109 \text{ months}$$

Programmed Solution

("BGN" mode)(Set P/Y = 12; C/Y = 4) 5.75 [I/Y] 0 [FV]

140 000 [±] [PV] 1650 [PMT] [CPT] [N] [108.323882]

Ted will be able to make withdrawals for 108 months from now, or nine years. His first withdrawal will be now.

E. Finding the rate of interest of a general annuity due

When the future value or present value, the periodic payment PMT and the term n of a general annuity due are known, you can find the nominal interest rate by entering the given values into a preprogrammed calculator. Retrieve the value of I/Y by being in "BGN" mode and pressing [CPT] [I/Y].

EXAMPLE 13.2G Compute the nominal annual rate of interest compounded monthly at which \$500 deposited at the beginning of every three months for ten years will amount to \$30 000.

SOLUTION FV(due) = 30 000.00; PMT = 500.00; n = 40; P/Y = 4; C/Y = 12;

$$c = \frac{12}{4} = 3$$

Programmed Solution

("BGN" mode) (Set P/Y = 4; C/Y = 12) 0 [PV] 30 000 [FV]

500 [±] [PMT] 40 [N] [CPT] [I/Y] [7.4845]

The nominal annual rate is 7.4845% compounded monthly.

EXERCISE 13.2

EXCEL NOTES If you choose, you can use Excel's Present Value (PV) function or Future Value (FV) function to answer the questions indicated below. Refer to PV and FV on MathXL to learn how to use these Excel functions.

EXCEL SPREADSHEET

A. For each of the following four annuities due, determine the unknown value represented by the question mark.

	Future Value FV(due)	Present Value PV(due)	Periodic Payment PMT	Payment Interval	Term	Nominal Rate of Interest	Conversion Period
1.	?	–	\$1500	6 months	10 years	5%	quarterly
2.	?	–	175	1 month	7 years	7	semi-annually
3.	–	?	650	3 months	6 years	12	monthly
4.	–	?	\$ 93	1 month	4 years	4	quarterly

EXCEL SPREADSHEET

B. Find the periodic payment for each of the following four annuities due.

	Future Value	Present Value	Payment Period	Term	Interest Rate	Conversion Period
1.	\$16 500	–	1 year	10 years	4%	quarterly
2.	\$ 9 200	–	3 months	5 years	5	semi-annually
3.	–	\$10 000	3 months	3 years	6	monthly
4.	–	\$24 300	1 month	20 years	9	semi-annually

EXCEL SPREADSHEET

C. Find the length of the term for each of the following four annuities due.

	Future Value	Present Value	Periodic Payment	Payment Period	Interest Rate	Conversion Period
1.	$32 000	–	$450	6 months	7.5%	monthly
2.	$ 7 500	–	150	3 months	11	annually
3.		$12 500	860	3 months	9	monthly
4.		$45 000	$540	1 month	4	semi-annually

EXCEL SPREADSHEET

D. For each of the following four annuities due, determine the nominal annual rate of interest.

	Future Value	Present Value	Periodic Payment	Payment Interval	Term	Conversion Period
1.	$ 6 400	–	$200	6 months	9 years	monthly
2.	$25 000	–	790	1 year	15 years	quarterly
3.		$ 7 500	420	3 months	5 years	monthly
4.		$60 000	450	1 month	25 years	semi-annually

E. Answer each of the following questions.

1. Bomac Steel sets aside $5000 at the beginning of every six months in a fund to replace equipment. If interest is 6% compounded quarterly, how much will be in the fund after five years? Reference Example 13.2A

2. Jamie Dean contributes $125 at the beginning of each month into an RRSP paying interest at 6.5% compounded semi-annually. What will be the accumulated balance in the RRSP at the end of 25 years?

3. What is the cash value of a lease requiring payments of $750 at the beginning of each month for three years if interest is 8% compounded quarterly? Reference Example 13.2B

4. Gerald and Marysia bought a property by agreeing to make semi-annual payments of $2500 for seven years. If the first payment is due on the date of purchase and interest is 9% compounded quarterly, what is the purchase price of the property?

5. A new owner purchased Alberni Fishing Lodge by contracting to make annual payments of $21 300 for eight years. If the first payment is due on the date of purchase and interest is 3.98% compounded quarterly, what is the purchase price of the property?

6. How much would you have to pay into an account at the beginning of every six months to accumulate $10 000 in eight years if interest is 7% compounded quarterly? Reference Example 13.2C

7. Teachers' Credit Union entered a lease contract valued at $5400. The contract provides for payments at the beginning of each month for three years. If interest is 5.5% compounded quarterly, what is the size of the monthly payment?

8. To expand his transmission shop, Hans needs to save $14 000 for new equipment. How much would he have to pay into an account at the beginning of every three months over three years if interest is 7% compounded semi-annually?

9. For their new manufacturing plant, Windsor Windows entered a lease contract valued at $64 000. With the contract, they must make payments at the beginning of each month for five years. If interest is 5.57% compounded quarterly, what is the size of the monthly payment?

10. Sarah Ling has saved $85 000. If she decides to withdraw $3000 at the beginning of every three months and interest is 6.125% compounded annually, for how long can she make withdrawals? Reference Example 13.2F

11. For how long must contributions of $1600 be made at the beginning of each year to accumulate to $96 000 at 10% compounded quarterly?

12. Sadie has subscribed to *Ingenue* magazine through a contract worth $242. If she pays $25 at the beginning of every three months and interest is 21% compounded monthly, for how many months will she receive issues of the magazine?

13. What is the nominal annual rate of interest compounded annually on a lease valued at $21 600 if payments of $680 are made at the beginning of each month for three years? Reference Example 13.2G

14. An insurance policy provides for a lump-sum benefit of $50 000 fifteen years from now. Alternatively, payments of $1700 may be received at the beginning of each of the next fifteen years. What is the nominal annual rate of interest if interest is compounded quarterly?

BUSINESS MATH NEWS BOX

Saving for a Child's Education

As tuition fees have risen, more students have relied on student loans to help finance their post-secondary education. According to the latest data from Statistics Canada, the majority of Canadian students (57%) expect to graduate with debt. And although those graduating in 2005 had an average debt load of $18 800, fortunately, similar studies have shown that post-secondary graduates have fared better in the labour market than those with less education.

With the cost of an undergraduate degree estimated at $60 000, it's essential that parents start to save for their children's education when their kids are young.

Registered Education Savings Plans (RESPs) allow for tax-sheltered growth and, through the Canada Education Savings Grant, the federal government contributes up to $7200 over the life of the plan, depending on your family income. RESPs can be used for tuition at universities, colleges, and trade and technical schools. The original capital can be withdrawn tax-free at any time, but the investment income and the grant are taxable at the beneficiary's (student's) rate of income tax, when withdrawn.

Contributing $100 a month to an RESP can grow to more than $30 000 by the end of 15 years (assuming a 7% annual rate of return).

But if parents haven't saved enough, there are other options to help. The federal government offers Canada Student Loans to full- and part-time post-secondary students in most provinces who demonstrate financial need. Students have a six-month grace period after they finish school before they must start to pay back the loan, although interest does start accumulating during this time. Alternatively, a student line of credit offers funds at a lower interest rate than a credit card, generally prime plus 1% to 3%. Payments must be made while the student is still in school, but can be spread over many years, and students generally require a cosigner (e.g., a parent or guardian).

The bottom line is that the RESP is likely the best means of accumulating money for post-secondary education, if the contribution is at least $2000 a year per child.

Source: May Luong, "The Financial Impact of Student Loans," *Perspectives on Labour and Income*, January 2010, **www.statcan.gc.ca/pub/75-001-x/2010101/article/11073-eng.htm**.

QUESTIONS

1. The advantage of the RESP is that the government will contribute $1 for every $5 parents put in, up to a maximum government grant of $500 per year per child. Assume the Wong family contributes $2000 per year over a 16-year period to an RESP earning 4.85% interest compounded semi-annually.
   a. Calculate the value the plan would have at the start of the 17th year.
   b. Calculate the value of annual contributions of $2000 into a non-RESP plan over a 16-year period at 4.85% interest compounded semi-annually.
   c. Determine the difference in plan values of the RESP plan and those of the non-RESP plan.
2. Assume that $1000 was contributed at the beginning of the year into an RESP plan for 10 years.
   a. If the rate of interest was 4% per annum compounded annually for the first 5 years, and 5.2% compounded quarterly for the last 5 years, calculate the amount of the plan.
   b. If the beneficiary's tax rate is 25% and the student uses this amount for a four-year degree, calculate the monthly value that can be used by the student.

13.3 ORDINARY DEFERRED ANNUITIES

A. Computation of an ordinary simple deferred annuity

A **deferred annuity** is one in which the first payment is made at a time *later* than the end of the first payment interval. The time period from the time referred to as "now" to the starting point of the term of the annuity is called the **period of deferment.** The number of compounding periods in the period of deferment is designated by the letter symbol d. The future value of a deferred ordinary simple annuity (designated by the symbol FV_n(defer)) is the accumulated value of the periodic payments at the end of the term of the annuity.

When the periodic payment amount PMT is known and the payments are deferred, you can find the present value PV_1 by first determining the present value of the term of the annuity. Then, using the present value of the annuity term as the future value of the deferment period, find the present value of the period of deferment PV_2.

EXAMPLE 13.3A Payments of \$500 are due at the end of each year for ten years. If the annuity is deferred for four years and interest is 6% compounded annually, determine the present value of the deferred annuity.

SOLUTION See Figure 13.3.

FIGURE 13.3 **Graphical Representation of Method and Data**

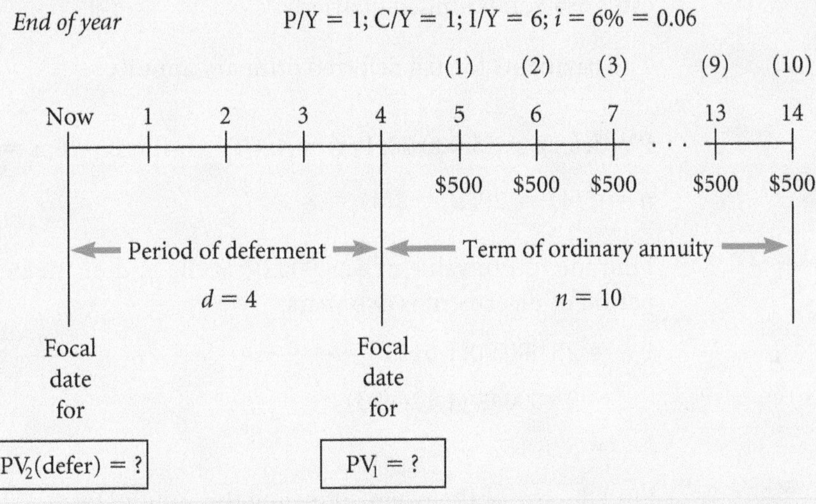

STEP 1 Focusing on the date that begins the term of the annuity, find the present value of the ordinary annuity of ten years PV_1.

$$PV_1 = 500.00\left(\frac{1 - 1.06^{-10}}{0.06}\right) \text{——— using Formula 11.2}$$

$$= 500.00(7.360087)$$

$$= \$3680.043526$$

STEP 2 With the focal date "now," and using the present value of the annuity term PV_1 as the future value of the deferment period, find the present value of the four-year period of deferment PV_2.

$$PV_2(\text{defer}) = PV = 3680.043526(1.06^{-4}) \text{——— using Formula 9.1C}$$

$$= 3680.043526(0.792094)$$

$$= \$2914.94$$

Programmed Solution

(Set P/Y = 1; C/Y = 1) 0 [FV] 500 [±] [PMT]

6 [I/Y] 10 [N] [CPT] [PV] [3680.043526]

[±] [FV] 0 [PMT] 6 [I/Y] 4 [N] [CPT] [PV] [2914.939157]

When a deferred payment amount PMT is to be calculated, and the present value PV of the deferment period is known, first determine the future value of the term of deferment. This value then becomes the present value of the annuity term, and the payment PMT is calculated.

EXAMPLE 13.3B

Find the size of the payment required at the end of every three months to repay a five-year loan of \$25 000 if the payments are deferred for two years and interest is 6% compounded quarterly.

SOLUTION

The payments form a deferred ordinary annuity

$$\text{PV(defer)} = 25\,000.00;\ \text{P/Y} = 4;\ \text{C/Y} = 4;\ \text{I/Y} = 6;\ i = \frac{6\%}{4} = 1.5\% = 0.015;$$

$$n = 5(4) = 20;\ d = 2(4) = 8$$

STEP 1

Find the future value of \$25 000.00 at the end of the period of deferment. The period of deferment is two years.

$$\text{FV} = 25\,000.00(1.015)^8 \quad \text{———— using Formula 9.1A}$$

$$= 25\,000.00(1.126493)$$

$$= \$28\,162.31466$$

STEP 2

Find the size of the payment during the annuity term of five years.

$$28\,162.31466 = \text{PMT}\left(\frac{1 - 1.015^{-20}}{0.015}\right) \quad \text{———— substituting in Formula 11.2}$$

$$28\,162.31466 = (17.168639)\text{PMT}$$

$$\text{PMT} = \frac{28\,162.31466}{17.168639}$$

$$\text{PMT} = \$1640.33$$

Programmed Solution

(Set P/Y = 4; C/Y = 4) [2nd] (CLR TVM) 25 000 [±] [PV] 0 [PMT] 6 [I/Y] 8 [N] [CPT] [FV] [28162.31466]

[±] [PV] 0 [FV] 6 [I/Y] 20 [N] [CPT] [PMT] [1640.334742]

The size of the required payment is \$1640.33.

When the length of annuity term n is to be calculated, the steps are similar to the method used in finding the periodic payment PMT.

EXAMPLE 13.3C For how long can you pay \$500 at the end of each month out of a fund of \$10 000, deposited today at 10.5% compounded monthly, if the payments are deferred for nine years?

SOLUTION The payments form a deferred ordinary annuity.

PV(defer) = 10 000.00; PMT = 500.00; P/Y = 12; C/Y = 12; I/Y = 10.5;

$$i = \frac{10.5\%}{12} = 0.875\% = 0.00875; \quad d = 9(12) = 108$$

STEP 1 Find the value of the \$10 000 at the end of the period of deferment. The period of deferment is nine years, or 108 months, because there is no payment made during those months.

$$\begin{aligned} FV &= 10\,000.00(1.00875)^{108} \\ &= 10\,000.00(2.562260) \\ &= 25\,622.59753 \end{aligned}$$

STEP 2 Find the number of monthly payments during the annuity period. The first payment is made at the end of the 109th month.

$$25\,622.59753 = 500.00\left(\frac{1 - 1.00875^{-n}}{0.00875}\right)$$

$$25\,622.59753 = 57\,142.85714(1 - 1.00875^{-n})$$

$$\frac{25\,622.59753}{57\,142.85714} = 1 - 1.00875^{-n}$$

$$0.448400 = 1 - 1.00875^{-n}$$

$$1.00875^{-n} = 0.551605$$

$$-n \ln 1.00875 = \ln 0.551605$$

$$-n(0.008712) = -0.594924$$

$$n = \frac{0.594924}{0.008712}$$

$$n = 68.288333$$

$$n = 69 \text{ (months)}$$

Programmed Solution

(Set P/Y = 12; C/Y = 12) 0 [PMT] 10 000 [±] [PV]

10.5 [I/Y] 108 [N] [CPT] [FV] [25622.59753]

[±] [PV] 0 [FV] 10.5 [I/Y]

500 [PMT] [CPT] [N] [68.288333]

Payments of \$500 can be made at the end of each of the first 68 months. For the 69th payment, the amount would be less than \$500.

Using the financial calculator, the steps to determine the nominal interest rate I/Y during the annuity term, when the payments are deferred, are similar to the methods used in finding either the periodic payment PMT or the annuity term n.

EXAMPLE 13.3D

Mr. Dhaliwal wants to receive payments of $800 at the end of each month for ten years after his retirement in seven years. If he invests $50 000 now to earn 6% compounded monthly until he retires, what monthly compounded nominal rate of interest must he earn after he retires?

SOLUTION

STEP 1 Find the accumulated value of the investment at retirement. The period of deferment is 7 years.

$PV_1 = 50\,000.00$; $PMT = 0$; $P/Y = 12$; $C/Y = 12$; $i = \frac{6\%}{12} = 0.5\% = 0.005$;
$d = 7(12) = 84$

$$\begin{aligned} FV_1 &= 50\,000.00(1.005^{84}) \\ &= 50\,000(1.520370) \\ &= \$76\,018.4818 \end{aligned}$$

STEP 2 Find the monthly payment amount, an ordinary annuity, for the period of ten years after retirement.

$PV_2 = 76\,018.4818$; $PMT = 800.00$; $P/Y = 12$; $C/Y = 12$; $n = 10(12) = 120$

Programmed Solution

(Set P/Y = 12; C/Y = 12) 50 000.00 [±] [PV] 0 [PMT] 6 [I/Y]

84 [N] [CPT] [FV] [76018.481804]

[±] [PV] 0 [FV] 800 [PMT]

120 [N] [CPT] [I/Y] [4.830216]

Mr. Dhaliwal's investments must earn 4.8302% compounded monthly.

B. Computation of an ordinary general deferred annuity

The same principles apply to an ordinary general deferred annuity as apply to an ordinary simple deferred annuity.

EXAMPLE 13.3E

Payments of $1000 are due at the end of each year for five years. If the payments are deferred for three years and interest is 10% compounded quarterly, what is the present value of the deferred payments?

SOLUTION

STEP 1 Find the present value of the term of the ordinary general annuity.

$PMT = 1000.00$; $n = 5$; $P/Y = 1$; $C/Y = 4$; $c = 4$; $I/Y = 10$;

$i = \frac{10\%}{4} = 2.5\% = 0.025$

The equivalent annual rate of interest

$p = 1.025^4 - 1 = 1.103813 - 1 = 0.103813 = 10.3813\%$

$$PV_1 = 1000.00\left(\frac{1 - 1.103813^{-5}}{0.103813}\right) \text{ ——— substituting in Formula 12.3}$$

$$= 1000.00(3.754149)$$

$$= \$3754.148977$$

Programmed Solution

(Set P/Y = 1; C/Y = 4) 1000 [±] [PMT] 0 [FV] 10 [I/Y]

5 [N] [CPT] [PV] [3754.148977]

STEP 2 Find the present value of PV_g at the beginning of the period of deferment.
FV = 3754.148977 is the present value of the general annuity PV_g;
$d = 3$ is the number of deferred payment intervals;
$p = 10.3813\%$ is the effective rate of interest per payment interval.

$$PV_2\text{ (defer)} = 3754.148977(1.103813^{-3}) \text{ ——— substituting in Formula 9.1C}$$

$$= 3754.148977(0.743556)$$

$$= \$2791.42$$

Programmed Solution

3754.148977 [FV] 10 [I/Y] 0 [PMT] 3 [N] [CPT] [PV] [-2791.419565]

The present value of the deferred payments is $2791.42.

EXAMPLE 13.3F Mr. Kovacs deposited a sales bonus of $31 500 in an income averaging annuity paying $375 at the end of each month. If payments are deferred for nine months and interest is 6% compounded quarterly, for what period of time will Mr. Kovacs receive annuity payments?

SOLUTION PV (defer) = 31 500.00; PMT = 375.00; $d = 9$; P/Y = 12; C/Y = 4;

$c = \frac{4}{12} = \frac{1}{3}$; I/Y = 6; $i = \frac{6\%}{4} = 1.5\% = 0.015$

The equivalent monthly rate of interest

$p = 1.015^{\frac{1}{3}} - 1 = 1.004975 - 1 = 0.004975 = 0.4975\%$

STEP 1 Find the accumulated value at the end of the period of deferment.

$$FV = 31\,500.00(1.004975)^9$$

$$= 31\,500.00(1.045678)$$

$$= 32\,938.86881$$

Programmed Solution

(Set P/Y = 12; C/Y = 4) 6 [I/Y] 0 [PMT]

31 500 [±] [PV] 9 [N] [CPT] [FV] 32938.86881

STEP 2 Find the number of payments for an ordinary annuity with a present value of \$32 938.86881.

$$32\,938.86881 = 375.00\left(\frac{1 - 1.004975^{-n}}{0.004975}\right)$$

$$32\,938.86881 = 75\,373.75928(1 - 1.004975^{-n})$$

$$0.437007 = 1 - 1.004975^{-n}$$

$$1.004975^{-n} = 0.562993$$

$$-n \ln 1.004975 = \ln 0.562993$$

$$-n(0.004963) = -0.574488$$

$$n = \frac{0.574488}{0.004963}$$

$$n = 115.757251$$

$$n = 116 \text{ months}$$

Programmed Solution

32 938.86881 [±] [PV] 0 [FV] 6 [I/Y] 375 [PMT] [CPT] [N] 115.757251

Mr. Kovacs will receive payments for 116 months, or nine years and eight months.

EXAMPLE 13.3G Harj and Sukie are considering the purchase of a plasma HDTV and home theatre system. The purchase price is \$2498 if they pay cash now. Alternatively, they can finance the purchase through the store's "Do not pay for 15 months" promotion. If they choose the promotion option, and wait 15 months to begin payments, they will then have 20 month-end payments of \$175.14. During the first 15 months, the loan charges interest at 7.2% compounded monthly. What service interest charge compounded monthly is being charged during the payment period?

SOLUTION

STEP 1 Find the equivalent value of the purchase price at the start of the payment period.

PV(defer) = 2498.00; PMT = 197.25; i = 0.6%; d = 15

$$FV = 2498.00(1.006^{15})$$

$$FV = 2798.00(1.096880)$$

$$FV = 2732.51$$

Programmed Solution

(Set P/Y = 12; C/Y = 12) 2498 [±] [PV] 7.2 [I/Y]

15 [N] [CPT] [FV] 2732.512421

STEP 2 Find the nominal interest rate for the payment period.

(Set P/Y = 12; C/Y = 12) 2732.51 [±] [PV] 175.14 [PMT]

20 [N] [CPT] [I/Y] 29.896464

Interest paid: 20(175.14) − 2498.00 = 3502.80 − 2498.00 = $1004.80

Harj and Sukie are paying an interest rate of 29.90% compounded monthly. They will have to pay an additional $1004.80 to finance the purchase through the promotion.

EXERCISE 13.3

EXCEL NOTES If you choose, you can use Excel's Present Value (PV) function to answer the questions indicated below. Refer to PV on MathXL to learn how to use this Excel function.

EXCEL SPREADSHEET

A. Find the present value of each of the following five ordinary deferred annuities.

	Periodic Payment	Made At:	Payment Period	Period of Deferment	Term	Interest Rate	Conversion Period
1.	$ 45	end	1 month	5 years	7 years	12%	monthly
2.	125	end	6 months	8 years	15 years	7	semi-annually
3.	2125	end	1 month	12 years	20 years	10.5	monthly
4.	720	end	3 months	4 years	10 years	12	monthly
5.	$1500	end	1 month	2 years	3 years	5	semi-annually

EXCEL SPREADSHEET

B. Answer each of the following questions.

1. Calvin Jones bought his neighbour's farm for $10 000 down and payments of $5000 at the end of every three months for ten years. If the payments are deferred for two years and interest is 8% compounded quarterly, what was the purchase price of the farm? Reference Example 13.3A

2. The Omega Venture Group needs to borrow to finance a project. Repayment of the loan involves payments of $8500 at the end of every three months for eight years. No payments are to be made during the development period of three years. Interest is 9% compounded quarterly.
   (a) How much should the Group borrow?
   (b) What amount will be repaid?
   (c) How much of that amount will be interest?

3. Zheng contracted to write a technical manual for a client. Upon completion of the manual, he agreed to accept $220.00 at the end of each month for three years. If the payments are deferred for fifteen months, and interest is 8.10% compounded monthly, what is the current value of the contract?

4. An annuity with a cash value of $14 500 earns 7% compounded semi-annually. End-of-period semi-annual payments are deferred for seven years, and then continue for ten years. How much is the amount of each payment?

Reference Example 13.3B

5. Josie won $8000 in an essay-writing contest. The money was deposited into a savings account earning 4.2% compounded monthly. She intends to leave the money for five-and-a-half years, then withdraw amounts at the end of each month for the next four years while she studies to become an entrepreneur. What will be the size of each withdrawal?

6. A deposit of $4000 is made today for a five-year period. For how long can $500 be withdrawn from the account at the end of every three months starting three months after the end of the five-year term if interest is 4% compounded quarterly?

Reference Example 13.3C

7. Greg borrowed $6500 at 6.4% compounded monthly to help finance his education. He contracted to repay the loan in monthly payments of $300 each. If the payments are due at the end of each month and the payments are deferred for four years, for how long will Greg have to make monthly payments?

8. Samantha wants to be able to withdraw $500 at the end of each month for two years while she travels, starting three years from now. If she invests $10 000 now to earn 4.68% compounded monthly until she begins to travel, what monthly compounded nominal rate of interest must she earn after she starts to travel?

Reference Example 13.3D

9. Paul is in the process of purchasing a new sound system for his car. The cash price is $1500, or he can sign a contract to "buy now and pay later." During the first year, the loan charges interest at 12.4% compounded monthly. The terms of the contract state that he would start making payments at the end of the month that is twelve months from now, paying $114 per month for eighteen months to fulfill the contract.
   (a) What monthly compounded nominal rate of interest would he be paying during the time he would be making payments?
   (b) How much extra would Paul be paying to "buy now and pay later?"

Reference Example 13.3E

10. On the day of his daughter's birth, Mr. Dornan deposited $2000 in a trust fund with his credit union at 5% compounded quarterly. Following her eighteenth birthday, the daughter is to receive equal payments at the end of each month for four years while she is at college. If interest is to be 6% compounded monthly after the daughter's eighteenth birthday, how much will she receive every month?

11. Mrs. Bell expects to retire in seven years and would like to receive $800 at the end of each month for ten years following the date of her retirement. How much must Mrs. Bell deposit today in an account paying 7.5% compounded semi-annually to receive the monthly payments?

12. Thomas is planning to withdraw $8000 from a savings account at the end of each quarter for four years. If the payments are deferred for five years and interest is 5.34% compounded semi-annually, what amount has to be invested now into the savings account?

Reference Example 13.3F

13. Asa has invested money from the settlement of an insurance claim. She plans to withdraw $600 from her savings account at the end of each month for four years. If the payments are deferred for two years and interest is 6% compounded quarterly, what was the amount of the insurance settlement?

14. Arianne borrowed $6200 to buy a vehicle to drive to school. She plans to study for three years, and then start her career using her education. Interest is charged on the loan at 7.64% compounded annually. If she starts making month-end payments of $230 when she begins working, how many payments will she have to make? Reference Example 13.3G

15. Jean inherited $25 000, where the terms of the inheritance state that she is to receive $1500 at the end of each quarter, starting in three years, until the money is completely withdrawn. If the money is placed in a savings account earning 2.75% compounded monthly, how long will the inheritance last?

16. Amir invested $12 000 in a three-year term investment earning 4.48% compounded semi-annually. He then invested the money in an investment earning 3.82% compounded semi-annually. How many quarterly $1000 withdrawals can he make?

17. An annuity purchased for $9000 makes month-end payments for seven years and earns interest at 5% quarterly. If payments are deferred for three years, how much is each payment? Reference Example 13.3H

18. Ed Ainsley borrowed $10 000 from his uncle to finance his postgraduate studies. The loan agreement calls for equal payments at the end of each month for ten years. The payments are deferred for four years and interest is 8% compounded semi-annually. What is the size of the monthly payments?

19. At Petruske's Warehouse, the forklift needs major repair. A new forklift can be purchased at a current cost of $28 000. If the new forklift is purchased, month-end payments of $679 would start in two years, and continue for five years. Interest for the first two years is charged at 8.32% compounded annually. What is the monthly compounded interest rate for the payment period?

20. Santini Construction is evaluating a project to build a bridge over the Salmon River. The project is currently worth $14 million. In one year, when the construction is 30% complete, there will be a one-time payment of $3 million. Over the next two years, quarterly payments of $1.62 million will be made. The job is scheduled to be completed within the three years. During the first year, money is worth 7.25% compounded annually. What is the annually compounded interest rate for the annuity period?

13.4 DEFERRED ANNUITIES DUE

A. Computation of a simple deferred annuity due

The same principles apply to a simple deferred annuity due as apply to a simple annuity due.

EXAMPLE 13.4A Mei Willis would like to receive annuity payments of \$2000 at the beginning of each quarter for seven years. The annuity term is to start five years from now and interest is 5% compounded quarterly.

(i) How much must Mei invest today?

(ii) How much will Mei receive from the annuity?

(iii) How much of what she receives will be interest?

SOLUTION

STEP 1 Find the present value of the annuity due (the focal point is five years from now).

(i) PMT = 2000.00; P/Y = 4; C/Y = 4; I/Y = 5; $i = \frac{5\%}{4} = 1.25\% = 0.0125$;

$n = 7(4) = 28$

$$\begin{aligned} PV_1(\text{due}) &= 2000.00\left[\frac{1 - 1.0125^{-28}}{0.0125}\right](1.0125) \\ &= 2000.00(23.502518)(1.0125) \\ &= 47\,005.03556(1.0125) \\ &= \$47\,592.60 \end{aligned}$$

STEP 2 Find the present value of \$47 592.60 (the focal point is "now").

FV = 47 592.598501; $i = 1.25\%$; $n = 5(4) = 20$

$$\begin{aligned} PV_2 &= 47\,592.5985(1.0125)^{-20} \\ &= 47\,592.5985(0.780009) \\ &= \$37\,122.63 \end{aligned}$$

Programmed Solution

("BGN" mode) (Set P/Y = 4; C/Y = 4) 0 [FV] 2000 [±] [PMT]

5 [I/Y] 28 [N] [CPT] [PV] [47592.598501]

[FV] 0 [PMT] 5 [I/Y] 20 [N] [CPT] [PV] [-37122.633667]

Mei will have to invest \$37 122.63.

(ii) Mei will receive 28(2000.00) = \$56 000.00.

(iii) Interest will be 56 000.00 − 37 122.63 = \$18 877.37.

EXAMPLE 13.4B What payment can be withdrawn at the beginning of each month for six years if \$5000 is invested today at 12% compounded monthly and the payments are deferred for ten years?

SOLUTION The payments form a deferred annuity due.

PV(defer) = 5000.00; P/Y = 12; C/Y = 12; I/Y = 12; $i = \frac{12\%}{12} = 1\% = 0.01$;

$n = 6(12) = 72$; $d = 10(12) = 120$

STEP 1 Find the value of the \$5000 at the end of the period of deferment,

$$FV = 5000.00(1.01)^{120}$$
$$= 5000.00(3.300387)$$
$$= \$16\,501.93447$$

STEP 2 Find the payment amount of the annuity.

$$16\,501.93447 = PMT\left(\frac{(1 - 1.01^{-72})}{0.01}\right)(1.01) \text{— substituting in Formula 13.2}$$

$$16\,501.93447 = PMT(51.150392)(1.01)$$
$$16\,501.93447 = (51.661896)\,PMT$$
$$PMT = \frac{16\,501.93447}{51.661896}$$
$$PMT = \$319.42$$

Programmed Solution

(Set P/Y = 12; C/Y = 12) 0 [PMT] 5000 [±] [PV]

12 [I/Y] 120 [N] [CPT] [FV] 16501.934473

("BGN" mode) 16 501.93447 [±] [PV] 0 [FV]

12 [I/Y] 72 [N] [CPT] [PMT] 319.421778

The monthly payment is \$319.42.

EXAMPLE 13.4C

A scholarship of \$2000 per year is to be paid at the beginning of each year from a scholarship fund of \$15 000 invested at 7% compounded annually. How long will the scholarship be paid if payments are deferred for five years?

SOLUTION

The annual payments form a deferred annuity due.

PV(defer) = 15 000.00; PMT = 2000.00; P/Y = 1; C/Y = 1; I/Y = 7;
$i = 7\% = 0.07$; $d = 5$

The value of the \$15 000 at the end of the period of deferment,

STEP 1

$$FV = 15\,000.00(1.07)^5$$
$$= 15\,000.00(1.402552)$$
$$= 21\,038.27596$$

STEP 2

$$21\,038.27596 = 2000.00\left(\frac{1 - 1.07^{-n}}{0.07}\right)(1.07)$$

$$21\,038.27596 = 30\,571.43(1 - 1.07^{-n})$$
$$0.688168 = 1 - 1.07^{-n}$$
$$1.07^{-n} = 0.311832$$

$$-n \ln 1.07 = \ln 0.311832$$
$$-0.067659n = -1.165290$$
$$n = \frac{1.165290}{0.067659}$$
$$n = 17.223081$$
$$n = 18 \text{ years}$$

Programmed Solution

(Set P/Y = 1; C/Y = 1) 0 PMT 15 000 ± PV

7 I/Y 5 N CPT FV 21038.27596

("BGN" mode) 21 038.27596 ± PV 0 FV

7 I/Y 2000 PMT CPT N 17.223081

The scholarship fund will provide 17 payments of $2000 and a final payment of less than $2000.

EXAMPLE 13.4D George Rich has set up a fund to help pay the expenses for a children's summer camp. The balance in the fund today is $50 000, and it will earn interest at 7% compounded annually. Starting ten years from now, $10 000 will be withdrawn from the fund at the beginning of every year for twelve years. What is the annually compounded interest rate for the fund during the final twelve years?

SOLUTION The withdrawals form a simple annuity due.

STEP 1 Find the present value of the simple annuity due ten years from now.

PMT = 0.00; P/Y = 1; C/Y = 1; I/Y = 7; $i = 7\% = 0.07$; $n = 10(1) = 10$;
So PV(due) = $50\ 000(1 + 0.07)^{10} = 50\ 000(1.967151357289566) = 98\ 357.56$.

Programmed Solution

(Set P/Y = 1; C/Y = 1) 50 000 ± PV 0 PMT 10 N 7 I/Y CPT

FV 98 357.56786

STEP 2 Find the nominal interest rate compounded annually during the annuity phase.

(Set P/Y = 1; C/Y =1) ("BGN"Mode) 98 357.56786 PV 0 FV 10000 ±

PMT 12 N CPT I/Y 3.841684

The nominal interest rate for the fund during the final 12 years is 3.8417% compounded annually.

B. Computation of a general deferred annuity due

The same principles apply to a general deferred annuity due as apply to a simple annuity due.

EXAMPLE 13.4E

Tom Casey wants to withdraw $925 at the beginning of each quarter for twelve years. If the withdrawals are to begin ten years from now and interest is 4.5% compounded monthly, how much must Tom deposit today to be able to make the withdrawals?

SOLUTION

PMT = 925.00; $n = 12(4) = 48$; $d = 10(4) = 40$; P/Y = 4; C/Y =12;

I/Y = 4.5; $c = \frac{12}{4} = 3$; $i = \frac{4.5\%}{12} = 0.375\% = 0.00375$

The equivalent quarterly rate of interest

$p = 1.00375^3 - 1 = 1.011292 - 1 = 0.011292 = 1.1292\%$

STEP 1 Find the present value of the general annuity due.

$$PV_1(\text{due}) = 925.00\left(\frac{1 - 1.011292^{-48}}{0.011292}\right)(1.011292)$$ ——substituting in Formula 13.4

$$= 925.00(36.898160)(1.011292)$$

$$= \$34\ 516.21131$$

Programmed Solution

(Set P/Y = 4; C/Y = 12) ("BGN" mode) 4.5 [I/Y] 0 [FV]

925 [±] [PMT] 48 [N] [CPT] [PV] [34516.21131]

STEP 2 Find the present value of $PV_g(\text{due})$ at the beginning of the period of deferment.

FV = 34 516.21131 is the present value of the general annuity $PV_1(\text{due})$
$d = 40$ is the number of deferred payment intervals
$p = 1.1292\%$ is the effective rate of interest per payment interval

$$PV_2(\text{defer}) = 34\ 516.21131(1.011292)^{-40}$$ ———— substituting in Formula 9.1C

$$= 34\ 516.21131(0.638165)$$

$$= \$22\ 027.04$$

Programmed Solution

[FV] 4.5 [I/Y] 0 [PMT] 40 [N] [CPT] [PV] [-22027.03920]

Tom must deposit $22 027.04 to make the withdrawals.

EXAMPLE 13.4F

A lease contract that has a cash value of $64 000 requires payments at the beginning of each month for seven years. If the payments are deferred for two years and interest is 8% compounded quarterly, what is the size of the monthly payment?

SOLUTION

PV(defer) = 64 000.00; $n = 7(12) = 84$; P/Y = 12; C/Y = 4;

$d = 2(12) = 24$; $c = \frac{4}{12} = \frac{1}{3}$; I/Y = 8; $i = \frac{8\%}{4} = 2\% = 0.02$

The equivalent monthly rate of interest

$p = 1.02^{\frac{1}{3}} - 1 = 1.006623 - 1 = 0.6623\%$

STEP 1 Determine the accumulated value of the cash value at the end of the period of deferment.

$$\begin{aligned} FV &= 64\,000.00(1.006623)^{24} \\ &= 64\,000.00(1.171659) \\ &= \$74\,986.20038 \end{aligned}$$

Programmed Solution

(Set P/Y = 12; C/Y = 4) 8 [I/Y] 0 [PMT]

64 000 [±] [PV] 24 [N] [CPT] [FV] [74986.20038]

STEP 2 Determine the periodic payment for the general annuity due whose present value is $74 986.20038.

$$74\,986.20038 = \text{PMT}\left(\frac{1 - 1.006623^{-84}}{0.006623}\right)(1.006623)$$

$$74\,986.20038 = \text{PMT}(64.267570)(1.006623)$$

$$74\,986.20038 = \text{PMT}(64.693195)$$

$$\text{PMT} = \$1159.10$$

Programmed Solution

("BGN" mode) 74 986.20038 [±] [PV] 0 [FV]

8 [I/Y] 84 [N] [CPT] [PMT] [1159.104917]

The monthly payment is $1159.10.

EXAMPLE 13.4G

By age 65, Janice Berstein had accumulated $120 000 in an RRSP by making yearly contributions over a period of years. At age 69, she converted the existing balance into an RRIF from which she started to withdraw $2000 per month. If the first withdrawal was on the date of conversion and interest on the account is 6.5% compounded quarterly, for how long will Janice Berstein receive annuity payments?

SOLUTION

PV(defer) = 120 000.00; PMT = 2000.00; $d = 4(12) = 48$

P/Y = 12; C/Y = 4; $c = \frac{4}{12} = \frac{1}{3}$; I/Y = 6.5; $i = \frac{6.5\%}{4} = 1.625\% = 0.01625$

The monthly effective rate of interest

$$p = 1.01625^{\frac{1}{3}} - 1 = 1.005388 - 1 = 0.005388 = 0.5388\%$$

Since payments are at the beginning of each month, the problem involves a deferred general annuity due.

STEP 1 Find the accumulated value at the end of the period of deferment.

$$\begin{aligned} FV &= 120\,000.00(1.005388)^{48} \\ &= 120\,000.00(1.294222) \\ &= \$155\,306.70 \end{aligned}$$

Programmed Solution

(Set P/Y = 12; C/Y = 4) 6.5 [I/Y] 0 [PMT]

120 000 [±] [PV] 48 [N] [CPT] [FV] [155306.6971]

STEP 2 Find the number of payments for an annuity due with a present value of $155 306.70.

$$\begin{aligned} 155\,306.70 &= 2000.00\left(\frac{1 - 1.005388^{-n}}{0.005388}\right)(1.005388) \\ 155\,306.70 &= 373\,223.60511(1 - 1.005388^{-n}) \\ 0.416122 &= 1 - 1.005388^{-n} \\ 1.005388^{-n} &= 0.583878 \\ -n \ln 1.005388 &= \ln 0.583878 \\ -n(0.005373) &= -0.538064 \\ n &= 100.139801 \\ n &= 101 \text{ months} \end{aligned}$$

Programmed Solution

("BGN" mode) 155 306.70 [±] [PV] 0 [FV]

6.5 [I/Y] 2000 [PMT] [CPT] [N] [100.139801]

Since the first payment is on the conversion date, Janice Berstein will receive payments of $2000 for 100 more months. The 101st payment will be less than $2000.

EXERCISE 13.4

EXCEL NOTES If you choose, you can use Excel's Present Value (PV) function to answer the questions indicated below. Refer to PV on MathXL to learn how to use this Excel function.

EXCEL SPREADSHEET

A. Find the present value of each of the following five deferred annuities due.

	Periodic Payment	Made At:	Payment Period	Period of Deferment	Term	Interest Rate	Conversion Period
1.	$850	beginning	1 year	3 years	10 years	7.5%	annually
2.	720	beginning	3 months	6 years	12 years	4	quarterly
3.	85	beginning	1 month	20 years	15 years	6	monthly
4.	145	beginning	6 months	3 years	5 years	8	quarterly
5.	$225	beginning	3 months	6 years	8 years	9	annually

EXCEL SPREADSHEET

B. Answer each of the following questions.

1. Arlene and Mario Dumont want to set up a fund to finance their daughter's university education. They want to be able to withdraw $400 from the fund at the beginning of each month for four years. Their daughter enters university in seven-and-a-half years and interest is 6% compounded monthly.
   (a) How much must the Dumonts deposit in the fund today?
   (b) What will be the amount of the total withdrawals?
   (c) How much of the amount withdrawn will be interest? Reference Example 13.4A

2. Edmonton Pizza borrowed money to redesign their restaurants. Payments of $1600 would be made at the beginning of each month for two years, starting in eighteen months. Interest on the loan is 7.12% compounded monthly.
   (a) How much must the company borrow today?
   (b) What will be the amount of the total payments?
   (c) How much of the amount paid will be interest?

3. An investment in a lease offers returns of $2500 per month due at the beginning of each month for five years. What investment is justified if the returns are deferred for two years and the interest required is 12% compounded monthly?

4. To finance the development of a new product, a company borrowed $50 000 at 7% compounded quarterly. If the loan is to be repaid in equal quarterly payments over seven years and the first payment is due three years after the date of the loan, what is the size of the quarterly payment?

5. Mike borrowed $14 000 at 6.5% compounded semi-annually. If the loan is to be repaid in equal semi-annual payments over three years and the first payment is due four years after the date of the loan, what is the size of the semi-annual payment?

6. Matt's Machine Shop purchased a computer to use in tuning engines. To finance the purchase, the company borrowed $12 000 at 8% compounded monthly. To repay the loan, equal monthly payments are made over five years, with the first payment due one year after the date of the loan. What is the size of each monthly payment?

7. An RRIF with a beginning balance of $21 000 earns interest at 10% compounded quarterly. If withdrawals of $3485 are made at the beginning of every three months, starting eight years from now, how long will the RRIF last? Reference Example 13.4C

8. A lease valued at \$32 000 requires payments of \$4000 every three months. If the first payment is due three years after the lease was signed and interest is 12% compounded quarterly, what is the term of the lease?

9. For his business, Nicholas leased equipment valued at \$23 000. The terms of the lease required payments of \$1800 every month. If the first payment is due nine months after the lease was signed and interest is 11% compounded monthly, what is the term of the lease?

10. Starting three years from now, Dustin plans to withdraw \$450 at the beginning of every three months for five years. If he has \$7200 now in his savings, and the account earns interest at 4% compounding quarterly during the first three years, what is the nominal interest rate compounded quarterly during the last five years? Reference Example 13.4B

11. Tina purchases a new computer by financing it on the "no payment until next year" plan. The cash price of the computer is \$1384. The financing agreement requires equal payments every month for two years. If the first payment of \$95 is due at the beginning of the month starting one year after the date of purchase, and interest is 28.8% compounded monthly during the first year, what is the monthly compounded nominal interest rate for the following two years?

12. Nuwan has invested a \$30 000 insurance settlement to earn interest at 4.18% compounded semi-annually for the next ten years. If he then makes withdrawals of \$850 at the beginning of every three months from the investment for twenty years, what quarterly compounded nominal interest rate is earned during the withdrawal period?

13. The sale of a property provides for payments of \$2000 due at the beginning of every three months for five years. If the payments are deferred for two years and interest is 9% compounded monthly, what is the cash value of the property? Reference Example 13.4F

14. Emerson developed a new style of camping trailer. He is considering a licensing agreement with Easy-Tow, who will manufacture the new trailer. They are proposing to pay him \$30 000 now, and \$15 000 at the beginning of each of the twelve years of the licensing agreement, starting in two years. If interest is 6.55% compounded semi-annually, what is the agreement worth today?

15. An annuity pays \$6000 at the beginning of every year for twelve years. If the payments are deferred for seven years and interest is 4.38% compounded monthly, what is the cash value of the property?

16. Dr. Young bought \$18 000 worth of equipment from Medical Supply Company. The purchase agreement requires equal payments every six months for eight years. If the first payment is due two years after the date of purchase and interest is 7% compounded quarterly, what is the size of the payments? Reference Example 13.4F

17. A business borrows $250 000 to finance an expansion. The loan agreement requires equal payments every three months for nine years. If the first payment is due two years after the date of purchase and interest is 8.3% compounded monthly, what is the size of the payments?

18. Mark and his partners have contracted to purchase the franchise rights, worth $75 000, to open and operate a specialty pizza restaurant called Pepperoni's. With a renewable agreement, the partners have agreed to make payments at the beginning of every six months for five years. To accommodate the renovation period, Pepperoni's corporate office has agreed to allow the payments to start in one year, with interest at 7.82% compounded annually. What is the amount of each payment?

19. Mrs. McCarthy has paid a single premium of $22 750 for an annuity, with the understanding that she will receive $385 at the beginning of each month. How long will the annuity last if it earns 5% compounded semi-annually, and the first payment period starts one year from now? Reference Example 13.4G

20. Bhupinder, who has just had his fifty-fifth birthday, invested $3740 on that day for his retirement. The investment earns 8% compounded monthly. For how long will he be able to withdraw $1100 at the beginning of each year, starting on his sixty-fifth birthday?

21. A property development agreement valued at $45 000 requires annual lease payments of $15 000. The first payment is due five years after the date of the agreement and interest is 11% compounded semi-annually. For how long will payments be made?

22. New vehicle lift equipment with a value of $82 000 has been purchased by Lockwood Automotive. Starting in 18 months, the company will make payments of $2200 at the beginning of every month over four years. If interest is 7.49% compounded quarterly during the first 18 months, what quarterly compounded interest rate is charged during the remaining four years?

23. Joe, Henry, and Noela, after graduating together, started a business with a $28 000 investment from their parents. For the first two years, they were charged interest at 6% compounded monthly, but no payments were required during that period. For the next five years, they would make payments of $625 at the beginning of every month, and the interest rate changed to semi-annual compounding. What is the nominal interest rate they were charged during the last five years?

24. A major property developer is concerned about lack of sales due to local economic conditions. To ensure that his condos are occupied, he offers a lease-to-purchase program in which, if people sign a lease by the end of March, they will not have to start making payments until March of the following year. The purchase price of the condo is $189 000. Payments of $1169.51 will be required at the beginning of each month over a 25-year amortization period. If interest is 5.29% compounded semi-annually during the first year, what is the semi-annually compounded interest rate during the payment period?

13.5 PERPETUITIES

A. Basic concepts

A **perpetuity** is an annuity in which the periodic payments begin on a fixed date and continue indefinitely (see Figure 13.4 for a graphical representation). Interest payments on permanently invested sums of money are prime examples of perpetuities. Dividends on preferred shares fall into this category, assuming that the issuing corporation has an indefinite life. Scholarships paid perpetually from an endowment fit the definition of perpetuity.

Since there is no end to the term, it is *not* possible to determine the future value of a perpetuity. However, the present value of a perpetuity *is* a definite value. This section deals with the present value of simple perpetuities.

B. Present value of ordinary perpetuities

We will use the following symbols when dealing with perpetuities:

PV = the present value of the perpetuity;
PMT = the periodic rent (or perpetuity payment);
i = the rate of interest per conversion period;
p = the effective rate of interest per payment period.

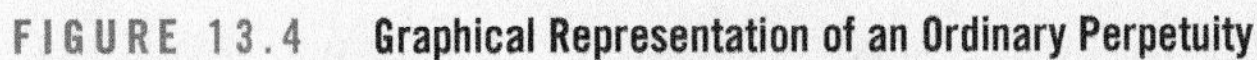
FIGURE 13.4 Graphical Representation of an Ordinary Perpetuity

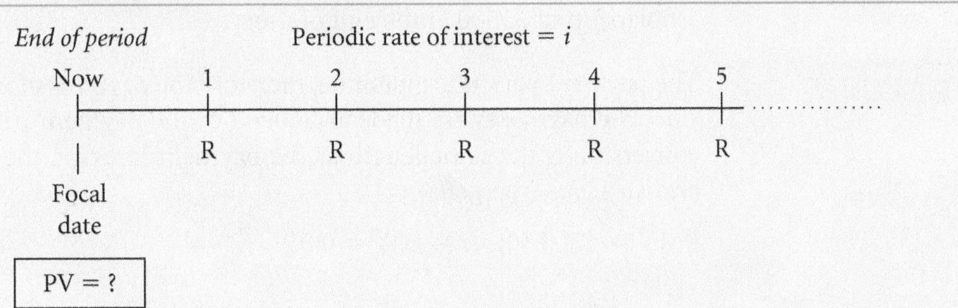

The **perpetuity payment** PMT, is the interest earned by the present value of the perpetuity in one interest period.

When n is determined, the present value of an ordinary simple annuity was calculated using the formula

$$PV_n = PMT\left[\frac{1-(1+i)^{-n}}{i}\right] \qquad \text{Formula 11.2}$$

As n in the formula increases and approaches infinity, the factor $(1 + i)^{-n}$ approaches 0.

Thus, the formula for finding the present value of an ordinary simple perpetuity is:

$$PV = \frac{PMT}{i}$$ ——— Formula 13.5

Remember that the i represents the periodic interest rate, calculated as the nominal interest rate divided by the number of conversion periods per year. That is, in the terms of the financial calculator, this represents the I/Y divided by the C/Y.

For an ordinary general perpetuity, the payment PMT is the interest earned by the present value of the perpetuity in one payment interval. That is,

$$PMT = pPV$$

Thus, the formula for finding the present value of an ordinary general perpetuity is:

$$PV = \frac{PMT}{p}$$

$$\text{where } p = (1 + i)^c - 1$$ ——— Formula 13.6

where

p = the equivalent rate of interest per payment interval;
c = the number of conversion periods per payment period.

EXAMPLE 13.5A

What sum of money invested today at 5% compounded annually will provide a scholarship of $1500 at the end of every year?

SOLUTION

The payment period is indefinite, therefore the payments form a perpetuity. Also, since the payments are made at the end of the payment period, and the interest conversion is the same length as the payment interval, the problem involves an *ordinary simple perpetuity.*

$PMT = 1500.00; \quad i = 5\% = 0.05$

$$PV = \frac{1500.00}{0.05} = \$30\,000.00$$ — substituting in Formula 13.5

EXAMPLE 13.5B

The maintenance cost for Northern Railroad of a crossing with a provincial highway is $2000 at the end of each month. Proposed construction of an overpass would eliminate the monthly maintenance cost. If money is worth 6% compounded monthly, how much should Northern be willing to contribute toward the cost of construction?

SOLUTION

The monthly maintenance expense payments form an *ordinary simple perpetuity.*

$PMT = 2000.00; \quad i = \frac{6\%}{12} = 0.005$

$$PV = \frac{2000.00}{0.005} = \$400\,000.00$$

Northern should be willing to contribute $400 000 toward construction.

EXAMPLE 13.5C What sum of money invested today at 8% compounded quarterly will provide for payments of $2500 to be paid at the end of each year indefinitely?

SOLUTION The payments form an *ordinary general perpetuity.*

$$PMT = 2500.00; \quad c = 4; \quad i = \frac{8\%}{4} = 2\% = 0.02$$

The equivalent annual rate of interest

$$p = 1.02^4 - 1 = 1.082432 - 1 = 0.082432 = 8.2432\%$$

$$PV = \frac{2500.00}{0.082432} = \$30\,327.97$$ ——— substituting in Formula 13.6

The required sum of money is $30 327.97.

EXAMPLE 13.5D A will gives an endowment of $50 000 to a university with the provision that a scholarship be paid at the end of each year indefinitely. If the money is invested at 11% compounded annually, how much is the annual scholarship?

SOLUTION $PV = 50\,000.00; \quad i = 11\% = 0.11$

By rearranging the terms of Formula 13.5, we get the equation $PMT = PVi$.

$$PMT = PVi = 50\,000.00(0.11) = \$5500.00$$

The annual scholarship is $5500.

EXAMPLE 13.5E The alumni of Centennial College collected $32 000 to provide a fund for ongoing bursaries. If the money is invested at 7% compounded annually, what is the size of the bursary that can be paid every six months?

SOLUTION $PV = 32\,000.00; \quad c = \frac{1}{2}; \quad i = 7\% = 0.07$

The equivalent semi-annual rate of interest

$$p = 1.07^{0.5} - 1 = 1.034408 - 1 = 0.034408 = 3.4408\%$$

By rearranging the terms of Formual 13.6, we get the equation $PMT = pPV$.

$$PMT = pPV = 0.034408(32\,000.00) = \$1101.06$$

The size of the bursary is $1101.06.

C. Present value of perpetuities due

A perpetuity due differs from an ordinary perpetuity only in that the first payment is made at the focal date. Therefore, a simple perpetuity due may be treated as consisting of an immediate payment, PMT, followed by an ordinary perpetuity. The formula for finding the present value of a simple perpetuity due is:

$$\text{PV(due)} = \text{PMT} + \frac{\text{PMT}}{i}$$ ——— **Formula 13.7**

A general perpetuity due can also be treated as consisting of an immediate payment, PMT, followed by an ordinary general perpetuity. Using the symbol PV(due) for the present value, the formula for finding the present value of a general perpetuity due is:

$$\text{PV(due)} = \text{PMT} + \frac{\text{PMT}}{p}$$
$$\text{where } p = (1 + i)^c - 1$$ ——— **Formula 13.8**

EXAMPLE 13.5F A tract of land is leased in perpetuity at $1250 due at the beginning of each month. If money is worth 7.5% compounded monthly, what is the present value of the lease?

SOLUTION

$$\text{PMT} = 1250.00; \quad i = \frac{7.5\%}{12} = 0.625\% = 0.00625$$

$$\text{PV} = 1250.00 + \frac{1250.00}{0.00625}$$ ——— substituting in Formula 13.7

$$= 1250.00 + 200\,000.00$$
$$= \$201\,250.00$$

EXAMPLE 13.5G What is the present value of perpetuity payments of $750 made at the beginning of each month if interest is 8.5% compounded semi-annually?

SOLUTION

$$\text{PMT} = 750.00; \quad c = \frac{2}{12} = \frac{1}{6}; \quad i = \frac{8.5\%}{2} = 4.25\% = 0.0425$$

The equivalent semi-annual rate of interest

$$p = 1.0425^{\frac{1}{6}} - 1 = 1.006961 - 1 = 0.006961 = 0.6961\%$$

$$\text{PV(due)} = 750.00 + \frac{750.00}{0.006961} = \$108\,492.18$$ ——— substituting in Formula 13.8

The present value of the perpetuity is $108 492.18.

D. Deferred perpetuities

The payments on a perpetuity may be deferred for a number of payment periods. To perform calculations for a deferred perpetuity, at least two calculations are needed.

To calculate the initial amount invested, first calculate the present value of the perpetuity, then calculate the present value of the amount at the beginning of the deferral period.

EXAMPLE 13.5H

How much money must be invested today in a fund earning 5.5% compounded annually to pay annual scholarships of $2000 starting

(i) at the end of the current year?
(ii) at the end of the year four years from now?
(iii) immediately?

SOLUTION

PMT = 2000.00; $i = 5.5\% = 0.055$

(i) The annual scholarship payments form an ordinary perpetuity.

$$PV_1 = \frac{2000.00}{0.055} = \$36\ 363.64$$

The required sum of money is $36 363.64.

(ii) The annual scholarship payments form an ordinary perpetuity. The first payment is at the end of the fourth year. During the deferral period, there are no payments for the first three years.

$$\begin{aligned} PV_2(\text{defer}) &= PV_1(1.055^{-3}) \\ &= 36\ 363.64(0.851614) \\ &= \$30\ 967.77 \end{aligned}$$

The required sum of money is $30 967.77.

(iii) The annual scholarship payments form a perpetuity due.

$$\begin{aligned} PV &= 2000.00 + \frac{2000.00}{0.055} \\ &= 2000.00 + 36\ 363.64 \\ &= \$38\ 363.64 \end{aligned}$$

The required sum of money is $38 363.64.

EXAMPLE 13.5I

What sum of money invested today in a fund earning 6.6% compounded monthly will provide perpetuity payments of $395 every three months starting

(i) immediately?
(ii) three months from now?
(iii) one year from now?

SOLUTION

$$PMT = 395.00; \quad c = \frac{12}{4} = 3; \quad i = \frac{6.6\%}{12} = 0.55\% = 0.0055$$

The equivalent quarterly rate of interest

$$p = 1.0055^3 - 1 = 1.016591 - 1 = 0.016591 = 1.6591\%$$

(i) Because the perpetuity payments are at the beginning of each payment interval, they form a *perpetuity due.*

$$PV_1(\text{due}) = 395.00 + \frac{395.00}{0.016591} = 395.00 + 23\,808.21 = \$24\,203.21$$

The required sum of money is $24 203.21.

(ii) Since the first payment is three months from now, the perpetuity payments form an *ordinary perpetuity.*

$$PV = \frac{395.00}{0.016591} = \$23\,808.21$$

The required sum of money is $23 808.21.

(iii) If you consider that the payments are deferred for one year, they form a *deferred perpetuity due.*

$$\begin{aligned} PV_2(\text{defer}) &= PV_1(\text{due}) \times (1.0055)^{-12} \\ &= 24\,203.21(0.936300) \\ &= \$22\,661.47 \end{aligned}$$

The required sum of money is $22 661.47.

Perpetuities Using a Texas Instruments BAII Plus

Perpetuities can be treated like any other annuity on the BAII Plus. While technically there are two missing variables, present value and payments can be calculated using arbitrary values for time and future value. The suggested values to use are a time of at least 300 years when calculating the value of n, and 0 for the future value. Using these values will allow the BAII Plus to mimic perpetuity and allow you to calculate perpetuity values the same way as you would any other annuity.

The process would be:

1. Set the calculator to beginning or end.
2. Set P/Y and C/Y.
3. Input the variables you know.
4. Compute the variable you want to know (present value or payments).

Note: When you are using this method, the answer may be marginally different from the formula due to the approximation used.

EXERCISE 13.5

EXCEL SPREADSHEET

Find the present value of each of the following eight perpetuities.

	Perpetuity Payment	Made At:	Payment Interval	Interest Rate	Conversion Period
1.	$1250	end	3 months	6.8%	quarterly
2.	3420	end	1 year	8.3	annually
3.	5600	end	6 months	12	monthly
4.	380	end	3 months	8	semi-annually
5.	985	beginning	6 months	4.5	semi-annually
6.	125	beginning	1 month	5.25	monthly
7.	2150	beginning	3 months	9	monthly
8.	$7250	beginning	1 month	10	quarterly

EXCEL SPREADSHEET

Answer each of the following questions.

1. Choosing to commute to work by driving a hybrid vehicle will save $32 each month in fuel. If money is worth 4% compounded monthly, how much extra money, over the price of a gas-powered vehicle, should be invested to purchase a hybrid?

2. How much can be paid in scholarships at the end of each year if $150 000 is deposited in a trust fund if interest is 4.5% compounded annually?

3. The Wambat Company pays a dividend of $4.25 every three months per preferred share. What is the expected market price per share if money is worth 8% compounded semi-annually? Reference Example 13.5A

4. Transcontinental Pipelines is considering a technical process that is expected to reduce annual maintenance costs by $85 000. What is the maximum amount of money that could be invested in the process to be economically feasible if interest is 7% compounded quarterly?

5. The municipal building for the City of Lethbridge is considering installation of a system of wind-powered generators. With the system, they can save $13 000 every six months in expenses. If interest is 4.75% compounded quarterly, how much is the amount they should invest to install the system? Reference Example 13.5D

6. Alain Dupre wants to set up a scholarship fund for his school. The annual scholarship payment is to be $2500 with the first such payment due four years after his deposit into the fund. If the fund pays 7.25% compounded annually, how much must Alain deposit?

7. Preferred shares of Western Oil paying a quarterly dividend are to be offered at $55.65 per share. If money is worth 6.2% compounded semi-annually, what is the minimum quarterly dividend to make investment in such shares economically feasible?

8. Aleena rents a suite and pays $1150 in monthly rent in advance. What is the cash value of the property if money is worth 6.6% compounded monthly?

9. Larry and John purchased a warehouse property for $836 000 that they are going to lease to several businesses, including a computer repair business. The property provides a net income of $3600 at the beginning of every month. What is the monthly compounded annual yield earned by the property?

10. Municipal Hydro offers to acquire a right-of-way from a property owner who receives annual lease payments of $2225 due in advance. What is a fair offer if money is worth 5.5% compounded quarterly? Reference Example 13.5F

11. What monthly lease payment due in advance should be charged for a tract of land valued at $35 000 if the agreed interest is 8.5% compounded semi-annually?

12. Western Pipelines pays $480 at the beginning of every half-year for using a tract of land. What should the company offer the property owner as a purchase price if interest is 8.6% compounded semi-annually?

13. Carla plans to invest in a property that after three years will yield $1200 at the end of each month indefinitely. How much should Carla be willing to pay if an alternative investment yields 9% compounded monthly?

14. The faculty of Eastern College collected $14 000 for the purpose of setting up a memorial fund from which an annual award is to be made to a qualifying student. If the money is invested at 7% compounded annually and the first annual award payment is to be made five years after the money was deposited, what is the size of the annual award payment?

15. Barbara Katzman bought an income property for $28 000 three years ago. She has held the property for the three years without renting it. If she rents the property out now, what should be the size of the monthly rent payment due in advance if money is worth 6% compounded monthly?

Go to MathXL at www.mathXL.com. You can practise many of this chapter's exercises as often as you want. The guided solutions help you find an answer step by step. You'll find a personalized study plan available to you too!

Review Exercise

1. What is the future value of monthly payments of $50 each for four years and two months at 4.62% compounded monthly if the payments form an annuity due?

2. Frank makes deposits into his savings account of $225 at the beginning of every three months. Interest earned by the deposits is 3% compounded quarterly.
   (a) What will the balance in Frank's account be after eight years?
   (b) How much of the balance will Frank have contributed?
   (c) How much of the balance is interest?

3. If you save $25 at the beginning of each month, and interest is 4% compounded quarterly, how much will you accumulate in thirty years?

4. What quarterly compounded nominal interest rate is earned on payments of $215 paid at the beginning of every month for nine years out of an investment of $18 000?

5. Home entertainment equipment can be purchased by making monthly payments of $82 for three-and-a-half years. The first payment is due at the time of purchase and the financing cost is 16.5% compounded monthly.
   (a) What is the purchase price?
   (b) How much will be paid in instalments?
   (c) How much is the cost of financing?

6. You have set a goal to save $10 000 in a savings account that earns interest at 2.54% compounded quarterly. How much must you deposit every three months for five years if the deposits are made at the beginning of each quarter?

7. Payments of $375 made every three months are accumulated at 3.75% compounded monthly. What is their amount after eight years if the payments are made
   (a) at the end of every three months?
   (b) at the beginning of every three months?

8. A property was purchased for quarterly payments of $1350 for ten years. If the first payment was made on the date of purchase and interest is 5.5% compounded annually, what was the purchase price of the property?

9. Arnie will receive payments of $850 at the beginning of every month from a trust account starting on his thirtieth birthday and continuing for twenty years. Interest is 5.04% compounded monthly.
   (a) What is the balance in the trust account on Arnie's fiftieth birthday?
   (b) How much interest will be included in the payments he receives?

10. How much must be deposited into an account to accumulate to $32 000 at 7% compounded semi-annually
    (a) at the beginning of each month for twenty years?
    (b) at the end of each year for fifteen years?

11. A six-year lease contract valued at $49 350 requires semi-annual payments. If the first payment is due at the date of signing the contract and interest is 9% compounded monthly, what is the amount of the payment?

12. How long will it take to build up a fund of $10 000 by saving $300 at the beginning of every six months at 4.5% compounded semi-annually?

13. Terry saves $50 at the beginning of each month for sixteen years. Beginning one month after his last deposit, he intends to withdraw $375 per month. If interest is 6% compounded monthly, for how long can Terry make withdrawals?

14. Debra is considering taking out a membership in her local fitness club. If she pays for a two-year membership in advance, the cost is $698. If she makes monthly payments over the same two years, she would have to pay $34 at the beginning of each month. What is the monthly compounded nominal rate charged for the payment plan?

15. Alex Sanchez won a $12 500 prize that he deposited in an account paying 5.95% compounded semi-annually for ten years. At the end of ten years, he reinvested the balance into an annuity that paid $500 at the beginning of each month starting with the date of reinvestment. If interest on the annuity is 5.16% compounded monthly, for how long will Alex receive monthly payments?

16. What is the nominal rate of interest compounded quarterly at which payments of $400 made at the beginning of every six months accumulate to $8400 in eight years?

17. FlexLabs borrowed funds to purchase a new blood analysis machine by signing a loan contract requiring payments of $1630 at the end of every three months for six years.

(a) How much is the cash value of the contract if money is worth 8.1% compounded quarterly?

(b) If the first three payments are missed, how much would have to be paid after one year to bring the contract up to date?

(c) If, because of the missed payments, the contract has to be paid out at the end of one year, how much money is needed?

(d) How much of the total interest paid is due to the missed payments?

18. A debt of $20 000 is repaid by making payments of $3500. If interest is 9% compounded monthly, for how long will payments have to be made?

(a) at the end of every six months?

(b) at the beginning of each year?

(c) at the end of every three months with payments deferred for five years?

(d) at the beginning of every six months with payments deferred for three years?

19. Tomac Swim Club bought electronic timing equipment on a contract requiring monthly payments of $725 for three years beginning eighteen months after the date of purchase. What was the cash value of the equipment if interest is 7.5% compounded monthly?

20. Aaron deposited $900 every six months for twenty years into a fund paying 5.5% compounded semi-annually. Five years after the last deposit he converted the existing balance in the fund into an ordinary annuity paying him equal monthly payments for fifteen years. If interest on the annuity is 6% compounded monthly, what is the size of the monthly payment he will receive?

21. A debt of $40 000 is to be repaid in instalments due at the end of each month for seven years. If the payments are deferred for three years and interest is 7% compounded quarterly, what is the size of the monthly payments?

22. Ty received a separation payment of $25 000 from his former employer when he was thirty-five years old. He invested that sum of money at 5.5% compounded semi-annually. When he was sixty-five, he converted the balance into an ordinary annuity paying $6000 every three months with interest at 6% compounded quarterly. For how long will the annuity continue to pay him?

23. George purchased an annuity that provides payments of $4500 at the end of every three months. The annuity is bought for $33 500 and payments are deferred for twelve years. If interest is 4.94% compounded monthly, for how long will payments be received?

24. Frank sold an antique car he had inherited, investing the proceeds of $15 000 to earn 4.84% compounded monthly. After 45 months, he converted his investment to an annuity, where he withdraws $335 at the end of each month over five years. What monthly compounded nominal rate of interest does the annuity earn during the annuity period?

25. Reagan O'Brien bought his parents' apple orchards for $200 000. The transfer agreement requires Reagan to make annual year-end payments of $35 000 for ten years. Money is worth 5.29% compounded annually. If the first payment is due in three years, what is the annually compounded nominal interest rate during the next ten years?

26. If the White Rock Fire Department invests now in new ladder systems for several of their trucks, they would save $3500 every six months in repair costs. What single cash investment made now is equivalent to the repair payments if interest is 8% compounded quarterly and the payments are made

(a) at the end of every six months for fifteen years?

(b) at the beginning of every six months for ten years?

(c) at the end of every six months for eight years but deferred for four years?

(d) at the beginning of every six months for nine years but deferred for three years?

(e) at the end of every six months in perpetuity?

(f) at the beginning of every six months in perpetuity?

27. Bonita contributed $450 at the beginning of every three months to an RRSP. Interest on the account is 6% compounded quarterly.

(a) What will the balance in the account be after seven years?

(b) How much of the balance will be interest?

(c) If Bonita converts the balance after seven years into an RRIF paying 5% compounded quarterly and makes equal quarterly withdrawals for twelve years starting three months after the conversion into the RRIF, what is the size of the quarterly withdrawal?

(d) What is the combined interest earned by the RRSP and the RRIF?

28. A church congregation has raised $37 625 for future outreach work. If the money is invested in a fund paying 7% compounded quarterly, what annual payment can be made for ten years from the fund if the first payment is to be made four years from the date of investment in the fund?

29. For their marketing class in sales techniques, the business students of Keewaten College raised $16 750 in scholarship donations. What sum of money can be withdrawn from the fund if the money is invested at 6.5% compounded semi-annually

(a) at the end of every three months for twelve years?

(b) at the beginning of each year for twenty years?

(c) at the end of each month for fifteen years but deferred for ten years?

(d) at the beginning of every three months for twelve years but deferred for twenty years?

(e) at the end of each month in perpetuity?

(f) at the beginning of each year in perpetuity?

30. Niagara Vineyards borrowed $75 000 to update their bottling equipment. They agreed to make payments of $6000 at the end of every three months. If interest is 7.31% compounded quarterly, how long will the company have to make the payments?

31. Keyes Farms bought a tractor priced at $20 000 and agreed to make payments of $1223 at the end of every three months. If interest is 7.8% compounded quarterly, how long will payments have to be made if the payments are deferred for two years and six months?

32. Pipeline Corporation's preferred share dividend of $1.45 is paid at the end of every six months. If comparable investments yield 5.6% compounded quarterly, what should be the selling price of these shares?

33. Western Railway leases land owned by the City of Regina, paying $11 000 at the beginning of each year. For what amount should Western offer to buy the land if interest is 6.5% compounded annually?

34. A scholarship fund is to be set up to provide annual scholarships of $4000. If the first payment is due in three years and interest is 4.82% compounded quarterly, what sum of money must be deposited in the scholarship fund today?

Self-Test

EXCEL SPREADSHEET

1. To support his handicapped niece, Tony made payments of $1800 into a fund at the beginning of every three months. If the fund earns interest at 5.24% compounded quarterly, how much will the balance in the fund be after eighteen years?

2. Find the present value of payments of $960 made at the beginning of every month for seven years if money is worth 6% compounded monthly.

3. Tim bought a boat valued at $10 104 by agreeing to make semi-annual payments for five years. If the first payment if due on the date of purchase and interest is 8.8% compounded semi-annually, what is the size of the semi-annual payments?

4. Bruce needs construction tools and equipment to start his new job. He has signed a lease contract valued at $5200, and will make payments of $270 at the beginning of every three months for six years. What is the nominal annual rate of interest compounded quarterly charged on the lease?

5. Through automatic transfer from her bank chequing account to her savings account, Lily has made deposits of $145 at the beginning of each month. The savings account earns interest at 2.12% compounded semi-annually. After twelve years, how much has she accumulated in her savings account?

6. A lease requires monthly payments of $950 due in advance. If interest is 12% compounded quarterly and the term of the lease is five years, what is the cash value of the lease?

7. J.J. deposited $1680 at the beginning of every six months for eight years into a fund paying 5.5% compounded semi-annually. Seven years after the first deposit, he converted the balance into an annuity paying him equal monthly payments for twenty years. If the payments are made at the end of each month and interest on the annuity is 6% compounded monthly, what is the size of the monthly payments?

8. Ken acquired his sister's share of their business by agreeing to make payments of $4000 at the end of each year for twelve years. If the payments are deferred for three years and money is worth 5% compounded quarterly, what is the cash value of the sister's share of the business?

9. The amount of $39 600 is invested at 3.5% compounded quarterly. After four years the balance in the fund is converted into an annuity. If payments of $6000 payments are made at the end of every six months for seven years, what is the nominal rate of interest compounded semi-annually on the annuity?

10. Elsie Shen wants to withdraw $6000 at the beginning of every three months for twenty years starting at the date of her retirement. If she retires in eighteen years and interest is 4.68% compounded quarterly, how much must she deposit into an account every quarter for the next eighteen years starting now?

11. The amount of $27 350 is invested at 6% compounded monthly for six years. After the initial six-year period, the balance in the fund is converted into an

annuity due paying $1600 every six months. If interest on the annuity is 4.96% compounded semi-annually, what is the term of the annuity in years?

12. New Brunswick bank pays a quarterly dividend of $0.75 per share. If comparable investments yield 4.16% compounded monthly, what is the sales value of the shares?

13. Mr. Smart wants to set up an annual scholarship by donating $50 000 to the scholarship fund of his university. If the first payment is to be made in five years and interest is 4% compounded annually, what is the amount of the annual scholarship?

14. What is the principal invested at 4.75% compounded semi-annually from which monthly withdrawals of $240 can be made

(a) at the end of each month for twenty-five years?
(b) at the beginning of each month for fifteen years?
(c) at the end of each month for twenty years but deferred for ten years?
(d) at the beginning of each month for fifteen years but deferred for twelve years?
(e) at the end of each month in perpetuity?
(f) at the beginning of each month in perpetuity?

Challenge Problems

1. A regular deposit of $100 is made at the beginning of each year for twenty years. Simple interest is calculated at *i*% per year for the twenty years. At the end of the twenty-year period, the total interest in the account is $840. Suppose that interest of *i*% compounded annually had been paid instead. How much interest would have been in the account at the end of the twenty years?

2. Herman has agreed to repay a debt by using the following repayment schedule. Starting today, he will make $100 payments at the beginning of each month for the next two-and-a-half years. He will then pay nothing for the next two years. Finally, after four-and-a-half years, he will make $200 payments at the beginning of each month for one year, which will pay off his debt completely. For the first four-and-a-half years, the interest on the debt is 9% compounded monthly. For the final year, the interest is lowered to 8.5% compounded monthly. Find the size of Herman's debt. Round your answer to the nearest dollar.

CASE STUDY 13.1 Planning for University

» Victor and Jasmine Gonzalez were discussing how to plan for their three young sons' university education. Stephen turned twelve years old in April, Jack turned nine in January, and Danny turned seven in March. Although university was still a long way off for the boys, Victor and Jasmine wanted to ensure enough funds were available for their studies.

Victor and Jasmine decided to provide each son with a monthly allowance that would cover tuition and some living expenses. Because they were uncertain about the boys' finding summer jobs in the future, Victor and Jasmine decided their sons would receive the allowance at the beginning of each month for four years. The parents also assumed that the costs of education would continue to increase.

Stephen would receive an allowance of $1000 per month starting September 1 of the year he turns eighteen.

Jack would receive an allowance that is 8% more than Stephen's allowance. He would also receive it at the beginning of September 1 of the year he turns eighteen.

Danny would receive an allowance that is 10% more than Jack's at the beginning of September of the year he turns eighteen.

Victor and Jasmine visited their local bank manager to fund the investment that would compensate the boys' allowances for university. The bank manager suggested an investment paying interest of 4.0% compounded monthly from now until the three boys had each completed their four years of education. Victor and Jasmine thought this sounded reasonable. So on June 1, a week after talking with the bank manager, they deposited the sum of money necessary to finance their sons' postsecondary educations.

QUESTIONS

1. How much allowance will each of the boys receive per month based on their parents' assumptions of price increases?
2. (a) How much money must Victor and Jasmine invest for each son on June 1 to provide them the desired allowance?
   (b) Create a timeline of events for each of the sons.
   (c) What is the total amount invested on June 1?

CASE STUDY 13.2 Setting Up Scholarships

» King's Cross University College recently launched a fundraising campaign for three new student bursaries. The Student Awards Committee of the college has been working with three community organizations to create and fund these bursaries: Friends of Education, Environmental Betterment Foundation, and Community Service Club. These organizations are all convinced that the best way to fund the bursaries is to make one large donation to the college. The donation would be invested so that it would grow over time, and regular, annual bursaries would be paid out indefinitely.

Friends of Education has agreed to donate a sum of money on September 1 that would allow its annual bursary of $1900 to be awarded immediately on September 1, and has agreed to allow the college to choose the best local student to receive its bursary every year.

Environmental Betterment Foundation would like to earn some interest on its September 1 donation before awarding its first bursary on December 1, three months later. The Foundation has agreed to award one bursary of \$2100 per year. It will choose the recipient from all applications received.

Community Service Club will make its donation on September 1, but it wants to award its bursary of \$1000 per year starting September 1 next year. This will give the club time to develop the criteria used to choose the recipient of the bursary.

QUESTIONS

1. What sum of money must Friends of Education invest on September 1 if its donation is expected to earn 3.6% compounded semi-annually?

2. What sum of money must Environmental Betterment Foundation invest on September 1 if its donation is expected to earn 4.1% compounded quarterly?

3. What sum of money must Community Service Club invest on September 1 this year if its donation is expected to earn 3.3% compounded monthly?

SUMMARY OF FORMULAS

Formula 13.1

$$FV_n(\text{due}) = PMT\left[\frac{(1+i)^n - 1}{i}\right](1+i)$$

Finding the future value of a simple annuity due

Formula 13.2

$$PV_n(\text{due}) = PMT\left[\frac{1-(1+i)^{-n}}{i}\right](1+i)$$

Finding the present value of a simple annuity due

Formula 13.3

$$FV_g(\text{due}) = PMT\left[\frac{(1+p)^n - 1}{p}\right](1+p)$$

Finding the future value of a general annuity due using the effective rate of interest per payment period

where $p = (1+i)^c - 1$

Formula 13.4

$$PV_g(\text{due}) = PMT\left[\frac{1-(1+p)^{-n}}{p}\right](1+p)$$

Finding the present value of a general annuity due using the effective rate of interest per payment period

where $p = (1+i)^c - 1$

Formula 13.5

$$PV = \frac{PMT}{i}$$

Finding the present value of an ordinary simple perpetuity

Formula 13.6

$$PV = \frac{PMT}{p}$$

Finding the present value of an ordinary general perpetuity

where $p = (1+i)^c - 1$

Formual 13.7

$$PV(due) = PMT + \frac{PMT}{i}$$

Finding the present value of a simple perpetuity due

Formual 13.8

$$PV(due) = PMT + \frac{PMT}{p}$$

Finding the present value of a general perpetuity due

where $p = (1 + i)^c - 1$

GLOSSARY

Annuity due an annuity in which the periodic payments are made at the beginning of each payment interval *(p. 504)*

Deferred annuity an annuity in which the first payment is made at a time later than the end of the first payment interval *(p. 528)*

General annuity due a general annuity in which the payments are made at the beginning of each payment interval *(p. 519)*

Period of deferment the period from the time referred to as "now" to the starting point of the term of the annuity *(p. 528)*

Perpetuity an annuity in which the periodic payments begin at a fixed date and continue indefinitely *(p. 547)*

Perpetuity payment the interest earned by the present value of the perpetuity in one interest period *(p. 547)*

USEFUL INTERNET SITES

www.tdcanadatrust.com/resp/edu_planning.jsp

RESPs Visit the TD Canada Trust's financial planning centre to read general information and FAQs about RESPs (Registered Education Savings Plans) and the products that TD Canada Trust offers.

www.smartmoney.com

SmartMoney.com SmartMoney has daily stock and mutual fund recommendations, hourly market updates, personal finance investing research tools and advice, and up-to-the-minute stock and mutual fund quotes and charts.

www.canadianbusiness.com

Canadian Business Magazine This Canadian site provides access to articles on current financial business issues, as well as tools for mutual funds, stocks, and personal finances.

APPENDIX I

Further Review of Basic Algebra

I.1 BASIC LAWS, RULES, AND DEFINITIONS

A. The fundamental operations

The fundamental operations of algebra are *addition*, *subtraction*, *multiplication*, and *division*. The symbols used to show these operations are the same as the symbols used in arithmetic.

For any two numbers a and b, the fundamental operations are as follows.

1. *Addition* is denoted by $a + b$ and referred to as the sum of a and b.
   If $a = 7$ and $b = 4$, then $a + b = 7 + 4 = 11$.
2. *Subtraction* is denoted by $a - b$ and referred to as the difference between a and b.
   If $a = 7$ and $b = 4$, then $a - b = 7 - 4 = 3$.
3. *Multiplication* is denoted by $a \times b$ or $(a)(b)$ or ab. a and b are called *factors* and ab is referred to as the product of a and b.
   If $a = 7$ and $b = 4$, then $ab = (7)(4) = 28$.
4. *Division* is denoted by $a{:}b$ or $\frac{a}{b}$ or a/b. a is the dividend, b is the divisor, and $\frac{a}{b}$ is the quotient.
   If $a = 7$ and $b = 4$, then $\frac{a}{b} = \frac{7}{4}$.

B. Basic laws

The basic laws governing algebraic operations are the same as those used for arithmetic operations.

1. The Commutative Laws for Addition and Multiplication

(a) When adding two numbers, the two numbers (addends) may be interchanged.

$$a + b = b + a \qquad \text{Formula I.1}$$

If $a = 7$ and $b = 4$, then $7 + 4 = 4 + 7 = 11$.

(b) When multiplying two numbers, the two factors may be interchanged.

$$ab = ba$$ — Formula I.2

If $a = 7$ and $b = 4$, then $(7)(4) = (4)(7) = 28$.

2. The Associative Laws for Addition and Multiplication

(a) When adding three or more numbers, the numbers (addends) may be combined in any order.

$$a + b + c = (a + b) + c = a + (b + c) = b + (a + c)$$ — Formula I.3

If $a = 7$, $b = 4$, and $c = 2$, then $7 + 4 + 2 = (7 + 4) + 2 = 7 + (4 + 2) = 4 + (7 + 2) = 13$.

(b) When multiplying three or more numbers, the numbers (factors) may be combined in any order.

$$abc = (ab)c = a(bc) = b(ac)$$ — Formula I.4

If $a = 7$, $b = 4$, and $c = 2$, then $7 \times 4 \times 2 = (7 \times 4) \times 2 = 7 \times (4 \times 2) = 4 \times (7 \times 2) = 56$.

3. The Distributive Law of Multiplication over Addition

The product of a times the sum of b and c is equal to the sum of the products ab and ac.

$$a(b + c) = ab + ac$$ — Formula I.5

If $a = 7$, $b = 4$, and $c = 2$, then $7(4 + 2) = 7 \times 4 + 7 \times 2 = 42$.

4. Special Properties of 1

(a) $a \times 1 = 1 \times a = a$

When any number a is multiplied by 1, the product is the number a.

If $a = 5$, then $5 \times 1 = 1 \times 5 = 5$.

(b) $\frac{a}{1} = a$

When any number a is divided by 1, the quotient is the number a.

If $a = 5$, then $\frac{5}{1} = 5$.

(c) $\frac{a}{a} = 1$

When any number a is divided by itself, the quotient is 1.

If $a = 5$, then $\frac{5}{5} = 1$.

5. Special Properties of 0

(a) *Addition with 0*

$a + 0 = 0 + a = a$

When 0 is added to any number *a*, the sum is the number *a*.

If $a = 5$, then $5 + 0 = 0 + 5 = 5$.

(b) *Subtraction with 0*

(i) $a - 0 = a$

When 0 is subtracted from any number *a*, the difference is the number *a*.

If $a = 5$, then $5 - 0 = 5$.

(ii) $0 - a = -a$

When any number *a* is subtracted from 0, the difference is the inverse value of *a*, that is, *a* with the sign changed.

If $a = 5$, then $0 - 5 = -5$.

(c) *Multiplication with 0*

$a \times 0 = 0 \times a = 0$

When 0 is multiplied by any number *a*, the product is 0.

If $a = 5$, then $5 \times 0 = 0 \times 5 = 0$.

(d) *Division with 0*

(i) $\frac{0}{a} = 0$

When 0 is divided by any number *a* other than 0, the quotient is 0.

(ii) $\frac{a}{0} = \text{undefined}$

Division by 0 has no meaning.

If $a = 5$, then $\frac{5}{0} = \text{undefined}$.

C. Definitions

1. An **algebraic expression** is a combination of numbers, variables representing numbers, and symbols indicating an algebraic operation.

   $7ab, 3a - 5b, x^2 - 3x + 4, \frac{3}{4}x - \frac{1}{5}y$ are algebraic expressions.

2. A **term** is a part of an algebraic expression separated from other parts by a positive (+) sign or by a negative (−) sign. The preceding (+) sign or (−) sign is part of the term.

   The terms for the algebraic expressions listed in part (1) are

   $7ab$; $3a$ and $-5b$; x^2, $-3x$, and $+4$; $\frac{3}{4}x$ and $-\frac{1}{5}y$

3. A **monomial** is an algebraic expression consisting of *one* term, such as $7ab$. A **binomial** is an algebraic expression consisting of *two* terms, such as

   $3a - 5b$ or $\frac{3}{4}x - \frac{1}{5}y$.

   A **trinomial** is an algebraic expression consisting of *three* terms, such as $x^2 - 3x + 4$. A **polynomial** is an algebraic expression consisting of *more than one* term.

4. A **factor** is one of the numbers that when multiplied by another number or other numbers yields a given product.

   The factors of the term $7ab$ are 7, a, and b.

5. A *factor of a term* is called the *coefficient* of the rest of the term.

   In the term $7ab$, 7 is the coefficient of ab,
   $7a$ is the coefficient of b,
   $7b$ is the coefficient of a.

6. The **numerical coefficient** is the part of a term formed by *numerals*.

   In the term $7ab$, the numerical coefficient is 7;
   in the term x^2, the numerical coefficient is *understood* to be 1 (1 is usually not written);
   in the term $-\frac{1}{5}y$, the numerical coefficient is $-\frac{1}{5}$ (the sign is considered to be part of the numerical coefficient).

7. The **literal coefficient** of a term is the part of the term formed with *letter* symbols.

   In the term $7ab$, ab is the literal coefficient;
   in the term $3x^2$, x^2 is the literal coefficient.

8. **Like terms** are terms having the *same* literal coefficients.

   $7a, -3a, a, -\frac{1}{3}a$ are like terms;

   $x^2, -2x^2, -\frac{1}{2}x^2, 5x^2$ are like terms.

9. **Combining like terms** or **collecting like terms** means *adding* like terms. Only like terms can be added.

10. **Signed numbers** are numbers preceded by a positive (+) or a negative (−) sign. Numbers preceded by a positive (+) sign are called **positive numbers**, while numbers preceded by a negative (−) sign are called **negative numbers.**

11. **Like signed numbers** are numbers that have the *same* sign, while numbers with *different* signs are called **unlike signed numbers.**

    +7 and +8 are like signed numbers;
    −7 and −8 are like signed numbers;
    +7 and −8 are unlike signed numbers;
    −7 and 8 are unlike signed numbers.

    Note: If no sign is written in front of a number, a plus (+) sign is understood to precede the number.

    6 means +6.

12. The **absolute value** of a signed number is the value of the number *without* the sign and is denoted by the symbol | | surrounding the number.

    The absolute value of $+5 = |+5| = 5$;
    the absolute value of $-5 = |-5| = 5$.

EXERCISE I.1

 Answer each of the following questions.

1. List the terms contained in each of the following expressions.

(a) $-3xy$ **(b)** $4a - 5c - 2d$

(c) $x^2 - \frac{1}{2}x - 2$ **(d)** $1.2x - 0.5xy + 0.9y - 0.3$

2. Name the numerical coefficient of each of the following terms.

(a) $-3b$ **(b)** $7c$ **(c)** $-a$ **(d)** x

(e) $12a^2b$ **(f)** $-3ax$ **(g)** $-\frac{1}{2}x^2$ **(h)** $\frac{x}{5}$

3. Name the literal coefficient of each of the following.

(a) $3x$ **(b)** ab **(c)** $-4y$ **(d)** $-xy$

(e) $-15x^2y^2$ **(f)** $3.5abx$ **(g)** $\frac{4}{3}x^3$ **(h)** $\frac{by}{6}$

I.2 FUNDAMENTAL OPERATIONS WITH SIGNED NUMBERS

A. Additions with signed numbers

1. *Addition of like signed numbers*

To add like signed numbers,

(i) add their absolute values, and

(ii) prefix the common sign.

EXAMPLE I.2A Add each of the following.

(i) -6 and -8

SOLUTION The absolute values are 6 and 8;
the sum of 6 and 8 is 14;
the common sign is $(-)$.
$(-6) + (-8) = -6 - 8 = -14$

(ii) $+6$, $+5$, and $+12$

SOLUTION The absolute values are 6, 5, and 12;
the sum of 6, 5, and 12 is 23;
the common sign is $(+)$.
$(+6) + (+5) + (+12) = +6 + 5 + 12 = +23$, or 23

SOLUTION

(iii) $-9, -3, -1$, and -15

The absolute values are 9, 3, 1, and 15;
the sum of the four numbers is 28;
the common sign is $(-)$.
$(-9) + (-3) + (-1) + (-15) = -9 - 3 - 1 - 15 = -28$

2. *Addition of unlike signed numbers*
To add unlike signed numbers,
(i) subtract the smaller absolute value from the larger absolute value, and
(ii) prefix the sign of the *larger* absolute value.

EXAMPLE 1.2B

Add each of the following.

(i) 8 and -5

SOLUTION

The absolute values are 8 and 5;
the difference between the absolute values is 3;
the sign of the larger absolute value is $(+)$.
$(+8) + (-5) = +8 - 5 = +3$, or 3

(ii) 4 and -9

The absolute values are 4 and 9;
the difference between the absolute values is 5;
the sign of the larger absolute value is $(-)$.
$(+4) + (-9) = 4 - 9 = -5$

(iii) $-6, +8, +3, -4$, and -5

When more than two numbers are involved and unlike signs appear, two approaches are available.

METHOD 1

Add the first two numbers and then add the sum to the next number and so on.

$$(-6) + (+8) + (+3) + (-4) + (-5)$$
$$= -6 + 8 + 3 - 4 - 5$$
$$= +2 + 3 - 4 - 5 \quad \text{——— add } -6 \text{ and } +8 \text{, which equals } +2$$
$$= +5 - 4 - 5 \quad \text{——— add } +2 \text{ and } +3 \text{, which equals } +5$$
$$= +1 - 5 \quad \text{——— add } +5 \text{ and } -4 \text{, which equals } +1$$
$$= -4 \quad \text{——— add } +1 \text{ and } -5 \text{, which equals } -4$$

METHOD 2

First add the numbers having like signs and then add the two resulting unlike signed numbers.

$$(-6) + (+8) + (+3) + (-4) + (-5)$$
$$= -6 + 8 + 3 - 4 - 5$$
$$= (-6 - 4 - 5) + (+8 + 3)$$
$$= (-15) + (+11)$$
$$= -15 + 11$$
$$= -4$$

B. Subtraction with signed numbers

The subtraction of signed numbers is changed to addition by using the inverse of the *subtrahend*. Thus, to subtract with signed numbers, change the sign of the subtrahend and add.

EXAMPLE 1.2C Perform each of the following subtractions.

(i) (+6) from (4)

SOLUTION

$(+4) - (+6)$
$= (+4) + (-6)$ — change the subtrahend (+6) to (−6) and change the subtraction to an addition
$= +4 - 6$
$= -2$ — use the rules of addition to add +4 and −6

(ii) (−12) from (+7)

$(+7) - (-12)$
$= (+7) - (+12)$ — change the subtrahend (−12) to (+12) and add
$= +7 + 12$
$= 19$

(iii) (+9) from (−6)

$(-6) - (+9)$
$= (-6) + (-9)$
$= -6 - 9$
$= -15$

C. Multiplication with signed numbers

The product of two signed numbers is positive or negative according to the following rules.

(a) If the signs of the two numbers are *like*, the product is *positive*.
$(+)(+) = (+)$
$(-)(-) = (+)$

(b) If the signs of the two numbers are *unlike*, the product is *negative*.
$(+)(-) = (-)$
$(-)(+) = (-)$

EXAMPLE 1.2D

(i) $(+7)(+4) = 28$ — the signs are like (both positive); the product is positive

(ii) $(-9)(-3) = 27$ — the signs are like (both negative); the product is positive

(iii) $(-8)(3) = -24$ — the signs are unlike; the product is negative

(iv) $(7)(-1) = -7$ — the signs are unlike; the product is negative

(v) $(-8)(0) = 0$ — the product of any number and 0 is 0

(vi) $(-7)(3)(-4) = (-21)(-4)$ — (-7) times (3) is (-21)
$= 84$

(vii) $(-2)(-1)(-4)(3) = (2)(-4)(3) = (-8)(3) = -24$

Note: Brackets around one or both numbers indicate multiplication.

D. Division with signed numbers

The quotient of two signed numbers is positive or negative according to the following rules.

(a) If the signs are *like*, the quotient is *positive*.
$(+) \div (+) = (+)$
$(-) \div (-) = (+)$

(b) If the signs are *unlike*, the quotient is *negative*.
$(+) \div (-) = (-)$
$(-) \div (+) = (-)$

EXAMPLE 1.2E

(i) $15 \div (+5) = 3$ — the signs are like; the quotient is positive

(ii) $(-24) \div (-4) = 6$ — the signs are like; the quotient is positive

(iii) $(-18) \div 2 = -9$ — the signs are unlike; the quotient is negative

(iv) $(12) \div (-1) = -12$ — the signs are unlike; the quotient is negative

(v) $0 \div (-10) = 0$ — 0 divided by any number other than 0 is 0

(vi) $(-16) \div 0 =$ undefined — division by 0 has no meaning

E. Absolute value of signed numbers

The absolute value of signed numbers, denoted by $|\ |$, is the value of the numbers without the signs.

EXAMPLE 1.2F

(i) $|-7| = 7$

(ii) $|-3 + 8| = |+5| = 5$

(iii) $|4 - 9| = |-5| = 5$

(iv) $|-9 - 4| = |-13| = 13$

(v) $|4(-7)| = |-28| = 28$

(vi) $|(-9)(-3)| = |27| = 27$

(vii) $|(-12) \div (4)| = |-3| = 3$

(viii) $|(-30) \div (-5)| = |+6| = 6$

EXERCISE I.2

A. Simplify.

1. $(+3) + (+7)$ **2.** $(+12) + (+6)$ **3.** $(-5) + (-9)$
4. $(-15) + (-12)$ **5.** $4 + (+5)$ **6.** $(+6) + 8$
7. $-8 + (-7)$ **8.** $(-18) - 7$ **9.** $+3 + 14$
10. $+12 + 1$ **11.** $-6 - 9$ **12.** $-14 - 3$
13. $-8 + 3$ **14.** $-12 + 16$ **15.** $8 - 12$
16. $0 - 9$ **17.** $1 - 0.6$ **18.** $1 - 0.02$
19. $(-4) + (6) + (-3) + (+2)$ **20.** $12 + (-15) + (+8) + (-10)$
21. $-3 - 7 + 9 + 6 - 5$ **22.** $10 - 8 - 12 + 3 - 7$

B. Simplify.

1. $(+9) - (+8)$ **2.** $(+11) - (+14)$ **3.** $(+6) - (-6)$
4. $(+11) - (-12)$ **5.** $(-8) - (-7)$ **6.** $(-9) - (-13)$
7. $(-4) - (+6)$ **8.** $(-15) - (+3)$ **9.** $0 - (-9)$
10. $1 - (-0.4)$ **11.** $1 - (-0.03)$ **12.** $0 - (+15)$
13. $6 - (-5) + (-8) - (+3) + (-2)$
14. $-12 - (-6) - (+9) + (-4) - 7$

C. Simplify.

1. $(+5)(+4)$ **2.** $11(+3)$ **3.** $(-4)(-6)$
4. $-7(-3)$ **5.** $(+7)(-1)$ **6.** $10(-5)$
7. $-3(12)$ **8.** $-9(1)$ **9.** $0(-6)$
10. $-12(0)$ **11.** $6(-4)(-3)(2)$ **12.** $-3(5)(-2)(-1)$

D. Simplify.

1. $(+18) \div (+3)$ **2.** $(32) \div (+4)$ **3.** $(+45) \div (-9)$
4. $(63) \div (-3)$ **5.** $(-28) \div (+7)$ **6.** $(-36) \div (+12)$
7. $(-16) \div (-1)$ **8.** $(-48) \div (-8)$ **9.** $0 \div (-5)$
10. $0 \div 10$ **11.** $(+4) \div 0$ **12.** $(-12) \div 0$

E. Simplify.

1. $|-9|$ **2.** $|+4|$ **3.** $|6 - 10|$ **4.** $|-5 + 12|$
5. $|-7 - 8|$ **6.** $|0 - 3|$ **7.** $|(-3) \times 3|$ **8.** $|4 \times (-5)|$
9. $|20 \div (-5)|$ **10.** $|(-35) \div (7)|$

I.3 COMMON FACTORING

A. Basic concept

In arithmetic, certain computations, such as multiplication and division involving common fractions, are helped by factoring. Similarly, algebraic manipulation can be made easier by the process of finding the factors that make up an algebraic expression.

Factoring an algebraic expression means writing the expression as a product in component form. Depending on the type of factors contained in the expression, the process of factoring takes a variety of forms. Only the simplest type of factoring applies to the subject matter dealt with in this text. Accordingly only this type, called *common factoring*, is explained in this section.

A **common factor** is one that is divisible without remainder into each term of an algebraic expression. The factor that is common to each term is usually found by inspection; the remaining factor is then obtained by dividing the expression by the common factor.

B. Examples

EXAMPLE 1.3A

Factor $14a + 21b$.

SOLUTION

By inspection, recognize that the two terms $14a$ and $21b$ are both divisible by 7.

The common factor is 7.
The second factor is now found by dividing the expression by 7.

$$\frac{14a + 21b}{7} = \frac{14a}{7} + \frac{21b}{7} = 2a + 3b$$

Thus the factors of $14a + 21b$ are 7 and $2a + 3b$.

$14a + 21b = 7(2a + 3b)$

EXAMPLE 1.3B

Factor $18a - 45$.

SOLUTION

By inspection, the highest common factor is 9;

the second factor is $\frac{18a - 45}{9} = 2a - 5$.

$18a - 45 = 9(2a - 5)$

Note: If 3 is used as the common factor, the second factor, $6a - 15$, contains a common factor 3 and can be factored into $3(2a - 5)$.

$$\begin{aligned} \text{Thus, } 18a - 45 &= 3[6a - 15] \\ &= 3[3(2a - 5)] \\ &= 9(2a - 5) \end{aligned}$$

When factoring, the accepted procedure is to always take out the *highest* common factor.

EXAMPLE 1.3C Factor $mx - my$.

SOLUTION The common factor is m;

the second factor is $\frac{mx - my}{m} = x - y$.

$mx - my = m(x - y)$

EXAMPLE 1.3D Factor $15x^3 - 25x^2 - 20x$.

SOLUTION The common factor is $5x$.

The second factor is $\frac{15x^3 - 25x^2 - 20x}{5x} = 3x^2 - 5x - 4$.

$15x^3 - 25x^2 - 20x = 5x(3x^2 - 5x - 4)$

EXAMPLE 1.3E Factor $P + Prt$.

SOLUTION The common factor is P.

The second factor is $\frac{P + Prt}{P} = \frac{P}{P} + \frac{Prt}{P} + 1 + rt$.

$P + Prt = P(1 + rt)$

EXAMPLE 1.3F Factor $a(x + y) - b(x + y)$.

SOLUTION The common factor is $(x + y)$.

The second factor is $\frac{a(x + y) - b(x + y)}{x + y} = \frac{a(x + y)}{x + y} - \frac{b(x + y)}{x + y} = a - b$.

$a(x + y) - b(x + y) = (x + y)(a - b)$

EXAMPLE 1.3G Factor $(1 + i) + (1 + i)^2 + (1 + i)^3$.

SOLUTION The common factor is $(1 + i)$.

The second factor is $\frac{(1 + i) + (1 + i)^2 + (1 + i)^3}{(1 + i)}$

$$= \frac{(1+i)}{(1+i)} + \frac{(1+i)^2}{(1+i)} + \frac{(1+i)^3}{(1+i)}$$

$$= 1 + (1+i) + (1+i)^2$$

$$(1+i) + (1+i)^2 + (1+i)^3 = (1+i)\,[1 + (1+i) + (1+i)^2]$$

EXERCISE I.3

A. Factor each of the following.

1. $8x - 12$ **2.** $27 - 36a$

3. $4n^2 - 8n$ **4.** $9x^2 - 21x$

5. $5ax - 10ay - 20a$ **6.** $4ma - 12mb + 24mab$

B. Factor each of the following.

1. $mx + my$ **2.** $xa - xb$

3. $m(a - b)+n(a - b)$ **4.** $k(x - 1) -3(x - 1)$

5. $\mathrm{P} + \mathrm{P}i$ **6.** $\mathrm{A} - \mathrm{A}dt$

7. $r - r^2 - r^3$ **8.** $(1 + i)^4 + (1 + i)^3 + (1 + i)^2$

I.4 GRAPHING INEQUALITIES

A. Basic concepts and method

A straight line drawn in a plane divides the plane into two regions:

(a) the region to the left of the line drawn in the plane;
(b) the region to the right of the line drawn in the plane.

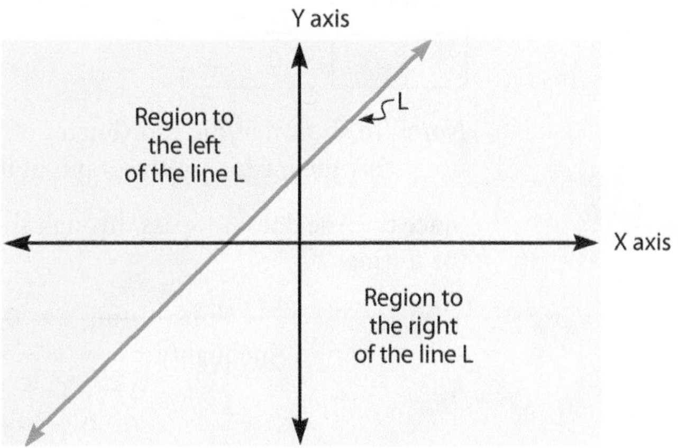

When a system of axes is introduced into the plane, each region consists of a set of points that may be represented by ordered pairs (x, y). Relative to the dividing line, the two sets of ordered pairs (x, y) that represent the points in the regions are defined by the two **inequalities** associated with the equation of the dividing line.

For the equation $x = 5$, the associated inequalities are $x < 5$ (x is less than 5) and $x > 5$ (x is greater than 5). For the equation $y = -3$, the associated inequalities are $y < -3$ and $y > -3$. For the equation $2x + 3y = 6$, the associated inequalities are $2x + 3y < 6$ and $2x + 3y > 6$.

Graphing an inequality means identifying the region that consists of the set of points whose coordinates satisfy the given inequality. To identify this region, use the following method.

1. *Draw* the graph of the equation associated with the inequality.
2. *Test* an arbitrarily selected point that is not a point on the line by substituting its coordinates in the inequality. The preferred point for testing is (0, 0). If (0, 0) is not available because the line passes through the origin, try the points (0, 1) or (1, 0).
3. **(a)** If substituting the coordinates of the selected point in the inequality yields a mathematical statement that is true, the selected point is a point in the region defined by the inequality. Thus, the region is identified as the area containing the selected point.

   (b) If substituting the coordinates of the selected point in the inequality yields a mathematical statement that is false, the selected point is not a point in the region defined by the inequality. Thus, the region defined by the inequality is the area that does not contain the point tested.

B. Graphing inequalities of the form $ax + by > c$ and $ax + by < c$

EXAMPLE 1.4A Graph each of the following inequalities.

(i) $x - y > -3$ (ii) $3x + 2y < -8$

SOLUTION (i) The equation associated with the inequality $x - y > -3$ is $x - y = -3$.

Table of values

x	0	−3	2
y	3	0	5

Note: To show that the coordinates of the points on the line $x - y = -3$ do not satisfy the inequality, the graph of the equation is drawn as a broken line.

Since the line does not pass through the origin, the point (0, 0) may be used for testing.

Substituting $x = 0$ and $y = 0$ in the inequality $x - y > -3$ yields the statement

$$0 - 0 > -3$$
$$0 > -3$$

Since the statement $0 > -3$ is true, the point (0, 0) is a point in the region. The region defined by the inequality $x - y > -3$ is the area to the right of the line as shown in the diagram below.

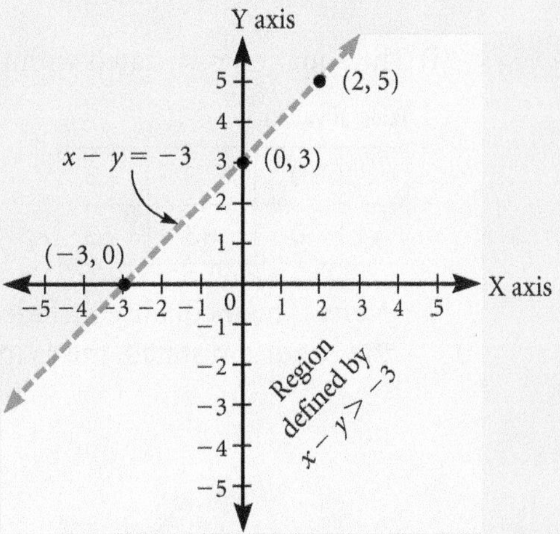

(ii) The equation associated with the inequality $3x + 2y < -8$ is $3x + 2y = -8$.

Table of values

x	0	−2	−4
y	−4	−1	2

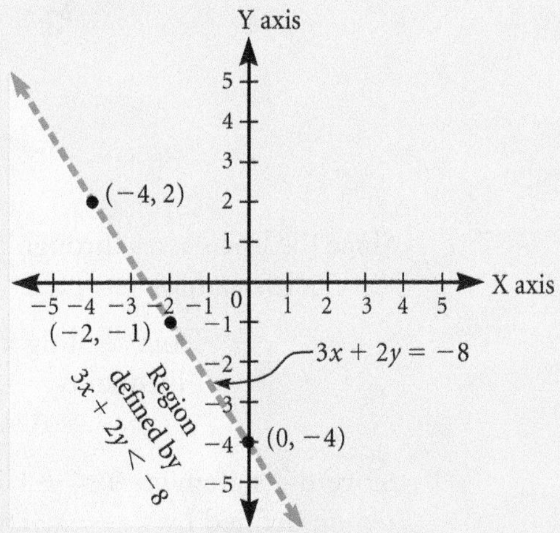

Testing the point (0, 0)

$$3(0) + 2(0) < -8$$
$$0 + 0 < -8$$
$$0 < -8$$

Since the statement $0 < -8$ is false, the point (0, 0) is not a point in the region defined by $3x + 2y < -8$. The region defined by the inequality is the area to the left of the line as shown.

C. Graphing inequalities of the form $ax > by$ or $ax < by$

EXAMPLE 1.4B Graph each of the following inequalities.

(i) $y \leq -x$ (ii) $3x < 2y$

SOLUTION (i) The equation associated with the inequality $y \leq -x$ is $y = -x$.

Table of values

x	0	3	−3
y	0	−3	3

Note: The inequality includes $y = -x$. Because the points on the line meet the condition stated, the graph of the equation is drawn as a solid line.

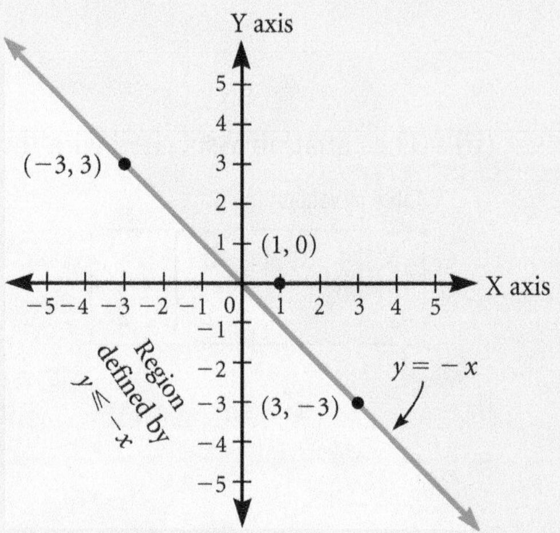

Since the line passes through the origin, the point (0, 0) cannot be used for testing. Instead, we test (1, 0).

Substituting $x = 1, y = 0$ in the inequality $y < -x$ yields the statement $0 < -1$.

Since the statement $0 < -1$ is false, the point (1, 0) is not a point in the region defined by $y \leq -x$. The region defined by the inequality is the area to the left of the line *including* the line.

(ii) The equation associated with the inequality $3x < 2y$ is $3x = 2y$.

Table of values

x	0	2	−2
y	0	3	−3

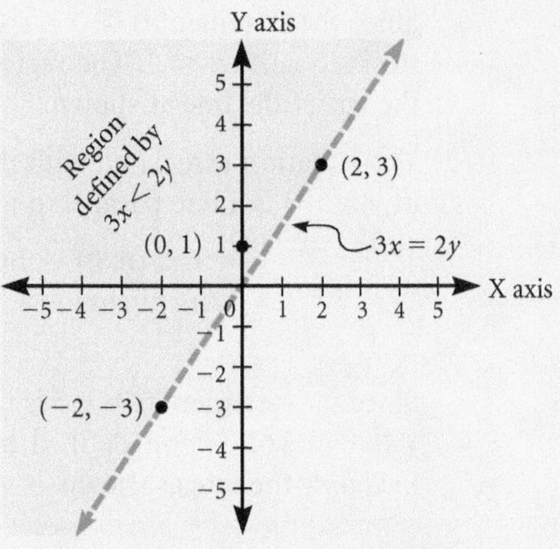

Since (0, 0) is on the line, test (0, 1). Substituting $x = 0, y = 1$ in the inequality $3x < 2y$ yields the statement

$$0 < 2.$$

Since the statement $0 < 2$ is true, the point (0, 1) is a point in the region defined by $3x < 2y$. The region defined by the inequality is the area to the left of the line as shown.

D. Graphing inequalities involving lines parallel to the axes

EXAMPLE 1.4C Graph each of the following inequalities.

(i) $x < 3$ (ii) $y \geq -3$

SOLUTION (i) The equation associated with the inequality $x < 3$ is $x = 3$. The graph of $x = 3$ is a line parallel to the Y axis three units to the right.

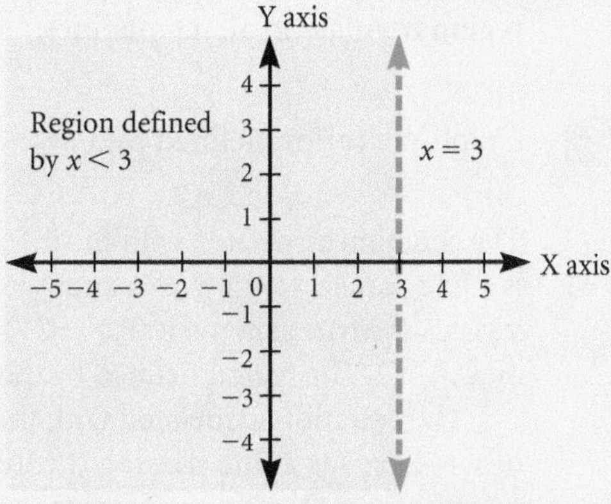

Test (0, 0). Substituting $x = 0$ in the inequality $x < 3$ yields the statement

$$0 < 3.$$

Since the statement $0 < 3$ is true, (0, 0) is a point in the region defined by the inequality $x < 3$. The region defined by the inequality is the region to the left of the line as shown.

(ii) The equation associated with the inequality $y \geq -3$ is $y = -3$. The graph of $y = -3$ is a line parallel to the X axis three units below it.

Test (0, 0). Substituting $y = 0$ in the inequality $y > -3$ yields the statement
$$0 > -3.$$

Since the statement $0 > -3$ is true, (0, 0) is a point in the region defined by $y \geq -3$. The region defined by the inequality is the area above the line *including* the line as shown.

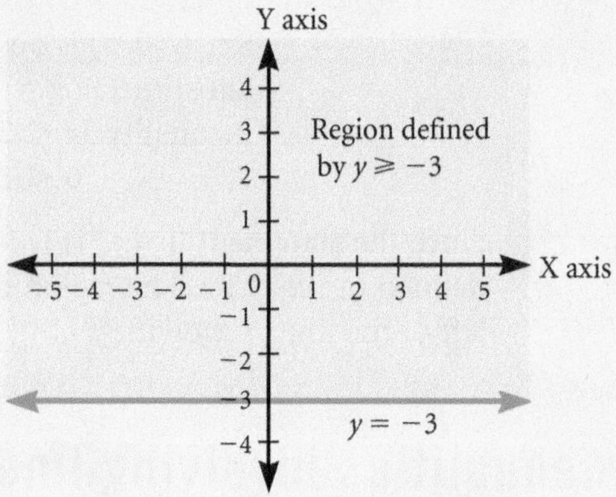

E. Graphing systems of linear inequalities

Systems consisting of two or more linear inequalities in two variables can be drawn by graphing each of the inequalities in the system. The graph of the system is the region *common* to all inequalities.

EXAMPLE 1.4D Graph the region defined by $x > -2$ and $y > x - 3$.

SOLUTION The equation associated with the inequality $x > -2$ is $x = -2$. The graph of $x = -2$ is a line parallel to the Y axis and two units to the left of it. The substitution of 0 for x yields the true statement $0 > -2$. The point (0, 0) is a point in the region defined by $x > -2$. The region defined by the inequality is the area to the right of the line.

The equation associated with the inequality $y > x - 3$ is $y = x - 3$. The graph of $y = x - 3$ is a line passing through the points (3, 0) and (0, −3). The substitution of $x = 0$ and $y = 0$ yields the statement $0 > 0 - 3$, or $0 > -3$. Since this statement is true, the point (0, 0) is a point in the region defined by the inequality $y > x - 3$. The region defined by the inequality is the area to the left of the line $y = x - 3$.

The region defined by the two inequalities is the area formed by the intersection of the two regions. The common region is shown in the diagram.

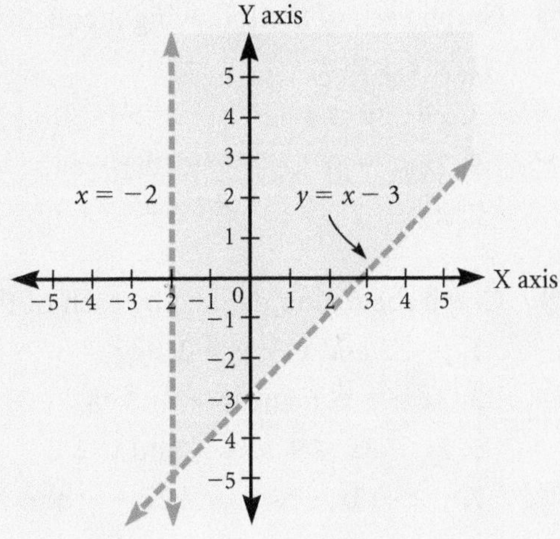

EXAMPLE 1.4E Graph the region defined by $y \geq 0$, $4x + 5y \leq 20$, and $4x - 3y \geq -12$.

SOLUTION The equation associated with the inequality $y \geq 0$ is $y = 0$. The graph of $y = 0$ is the X axis. The region defined by the inequality $y \geq 0$ is the area above the X axis and includes the points forming the X axis.

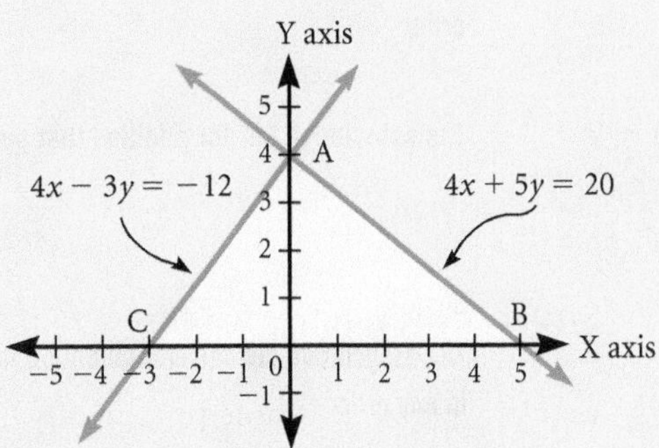

The equation associated with the inequality $4x + 5y \leq 20$ is $4x + 5y = 20$. The graph of the equation is the line passing through the points A(0, 4) and B(5, 0). The true statement $0 < 20$ shows that the origin is a point in the region defined by the inequality. The region defined by $4x + 5y \leq 20$ is the area to the left of the line and includes the line itself.

The equation associated with the inequality $4x - 3y \geq -12$ is $4x - 3y = -12$. The graph of this equation is the line passing through the points A(0, 4) and C(−3, 0). The true statement $0 > -12$ shows that the origin is a point in the region defined by the inequality. The region defined by $4x - 3y \geq -12$ is the area to the right of the line, including the line itself.

The region defined by the three inequalities is the area formed by the intersection of the three regions. It is the triangle ABC shown in the diagram.

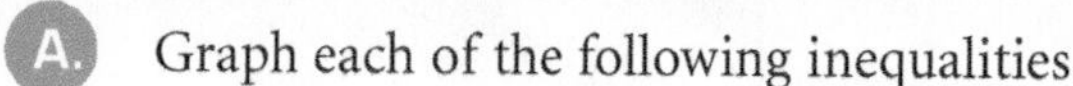

EXERCISE I.4

A. Graph each of the following inequalities.

1. $x + y > 4$

2. $x - y < -2$

3. $x - 2y \leq 4$

4. $3x - 2y \geq -10$

5. $2x < -3y$

6. $4y \geq 3x$

7. $x \geq -2$

8. $y < 5$

B. Graph the region defined by each of the following linear systems.

1. $y < 3$ and $x + y > 2$

2. $x - 2y < 4$ and $x > -3$

3. $3x - y \leq 6$ and $x + 2y > 8$

4. $5x > -3y$ and $2x - 5y \geq 10$

5. $2y - 3x \leq 9$, $x \leq 3$, and $y \geq 0$

6. $2x + y \leq 6$, $x \geq 0$, and $y \geq 0$

7. $y \geq -3x$, $y \leq 3$, and $2x - y \leq 6$

8. $2x \leq y$, $x \geq -3y$, and $x - 2y \geq -6$

SUMMARY OF FORMULAS (LAWS)

Formula I.1

$a + b = b + a$ — **The commutative law for addition that permits the addition of two numbers in any order**

Formula I.2

$ab = ba$ — **The commutative law for multiplication that permits the multiplication of two numbers in any order**

Formula I.3

$$a + b + c = (a + b) + c = a + (b + c) = b + (a + c)$$

The associative law for addition that permits the addition of three or more numbers in any order

Formula I.4

$$abc = (ab)c = a(bc) = b(ac)$$

The associative law for multiplication that permits the multiplication of three or more numbers in any order

Formula I.5

$a(b + c) = ab + ac$ — **The distributive law of multiplication over addition that provides the basis for the multiplication of algebraic expressions**

GLOSSARY

Absolute value the value of a number without its sign *(p. 721)*

Algebraic expression a combination of numbers, variables representing numbers, and symbols indicating an algebraic operation *(p. 720)*

Binomial an algebraic expression consisting of two terms *(p. 720)*

Collecting like terms adding like terms *(p. 721)*

Combining like terms *see* **Collecting like terms**

Common factor a factor that is divisible without remainder into each term of an algebraic expression *(p. 727)*

Factor one of the numbers that when multiplied with the other number or numbers yields a given product *(p. 727)*

Inequality a mathematical statement involving relationships between variables described as "greater than" or "less than" *(p. 730)*

Like signed numbers numbers having the same sign *(p. 721)*

Like terms terms having the same literal coefficient *(p. 721)*

Literal coefficient the part of a term formed with letter symbols *(p. 721)*

Monomial an algebraic expression consisting of one term *(p. 720)*

Negative numbers signed numbers preceded by a minus (−) sign *(p. 721)*

Numerical coefficient the part of a term formed with numerals *(p. 721)*

Polynomial an algebraic expression consisting of more than one term *(p. 720)*

Positive numbers signed numbers preceded by a plus (+) sign *(p. 721)*

Signed numbers numbers preceded by a plus (+) or by a minus (−) sign *(p. 721)*

Term a part of an algebraic expression separated from other parts by a plus (+) sign or by a minus (−) sign *(p. 720)*

Trinomial an algebraic expression consisting of three terms *(p. 720)*

Unlike signed numbers numbers having different signs *(p. 721)*

APPENDIX II

Instructions and Tips for Three Preprogrammed Financial Calculator Models

Different models of financial calculators vary in their operation and labelling of the function keys and face plate. This appendix provides you with instructions and tips for solving compound interest and annuity problems with these financial calculators: Texas Instruments BAII Plus, Sharp EL-733A, and Hewlett-Packard 10B. The specific operational details for each of these calculators are given using the following framework:

A. Basic Operations

1. Turning the calculator on and off
2. Operating modes
3. Using the Second function
4. Clearing operations
5. Displaying numbers and display formats
6. Order of operations
7. Memory capacity and operations
8. Operating errors and calculator dysfunction

B. Pre-Calculation Phase (Initial Set-up)

1. Setting to the financial mode, if required
2. Adjusting the calculator's interest key to match the text presentation, if required
3. Setting to the floating-decimal-point format, if required
4. Setting up order of operations, if required

C. Calculation Phase

1. Clearing preprogrammed registers
2. Adjusting for annuities (beginning and end of period), if required
3. Entering data using cash flow sign conventions and correcting entry errors
4. Calculating the unknown variable

D. Example Calculations

1. Compound interest
2. Annuities

E. Checklist for Resolving Common Errors

Go to the section of this appendix that pertains to your calculator. You may want to flag those pages for easy future reference.

II. 1. Texas Instruments BAII Plus Advanced Business Analyst, page 739

II. 2. Sharp Business/Financial Calculator EL-733A, page 743

II. 3. Hewlett-Packard 10B Business, page 746

II.1 TEXAS INSTRUMENTS BAII PLUS

A. Basic operations

1. Turning the calculator on and off

The calculator is turned on by pressing [ON/OFF]. If the calculator was turned off using this key, the calculator returns in the standard-calculator mode. If the Automatic Power Down (APD) feature turned the calculator off, the calculator will return exactly as you left it—errors and all, if that was the case. The calculator can be turned off either by pressing [ON/OFF] again or by not pressing any key for approximately 10 minutes, which will activate the APD feature.

2. Operating modes

The calculator has two modes: the standard-calculation mode and the prompted-worksheet mode. In the standard-calculation mode, you can perform standard math operations and all of the financial calculations presented in this text. This is the default mode for your calculator. Refer to your calculator's *Guidebook* to learn more about the worksheet mode, since it is not addressed in this appendix.

3. Using the Second function

The primary function of a key is indicated by a symbol on its face. Second functions are marked on the face plate directly above the keys. To access the Second function of a key, press [2nd] ("2nd" will appear in the upper-left corner of the display) and then press the key directly under the symbol on the face plate ("2nd" will then disappear from the display).

4. Clearing operations

[→] clears one character at a time from the display, including decimal points.

[CE/C] clears an incorrect entry, an error condition, or an error message from the display.

[2nd] (QUIT) clears all pending operations in the standard-calculation mode and returns the display to 0.

[CE/C] [CE/C] clears any calculation you have started but not yet completed.

[2nd] (CLR TVM) sets the financial function registers to 0 and returns to standard-calculation mode.

5. Displaying numbers and display formats

The display shows entries and results up to 10 digits but internally stores numeric values to an accuracy of 13 digits. The default setting in the calculator is 2 decimal places. To change the number of fixed decimal places, press 2nd (FORMAT) along with a number key for the decimal places desired. Then press ENTER to complete the installation. For a floating-decimal-point format, press 2nd (FORMAT) 9 ENTER. Return to standard-calculation mode by pressing 2nd (QUIT).

6. Order of operations

The default for the BAII Plus is Chn. To change to AOS, which will have the calculator do all mathematical calculations in the proper order according to the rules of mathematics, press 2nd (FORMAT), arrow down four times, and with display on Chn press 2nd SET. Press 2nd (QUIT) to go back to the standard-calculation mode.

7. Memory capacity and operations

The calculator has 10 memory addresses available, numbered 0 through 9. To store a displayed value in a memory address (0 through 9), press STO and a digit key 0 through 9. To recall a value from memory and display it, press RCL and a digit key 0 through 9. The numeric value is displayed but is also retained in that memory address.

To clear each memory address individually, store "0" in each selected memory. To clear all of the addresses at the same time, press 2nd (MEM) 2nd (CLR WORK).

Memory arithmetic allows you to perform a calculation with a stored value and then store the result with a single operation. You may add, subtract, multiply, divide, or apply an exponent to the value in the memory. Use this key sequence:

(number in display) STO + (or − or × or ÷ or x^{-1}) and a digit key 0 to 9 for the memory address.

8. Operating errors and calculator dysfunction

The calculator reports error conditions by displaying the message "Error n," where n is a number that corresponds to a particular error discussed in the calculator's *Guidebook* on pages 80–82. Errors 4, 5, 7, and 8 are the most common financial calculation errors. A list of possible solutions to calculator dysfunction is given on page 87 of the *Guidebook*. Generally, if you experience difficulties operating the calculator, press 2nd (RESET) ENTER to clear the calculator, and repeat your calculations.

B. Compound interest and annuity calculations

The BAII Plus calculator can be used for virtually all compound interest calculations using the third row of the calculator *after* the payment and interest schedules have been set up in the Second function area of the calculator. Each key represents one of the variables in the formula. The variables are:

- N—Represents time. The value is arrived at by taking the number of *years* involved in the transaction and multiplying it by the value set up in P/Y.
- I/Y—The stated or nominal yearly interest rate.
- PV—The amount of money one has at the beginning of the transaction.
- PMT—The amount of money paid on a regular basis.
- FV—The amount of money one has at the end of the transaction.

To perform compound interest or annuity calculations, the process will be to input the variables that are known and to compute the unknown variable.

For compound interest, the process will be:

1. Set up the payment and interest schedules in the Second function of the calculator. This is done by pressing **2nd** (P/Y) and inputting the payment and interest schedules as prompted. Since the transaction will not have any payments, simply make the payment and interest schedules the same. For example, if there are no payments and interest is compounded quarterly, the process would be **2nd** (P/Y), 4, **Enter** **2nd** (QUIT). This will set up the proper schedules in both P/Y and C/Y and take you back to the calculator mode.
2. Clear out any old information with **2nd** (CLR TVM).
3. Input the variables you know.
4. Compute the variable you need to find.

For annuity calculations, the process will be:

1. Set up the calculator for either an ordinary annuity (payments made at the end) or an annuity due (payments made at the beginning). This is done by hitting **2nd** (BGN) and then setting up the display to END or BGN. **2nd** (SET) will allow you to switch between the two options. **2nd** (QUIT) will take you back to the calculcator. Note: if the calculator is in END mode, the display will be clear in the upper-right-hand corner of the display; if it is in BGN mode, the letters BGN will appear in the upper-right-hand corner.
2. Set up the payment and interest schedules in the Second function of the calculator. This is done by pressing **2nd** (P/Y) and inputting the payment and interest schedules as prompted. For example, if the transaction had monthly payments with quarterly compounding, the process would be **2nd** (P/Y) 12, **Enter**, **↓**, 4, **Enter**, **2nd** (QUIT). This would set up monthly payments with interest compounded quarterly.
3. Clear out the old information with **2nd** (CLR TVM).
4. Input the variables you know.
5. Compute the variable you need to find.

C. Calculation phase

1, 2. The steps required to perform calculations and an example calculation appear on pages 338–340 in Chapter 9. The steps required for annuities and sample annuity calculations appear on pages 476–477 in Chapter 12.

3. Entering data using cash flow sign conventions and correcting entry errors

Data can be entered in any order, but you *must* observe the cash flow sign conventions. For compound interest calculations, always enter PV as a negative number and all other values (N, I/Y, FV) as positive numbers. An error message will be displayed when calculating I/Y or N if both FV and PV are entered using the same sign. For annuity calculations, enter either PV or PMT as negative numbers and all other values (N, I/Y, FV) as positive numbers. When PV = 0, designate PMT as the negative number and all other values (N, I/Y, FV) as positive numbers. Failure to observe this sign convention will result in either an error message in the display when calculating I/Y values or an incorrect negative number when calculating values of N.

Data entry errors can be corrected one character at a time by using [→] or the entry, and error messages can be cleared from the display by using [CE/C]

4. Calculating the unknown variable

Press [CPT] and the financial key representing the unknown variable after all the known variable data are entered (including 0 for PV or FV if required). Successive calculations are possible because numerical values stored in the function key registers remain there until cleared or replaced. The value stored in any of the function key registers can be determined without altering its value by pressing [RCL] and the function key.

D. Example calculations

1. Compound interest

See pages 338–340 in Chapter 9 for an example of a compound interest calculation using this calculator.

2. Annuities

See pages 476 and 479 in Chapter 11 for examples of annuity calculations using this calculator.

E. Checklist for resolving common errors

1. Confirm that the P/Y and C/Y are properly set.
2. Confirm that the decimal place format is set to a floating decimal point.
3. If attempting annuity calculations, check to see that the calculator is in the appropriate payment mode ("END" or "BGN").
4. Clear all function key registers before entering your data.

5. Be sure to enter a numerical value, using the cash flow sign convention, for all known variables before solving for the unknown variable, even if one of the variables is 0.

II.2 SHARP EL-733A BUSINESS/FINANCIAL CALCULATOR

A. Basic operations

1. Turning the calculator on and off

[C·CE] turns the calculator on. [OFF] turns the calculator off. To conserve battery life, the calculator will turn itself off automatically 9 to 13 minutes after the last key operation.

2. Operating modes

The available operational modes are financial (FIN), statistical (STAT), and Normal (no message). The message FIN, STAT, or no message appears in the upper right corner of the display to indicate the current mode. Change the mode by pressing [2nd F] (MODE) until the desired mode is displayed.

3. Using the Second function

The primary function of a key is indicated by a symbol on the face of the key. Second functions are marked on the face plate directly above the keys. To access the Second function of a key, press [2nd F] ("2ndF" will appear in the upper-left corner of the display), and then press the key directly under the symbol on the face plate ("2ndF" will then disappear from the display).

4. Clearing operations

[2nd F] (CA) clears the numerical values and calculation commands including data for financial calculations. The contents of memory register storage are not affected.

[C·CE] [x→M] clears the memory.

[C·CE] clears the last entry.

[C·CE] [C·CE] clears the calculator of all data *except* the data for financial calculations.

[→] clears the last digit entered.

5. Displaying numbers and display formats

The display shows entries and results up to 10 digits. The default setting in the calculator is the floating decimal. To change the number of fixed decimal places, press [2nd F] (TAB) along with a number key for the decimal places desired. For a floating-decimal-point format, press [2nd F] (TAB) [•]. The number of decimal places is retained even when the power is turned off.

Various messages can appear in the display from time to time. Refer to page 73 of the *Operation Manual and Application Manual* for a complete list.

6. Memory capacity and operations

This calculator has one memory address. To store a displayed value in memory, press [x→M].

To clear the memory of values other than zero, press [C·CE] [x→M].

To recall a value from memory and display it, press [RM].

To add a displayed amount to the value in the memory, press [M+]. To subtract a displayed amount to the value in the memory, press [±] [M+].

7. Operating errors and calculator dysfunction

Operational errors are indicated by the symbol **E** in the lower-left corner of the display. See pages 74–77 of the *Operation Manual and Application Manual* for a complete description of errors and error conditions that may affect the operation and functioning of your calculator. The error symbol is cleared from the display by pressing [C·CE].

B. Pre-calculation phase

With the calculator on, set the financial mode by pressing [2nd F] (MODE) until the FIN message appears in the upper-right corner of the display. The calculator requires no change to a register or mode in order to match the text presentation. To set the calculator to the floating-decimal-point format, press [2nd F] (TAB) [•].

C. Calculation phase

1. Clearing preprogrammed registers

[2nd F] (CA) clears the preprogrammed registers of numerical values and sets them to 0 for financial calculations.

2. Adjusting for annuities (beginning and end of period)

The default mode for annuity calculations is "end of period." If "beginning of period" calculations are required, press [BGN]. "BGN" will appear in the upper-right corner of the display. To return to "end of period" mode, press [BGN] again. "BGN" will disappear from the display.

3. Entering data using cash flow sign conventions and correcting entry errors

Data can be entered in any order but you must observe the cash flow sign conventions to avoid operational errors and incorrect answers. For compound interest calculations, *always* designate PV as a negative number and all other values (N, *i*, FV) as positive numbers. If you do not observe this sign convention when you enter data, your answer will be the same numerical value but the opposite sign of the answer in the text. An error message will be displayed when calculating *i* or N if both FV and PV are entered using the same sign. For annuity calculations, when FV = 0, designate PV as a negative number and all other values (N, *i*, PMT) as positive numbers. When PV = 0, designate PMT as the negative number and all other values (N, *i*, FV) as positive numbers. Failure to observe this sign convention will result in either an error message in the display when calculating *i* values or an incorrect negative number when calculating values of N.

4. Calculating the unknown variable

Press [COMP] and the financial key representing the unknown variable after all the known variable data are entered (including 0 for PV or FV if required). Successive calculations are possible because numerical values stored in the function key registers remain there until cleared or replaced. The value stored in any of the function key registers can be determined without altering its value by pressing [2nd F] (RCL) and the function key.

D. Example calculations

1. Compound interest (Example 9.2A, page 335)

Key in	*Press*	*Display shows*	
	[2nd F] (CA)	no change	clears all registers
6000	[±] [PV]	−6000	this enters the present value P (principal) with the correct sign convention
1.0	[i]	1.0	this enters the periodic interest rate *i* as a percent
20	[N]	20	this enters the number of compounding periods *n*
	[COMP] [FV]	7321.14	this computes and displays the unknown future value S

2. Annuities (Example 11.2D, pages 426–428)

Key in	*Press*	*Display shows*	
0	PV	0	a precaution to avoid incorrect answers
10	± PMT	−10	this enters the periodic payment, PMT
6.0	*i* I/Y	6.0	this enters the interest rate per year
60	N	60	this enters the number of payments, *n*
	CPT FV	697.700305	this retrieves the wanted amount, FV

E. Checklist for resolving common errors

1. Check to see that your calculator is in the financial (FIN) mode.
2. Check to see that the calculator is in the appropriate payment mode (BGN or end mode).
3. Clear all registers before entering your data by pressing 2nd F (CA).
4. Be sure to enter values for all variables except the unknown variable, before solving for the unknown variable, even if one of the variables is 0.
5. Observe the cash flow sign conventions (discussed above) when entering the data to avoid unwanted negative signs, display errors, or incorrect answers.

II.3 HEWLETT-PACKARD 10B II BUSINESS CALCULATOR

A. Basic operations

1. Turning the calculator on and off

Turn the calculator on by pressing ON . Turn the calculator off by pressing the ▭ (SHIFT) OFF .

To conserve energy, the calculator turns itself off automatically approximately 10 minutes after you stop using it. The calculator has a continuous memory, so turning it off does not affect the information you have stored in the memory.

2. Operating modes

You can perform all of the financial calculations presented in this text as soon as you turn on the calculator. No mode adjustment is required for financial-, statistical-, or standard-mode calculations.

3. Using the SHIFT function

The primary function of a key is indicated by a symbol on the top face of the key. SHIFT functions are marked on the bottom face of the key. To access the SHIFT function of a key, press [ ] (SHIFT) ("SHIFT" will appear in the lower-left corner of the display), and then press the key with the symbol on the lower face of the key ("SHIFT" will then disappear from the display).

4. Clearing operations

[ON] [N] [FV], all held down at the same time, clears all memory and resets all modes.

[ ] [C ALL] (CLEAR ALL) clears all memory, but does not reset the modes.

[←] [C] clears the message and restores the original constants.

[C] clears the entered number to 0.

[←] clears the last digit entered.

5. Displaying numbers and display formats

The display shows entries and results up to 12 digits. Brightness is controlled by holding down [ON] and then pressing [+] or [−]. The default setting is 2 decimal places. Regardless of the display format, each number entered is stored with a signed 12-digit number and a signed 3-digit exponent. To change the number of fixed decimal places, press [ ] [DISP] and a number key for the number of decimal places desired. For a floating decimal point, press [ ] [DISP] [•]. To temporarily view all 12 digits, press [ ] [DISP] and hold [=].

Graphics in the display are used to indicate various settings, operating modes, error conditions, and calculator dysfunctions. Refer to the *Owner's Manual*, pages 137–138, for a complete list.

6. Memory capacity and operations

This calculator has 10 numbered registers available to store numbers, as well as a single storage register called the M register.

To store a number in the M register, press [→M].

To recall a value from the M register and display it, press [RM].

To add a displayed amount to the value in the M register, press [M+]. To subtract a displayed amount to the value in the memory, press [±] [M+].

To store a displayed value in a numbered memory register (numbered 0 to 9), press [ ] [STO] and a digit key [0] through [9].

To recall a number from a numbered memory register, press [RCL] and the digit key for the memory register number.

7. Operating errors and calculator dysfunction

Operational errors are indicated by an error message appearing in the display. For a complete description of the error messages, refer to pages 137–138 of the *Owner's*

Manual. For calculator dysfunctions, refer to pages 121–122 of the *Owner's Manual.*

No additional adjustment is required to set the calculator to the financial mode. Begin calculations as soon as you turn on your calculator.

B. Calculation phase

1. Clearing preprogrammed registers

[ ] [C ALL] sets all key numerical registers to 0 and momentarily displays the P/YR value.

2. Adjusting for annuities (beginning and end of period)

The default mode for annuity calculations is "end of period." If "beginning of period" calculations are required, press [ ] [BEG/END]. "BEGIN" will appear in the lower middle portion of the display. To return to "end of period" mode, press [ ] [BEG/END] again. "BEGIN" will disappear from the display.

3. Entering data using cash flow sign conventions and correcting entry errors

Data can be entered in any order using the financial function keys. To confirm the values already in the registers or to validate your data entry, press [RCL] and the desired function key.

You must observe the cash flow sign conventions to avoid errors like "no solution" or incorrect answers when calculating N. For compound interest calculations, *always* enter PV as a negative number and the other variables as positive numbers. For annuity calculations, when FV = 0, enter PV as a negative number and all other values (N, I/YR, PMT) as positive numbers. However, when PV = 0, enter PMT as a negative number and all other values (N, I/YR, FV) as positive numbers. If you do not observe the sign convention, the numerical value you calculate will be identical to that of this text except when calculating N (your answer will be incorrect) or when calculating I/YR (an error message may appear in the display).

Data entry errors can be corrected character by character by pressing [←] or the entry can be cleared from the display by pressing [C].

4. Calculating the unknown variable

Press the financial key representing the unknown variable after all the known variable data are entered (including 0 for PV or FV if required). Successive calculations are possible because numerical values stored in the function key registers remain there until cleared or replaced. The value stored in any of the function key registers can be determined without altering its value by pressing [RCL] and the function key.

C. Example calculations

1. Compound interest (Example 9.2A, page 335)

Key in	*Press*	*Display shows*	
	[ ] [C ALL]	0	clears the function key registers and confirms the value in the P/YR register
6000	[±] [PV]	−6000	this enters the present value P (principal) with the correct sign convention
4	[I/YR]	4	this enters the periodic interest rate *i* as a percent
4	[ ] [P/YR]	4	
20	[N]	20	this enters the number of compounding periods *n*
	[FV]	7321.14	this computes and displays the unknown future value S

2. Annuities (Example 11.2D, pages 428–429)

Key in	*Press*	*Display shows*	
	[ ] [C ALL]	0	a precaution to avoid incorrect answers
10	[±] [PMT]	−10	this enters the periodic payment, PMT
6.0	[I/YR]	6.0	this enters the interest rate per year
60	[N]	60	this enters the number of payments, *n*
	[FV]	697.700305	this retrieves the wanted amount, FV

D. Checklist for resolving common errors

1. Confirm that P/YR is properly set.
2. Clear all registers before entering your data by pressing [ ] [C ALL].
3. Check to see that the calculator is in the appropriate payment mode (BEGIN or END mode).
4. Be sure to enter values for all variables except the unknown variable, before solving for the unknown variable, even if one of the variables is 0.
5. Observe the cash flow sign conventions (discussed above) when entering the data to avoid unwanted negative signs, display errors, or incorrect answers.

ANSWERS TO ODD-NUMBERED PROBLEMS, REVIEW EXERCISES, AND SELF-TESTS

CHAPTER 1

Exercise 1.1

A. **1.** 14
3. 53
5. 4
7. 68
9. 0.2
11. 4
13. 0.17
15. 8300

Exercise 1.2

A. **1.** $\frac{2}{3}$
3. $\frac{7}{12}$
5. $\frac{8}{5}$
7. $\frac{2}{5}$
9. $\frac{5}{73}$
11. $\frac{5}{1}$

B. **1.** 1.375
3. $1.\dot{6}$
5. $1.8\dot{3}$
7. $1.08\dot{3}$

C. **1.** 3.375
3. $8.\dot{3}$
5. $33.\dot{3}$
7. $7.\dot{7}$

D. **1.** 5.63
3. 18.00
5. 57.70
7. 13.00

E. **1.** $730
3. $630.70
5. $220 364.90
7. 34 426.47022
9. 31 500
11. 29 000
13. 0.586

Exercise 1.3

A. **1.** 0.64
3. 0.025
5. 0.005
7. 2.5
9. 0.75
11. 0.0625
13. 2.25
15. 0.0825
17. 1.125
19. 0.0075
21. 0.004
23. 0.00025
25. 0.00625
27. 0.0225
29. $1.1\dot{6}$
31. $0.8\dot{3}$

B. **1.** $\frac{1}{4}$
3. $\frac{7}{4}$
5. $\frac{3}{8}$
7. $\frac{1}{25}$
9. $\frac{2}{5}$
11. $\frac{5}{2}$
13. $\frac{1}{8}$
15. $\frac{9}{400}$
17. $\frac{1}{800}$
19. $\frac{3}{400}$
21. $\frac{1}{16}$
23. $\frac{1}{6}$
25. $\frac{3}{400}$
27. $\frac{1}{1000}$
29. $\frac{1}{40}$
31. $\frac{11}{6}$

C. **1.** 350%
3. 0.5%
5. 2.5%
7. 12.5%
9. 22.5%
11. 145%
13. 0.25%
15. 9%
17. 75%
19. $166.\dot{6}\%$
21. 4.5%
23. 0.75%
25. 1.125%
27. 37.5%
29. $133.\dot{3}\%$
31. 65%

Exercise 1.4

A. **1.** $10 734.37
3. $1147.50
5. $ 48.00
45.00
27.00
56.00
$176.00

B. **1.** 41¢
3. 2.9
5. **(a)** $10.45
(b) 115.899
(c) $10.35
(d) $1379.20

Exercise 1.5

A. **1.** **(a)** $1326
(b) $17
(c) $1606.50
3. **(a)** $7.26
(b) $1185.50
5. **(a)** $16.47
(b) $875.94
7. $1568.06
9. **(a)** $825
(b) $932.25
11. 5.25%
13. $19 680
15. $584.79
17. $10.26

Exercise 1.6

A. **1.** Cook's owes the government $27 728.50.
3. $39.00
5. $0.74
7. $2843.88
9. 14.497857

Review Exercise

1. **(a)** 29
(b) −8
(c) 11
(d) 8
(e) 1500
(f) 0.15
(g) 339.73
(h) 950.68
(i) 625.45
(j) 1250
3. **(a)** $\frac{1}{2}$
(b) $\frac{3}{8}$
(c) $\frac{1}{6}$
(d) $\frac{5}{3}$
(e) $\frac{1}{200}$
(f) $\frac{3}{40}$
(g) $\frac{3}{400}$
(h) $\frac{1}{160}$
5. **(a)** $20.208\dot{3}$ kg
(b) $24.25
(c) 5.05 kg
(d) $6.06
7. **(a)** $11.99
(b) $10.71
9. $13 680
11. **(a)** $845.52
(b) $10.84
(c) $1048.77
13. **(a)** $481.95
(b) $33.15
15. **(a)** $398.65
(b) $11.39
17. $21 750
19. **(a)** $13.40
(b) 8.15
21. $10.56
23. $3052.00
25. $18.68
27. **(a)** 46.71143
(b) $1634.90
(c) 2.050231
(d) $71.76

Self-Test

1. **(a)** 4415.87
(b) 93.21
(c) 2610.15
(d) 4623.33
(e) 5489.46

3. **(a)** $\frac{1}{40}$
(b) $\frac{7}{6}$

5. \$7080
7. \$7.35
9. \$650
11. \$2382.41
13. \$12.12
15. \$9.00
17. \$45 500.00

CHAPTER 2

Exercise 2.1

A. **1.** $19a$
3. $-a - 10$
5. $-2x - 4y$
7. $14f - 4v$
9. $0.8x$
11. $1.4x$
13. $2.79x$
15. $-x^2 - x - 8$
17. $x - 7y$
19. $4b + 2c + 2$
21. $-m^2 + 6m + 1$
23. $10a - 14b$

B. **1.** $-12x$
3. $-10ax$
5. $-2x^2$
7. $60xy$
9. $-2x + 4y$
11. $2ax^2 - 3ax - a$
13. $35x - 30$
15. $-20ax + 5a$
17. $3x^2 + 5x - 2$
19. $x^3 + y^3$
21. $7x^2 + 3x + 39$
23. $4ab$
25. $4x$
27. $10m - 4$
29. $-2x^2 + 3x + 6$

C. **1.** -5
3. 5500
5. 0.586
7. \$378
9. \$3000
11. \$901.99
13. \$1400.06

Exercise 2.2

A. **1.** 81
3. 16
5. $\frac{16}{81}$
7. $-\frac{1}{64}$
9. 0.25
11. -0.001
13. 1
15. $\frac{1}{9}$
17. $-\frac{1}{125}$
19. 125
21. $\frac{1}{1.01}$

B. **1.** 2^8
3. 4^3
5. 2^{15}
7. a^{14}
9. 3^{11}
11. 6
13. $\frac{3^{11}}{5^{11}}$
15. $\frac{(-3^{11})}{2^{11}}$
17. 1.025^{150}
19. 1.04^{80}
21. $(1 + i)^{200}$
23. $(1 + i)^{160}$
25. a^5b^5
27. $m^{24}n^8$
29. 2^4
31. $\frac{b^8}{a^8}$

Exercise 2.3

A. **1.** 72
3. 3
5. 1.075886
7. 1.013300

B. **1.** 55
3. 12.25
5. 1.071122
7. 0.629961
9. 163.053437
11. 2.158925
13. 1630.176673
15. 1139.915716
17. 5000.00
19. 0.029998
21. 0.04

Exercise 2.4

A. **1.** $9 = \log_2 512$
3. $-3 = \log_5 \frac{1}{125}$
5. $2j = \ln 18$

B. **1.** $2^5 = 32$
3. $10^1 = 10$

C. **1.** 0.693147
3. -2.253795
5. 6.825303

Exercise 2.5

A. **1.** $x = 3$
3. $x = 80$
5. $x = 18$
7. $x = -35$
9. $x = -4$
11. $x = -8$
13. $x = 5$
15. $x = 20$
17. $x = 200$

B. **1.** $x = 4$; LS = 17 = RS
3. $x = 0$; LS = -7 = RS
5. $x = 5$ LS = 29 = RS
7. $x = 21$ LS = 92 = RS

Exercise 2.6

A. **1.** $x = -10$; LS = 320 = RS
3. $x = -3$; LS = -15 = RS
5. $x = 3$ LS = 18 = RS
7. $x = 14$ LS = 32 = RS

B. **1.** $x = 20$
3. $x = -1$
5. $x = \frac{1}{2}$

C. **1.** $x = -1$
3. $x = \frac{5}{6}$

D. **1.** $x = \frac{y - b}{m}$
3. PMT = PVi
5. $r = \frac{A-P}{Pt}$

Exercise 2.7

A. **1.** \$28.28
3. \$35.00
5. 192
7. \$670
9. \$89.00
11. 1300
13. 20 units
15. 30 \$ 12 tickets
100 \$ 8 tickets
21 \$ 15 tickets

Review Exercise

1. **(a)** $-2x - 7y$
(b) $1.97x$
(c) $6a - 7$
(d) $x + 3y$
(e) $9a^2 - 4b - 4c$
(f) $-x^2 + 3x + 1$

3. **(a)** -47
(b) $6\frac{1}{3}$
(c) 0.16
(d) 200
(e) \$644.40
(f) 2500

5. **(a)** 0.96
(b) 1.012126
(c) 1.07
(d) 0.968442
(e) 1.098612
(f) -2.995732
(g) 7.087540
(h) 9.871647

7. **(a)** $x = -7$; LS = -203 = RS
(b) $x = 5$ LS = -32 = RS
(c) $x = -3$; LS = $-\frac{23}{14}$ = RS
(d) $x = -\frac{7}{12}$ LS = $\frac{11}{9}$ = RS

(e) $x = 7$
LS = 25 = RS
(f) $x = -\frac{1}{3}$
LS = −1 = RS
(g) $x = -\frac{1}{2}$
LS = $-\frac{31}{6}$ = RS

9. (a) 138
(b) \$63 350
(c) \$117
(d) \$44 500
(e) heat, \$814; power, \$1056; water, \$341
(f) \$37 500
(g) 35 minutes
(h) superlight, 27; ordinary, 45
(i) 164

Self-Test

1. (a) $-2 - 8x$
(b) $-2x - 9$
(c) $-16a - 7$
(d) $-6x^2 + 6x + 12$

3. (a) −8
(b) $\frac{4}{9}$
(c) 1
(d) 2187
(e) $\frac{9}{16}$
(f) $-x^{15}$

5. (a) $n = 6$
(b) $n = 5$

7. (a) $P = \frac{I}{rt}$
(b) $d = \frac{S - P}{St}$

CHAPTER 3

Exercise 3.1

A. 1. (a) 3:8
(b) 3:2
(c) 5:8:13
(d) 3:6:13

3. (a) $\frac{5}{16}$
(b) $\frac{2}{7}$
(c) 2:7:11
(d) 23:14:5
(e) 5:4
(f) 25:21
(g) 9:16:18
(h) 28:40:25
(i) 32:60:25
(j) 9:7:17
(k) 69:92
(l) 28:55
(m) 8:15
(n) 9:10

B. 1. $\frac{8}{7}$
3. 2:3:12
5. 1:29

C. 1. \$2295; \$510; \$255
3. \$5250; \$2800; \$1400
5. \$4400000; \$2200000; \$4950000

Exercise 3.2

1. 4
3. 56
5. 7.4
7. 2.4
9. $\frac{7}{10}$
11. 1

B. 1. 21
3. 600 km
5. (a) \$3600
(b) \$9000
7. \$100 800

Exercise 3.3

A. 1. 36
3. 300
5. 18
7. 6
9. 0.5
11. 2
13. 7.5
15. 17.5

B. 1. \$16
3. \$1950
5. \$9
7. \$200
9. \$600
11. \$49
13. \$135
15. \$60
17. \$44 800
19. \$900

C. 1. 60%
3. 115%
5. 5%
7. 600%
9. $166\frac{2}{3}$%

D. 1. 200
3. 3.60
5. 3.06
7. 200
9. 1.10
11. 240
13. 300

E. 1. \$28
3. \$1500
5. \$45 000
7. \$60 000
9. \$6

Exercise 3.4

A. 1. 168
3. 1140
5. 88

B. 1. 50%
3. 200%
5. 2%

C. 1. $x = 20$
3. $x = 440$
5. $x = 36$
7. $x = 30$

D. 1. 32
3. \$130
5. \$4.40

Exercise 3.5

A. 1. 27
3. 12.5%
5. \$4320
7. (a) \$180 000
(b) \$225 000

B. 1. \$14.52
3. \$130
5. \$83.62
7. \$5000
9. $83\frac{1}{3}$%
11. 325%
13. \$96.69
15. \$680

Exercise 3.6

A. 1. U.S. \$706.58
3. C\$321.51

B. 1. C\$359.38
3. 187.11 Swiss francs
5. C\$754.00

Exercise 3.7

A. 1. bread, 103.6145; bus pass, 110.5528; clothing, 96.9697
3. (a) 2006 relative to 2002, 0.9166; 2009 relative to 2002, 0.8741
(b) 0.9537
5. \$81 889.51

Exercise 3.8

A. 1. \$8011.10
3. \$8268.50

Review Exercise

1. (a) 5:6
(b) 6:1
(c) 9:40
(d) 6:1
(e) 240:20:1
(f) 15:4:3

3. (a) 210
(b) 7.2
(c) 195
(d) 3.6

5. (a) \$6.66
(b) \$8.30
(c) \$90.00
(d) \$27.72

7. (a) \$18
(b) \$1955
(c) $16\frac{2}{3}$%
(d) 550%
(e) \$56
(f) \$340
(g) \$140

9. Department A, \$2400;
Department B, \$4200;
Department C, \$4800

11. Company 1, \$75 000;
Company 2, \$50 000;
Company 3, \$60 000

13. \$182 000

15. 540

17. Bonds, \$56 250;
Common stock, \$84 375;
Preferred shares, \$9375

19. **(a)** \$400 000
(b) \$280 000

21. **(a)** 7.5%
(b) $16\frac{2}{3}\%$

23. **(a)** $166\frac{2}{3}\%$
(b) $266\frac{2}{3}\%$

25. \$165

27. \$15 000

29. **(a)** \$80 000
(b) \$250 000
(c) 312.5%

31. U.S.\$201.87

33. \$15 551.46

Self-Test

1. **(a)** \$350
(b) \$76.05
(c) \$145.00
(d) \$13.20

3. 45%

5. \$10 000

7. First bonus, \$16 875;
Second bonus, \$11 250;
Third bonus, \$6750;
Fourth bonus, \$5625

9. \$32.50

11. 180

13. **(a)** AUD\$1.1084
(b) AUD\$554.20

15. \$0.880282

CHAPTER 4

Exercise 4.1

A. **1.** LS = −9 = RS;
LS = −7 = RS

3. LS = 74 = RS;
LS = 46 = RS

5. LS = 3 = RS;
LS = −3 = RS

B. **1.** LS = −13 = RS;
LS = −19 = RS

3. LS = −22 = RS;
LS = 5 = RS

5. LS = 36 = RS;
LS = 0 = RS

C. **1.** $x = 12, y = 8$

3. $x = 1.5, y = 2.5$

5. $x = 6, y = 10$

7. $x = \frac{1}{2}, y = \frac{3}{4}$

Exercise 4.2

A. **1.** A (−4, −3)
B (0, −4)
C (3, −4)
D (2, 0)
E (4, 3)
F (0, 3)
G (−4, 4)
H (−5, 0)

3. **(a)**

x	−5	−4	−3	−2	−1	0	1	2	3
y	−3	−2	−1	0	1	2	3	4	5

(b)

x	3	2	1	0	−1	−2
y	5	3	1	−1	−3	−5

(c)

x	3	2	1	0	−1	−2	−3
y	6	4	2	0	−2	−4	−6

(d)

x	−5	−4	−3	−2	−1	0	1	2	3	4	5
y	5	4	3	2	1	0	−1	−2	−3	−4	−5

B. **1.**

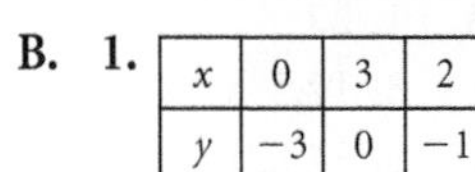

x	0	3	2
y	−3	0	−1

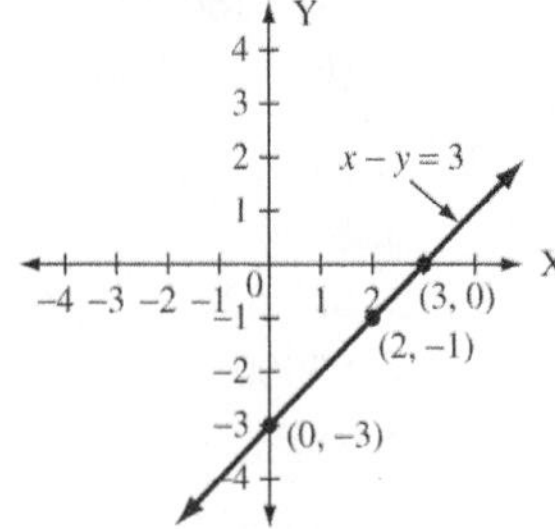

3.

x	0	−2	2
y	0	2	−2

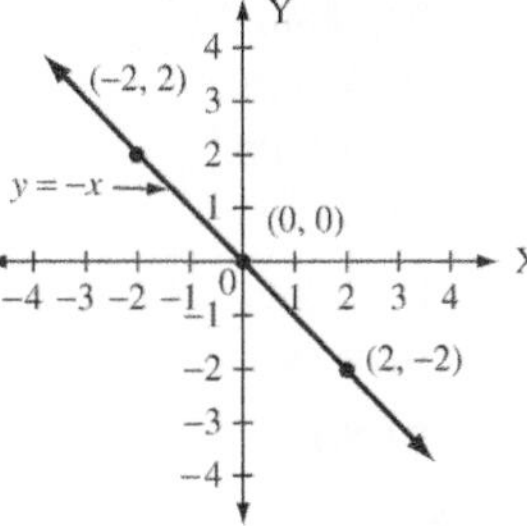

5.

x	0	4	−4
y	−3	0	−6

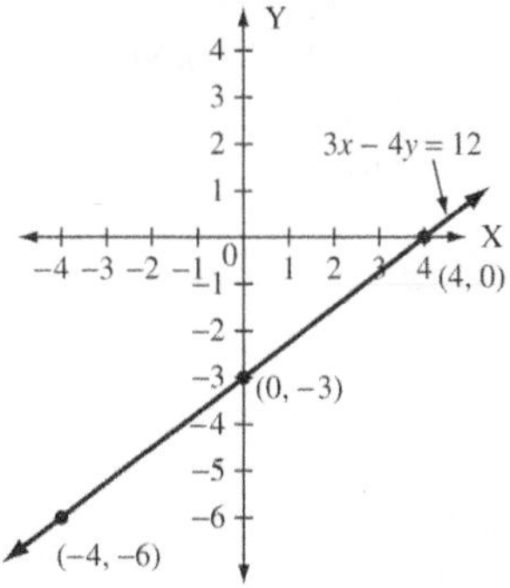

7.

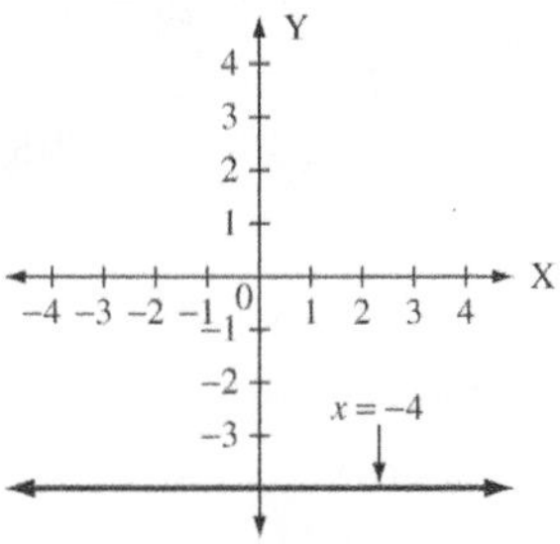

9. For
$y = 2x - 3$
slope, $m = 2$
y-intercept, $b = -3$

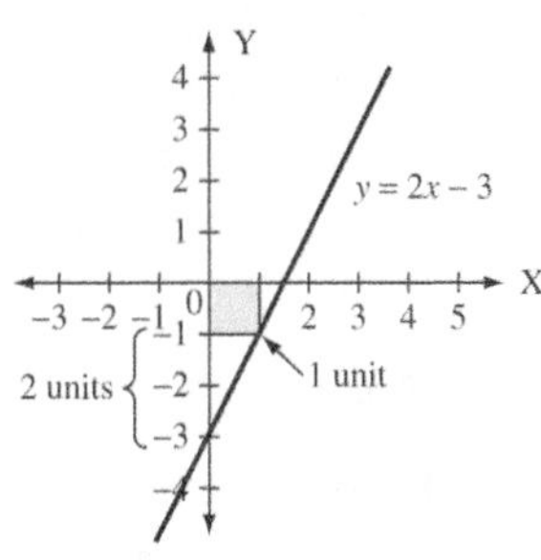

C. **1.** For $y = 3x + 20$

x	0	20	40	
y	20	80	140	

or $m = 3$
$b = 20$

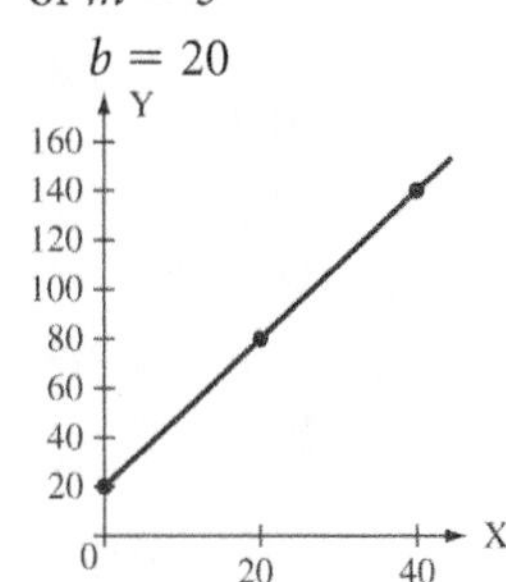

3. For $3x + 4y = 1200$

x	0	200	400
y	300	150	0

or $m = -\frac{3}{4}$

$b = 300$

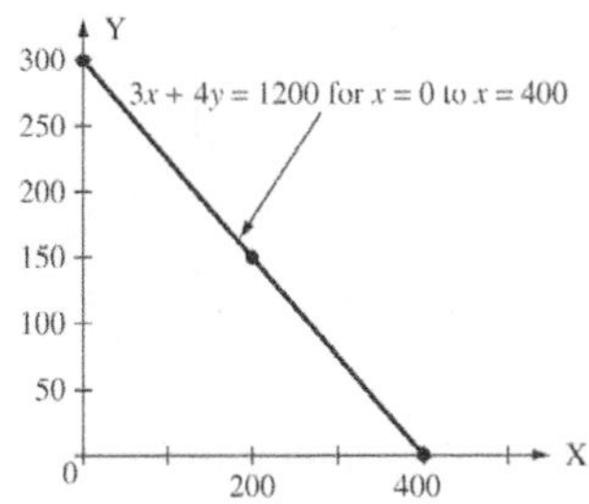

Exercise 4.3

A. 1.

$x - y = -4$ $x + y = 4$ (0, 4)

(0, 4) is the solution.

3. $x = 2y - 1$

x	3	−1	−5
y	2	0	−2

$y = 4 - 3x$

x	0	2	1
y	4	−2	1

(1,1) is the solution.

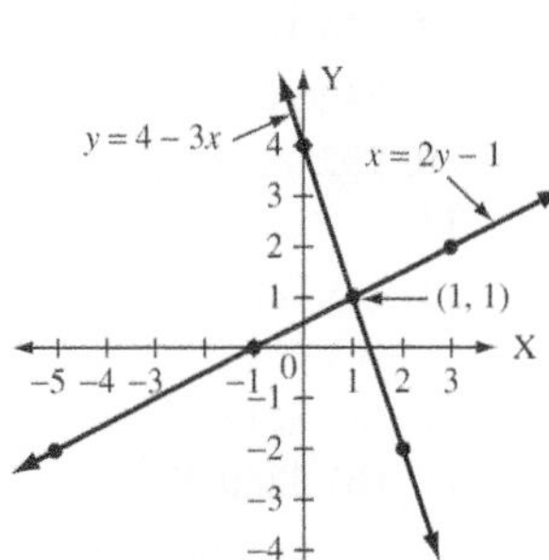

5. $3x - 4y = 18$

x	6	2	−2
y	0	−3	−6

$2y = -3x$

x	0	2	−2
y	0	−3	3

(2, −3) is the solution.

$2y = -3x$ $3x - 4y = 18$ (2, −3)

7. $5x = 2y = 20$

x	4	2	6
y	0	−5	5

(6, 5) is the solution.

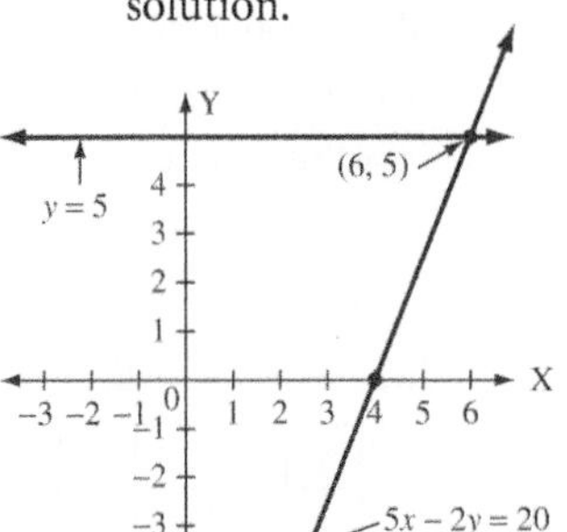

B. 1. For $y - 4x = 0$

x	0	5000	10 000
y	0	20 000	40 000

For $y - 2x - 10\,000 = 0$

x	0	5000	10 000
y	10 000	20 000	30 000

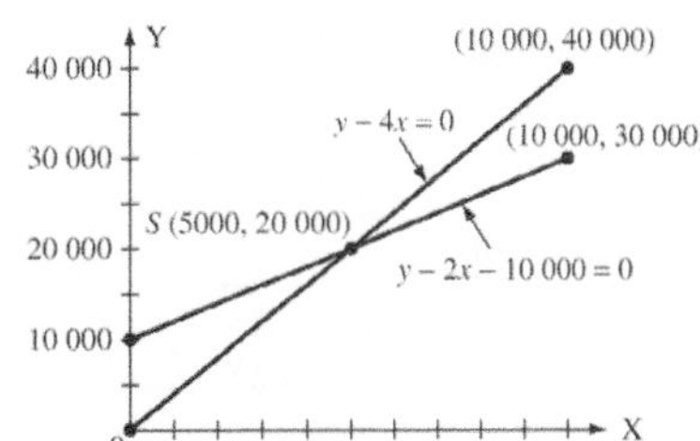

3. For $3x + 3y = 2400$

x	0	400	800
y	800	400	0

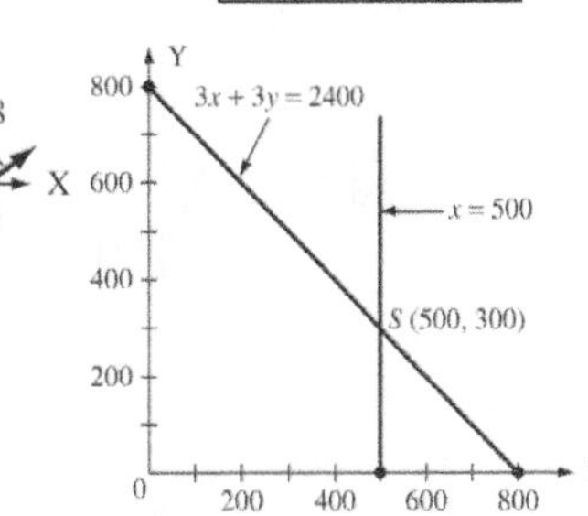

Exercise 4.4

A. 1.

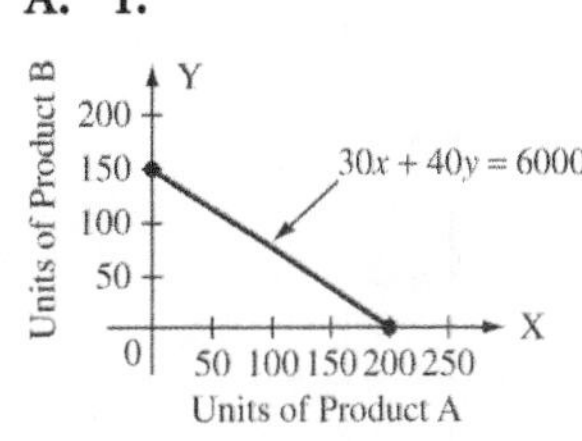

3.

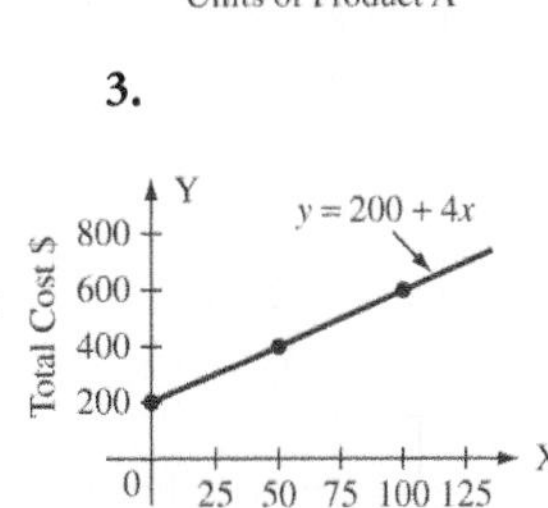

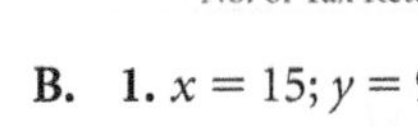

B. 1. $x = 15$; $y = 9$

3. Brand X, 90; No-Name, 50

5. Kaya, \$31 500; Fred, \$23 500

7. Type A, 42; Type B, 18

9. 55 quarters; 72 loonies

Review Exercise

1. (a) $m = -\frac{7}{3}, b = 2$

(b) $m = \frac{1}{2}, b = 0$

(c) $m = \frac{3}{2}, b = 4$

(d) $m = -6, b = 10$

(e) m is undefined, there is no y-intercept

(f) $m = \frac{1}{3}, b = -3$

(g) $m = \frac{1}{4}, b = -1$

(h) $m = 0, b = 5$

3. (a) $3x + y = 6$ and $x - y = 2$

x	0	2	4
y	6	0	−6

x	0	2	4
y	−2	0	2

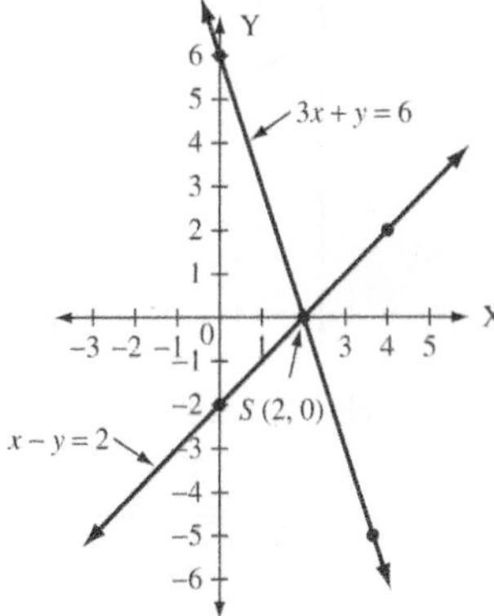

(b) $x + 4y = -8$ and $3x + 4y = 0$

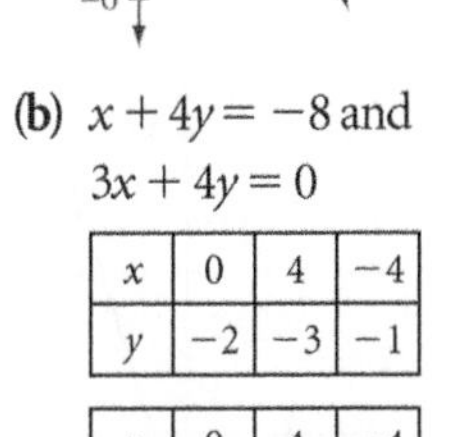

x	0	4	−4
y	−2	−3	−1

x	0	4	−4
y	0	−3	3

$3x + 4y = 0$ $x + 4y = -8$ S(4, −3)

(c) $5x = 3y$ and $y = -5$

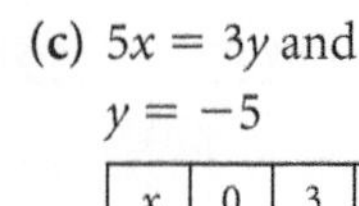

x	0	3	−3
y	0	5	−5

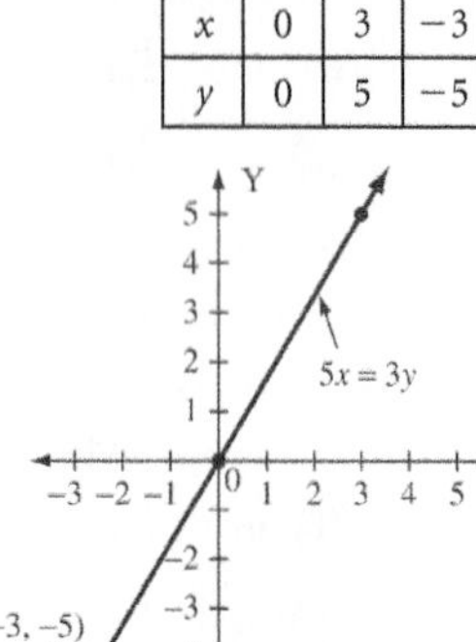

(d) $2x + 6y = 8$ and $x = -2$

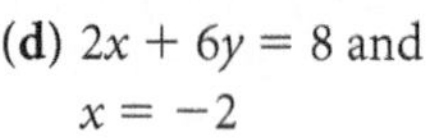

x	4	−2	1
y	0	2	1

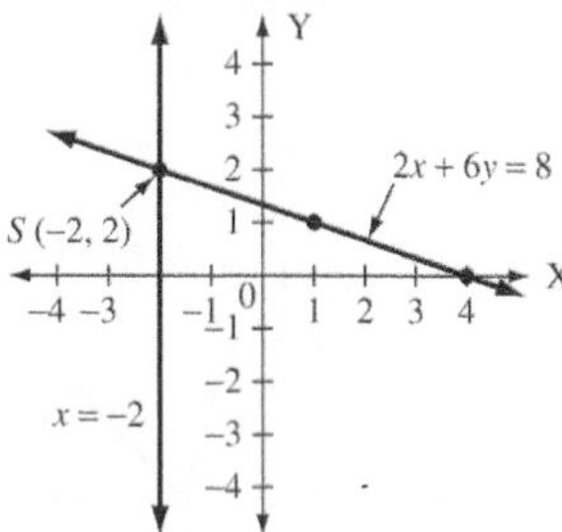

(e) $y = 3x - 2$ and $y = 3$

x	0	$\frac{5}{3}$	−1
y	−2	3	−5

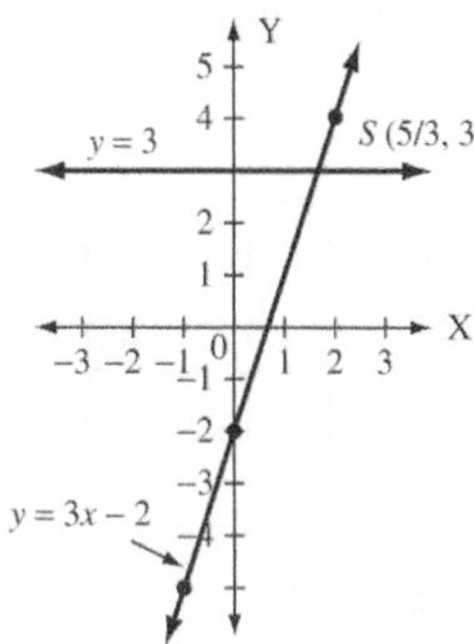

(f) $y = -2x$ and $x = 4$

x	0	4	−2
y	0	−8	4

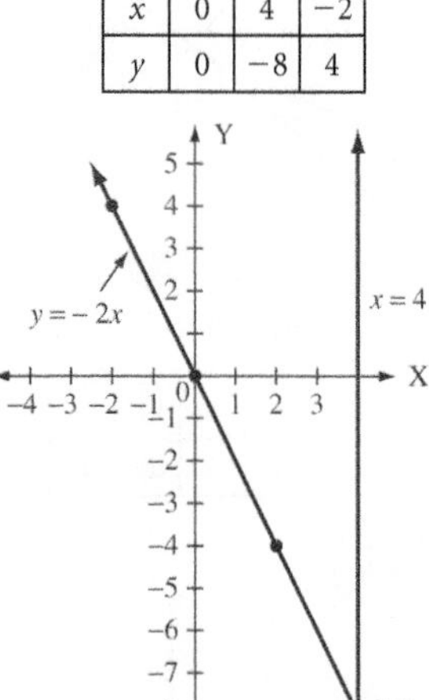

(g) $x = -2$ and $3x + 4y = 12$

x	0	−2	4
y	3	4.5	0

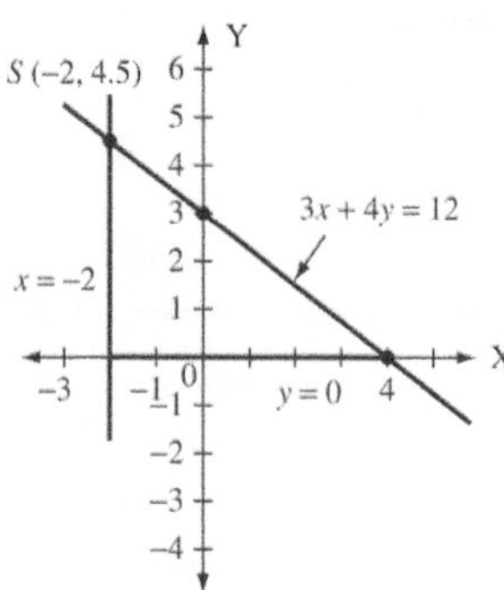

(h) $y = -2$ and $5x + 3y = 15$

x	3	0	4.2
y	0	5	−2

5. (a)

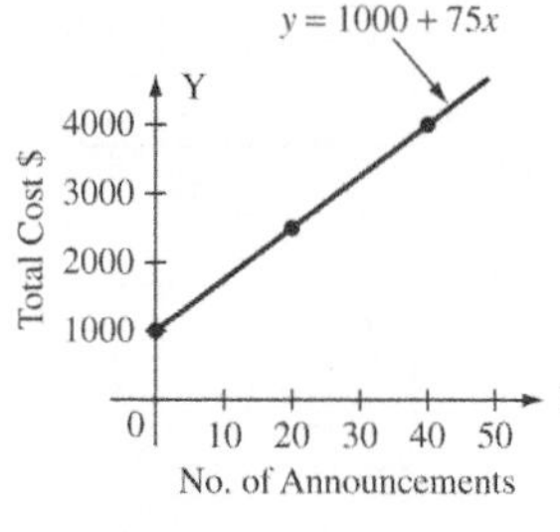

(b)

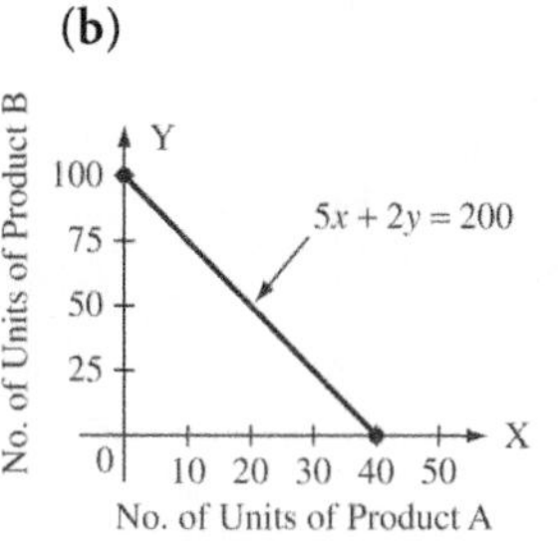

Self-Test

1. (a) $m = 0$, $b = -\frac{11}{3}$

(b) $m = 6$, $b = -9$

(c) $m = -\frac{1}{3}$, $b = 0$

(d) $m = 0, b = -3$

(e) m is undefined, there is no y-intercept

(f) $m = -\frac{a}{b}, b = \frac{c}{b}$

3. (a) For $-x = -55 + y$

x	0	25	55
y	55	30	0

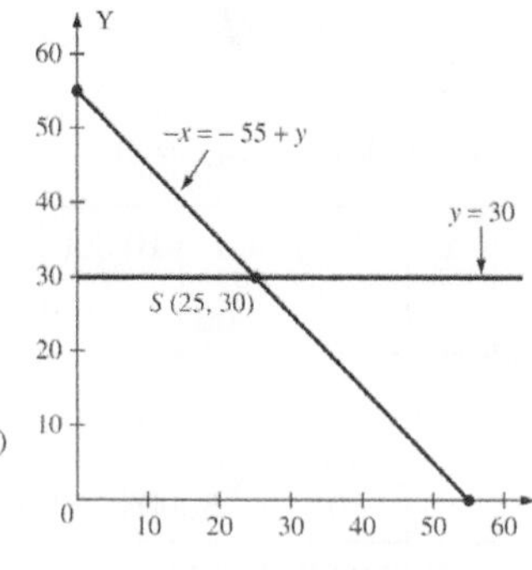

(b) For $3x + 2y + 600 = 0$

x	0	100	200
y	−300	−450	−600

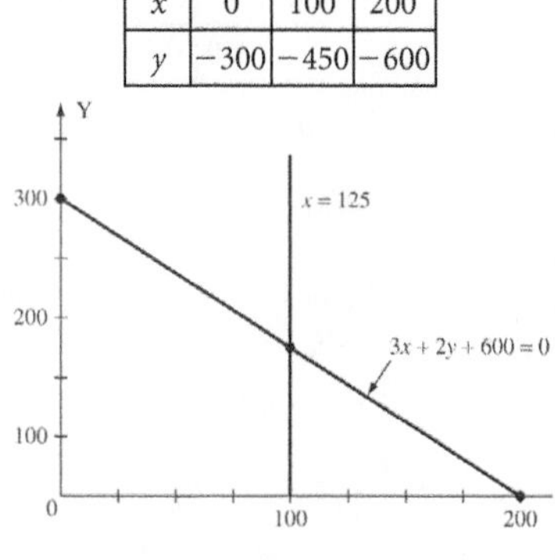

5. \$8000 is invested at 4%, \$4000 is invested at 6%

CHAPTER 5

Exercise 5.1

A. 1. Discount = \$11.07, Net = \$13.53
3. Discount = \$25.65, Rate = 33.3%
5. List = \$252.60, Rate = 15%
7. List = \$133.36, Net = \$50.01
9. List = \$134.96, Discount = \$50.61

B. 1. Net = \$30.24, Single rate = 32.5%
3. Net = \$137.89, Single rate = 48.55%
5. L = \$1583.33, Single rate = 61%

C. 1. \$78.53
3. \$3200
5. \$74.10
7. \$426.00
9. 15.9%
11. 41.6%
13. (a) 38.75% **(b)** 48.26%
15. (a) \$318.67 **(b)** \$280.33 **(c)** 46.8%
17. (a) \$443.79 **(b)** \$342.41 **(c)** 43.552%

19. 15%
21. 5%
23. $180.00
25. 15%
27. 8.7%

Exercise 5.2

A. 1. $640.00
3. $776.11
5. $1160
7. $4581.50

B. 1. Net = $582.00, Balance due = $850.00
3. Credit = $564.50, Net received = $536.28
5. Credit = $810.00, Balance due = $810.00

C. 1. (a) May 23
(b) $2449.02
3. (a) $799.90
(b) $825.16
(c) $842.00
5. $2507.19
7. $2184.00
9. (a) August 22
(b) $5276.85
(c) $103.20
11. (a) $1164.00
(b) $733.54
(c) Amount paid on October 25 is $600.00.
13. (a) $1925.00
(b) $3400.00
15. (a) $1.96
(b) 3.5%

Exercise 5.3

A. 1. (a) $6.00
(b) $3.84
(c) $2.16
(d) 25%
(e) 20%
3. (a) $35.00
(b) $31.50
(c) $3.50
(d) $66.\dot{6}\%$
(e) 40%
5. (a) $10.50
(b) $12.75
(c) ($2.25)
(d) $38.\dot{8}$
(e) 28%

B. 1. M = $6.25; Rate of M based on C = 25%; Rate of M based on S = 20%
3. S = $102.40; Rate of M based on C = 60%; Rate of M based on S = 37.5%
5. M = $21.70; S = $75.95; Rate of M based on S = 28.5714%
7. C = $44.24; M = $22.12; Rate of M based on S = $33.\dot{3}\%$
9. S = $78.10; M = $46.86; Rate of M based on C = 150%
11. S = $133.56; C = $111.30; Rate of M based on C = 20%

C. 1. $13.60
3. $3.00
5. $102.08
7. (a) 150%
(b) 60%
9. (a) $36.50
(b) $29.93
(c) 21.9512%
11. (a) $1.65 per litre
(b) $66.\dot{6}\%$
13. (a) $234.20
(b) 47.3684%
15. (a) $140.00
(b) $66.\dot{6}\%$
17. (a) $16.80
(b) $27.\dot{2}\dot{7}\%$

Exercise 5.4

A. 1. $51.00; $59.00; ($8.00)
3. $96.40; $30.65; $7.91
5. $160.00; 12%; $124.20

B. 1. (a) $21.99
(b) $17.59
(c) −$1.98
3. 20.0803%
5. 16%
7. (a) $7.00
(b) $21.\dot{2}\dot{1}\%$
9. (a) $17.79
(b) $25.44
(c) 12.2759%
(d) 38.6552%

Exercise 5.5

A. 1. (a) $267.30
(b) $160.36
(c) $12.56
3. (a) 40%
(b) −$8.00
(c) 10.2941%
(d) $9.\dot{3}\%$
5. −$2.23
7. (a) normal quality = $14.85
seconds = $9.90
substandard = $6.60
(b) $957.00
(c) 34.4978%
9. (a) $72.00
(b) $54.00
(c) 25%
11. −$6.50
13. −$7.00
15. −$82.50

Review Exercise

1. (a) $31.92
(b) $24.08
(c) $43%
3. 45.66%
5. 15%
7. $30.00
9. August 25; $25 117.40
11. (a) $1940.00
(b) $2813.00
13. (a) $1645.00
(b) $1500.00
15. (a) $90.00
(b) $58.50
(c) 53.8462%
(d) $74.88
(e) −$6.48
17. (a) $77.50
(b) 42.8571%
19. $240.00
21. (a) −$0.60
(b) 26.9841%
23. (a) −$13.20
(b) 25%
25. (a) $240.00
(b) $168.00
(c) −$21.00
27. (a) $2152.40
(b) 69.4323%
(c) 40.9794%

Self-Test

1. $295.77
3. 50.5%
5. $1635.04
7. $1450.00
9. $240.00
11. $348.36
13. 180%
15. 23.3974%
17. −$660.45

CHAPTER 6

Exercise 6.1

A. 1. (a)
(i) TR = $120x$
(ii) TC = $2800 + 50x$
where x represents the number of units per period
(b) (i) 40 units
(ii) $4800
(iii) 40%

(c)

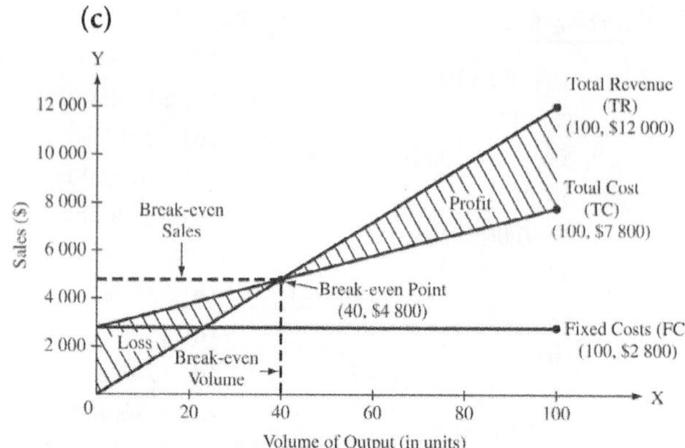

3. (a) (i) TR = $1x
 (ii) TC = 220 000 + 0.45x
 (b) (i) 400 000 units
 (ii) $400 000
 (iii) 50%
 (c)

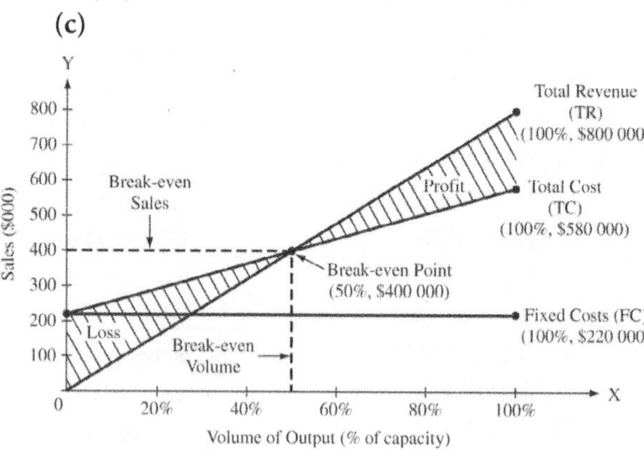

B. 1. 600 units
 3. 45 units
 5. $18 000
 7. $9.95
 9. (a) $1600
 (b) $700
 11. (a) 28 units
 (b) $2.44

Exercise 6.2

A. 1. (a) $72
 (b) 48%
 (c) 82 units
 (d) $12 300
 3. (a) $46
 (b) $46.4\dot{6}\%$
 (c) 11 units
 (d) $1089

B. 1. (a) $438 600
 (b) 43%
 (c) $372 094 units
 3. (a) $97 500
 (b) 75%
 (c) $113 334 units

C. 1. 27 units
 3. 169 units
 5. (a) 80 units
 (b) $1610.00
 7. $726 250
 9. $1 218 518.52
 11. 228 000 units

Exercise 6.3

1. (a) 164 units
 (b) 246 units
 (c) 250 units
 (d) $13
3. (a) 975 units
 (b) 1034 units
 (c) $2094
 (d) 1338 units
5. (a) 76%
 (b) 773 685 units
 (c) 803 948 units
 (d) $178 260

Review Exercise

1. (a) (i) $28.00
 (ii) 15.135%
 (b) (i) 112 units
 (ii) 35%
 (iii) $20 720
 (c) Revenue = 185x; Total cost = 3136 + 157x

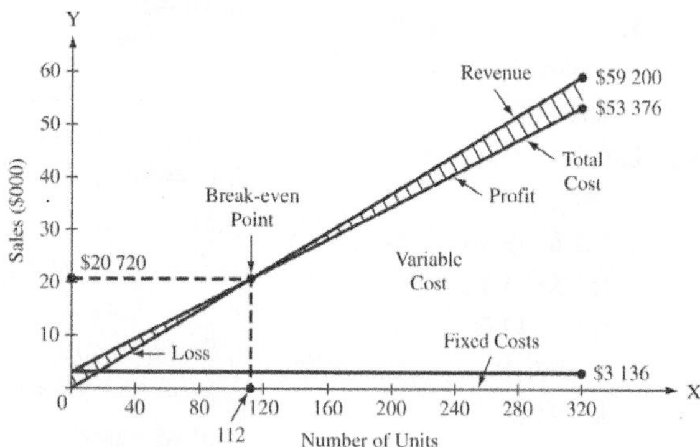

 (d) (i) 30%
 (ii) 38.75%
 (iii) 70%
3. (a) (i) 140 000
 (ii) 35%
 (b) (i) 60%
 (ii) $300 000
 (c) Total cost = 105 000 + 0.65x

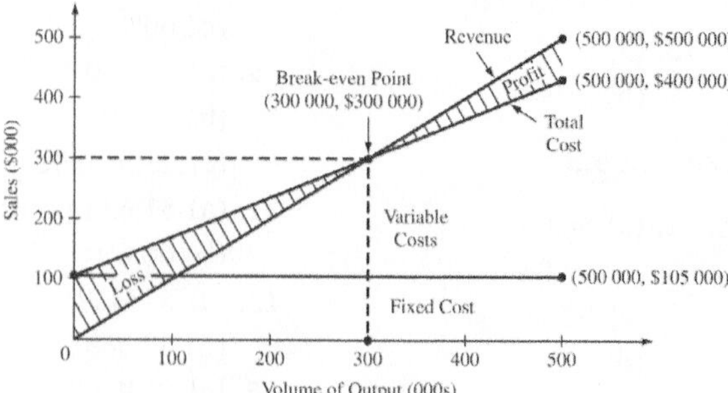

 (d) $335 000
5. 802

Self-Test

1. (a) (i) $3.00
   (ii) 30%
   (b) (i) 6000
   (ii) $60 000
   (iii) 40%
   (c) Revenue = $10x$
   Cost = $18\ 000 + 7.00x$

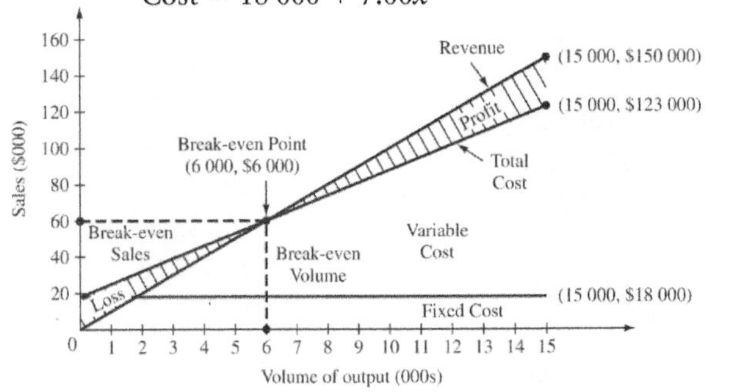

Sales ($000)
160
140
120
100
80
60
40
20
0
Revenue
(15 000, $150 000)
Profit
(15 000, $123 000)
Break-even Point
(6 000, $6 000)
Total
Cost
Break-even
Sales
Break-even
Volume
Variable
Cost
Loss
(15 000, $18 000)
Fixed Cost
1 2 3 4 5 6 7 8 9 10 11 12 13 14 15
Volume of output (000s)

   (d) 5600 units
   (e) 5500 units

CHAPTER 7

Exercise 7.1

A. 1. 0.035; $\frac{7}{12}$
   3. 0.0825; $\frac{183}{365}$

B. 1. $406.25
   3. $40.80
   5. $75.34
   7. $10.87
   9. $21.76
   11. $26.44

C. 1. $88.77
   3. $153.79

Exercise 7.2

A. 1. $1224.00
   3. 10.75%
   5. 14 months
   7. 144 days

B. 1. $3296.00
   3. 9.5%
   5. 8.4%
   7. 11 months
   9. 126 days
   11. $876.00
   13. $400 000
   15. 9%
   17. 41 days

Exercise 7.3

A. 1. $490.13
   3. $768.75
   5. $849.21

B. 1. $2542.53
   3. $13 800.00
   5. (a) $51 975
   (b) $51 943.53
   (c) 3.8871%

Exercise 7.4

A. 1. $266.00; $13.30
   3. $517.50; $547.17
   5. $2025.00; 292 days

B. 1. $1222.00
   3. $1704.60
   5. $644.00
   7. $6947.60
   9. $23 000.00

Exercise 7.5

A. 1. $829.33
   3. $617.50
   5. $1103.37
   7. $856.47
   9. $777.81
   11. $1070.39

B. 1. $1156.80
   3. $2248.66
   5. $1722.00
   7. $519.48
   9. $569.45
   11. $379.15
   13. $811.93
   15. $1408.21

Review Exercise

1. $63.98
3. 7.5%
5. 265 days
7. $3000.17
9. 8.25%
11. 196 days
13. $1601.89
15. $3200.00
17. $1736.47
19. $2664.00
21. $5119.89
23. $3560.00
25. $1614.74

Self-Test

1. $21.40
3. 6.5%
5. $6187.50
7. $4306.81
9. 359 days
11. $7432.80
13. $2910.69
15. $1163.85

CHAPTER 8

Exercise 8.1

A. 1. December 30, 2012
   3. $530.00
   5. 154 days
   7. $544.54

B. 1. (a) March 3, 2012
   (b) 155 days
   (c) $21.40
   (d) $861.40

C. 1. $631.24
   3. $837.19
   5. $856.35
   7. $10 413.71

D. 1. $2464.70
   3. $3615.69

Exercise 8.2

A. 1. $49 329.12
   3. 2.73%
   5. (a) 2.72%
   (b) $99 636.18
   (c) 2.71%

Exercise 8.3

A. 1. $278.14
   3. $3785.67
   5. $1825.63
   7. $178.66

Exercise 8.4

A. 1. (a) $0.16
   (b) $4.05
   (c) $1.24
   (d) $10.00
   (e) −$956.34

Exercise 8.5

A. 1. Amount paid, $1233.69; Interest paid, $33.69; Principal repaid, $1200.00
   3. Amount paid, $922.36; Interest paid, $22.36; Principal repaid, $900.00

Review Exercise

1. (a) November 2
   (b) $35.62
   (c) $1635.62
3. $1500.00
5. $5125.75
7. $814.17
9. $1269.57
11. 6.15%
13. $474.19
15. (a) July 31, $54.57; August 31, $62.49; September 30, $70.82; October 31, $74.11; November 30, $70.81
   (b) −$10 627.80

Self-Test

1. \$19.79
3. \$1160.00
5. \$1664.66
7. (a) \$98 116.43
   (b) 3.68%
9. \$340.26
11. Amount paid, \$4070.41; Interest paid, \$70.41; Principal repaid, \$4000.00

CHAPTER 9

Exercise 9.1

A. 1. $m = 1; i = 0.12; n = 5$
3. $m = 4; i = 0.01375; n = 36$
5. $m = 2; i = 0.0575; n = 27$
7. $m = 12; i = 0.00\dot{6}; n = 150$
9. $m = 2; i = 0.06125; n = 9$

B. 1. $(1 + 0.12)^5 = 1.762342$
3. $(1 + 0.01375)^{36} = 1.634975$
5. $(1 + 0.0575)^{27} = 4.524495$
7. $(1 + 0.006)^{150} = 2.452998$
9. $(1 + 0.06125)^9 = 1.707495$

C. 1. (a) 48
   (b) 2.5%
   (c) 1.025^{48}
   (d) 3.271490

Exercise 9.2

A. 1. \$713.39
3. \$2233.21
5. \$5468.38
7. \$6639.51
9. \$6259.48
11. \$4152.58
13. \$2052.74

B. 1. FV = \$5947.22; I = \$947.22
3. \$1221.10
5. (a) \$180.61
   (b) \$181.40
   (c) \$181.80
   (d) \$182.08
7. (a) FV = \$124.46; I = \$24.46
   (b) FV = \$154.90; I = \$54.90
   (c) FV = \$239.93; I = \$139.93
9. FV = \$7789.13; I = \$2791.10
11. \$761.75
13. \$17 116.96
15. \$183.24
17. (a) The bank investment gives more interest.
    (b) \$33.57

C. 1. \$2541.37
3. \$1452.78
5. \$4126.47
7. \$1102.13
9. \$1444.24
11. \$10 658.73

Exercise 9.3

A. 1. \$574.37
3. \$371.86
5. \$409.16
7. \$500.24
9. \$749.91
11. \$4344.21

B. 1. \$1338.81; \$261.19
3. \$762.84
5. \$3129.97
7. \$1398.85
9. two payments; \$4835.49
11. one payment

Exercise 9.4

A. 1. \$1951.22; \$48.78
3. \$4839.99; \$160.01
5. \$2642.50; \$557.50
7. \$1390.58; \$293.38
9. \$2310.82; \$720.62
11. \$2036.86; \$540.42
13. \$1332.82; \$261.78

B. 1. \$4589.47
3. \$1345.06
5. \$3800.24
7. \$1561.49

C. 1. \$8452.52
3. \$2346.36
5. \$3488.29
7. \$1074.71
9. \$1972.80
11. \$1492.15

Exercise 9.5

A. 1. \$5983.40
3. \$2537.13
5. \$1673.49
7. \$641.36

B. 1. (a) \$2851.94
   (b) \$3265.19
   (c) \$4000.00
   (d) \$5610.21
3. \$6805.31
5. \$655.02
7. \$2464.35
9. \$1955.51
11. \$4379.98
13. \$2707.08
15. \$3076.33
17. \$987.93

Review Exercise

1. (a) \$1198.28
   (b) \$1221.61
   (c) \$1227.05
3. (a) \$2378.89
   (b) \$378.89
5. (a) \$3185.63; \$1385.63
   (b) \$1299.71; \$49.71
7. \$10 681.77
9. \$11 102.50
11. \$4194.33
13. \$9791.31
15. \$3190.63
17. \$9294.86
19. \$1035.70
21. \$2838.62
23. \$2079.94
25. \$110 440.03
27. \$26 048.42
29. (a) \$2742.41
    (b) \$2911.55
    (c) \$3281.79
31. \$4857.56
33. \$1820.32
35. \$3574.57

Self-Test

1. \$2129.97
3. 2.711878
5. \$6919.05
7. \$14 711.80
9. \$4504.29
11. \$10 138.19
13. \$2661.85
15. \$848.88

CHAPTER 10

Exercise 10.1

A. 1. (a) 13.4 (years)
   (b) 28 (quarters)
   (c) 117.76 (months)
   (d) 8 (half-years)
   (e) 37.31 (quarters)
   (f) 37.17 (half-years)

B. 1. 18.66 half-years
3. 17.5 years
5. 5.62 years
7. October 31, 2010
9. 21 months before the due date

11. 33.79 months from now
13. 6.77 half-years

Exercise 10.2

A. **1.** 4.5%
3. 9.6050%
5. 9.7779%

B. **1.** 9.2366%
3. **(a)** 10.4018%
(b) 7.5855%
5. 3.4999%
7. 4.7713%

Exercise 10.3

A. **1.** **(a)** 12.8906%
(b) 6.1678%
(c) 7.3967%
(d) 10.6906%
3. **(a)** 8.9010%
(b) 6.4651%
(c) 7.3854%
(d) 4.2726%

B. **1.** 6.9913%
3. 4.6561%
5. 8.9454%
7. 6.2196%
9. 7.3854%
11. **(a)** $714.57
(b) $114.57
(c) 3.5567%
13. **(a)** $1831.40
(b) $631.40
(c) 4.3182%

Review Exercise

1. 5.592%
3. 19.60 months from now
5. 22.52 half-years
7. 6.0305%
9. **(a)** 5.9184%
(b) 14.3547%
(c) 8.8334%
(d) 8.2432%
11. **(a)** 4.5940%
(b) 5.9634%
13. 8.4405%
15. **(a)** 4%
(b) 3.7852%
(c) 3.5462%
(d) 3.2989%
He should choose 4% compounded annually.
17. 7.33 quarters from now
19. 18.81 months from now
21. 14.76 quarters

Self-Test

1. 3.3 years
3. 5.5357%
5. 7.3522%
7. 10%
9. 3.95% compounded semi-annually

CHAPTER 11

Exercise 11.1

A. **1.** **(a)** annuity certain
(b) annuity due
(c) general annuity
3. **(a)** perpetuity
(b) deferred annuity
(c) general annuity
5. **(a)** annuity certain
(b) deferred annuity
(c) simple annuity

Exercise 11.2

A. **1.** $54 193.60
3. $59 185.19
5. $17 915.08

B. **1.** $13 045.68
3. $32 434.02
5. **(a)** $8531.12
(b) $4500.00
(c) $4031.12
7. **(a)** $20 090.19
(b) $15 000.00
(c) $5090.19
9. $2536.75

Exercise 11.3

A. **1.** $9515.19
3. $30 941.11
5. $10 544.91

B. **1.** $6897.02
3. **(a)** $9906.20
(b) $2093.80
5. **(a)** $2523.82
(b) $372.06
7. **(a)** $27 947.10
(b) $4980.90
(c) $27 809.29
9. Wayne's price, $1629.60; Roberto's price, $1818.63; Wayne paid less.
11. **(a)** $13 683.13
(b) $1428.88
(c) $14 183.17
(d) $500.04
(e) $21.28

Exercise 11.4

A. **1.** $821.39
3. $1117.37
5. $272.73
7. $232.54
9. $1653.70

B. **1.** $207.87
3. $591.66
5. $255.36
7. $109.89
9. $665.25
11. $290.55
13. $1092.48
15. $64 559.08
17. $428.18
19. $1673.54

Exercise 11.5

A. **1.** 14 years, 8 months
3. 7 years, 10 months
5. 8 years
7. 8 years
9. 6 years

B. **1.** 75 months
3. 18 deposits
5. 3 years
7. 2 years, 4 months
9. 4 years
11. 6 years, 6 months
13. 10 months

Exercise 11.6

A. **1.** 5.0001%
3. 9.0002%
5. 7.6013%
7. 11.3679%

B. **1.** 12.5%
3. 3.0356%
5. 7.1983%
7. 7.685%
9. 8.8899%

Review Exercise

1. **(a)** $26 734.60
(b) $17 280.00
(c) $9454.60
3. $5232.46
5. 13 years
7. $1906.28
9. $16 655.75
11. 5 years, 6 months
13. 7.2505%
15. $34 031.63
17. 7 years
19. $13 181.14

Self-Test

1. $35 786.08
3. 10.9002%
5. 47 months
7. $40 385.38
9. $3268.62

CHAPTER 12

Exercise 12.1

A. **1.** $45 855.46
3. $16 317.77
5. $63 686.72
7. $32 876.06

B. **1.** $3810.79
3. $2326.66
5. **(a)** $13 265.50
(b) $3265.50
7. $31 293.63
9. $6927.06

Exercise 12.2

A. **1.** $47 583.23
3. $42 505.49
5. $5106.97
7. $34 627.97

B. **1.** $10 041.88
3. $31 736.57
5. **(a)** $29 829.02
(b) $5170.98
7. $116 126.62
9. $46 568.95
11. The lump-sum cash offer is $223.27 higher than the quarterly payments offer.

Exercise 12.3

A. **1.** $823.60
3. $1121.26
5. $273.20
7. $1426.84
9. $156.68

B. **1.** $124.41
3. $799.39
5. $776.11
7. $117.26
9. $41.85

Exercise 12.4

A. **1.** 15 years
3. 7 years, 9 months
5. 30 years
7. 8 years
9. 33 years, 7 months

B. **1.** 3 years, 9 months
3. 3 years, 4 months
5. 13 years, 8 months
7. 1 year, 10 months
9. 10 years

Exercise 12.5

A. **1.** 6.007%
3. 6.861%
5. 12.4076%
7. 4.4017%

B. **1.** 5.0895%
3. 7.3071%
5. 8.8248%
7. 10.7784%
9. 7.856%
11. 18.6169%

Exercise 12.6

A. **1.** **(a)** $1016.40
(b) $18 229.63
3. **(a)** $27 748.40
(b) $35 011.37
(c) $1413.54
(d) $7262.97

B. **1.** $17 790.55
3. $107 789.17

Review Exercise

1. $13 509.62
3. $82 901.70
5. $75 962.59
7. $1979.24
9. **(a)** 7 years, 9 months
(b) 14 years
11. **(a)** 6 years, 6 months
(b) 24 years
13. 4 years, 3 months
15. 9 years
17. **(a)** $16
(b) $333.29
(c) $3913.29
(d) $622.92
19. 8 years, 1 month
21. $160 296.97

Self-Test

1. $55 246.47
3. 4 years, 6 months
5. $2801.41
7. 8 years
9. $246.97
11. $302 131.40

CHAPTER 13

Exercise 13.1

A. **1.** $135 334.71; $71 813.10
3. $69 033.69; $35 581.67
5. $43 738.24 $7278.61

B. **1.** $204.80
3. $909.95

C. **1.** 9 years, 5 months
3. 8 years

D. **1.** 7.125%
3. 12.4984%

E. **1.** $31 378.29
3. **(a)** $9222.21
(b) $742.21
(c) $2539.32
5. $6245.85
7. **(a)** $1618.41
(b) $2241.00
(c) $622.59
(d) $59.08
9. $84.97
11. $4565.36
13. 1 year, 8 months
15. 4 years, 6 months
17. 7.0001%
19. 8.5803%

Exercise 13.2

A. **1.** $39 342.74
3. $11 304.97

B. **1.** $1316.98
3. $903.61

C. **1.** 17 years, 6 months
3. 4 years, 6 months

D. **1.** 11.2802%
3. 4.8856%

E. **1.** $59 113.10
3. $24 111.08
5. $148 955.96
7. $162.26
9. $1218.16
11. 20 years
13. 9.1776%

Exercise 13.3

A. **1.** $1403.20
3. $60 706.09
5. $45 376.38

B. **1.** $126 738.19
3. $6337.39
5. $228.38
7. 2 years, 7 months
9. **(a)** 24.9751
(b) $552.00
11. $40 456.61
13. $22 692.59
15. 5 years
17. $147.55
19. 8.8132%

Exercise 13.4

A. **1.** $5048.76
3. $3058.17
5. $3135.48

B. **1.** **(a)** $10 926.71
(b) $19 200.00
(c) $8273.29
3. $89 397.79
5. $3259.68
7. 3 years, 9 months
9. 1 year, 3 months
11. 1.9638%
13. $27 246.86
15. $42 162.27
17. $11 499.21
19. 6 years
21. 7 yearly payments
23. 7.3684%

Exercise 13.5

A. **1.** $73 529.41
3. $91 027.09

5. $44 762.78
7. $96 992.46

B. 1. $9600.00
3. $214.60
5. $343 446.85
7. $0.57
9. 5.1898%
11. $241.95
13. $122 263.83
15. $166.70

Review Exercise

1. $27 616.11
3. $17 367.79
5. (a) $2638.84
(b) $3444.00
(c) $805.16
7. (a) $13 925.54
(b) $14 056.50
9. (a) $128 905.47
(b) $75 094.53
11. $5199.99
13. 4 years, 1 month
15. 4 years, 2 months
17. (a) $30 742.57
(b) $6720.73
(c) $33 309.38
(d) $200.73
19. $21 116.58
21. $742.45
23. 2 years
25. 9.296%
27. (a) $15 749.42
(b) $3149.42
(c) $438.32
(d) $8439.36
29. (a) $503.87
(b) $1437.96
(c) $275.12
(d) $1782.29
(e) $89.52
(f) $1037.88
31. 6 years, 6 months
33. $180 230.77

Self-Test

1. $216 115.89
3. 1217.11
5. $23 780.54
7. $244.42
9. 18.927%
11. 18.5 years
13. $2339.72

CHAPTER 14

Exercise 14.1

A. 1. (a) $549.22
(b) $5633.76
(c) $140.84
(d) $408.38
3. (a) $1103.73
(b) $4913.52
(c) $196.54
(d) $907.19

B. 1. (a) 19.48 quarters
(b) $2493.97
3. (a) 14.53 half-years
(b) $8035.94

C. 1. (a) $920.57
(b) $15 053.02
(c) $59 234.20
(d) $23 234.20
3. (a) $136.87
(b) $4199.43
(c) $31.50
(d) $105.37
5. (a) $73 353.95
(b) $50 833.74
(c) $5079.79
(d) $22 520.21
7. PMT = $1904.33
9.

Payment number	*Amount paid*	*Interest paid*	*Principal repaid*	*Outstanding principal*
0				9,200.00
1	2,000.00	1,012.00	988.00	8,212.00
2	2,000.00	903.32	1,096.68	7,115.32
3	2,000.00	782.69	1,217.31	5,898.01
4	2,000.00	648.78	1,351.22	4,546.79
5	2,000.00	500.15	1,499.85	3,046.93
6	2,000.00	335.16	1,664.84	1,382.09
7	1,534.12	152.03	1,382.09	—
Total	13,534.12	4,334.13	9,200.00	

11. $491.56
13. $1315.03
15. (a) $3621.90
(b) $1035.28
(c) $2799.85
(d) $10 445.20
17. (a) 14.02 half-years
(b) $957.79
(c) $1910.53
(d) $4665.00

Exercise 14.2

A. 1. (a) $1829.69
(b) $20 286.24
(c) $819.56
(d) $1010.13
3. (a) $164.04
(b) $4563.42
(c) $22.54
(d) $141.50

B. 1. (a) 17.13 quarters
(b) $2685.85
3. (a) 14.894762 quarters
(b) $1584.97

C. 1. (a) $2790.38
(b) $34 892.31
(c) $1599.89
(d) $1190.49
3. (a) $252.15
(b) $34 199.92
(c) $7277.32
(d) $294.24
5. (a) 13.24 half-years
(b) $1107.06
(c) $2507.06
7. $3212.01
9. $752.68
11. (a) $26 387.44
(b) $12 151.71
(c) $14 235.73
(d) $3044.27
13. (a) $883.28
(b) $8024.59
(c) $621.39
(d) $932.94

Exercise 14.3

A. 1. $1006.24
3. $348.26
5. $1112.30

B. 1. (a) 30 payments
(b) $157.47
3. (a) 48 payments
(b) $722.00
5. $234.54
7. $301.40
9. $1152.88
11. (a) 62 payments
(b) $724.46
(c) $84 599.46
(d) $68 599.46

Exercise 14.4

A. 1. (a) $978.11
(b) $158 698.67
(c) $1008.85
3. (a) 108.36 months or 109 payments
(b) $178.13
(c) $1667.47
5. 5.42%
7. (a) $83 293.76
(b) 171 payments
(c) $10 365.10
9. $378.81

11. Mortgage statement:

PMT = 190.00; annual rate of interest = 12(0.45317%) = 5.4380%

Payment date	*Number of days*	*Amount paid*	*Interest paid*	*Principal*	*Balance repaid*
June 1					40 000.00
16	15	190.00	89.39	100.61	39 899.39
July 1	15	190.00	89.17	100.83	39 798.56
16	15	190.00	88.94	101.06	39 697.50
Aug 1	16	190.00	94.63	95.37	39 602.13
16	15	190.00	88.50	101.50	39 500.63
Sept 1	16	190.00	94.16	95.84	39 404.79
16	15	190.00	88.06	101.94	39 302.85
Oct 1	15	190.00	87.83	102.17	39 200.68
15	15	190.00	87.61	102.39	39 098.29
Nov 1	16	190.00	93.20	96.80	39 001.49
15	15	190.00	87.16	102.84	38 898.65
Dec 1	15	190.00	86.93	103.07	38 795.58

The mortgage statement balance on December 1 of \$38 795.58 differs from the amortization schedule balance of \$38 794.01 by \$1.57. The difference is reduced from \$3.01 in the answer to Question 10 by \$1.44 due to making semi-monthly payments.

Review Exercise

1. **(a)** \$1491.37
(b) \$12 723.84
(c) \$15 771.79
(d) \$338.49
(e) \$1247.91
(f) \$4300.99; totals are \$47 723.89; \$12 723.89; \$35 000.00

3. **(a)** 25 quarters
(b) \$28 940.21
(c) \$426.66
(d) \$1807.58
(e) \$5477.30; totals are \$49 664.30; \$9664.30; 40 000.00

5. **(a)** \$735.80
(b) \$280.57
(c) \$23 981.71
(d) \$1000.87
(e) \$15 899.97; totals are \$24 843.52; \$11 087.46 \$13 756.06

7. **(a)** 10 payments
(b) \$1139.87

9. **(a)** 12 quarters
(b) \$3211.27

11. **(a)** \$1313.76
(b) \$206 661.46
(c) \$1358.02

13. **(a)** 118 payments
(b) \$736.39
(c) \$389.21

15. **(a)** \$161.75
(b) \$1264.00
(c) \$5086.64
(d) \$21.41
(e) \$478.21; totals are 7764.16; 1264.16; 6500.00

17. 5.38%

19. **(a)** \$601.20
(b) \$1650.96
(c) \$25 597.94
(d) \$638.93

Self-Test

1. \$5887.85

3. \$6070.22

5. **(a)** 171 payments
(b) \$441.89
(c) \$2911.71

7. 10.0%

CHAPTER 15

Exercise 15.1

A. **1.** \$11 169.09
3. \$23 634.93
5. \$52 193.60
7. \$7173.32

B. **1.** \$466.70
3. \$14 560.07
5. \$10 350.30
7. \$4 778 270.32
9. \$42 940.38
11. \$1161.31
13. **(a)** \$29 546.64
(b) \$792.35
(c) \$30 338.99

Exercise 15.2

A. **1.** **(a)** \$4877.98
(b) \$20 122.02
3. **(a)** \$1119.82
(b) \$8880.18

B. **1.** **(a)** Premium, \$14 304.00; Purchase price, \$114 304.00
(b) Premium, \$6359.60; Purchase price, \$106 359.60
3. **(a)** Premium, \$2800.72; Purchase price, \$27 800.72
(b) Premium, \$2458.66; Purchase price, \$22 541.34
5. \$4 569 384.71
7. \$103 723.59

Exercise 15.3

A. **1.** Discount, −\$77.15; Purchase price, \$4922.85

Schedule of Accumulation of Discount

Payment interval	*coupon b = 3%*	*Interest on book i = 3.25%*	*Discount accumulated*	*Book value*	*Discount balance*
0				4922.85	77.15
1	150.00	159.99	9.99	4932.84	67.16
2	150.00	160.32	10.32	4943.16	56.84
3	150.00	160.65	10.65	4953.81	46.19
4	150.00	161.00	11.00	4964.81	35.19
5	150.00	161.36	11.36	4976.17	23.83
6	150.00	161.73	11.73	4987.90	12.10
7	150.00	162.10	12.10	5000.00	—
Total	1050.00	1127.15	77.15		

3. Premium, $32.36; Purchase price, $1032.36

B. 1. $242.12
3. $387.55

Exercise 15.4

1. 5.8681%
3. 7.901%
5. 9.2566%

Exercise 15.5

A. 1. (a) $558.24
(b) $6399.60
3. (a) $22.03
(b) $3104.14

B. 1. (a) $500.00
(b) $265.25
(c) $765.25
(d) $10 868.38
3. (a) $62.50
(b) $143.33
(c) $205.83
(d) $2246.16

C. 1. (a) $2699.00
(b) $64 776.00
(c) $10 224.00
3. $2419.29; totals are $16 935.03; $3064.99; $20 000.02
5. $2840.83
7. (a) $495.27
(b) $9598.44
9. (a) $4275.00
(b) $1124.00
(c) $5399.00
(d) $36 976.00
11. (a) $302.01
(b) $21 903.91
(c) $257.62
(d) $764.19
(e) $97 252.61; totals are $54 361.80; $45 637.43; $99 999.23
13. (a) $24 750.00
(b) $8604.00
(c) $33 354.00
(d) $13 931.00
(e) $107 196.00
(f) $232 277.00; totals are $172 073.00; $127 927.00; $300 000.00

Review Exercise

1. (a) $5751.14
(b) $4776.44
3. $26 174.35
5. Premium, $1129.61; Purchase price, $21 129.61
7. (a) −$15 620.41
(b) $84 379.59
(c) $85 664.12
9. $4527.65
11. $12.5685%
13. Discount, −$272.16; Purchase price, $4727.84
15. Gain of $1899.18
17. $7.6478%
19. (a) $44 248.79
(b) $48 017.12
(c) Gain of $1795.38
21. (a) $9268.75
(b) $28 862.02
(c) $1873.21
(d) Totals are $92 687.50; $17 312.54; $110 000.04
23. (a) $13 750.00
(b) $8279.90
(c) $22 029.90
(d) $72 194.23
(e) $5989.29
(f) Totals are $66 239.23; $33 760.77; $100 000.00
25. (a) $2469.40
(b) $10 612.00
(c) $21 194.78
(d) $788.92
27. (a) 27 payments
(b) $28 983.13

Self-Test

1. $9269.43
3. Premium $367.77
5. $4596.98
7. 12.4614%
9. 12.9369%
11. $240.24
13. $603 102.20

CHAPTER 16

Exercise 16.1

A. 1. Alternative 1, $44 634; Alternative 2, $53 448; Alternative 2 is preferred at 12%.
3. Alternative 1, $22 205; Alternative 2, $23 384; Alternative 1 is preferred.
5. Alternative 1, $2000; Alternative 2, $2393; Alternative 1 is preferred.

B. 1. At 6%, Alternative 2 is preferred.
3. At 10%, Offer A is preferred.
5. The warehouse should be purchased.

Exercise 16.2

A. 1. Reject; NPV is −$5367
3. NPV Alternative 1, $234; NPV Alternative 2, $203, Alternative 1 is preferred.
5. NPV Alternative 1, $1666; NPV Alternative 2, $352, Alternative 1 is preferred.

B. 1. Project B is preferred at 12%.
3. No; NPV is −$8561
5. Yes; NPV $5696. The new product provides the required return on investment of 20% and should therefore be distributed.
7. Yes; NPV $5142. The investment will return more than 12% on the investment and should therefore be distributed.

Exercise 16.3

A. 1. 25.3%
3. 20.7%

B. 1. 19.9%
3. 19.9%
5. 22.2%

Review Exercise

1. Alternative B is preferred.
3. Alternative A is preferred.
5. −$22 227
7. 26.3%
9. 17.4%
11. 25.8%
13. The company should chose Project B.
15. −$1215
17. The product should be marketed.

Self-Test

1. Alternative A is preferred.
3. 16.9%
5. Project B is preferred at 20%.

INDEX

C

F

G

S

T

Study Card for *Contemporary Business Mathematics with Canadian Applications*, Ninth Edition

S. A. Hummelbrunner K. Suzanne Coombs

PEARSON

LIST OF FORMULAS

Formula 2.1A	$a^m \times a^n = a^{m+n}$	The rule for multiplying two powers having the same base
Formula 2.2	$a^m \div a^n = a^{m-n}$	The rule for dividing two powers having the same base
Formula 2.3	$(a^m)^n = a^{mn}$	The rule for raising a power to a power
Formula 2.4	$(ab)^m = a^m b^m$	The rule for taking the power of a product
Formula 2.5	$\left(\frac{a}{b}\right)^m = \frac{a^m}{b^m}$	The rule for taking the power of a quotient
Formula 2.6	$a^{-m} = \frac{1}{a^m}$	The definition of a negative exponent
Formula 2.7	$\left(\frac{y}{x}\right)^{-m} = \left(\frac{x}{y}\right)^m$	The rule for a fraction with a negative exponent
Formula 2.8	$a^{\frac{1}{n}} = \sqrt[n]{a}$	The definition of a fractional exponent with numerator 1
Formula 2.9	$a^{-\frac{1}{n}} = \frac{1}{a^{\frac{1}{n}}} = \frac{1}{\sqrt[n]{a}}$	The definition of a fractional exponent with numerator −1
Formula 2.10	$a^{\frac{m}{n}} = \sqrt[n]{a^m} = \left(\sqrt[n]{a}\right)^m$	The definition of a positive fractional exponent
Formula 2.11	$a^{-\frac{m}{n}} = \frac{1}{a^{\frac{m}{n}}} = \frac{1}{\sqrt[n]{a^m}}$	The definition of a negative fractional exponent
Formula 2.12A	$\ln(ab) = \ln a + \ln b$	The relationship used to find the logarithm of a product
Formula 2.13	$\ln\left(\frac{a}{b}\right) = \ln a - \ln b$	The relationship used to find the logarithm of a quotient
Formula 2.14	$\ln(a^k) = k(\ln a)$	The relationship used to find the logarithm of a power
Formula 3.1A	PERCENTAGE = RATE × BASE or NEW NUMBER = RATE × ORIGINAL NUMBER	The basic percentage relationship
Formula 3.2	ORIGINAL NUMBER $\begin{matrix}+\text{ INCREASE}\\-\text{ DECREASE}\end{matrix}$ = NEW NUMBER	The relationship to use with problems of increase or decrease (problems of change)
Formula 3.3	$\text{RATE OF CHANGE} = \frac{\text{AMOUNT OF CHANGE}}{\text{ORIGINAL NUMBER}}$	The formula for finding the rate of change (rate of increase or decrease)
Formula 3.4	$\text{REAL INCOME} = \frac{\text{INCOME IN CURRENT DOLLARS}}{\text{CONSUMER PRICE INDEX}}$	The formula for eliminating the effect of inflation on income
Formula 4.1	$y = mx + b$	Slope-*y*-intercept form of a linear equation
Formula 5.1A	AMOUNT OF DISCOUNT = LIST PRICE × RATE OF DISCOUNT	Finding the amount of discount when the list price is known
Formula 5.2	NET PRICE = LIST PRICE − AMOUNT OF DISCOUNT	Finding the net amount when the amount of discount is known
Formula 5.3A	NET PRICE FACTOR (NPF) = 100% − % DISCOUNT	Finding the net price factor (NPF)

Copyright © 2012 Pearson Canada Inc.

Formula 5.4A NET PRICE = LIST PRICE × NET PRICE FACTOR (NPF) — Finding the net amount directly without computing the amount of discount

Formula 5.5A NET PRICE FACTOR (NPF) FOR A DISCOUNT SERIES = NPF FOR THE FIRST DISCOUNT × NPF FOR THE SECOND DISCOUNT × . . . × NPF FOR THE LAST DISCOUNT

Formula 5.6A NET PRICE = LIST PRICE × NET PRICE FACTOR FOR THE DISCOUNT SERIES — Finding the net amount directly when a list price is subject to a series of discounts

Formula 5.7 SINGLE EQUIVALENT RATE OF DISCOUNT FOR A DISCOUNT SERIES
= 1 − NPF FOR THE DISCOUNT SERIES
$= 1 - [(1 - d_1)(1 - d_2)(1 - d_3) \ldots (1 - d_n)]$
— Finding the single rate of discount that has the same effect as a given series of discounts

Formula 5.8A SELLING PRICE = COST OF BUYING + EXPENSES + PROFIT
or
$S = C + E + P$
— Basic relationship between selling price, cost of buying, operating expenses (or overhead), and profit

Formula 5.9 MARKUP = EXPENSES + PROFIT
or
$M = E + P$
— Basic relationship between markup, cost of buying, operating expenses (or overhead), and profit

Formula 5.10
$$\text{RATE OF MARKUP BASED ON COST} = \frac{\text{MARKUP}}{\text{COST}} = \frac{M}{C}$$
— Finding the rate of markup as a percent of cost

Formula 5.11
$$\text{RATE OF MARKUP BASED ON SELLING PRICE} = \frac{\text{MARKUP}}{\text{SELLING PRICE}} = \frac{M}{S}$$
— Finding the rate of markup as a percent of selling price

Formula 6.1A (PRICE × VOLUME) − (VARIABLE COST PER UNIT × VOLUME) − FIXED COST = PROFIT — Formula for finding profit when separating fixed and variable costs

Formula 6.2A CONTRIBUTION MARGIN PER UNIT = SELLING PRICE PER UNIT − VARIABLE COST PER UNIT
or
CM PER UNIT = P − VC
— Formula for finding contribution margin per unit

Formula 6.3
$$\text{BREAK-EVEN VOLUME (in units)} = \frac{\text{FIXED COST}}{\text{UNIT CONTRIBUTION MARGIN}}$$
or
$$X = \frac{\text{FC}}{\text{CM per unit}}$$
— Formula for finding break-even volume in units based on the unit contribution margin

Formula 6.4
$$\text{CONTRIBUTION RATE} = \frac{\text{UNIT CONTRIBUTION MARGIN}}{\text{UNIT SELLING PRICE}}$$
or
$$\text{C RATE} = \frac{\text{CM per unit}}{\text{P}}$$
— Formula for finding contribution rate

Formula 6.5
$$\text{BREAK-EVEN SALES (in sales dollars)} = \frac{\text{FIXED COST}}{\text{CONTRIBUTION RATE}}$$
or
$$\text{SALES} = \frac{\text{FC}}{\text{C RATE}}$$
— Formula for finding break-even sales based on contribution rate

Formula 7.1A $I = Prt$ — Finding the amount of interest when the principal, the rate, and the time are known
Finding the amount of interest on promissory notes

Copyright © 2012 Pearson Canada Inc.

Formula 7.2	$S = P + I$	Finding the future value (maturity value) when the principal and the amount of interest are known
Formula 7.3A	$S = P(1 + rt)$	Finding the future value (maturity value) at simple interest directly when the principal, rate of interest, and time are known Finding the maturity value of promissory notes directly
Formula 9.1A	$S = P(1 + i)^n$ restated as $FV = PV(1 + i)^n$	Finding the future value (or maturity value) when the original principal, the rate of interest, and the time period are known Finding the future value of a sum of money when *n* is a fractional value using the exact method Finding the future value of a compound amount (maturity value) when the original principal, the rate of interest, and the time period are known
Formula 9.2	$i = \frac{j}{m}$	Finding the periodic rate of interest
Formula 10.1	$f = (1 + i)^m - 1$	Finding the effective rate of interest, *f*, for a nominal annual rate compounded *m* times per year
Formula 11.1	$FV_n = PMT\left[\frac{(1 + i)^n - 1}{i}\right]$	Finding the future value (accumulated value) of an ordinary simple annuity
Formula 11.2	$PV_n = PMT\left[\frac{1 - (1 + i)^{-n}}{i}\right]$	Finding the present value (discounted value) of an ordinary simple annuity
Formula 12.1	$p = (1 + i)^c - 1$	Finding the equivalent rate of interest per payment period *p* for a nominal annual rate of interest compounded *c* times per payment interval
Formula 12.2	$FV_g = PMT\left[\frac{(1 + p)^n - 1}{p}\right]$ where $p = (1 + i)^c - 1$	Finding the future value of an ordinary general annuity using the effective rate of interest per payment period
Formula 12.3	$PV_g = PMT\left[\frac{1 - (1 + p)^{-n}}{p}\right]$	Finding the present value of an ordinary general annuity using the effective rate of interest per payment period
Formula 12.4	SIZE OF THE *n*TH PAYMENT = $PMT(1 + k)^{n-1}$	Finding the size of the *n*th payment of a constant-growth annuity
Formula 12.5	SUM OF THE PERIODIC CONSTANT-GROWTH PAYMENTS = $\frac{PMT\,(1 + k)^{n-1}}{k}$	Finding the sum of the periodic payments of a constant-growth annuity.
Formula 12.6	$FV = PMT\frac{(1 + i)^n - (1 + k)^n}{i - k}$	Finding the future value of an ordinary simple constant-growth annuity
Formula 12.7	$PV = PMT\left[\frac{1 - (1 + k)^n (1 + i)^{-n}}{i - k}\right]$	Finding the present value of a series of payments forming a constant-growth annuity
Formula 12.8	$FV = n\,(PMT)(1 + i)^{n-1}$	Finding the future value of an ordinary simple constant-growth annuity when the constant-growth rate and the number of conversion periods are the same
Formula 12.9	$PV = n\,(PMT)(1 + i)^{-1}$	Finding the present value of an ordinary simple constant-growth annuity when the constant-growth rate and the number of conversion periods are the same
Formula 13.1	$FV_n(\text{due}) = PMT\left[\frac{(1 + i)^n - 1}{i}\right](1 + i)$	Finding the future value of a simple annuity due

Copyright © 2012 Pearson Canada Inc.

Formula 13.2

$$PV_n(\text{due}) = PMT\left[\frac{1-(1+i)^{-n}}{i}\right](1+i)$$

Finding the present value of a simple annuity due

Formula 13.3

$$FV_g(\text{due}) = PMT\left[\frac{(1+p)^n - 1}{p}\right](1+p)$$

where $p = (l + i)^c - 1$

Finding the future value of a general annuity due using the effective rate of interest per payment period

Formula 13.4

$$PV_g(\text{due}) = PMT\left[\frac{1-(1+p)^{-n}}{p}\right](1+p)$$

where $p = (l + i)^c - 1$

Finding the present value of a general annuity due using the effective rate of interest per payment period

Formula 13.5

$$PV = \frac{PMT}{i}$$

Finding the present value of an ordinary simple perpetuity

Formula 13.6

$$PV = \frac{PMT}{p}$$

where $p = (1 + i)^c - 1$

Finding the present value of an ordinary general perpetuity

Formula 13.7

$$PV(\text{due}) = PMT + \frac{PMT}{i}$$

Finding the present value of a simple perpetuity due

Formula 13.8

$$PV(\text{due}) = PMT + \frac{PMT}{p}$$

where $p = (l + i)^c - 1$

Finding the present value of a general perpetuity due

Formula 15.1

$$PP = FV(1+i)^{-n} + PMT\left[\frac{1-(1+i)^{-n}}{i}\right]$$

Basic formula for finding the purchase price of a bond when the interest payment interval and the yield rate conversion period are equal

Formula 15.2

$$PP = FV(1+p)^{-n} + PMT\left[\frac{1-(1+p)^{-n}}{p}\right]$$

where $p = (1 + i)^c - 1$

Basic formula for finding the purchase price of a bond when the interest payment interval and the yield rate conversion period are different

Formula 15.3

$$\text{PREMIUM OR DISCOUNT} = (b \times \text{FACE VALUE} - i \times \text{REDEMPTION PRICE})\left[\frac{1-(1+i)^{-n}}{i}\right]$$

Direct formula for finding the premium or discount of a bond (a negative answer indicates a discount)

Formula 15.4

$$\text{APPROXIMATE VALUE OF } i = \frac{\text{AVERAGE INCOME PER INTEREST PAYMENT INTERVAL}}{\text{AVERAGE BOOK VALUE}}$$

where

$$\text{AVERAGE BOOK VALUE} = \frac{1}{2}(\text{QUOTED PRICE} + \text{REDEMPTION PRICE})$$

and

$$\text{AVERAGE INCOME PER INTEREST PAYMENT INTERVAL} = \frac{\text{TOTAL INTEREST PAYMENTS} \begin{matrix} - \text{PREMIUM} \\ + \text{DISCOUNT} \end{matrix}}{\text{NUMBER OF INTEREST PAYMENT INTERVALS}}$$

Basic formula for finding the yield rate using the method of averages

Formula 16.1

$$\underset{(\text{NPV})}{\text{NET PRESENT VALUE}} = \text{PRESENT VALUE OF INFLOWS} - \text{PRESENT VALUE OF OUTLAYS}$$

Formula for finding the difference between the present value of cash inflows and the present value of cash outflows, known as the net present value

Formula 16.2

$$\text{PROFITABILITY INDEX} = \frac{\text{PRESENT VALUE OF INFLOWS}}{\text{PRESENT VALUE OF OUTLAYS}} = \frac{PV_{IN}}{PV_{OUT}}$$

Formula for finding the relationship by dividing the present value of cash inflows by the present value of cash outflows, known as the profitability index

Copyright © 2012 Pearson Canada Inc.

"AS IS" LICENSE AGREEMENT AND LIMITED WARRANTY

READ THIS LICENSE CAREFULLY BEFORE OPENING THIS PACKAGE. BY OPENING THIS PACKAGE, YOU ARE AGREEING TO THE TERMS AND CONDITIONS OF THIS LICENSE. IF YOU DO NOT AGREE, DO NOT OPEN THE PACKAGE. PROMPTLY RETURN THE UNOPENED PACKAGE AND ALL ACCOMPANYING ITEMS TO THE PLACE YOU OBTAINED THEM. THESE TERMS APPLY TO ALL LICENSED SOFTWARE ON THE DISK EXCEPT THAT THE TERMS FOR USE OF ANY SHAREWARE OR FREEWARE ON THE DISKETTES ARE AS SET FORTH IN THE ELECTRONIC LICENSE LOCATED ON THE DISK:

1. GRANT OF LICENSE and OWNERSHIP: The enclosed computer programs and any data ("Software") are licensed, not sold, to you by Pearson Canada Inc. ("We" or the "Company") in consideration of your adoption of the accompanying Company textbooks and/or other materials, and your agreement to these terms. You own only the disk(s) but we and/or our licensors own the Software itself. This license allows instructors and students enrolled in the course using the Company textbook that accompanies this Software (the "Course") to use and display the enclosed copy of the Software for academic use only, so long as you comply with the terms of this Agreement. You may make one copy for back up only. We reserve any rights not granted to you.
2. USE RESTRICTIONS: You may not sell or license copies of the Software or the Documentation to others. You may not transfer, distribute or make available the Software or the Documentation, except to instructors and students in your school who are users of the adopted Company textbook that accompanies this Software in connection with the course for which the textbook was adopted. You may not reverse engineer, disassemble, decompile, modify, adapt, translate or create derivative works based on the Software or the Documentation. You may be held legally responsible for any copying or copyright infringement that is caused by your failure to abide by the terms of these restrictions.
3. TERMINATION: This license is effective until terminated. This license will terminate automatically without notice from the Company if you fail to comply with any provisions or limitations of this license. Upon termination, you shall destroy the Documentation and all copies of the Software. All provisions of this Agreement as to limitation and disclaimer of warranties, limitation of liability, remedies or damages, and our ownership rights shall survive termination.
4. DISCLAIMER OF WARRANTY: THE COMPANY AND ITS LICENSORS MAKE NO WARRANTIES ABOUT THE SOFTWARE, WHICH IS PROVIDED "AS-IS." IF THE DISK IS DEFECTIVE IN MATERIALS OR WORKMANSHIP, YOUR ONLY REMEDY IS TO RETURN IT TO THE COMPANY WITHIN 30 DAYS FOR REPLACEMENT UNLESS THE COMPANY DETERMINES IN GOOD FAITH THAT THE DISK HAS BEEN MISUSED OR IMPROPERLY INSTALLED, REPAIRED, ALTERED OR DAMAGED. THE COMPANY DISCLAIMS ALL WARRANTIES, EXPRESS OR IMPLIED, INCLUDING WITHOUT LIMITATION, THE IMPLIED WARRANTIES OF MERCHANTABILITY AND FITNESS FOR A PARTICULAR PURPOSE. THE COMPANY DOES NOT WARRANT, GUARANTEE OR MAKE ANY REPRESENTATION REGARDING THE ACCURACY, RELIABILITY, CURRENTNESS, USE, OR RESULTS OF USE, OF THE SOFTWARE.
5. LIMITATION OF REMEDIES AND DAMAGES: IN NO EVENT, SHALL THE COMPANY OR ITS EMPLOYEES, AGENTS, LICENSORS OR CONTRACTORS BE LIABLE FOR ANY INCIDENTAL, INDIRECT, SPECIAL OR CONSEQUENTIAL DAMAGES ARISING OUT OF OR IN CONNECTION WITH THIS LICENSE OR THE SOFTWARE, INCLUDING, WITHOUT LIMITATION, LOSS OF USE, LOSS OF DATA, LOSS OF INCOME OR PROFIT, OR OTHER LOSSES SUSTAINED AS A RESULT OF INJURY TO ANY PERSON, OR LOSS OF OR DAMAGE TO PROPERTY, OR CLAIMS OF THIRD PARTIES, EVEN IF THE COMPANY OR AN AUTHORIZED REPRESENTATIVE OF THE COMPANY HAS BEEN ADVISED OF THE POSSIBILITY OF SUCH DAMAGES. SOME JURISDICTIONS DO NOT ALLOW THE LIMITATION OF DAMAGES IN CERTAIN CIRCUMSTANCES, SO THE ABOVE LIMITATIONS MAY NOT ALWAYS APPLY.
6. GENERAL: THIS AGREEMENT SHALL BE CONSTRUED AND INTERPRETED ACCORDING TO THE LAWS OF THE PROVINCE OF ONTARIO. This Agreement is the complete and exclusive statement of the agreement between you and the Company and supersedes all proposals, prior agreements, oral or written, and any other communications between you and the company or any of its representatives relating to the subject matter.

Should you have any questions concerning this agreement or if you wish to contact the Company for any reason, please contact in writing: Permissions, Pearson Education Canada, a division of Pearson Canada Inc., 26 Prince Andrew Place, Toronto, Ontario M3C 2T8.